ULTIMATE GUIDE

BARNS, SHEDS & OUTBUILDINGS

UPDATED 4TH EDITION

ULTIMATE GUIDE

BARNS, SHEDS & OUTBUILDINGS

PLAN / DESIGN / BUILD

STEP-BY-STEP BUILDING AND DESIGN INSTRUCTIONS
PLUS PLANS TO BUILD MORE THAN 100 OUTBUILDINGS

UPDATED 4TH EDITION

CREATIVE
HOMEOWNER®

Content on pages 256-287 provided by Design America, Inc., St. Louis, MO.

Ultimate Guide: Barns, Sheds & Outbuildings, Updated 4th Edition
Vice President-Content: Christopher Reggio
Editor: Laura Taylor
Technical Editor: David Schiff
Designer: David Fisk
Indexer: Jay Kreider

ISBN 978-1-58011-799-9

The Cataloging-in-Publication Data is on file with the Library of Congress.

We are always looking for talented authors. To submit an idea, please send a brief inquiry to acquisitions@foxchapelpublishing.com.

Printed in China

Current Printing (last digit)
10 9 8 7 6 5 4 3 2 1

Creative Homeowner®, *www.creativehomeowner.com*, is an imprint of New Design Originals Corporation and distributed exclusively in North America by Fox Chapel Publishing Company, Inc., 800-457-9112, 903 Square Street, Mount Joy, PA 17552, and in the United Kingdom by Grantham Book Service, Trent Road, Grantham, Lincolnshire, NG31 7XQ.

SAFETY

Although the methods in this book have been reviewed for safety, it is not possible to overstate the importance of using the safest methods you can. What follows are reminders—some do's and don'ts of work safety—to use along with your common sense.

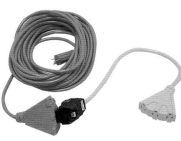

- **Always** use caution, care, and good judgment when following the procedures described in this book.

- **Always** be sure that the electrical setup is safe, that no circuit is overloaded, and that all power tools and outlets are properly grounded. Do not use power tools in wet locations.

- **Always** read container labels on paints, solvents, and other products; provide ventilation; and observe all other warnings.

- **Always** read the manufacturer's instructions for using a tool, especially the warnings.

- Use hold-downs and push sticks whenever possible when working on a table saw. Avoid working short pieces if you can.

- **Always** remove the key from any drill chuck (portable or press) before starting the drill.

- **Always** pay deliberate attention to how a tool works so that you can avoid being injured.

- **Always** know the limitations of your tools. Do not try to force them to do what they were not designed to do.

- **Always** make sure that any adjustment is locked before proceeding. For example, always check the rip fence on a table saw or the bevel adjustment on a portable saw before starting to work.

- **Always** clamp small pieces to a bench or other work surface when using a power tool.

- **Always** wear the appropriate rubber gloves or work gloves when handling chemicals, moving or stacking lumber, working with concrete, or doing heavy construction.

- **Always** wear a face mask when you create dust by sawing or sanding. Use a special filtering respirator when working with toxic substances and solvents.

- **Always** wear eye protection, especially when using power tools or striking metal on metal or concrete; a chip can fly off, for example, when chiseling concrete.

- **Never** work while wearing loose clothing, open cuffs, or jewelry; tie back long hair.

- **Always** be aware that there is seldom enough time for your body's reflexes to save you from injury from a power tool in a dangerous situation; everything happens too fast. Be alert!

- **Always** keep your hands away from the business ends of blades, cutters, and bits.

- **Always** hold a circular saw firmly, with both hands, if practical.

- **Always** use a drill with an auxiliary handle to control the torque when using large-size bits.

- **Always** check your local building codes when planning new construction. The codes are intended to protect public safety and should be observed to the letter.

- **Never** work with power tools when you are tired or when under the influence of alcohol or drugs.

- **Never** cut tiny pieces of wood or pipe using a power saw. When you need a small piece, saw it from a securely clamped longer piece.

- **Never** change a saw blade or a drill or router bit unless the power cord is unplugged. Do not depend on the switch being off. You might accidentally hit it.

- **Never** work in insufficient lighting.

- **Never** work with dull tools. Have them sharpened, or learn how to sharpen them yourself.

- **Never** use a power tool on a workpiece—large or small—that is not firmly supported.

- **Never** saw a workpiece that spans a large distance between horses without close support on each side of the cut; the piece can bend, closing on and jamming the blade, causing saw kickback.

- When sawing, **never** support a workpiece from underneath with your leg or other part of your body.

- **Never** carry sharp or pointed tools, such as utility knives, awls, or chisels, in your pocket. If you want to carry any of these tools, use a special-purpose tool belt that has leather pockets and holders.

CONTENTS

INTRODUCTION

Adding a barn, a backyard shed, a new detached garage, or some other type of outbuilding not only improves the functionality of your home but also adds value to your property. Written with the do-it-yourselfer in mind, *Ultimate Guide: Barns, Sheds, and Outbuildings* gives you the information you need to enhance your property by constructing one of these buildings. Whether you are a novice builder or seasoned pro and plan to do the work yourself or you just want to know the basics before you hire the work out to someone else, the book provides information on planning, building, and finishing in clear text aided by easy-to-follow photographic sequences. For those who wish to build an existing design, there are projects and blueprints available.

GUIDE TO SKILL LEVEL

 Easy. Made for beginners.

 Challenging. Can be done by beginners who have the patience and willingness to learn.

 Difficult. Can be handled by most experienced do-it-yourselfers who have mastered basic construction skills. Consider consulting a specialist.

Part 1: Design

Part 1 covers the planning stage of your project. You will find information to help you locate your building properly, decide on its design, and decipher architectural plans and building codes. This section also introduces you to the tools and materials you will be using to construct your project. For the most part, you will be able to build the typical barn, shed, or other outbuilding using basic tools and buying the materials you will need at the local home center or lumberyard.

Part 2: Building Basics

In this section, individual chapters detail the basics of building. Each chapter covers a specific area of construction, beginning with foundations. In this chapter, you will learn how to construct everything from simple shed foundations to poured concrete slabs. There is a chapter on framing, including extensive sections on pole buildings and old-fashioned timber-framing techniques— the way all barns were built in the past. This is followed by

chapters on closing in the framing, including information on all types of roofing and siding, and installing doors and windows.

To let you include some of the comforts of home, other chapters cover the basic wiring and plumbing needs of your building, and your options for interior and exterior finish and trimwork.

All of the building chapters guide you through the construction process. Step-by-step photo sequences will have you building like a pro.

Part 3: Projects and Plans

While Parts 1 and 2 supply the basics you need to know for building a barn, shed, or other type of outbuilding, Part 3 provides you with inspiration in the form of already designed buildings.

Starting on page 184, you will find designs for structures you can build, including sheds, barns for a variety of purposes, garages, and other utility buildings, including four simple backyard sheds. The range of buildings should meet the needs and the capabilities of most homeowners. The designs are flexible, meaning you can adjust the dimensions to meet your needs.

On pages 256 to 287, you will find plans for popular utility building designs. They range from large barns suitable for raising livestock to yard and garden sheds and one-car garages. Many of the larger garages, feature added living spaces. If you like the designs, you can purchase a complete set of blueprints for construction.

Full-size barns, opposite, can be used for livestock care or for extra storage. Be sure to plan your barn to fit your needs.

Yard and garden sheds, above, come in handy for storing gardening equipment, toys, or swimming pool accessories.

Garages, right, not only protect our cars from the elements but also provide extra storage space.

PART I

DESIGN

PLANNING

Begin planning your barn, shed, or other outbuilding by deciding how you will use the building. Don't forget to allow for expanded use in the future. Before purchasing plans or creating your own design, check with the local building department about codes and restrictions governing the project. It is also a good idea to have a building site and orientation picked out before settling on a final design. This chapter covers the basics of prebuilding planning, including understanding building codes, evaluating the site, developing a design, and reading and interpreting construction drawings.

BUILDING PERMITS & CODES

Getting Permits

Most towns, cities, and counties require permits for buildings over a certain size or for any structure with a permanent foundation. In some cases, plans to build a small garden shed do not require a permit, but always check with the local building inspector early in the planning process to be safe. To find the phone number, look under your town's name in the phone book, and search for either "permits," "building inspector," or "inspector." Then call and describe the type of structure you plan to build and the size and basic characteristics of your lot. Ask whether you are required to submit a building plan, how long before beginning you must submit it, how long the review process takes, and whether you may reapply on appeal.

Also ask what a complete permit package contains. Some municipalities want just a site plan and two elevations (side views); others may want floor plans and detailed building specifications as well. If zoning is particularly restrictive in your town, they may even want to know the type of roof you plan to use and the color of the barn. Also, your permit application may require the opinions of a soil specialist or an engineer. You can get all this information by phone and then start to assemble your permit package using the pieces outlined in the sections below, including a site plan, floor plans, elevations, sections, and specifications, which combined are sometimes simply called drawings or construction drawings.

Restrictions

Many municipalities have restrictions that limit where you can build a new structure. A setback is the minimum distance between a building and the property line. An easement is the legal right for another property owner (or often a utility company) to cross or have limited use of another's property. Height and lot coverage restrictions limit how high you can build and what percentage of your lot can be covered by structures (including your house).

If local zoning permits you to maintain livestock, you will probably be restricted as to how close to your property lines you can locate a livestock structure. Always check with the local building department. You may find that your particular zoning does not allow livestock at all or restricts their numbers.

Codes

No matter how lenient the permit requirement may appear, it cannot exempt you from building your structure to conform with area building codes. These codes are the minimum building specifications required by law and are enforced by your local building inspector.

Codes ensure that standard building practices are used to make your building structurally sound and safe. To find out more about building codes, you can consult the many code handbooks available, even though every effort has been made in this book to represent common building practices that pass code inspections. That said, note that codes vary even regionally. The local building inspector is the expert in this regard, so ask about the code requirements.

TYPICAL CODE AND ZONING RESTRICTIONS

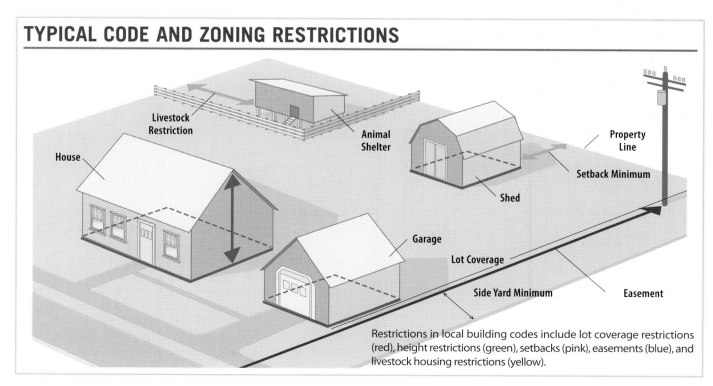

Restrictions in local building codes include lot coverage restrictions (red), height restrictions (green), setbacks (pink), easements (blue), and livestock housing restrictions (yellow).

TYPICAL GARAGE DIMENSIONS

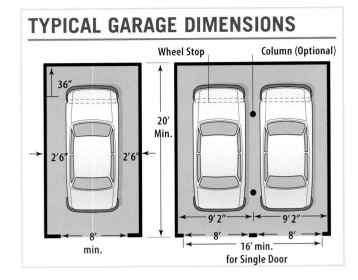

TYPICAL POTTING SHED

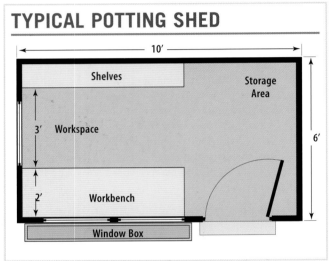

TYPICAL EQUIPMENT SHED

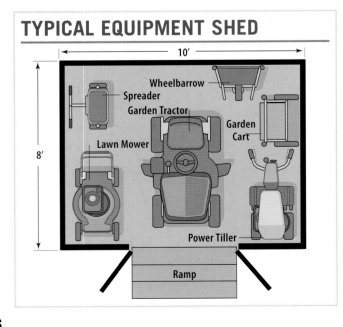

DESIGN GUIDE

Take your time when deciding on the layout, size, and overall design of your barn or shed. A great deal of effort goes into constructing a building—not just physical work but permits and financing as well. It is often worth the relatively minor effort and expense to expand a barn beyond what you expect to use today, just on the possibility that you'll need the space later. Ten years from now, for example, you may need an extra-large door for larger garden equipment.

If you already have a shed and need more space, it's not that expensive to build a second small shed or buy a prebuilt metal one. But if you're going to the trouble of building a large primary garden shed from scratch, you should think about the details you might want to add, such as wide, barn-style double doors and a sturdy ramp. If the shed will double as a workspace, you may want to add one or two windows, lights, and electrical outlets—or even a utility sink.

Designing for the Building's Purpose

The best thing to do when designing your structure is to list all possible uses you and your family can anticipate. Then sit down with this list and some graph paper, and figure out your space requirements.

For a storage shed, measure the equipment that you will need to store, and add at least a 12-inch buffer zone around the equipment so that you have room to walk around. If you want one room of an outbuilding to be a ceramics shop, for example, measure the potter's wheel, determine how much space you'll need to use it comfortably and safely, and be liberal when deciding on storage space.

For any kind of shop, whether you'll be working on cars or building furniture, you should mentally walk yourself through various projects to make sure you've allowed enough working space. For instance, in a woodworking shop where you'll need to rip a 4 x 8-foot sheet of plywood, you'll need at least 8 feet of clearance space in front of and behind the table saw.

Wiring & Plumbing

Also keep in mind your potential needs for electricity and water. If your eventual plan is to use part of a barn for living space or for keeping livestock, it makes sense to rough in some of the plumbing and heating—especially if it will be installed within a slab—so that the disruption is minor when you convert the barn to a heated structure. Adding wiring after you've finished the building may not be as disruptive as adding plumbing and heating, but if your building will have interior walls, you'll want to rough in the wiring before the walls are installed.

If you will be finishing furniture in your new shop, you will want to plan on an adequate ventilation system. And don't forget about a built-in vacuum system for removing dust from sanding and finishing. And if you will be spending a lot of time in your new outbuilding, you may want to include wiring for a sound system and perhaps even some sort of internet access.

Plan for the way the building will be used. Here, clear glazing over part of the roof framing turns this potting shed into a greenhouse/potting shed. Note how runoff from the roof will flow into the flower box that runs along the eave of the building.

Accommodating Expansion

Be sure to position entryways carefully, and keep in mind that although second-floor access may not be an issue today, it may be necessary in coming years. Think about how to design your structure to accommodate expansion. You may find it worth building an oversize header into one wall so that you can add a wing onto this side of the barn later and allow for a wide entryway. The same is true for window and door headers. It is messy work to install window and door headers after a building is built. But it is a cinch to install a header in the initial framing that could serve an additional window or door later. Just be sure to note these hidden elements in your plans for future reference.

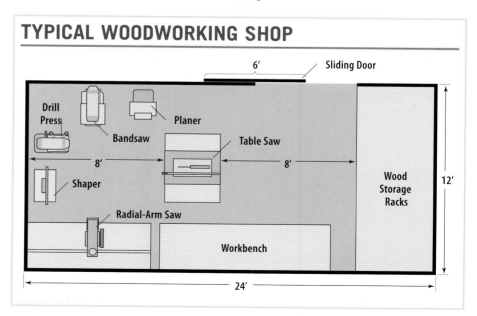

TYPICAL WOODWORKING SHOP

6′ — Sliding Door

Drill Press

Bandsaw

Planer

Table Saw

8′

Shaper

8′

Radial-Arm Saw

Wood Storage Racks

12′

Workbench

24′

In addition to housing animals, barns and other outbuildings can enhance the landscape. This eye-catching structure also provides valuable vertical space for climbing plants.

SMART TIP

FEED STORAGE

Controlling rodents at the feed storage area is crucial. This can be as simple as storing food in a sealed garbage can. But if you use feed bins, it's going to take some planning to line them properly to keep out rodents.

If your barn has a dirt floor, you should pour a minimum 4-inch-thick concrete floor slab in a storage room to help control pests. Purchase bags of premixed concrete, and mix it on-site using a rented mixer or (for very small rooms) hand tools and a wheelbarrow.

TYPICAL HORSE BARN

12' x 12' Stall	12' x 12' Stall
12' x 10' Stall	Tack Room (12' x 24')
Feed Room (12' x 8')	6' Aisle

30' × 30'

Horse barns have a central aisle, which makes it easier to clean the stalls. There should be sufficient stall space for the type of horse, and a large tack room for saddles and other equipment.

Guidelines for Animals

Animals have specific minimum space requirements, which are given in the table on the opposite page. When building a barn for animals, you'll also need to consider storage space for feed, as well as providing sufficient water and perhaps electricity. Don't forget manure: if you have animals in stalls much of the time, you will want enough space near the stalls to drive in some type of tractor.

When you have animals in a barn, you also need to provide sufficient ventilation so that your barn is free of noticeable levels of ammonia and methane fumes. For a barn that doesn't vent well naturally, you may have to install a fan that provides for a minimum of four air changes per hour in winter and up to 40 air changes per hour in summer to keep the air clean, depending on how many animals you have.

Horses. In most climates, horses can be kept outside year-round, as long as they are provided with a three-sided shelter from storms. If you want to stall your horses, the barn should be designed to be warm in winter, cool in summer, and easy to muck out. A wide aisle between two rows of stalls works well. A dirt floor is the cheapest option, but it must be well-drained and kept covered in sawdust or straw. If your barn site is low or has drainage problems, excavate from 8 to 12 inches and then fill the hole with crushed rock. Cover this with a layer of tamped clay.

Cattle. For calves, milk cows, and beef cattle (cows, steers, or bulls), a three-sided open-front barn with access to the outside and individual feeding stalls is a minimum requirement. In most climates, cattle don't need to be kept warm in winter, but (like horses) they do require a windbreak and protection from rain and

Animals require not only sufficient space inside a barn, but also enough area and properly fenced pasture outside to provide them with grass and room to exercise.

snow. An indoor pen for cows and their calves can have a dirt floor. Keep in mind when site planning that full-grown dairy cows or beef cattle may each need about 3 acres of forage pasture.

Pigs. For pigs, access to outside pastures is essential, along with an insulated, ventilated hutch for resting. In summer, pigs will need at least a roofed area to protect them from the sun. In cold winters, they'll need an enclosure to shield them from cold winds.

Sheep & Goats. Sheep and goats generally don't need any housing at all, unless they will be birthing during the winter. A 6 x 6-foot pen inside a larger barn generally is more than enough space for a doe or ewe and her offspring. A free space in the barn for shearing sheep will come in handy; if you plan on milking goats, allow an area for a milking station.

Poultry. Chickens, turkeys, and other domestic fowl require a closed-in building of their own, or a pen within a closed barn to protect them from wind, cold, and precipitation. The living area density for chickens should be no greater than 2 square feet per bird. Chicks need warmth and feeding space big enough so that half of them can eat at any one time. Turkeys require at least 3 square feet of housing per hen and 5 square feet per tom.

Because requirements vary for animals region to region (and even among breeds), always consult the local Cooperative Extension Service and code authorities on your plans.

SPACE REQUIREMENTS

REQUIREMENTS FOR ANIMALS

Horses	Stall Size (feet)	
Mare/gelding	10 x 10	
Brood mare	12 x 12	
Stallion	14 x 14	
Pony	9 x 9	

Cattle	Pen Size	Stall Size (feet)
Cow	50 sq. ft./cow	9 x 9 minimum
Cow and calf	75 sq. ft.	10 x 10
Steer	75 sq. ft.	10 x 10

Swine	Pen Area	Outdoor Area
Sow	15 sq. ft.	35 sq. ft.
Sow and litter	30 sq. ft.	80 sq. ft.

Goats	Pen Size	
Does	25 sq. ft./doe	
Buck	8 x 8 stall plus 100-sq.-ft. pen	
Kids	5 sq. ft./kid	

Poultry	Floor Space	
Chickens: Layer	2–3 sq. ft.	
Broiler	1 sq. ft.	
Roaster	2–3 sq. ft.	
Chicks	1 sq. ft./chick before 10 weeks	
Turkeys	3–4 sq. ft.	
Ducks	3 sq. ft. (6 sq. ft. for confined breeders)	
Geese	2 sq. ft. (5 sq. ft. for confined breeders)	

Rabbits	Pen Size	
	1 sq. ft. x 18 in. high per rabbit	

REQUIREMENTS FOR FEED/BEDDING STORAGE

Item	Storage Space Needed
Hay	
Two-wire, 14 x 18 x 36-in. bales	5.25 cu. ft./bale (100 bales = 525 cu. ft.)
Three-wire, 17 x 24 x 40-in. bales	9.44 cu. ft./bale (100 bales = 944 cu. ft.)
Grass hay (loose), 1 ton	450–600 cu. ft.
Alfalfa (loose), 1 ton	450–500 cu. ft.
Straw (loose), 1 ton	650–1000 cu. ft.
Feed	
Shelled corn, 100 lbs.	2.2 cu. ft.
Ear corn, 100 lbs.	3.6 cu. ft.
Oats, 100 lbs.	3.9 cu. ft.
Barley, 100 lbs.	2.6 cu. ft.
Soybeans, 100 lbs.	2.1 cu. ft.

This information is adapted from the MidWest Plan Service's Structures and Environment Handbook.

Construction drawings not only provide the local building department with information about your project, they also help you keep everything organized during the planning and building phases.

CONSTRUCTION DRAWINGS

Drawings are simply a set of plans or blueprints that you'll follow when building your project. Basic barn and shed plans are readily available in home centers, lumberyards, bookstores, and the like. If you don't find a barn plan that fits your needs, consider creating a customized version of one of the designs in the back of this book. If you try your hand at drawing plans yourself, be sure to hire an engineer or architect to review them for structural integrity.

Blueprints are drawn to scale; typically, a ¼-inch space on a blueprint represents a 1 foot space in the structure. Though the ¼-inch scale is common, some blueprints use a ³⁄₃₂-inch or ½-inch scale. Check the requirements of the local building department including the type and number of drawings you must submit.

Order Plans to Build Your Own Barn, Shed, or Outbuilding
To view designs and order plans for a variety of barns, sheds, and other types of outbuildings, turn to page 184.

Many Plans, One Building

If designers and architects were to put all the features of a building onto one sheet of the blueprint, it would be difficult to read and too complicated to follow. So at the design stage, an architect or engineer breaks the building down into different plans: a site plan, floor plan, elevation, wall sections, and the like

COMMON CONSTRUCTION DRAWINGS

SITE PLAN

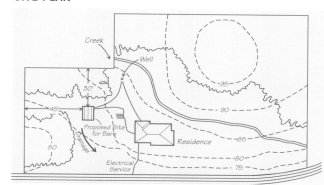

Site plans show from a bird's-eye view what your lot will look like with the new structure and any new roads or landscaping. Site plans need to show your property lines and how far the barn will be from each line. They will typically also show orientations to north, easements and right of ways, and existing structures.

FLOOR PLAN

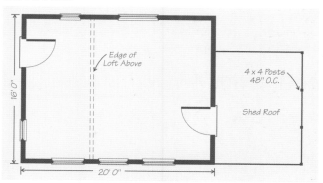

Floor plans give the location of exterior and interior walls and the location of windows and doors. If they're included in your project, the floor plans will also include location and types of major appliances, plumbing fixtures, and wiring, as well as exterior features such as stairs or a porch.

ELEVATION

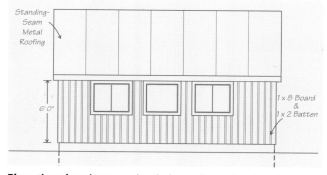

Elevation drawings are detailed one-dimensional renderings of the sides of a building. If two sides are identical (for example, the east and west walls), one drawing will suffice. Like floor plans, these can be a great aid when maintaining design and construction consistency during the building process.

SECTION

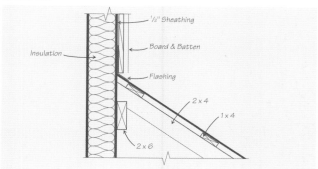

Sections are cutaway views of a wall, roof, or foundation that show what is contained within the structure. Sections can be helpful to show structures that are difficult to read on other building plans. Some inspectors may demand wall sections to see what will be within your finished walls.

UNDERSTANDING BLUEPRINTS

Blueprints may look confusing at first glance, but if you know the basics of how to read them, they eventually will become clear. First, learn how to read the lines, because it is with various types of lines that a blueprint represents a structure's component parts. Then turn your attention to the symbols commonly used so you can have a complete understanding of what is shown. Bear in mind that some architects and engineers litter blueprints with construction notes.

Blueprint Lines

A solid line on a blueprint indicates an object's visible outline. You would see a solid line along both edges of a concrete wall where it meets the floor because those edges would be visible. A broken line indicates a hidden object. When a basement slab hides the footing below, a broken line can indicate the shape of that structure.

Aspects of a building, such as a window or door, often have to be located precisely in a wall or floor. This positioning is often handled with a centerline to establish the center point of an area. A centerline is indicated by a C and a broken line drawn perpendicular to the wall or window frame.

A section line indicates where an aspect of the building is shown in cross section. It indicates the point at which the structure is sliced and the section view is shown. A break line indicates a shortened view of an aspect of the building that has a uniform and predictable shape. A leader line simply points from a specific measurement or note on the side about a detail or other aspect of the building to that part of the building.

Blueprints also give dimensions, or distances between various points of a building. Lines play a role here, too. If the distance between two walls is 10 feet, the dimension 10'-0" interrupts a solid line with arrows pointing outward on both ends. Sometimes a dimension line has dots or slanted lines instead of arrows at its ends. An extension line establishes a reference away from the building lines where dimensions are noted.

Utility Symbols. To maintain consistency in the construction industry and avoid confusion, blueprint floor plans use standard symbols to show the positions of heating and plumbing components (such as radiators, thermostats, and water heaters) as well as parts of the electrical system (such as outlets, switches, utility panels, and smoke detectors).

BLUEPRINTS

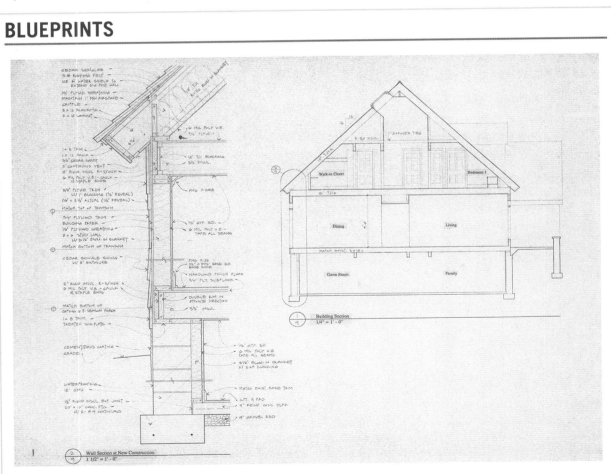

Twin peaks, matching doors, and a small side porch are included in the whimsical design of this small outbuilding, left. Many such buildings mimic design features found on the main house.

This three-story barn is unusual in that it has a concrete-block first floor topped with conventionally framed second and third floors. The block will keep the interior cool in summer.

UTILITY SYMBOLS

To maintain consistency in the construction industry and avoid confusion, blueprint floor plans use standard symbols to show the positions of heating and plumbing components (such as radiators, thermostats, and water heaters) as well as parts of the electrical system (such as outlets, switches, utility panels, and smoke detectors).

UTILITY SYMBOLS

Blueprints include special symbols to represent features of utility and mechanical systems in the building.

Soil Line	Reducer
Cold Water	Stop Cock
Hot Water	Return/Exhaust duct
Gas Line	Supply duct
Vent Line	Tank-type W.C.
Sprinkler Main	Water Closet
Drain Line	Lavatory
Fuel Oil Line	Tub
Check Valve	Corner Tub
Cleanout	Shower
Hose Bibb	Urinal
Floor Drain	Fuel Tank
90° Elbow	Shower Head
45° Elbow	Expansion Valve
Tee Connection	Scale Trap
Cross Connection	Compressor
Wiring in Wall	Blanked Outlet
Wiring in Floor	Junction Box
Exposed Wiring	Single-Pole Switch
Conduit	Three-Pole Switch
Weather Head	Lock Switch
GFCI Outlet	Pilot Light Switch
Main Panel	Switch and Duplex receptacle
Duplex Receptacle	Ceiling Fan
Triplex Receptacle	Clock Receptacle
Duplex Split	Telephone
Special Outlet	Signal Button
Range Outlet	Buzzer
Ceiling Light	Bell
Wall Bracket Light	Smoke Detector
Fluorescent	Intercom Station
Pull-Chain	Sound System

WALL SYMBOLS

Blueprints also sometimes include graphic patterns to indicate materials. When a structure is drawn on a blueprint, the walls are represented as a line. But that line can be a brick wall, a wood wall, or even stucco over a wood frame.

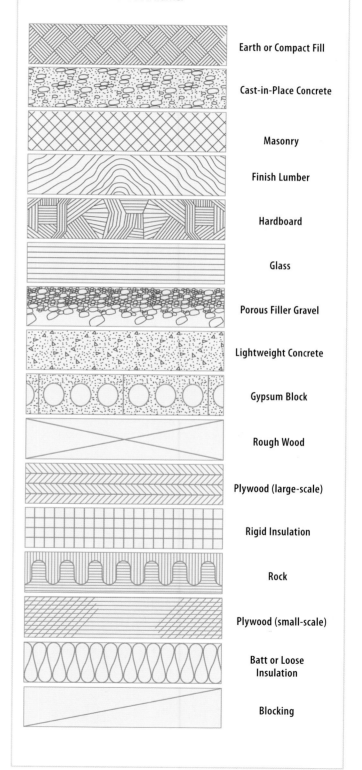

- Earth or Compact Fill
- Cast-in-Place Concrete
- Masonry
- Finish Lumber
- Hardboard
- Glass
- Porous Filler Gravel
- Lightweight Concrete
- Gypsum Block
- Rough Wood
- Plywood (large-scale)
- Rigid Insulation
- Rock
- Plywood (small-scale)
- Batt or Loose Insulation
- Blocking

EVALUATING THE SITE

There are four main things to consider about a potential site for your barn or outbuilding: access to both roads and utilities, soil type, drainage, and topography. If a number of places on your property satisfy these criteria, you might also consider other factors, such as solar orientation, weather protection, and the direction of prevailing winds.

Access to Roads

Good roads are expensive to engineer and build—even thousands of dollars per mile if you have to blast bedrock. They involve excavation, design for proper drainage, and careful selection of materials. You cannot just dump loads of gravel onto grass or bare earth and expect it to serve as a sound road surface for very long.

Also, once a road is in place, it has to be maintained. Gravel needs to be dressed every other year or so because the finer pieces sift down into the larger rocks. Blacktop cracks need to be sealed to prevent frost heaving that can tear apart all your costly work.

If you can position your barn so that it doesn't need a new road built to it, all the better. If you want to build your barn away from existing roads and your region endures winter weather (and a muddy spring), you will likely struggle with access over rutty roads and mud unless you construct a solid road bed. You will have to decide whether that's a price you're willing to pay to put off spending what it takes to build a good road.

Access to Utilities

You should always consult a licensed electrician in the planning stages. Depending on your circumstances, you may also need to contact the power company. Local utilities often regulate the maximum distance between a meter and a breaker panel, so check requirements. You should also check to determine whether you can run an outdoor circuit to your barn directly from your house's main service panel or whether you need to have a separate subpanel installed in the barn.

Whether or not your local government requires it, all work should conform to the requirements of the National Electrical Code (available in local libraries). If you will be keeping livestock, bringing water to your barn is an absolute necessity. You're probably not going to want the expense of a new water main and septic system just for your barn; you'll want to hook it into your house's system, if possible. In regions with cold winters, water-supply pipes need to be buried 4 feet or more in the ground; the closer you are to your well and septic system, or to the municipal water and sewage lines, the less time-consuming (and costly) this digging will be. Remember that some areas impose very strict standards for septic systems, and require perc tests, special permits, and inspections.

Soil

If you have a garden, you may already have an idea of what type of soil you have on your property—whether it's mostly sand, clay, silt, or loam. Before building a large structure, however, obtain a copy of a local soil survey map, which is available from the Cooperative Extension Service, to find out exactly what type of soil on which you'll be building. (A sample of what these maps look like is shown below.) The soil types are drawn onto aerial photographs with a key that explains the qualities of each soil type, including engineering properties and how suitable it is for different types of construction methods.

Soils are rated for their load-bearing capacity—that is, how much weight per square foot they can support without having

County soil maps are available from your Cooperative Extension Service office. They include aerial photos of the county with an overlay of coded soil types.

ACCESS ROAD CONSTRUCTION

Topsoil
Drainage Ditch
Compacted or Undisturbed Subsoil
Fine Gravel (or Asphalt) Finish
Slope
Compact Coarse Gravel

LOAD-BEARING VALUES OF SOILS

Class of Material	Load-bearing pressure (lbs. per sq. ft.)
Crystalline bedrock	12,000
Sedimentary rock	6,000
Sandy gravel or gravel	5,000
Sand, silt sand, clayey sand, silty gravel, and clayey gravel	3,000
Clay, sandy clay, silty clay, and clayey silt	2,000

Details make the difference when it comes to building design. The curved-top double garage doors aren't the only components that stand out on this detached garage—note the panel door in the gable and the leaded-glass window.

DRAINAGE

SOIL MUST DRAIN THOROUGHLY, especially in areas where the weather reaches freezing temperatures. Otherwise, moisture retained in the soil will freeze and cause frost heaving. Frozen soil can increase in volume as much as 25 percent, which presses the soil (and your barn's foundation) upward. In cold climates, prevent damage from heaving by installing your footings below the average frost depth, which is available from your local building department.

It's also important to have good drainage around your structure for water that runs off the roof and groundwater that may run downhill and be blocked from its normal path by your structure. The soil around your structure should slope away from the foundation, generally at ¼ inch or more per foot for at least 6 feet. If needed, a swale, or shallow depression, can be used to direct surface water. A perimeter drain made of perforated pipe can be used to direct groundwater away from your building into a drainage ditch or collection pond.

A typical perimeter drain has several inches of gravel in the bottom, a perforated drain pipe to carry away water, and more gravel topped with filter fabric.

To keep perforated drain pipes from clogging, cover the gravel trench with filter fabric, or slip on a filter-fabric sleeve that lets water through but keeps out dirt.

to be modified with soil stabilizers such as gravel, stepped landscaping, or retaining walls.

Bedrock, the most stable building surface, has the greatest load-bearing pressure rating. Sedimentary stone, such as sandstone, and gravel support slightly less weight; sand, silt, and clay soil support much less. Depending on your soil type, you can increase the width of the foundation footings to spread the load or even modify the soil itself by bringing in fill from elsewhere—an expensive option.

If you have any doubts about the bearing capacity of your soil, consult a soil engineer and the Cooperative Extension Service. Building on soil that can't support your structure will cause it to settle, crack the foundation, and rack the walls.

Topography

The topography of your site is the three-dimensional shape of your lot including major physical characteristics, such as standing water, large rocks, and trees. You can alter the topography of your lot, but it's expensive. Generally, it's better to adjust your barn to the topography.

A sloped site presents challenges when designing your foundation slabs. For example, you must excavate a flat pad, which could mean building a retaining wall. For walls, you can excavate the slope or use a stepped foundation. However, a sloped site isn't always a bad thing. If the lot slopes to the south, for instance, you

will have a site that's warmer than surrounding flat areas because ground sloping 10 degrees to the south receives the same amount of solar radiation as level ground 700 miles to the south. Plus, mildly sloped sites are good for drainage, so if you prepare your barn's perimeter drains and swales properly, you will have a well-drained site and a dry barn.

LEVELING A SLOPE

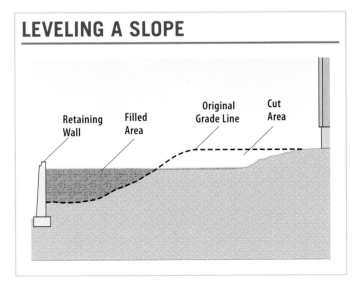

Retaining Wall

Filled Area

Original Grade Line

Cut Area

Sun & Wind

In the Northern Hemisphere, the climate is slightly warmer on south-facing slopes and slightly colder on north-facing ones. To reap gains from passive solar heating, buildings should have the longest dimensions running approximately east and west with most windows on the south side and few on the north. In that way, the winter sun can help heat the building. (See how the sun's path during different part of the year in "Winter Solar Path," right.) In hot climates, you'll want to do just the opposite to prevent solar gain. Of course, other elements in your environment may not permit you to orient your barn this way.

When you position your barn, note that positive pressure from wind will drive cold air into the barn, and negative pressure on the far side will suck warm air out of it. As you orient your barn for sun and wind, keep in mind that, for the winter, you want to expose the wall with the most glazing to the south to collect solar heat while exposing the fewest openings to the ends of the barn that are perpendicular to the prevailing wind.

As for trees, there are different scenarios for dealing with either year-long prevailing winds that come from one direction or prevailing winter winds that shift from north to south between the winter and summer seasons.

The arrangement of trees is important, but so is the type of tree you plant. Deciduous trees bear leaves in the summer but lose them during the cold winter months. These trees are excellent for the south side of a barn because their leaves will shield the roof from the harsh summer sunlight and heat and—when the leaves drop—admit sunlight and heat in the winter. Carefully placed after close observation of prevailing winds, deciduous and coniferous trees can be used to direct cooling breezes toward your structure in the summer and block cold winds in the winter.

WINTER SOLAR PATH

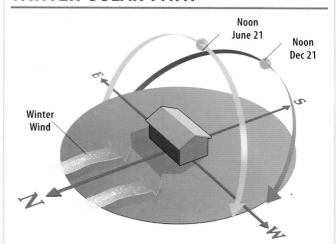

In northern climates, larger buildings that will house livestock or people should be built facing toward the sun and away from prevailing winds to take advantage of solar heating.

SMART TIP

THE RIGHT WINDOWS
Use windows to help control your building's environment. To keep heat in, choose windows with low U-factors. To let in the most light, look for windows with high visible transmittance ratings—the closer to 1 the better.

WIND DIRECTION

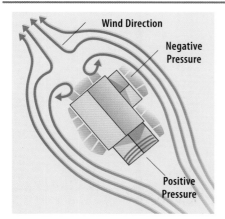

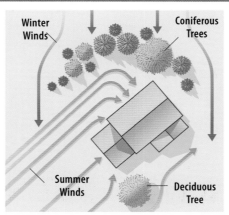

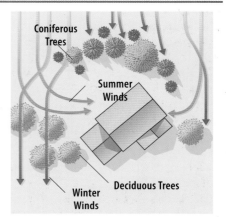

The direction of the wind and the pressures it creates affect how you should orient your building. The shortest side with the fewest windows should face into the prevailing wind.

If seasonal winds blow from opposite directions, plant any type of tree where it will help channel summer breezes, but only put evergreens where they will deflect winter winds.

If winter and summer winds blow from the same direction, plant tree types that will direct cooling summer breezes toward the building but direct winter winds away from the building.

POWER TO THE SITE

You can often bring power to saws and drills by running a power cord from a nearby house. Just be sure the cord is a heavy enough gauge to support the amp rating on your tool. An undersize cord can deprive a tool of the needed power and ruin the tool. This is because power encounters resistance in the cord and drops off over longer distances. You decrease this resistance by using heavier gauge wire. Generally use 10- or 12- gauge cords. They are not as flexible and light, but they will protect your tools in the long run. (For more information, see "Recommended Extension-Cord Wire Gauges," opposite bottom.)

If you can't get power nearby, you have two choices: make power with a generator, or install a temporary power pole. This setup includes a conduit mast, a meter base and meter, a turn-off switch, GFCI breakers, some outlets, and a rod hammered into the ground to act as a ground. Some utility companies will set up these poles for you for an installation fee and monthly power consumption charge. They will often have a minimum charge. An electrician can make one for you, but it will still have to be inspected by the utility company before the power is turned on. The building inspector may also want to take a look before it's approved for use.

If you do the work yourself, be sure to check specs with the local utility because there are often strict requirements about weatherproofing, pole height and depth in the ground, minimum distances from the service to the center of the street, and pole placement on the site. After you have the pole approved and power is flowing, you'll have to distribute it throughout the site through GFCI-protected cords and weatherproof outlet boxes.

There are a number of reasons to run electricity to your outbuilding. The most obvious is to provide light and power to the building itself, but outbuildings can also help you light remote areas of your property. Note the security light on the building above.

TEMPORARY SERVICE PANEL

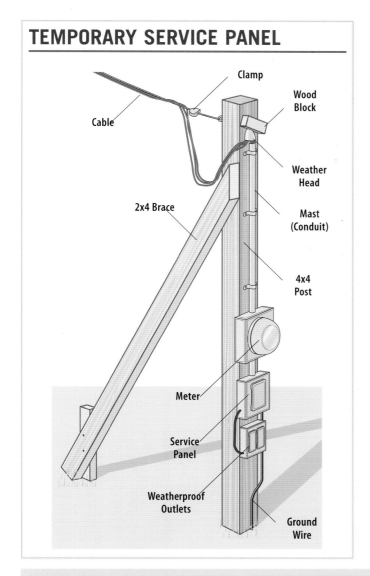

- Clamp
- Cable
- Wood Block
- Weather Head
- Mast (Conduit)
- 2x4 Brace
- 4x4 Post
- Meter
- Service Panel
- Weatherproof Outlets
- Ground Wire

A portable generator can supply power on a remote site. Fill it with oil and gasoline (top); start it; and plug in your cords (bottom). Buy or rent a model with enough power to run your equipment.

RECOMMENDED EXTENSION-CORD WIRE GAUGES

| For 110V: | | 25 ft. | 50 ft. | 100 ft. | 150 ft. | 200 ft. | 250 ft. | 300 ft. | 400 ft. | 500 ft. |
For 220V:		50 ft.	100 ft.	200 ft.	300 ft.	400 ft.	500 ft.	600 ft.	800 ft.	1000 ft.
Amp	0–2	18	18	18	16	16	14	14	12	12
Rating	2–3	18	18	16	14	14	12	12	10	10
of	3–4	18	18	16	14	12	12	10	10	8
Power	4–5	18	18	14	12	12	10	10	8	8
Tool	5–6	18	16	14	12	10	10	8	8	6
	6–8	18	16	12	10	10	8	6	6	6
	8–10	18	14	12	10	8	8	6	6	4
	10–12	16	14	10	8	8	6	6	4	4
	12–14	16	12	10	8	6	6	6	4	2
	14–16	16	12	10	8	6	6	4	4	2
	16–18	14	12	8	8	6	4	4	2	2
	18–20	14	12	8	6	6	4	4	2	2

A lived-in look adds to the charm of this small outbuilding tucked into the corner of the yard, left. Note the full-size door on the building's side.

Working barns, below, usually rely on natural ventilation such as the cupola on the roof and the large louvered vents on the sides of the building.

A garden shed, above, is indispensable for storing tools and gardening supplies close to where the work takes place.

The detached garage, right, provides parking spaces and presents the opportunity for annexing additional living space on the second floor.

Even small outbuildings, below, increase the overall storage capacity of most homes.

TOOLS AND MATERIALS

To construct a durable building you will first need to select the correct tools and materials for the job. Good tools are essential for any building project, but you don't need to invest in top-of-the-line tools—good-quality midpriced tools will go a long way in helping you work efficiently and safely. This chapter discusses the basic tools you will need for this type of construction project, including tools for layout, cutting, attachment, and working safely. You will also learn how to select the right materials, including distinguishing from among the different types of lumber available.

TOOLS

Construction Levels

It is essential to build any structure plumb, level, and square. To do that, you will at least want to have a 4-foot spirit level for checking framing, and a line level and mason's string for checking long spans.

Spirit Levels. Spirit levels come in many lengths. A 4-foot model is best for working with framing. You can also extend its useful range by resting it on a long straight 2x4.

Digital Levels. Unlike spirit levels, digital levels beep when they are level or plumb. The tools never go out of whack because you can reset them electronically. Some electronic levels also work as inclinometers to give you the angle of rafters. That feature can be handy when you have to match roof pitches in separate, distant locations.

Water Level. A water level is basically colored water in a long clear tube with gradation marks on both ends. Because water seeks its own level no matter what the distance or terrain, you can use the tool for long-distance level checks. Once any air bubbles are removed, stretch the hose from one place to another (even up and down over rough terrain) and the water line at both ends will be level.

For grading sloped land and laying out level foundations, you'll need to use a transit, a builder's level, or a laser level. These tools allow you to sight a level line across large distances. These are expensive items, so you should rent them.

Spirit levels are indispensable tools for carpentry. A 4-ft. level is needed for many aspects of framing and finishing; smaller levels are good for doors and windows.

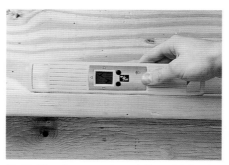

Digital levels are used much like spirit levels, but they have a digital readout. Most kinds will also emit a beep when they are held at level or plumb.

A water level is used for marking level points across long distances. They are especially useful for checking formwork before pouring a foundation.

SAFETY TOOLS

COMMON SENSE SHOULD TELL YOU not to do construction work without first having some basic safety equipment, such as eye and ear protection. Wear goggles or safety glasses that have aerated side guards whenever you work with power tools. The U.S. Occupational Safety and Health Administration (OSHA) recommends that hearing protection be worn when the noise level exceeds 85 decibels (dB) for an eight-hour workday. When you consider that a circular saw emits 110 dB, however, it is clear that even much shorter exposure to loud noises can contribute to hearing impairment. Both insert and muff-type ear protectors are available; whichever you choose, be sure it has a noise reduction rating (NRR) of a least 20 dB.

Wear a dust mask when creating sawdust, especially when cutting pressure-treated wood. Two basic kinds of respiratory protection are available: disposable dust masks and cartridge-type respirators. A dust

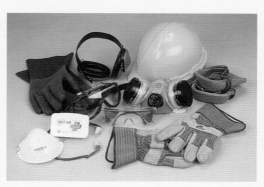

mask will allow you to avoid inhaling dust and fine particles. Respirators have a replaceable filter. Both are available for protection against nontoxic and toxic dust and mist. Whichever you buy, look for a stamp indicating that the National Institute for Occupational Safety and Health/Mine Safety and Health Administration (NIOSH/MSHA) has approved it for your specific job. When you can taste or smell the contaminant or when the mask starts to interfere with normal breathing, it's time for a replacement.

Work gloves are also advisable, at least when you're moving wood or doing other rough jobs. Similarly, heavy-duty work boots will protect your feet. Steel toes will prevent injuries to your toes from dropped boards or tools, and flexible steel soles will protect your feet from a puncture by a stray nail. Lastly, wear a hard hat when you're working in the basement or others are working above you.

Masonry Tools

Whether you're working with concrete, brick, or unit masonry, you'll need many of the same basic masonry tools. You can easily rent many expensive items, so check before you buy a tool that you may not use often.

You'll need trowels and floats for the placing and finishing of concrete, and a bull float (made of magnesium or steel) or a darby (made of wood) to finish the upper layer of curing concrete. With a finishing trowel, you can create a smooth surface once the concrete is leveled; then you'll use edging and jointing trowels on the surface of the smooth concrete. An edging trowel makes a rounded edge on a concrete slab, which is safer and more durable than a sharp edge. A groover has a ridge down the center of its blade to form grooves or control joints. Jointers are metal rods (round or square) attached to a handle that you use to create various mortar joints when working with brick and concrete block.

Driving Nails and Screws

Hammers. Pros often use a 20- to 24-ounce waffle-head, or serrated, straight-claw framing hammer. Wooden (hickory) handles tend to absorb vibration better than fiberglass handles, so some people think wooden handles lessen your chances of developing repetitive motion ailments like carpal tunnel syndrome. If you're not used to manual labor, a 24-ounce hammer may be too heavy for you, and you'll probably be better off with the 20- or 16-ounce size.

Nail Gun. A pneumatic, or air-driven, nail gun, which uses a magazine that holds up to 100 or more nails, can take much of the tedium out of repetitive nailing. But you pay a price: nail guns are expensive and heavy, and you need compressors and hoses to run them. Nail guns really don't pay for themselves—purchased or rented—unless you have a great amount of nailing to do all at one time.

Most guns handle 6d through 16d nails. You'll need a compressor, gasoline or electric, and at least 100 feet of air hose. If

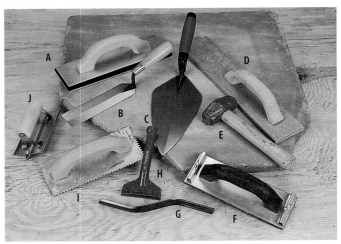

Masonry Tools. Rubber float (A), striking tool (B), mason's trowel (C), wood float (D), 5-lb. hammer (E), magnesium float (F), jointer (G), brickset (H), notched trowel (I), and groover (J).

A framing hammer has a straight claw and a heavy head. It is used to drive nails. Lighter hammers are best for siding and finishing work.

An air-powered nail gun has a clip of banded nails that feed into the gun and are fired with a trigger squeeze. While handy, it is not cost-effective for the occasional builder of small projects.

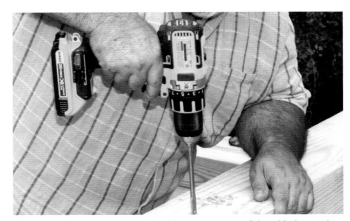

The batteries in today's drills/drivers are powerful and lightweight, and they hold a charge for a long time. As a result they have replaced corded drills for most jobs.

you have a choice, go with the quieter electric compressor. Also, make sure you set the compressor's in-line regulator to the pressure required for the tool you'll be using.

Power Drill. A corded or battery-powered drill is essential not only for driving wood screws but also for quickly and precisely drilling holes. If cost is an issue, buy a plug-in heavy-duty 3/8-inch drill with variable speeds. If you can afford the extra cost, you'll find a cordless drill even handier. Cordless drills come in an array of voltage ratings; the higher the voltage, the more powerful the drill. A 12-volt drill generally is powerful enough to fill all your needs.

Other Basic Tools

Drill Bits. The standard twist drill bit bores holes in wood, plastic, or metal. Spade bits quickly make large holes in wood, but not as cleanly as other bits. Masonry bits drill holes into brick and concrete. Hole saws make large, accurate holes up to several inches in diameter. Single-twist auger bits have a small cone-shaped

point at the tip to make them more accurate than traditional bits. Forstner bits cut holes with very little tear-out. An adjustable screw pilot bit will stop at a predetermined depth and cut a countersink.

Wrenches. Combination wrenches, adjustable wrenches, nut drivers, and socket wrenches have countless applications. You'll use pipe and spud wrenches when working with plumbing. For wiring, electrician's pliers, the multipurpose tool, and the cable ripper come in handy. Slip joint, diagonal-cutting, and needle-nose pliers have many practical uses.

Woodworking Tools. Use a tool belt when carrying nails and screws. Sanders, planes, and files help even out surfaces. Use measuring tapes to lay out the site and plan for cuts. Use knives and chisels to cut small amounts of material in places where a saw is not practical. You can use a pry bar as a lever. A screwdriver is often the only practical means of driving a screw.

Drill Bits. This basic collection includes a standard twist drill bit (A), spade bit (B), masonry bit (C), hole saw (D), single-twist auger bit (E), Forstner bit (F), and adjustable screw pilot bit (G).

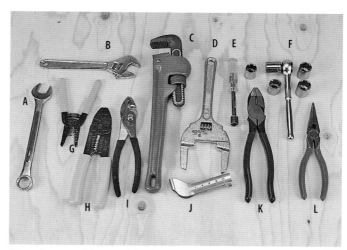

Wrenches: combination (A), adjustable (B), pipe (C), spud (D), nut driver (E), and socket (F). Wire stripper (G), wire cutter/stripper (H), slip-joint pliers (I), cable stripper (J), cutting pliers (K), and needle-nose pliers (L).

A **socket wrench kit** or a set of combination wrenches is necessary for driving lag screws as well as nuts onto bolts. If you're building a pole barn, buy extra-deep sockets.

Woodworking Tools: Tool belt (A), belt sander (B), plane (C), scrap-er (D), reel-type tape (E), screwdrivers (F), utility knife (G), measuring tape (H), sandpaper (I), wood chisels (J), wood files (K), pry bar (L).

SQUARES

FOR ACCURATE RAFTER LAYOUT, you'll need a framing square. It's etched for layout of plumb and seat cuts for common rafters or hip rafters. A rafter square, often referred to by the brand name Speed Square, is a heavy-duty aluminum right triangle that fits in your tool belt. It's great for striking cut lines and guiding your circular saw. A combination square and a sliding T-bevel are also used to mark cut lines on framing lumber.

FRAMING SQUARE. A framing square is an L-shaped tool made of steel or aluminum. It is indispensable when cutting rafters, marking cut lines on lumber, and making sure corners are square. It is etched with tables that will help you calculate rafter lengths.

COMBINATION SQUARE. A combination square is a ruler with a sliding bracket mounted to it at 90 degrees. The bracket has a second surface, which you can use to make 45-degree cut lines on lumber. Some squares have a pointed metal scribe to mark work for cutting. This tool is handy, but the rafter square will serve most of your needs.

SLIDING T-BEVEL. Often called a bevel square or bevel gauge, this tool is useful for some complicated framing problems. You can set a sliding T-bevel at any angle and use it to transfer the same angle from one place to another.

A framing square is a useful tool for checking stud layout, squaring up corners, and marking long cuts. For roof framing, a framing square with rafter tables is a useful addition to your toolkit.

A combination square has a sliding blade, ideal for making short measurements, checking right angles, and marking lumber cuts. Some combination squares have a spirit level embedded in the tool.

A sliding T-bevel has an adjustable pivot point between the blade and the handle. This enables you to mark angled cuts commonly needed on rafters and the framing for skylights.

PREVENTING DANGEROUS KICKBACK

THE WORKPIECE MUST BE FIRMLY SUPPORTED, typically on sawhorses or some other stable surface, before you cut it with a circular saw. The offcut must be able to fall freely away at the end of the cut. If you support a board on both sides of the cut, the kerf will fold in as the cut ends, causing the blade to bind, potentially resulting in kickback—a dangerous occurrence in which the saw jumps back at you. Kickback can also happen if you try to rush the cut. When ripping on a table saw, kickback can be caused by tension in the wood that causes the kerf to close around the blade.

You can buy anti-kickback blades, which have modified tooth designs, but you can best reduce kickback by not rushing a cut and by stabilizing your work. Never stand directly behind a circular saw, and don't remove the saw from the workpiece until the blade has stopped. Keep your hands as far as possible from the cut, and clearly sight your cut line to make sure it's free of obstructions such as nails or extension cords. Firmly place wood on a cutting surface; never cut wood held in your hand.

SAWS

FRAMING DOESN'T DEMAND THE PRECISE CUTS that finish carpentry does, but you still need high-quality saws with sharp blades. With power saws, a 7¼-inch circular saw is a practical choice. Look for one with good balance that is light enough for you to maneuver and easy to adjust for angle and depth. Make sure it has a comfortable handle. A table saw also adds tremendous capability because you can rip sheets of plywood and boards quickly and accurately.

HANDSAWS. Crosscut saws are versatile handsaws about 24 inches long, with seven or eight teeth per inch. You can also buy specialized trim saws and rip saws. Backsaws—shorter, stiffer, and broader than crosscut saws, with finer teeth—are good for detail and trimwork. Hacksaws are essential for cutting pipe, nails, and other materials too tough for a wood saw. Keyhole saws have a narrow-point blade handy for making small cutouts; stubbier versions with coarser teeth are called utility saws and are good for cutting outlet and other openings in drywall. Coping saws are used mainly to join curved-profile moldings.

CIRCULAR SAW. A circular saw is capable of quickly crosscutting, ripping, and beveling boards or sheets of plywood. The most popular saws are those that take a 7¼ inch blade. With this blade size you can cut to a maximum depth of about 2½ inches at 90 degrees. Some contractors use circular saws with larger blades for cutting posts in one pass, but a 7¼-inch circular saw is easier to control, and it allows you to cut anything as large as a 6x6 with a second pass. Smaller saws are also available, some of which are battery powered. These saws are often referred to as trim saws. Battery-driven models can be useful in situations when extension cords would get in the way.

Don't judge power saw performance by horsepower rating alone. Also look at the amperage that the motor draws. Low-cost saws may have 9- or 10-amp motors with drive shafts and arbors running on rollers or sleeve bearings. A contractor-grade saw generally is rated at 12 or 13 amps and is made with more-durable ball bearings. Plastic housings are no longer the mark of an inferior tool; however, a flimsy base plate made of stamped metal is. A thin base won't stay as flat as an extruded or cast base. To minimize any chance of electric shock, be sure that your saw is double insulated. Most saws have a safety switch that you must depress before the trigger will work.

POWER MITER SAW. For angle cuts, you'll want to use a power miter saw, also called a chop saw. This tool is simply a circular saw mounted on a pivot assembly, which enables you to make precise straight and angled crosscuts in boards. You can buy chop saws that handle 10- to 15-inch blades. A 12-inch saw is often the best value for the money. Use a 60-tooth combination-cut carbide blade for all-around work.

RECIPROCATING SAW. This saw comes in handy for cutting rough openings in sheathing, fixing framing errors, cutting nail-embedded wood, or cutting the last ½ inch that your circular saw can't get to when you cut to a perpendicular line. Buy plenty of wood- and metal-cutting blades, but don't confuse the two. Wood blades have larger teeth than the small-toothed metal-cutting blades.

You'll need a variety of handsaws for framing and finish work: crosscut saws are useful for making cuts where it's impractical to maneuver a circular saw.

A 7¼-in. midpriced circular saw is the best model for most do-it-yourselfers. Battery-powered models are available for sites located far from a source of electricity.

A power miter saw makes cross cuts at any angle with more precision than a circular saw. For trim work, it's quicker and easier to use than a hand miter saw. Used with a stop, it can speed up production if you have to make multiple cuts of the same length.

A reciprocating saw is a versatile tool that's very handy for demolition work. Blades are available that can cut through wood and nails. It can be fitted with a metal-cutting blade that can saw through old plumbing pipes. It's also handy for cutting openings for windows, doors, skylights, or roof vents.

LADDERS, SCAFFOLDS & FALL PROTECTION

Most accidents in the construction industry and on any construction project, including do-it-yourself projects are a result of falling. The risks increase as you move higher on a building. However, you can work safely by using the ladders, scaffolds, and fall-arrest devices on the market today and following some simple safety rules. When you use these systems properly, you can protect yourself and anyone else working on your project, and increase productivity.

FALL-ARREST SYSTEMS

ONE EFFICIENT WAY TO PROTECT AGAINST FALLS from a roof is a personal fall-arrest system. A full-body harness with a ring at the center of its back clips into one end of a lanyard, or tether. The other end of the lanyard clips into a rope-grab ascender, a one-way clamp that catches the rope if there is any downward pull, so you can go up but not down. You can release the ascender to descend. To use an ascender, clamp it onto a rope, and clip the rope into an anchor that's securely fastened into the ridgeboard or framing member.

LADDERS

THERE ARE THREE BASIC KINDS OF LADDERS: stepladders, fold-up (articulated) ladders, and extension ladders. Stepladders are stable on a level surface, but you should never use one on a slope. The hazard with a stepladder is that the higher you go, the more unstable the ladder is. If you find you're working with your feet on or near the top three steps, you should move to a scaffold work platform or extension ladder.

Fold-up ladders are great for working mid-distances between 4 and 12 feet off the ground. These ladders are handy because you can extend the ladder and lock it straight to act as a standard, one-section ladder, lock it in an A position to act as a stepladder, or fold it into an M shape or into an upside-down U shape as a mini-scaffold on which you can place certified scaffold planks.

Extension ladders are used mostly for high outdoor work. Depending on the performance rating you use, these ladders will support the weight of a worker plus material (shingles, lumber, one end of a beam). Extension ladders are available in a wide range of sizes, typically from 20 to 50 feet.

You'll find each kind of ladder in metal (usually aluminum) or fiberglass, and many stepladders and extension ladders made of wood. The type you'll choose depends on the work at hand and how much you want to spend.

RATINGS. Ladders are rated for the weight they can hold. You'll see a sticker on most ladders identifying their type. Type III ladders are light-duty and can carry 200 pounds per rung or step. Type II are medium-duty and can carry 225 pounds per rung or step. Type I ladders are heavy-duty industrial ladders and can hold 250 pounds per rung. Type IA ladders are extra heavy-duty and can hold 300 pounds per rung. Type I ladders are well worth the extra money for their greater safety margin.

SAFE USE. When you use a straight ladder, set it against a vertical surface at the proper angle. As a rule of thumb, the distance between the base of the ladder and the structure should be one-quarter the ladder's extension. If your ladder extends 16 feet, for example, it should be about 4 feet from the wall. Anything steeper increases the risk that the ladder will topple backward when someone is on it, especially near the top. Anything shallower risks that the ladder may kick out or slide. Bear in mind these two rules for safety: allow the top of the ladder to extend about 3 feet past your work area; and if you're working near electrical lines, use a fiberglass ladder.

Extension Ladder

Stepladder

Fold-Up Ladder

If you fall when wearing a personal fall-arrest system, you'll fall only as far as the slack of the lanyard and rope. A fall-arrest system costs around $350 for a starter kit, which includes all you'll need for most jobs.

As a practical matter, most novice do-it-yourselfers should work only on walkable roofs. These are roofs with a relatively low slope that you can negotiate safely without special fall-arrest systems.

SCAFFOLD SYSTEMS

PREFABRICATED SCAFFOLDS are aluminum- or steel-tube-framed structures that you assemble on site. You can make your own wooden scaffold, but prefabricated units are generally safer. Scaffolds provide an ideal working surface for such tasks as installing exterior sheathing or siding. Scaffolding is certainly good to have on site, but it's expensive to rent and prohibitive to buy. You may find other ways to work at heights—such as pump jacks in particular—that are more cost-effective for your project.

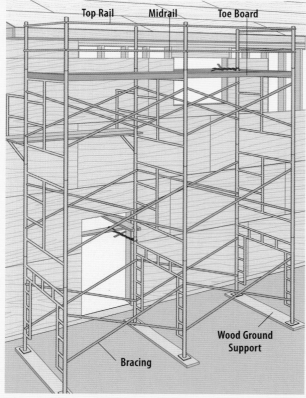

An OSHA-approved scaffold system includes a top rail, midrail, toe board (top), and wood supports beneath the baseplates (bottom).

PLATFORM JACKS

IT'S OFTEN MORE PRACTICAL to work from a platform rather than a ladder when you're framing. You can create a sturdy work platform using various kinds of brackets, called jacks, attached to a ladder, the roof, or vertical 4x4 posts.

ROOF JACKS. Roof jacks are nailed directly through sheathing into rafters, allowing them to sit on the roof surface. The arms of the roof jacks that support a plank are adjustable, so you can level scaffold planks for roofs of various pitches.

Roof Jack

LADDER JACKS. These metal brackets that hook onto extension ladders provide stable, level support for 2x10 scaffold planks or an aluminum platform. To use the jacks, you need two ladders, one for each end of the plank or work surface. There are two configurations for scaffold ladder jacks: inside-bracket and outside-bracket types. Inside ladder jacks suspend a plank or work platform beneath the ladders as they

Ladder Jack

rest against a structure. Outside ladder jacks support a plank on the front face of the ladders as they rest against a structure.

PUMP JACKS. Pump jacks are metal brackets that travel up and down on 4x4 posts. The vertical part of the L hugs the post and the horizontal part supports a plank or work surface. Other brackets, which you attach to structural members of the wall, hold the 4x4 uprights to the structure. To raise the work platform, you pump the L-shaped jacks with your foot. To lower the platform, you turn a crank.

OSHA rules require rails on the back side of a pump-jack platform (the side against which a worker leans back). You need a 42-inch-high top rail, a 21-inch midrail, and a 4-inch toe board.

The work platform can span a maximum of 10 feet. At their bases, the upright supports must bear on feet that keep them from sinking into the ground. If people are expected to be working below the pump-jack platform at any time, you must string plastic netting on the guard rails to keep things like dropped tools and materials from falling.

Pump Jack

LUMBER

Wood is one of the most important materials you'll buy for your project, so you should purchase the best quality you can afford.

Hardwood & Softwood

Wood is generally divided into two broad categories: hardwood and softwood. Common hardwoods include ash, birch, cherry, poplar, black walnut, maple, northern red oak, and white oak. Hardwoods come from slow-growing deciduous trees (trees that lose their leaves in winter); they are expensive and generally quite strong. Many hardwoods have beautiful grain patterns and are well suited to woodworking. But they are only used in the most expensive timber-frame construction.

Softwoods come from fast-growing, cone-bearing trees called conifers, or evergreens. Usually much less expensive than hardwoods and widely available at lumberyards, softwoods account for nearly all the lumber used in framing and construction. Though hardwoods are normally stronger because they're more dense, softwoods are certainly more than strong enough for utility framing.

Douglas fir, hemlock, eastern white pine, southern yellow pine, and spruce are all softwoods commonly used for framing. Douglas fir is used for most rough construction, especially along the Pacific Coast, where it is milled. In the South and East you're more likely to find southern pine. There are two other softwoods you might see, redwood and western red cedar, which aren't normally used for framing because of their expense. These species are excellent for exterior siding, trim, and decks because of their exceptional durability and natural resistance to decay.

Sawmills cut softwoods into standard dimensions and lengths. That's why the lumber is sometimes called dimension lumber. Unlike ordering hardwood, ordering softwood framing lumber generally doesn't require that you ask for a specific species of wood. You simply order by dimension and grade. The lumberyard has already made a softwood choice for you by buying whatever wood is available for your region. The lumber is often simply stamped SPF for spruce, pine, fir; it can be any one of these softwood species.

Sapwood & Heartwood

There are two kinds of wood in all trees: sapwood and heartwood. Sapwood, as its name implies, carries sap to the leaves. The heartwood is the dense center of the tree. Trees that grow quickly (softwoods) tend to have disproportionately more sapwood. In fact, young trees consist of almost all sapwood. This is important to know when you buy lumber because sapwood and heartwood function differently in buildings. Heartwood, for instance, is used in exposed conditions or for special structural members because it is stronger and more durable. Sapwood is better suited for use as planks, siding, wall studs, and most other building components. And unless it's treated, sapwood lumber is more susceptible to decay than heartwood lumber.

GRADES

BESIDES SAPWOOD AND HEARTWOOD DISTINCTIONS, many other wood features come into play, including moisture content, strength, number of knots, and appearance. A standardized system of grading rates wood for many of these qualities. The lower the grade, the poorer the quality.

Lumber grading for structural-grade lumber is complex, with categories, grades, and subgrades. For most framing, you'll find four lumber categories: select structural, No. 1, No. 2, and No. 3. The higher the number, the weaker the wood; the weaker the wood, the less distance you can span. A 2x8 hemlock-fir marked select-structural used as a joist and framed 16 inches on center might span 14 feet 2 inches, for instance, but a No. 3 grade only 11 feet. The wood gets weaker because there are more knots and less consistent grain as you move away from the select-structural grade. You also pay more for stronger wood. For structural framing the typical lumber grade is No. 2.

When evaluating 2x4s, you'll find that there are three other names for the No. 1, No. 2, and No. 3 categories. Construction grade corresponds to No. 1; Standard-Better to No. 2; and Utility to No. 3. (A final category, Economy, is for nonstructural use.) For wall framing, use No. 2 (Standard or Better) for load-bearing and most other walls. Many yards don't stock weaker No. 3 (Utility). Because it's hard to sort this all out, and using utility lumber yields only marginal savings, you can safely buy No. 2 lumber and use it for your entire project.

All lumber has a high moisture content when it is milled. So it is either air-dried or kiln-dried for construction use. The acceptable maximum moisture content for framing wood is 19 percent. Often the grade stamp for construction lumber will say "KD-19" (kiln-dried 19 percent).

LUMBER GRADES AND CUTS

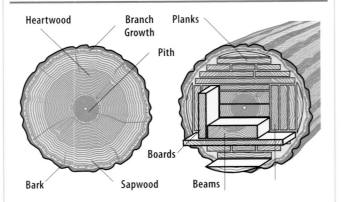

Two types of wood grow within all trees: sapwood and heartwood. Studs are typically sawed from the sapwood area, large-dimension and higher-grade boards and planks from the inner areas, and beams from the heartwood area.

Rough-Sawn Native Green Lumber

Available from some local sawmills, native green lumber's moisture content is usually high because it's sold unseasoned. Also, it's not cut as precisely as standard lumber. A 2x8 can be 2¼ x 8½ inches, for instance, or 2 x 7¼ inches. Additionally, native green lumber is not as structurally stable as kiln-dried or air-dried dimension lumber.

Pressure-Treated Lumber

Pressure-treated (PT) wood is lumber that's been soaked under pressure with an insecticide and a fungicide, which ward off pests and decay, respectively. It's intended for use anywhere the wood contacts the ground (decks and piers), experiences sustained moisture levels (sills, outdoor stairs), or is subject to insect infestation (any exposed part of your structure in termite areas). PT lumber is mostly southern yellow pine, although some other pines, firs, and hemlocks are used.

MILLED DIMENSIONS

NOMINAL SIZE VERSUS ACTUAL SIZE: When a 2x4 is first cut from the log, it's 2 inches thick and 4 inches wide. However, when it's planed to final size, it measures 1 ½ inches x 3 ½ inches. Lumber nominal and actual lengths, however, are the same. So a nominal 10-foot 2x10, is actually 10 feet long plus an inch or so, so you can square the ends. Lumberyards sell softwood and usually a limited selection of milled dimensioned hardwood species by the unit, so you might order twelve 2x6x10s. For a greater variety of hardwood species you'll need to visit a sawmill where you will find rough-sawn wood sold by the board foot. To calculate the board-foot price of a piece, take the nominal thickness, multiply it by the nominal width and the length, and divide by 12. A 10-foot 2x6 (usually written 2x6x10 in the industry) would be 10 board feet.

NOMINAL AND ACTUAL LUMBER SIZES

Nominal Size (in.)	Actual Size (in.)	Nominal Size (in.)	Actual Size (in.)
1x2	¾ x 1½	2x2	1½ x 1½
1x4	¾ x 3½	2x4	1½ x 3½
1x6	¾ x 5½	2x6	1½ x 5½
1x8	¾ x 7¼	2x8	1½ x 7¼
1x10	¾ x 9¼	2x10	1½ x 9¼
1x12	¾ x 11¼	2x12	1½ x 11¼
5/4x2	1 x 1½	4x4	3½ x 3½
5/4x4	1 x 3½	6x6	5½ x 5½

GRADE STAMPS

A TYPICAL GRADE STAMP identifies the mill, the grading service's name, the moisture content, the grade, and the species.

The mill identification number isn't really important. The same with the grading service. The species mark is mostly a curiosity, too. But look closely at the biggest word in the grading stamp. You should see a word like STAND, which stands for Standard, the grade you'll use for standard residential-grade light framing. Next, look at the moisture designation. Here's where you'll see KD for kiln-dried, S-DRY, MC, or S-GRN. These are the moisture content ratings mentioned in the text below.

But no matter how much you know, the lumberyard will have already made most framing lumber choices for you, at least in terms of species. You'll simply specify the grade. Check the grading stamp at the yard to make sure you've picked up the right kind of wood.

TYPICAL GRADE STAMP

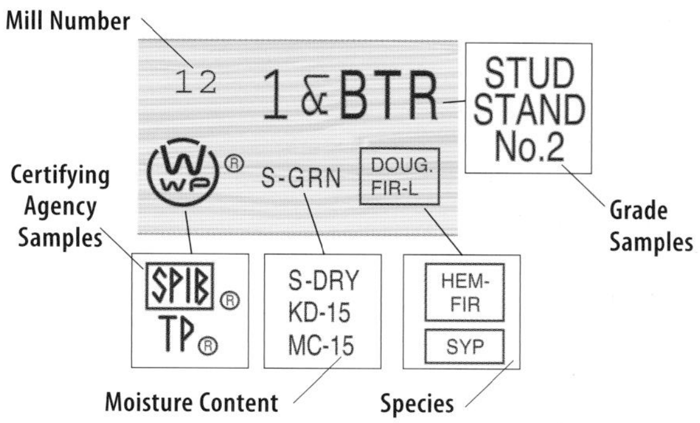
Mill Number
12
1&BTR
STUD
STAND
No.2
Certifying Agency Samples
S-GRN
DOUG. FIR-L
SPIB
TP
S-DRY
KD-15
MC-15
HEM-FIR
SYP
Grade Samples
Moisture Content
Species

Rough-sawn green lumber (at right) can be ordered from some lumberyards and sawmills. It is beefier (a 2x4 being much closer to 2 inches thick), rougher, more irregular, and less expensive than finished lumber (at left).

TYPES OF PRESSURE-TREATED LUMBER. In the past, the most common kind of PT wood was treated with chromated copper arsenate (CCA), a compound that chemically bonds with the wood. CCA-treated lumber has a green tint from the oxidation of the copper.

CCA (and to some extent, all chemical treatments) is controversial: some studies have shown that the arsenic in it dissolves back into the environment under certain circumstances. Manufacturers of these products have voluntarily withdrawn all CCA-treated lumber from the residential market. To fill the void, manufacturers have replaced CCA products with those treated with nonarsenic copper compounds. Most companies have proprietary formulas and market the products under different brand names.

CAUTIONS. Check product data sheets for proper uses of the new treated lumber. One difference you will notice right away is that the signature green tint of CCA-treated lumber is replaced by a more brownish color that eventually weathers to a gray color.

The other major difference is that there is some evidence that the chemicals used to treat lumber are more corrosive than CCA. This could be a problem with some fasteners. Again, check with the manufacturer about fastener selection. Some studies have shown that stainless-steel fasteners offer the best resistance to corrosion. A second choice may be nails and screws finished with a polymer coating.

Pressure-treated CCA lumber (PT) was easily recognized by its green tint and commonly used on foundation sills.

COMMON LUMBER PROBLEMS

AS WITH ANY ORGANIC MATERIAL that gains and loses water, wood swells when it is moist and shrinks as it dries. This can lead to warping (uneven shrinking during drying), checking (cracks along growth rings), bowing (end-to-end deviation from the plane of the board's wide face), twisting (spiral or torsional distortion), and cupping (deviation from a flat plane, edge to edge). Softwoods are particularly vulnerable.

Given the demand on the nation's forests for wood, many lumber companies have shortened their harvesting cycles or have planted fast-growing trees. When these trees are harvested, they yield juvenile wood, which can give you problems. Juvenile wood encompasses the first 5 to 20 annual growth rings of any tree, and when it's used for lumber, it doesn't have the same strength as mature wood. You may get bouncy floors, buckled walls, weakened joints, and poorly fitting windows and doors. Even kiln-dried juvenile wood can warp because of nonuniform growth-ring distribution. Inspect the lumber you're buying, and look for telltale signs of juvenile wood, such as uneven grain distribution and warping, and refuse wood that is not up to par.

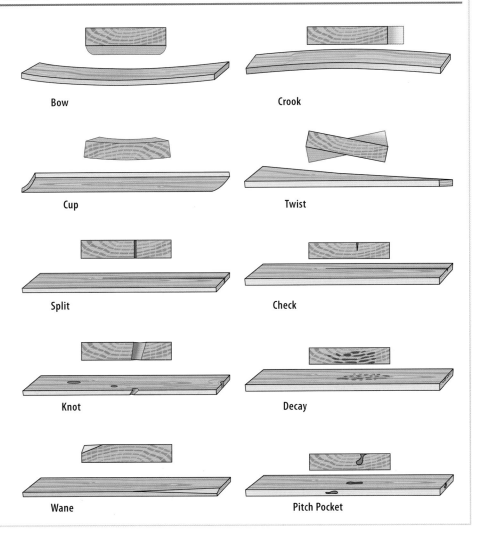

Bow

Crook

Cup

Twist

Split

Check

Knot

Decay

Wane

Pitch Pocket

ENGINEERED FRAMING PRODUCTS

SOME ENGINEERED WOOD PRODUCTS were created in response to declining wood quality and rising costs. High-quality long beams of Douglas fir are expensive and few lumberyards will stock them. Engineered products using smaller pieces of lumber were created to fill the gap. You must use engineered products in strict accordance with manufacturers' span specifications. In addition, you must install them with specified techniques and, in some cases, special connectors.

GLUE-LAMINATED LUMBER. A glue-laminated beam is made up of smaller pieces of wood glued together lengthwise with waterproof glue. Glue-laminated lumber can be as long as you like—25 feet or longer. Each beam is specifically engineered to support an intended load. No matter what kind of glue-laminated lumber you install, you can't just nail it in place. You'll need framing connectors, shear plates, threaded rods, nail-on clips, or hangers at the connections.

LAMINATED-VENEER LUMBER (LVL). LVL can replace steel or an oversize glue-laminated beam. It is made, as the name implies, by laminating ¼-inch-thick plies together to a thickness of 4½ inches. You'll have to consult with the manufacturers' span charts to determine the size LVL to use on your job. Be sure to use connectors approved for LVLs. Avoid drilling or notching LVLs for pipes, wires, and heating or air-conditioning ducts, if possible. If you must drill or notch, be sure to strictly follow manufacturer's guidelines to prevent compromising the LVL's structural integrity.

PARALLEL-STRAND LUMBER. Parallel-strand lumber is a kind of engineered beam, between 1¾ and 7 inches thick, made of thin strands of Douglas fir and/or southern yellow pine. The strands are glued together running parallel with one another. These beams are more dimensionally stable than LVLs or glue-laminated lumber beams, and they serve in the same applications. Parallel-strand lumber resists cupping and twisting when stored, which is a potential problem with some glue-laminated beams and LVLs.

WOOD I-JOISTS. Wood I-joists are straight, dimensionally stable, and ideal for longer spans. I-joists are light and easy to install. The web, or center, of a wood I-joist is typically ½-inch plywood or oriented-strand board (OSB), and the 2-inch rails at the top and bottom are fir. Wood I-joists come in four sizes: 9½, 11⅞, 14, and 16 inches deep. Some connections may require special hardware.

Glue-laminated lumber is built up of finger-jointed dimensional lumber that must be sized for your application. The lumber is usually used as ridge beams, purlins, headers, and floor girders. Cambered beams are also available.

Parallel-strand lumber, similar to glue-laminated lumber, is made from individual strands of softwood lumber and an adhesive. These engineered beams may be up to 7 in. thick; you can order them in lengths up to 60 ft.

Laminated-veneer lumber (LVL) is a beam composed of wooden plies (like the layers of a plywood panel) glued together. The beams can be ordered in depth from 9¼ to 18 in. and anything up to 60 ft. long.

Wood I-joists can take the place of lumber joists in floors and ceilings. They are made with solid- or engineered-wood rails (the upper and lower part of the I) and ½-in. plywood or OSB webs. Web stiffeners and framing connectors may be required.

PLYWOOD & PANEL PRODUCTS

Depending on your design, you might need plywood for floor decking and wall and roof sheathing. Plywood comprises an odd number of thin veneer layers of wood, called plies. The veneers are cross-laminated so the grain of one ply runs perpendicular to another. The veneers are glued and sandwiched together and then heated to over 300°F under 200 pounds per square inch (psi) of pressure. Standard plywood thicknesses are $\frac{5}{16}$, $\frac{3}{8}$, $\frac{7}{16}$, $\frac{15}{32}$, $\frac{1}{2}$, $\frac{5}{8}$, $\frac{23}{32}$, $\frac{3}{4}$, and $\frac{11}{8}$ inches. If you order $\frac{1}{2}$- and $\frac{3}{4}$-inch plywood for your job, you'll most likely get $\frac{15}{32}$- and $\frac{23}{32}$-inch plywood, respectively. Panels are almost always 4 x 8 feet after factory trimming. Corner to corner, panels sometimes can be slightly out of square, but not enough to be problematic.

Every piece of plywood has a face veneer and a back veneer. These are the outside plies. The plies under the face and back veneers are called crossbands, and the center ply is called the core. The core can be either veneer or solid lumber. Some plywoods even have fiberglass or particleboard at their cores. Veneer-core plywood is stronger than lumber-core plywood, but lumber-core plywood can hold screws better at its edges.

Used in the right applications, plywood is strong and adds stiffness to walls and strength to floors. Besides conventional sheathing plywood, you can buy treated, fire-retardant, and waterproof plywood for special applications. Plywood with hardwood face veneers is available for fine cabinetry and furniture applications.

Common Plywood Types

For most outbuilding projects you'll be using $\frac{1}{2}$-inch or $\frac{5}{8}$-inch BC or CDX plywood—Exposure 1 for wall and roof sheathing and Exposure 2 for subfloors. If you're finishing a barn or shed with plywood alone, you may want to consider AC, which has one "good" side without any repair plugs or major defects.

Another alternative is Texture 1-11 siding plywood, which has grooves cut into it to resemble board siding. T1-11 comes in 4 x 8-foot and larger panels. At corners, and at seams between top and bottom courses on high walls, you'll need to cover joints with trim to maintain the illusion of board siding.

OTHER PANEL PRODUCTS

PANEL PRODUCTS OTHER THAN PLYWOOD, called nonveneer or reconstituted wood-product panels, are sometimes used for sheathing. (Check this with your local building department.) Some of these panels are just as strong—and cheaper—than plywood. The products are called reconstituted because they're made from wood particles or wood strands that are bonded together.

STRUCTURAL PARTICLEBOARD. Also called flakeboard or chipboard, particleboard is simply a panel of wood particles held together by hot-pressed resin. Some exterior-rated products have a layer of resin or wax on the outside to repel water. The glue used in these products is urea formaldehyde or phenol-formaldehyde adhesive. Some building-code organizations allow you to use structural particleboard as underlayment, subflooring, and/or sheathing.

ORIENTED-STRAND BOARD. Usually called OSB, this product also uses strands of wood, but the layers are crossed so that the direction of the grain of each layer is at 90 degrees to the previous layer, just as plywood is cross-laminated to give it strength. The three to five layers of strands in OSB are bonded together with phenolic resin. These panels have a smooth face and are often rated for structural applications. Waferboard, sometimes called strand board, is a similar product, but without the alternating layers of OSB.

COMPOSITE BOARD. Basically a hybrid of plywood and particleboard, composite board has a reconstituted-wood-particle center but a face and back of plywood veneer. Where codes allow, you can use composite board as underlayment, subflooring, and/or sheathing.

COMMON WOOD PANEL PRODUCTS

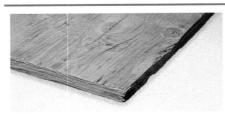

Plywood consists of several thin layers glued together with their grains running in alternating directions. Plywood comes in several thicknesses, grades, and ratings that indicate its use.

Structural particleboard is made from wood chips and sawdust glued together, typically with urea formaldehyde resin, into 4 x 8-ft. sheets. Its uses are often restricted by local building codes.

Oriented-strand board (OSB) is made from opposingly placed strips of scrap wood, held together with waterproof adhesives. OSB is allowed by many codes as subflooring and sheathing.

RATING PANEL PRODUCTS

WHEN YOU PURCHASE STRUCTURAL PANELS, a grading label tells you what you're buying. The leading grading association is the American Plywood Association (APA), and you're most likely to see its stamp.

PANEL GRADE. Panel products are rated in a number of categories. If you look at a typical APA grade stamp, you'll see the panel grade on the top line. This entry designates the proper application for the panel—rated sheathing, rated flooring, rated underlayment, and the like.

SPAN RATING. Next you'll see a large number or numbers, indicating the span rating. This rating is the recommended center-to-center spacing in inches of studs/joists/rafters over which you can place the panel. If you see numbers like $^{32}/_{16}$, the left number shows the maximum spacing in inches of the panel when used in roofing—32 inches of allowable span with three or more supports—and the right number gives the maximum spacing when the panel is used as subflooring—16 inches of

TYPICAL PLYWOOD GRADE

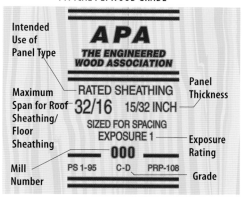

Intended Use of Panel Type

Maximum Span for Roof Sheathing/Floor Sheathing

Mill Number

APA THE ENGINEERED WOOD ASSOCIATION

RATED SHEATHING
32/16 15/32 INCH
SIZED FOR SPACING
EXPOSURE 1
000
PS 1-95   C-D   PRP-108

Panel Thickness

Exposure Rating

Grade

Grade stamp information includes the panel's use, thickness, grade, exposure rating, and mill identification.

allowable span with three or more supports.

THICKNESS. The grade stamp also identifies the thickness of the panel—$^3/_8$ inch, $^7/_{16}$ inch, $^{15}/_{32}$ inch, $^{23}/_{32}$ inch, and so on.

EXPOSURE. The stamp also lists the exposure classification for plywood. Exterior indicates that permanent exposure to weather is allowed. Exposure 1 is for temporary water exposure such as sheathing that may get rained on during construction. Exposure 3 is for interior use such as subfloors that will be exposed to little moisture.

MILL & STANDARDS NUMBERS. The mill number simply identifies the manufacturer. The remaining numbers on the label—the national evaluation report (NER) and performance-rated panel standard (PRP)—indicate that the panel meets all construction requirements and requisite codes.

VENEER GRADES. Plywood is also rated for veneer grades, and that rating appears on the edge of the plywood in combinations of letters. There are six categories in veneer ratings: N, A, B, C Plugged, C, and D, indicating descending order of quality. N is a smooth surface of select woods with no defects, but you won't be using N in framing. It's for use in cabinetry. For construction-grade plywood, the face-and-back-veneer grades are combinations of letters. B-C, for example, is suitable for sheathing, while you'd use A-B when both the face and back veneers will show. A-C or A-D is suitable when only the A side will show, and C-D is used for concrete forms.

TIPS ON MATERIALS, DELIVERIES & STORAGE

STAGE DELIVERIES so that your materials aren't backlogged, and you'll never run short of what you need. A good approach is to produce all your cut lists at the beginning of the job, break them down into work stages (foundation, rough framing, rafters, sheathing, roofing, windows and doors, siding, and interior finish), and assign delivery dates for the materials needed for each work stage.

Using your site plan, with a clear outline of the footprint of your barn, designate some material drops. Lumber is heavy, so have it dropped close by. If you use trusses, which are fragile until set in place, don't schedule delivery until your truss crew is on hand. Windows and doors can go into a nearby garage. Trim lumber or siding should be set in a clean, dry area up on blocks.

Though it may be sunny and dry when materials are delivered, you should protect your deliveries against the elements. Many lumberyards have pallets that they will offer for free to keep the wood off the ground. Covering it with plastic is a good idea, but leave the ends of the wood open to breathe.

Finally, plan your deliveries to take advantage of any labor-saving tools the lumberyards offer. If the delivery truck has a lift, have them place rafter lumber on the second-floor deck.

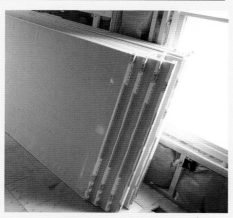

Have drywall delivered after the exterior has been sheathed and windows have been installed. Store it indoors so that moisture will not affect it.

FASTENERS

NAILS

THE TRICK TO CHOOSING NAILS is to match the nail to the task. Codes often specify sizes of common nails for framing because they have an extra-thick shank and a broad head. You should use duplex, or double-headed, nails when you know you'll be removing the nail—in temporary sheathing, for example. Duplex nails allow you to snug the bottom nailhead up tight, but still give your hammer claw purchase to pull them out easily.

Besides common nails, you're likely to use ring-shank nails for subflooring; roofing nails and staples for applying felt paper, roofing shingles, and air-infiltration barriers (housewrap); and finishing nails for window- and door-jamb installations. Ring-shank nails have ridges on their shafts for extra holding power. Roofing nails have large heads to hold roofing paper securely. Finishing nails are thin, with small heads that you can easily drive beneath the surface of the wood with a nail set.

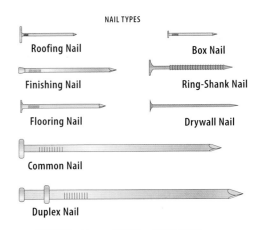

NAIL TYPES

Roofing Nail

Box Nail

Finishing Nail

Ring-Shank Nail

Flooring Nail

Drywall Nail

Common Nail

Duplex Nail

NAIL SIZES AND WEIGHTS

Pennyweight	Length (in.)	Nails/lb. (Common)
2d	1	876
3d	1¼	568
4d	1½	316
5d	1¾	271
6d	2	181
7d	2¼	161
8d	2½	106
10d	3	69
12d	3¼	63
16d	3½	49
20d	4	31
30d	4½	24
40d	5	18
60d	6	14

SCREWS

THERE ARE MANY TYPES OF SCREWS, but you'll probably use only a few in a barn project: wood screws or deck (buglehead) screws for joining lumber, and lag screws for making heavy-duty wood-to-wood attachments. Lag screws, sometimes called lag bolts because of their bolt-like heads, are heavy-duty screws that you drive with a socket wrench. They have wide threads for biting into wood like a screw but a hex-shaped head like a bolt. Lag screws are sized according to the diameter of their shanks: usually ⁵⁄₁₆, ⅜, or ½ inch.

Wood and deck screws are generally slotted or Phillips head, although there are other, less common head types. These screws are sized by their thickness, referred to by number. A screw's number indicates the diameter of its shank, the solid shaft of the screw measured at the base of the threads near the head. Common sizes are #6, #8, and #10. The length for any of these screws can vary. A #8 screw, for example, can be nearly any length up to about 3½ inches. The heavier the gauge, the more likely you are to find it in longer lengths.

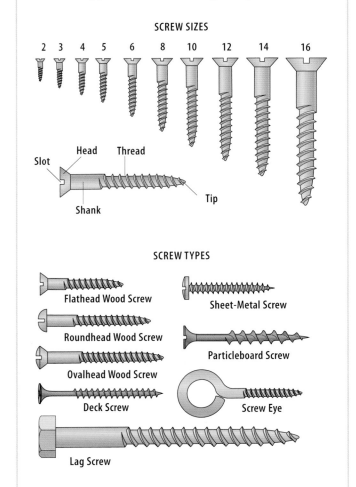

SCREW SIZES

2   3   4   5   6   8   10   12   14   16

Slot   Head   Thread

Shank   Tip

SCREW TYPES

Flathead Wood Screw

Sheet-Metal Screw

Roundhead Wood Screw

Particleboard Screw

Ovalhead Wood Screw

Deck Screw

Screw Eye

Lag Screw

BOLTS

BOLTS FALL INTO THREE MAIN CATEGORIES: carriage bolts, machine bolts, and stove bolts. Specialty bolts add many more categories.

You probably won't find many framing applications for machine or stove bolts. But carriage bolts, which have unslotted oval heads, can be effective when attaching structural lumber face-to-face or major timbers to posts. Carriage bolts have a square shoulder just beneath the head that digs into the wood as you tighten the bolt, which prevents it from slipping and spinning in the hole. They are sized according to the diameter of their shanks and their length.

Another bolt you're likely to use, the anchor bolt, attaches the sill plate to the top of a foundation. Wedge-type bolts and J-bolts are the most common types.

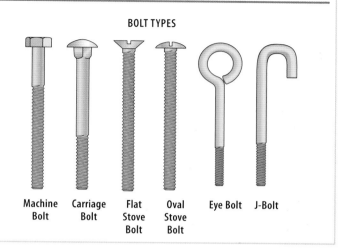

BOLT TYPES

Machine Bolt | Carriage Bolt | Flat Stove Bolt | Oval Stove Bolt | Eye Bolt | J-Bolt

FRAMING CONNECTORS

MAJOR JOINTS IN FRAMING, by code, need hangers, ties, anchors, or other metal supports for reinforcement. There often are special requirements in earthquake- or hurricane-prone areas. You can buy hangers and ties for a wide range of applications and for nearly every type of framing joint. For example, there are rafter ties for the joint between rafters and top plates, and joist hangers for joining ceiling or floor joists to header joists. Other commonly used fasteners include post anchors, which attach posts to concrete piers; truss plates,

which hold together prebuilt roof trusses; panel clips, which join adjacent sheathing panels; and nail-stopping plates, which prevent drywall nails from being driven into pipes, wires, or ductwork.

Some connectors have nailing clips or teeth stamped into them, but these have little structural value and are used only to hold the hanger while you nail it in place. Some hangers require special nails; most use common nails.

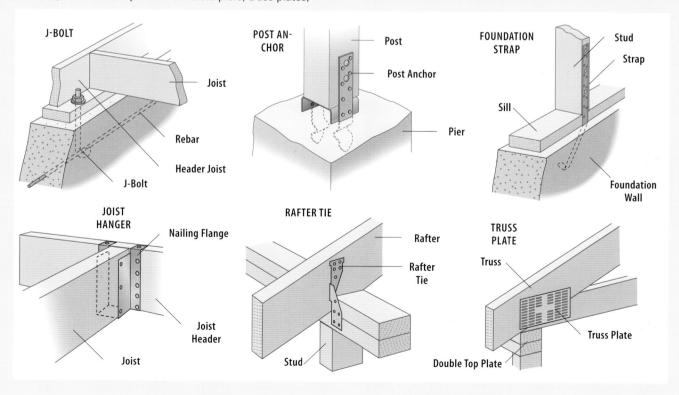

PART II
BUILDING BASICS

All well-constructed buildings start with well-designed and properly built foundations. There are different types of foundations, and the type you need for your building depends on a number of factors, including the design, size, and intended use of your building; the type of soil on your site; and the depth of frost penetration in the area in which you intend to build. In this chapter, you'll find information on installing perimeter footings, concrete slabs, piers and posts, and wall foundations made of poured concrete, concrete blocks, or treated wood.

FOUNDATION TYPES

Barns and sheds often require different foundations than houses. Many houses, at least in the northern half of the United States and Canada, have perimeter wall foundations made from concrete block or poured concrete, providing a basement or crawl space underneath the house. While you could build a barn with a full basement if you wanted to—big nineteenth century dairy barns often have a floor at least partially below grade—it is an extra expense almost never undertaken in outbuildings. Depending on the size and type of outbuilding, you're likely to use one of these foundations.

Concrete Slabs & Footings. A slab is a thick layer (often 4 to 6 inches) of poured concrete reinforced with welded wire. You can combine slabs with foundations to hold up buildings by pouring a thickened edge (basically a footing and foundation in one) that is reinforced with steel bars. A slab is laid directly over a layer of compacted gravel in many barns to provide the finished floor. If you don't need a finished floor, you can pour a concrete perimeter foundation and leave a dirt floor.

Skids. Pressure-treated timbers, such as 6x6s, often can handle sheds under 100 square feet that won't have to bear heavy loads. The skids should rest on trenches filled with compacted gravel to prevent excessive movement.

Wall Foundations. You can use poured concrete or stacked concrete block reinforced with rebar. Less common wood-wall foundations, generally called permanent wood foundations, are used in regions with cold winters, particularly in Canada, because they can be built in weather too cold to pour concrete. Pressure-treated wood rated for ground contact is used for this foundation.

Pier & Beam. This system is simply a combination of a footing with some type of foundation wall bridged by beams to support a floor.

Poles. This unique system is one of the most efficient ways to build large barns. It consists of large-diameter poles commonly set below frost depth on concrete footings.

TYPES OF FOUNDATIONS

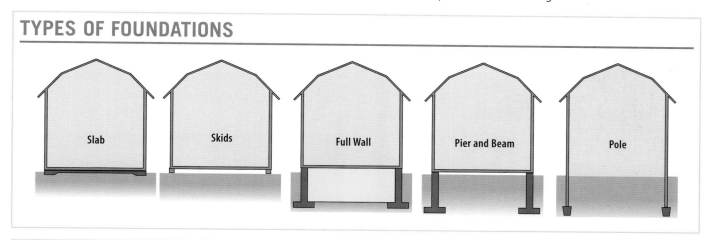

Slab   Skids   Full Wall   Pier and Beam   Pole

PLUMBING AND ELECTRICAL

IF YOUR OUTBUILDING will have plumbing or electrical wiring, you need to make preparations for these systems before you begin to build the foundation. You'll need to dig trenches and install your below-grade pipes for your water-supply lines and drainpipes, as well as underground conduit for wires, before you place any rebar or wire-mesh reinforcement. If you want footing drains to deal with runoff, this is the time to install them. Local building codes will dictate the types of pipe and conduit permitted and how deep these pipes need to be. Wires can usually be 12 to 18 inches below grade; in areas with cold winters, plumbing pipes generally will have to be at least 48 inches below grade.

If you're pouring a slab foundation, use plastic pipe to create spaces in the concrete slab for toilet flanges, floor drains, and other mechanical fittings. Even if you won't be pouring a slab, you'll still want to install the plumbing and wiring before you begin construction. If you're pouring a foundation, insert plastic pipes through the forms to provide mechanical access.

Provide mechanical access by cutting through plywood foundation forms and inserting plastic pipe before pouring concrete.

PREPARING THE SITE

The amount of site preparation required varies with the project. A dirt-floor pole barn located in a flat, well-drained area on stable soil might only need weeds cleared before you excavate. A slab-on-grade foundation on a sloped spot in a heavily wooded part of your property that also has poorly draining soil will require a great deal of work involving chain saws and heavy equipment. In areas with poor drainage, you will need to excavate enough soil to accommodate a layer of tamped gravel. If there's any doubt in your mind about your site, have an engineer test the soil. Improper site preparation will inevitably lead to uneven settling or heaving.

Marking a Layout

To lay out the rough corners of a basic building, you'll need four 2x4 stakes and a 50- or 100-foot measuring tape. To find the location of your building's corners, measure from your property line or from an existing structure on your property. To make sure your layout is square, measure the diagonals (they will be the same length in a square or rectangle), or use the 3-4-5 triangulation method. To lay out large foundations, especially those being built on a slope, it's wise to use a transit level or builder's level.

If you're not going to need excavation with heavy machinery, you can tie mason's string to nails on the corner boards and keep these lines as your layout marks. Once the layout is square, if the strings will get in your way, use spray paint to mark the ground beneath the lines. If you need to excavate the site, however, you'll need to build batter boards, which move the stakes outside of the building layout. Otherwise, a bulldozer or backhoe will excavate your corner boards along with the dirt.

Excavation

You can excavate for a foundation or a small slab with just a shovel or posthole digger and a lot of backbreaking work. Extensive excavation is best left to a contractor with the necessary heavy equipment. Although a professional operator can dig a hole with accuracy, machinery also can damage your yard. It pays to mark a particular route you want the operator to take to the site and to label trees or bushes that you don't want knocked down or damaged.

Always have the local utility company inspect the site and locate and mark all the utility lines you'll need to avoid. Also, be sure your contract is explicit about soil and trees that are removed. Never bury stumps and wood scraps near the foundation because that may cause termite problems.

PREPARING AND LEVELING A SITE

For most slab construction or to cut into a slope, you'll need to hire a contractor to operate a bulldozer or backhoe.

A 4x4 post, powered by elbow grease, makes an effective hand tamper to compact soil and gravel in a foundation.

Rent a gasoline-powered vibration compactor for large jobs. These machines solidify ground and gravel under concrete.

Begin excavating the soil within your string lines by undercutting and rolling up sod, which you can use elsewhere.

TRANSITS AND LASER LEVELS

EVEN THOUGH YOU MIGHT NOT BE FAMILIAR WITH THEM, it may be worth your while to rent a transit or a laser level and gain some experience with one of these tools. Their accuracy is the best way to be sure that your foundation is level and square.

TRANSITS. A transit looks like a short telescope attached to a scale that is mounted on a plate on top of a tripod. The scope pivots both vertically and horizontally—unlike a builder's level (sometimes called a dumpy level), which only pivots horizontally and therefore can't be used to calculate a slope.

With a perfectly leveled transit you can sight a level line in a full circle, sight perfectly right-angled (90-degree) corners from a fixed spot, or exactly lay out a 1-percent slope for a trench that will hold a drainpipe.

To use a transit, you'll need to level the scope because even a minuscule error in leveling can be amplified to a significant amount over the length of your layout line. When you set the tripod into the ground, adjust the plate on which the transit sits (called the leveling plate) as close to level as you can, either by eye or with a spirit level built into the transit. Lock the plate so that the Vernier scale (which measures vertical tilt) reads in a level position. Aim the transit at 0 on the horizontal scale, and then use the leveling screws to further adjust the transit until it reads level. Repeat this process at 90, 180, and 270 degrees, releveling the plate each time. Once you've leveled it in the fourth direction, the transit should be perfectly straight.

To mark level points with a transit, you'll need to have all four batter boards set up. The simplest way to do it is to sight all four batter boards in the scope, and then have a helper make a mark where the crosshairs intersect. Measuring down uniformly from these marks will always give you points at the same level. You can use this method to check whether form boards are level and deep enough to contain your pour.

LASER LEVELS. Laser levels also pivot horizontally and vertically, enabling you to mark a level plane or sight perfect corners. However, a laser level doesn't require a second person to make marks. It sends a beam of light allowing the user to work alone.

LAYING OUT CORNERS. To lay out the four corners of a building, attach a plumb bob under the tripod head, and set the transit directly over where you have set your first corner. Sight the transit along a string (after unlocking the vertical pivot screw) until the string is lined up in the scope's crosshairs. Set the horizontal scale to 0, and then rotate the scope to exactly 90 degrees. Have a helper place a batter board along where you've sighted, and mark on the board where the crosshairs line up. This creates a line at an exact right angle to the string line you first sighted. From this perfect corner, you can lay out the remaining two sides of the building by measuring them. All four angles will be exactly 90 degrees.

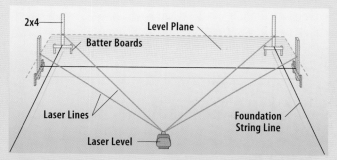

To level a site, rotate the scope of a transit or laser level and mark level points on poles at the corners. Batter boards set at a fixed distance below these marks indicate the new grade.

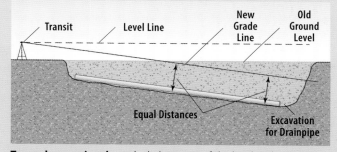

To mark a precise slope, lock the scope of the level at the incline desired, for example, on a drainage pipe. Use a pole to make marks on stakes a fixed distance below the sloped line.

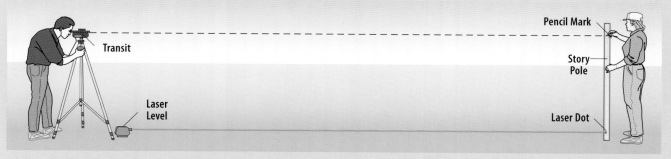

To use a transit, one person sights through the scope, while another makes reference marks where the first person indicates. A laser level, which casts a beam of light, can be used by one person. Both are accurate to distances up to 200 ft.

SQUARING CORNERS

A SIMPLE SYSTEM for creating a perfectly square building layout is the 3-4-5 method of triangulation. Starting at corner A, measure 3 feet along one guideline and mark point B. Starting again from corner A, measure 4 feet along the guideline perpendicular to the first one, and mark point C. Adjust the AC line until the distance BC is exactly 5 feet. Angle BAC is now a true 90-degree angle. You can double-check the squareness of corners and the overall layout by measuring the diagonals between opposite corners. The two distances should be equal if the layout is square.

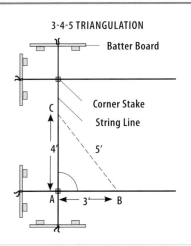

3-4-5 TRIANGULATION

Batter Board
Corner Stake
String Line
C
4'
5'
A — 3' — B

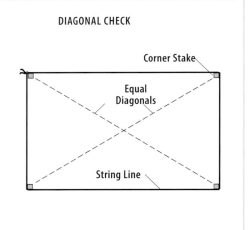

DIAGONAL CHECK

Corner Stake
Equal Diagonals
String Line

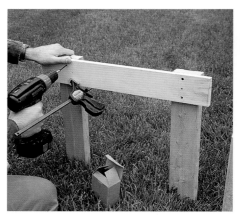

PROJECT:
MAKING BATTER BOARDS

TOOLS & MATERIALS

- Work gloves
- Safety glasses
- Measuring tape
- 2x4 stakes
- 1x4 boards
- Circular saw Sawhorse
- Short sledgehammer
- Clamps
- Power drill-driver
- 1-inch drywall screws
- Spirit level
- Line level

1 Cut 16 stakes (4 for each corner) from 2x4s, about 3 ft. long, with pointed ends. These stakes support the horizontal batter boards.

2 Set pairs of 2x4 stakes at roughly right angles to each other, 2 or more feet outside the corners and parallel with the lines of the foundation.

3 Make batter boards by cutting 2-ft. 1x4s. Screw the batter boards to the stakes, using clamps to hold the boards in position.

4 Use a level to check the batter boards. This allows you to stretch level string lines along the perimeter of the building foundation.

5 After determining where lines will cross at 90 degrees, tack nails into the batter boards to fix them in position.

CLIMATE AND PEST CONSIDERATIONS

FROST DEPTH & FROST HEAVING

Water expands in volume by about 10 percent when it freezes, which can exert enough pressure to break apart concrete from below. To avoid this problem, called frost heave, piers and footings need to reach below the frost line, which is the average maximum depth of frost penetration. This map shows the average depth of frost throughout the U.S. In the western and northern parts of the country, as well as in Canada, freezing patterns vary so much that zoning is all but impossible. Even within zones, frost depths can vary depending on local weather patterns, altitude, and soil. Local building codes strictly regulate foundation depth and construction. To be safe, you should always consult the building inspector before starting a foundation project.

VAPOR BARRIERS

To avoid problems with condensation and moisture buildup on your foundation, you should lay a vapor-retarding ground cover over the grade before you fill in your excavation with gravel. This is recommended particularly for the areas in dark green on the map at right. The barrier should be 6-mil-thick polyethylene sheeting, which is available at most home centers. Lay the barrier in the bottom of the excavation, and cover it with a few inches of sand to prevent the gravel from tearing holes in it. Individual sheets should overlap one another by at least 6 inches to prevent leaks. In areas with severe termite problems, you might want to replace the sand with special termite sand or add some kind of chemical- based termite protection.

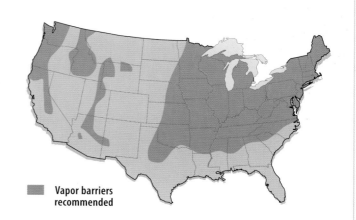

Vapor barriers recommended

TERMITE PROTECTION

In regions where termite infestation is a problem, steps must be taken to block the termites between the ground and the wood (typically the sill) at the foundation. Never bury any wood debris near a building, and make sure that you've cleared away grade stakes and footing forms. Place metal termite shields between the foundation and the sill for wall foundations. For slabs, a few inches of termite sand or diatomaceous earth on top of your vapor barrier should deter any termites from living underneath your floor. In some regions, the sand must be treated with an insecticide; consult with the building inspector.

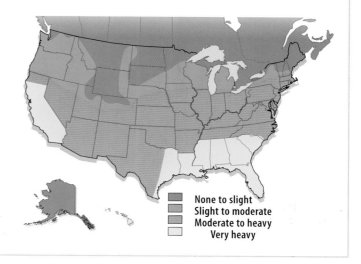

None to slight
Slight to moderate
Moderate to heavy
Very heavy

WORKING WITH CONCRETE

Concrete is a mixture of portland cement, sand, gravel, and water. You can purchase the dry ingredients separately or buy them premixed, generally in 80-pound bags.

Mixing Options

For large-scale projects, however, you should order ready-mix concrete. It is sold by the cubic yard and delivered in a truck ready to pour. For smaller jobs—say, form-tube piers for a small storage shed—you can mix your own concrete by adding water according to the instructions of the bag or by following the table, "Concrete Ingredients by Proportion," at right.

But don't get too ambitious. One cubic yard, only enough for an 8 x 10-foot 4-inch slab, would require about 40 of those 80-pound bags. For mid-size jobs or those that a concrete truck can't drive to, it makes sense to rent a portable power mixer. For estimating purposes, you can make about 1 cubic yard of concrete with five 94-pound bags of portland cement, 14 cubic feet of sand, and 21 cubic feet of gravel.

Ordering Concrete

Before you call, have an estimate for your order. Most ready-mix contractors will require only a day's notice. It's important to double-check your measurements of length times width times depth (and your calculations) to specify the order in cubic yards. Always round up your numbers so that you don't run short of material.

Mix Variations

When hand-mixing, you may be tempted to adjust the mix proportions—say, by adding more water to make the concrete easier to mix and pour. However, as water content can drastically affect strength, the best policy is to order ready-mix concrete or precisely follow directions on the bags.

PROJECT:
MIXING CONCRETE

TOOLS & MATERIALS
- Work gloves
- Wheelbarrow
- Concrete mix
- Water
- Mason's hoe
- Shovel

1 If concrete is too wet, ridges made in the mix with a trowel won't hold their shape. The concrete will not provide its rated strength.

2 If concrete is too dry, you won't be able to make any ridges in the mix, making it difficult to work. This concrete will not cure properly.

3 When the concrete is mixed correctly, the ridges will hold most of their shape; only a little water will be visible on the surface.

PROJECT:
CURING CONCRETE

TOOLS & MATERIALS
- Garden hose
- Paint roller
- Curing compound
- Tarpaulin/ plastic sheeting or straw

1 To keep concrete sufficiently moist during the curing process, you can periodically spray the finished surface lightly but thoroughly with water from a garden hose.

2 A chemical curing compound, applied to concrete with a paint roller or paint sprayer, is one way to prevent water loss during curing. Apply it after the surface has set up.

3 Prevent concrete from drying prematurely by covering the slab with plastic sheeting held down with lumber or bricks. Burlap or straw, kept moist, can also be used.

The standard proportion of water to cement produces concrete with a compressive strength of 3,000 to 4,000 pounds per square inch (psi). Adding less water makes mixing more difficult and could weaken the mix.

Ready-mix concrete is also available with additives unavailable to the DIYer. One type produces microscopic air bubbles. This air-entrained concrete is more resistant to cracking than concrete you mix on site. There are also additives that accelerate the curing time for concrete poured in cold weather. You can order ready-mix concrete to a greater compressive strength than hand-mixed concrete, to support a greater building load.

Curing

The process of hardening concrete and bringing it to its full strength is called curing. Concrete begins to harden as soon as it is mixed, and can support your weight within a few hours. Most of the curing takes place in the first two weeks, but it takes a month to reach near its peak hardness. Most concrete needs to be kept moist over seven consecutive days above 50° F to cure properly. If the temperature is above 70° F, the concrete may cure in five days; high-early-strength concrete needs only three. Curing concrete can be sprinkled periodically with water and covered with plastic sheeting, burlap, canvas, or straw to limit dehydration. There are also liquid curing compounds that you can roll or spray onto concrete.

CURING IN EXTREME HEAT. Concrete will dehydrate too quickly in hot weather, robbing it of the water it needs to cure. In extreme cases, a steady hot, dry breeze can accelerate evaporation so that the surface begins to set before it can be smoothed. There are some solutions, such as adding flaked ice or cooling down the aggregates with a sprinkler before adding them to the mix. To eliminate the risk of wasting your efforts on a job that doesn't last, don't pour in temperatures over 90°F. It's also important to remember that if the mix makes contact with a hot surface, moisture may burn off. It's wise to spray some cool water on forms that are sitting in the sun, as well as on the reinforcing bar, which can get quite hot to the touch.

CONCRETE FINISHES

FLOATING CONCRETE after jointing and edging will drive the large aggregate below the surface and further smooth the concrete. Different tools—a wooden float, metal float, or a stiff-bristled broom—will leave behind very different finishes. Steps and walkways can be given additional color and texture with extra aggregate added to the surface. But don't overwork the surface of air-entrained concrete. This can impair the concrete's frost resistance by removing air near the surface.

A wooden-float finish is slightly rough, just enough to be slip-resistant for safety, and also glare-free.

A steel-trowel finish is smooth and is best suited for interior applications such as finished floor slabs.

A broomed surface is rough and very slip-resistant; this finish is ideal for outdoor steps and walkways.

CONCRETE INGREDIENTS BY PROPORTION

Maximum Size of Course Aggregate Inches	AIR-ENTRAINED CONCRETE Number of Parts per Ingredient				CONCRETE WITHOUT AIR Number of Parts per Ingredient			
	Cement	Sand*	Coarse Aggregate	Water	Cement	Sand*	Coarse Aggregate	Water
⅜	1	2¼	1½	½	1	2½	1½	½
½	1	2¼	2	½	1	2½	2	½
¾	1	2¼	2½	½	1	2½	2½	½
1	1	2¼	2¾	½	1	2½	2¾	½
1½	1	2¼	3	½	1	2½	3	½

Note: 7.48 gallons of water equals 1 cubic foot. One 94-pound bag of portland cement equals about 1 cubic foot.
* *"Wet" sand sold for most construction use.*
The combined finished volume is approximately two-thirds the sum of the bulk volumes.

CONCRETE FOOTINGS

For larger structures and in areas subject to frost heave, footings are the first step to a complete perimeter wall foundation or floor slab. (Some slabs are monolithic, which means that both footing and slab are poured at once.)

Assembling the Forms

Using your batter boards and strings as guides, dig the footing to the required width and depth. In some cases, part of the footing may extend above grade. If the soil is loose at the bottom of the trench, compact it with a tamper to prevent the concrete from settling. If you remove large rocks, fill the depressions and tamp them down firmly.

Drive stakes for the forms 18 to 24 inches apart. Clamp on the form boards before fastening them. Attach 1x2 braces across the top of the forms every 2 feet or so to keep them from spreading when you pour the concrete. To keep cracks from forming, place steel reinforcing bars (#4 rebar) horizontally. You may need several rows for deep footings. Before you pour the concrete, make sure the form boards are level and plumb. Brush the insides of the forms with a light coat of motor oil or form oil; this will make them easier to remove later.

Pouring the Concrete

Pour or shovel wet concrete into the forms, flush to the top. As you pour, use a shovel or mason's hoe to work out any air pockets. Use a wood float, flat trowel, or short length of 2x4 to smooth the top surface of the footing. After pouring the concrete into the forms and smoothing and leveling it, set anchor bolts into the concrete 1 foot from the ends of each wall and 6 feet on center. The bolts are used to secure the sill plate that anchors the structural frame to the foundation. If the footing will support a block wall, you'll need to add vertical rebar to tie the wall to the footing.

PROJECT: BUILDING FOOTING FORMS

TOOLS & MATERIALS

- 2x4 stakes
- 1x4 batter boards
- Short sledgehammer
- Mason's twine
- Handsaw
- Measuring tape
- Duplex nails
- Hammer
- Clamps
- Shovel
- Two-by formwork boards
- 4-foot spirit level
- Galvanized screws
- Plywood gussets
- Power drill with screwdriver bit
- 1x2 spreaders
- Form oil or motor oil

1 After setting up batter boards and marking the perimeter, begin excavating the soil within your string lines. Remember, the footings must rest below the local frost-depth line.

2 Drive in the stakes to support the form boards. You can build them from 1x4s or 2x4s, with an angle cut into the tip. Most footings are twice the width of the wall.

3 Use a clamp to fasten the form boards to the stakes temporarily. Check the boards for level; adjust them as needed; and then nail or screw the boards to the stakes.

4 Secure any butt joints in the formwork with ½-in.-thick plywood gussets. Use a power drill and 1½-in. screws to fasten these in place across the exterior face of each joint.

5 Use 1x2 spreaders to bridge the forms every few feet. These braces ensure that the weight of the concrete as it is poured will not cause the forms to bulge.

PROJECT: POURING CONCRETE FOOTINGS

TOOLS & MATERIALS
- Rebar
- Wire
- Wire cutters
- Bricks, blocks, or wire chairs
- Pliers
- Hacksaw
- Concrete mix
- Mason's hoe
- Wheelbarrow or mixing tub
- Shovel
- Mason's trowel
- 2x4 screed
- Measuring tape or ruler
- Anchor bolts

1 Support rebar at the proper height—generally at least an inch or two off the ground—with pieces of brick. Wire supports called chairs work better than bricks if you can find them.

2 Secure the rebar to the chairs or supports with wire ties, twisted tightly with pliers. This keeps the supports from being forced out of position by the concrete during the pour.

3 You'll need to bend the rebar around corners. Adjoining pieces of rebar should be lapped by several inches to provide unbroken support. Secure the laps together with wire ties.

4 Transport the concrete to the formwork using a wheelbarrow, bucket, or other container, and pour it into place. Use a shovel to distribute the concrete evenly throughout the form.

5 Fill the forms completely, using a hoe or shovel to spread it around evenly. Tamp the concrete as you work in order to eliminate any voids or air bubbles, particularly in corners.

6 To ensure a smooth and durable edge to the footing once it has cured, use a mason's trowel to fill corners, working along the inside edges of the form boards.

7 Use a 2x4 screed board, cut a few inches longer than the total width of the footing, to fill the forms evenly and strike off any excess concrete above the level of the formwork.

8 Embed steel anchor bolts—usually 6-in. J-bolts—into the screeded concrete at 6 ft. on center and within 1 ft. of each corner or door opening. These bolts will hold the sill.

CONCRETE SLABS

The concrete slab, often called a slab-on-grade (the grade being the surface of the ground), is a monolithic piece of concrete, usually 4 to 6 inches thick, poured onto the ground over a bed of gravel within forms. Local codes specify the thickness of slabs for different building purposes.

Soil preparation beneath a slab is crucial. Before you form a slab, prepare the soil to ensure proper drainage around and beneath it. In cold climates, this might mean replacing the soil to 50 percent of the frost depth with gravel. In some parts of the country, a polyethylene vapor barrier should be placed between the soil and the gravel base.

Formwork

Around the edges, a slab is formed by boards: 2x6s, 2x8s, 2x10s, 2x12s, or a combination of these, depending on the slab thickness and desired height above grade. Use 2x4 scab boards to hold the form boards together as you place them around the perimeter. Be careful to keep them plumb: check periodically with a spirit level. Brace and stake the boards in place using 2x2s or 2x4s, either driven into the ground or run diagonally as kickers. Also use a water level or transit to check that the forms are level across their tops.

When positioning the slab form boards, use mason's string as a guide. A batter-board system for defining form placement works well and provides a precise string outline to follow when forming the slab perimeter.

Reinforcement

You must reinforce concrete slabs with #10 steel welded wire reinforcing mesh. If the footing is integrated into the slab, lay horizontal pieces of #4 rebar in the footing and wire-tie them to vertical pieces that have been bent to overlap the slab mesh. Tie these pieces to the slab.

After pouring the concrete, insert J-bolts into the footing. The J-bolts will be used to attach the sill plates to the footing as the first step in framing the building.

Most codes call for J-bolts to be no more than 6 feet apart. Be careful not to put J-bolts where doorways will be.

Slab Footings

In many cases, the slabs and footings are integrated into the same concrete pour—the slab is made deeper along the perimeter where it will carry the building load. To create an integrated footing, simply dig deeper around the perimeter. If you have sandy soil that won't allow you to do this, you can use 2x8s or 2x10s to form the sides of the footing.

SLAB FOOTING ANATOMY

Concrete slabs need to be built on a bed of compacted soil and 4 to 6 in. of gravel. Rebar and welded-wire mesh add strength and tie the thinner slab to the thicker footings.

Welded wire comes in rolls that you can spread out over the excavation between forms. Overlap and wire-tie together sections of welded wire required to cover a large slab.

Anchor bolts are set into the top course of block or into concrete. When installing sill plates after the concrete cures, measure from the outside edge of the block or slab to the bolt; then mark that distance in from the sill's edge.

PROJECT:
POURING A SLAB

TOOLS & MATERIALS

- Shovel and earth-moving tools
- Compactor Mason's twine
- 2x4 or 1x4 stakes Line level
- Measuring tape Form boards
- Duplex nails Gravel Rebar Rebar chairs Wire ties
- Welded or woven-wire mesh
- Bricks, blocks, or wire chairs
- Sledgehammer Wheelbarrow
- Concrete Broom Screed Float Edging trowel
- Jointing trowel

1 To strengthen the concrete, lay welded wire within the slab, generally on short supports called chairs. You can also use bricks to keep the wire above the soil.

2 Large slabs can be formed to be poured in sections. Control joints can be formed into the sections to hide and control cracks. Alternately, control joints can be made after the pour using a jointing tool.

3 As concrete pours from the ready-mix truck, use hoes and shovels to spread it evenly throughout the slab forms. You'll need several helpers to do this while the mix is still plastic.

4 After you have evenly distributed the concrete throughout the form, loosen a screed board to strike off the excess and fill in the hollows. Use a 2x4 slightly longer than the width of the slab.

5 Depending on the slab's use, you can smooth (with a float) the rough surface left by screeding (such as for a floor slab) or texture it with a broom for better traction (for a patio).

ESTIMATING

CONCRETE FOR SLABS

To figure out how much concrete to mix or order, you can use the chart at right. If you prefer, total up the volume inside the forms in cubic feet (length x height x width); then divide this figure by 27 to convert it into the ordering standard of cubic yards. To avoid a shortfall, it's smart to build in a reasonable excess factor of about 8 percent by changing the conversion factor to 25. Remember that an 80-pound bag of concrete mix will make only two-thirds of a cubic foot. Large orders measured in cubic yards will require a rented power mixer (and many bags of premixed concrete) or delivery from a concrete truck.

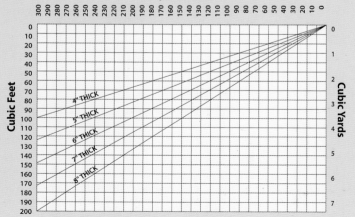

PIERS & POSTS

Pier or tube-form foundations are concrete pillars that support wood posts or girders. You will often find these foundations supporting decks on houses, but they work on outbuildings as well. Piers are susceptible to shifting out of plumb in areas that experience freeze-thaw cycles or shifting soil. So whether you use formless piers or tube forms, prepare the soil where they sit with the proper gravel and drainage to reduce the danger of frost heaving, and be sure to use the correct anchor, bracket, or strap to keep your framing in place on the pier.

To avoid frost heave, which can crack concrete and disrupt the structure above, piers must extend below where groundwater usually freezes in the winter—the average frost depth. In much of the country, this depth varies from region to region; it even varies with regions as shown in "Frost Depth & Frost Heaving," page 57. To check for the depth in your area, contact the local building department or building inspector.

Holes for piers need to be deep and narrow. They are best dug with a power auger, either one that runs off a tractor's power take off or a rented portable unit. Otherwise, use a posthole digger—a shovel will dig a hole with too wide a mouth. Minimize settling by digging down to the required depth and pounding the dirt at the bottom of the hole with the end of a 2x4. The concrete pier must rest on a solid base.

Pouring Piers

To avoid mixing dirt and concrete, weakening the pier, use lightweight form tubes that are available at lumberyards and masonry-supply yards. You cut them to the height you need, which is a few inches above grade, and backfill them securely in the ground. Fill with concrete; insert a J-bolt; and attach an post anchor to the bolt. If the sides of the holes aren't crumbling, you could use them as rough forms and pour the concrete directly into the hole. In that case, insert hardware into the concrete to attach the framing to the top of the concrete pier.

PROJECT:
SETTING PIERS WITH FORM TUBES

TOOLS & MATERIALS

- Work gloves
- Shovel
- Posthole digger or power auger
- Gravel
- Fiber tube
- Handsaw
- Spirit level
- Concrete mix
- Mason's hoe
- Wheelbarrow or plywood
- J-bolt with washer and nut
- Mason's trowel
- Wrench
- Post base anchors

1 Dig holes for your piers with a post-hole digger or power auger to below the frost depth. Rocky or wooded soil will be difficult to work. Fill the bottom with 2 in. of gravel for support and drainage.

2 Insert a fiber form tube into the hole. It should protrude from the soil level about 6 in. Cut off any excess with a handsaw. Plumb the inside of the form with a spirit level to ensure straightness.

3 Check the form tube for level with a spirit level. Then backfill around the form with soil and check again for plumb and level. Remove large rocks from the fill; small rocks can be added near the bottom of the hole.

4 Pour concrete from a wheelbarrow directly into the form. Before the concrete hardens, insert a J-bolt into the center, allowing the threads to protrude above the concrete surface.

5 After the concrete sets, attach post-base hardware using washers and nuts. The post sits on a metal standoff that allows for drainage and keeps the bottom of the post dry.

PIER ANATOMY

Girder

6x6 Post

Post Anchor

J-Bolt

Fiber Tube

Concrete below frost line

ESTIMATING

CONCRETE FOR PIERS
Piers don't require much concrete. You can mix one batch at a time, or use no-mix concrete that you simply dump into the form and then add water.

BOX FORMS: To determine the cubic footage of a box, multiply the length times the width times the depth (all in inches), and divide the result by 1,728.

$$(l \times w \times d) \div 1{,}728 = \text{cu. ft.}$$

CYLINDER FORMS: To determine the cubic feet in a cylinder, multiply the radius (half the diameter) by itself (square it), and then multiply by its height and 3.14. Divide the result by 1,728.

$$(r \times r \times h \times 3.14) \div 1{,}728 = \text{cu. ft.}$$

PROJECT: SETTING FORMLESS PIERS

TOOLS & MATERIALS
- Posthole digger or power auger
- Tamper, 2x4, or 4x4
- Measuring tape
- Shovel
- Wheelbarrow or mixing tub
- Concrete mix
- Post hardware
- Spirit level

1 Use a posthole digger—or to save time, a rented power auger—to excavate a hole for a formless pier. The earthen walls of the hole serve as the formwork.

2 Measure the depth of the hole carefully to make sure that the base of the pier will rest on undisturbed or compacted soil that is below the minimum frost depth for your region.

3 Fill the hole with the required concrete mix. The bottom of the hole should be tamped down with a tamper or the end of a 2x4 or 4x4

4 Insert a metal base for a post or girder into the concrete when the mix is just firm enough to hold it, but not yet hardened. This hardware will attach the framing to the pier.

5 Adjust the hardware so that it is level, plumb, and properly oriented to support the structural post or beam, which will be installed later. Once the concrete has set, it can't be adjusted.

WALL FOUNDATIONS

Full-wall foundations are generally only found on houses in colder climates. They are expensive to dig and build, and subject to an array of moisture problems. Other than a huge dairy barn, you'll rarely see a full-wall foundation on a utility building. However, a short-wall foundation with a small wall of either poured concrete or concrete block is a possibility for some designs.

Short-Wall Foundations

A short-wall foundation is a concrete block half-wall that sits on a concrete footing. Concrete blocks are stacked one on top of another until the wall's desired height is reached. On top of the last tier of blocks, you can install 4-inch cap blocks to close off the hollow cores or, more typically, fill the voids and add anchor bolts and a sill. If you want a crawl space, frame the floor on top of the half-wall. The minimum allowable floor-joist-to-ground space generally is 18 inches. If you use girders beneath the joists, the minimum distance between the outside bottom of the wood structure and the ground is usually 8 inches.

Footings beneath these foundations serve the same purpose wider sections of slabs serve: they spread the building's live and dead loads over a wider footprint, distributing the building's weight to the ground and stabilizing the building. Prepare the soil beneath the footing to ensure proper drainage, just as with a slab.

Permanent Wood Foundations

Permanent wood foundations are popular in cold areas. They use prefabricated sections of pressure-treated lumber and sheathing that are lowered onto a concrete slab or a stable bed of compacted gravel. The walls are braced before plastic sheeting or additional protection is applied outside the wood walls. You can also use pressure-treated joists in place of the slab, eliminating concrete entirely. The system (without concrete) can be installed even in subfreezing temperature.

WALL FOUNDATION ALTERNATIVES

Stud
Drip Edge
4" Floor Slab
2" Rigid Foam
J-Bolt
2" Rigid Foam
Pressure-Treated Plywood
Gravel
Backfill
Mortar
Concrete Block
Concrete Footing

Joist
Joist Header
Top Plates
Treated Plywood Cover Plate
Midwall Blocking
Backfill
Treated Wall Sheathing
Poly Sheeting
2x6 Stud
Slab Floor
Soleplate
Footing Plate
Gravel

PROJECT: 🐾🐾🐾
LAYING CONCRETE BLOCK

TOOLS & MATERIALS
- Work gloves
- Trowels
- Mortar
- Brickset & hammer
- Concrete blocks
- Mason's string
- Jointing tool

1 Once the footing is cured, use a string and a line level to keep the wall straight. Spread mortar using a trowel, and lay the courses of blocks, staggering the joints. Check that every course is level.

2 When the wall is at full height, you can finish the top of the wall with cap blocks. More often, voids are filled with concrete, and J-bolts are added to secure a building sill

3 Use a jointing tool to smooth the mortar on the outside of the wall into a slightly concave shape. This shape sheds water and keeps the mortar from deteriorating.

SKID & TRENCH FOUNDATIONS

A small shed—one of less than 100 square feet—can usually sit on a foundation constructed of pressure-treated 4x4 skids or concrete blocks that have been cut into the soil and set level. The use of this type of foundation is subject to local code restrictions, so check with the building department before you start building, even if you are planning on constructing a small shed.

Skids

Some jurisdictions may consider wooden skids to be nonpermanent foundations, and this may eliminate the need for a building permit. Or it may be illegal to build a structure of any size on this type of foundation. If you can do it, make sure you use pressure-treated wood that has been rated for ground contact—at least 0.40 pound per cubic foot, 0.60 if it is available.

The key to a good skid foundation is to prepare a stable base with good drainage. Because slight movement will not affect the foundation's stability, you don't need to remove soil to the frost line. You will need to dig out 4 or 5 inches of soil for the shed's entire footprint, however, and replace it with gravel so that the runoff does not sit underneath the shed and rot the floor of the structure. A layer of 6-mil perforated polyethylene sheeting or landscape fabric under the gravel will aid in drainage as well.

Trenches

If there is minimal or no frost heave in your area, you can also make a rudimentary concrete perimeter foundation in a trench. Pour concrete into parallel trenches 8 to 10 inches wide and 12 inches deep. Depending on how firm your soil is, you may or may not need to use form boards. Lay rebar on chairs or on bricks in the bottom of the trench for additional strength. Depending on the kind of shed you are building, you can add anchor bolts to the foundation to attach a sill or just build pressure-treated floor framing right on the concrete. Again, check local requirements before building.

PROJECT: BUILDING A SKID FOUNDATION

TOOLS & MATERIALS
- Shovel
- Tamper
- Landscape fabric or polyethylene sheeting
- Pea gravel
- Circular saw
- 4x4 or 6x6 pressure-treated lumber
- Spirit level

1 After laying out the outline of your shed on the ground, use a shovel to excavate out the first 4 or 5 in. of soil. Tamp the remaining subgrade firm with a hand tamper or the end of a 2x4.

2 Cover the hole with landscape fabric or 6-mil perforated polyethylene sheeting, and fill it in with gravel. Form the edges of the foundation by aligning two 4x4 or 6x6 PT timbers parallel with each other.

3 Check the timbers for level, and add or subtract gravel as needed. Use a straight 2x4 longer than the width of the shed to make sure that the timbers are level with each other.

SKID AND TRENCH ANATOMY

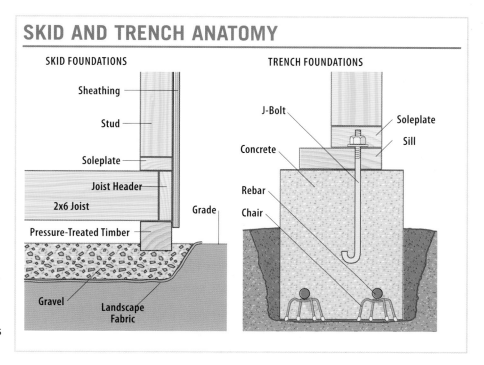

SKID FOUNDATIONS
- Sheathing
- Stud
- Soleplate
- Joist Header
- 2x6 Joist
- Pressure-Treated Timber
- Grade
- Gravel
- Landscape Fabric

TRENCH FOUNDATIONS
- J-Bolt
- Soleplate
- Sill
- Concrete
- Rebar
- Chair

FRAMING FUNDAMENTALS

The framing portion of your project allows you to see the plans you've made finally begin to take shape. There are many ways to frame a building. The most common is called stick framing, where 2x4 studs form the skeleton of walls and two-by lumber of various sizes is used to support floors and the roof. It is the method used to build most houses, and most barns and outbuildings for that matter. But there are other methods. You can also use a grid of structural poles or try the old-fashioned but challenging system of timber framing.

APPROACHES TO FRAMING

You can construct a utility building with steel and concrete, adobe, or even straw bales and rebar. But in most areas—and for barns and other outbuildings—the most common way to build is by framing with wood. Small sheds are often built like houses, piece by piece, using a system known as stick framing. With this approach, you typically install a foundation or footing piers, build a platform of girders and floor joists, and cover the platform with plywood before raising walls right on the floor platform.

The old-fashioned way of doing this, called post-and-beam building or timber framing, uses fewer but larger timbers in the structure. The heavy-timber system, which can require a crane or special rigging to set large beams, is practiced mainly by professional contractors. Another option, called pole framing, is often used on barns because it provides large clear-span areas inside the building. But poles for a large structure can be heavy and unwieldy, and they require professional installation.

Stick Framing

Stick framing refers to two types of construction. Platform framing consists of a skeletal web of milled two-by lumber that makes up the frame of the floor, walls, ceilings, and roof. Walls are often framed on the deck (made of floor joists and plywood) and then raised into place. An older method, called balloon framing, doesn't divide the stories into platforms but uses long studs to frame the entire structure. Platform framing is easier and safer to build because it provides a deck for raising the second floor and also has the advantage of using shorter more readily available studs. As a result, balloon framing is rarely used anymore.

Timber Framing

Traditional timber framing requires a high level of traditional carpentry skills including making tight-fitting mortise-and-tenon joints. The large timbers required are costly, difficult to transport, and require a large crew to assemble. The reward is an especially strong and handsome frame. But a well-built timber frame is stronger than a stick-framed structure. Also, this system has the authentic appeal of an old barn, which you can preserve by leaving the huge posts and beams exposed inside and cladding the structure with prefabricated roofing and siding panels. A post-and-beam frame may consist of only a hundred or so individual pieces that make an elegant frame. But making the complex joints and erecting the frame generally takes much more time and skill than conventional stick framing.

Pole Framing

A pole building is similar in many ways to a commercial building made with steel. A pole-frame structure doesn't rest on the ground with a full foundation but hangs from a grid of poles. Chemically treated poles (or square pressure-treated posts) are connected with large timbers or pairs of timbers that are bolted in place. These timbers serve to support floor joists, walls, and rafters, but all of the building loads travel down the poles.

FRAMING SYSTEM OPTIONS

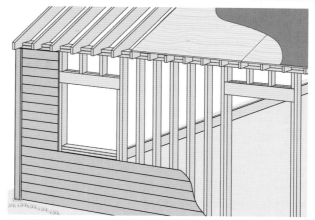

A stick-frame structure has walls built from 2x4s or 2x6s set 16 or 24 in. on center. They are often built on the deck and tipped up into position. Floors and roofs are framed with heavier lumber.

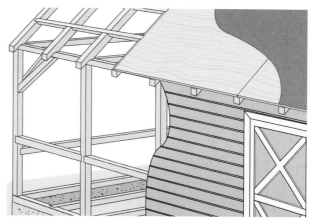

Timber framing with a small number of large beams was the norm until the twentieth century when it gave way to stick-framing systems that use two-by milled lumber.

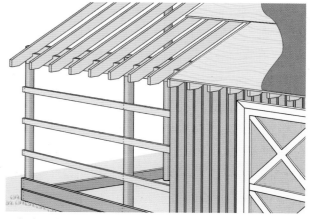

Pole framing is especially popular for livestock barns, which need a large, open central space. For smaller projects, pressure-treated posts can be substituted for heavy poles.

BUILDING LOADS

Your barn design must take structural loads into account—the weight of the building itself, what goes inside it, and the elements outside, such as wind and snow.

A framing system is like a network of streams along which building loads flow: from the roof, through the building and foundation, and ultimately into the ground. Like water, loads tend to take the path of least resistance to the lowest point, in accordance with the law of gravity—the load from a rafter flows down the rafter to the support wall framing, for example.

Load Paths. Loads must be carried from the top of the structure to the foundation without interruption. If there is a break in the system—for example, if you fail to install an adequate header over a door—weight from above will cause deflection on top of the door frame, and the door will stick. Even minor structural weaknesses can pop nails in drywall or siding, bind windows, crack trim, and create other problems.

Load-bearing and Nonload-bearing Elements. Major structural elements such as floors, posts, columns, roof framing, and all exterior walls are load-bearing. They carry the weight of the structure and everything in it (such as people) or on it (such as shingles). Many interior walls are not load-bearing. These partition walls simply divide up space. You can cut through a partition to create a doorway, or remove the wall altogether. But wherever you cut into a bearing wall, you need to account for the load it carries by installing a structural header.

TYPES OF LOADS

STRUCTURAL LOADS consist of dead loads, such as the weight of the building materials and mechanical equipment, and live loads, such as the weight of people, furnishings, stored materials, and snow on the roof. Another type of load, shear load, is the force the building encounters when the wind gusts, the earth quakes, or the foundation shifts because of events like soil washout. A point load is the downward force exerted by a single heavy thing inside or on top of the structure, such as a fireplace, hot tub, or water heater. Lastly, there is the spread load, the outward force on walls caused by the downward-and-outward force of rafters, usually because of heavy snow pressing down on the roof.

The architect's or engineer's job is to anticipate all conditions that could reasonably be expected at the site. In residential design, potential loads and stresses are typically provided by local building codes. For example, floor systems are generally designed to support 40 pounds of live load per square foot. Because wood is resilient, the frame can absorb the extra strain as you move around or concentrate heavy furniture in one room.

In a wood frame there is bound to be some movement, particularly on the floor where joists span from one support to another. But the standard limit of movement, called deflection, is $\frac{1}{360}$ of the length of the span. That means if the floor joists were 360 inches long, they would have to be strong enough to deflect no more than 1 inch when loaded with people and furniture.

Although even a small shed has building loads, 2x4s generally are more than enough to handle them. In a large barn, however, your plans will have to conform to the guidelines on approved span tables and be checked by the local building department. Inspectors will check both the size and spacing of the girders, joists, and rafters.

BUILDING LOADS

Snow Load
Spread Load
Shear Load
Live Load
Live Load
Point Load
Uneven Settling
Dead Load
Ultimate Foundation Load

The total load includes the weight of materials, people, furnishings, and environmental loads, such as the forces of wind and snow. The structure must meet local codes for all loads.

SNOW LOAD MAP

	45
	40-45
	35–40
	30–40
	25–30
	20–25
	15–20
	10–15
	5–10
	0–5
	0

Snow loads affect the design of your building. The map above shows in lbs. per sq. ft. the minimum design values. White areas vary too greatly to be mapped accurately.

SPAN TABLES

THE ALLOWABLE SPANS for joists, rafters, girders, and other load-bearing elements of a building frame are all subject to local building codes. Codes specify the loads that framing members must bear in each location. For example, 40 pounds per square foot for floor joists in living space. They also set deflection limits, given as span in inches (L) over a given number. For example, an L/360 limit for joists means a 10-foot joist can bend a maximum of 120 inches divided by 360, or ⅓ inch, under the load.

READING A SPAN TABLE. Span tables are organized by wood species and grade because they have different strengths. Different sizes for each grade are given different maximum span lengths in feet and inches for the most common on-center spacings. For example, looking at the table at top right, if you wanted to span 13 feet with southern pine 2x8s, you would need to use at least No. 1 grade at 16 inches on center. If No. 1 were unavailable, you would have the choice of using thicker lumber (such as 2x10s), or spacing No. 2 grade 2x8s at 12 inches on center.

Some codes use two tables. One gives the design values for each grade of wood—measurements of fiber strength in bending (Fb) and a ratio of stress to strain called the modulus of elasticity, or the E-value. Another gives span lengths according to these values. You first determine which size lumber will work for your span. Looking at the middle table, if you had a span of 14 feet, 6 inches, you'd need to use at least 2x10s—ones made from a wood with a minimum E-value of 1.2 (spaced at 16 inches on center) and an Fb of 1,036. The bottom table shows the design value for one type of wood (hemlock/fir) for this thickness. By matching the E-values and Fb ratings, you find that you can use No. 2 hemlock/fir (or any better grade).

It is possible for do-it-yourselfers to determine lumber sizes and spans. But final determinations are best left to an architect or structural engineer unless you use code-approved plans that pass muster at the local building department.

FLOOR JOIST SPAN RATINGS

Strength: For 40 psf live load 10 psf dead load.
Deflection: Limited in span in inches divided by 360 for live load only.

Species	Grade	2x8 Spacing On-Center			
		12"	16"	19.2"	24"
Douglas Fir-Larch	Select structural	15'	13' 7"	12' 10"	11' 11"
	No. 1 and better	14' 8"	13' 4"	12' 7"	11' 8"
	No. 1	14' 5"	13' 1"	12' 4"	11' 0"
	No. 2	14' 2"	12' 9"	11' 8"	10' 5"
	No. 3	11' 3"	9' 9"	8' 11"	8'

Excerpted from Western Wood Products Association, Western Lumber Span tables

FLOOR JOIST SPAN RATINGS

With L/360 deflection limits. For 40 psf live load.

Joist Size	On-Center Spacing	E-Value (in million psi)			
		0.8	1.0	1.2	1.4
2x6	12"	8' 6"	9' 2"	9' 9"	10' 3"
	16"	7' 9"	8' 4"	8' 10"	9' 4"
	24"	6' 9"	7' 3"	7' 9"	8' 2"
2x8	12"	11' 3"	12' 1"	12' 10"	13' 6"
	16"	10' 2"	11' 0"	11' 8"	12' 3"
	24"	8' 11"	9' 7"	10' 2"	10' 9"
2x10	12"	14' 4"	15' 5"	16' 5"	17' 3"
	16"	13'	14'	14' 11"	15' 8"
	24"	11' 4"	12' 3"	13' 0"	13' 8"
Fb	12"	718	833	941	1,043
	16"	790	917	1,036	1,148
	24"	905	1,050	1,186	1,314

Excerpted from American Wood Council

DESIGN VALUES FOR JOISTS AND RAFTERS

Species & Grade	Size	Design Value in Bending (Fb)		E-Value (in million psi)
		Normal	Snow Loading	
Hemlock/fir	2x10			
Select structural		1,700	2,035	1.6
No. 1 and better		1,390	1,600	1.5
No. 1		1,235	1,420	1.5
No. 2		1,075	1,235	1.3
No. 3		635	725	1.2

Excerpted from American Wood Council

FRAMING FLOORS

If your barn or shed will have a dirt or concrete-slab floor, you won't be building floor framing. However, you will have to install a sill (sometimes called a sill plate) of pressure-treated wood around the perimeter of your foundation.

If you want your building to have a finished floor, however, a framework of floor joists, made from 2x6s or larger lumber set on end, will sit on top of the sill. You will then add a subfloor, generally made of plywood, on top of the joists. The subfloor will be used to support a finished floor or serve as the floor itself, as is in a work space such as a shop or potting shed.

Floor Frame Options

How you frame the floor depends on the type of foundation and the desired height of the floor above ground. Joists are spaced 16 or 24 inches on center, depending on their thickness and the load

they support. They generally run parallel with the shortest side of the building, so a 8 x 12-foot shed would have 8-foot-long joists.

For small buildings, 2x6 floor joists are often strong enough to run unsupported for 8 to 10 feet. If they will run more than 10 feet, you will need to use 2x8s or 2x10s, or support the joists midspan with a girder. It also helps to install bridging between joists.

You may need to install tie-down hardware to prevent overturn; check local codes for requirements in your area. Another option, generally reserved for houses, is to use manufactured joists in the shape of an I-beam. They can span even greater lengths than a standard dimensional timber of the same thickness. These should be specified by a structural engineer.

In any case, you should consult a floor joist span table and the local building department to determine the type and size of wood you will need to span between supports.

FLOOR FRAMING ON PIER FOUNDATIONS

A STRUCTURE BUILT ON PIERS doesn't have a continuous foundation on which to lay a sill. With piers, you generally attach the beams or joists to a framing connector sunk into the concrete. This keeps the floor as low as possible. If you want to elevate the floor more than a foot or so above the ground, such as when building on a sloping site, you can attach 4x4 posts to the piers using different metal connectors, and then attach the beams to the posts. Otherwise, you can use one of these two methods, adjusting sizes as required.

4X6 OR DOUBLED 2X6 HEADER. Attach a 4x6 beam—or a rim joist made out of doubled 2x6s—to the pier blocks on each long side of the building. If you use precast concrete piers, you

can bolt pressure-treated blocks to the piers and attach the beam to the blocks with 16d galvanized nails. For cast concrete piers, attach the beams to framing connectors. Once you attach the beams, hang intermediate joists between the beams with metal joist hangers. The two end joists (stringer joists) are nailed to the ends of 4x6s or doubled 2x6s at each corner with 16d galvanized nails. Some inspectors may require hardware on all floor frame connections.

HEADER ON BEAM. You still attach beams directly to the piers. Then you build the grid of header joists and intermediate joists on the top of the beams. This will provide more ground clearance.

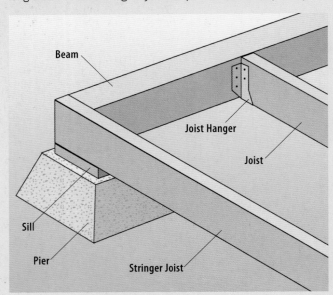

To frame a floor on piers, attach a pressure-treated beam to serve as both girder and header joist. Hang joists directly off the beam and nail stringer joists to the ends of the beam.

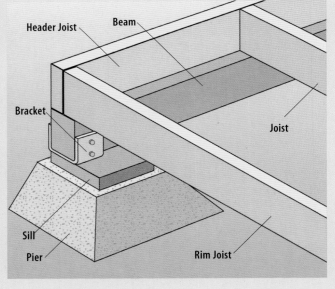

Another option is to set the joists on top of the girder, and in some cases, project them beyond the support. But this arrangement will increase the height of the floor.

Attaching Sills to Concrete Foundations

You attach a pressure-treated 2x6 sill to a concrete slab or perimeter foundation using anchor bolts placed every 4 to 6 feet in concrete or concrete-filled voids of foundation block. In houses, a thin sealer strip of foam is installed under the sill mainly for energy efficiency, which may not be an issue in an unheated barn. In regions prone to termite damage, you may want to install a metal termite shield on top of the foundation before you install the sill. The metal shield prevents termites from reaching the wooden parts of the building.

Laying down the sill is your last chance to straighten a crooked foundation. When you set the sill over the anchor bolts, the outside edge of the sill should align with the outside edge of the slab or wall—unless the foundation is out of square. In that case, take the time to make small adjustments as needed to square up the sill on which the building will sit.

SQUARING A SILL

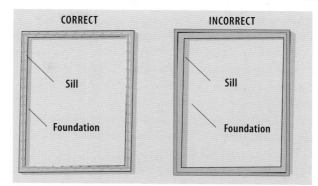

CORRECT

Sill

Foundation

INCORRECT

Sill

Foundation

When squaring a sill to a crooked foundation, increase the sill size as needed to overhang the foundation up to ½ in. or water will collect on top of the foundation and leak into the building.

PROJECT:
INSTALLING A SILL

TOOLS & MATERIALS
- Pressure-treated two-by sill
- Measuring tape
- Pencil
- Combination square
- Circular saw
- Power drill with ⅜-inch bit
- Sill sealer
- Wire brush
- ½-inch anchor-bolt nuts and washers
- Socket wrench
- Termite shield (optional)

SMART TIP

Protect the threads of anchor bolts during construction by wrapping them with duct tape.

1 After sweeping the top of the foundation clean, set the sill—typically a pressure-treated 2x6—on the foundation, and use a combination square to mark the locations of anchor bolts.

2 Measure along your mark to duplicate the distance of the bolt from the outside of the foundation. Use a ⅝-in. bit to drill a hole through the sill—this will make it easier to fit over the ½-in. bolts.

3 Thin sill sealer fills the slightly irregular space between the foundation and the sill if needed for energy efficiency. Local codes may call for a metal termite shield under the sill.

4 The threads of anchor bolts often become clogged with concrete. They need to be wire-brushed before you install the sill and try to tighten down the nuts.

5 Set the sill board onto the sealer, and leave the anchor bolts protruding. Slip a large washer on each one; make sure the sill is square; and tighten the nuts with a socket wrench.

Framing a Floor

After installing the sill, you may need to install girders, which are beams that support joists over long spans. (See "Girders," below.) The next step is to install the floor joists and cover them with sheets of plywood, called the subfloor or the deck.

Before placing joists on the sill, measure and mark your joist layout, generally spacing the joists 16 inches on center. This layout will allow the edges of the plywood sheets to fall along the middle of a joist—two edges of two sheets will share one joist. The exception is the first sheet in line along the edge of the building. You have to adjust the layout so that its edge covers the entire joist, which is an extra ¾ inch beyond the centerline of the outermost joist. If you are not very experienced with construction layout, it's wise to lay a starter sheet in position temporarily to be sure that you have the joists in the right places.

When determining joist length, deduct the thickness of the header, or rim, joists—the boards nailed across the ends of the floor joists. Header joists (with joist hangers attached) secure the floor joists upright. They also provide a clean edge for attaching subflooring. You can cut all the joists to size ahead of time, or let cantilevered joists run long, snap a line across the ends to create a perfectly straight line, and trim them in place.

FRAME ON FOUNDATION

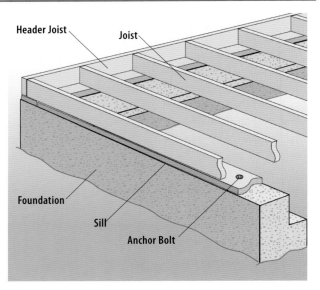

Header Joist · Joist · Foundation · Sill · Anchor Bolt

Basic floor framing is made up of header, or rim, joists and a grid of floor joists set at 16 or 24 in. on center that rests on foundation sills. Long spans may require a girder at midspan.

GIRDERS

CONTEMPORARY BARN DESIGNS often call for big floor spans with no walls or columns to break up the space. In these cases, the entire floor load must be transferred to the perimeter walls and structural framing configurations have to be beefed up to accommodate longer spans.

Let's say you have a basement workshop that is 30 feet long and 20 feet wide. It would be easy to divide up this space by running a load-bearing wall across the room, making 15 feet the longest span (if joists were running lengthwise). Fifteen feet is a span that can easily be handled by readily available framing lumber. But if you want that space open, you won't want to divide it with a load-bearing wall down the center. Instead, you can install a beam, known as a girder, beneath the floor joists to split the span in half and carry a lot of the load. Each end of the girder can sit in a pocket in the foundation wall, on pilaster extensions, or the foundation itself. Steel I-beams are the strongest and can span greater distances. Wood girders—whether glue-laminated, made from two-bys, or manufactured wood I-beams—are easier to install and less expensive.

Girders on first floors are often supported in pockets cut or formed into opposite ends of the foundation. Most codes require these pockets to be a minimum of 4 inches deep to bear the load. You also need to guard against wood rot by setting the girder on a piece of steel baseplate and allowing ½ inch of space on both sides of the girder for ventilation. If pockets won't provide enough support for your design, you can raise girders to the sill or set them on masonry pilasters built onto the foundation.

On many girder designs, there is a point of diminishing returns. You can keep adding boards to the girder to increase its width so that the girder can create an unsupported span. But once you get to the point of using three 2x12s, it's generally more economical to install a post. You can use wood or steel posts. Some steel columns have an adjustable cap for sagging girders.

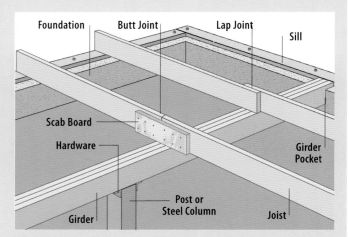

Foundation · Butt Joint · Lap Joint · Sill · Scab Board · Hardware · Girder Pocket · Post or Steel Column · Girder · Joist

Girders support floor joists over long spans. You can butt joists where they meet over a girder, and add a scab board to keep them aligned, or lap them with each joist bearing fully on the girder. But this approach will offset your subfloor nailing pattern.

PROJECT:
FRAMING A FLOOR

TOOLS & MATERIALS
- Circular saw or hand saw
- Two-by lumber for joists and bridging
- Framing square
- Framing hammer
- 16d and 12d common nails
- Measuring tape
- Carpenter's pencil
- Combination square
- Bar clamp (if needed)
- Joist hangers and joist-hanger nails (optional)

1 Place the rim joists on top of the sill (with both slab and wall foundations) or the beam (on pier foundations for a small shed as shown here). Square them up with a framing square.

2 Tack the joists in place, and stop to check the perimeter frame to make sure it's square. Use a framing square at the corners, and measure the overall diagonals, which should be equal.

3 End-nail the rim joists and end joist together with three 16d common nails. Check that they are tight against the sill. You may want to predrill nail holes near the ends to prevent splitting.

4 Mark your layout on opposite headers using 16-in. on-center marks, depending on the span and load. You may want to make duplicate layouts on both boards before installing them

5 Set each joist in place at the marks. You can check the joists for square against the rim joist with a large framing square; use a combination square to check vertical alignment.

6 Once they are square, you can end-nail the joists through the rim joist with three 12d common nails. Local codes generally require that you set joists into metal joist hangers.

7 If your code requires joist hangers, nail them through one pair of flanges to the header and through the other pair into the joist. Be sure that the top of the joist is flush with the rim joist.

8 To stiffen the floor overall and prevent exposed joists from twisting, add solid bridging made from floor joist material, or use premolded X-shaped metal bridging.

INSTALLING SUBFLOORS

With the floor joists in place, it's time to put down the subfloor, or floor deck. In houses, the subfloor forms the base for floor coverings such as carpet or finished wood and often is covered with another layer of material, called underlayment, before finish materials are installed. In sheds, barns, and other utility buildings, you'll probably leave the subfloor unfinished, if you install a floor at all. Barns, especially livestock barns, are often best left with a bare-earth floor.

Materials

CDX plywood is most typically used for subfloors, although if code permits you may also use waferboard, oriented-strand board (OSB) or other sheet materials. For joists 16 inches on center, most codes require the subfloor to be at least ½-inch thick; for joists spaced 24 inches on center, the subflooring must be at least ¾-inch thick. However, if you are not planning to put a finished floor over the plywood, it's a good idea to make the subfloor at least ¾-inch thick or even use two layers of ½-inch plywood if you plan to store heavy machinery or tools.

Installation

You can nail plywood decking, but for maximum strength apply a bead of construction adhesive to the tops of the joists, and fasten the sheets with screws. Lay down the subfloor by staggering panel edges so that the seams don't line up across the floor over one joist. If you start the first row with a full panel, start the second with a half panel. Leave a gap of ⅛ inch between panels to prevent buckling if the panels expand. You can use a couple of 8d common nails as spacer gauges.

If you use an adhesive, nail or screw the subflooring every 12 inches along the edges and in the field of the plywood. If you don't use adhesive, you will need to add more fasteners. In this case, nail or screw every 6 inches on the outside edges and 10 inches in the field. Remember that basic ½-inch sheets may satisfy local codes but bend under the weight of a heavy lawn mower or a stack of lumber. Be sure to build based on the purpose of the building. If you use ¾-inch panels, attach them with adhesive and screws.

PROJECT:
INSTALLING A SUBFLOOR

- Caulking gun
- Subfloor adhesive
- Plywood or OSB panels
- Hammer or power drill with screwdriver bit
- 8d ring-shank nails or
- 2-inch deck screws
- Circular saw or table saw
- Measuring tape
- 2-pound sledgehammer

1 Although it is not a requirement, gluing down the subfloor will increase the floor's stiffness and decrease nail popping. Run a ¼-in.-dia. bead of subfloor adhesive down each joist.

2 Nail panels to the joists with 8d nails, spaced every 6 in. along the edge and every 12 in. elsewhere. Install panels with the face-grain perpendicular to the joists and stagger panel joints.

3 If you're using ordinary square-end panels instead of tongue-and-groove subflooring, leave about a ⅛-in. space between the panels to allow for expansion without buckling.

4 If you started with a half panel in your first course, start the second course with a full panel. This keeps the panel seams from aligning over one joist and makes for a stronger floor

5 You can use a scrap board, such as a 2x4, to work a panel into position. But this technique is more often used to fit together sheets of interlocking tongue-and-groove plywood.

STAIR OPENINGS

Many framed floors have openings for stairways, chimneys, and other features. The basic idea is to install double headers at each end of the opening and double joists (a standard joist plus a trimmer) along the sides. This creates a strong box around the opening that can carry the loads normally carried by full-length joists. The extra framing should be the same size as the surrounding joists. In most regions, you need to use metal hangers on these connections.

Building the Opening

To make a rough opening in floor framing, first measure the dimensions of the opening on the plan, and then cut the lumber accordingly. Double up joists on both sides of the rough opening; anchor them at the ends; and face-nail the trimmers every 16 to 24 inches with three 12d nails. You also can use 16d nails (3½ inches long) driven at a slight angle to prevent the sharp points from protruding through the 3½ inches of lumber.

To install the header joists, mark the header positions on inside trimmer joists at both ends of the rough opening. Install the headers by running a double thickness of joist lumber perpendicular to the floor joists.

In most installations, you'll need short joists called tail joists to span from the headers to the outer joists of the floor frame. Space the tail joists at the standard on-center spacing of regular floor joists to maintain nailing surfaces.

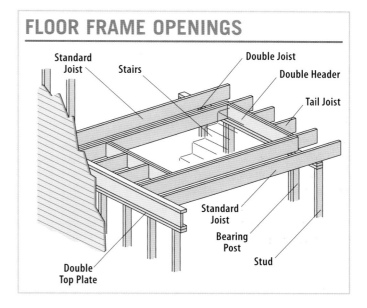

FLOOR FRAME OPENINGS

Standard Joist • Stairs • Double Joist • Double Header • Tail Joist • Standard Joist • Bearing Post • Stud • Double Top Plate

FRAMING SECOND FOORS & LOFTS

IF YOUR DESIGN calls for a second floor or a loft, you will need to add ceiling joists supported by the exterior and interior load-bearing walls. Ceiling joists are usually spaced 16 inches on center. If there's no second-floor living space, the joists can be smaller because they bear a smaller load—generally 30 pounds per square foot or less anticipating light storage, as compared to 40 pounds per square foot in living areas.

The loads they will carry and the length of the unsupported span determine the size of joists you must use. If the house will have a truss roof, the bottom chord of the truss will substitute for the ceiling joists. It may be small in size but is reinforced by the internal braces of the truss. Of course, many barn designs don't include a second-floor frame and leave the rafters open.

Most often, ceiling joists run parallel with the shorter side of the building and are toenailed to the tops of exterior and interior load-bearing walls. When the roof is framed, the roof rafters are face-nailed to the ceiling joists.

If room dimensions are too large for the length of normal ceiling joists, you will need to add a girder or bearing wall, generally at midspan, or use larger joists.

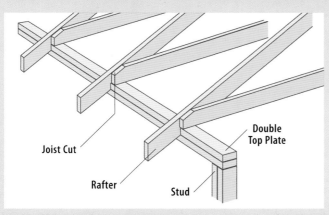

Ceiling joists in a load-bearing attic floor should be laid out so that they rest against the rafters. You can toenail the joists to the double plate and also nail them to the rafters.

Joist Cut • Double Top Plate • Rafter • Stud

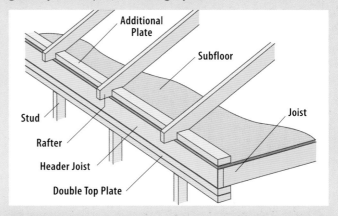

Another option is to frame a new deck with header joists on top of the walls. This approach works well on mansard-style roofs with usable floor space along the eaves.

Additional Plate • Subfloor • Stud • Rafter • Header Joist • Double Top Plate • Joist

FRAMING WALLS

Stick-built walls are constructed on a modular system designed to provide a combination of structural strength and nailing surfaces for sheathing materials inside and out. Adding windows and doors generally requires extra studs because the openings don't normally fall exactly into the modular plan.

The base of the wall is a horizontal 2x4 (or a 2x6 in some cases) called a soleplate, or shoe. Studs sit on the shoe, generally every 16 inches on center. The top of the wall is capped with two more horizontal 2x4s called a top plate.

There are three kinds of studs in most walls. Full-height studs, sometimes called king studs, run from the soleplate to the top plate. Jack studs, also called trimmer studs, run from the shoe up alongside a full stud at rough openings. The top of the jack stud rests under the header over a window or door. Cripple studs are short 2x4s that fill in the spaces above and below a rough opening, for example, from the soleplate to the sill of a window. They transfer the load to top plates and windowsills, and they maintain the modular layout to provide nailing surfaces for siding and drywall or other surface materials.

The load-bearing walls in a frame are typically made of 2x4s although some codes require 2x6 framing to allow room for more insulation. Although each 2x6 stud costs more than a comparable 2x4, the overall cost is only marginally different because fewer 2x6s are needed. (Building codes usually allow them to be placed 24 inches on center.) For any framing jobs in uninsulated buildings, such as sheds, barns, and garages, 2x4 studs are the most economical.

Assembling a Wall

Start by marking the plate and shoe according to the wall layout in your plans. Then you can cut the studs. A power miter box makes this job go quickly. King studs will be full length—generally 91½ inches for 8-foot ceilings. Jack studs will be king-stud length minus the combined height of the header and cripples above. You can cut the cripples and sills to length after you put the jack studs and headers in place. Some builders prefer to build rough openings after the wall has been raised.

One efficient way to build walls is to assemble the components on the deck and tip them into position. On long walls you'll need some help raising the structure, and on all walls you have to plan the framing carefully before nailing through the shoe and first plate and into the ends of the studs.

STICK-FRAMED WALL

Double Top Plate · Cripple Stud · Wall Stud · Window Header · Full Stud · Jack Stud · Door Header · Window Sill · Jack Stud · Full Stud · Cutout · Full Stud · Jack Stud · Soleplate · Cripple Stud · Subfloor

A stick-framed wall consists of studs—vertical 2x4s or 2x6s—between a single horizontal soleplate, often called a shoe, and a double top plate. Windows and doors have framed headers and extra jack and cripple studs to account for the missing full studs.

Squaring a Wall

Check walls to make sure they're square before you stand them in place, and again after you raise them. You can check the diagonals, which should be equal if the wall is square. It also helps to lock up the position by tacking diagonal braces along the wall. Some builders install sheathing before raising, although this makes the wall heavier.

BRACING OPTIONS

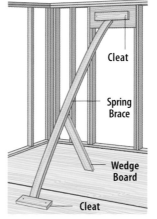

Cleat · Spring Brace · Wedge Board · Cleat

Temporary Corner Brace

Apply a spring brace to fix a bow in a stud wall. Nail a flat brace (at least 8 ft. long) to cleats on the floor and wall.

To brace a corner, lock it in place with a 2x4. Leave the brace in place until the whole wall is finished.

Raising a Wall

Before erecting any wall, snap a chalk line along the subfloor or slab to establish a reference guide for positioning the inside edge of the wall soleplate. On a subfloor, also nail a few 2x4 cleats to the outside of the header joist to keep the wall from slipping off the deck as you raise it. With as many helpers as you need, slide the wall into position so that when you raise it, it will stand close to the guideline. Erect the wall, and align it to the chalk line.

Using a 4-foot spirit level, get the wall as close to plumb as possible. You'll fine-tune it for plumb when you install the adjacent wall. Run braces from studs to cleats that are nailed into the subfloor, or on corners, to the outsides of the floor joists. When the wall is plumb, have a helper nail the braces to the cleats. With the bottom soleplate properly positioned, nail into the rim joists and floor joists with 16d nails. You can plumb a small wall by yourself. The trick is to nail an angled brace to a cleat on the deck and clamp it to the wall. Check with a level, adjust and reclamp as needed, and tack the brace to hold the wall plumb. On long walls of 20 feet or so, brace each corner and several interior studs.

To check for plumb, hold a 4-foot level against a straight 2x4. Pay particular attention to corners. If the wall is leaning in or out, release any braces and adjust the wall. Apply force to the braces to push the wall out. To bring the wall in, attach a flat brace between two cleats (one attached to the wall and one to the floor) and use a two-by as a kicker to bow the brace and force the wall inward. You can also apply braces staked outside the building. Retack the braces to hold the wall in its proper position.

Top Plates

When adjoining walls are in proper position you can add the second top plate and tie the walls together. The top plate on one wall overlaps the bottom plate of the adjoining wall. Where partitions join exterior bearing walls, the top plate of the partition should lap onto the top plate of the exterior wall. Secure all laps with at least two 16d nails.

LAYING OUT THE WALLS

TO LAY OUT THE SOLEPLATE and top plates of a wall, first cut a pair of straight 2x4s (or 2x6s) to length. Tack the soleplate to the subfloor and set the top plate flush against it. Make your first mark ¾ inch short of your on-center spacing (15¼ inches), and make an X past that mark. This will place center of the first stud 16 inches from the corner. Measure down the length of the plates, and mark where the common, full-length studs will fall, every 16 or 24 inches, and mark each of these studs with an X. You can also measure and mark the locations of cripple studs (C) and jack studs (O).

Avoid layout confusion by marking the shoe and the top plate the same way in a step-ahead system. You may want to mark the soleplate and top plate at the same time with a combination square or rafter square.

Once the square line is drawn, step ahead of the line to mark the location of a stud with an X. You can also use the tongue of a framing square, which is 1½ inches wide, to mark the full width.

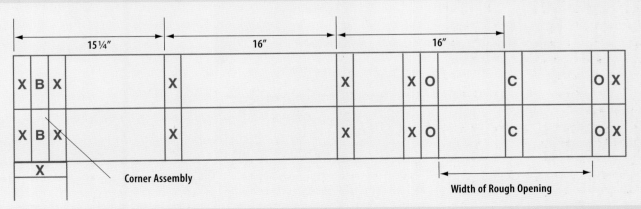

Lay out corners and rough openings on your plates as indicated on your plans. Mark all full-length studs with an X, jack studs (also called trimmers) with an O, blocking with a B, and cripples with a C.

PROJECT: 🐾🐾🐾
FRAMING WALLS

TOOLS & MATERIALS

- Safety goggles and work gloves
- 2x4 or 2x6 lumber
- Measuring tape
- Circular saw or table saw
- Carpenter's pencil
- Combination square
- Hammer
- 16d and 12d common nails
- Framing square
- 4-foot spirit level

1 Start by marking the layout on both the soleplate and one of the two top plates at the same time—this ensures that the studs will line up when the wall is erected and squared.

2 Work on the subfloor (or the surface of the slab) to assemble the frame. Position each stud; stand on it to prevent shifting; and nail through the soleplate with two 16d common nails.

3 When the soleplate is nailed on, shift to the top of the wall, and follow the same procedure to nail on one of the top plates. Before nailing, check the stud position for square.

4 Check the overall frame by comparing diagonal measurements. If the wall is square, the diagonals should be equal. Once the wall has been adjusted, you can nail on a temporary brace.

5 Small shed walls can be raised by one person; larger walls may require three or more. The wall components are nailed to the floor framing with 16d nails and then braced.

6 Once the wall is braced, use a 4-ft. level to check several studs for plumb. It's easiest to assemble corner posts that may include short pieces of blocking on the deck and add them later.

7 With the walls straightened and the corner posts in place, you can install the second top plate, also called the cap plate. Stagger the joints over the corner in order to tie one wall to another.

8 Nail on the cap plate with 12d or 16d nails. Once all the exterior walls are in place, you can add sheathing and remove the temporary bracing as you nail on the sheets.

PROJECT:
INSTALLING LET-IN BRACING

TOOLS & MATERIALS
- Chalk-line box
- Circular saw
- Measuring tape
- Metal bracing or 1x4 lumber
- Hammer
- 6d common nails

SMART TIP

Let-in bracing won't be necessary if you are siding or sheathing with plywood panels. However it can add rigidity to buildings with no sheathing and board. For buildings that will not have interior finished walls, bracing can simply be 2x4s nailed diagonally inside the framing instead of let in as shown here.

1 Many do-it-yourselfers will find metal bracing easier to install than wood bracing. Start by snapping a chalk line from the top of the corner on a diagonal down and across several studs.

2 As with wood bracing, set your saw blade to cut only as deep as one side of the L-shaped metal brace. Then make one straight cut through the studs along the chalk line.

3 Metal let-in bracing is L-shaped. You simply set one edge into the straight line of cuts angled from the top of the corner to the sill. The cuts must form a straight line for the brace to fit.

4 The metal bracing is perforated, so it's easy to nail it in place at each stud. Installing braces (either metal or wood) strengthens walls and helps to keep them square.

5 To install wood 1x4 bracing instead of metal, you'll need to snap two chalk lines and cut two kerfs in the stud faces. Then use a hammer and chisel to make a ¾ x 3½-in. channel.

STUD CONFIGURATIONS AT CORNERS

YOU HAVE SEVERAL CHOICES when it comes to framing corners. Stud-and-block corners use the most material, but they are the most rigid. The three-stud corner saves time and a little material because you don't need the blocking. Both provide interior and exterior nailing surfaces. The two-stud corner may be fine for a small shed but does not provide for interior nailing on both walls.

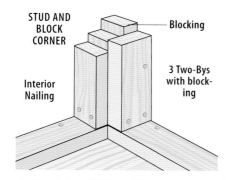

STUD AND BLOCK CORNER — Blocking
Interior Nailing
3 Two-Bys with block-ing

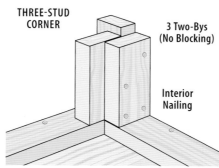

THREE-STUD CORNER
3 Two-Bys (No Blocking)
Interior Nailing

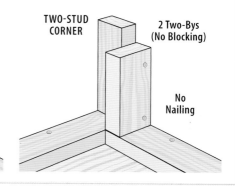

TWO-STUD CORNER
2 Two-Bys (No Blocking)
No Nailing

WINDOWS & DOORS

Stud placement is crucial for rough openings in walls where you insert doors and windows. The rough opening size is listed in window and door catalogs, and generally allows ½ to ¾ inch of shimming space around the unit. This allows you to plumb and level the window or door even when the adjacent wall frame is out of kilter. Each side of the opening has a full-height stud. Inside those studs are shorter jacks that supports the header, and, in the case of windows, the sill. The distance from jack to jack, allowing for shimming space, is the rough opening.

On windows, one set of jacks is cut to a height to fit between the sole plate and the sill. Then the sill is installed and another set of jacks is cut to fit between the sill and the header. Cripple studs between sole plate and sill and between header and top plate help support the sill and top plate and provide nailing for drywall and sheathing. You can rest the jacks on the soleplate, or you can run them down to the plywood deck.

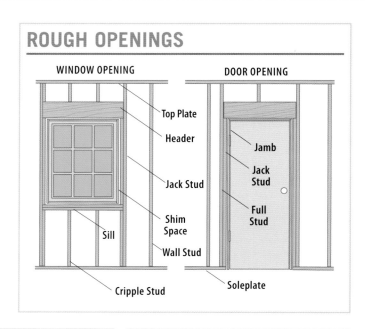

ROUGH OPENINGS

WINDOW OPENING — Top Plate, Header, Jack Stud, Shim Space, Sill, Wall Stud, Cripple Stud

DOOR OPENING — Jamb, Jack Stud, Full Stud, Soleplate

PROJECT:
BUILDING ROUGH OPENINGS

TOOLS & MATERIALS
- Safety goggles
- Circular saw
- 2x4 or 2x6 studs
- Measuring tape
- Pencil
- Combination square
- Hammer
- Common nails
- 4-foot spirit level
- Two-by headers

SMART TIP

Toenailing and face nailing are both effective ways to join lumber. However, face nailing at a right angle through one board into another is easier. Building walls on the deck lets you face nail through the soleplate into the studs instead of having to toenail the studs to soleplates that already are installed.

1 At each side of the rough opening, nail a jack stud into the soleplate and adjacent full-height stud. In 2x4 walls, use two 10d nails every foot or so to create the structural equal of a 4x4 post.

2 A small window doesn't weigh enough to need a double sill, but it's wise to nail two 2x4s on the flat to jack studs and side studs to provide adequate nailing for sheathing and drywall. End-nail through the full-height studs.

3 Continue additional jack stud sections along both sides of the window opening. These framing members will help to support the weight carried by the header across the opening.

4 Make up a header with two 2x6s, sandwiching a sheet of 1/2-in. plywood that packs out the header to the wall thickness. Wider openings will require larger headers.

5 Add cripple studs above the header and below the sill to maintain the on-center layout of the wall. You need the cripples for nailing surfaces (and strength) under surface materials.

RIB CONSTRUCTION FOR SHEDS

This method of building small barn-style sheds (generally 10 feet wide or less) involves constructing complete framing units called ribs. These include not only roof members but studs and floor joists as well. Studs are added to the rear wall rib to provide a nailing surface for sheathing and siding, and a door is framed in the front rib. Plywood sheathing joins the ribs together, and the ribs themselves are reinforced at the joints with plywood gussets and galvanized hardware.

The drawings below show typical ribs for 8- or 10-foot-wide sheds. The length of the shed depends on the number of interior ribs. Ribs on small gable structures generally need no additional bracing. Gambrel designs may need bracing due to the built-in weak spot between rafter sections. Even small sheds must conform to building codes.

Bear in mind that the rib floor joists should be made of pressure-treated wood. It's best to elevate the structure on beams and concrete piers, or attach it to pressure-treated skids set into the ground, if code allows.

Installing Ribs

You can't nail up sheathing as you erect the ribs, because you have to check and recheck that the ribs are plumb, are the same distance apart at either end, and are squared up to the foundation and to one another. It's better to follow the same installation technique used on roof trusses. Erect one rib, and temporarily nail up some 2x4 braces staked to the ground. As you erect the next rib, nail some strapping rib to rib as you bring it into plumb position to hold it in place.

To keep the ribs secure as you continue working, you should anchor the first rib with several braces. Be sure it is braced solidly side to side as well as end to end. And as you erect, plumb, and square up each rib in turn, leapfrog the strapping so that each strap spans two or three ribs with overlapping coverage.

Building individual ribs is a simple way to construct a small garden shed or toolshed. Each rib is a complete cross section of the building that is tied together with plywood sheathing.

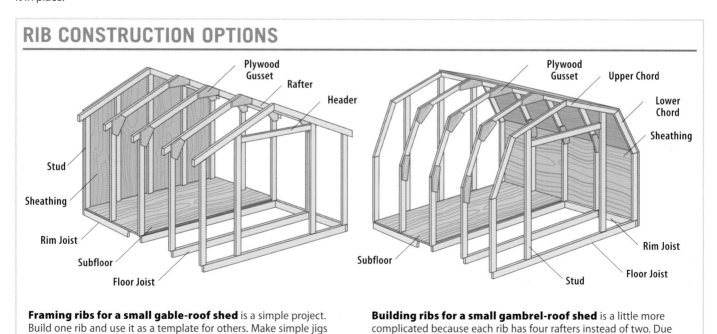

RIB CONSTRUCTION OPTIONS

Plywood Gusset · Rafter · Header · Stud · Sheathing · Rim Joist · Subfloor · Floor Joist

Plywood Gusset · Upper Chord · Lower Chord · Sheathing · Rim Joist · Floor Joist · Stud · Subfloor

Framing ribs for a small gable-roof shed is a simple project. Build one rib and use it as a template for others. Make simple jigs to help you mark and cut the lumber and gusset components. All nongusset joints should be reinforced with hardware.

Building ribs for a small gambrel-roof shed is a little more complicated because each rib has four rafters instead of two. Due to the two-part rafters, you may need extra pieces to reinforce the rafters and effectively turn part of the rib into a roof truss.

POLE BARNS

Building on poles driven into the ground is one of the oldest construction techniques. It has endured because poles (in the form of unmilled trees) are everywhere, and the construction is highly practical. And by elevating a structure off the ground on poles, you avoid floods and vermin.

Furthermore, when you stick a quarter or even a third of a pole into the ground, the portion rising out of the ground has great stability and strength. Pole buildings generally have great resistance to racking, good wind resistance, and—when the poles are sized properly—excellent overall strength. Additionally, a well-engineered pole barn has structural components that interlock and absorb force and distribute loads across the entire frame—unlike stick-frame structures, where an isolated portion of the structure absorbs forces and has limited force-distribution paths. Pole barns are highly adaptable to most sites; they work much better for sloped sites than stick framing.

Parts of a Pole Barn

Vertical members can be either poles (round) or posts (square). Most of the horizontal members, which are usually dimensional lumber, are called girts. Depending on where a girt is positioned, it might be a floor girt (what a stick framer would call a header or rim joist), a siding girt (the horizontal backing for siding), an eaves girt, or a ridge girt, both of which support rafters.

Once a pole frame is up, you can pour a slab for the floor, leave a dirt floor, or frame a floor suspended on the poles. Because you are not platform framing, with one floor depending on the floor beneath it, you can hang floors and ceilings off the poles at any elevation.

Choosing Poles

If you think that round poles don't live by the same rules as dimensional lumber, think again. Poles are subject to the laws of loads, spans, and stresses, just like timbers and beams. You will find, however, that poles are stronger than comparable dimensional timbers. This is because the tree, engineered by nature, naturally grows certain parts of its layers in compression and certain ones in tension. A pole that is simply a debarked tree, unmilled, is stronger than a timber milled to the same size because the timber loses these tension-compression relationships.

Poles are rated in classes by the American Wood Preservers Association. The different classes take into account the diameter and circumference at the top and the length of the pole in feet. (See "Common Pole Classes" at right.) Poles within classes are rated for their load-bearing capacity (for loads delivered on a vertical pole) and for span (for loads on a horizontal pole or girt). The upshot is that poles need to be engineered for your specific structure with careful consideration given to wind and snow loading, the dead load of the building (the weight of the material it is made from),

TYPICAL POLE BARN CONSTRUCTION

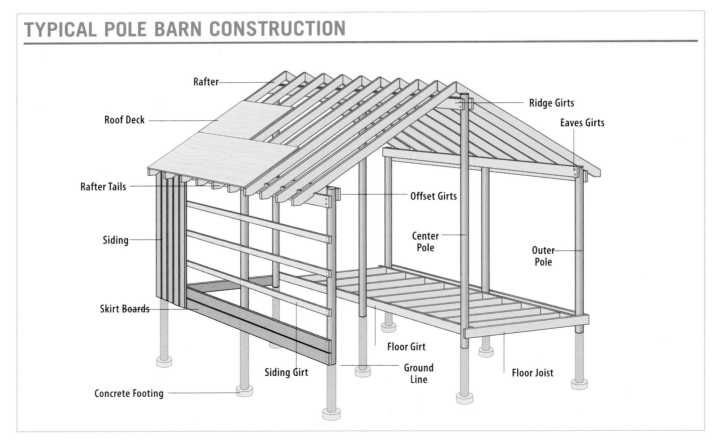

Rafter

Roof Deck

Ridge Girts

Eaves Girts

Rafter Tails

Offset Girts

Siding

Center Pole

Outer Pole

Skirt Boards

Floor Girt

Siding Girt

Ground Line

Floor Joist

Concrete Footing

FLOOR FRAMING FOR A POLE BARN

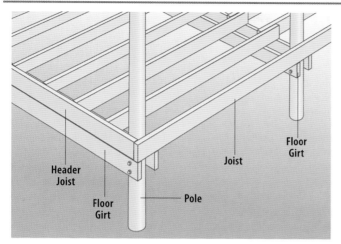

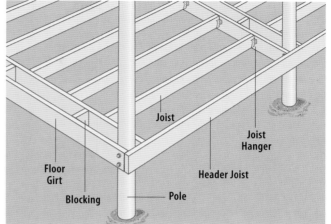

To frame a floor for a pole building, you can bolt double girts to the poles and frame your joist members on top of them the way you would add joists over a girder.

Another way to frame a pole building floor is to use the double girts as part of the finished floor frame, hanging joists between the girts on galvanized joist hangers.

and the live load of the building (weight of the things you put into the barn once it is built). If you're not working from code-approved plans, consult an architect, engineer, pole suppliers, or the trade associations that represent them.

Pole Treatments

Poles need to be treated with preservative just like any other wood that comes in sustained contact with the ground. The majority of pressure-treated wood has a recommended ground-contact concentration of preservatives. You need to be sure that the preservative is safe and approved by code. It's wise to check with the pole supplier and local inspectors to be sure that your poles are properly treated. In the past, building poles were treated with chromated copper arsenate (CCA) and this is still an approved preservative for some applications, but its use is restricted, and other products exist. For lumber and timbers that are structural and in contact with soil or fresh water, look for a CCA concentration of 0.60.

Using Posts

You probably won't find a local home center or even a big lumberyard that carries unmilled poles. Most likely you will need to special-order them from a lumberyard that specializes in pole buildings. (Cutting down trees and chemical-treating them yourself is dangerous and not recommended.)

However, in the absence of poles, 6x6 or 8x8 pressure-treated posts work well for most small projects. Many lumberyards carry 12- and 16-foot 6x6s, which would be long enough for a building with an 8-foot wall height and a 4-foot frost depth. In fact, it is much easier to attach girts to the square side of a post than the round edge of a pole. But oversize posts like this can be quite expensive.

Poles for construction are usually dark brown or green from chemical treatments that protect the wood from rotting.

COMMON POLE CLASSES

CLASS	1	2	3	4	5	6
Diameter at top	8½"	8"	7¼"	6¾"	6"	5½"
Minimum top circumference	27"	25"	23"	21"	19"	17"
Length of pole	Minimum circumference at 6 ft. from butt					
20'	–	–	–	–	–	21"
25'	–	–	–	–	–	23"
30'	–	34"	32"	29½"	27½"	25"
35'	–	36½"	34"	31½"	29"	27"
40'	41"	38½"	36"	33½"	31"	28½"
45'	43"	40½"	37½"	35"	32½"	–

Check classes and sizes with the local building department.

Setting Poles

On small pole buildings, you may be able to tip up poles or posts with a few helpers. On most large barns that require very large poles, you need a crane or a special setup called a gin pole, which is a type of site-built hand-powered crane held with guy wires on a hinged base. Similar systems using a tripod array and block and tackle are generally well beyond the scope of do-it-yourselfers. But on a large barn project, you might prepare the site, dig the holes, and have a professional crew set and brace the poles before continuing with sheathing and roofing on your own. Even on a modest project, you'll need one person to hold and brace the pole while another checks for plumb.

Raising the Pole

Before raising a pole, it helps to place a rough lumber plank on the side of the excavation that the pole will bear against on its way into the hole. This will keep the pole from caving in a lot of dirt. Once a pole is vertical, you need to hold it in place with at least two angled braces securely staked to the ground. Remember, poles are heavy. You can clamp the braces temporarily as you adjust for plumb and fine-tune the placement of the pole. Then nail the braces securely before you backfill the hole with soil or concrete.

PREPARING THE HOLE

THE HOLE DEPTH depends on your frost line and how you will set the pole. Whether you embed the pole in the ground, or use the common system of setting poles with hardware aboveground on piers, the base of the pole or pier needs to be set below the frost line. Otherwise, freezing subsurface water could cause shifting. The local building inspector can provide (and likely will check) the required depth.

The way you dig depends on the number of poles, their depth, and whether your soil is rocky. If you're building a small shed or workshop, a small number of 2-foot holes in sandy soil can be dug with a shovel and a posthole digger. Many deep holes call for a rented power auger. A narrow, 4-foot-deep hole will be almost impossible to dig without one. Extremely rocky soil will make digging tough, even with a handheld power auger. It's worth spending money to save time (and maybe spare you a few bruised ribs) by hiring someone to dig your holes with a tractor equipped with a power-driven auger bit. If you don't have any willing farmers in your area, try a fencing company.

In loose or sandy soil, you can rent a two-person gasoline-powered auger so that you (and a helper) can dig deep holes a lot faster than you can with a shovel and a posthole digger.

FOUR WAYS TO SET POLES

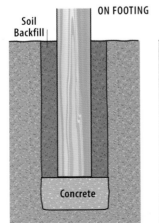
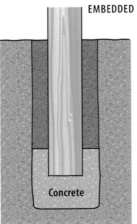
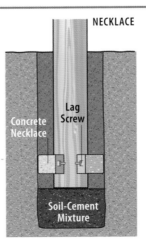
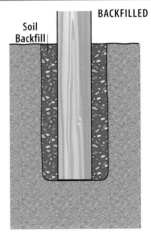

There are several ways to support a pole in the ground, including on a concrete footing, embedded in a concrete footing, on a soil-cement mixture with a concrete ring, called a necklace, poured around lag screws, or in a hole backfilled with soil or a soil-cement mixture. Poles also are commonly installed with hardware on aboveground concrete piers.

PROJECT: RAISING, SETTING & BRACING POLES

TOOLS & MATERIALS
- Posthole digger or power auger
- One-by boards
- Poles or posts
- Power drill/driver
- 6-inch (or longer) bolts
- 4-foot spirit level
- 2x4s for bracing
- Concrete
- Shovel

1 You'll need to dig a hole below the frost line for each pole. For small buildings, try digging with a posthole digger. For many poles, deep frost lines, or rocky soil, rent a power auger.

2 Place a few one-by boards on one side of the hole to keep the pole from dragging down dirt from the sides of the hole and making the hole shallower than it should be.

3 For greater stability (if you'll be pouring concrete into the hole), fasten a few large bolts or lag screws at the bottom of the pole (or post as shown here) so that they stick out a few inches.

4 A 12-ft. 6x6 post can easily be raised into position by two people; longer, heavier poles may require four or six people—or even a crane—to get them upright safely.

5 One or more workers should hold the pole or post in position while another checks it for plumb. Once it is straight, it can be secured in position with braces staked to the ground.

6 Use two sets of 2x4 braces and stakes to keep the post plumb while you pour the concrete or backfill the hole. Check it again as you work and readjust as needed.

7 Once all the poles are braced, fill the bottom of each hole with enough concrete to reach past the bolts. Other embedding systems use soil or a mix of soil and cement.

8 Once the concrete necklace has cured, you can backfill the hole with soil. Other systems use aboveground piers that keep the poles off the ground. Check local codes for preference.

Wall & Roof Framing

In most pole barn plans, poles or posts serve only as the vertical framing members that support dimensional lumber or rough-cut timbers. These pieces of lumber in turn support the siding and roofing. There are a number of different ways to fasten girts, joists, and rafters to the grid of vertical poles or posts. The best one depends on several factors, for example, whether you are using round poles or square posts, how large the timbers are, and what fasteners are favored by the local building department.

Lumber-to-Pole Connections

When connecting lumber to poles, you have four main choices: spikes, lag screws, machine bolts, and a spike grid. If you're using posts, it's easy to fasten the flat sides of girts against the flat surfaces of the posts. The two timbers rest against each other and provide more than enough bearing for a secure connection. But if you're using poles, only a narrow strip of a girt will rest against the pole because the pole is round. To improve this situation and gain more bearing in the connection, many builders recess the girts into the poles using a process called dapping.

The idea is to cut a shallow notch in the face of the pole and let in the girt, generally by about half its thickness. This way, the girt bears partially on the pole instead of hanging completely on the fasteners. Make the notch by setting the depth of cut on a circular saw and cutting several parallel kerfs into the outer face of the post. Then knock out the wood between kerfs with a hammer or hatchet, and smooth out the surface with a chisel. The result is that the girt now nestles into the pole, creating a stronger connection.

PROJECT:
ATTACHING SIDING & EAVES GIRTS

TOOLS & MATERIALS
- Pressure-treated 2x6s for skirt boards
- Bar clamps
- 4-foot spirit level
- Power drill/driver or framing hammer
- Nails or screws
- Measuring tape
- Water level or line level and mason's twine
- 2x4s for siding girts

1 Install skirt boards made of pressure-treated 2x6s. The bottom skirt board runs along the ground. Check for level, and then screw or nail them into the support poles or posts

2 Horizontal girts provide a nailing surface for the siding. Most designs call for one every 24 in. Measure up from the top skirt board on the first post, and make a mark.

3 Mark all the posts for the siding girts using a line level, transit, or water level. Run the line along the posts, adjusting it to level all around the perimeter of the building.

4 A water level indicates level readings over large areas, even when the tube runs up and down across a construction site. The level at one end of the tube is level with the water at the other end.

5 Siding girts are usually 2x4s face-nailed (or screwed) to posts. For poles, they may be partially recessed into the face of the poles (a process called dapping) for extra support.

The trick to this process is holding the saw flat even when you're cutting a pole that is round. It takes some practice to create an even series of kerfs that you can break out easily. You will find that it pays to make more cuts with kerfs closer together. This reduces the time needed to chip out and smooth the notch.

Four Ways to Make Connections

- **Spikes.** You can attach lumber to a pole using 8-inch ring nails called pole spikes, generally four per connection. This connection won't support much load, around 2,500 pounds, and nails can loosen, so you should use this system only for small structures.
- **Lag Screws.** Using two 4- to 6-inch-long rust-resistant lag screws can provide a connection that will support about 5,500 pounds. The screw threads won't loosen or pull out the way nails can.
- **Machine or Carriage Bolts.** By predrilling the dimension lumber and pole and through-bolting the notched joint with stainless-steel machine or carriage bolts, washers, and nuts, you can achieve a solid structural connection capable of carrying about 8,000 pounds. Through-bolting, generally two bolts per girt connection, is often the best balance of efficiency and strength, and should meet local codes.
- **Spike Grid.** Some builders use spike grids between poles and dimensional lumber instead of, or in addition to, through-bolting. There are several types, including shaped grids that fit between curved poles and squared lumber. Be sure to check not only lumber sizes, but lumber connections as well, with the local building inspector.

CONNECTOR OPTIONS

ATTACH GIRTS TO POLES with one of these four types of connectors. Eight-inch ring-nail spikes can be used for smaller structures. Lag screws, machine bolts, and spike grids have more holding power. You can't rely on nails that are used on stick-built house frames.

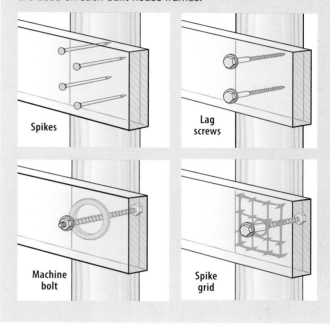

Spikes

Lag screws

Machine bolt

Spike grid

HOLDING UP THE ROOF

ROOF STRUCTURES on pole barns are subject to the same stresses and loads as those built over a stick-frame structure. But in a pole building, the rafters (or trusses) are supported differently.

One option is to use double girts on the outer poles. This provides two points of support for conventional rafters and decreases the span somewhat. Another option is to use double girts bolted on the outside of the poles. The double-width top edge creates a support platform for rafters that is similar to the double top plate of a stick-built wall frame. And double girts can be designed to support rafters between poles. On small structures, you can join rafters at a central ridgeboard. Depending on the slope of the roof and the rafter setup, you may also need the extra strength of collar ties.

On large structures with a line of poles at midspan, the upper ends of the rafters can rest on girts bolted to the center poles. (The central girts take the place of a ridgeboard.) If you plan to install roof trusses, you need a level platform for the bottom chord to rest on.

TWO GIRTS SANDWICH POLE

TWO GIRTS ON ONE SIDE

TRUSS ON TWO GIRTS

PROJECT: 🐿🐿🐿
ATTACHING RAFTER GIRTS

TOOLS & MATERIALS

- Measuring tape
- Line level with twine or water level
- 2x4 scraps for scab boards
- Power drill with screwdriver bit
- 2x10s or 2x12s for rafter girts
- Bar clamps
- 4-foot spirit level
- Circular or chain saw
- Hatchet, 2-inch wood chisel
- Paint brush
- Wood preservative
- Spade, auger, and/or Forstner bits
- ½-inch bolts or threaded rods with nuts and washers
- Socket wrench
- Reciprocating saw

1 The top of the rafter girts represent your wall height. Measure up on one pole from the level skirt boards, and then transfer this mark to the other poles using a line level or water level.

2 Make another mark below this, representing the bottom edge of the girt. Screw on a temporary scab board at this mark to hold the girts in place against the pole while you mark them.

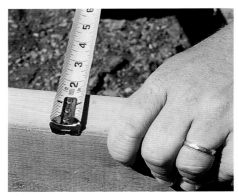

6 After removing the girts, double-check the thickness. Although two-by lumber is usually 1½ in. thick, pressure-treated 2x10s and 2x12s may vary and are often thinner.

7 Set your circular saw blade to the depth of about one-half the girt thickness and make a series of closely spaced cuts across the face of the pole between the marks.

8 An alternative to using a circular saw is to make the kerfs with a chain saw. It's more difficult to control the depth of cut with a chain saw, which must be used with extreme caution.

12 Most rafter girts are held up by carriage bolts centered on the pole about 2 to 3 inches from the top and bottom of the girt. Use a bit with the same diameter as the bolt head to drill shallow counterbores so the heads will be recessed below the surface.

13 Next, drill into the center of the counterbores all the way through the girt (or girts) and the pole. You'll need an extra-long bit for this job.

14 Once you drill all the holes, drive the bolts through (from the outside of the wall) with a hammer. Set them so that the top of the bolt head is flush with the surface of the wood.

3 Rest the rafter girts on the scab boards, and clamp them into place on the poles. Place one set of clamps at the end of each board; long girts should have a set in the center.

4 Once all the girts have been installed, check them for level with a 4-ft. (or longer) level. Make adjustments as needed by removing and replacing the scab boards one at a time.

5 Once all the girts are level, carefully mark the pole at the top and bottom of each girt. These marks indicate the top and bottom of the dapping detail.

9 When you've cut kerfs about ½ in. apart between the marks, chop out the wood between the cuts using a hammer or small hatchet. Then smooth the surface of the dap with a wood chisel.

10 Before resetting the girts, coat the notch with a wood preservative as a precautionary measure, even if the support pole or post is made of pressure-treated lumber.

11 Set the girts into the notches and clamp them. One clamp at each end should be enough to hold them. Be careful not to place the clamp where you'll be drilling the bolt holes.

15 For buildings with thick poles and two girts, there may not be a bolt long enough. In these cases, insert threaded rods and use nuts and washers at both ends.

16 Tighten the bolts with a socket wrench. Deep sockets are available for bolts where an inch or more protrudes from the girt. Trim excess length after the bolts are tightened.

17 Once the rafter girts are set, you can cut off the tops of the poles using a reciprocating saw. A chain saw is faster, but must be used very carefully from a safe and secure working position.

TIMBER-FRAME BARNS

Timber framing is one of the oldest but most refined and durable forms of construction. In fact, you can travel the world and see straight and true timber-frame buildings dating back before the fifteenth century. Some archaeologists have dated timber-frame construction to 200 B.C.

Timber framing is not an easy trade; it will take some real practice before you can make timber-frame joints as tight and snug as they ought to be. There are several timber-framing schools where do-it-yourselfers can spend a few weeks learning the basics and actually erect a small timber-frame building.

You'll find that even modest projects often involve a lot of people, allthough a crane can greatly reduce the size of the crew required. Tackling a timber-frame project on your own isn't practical unless you plan to build a very small structure with timbers you can handle by yourself. The upshot is that this section of the book is just a primer that provides an overview that is designed to help you get a running start when working with an experienced timber framer who is handling the construction.

Timber Framing versus Stick Framing

With a stick-built structure, you can raise one wall or even one stud at a time. Timber-frame walls are generally raised in complete cross sections of the building, called bents. (See "Bent Configurations," opposite.) They can be very heavy, and often have to be raised with a complicated system of ropes and pulleys, or even with a crane. In old-fashioned barn-raisings, large groups of people would hoist and push up the walls. But today that's a job for an experienced crew led by an experienced builder. And once heavy timber-frame sections are in place, you need heavy-duty bracing to keep the components in place.

Also, unlike stick-frame structures, timber frames are not built with wood cut on-site. The frames are often measured and cut at a shop based on a detailed plan that includes complex (and sometimes machine-controlled) cuts for the array of joints. Sometimes the frame is assembled, marked, and only then transported to the building site and erected.

TYPICAL TIMBER-FRAME CONSTRUCTION

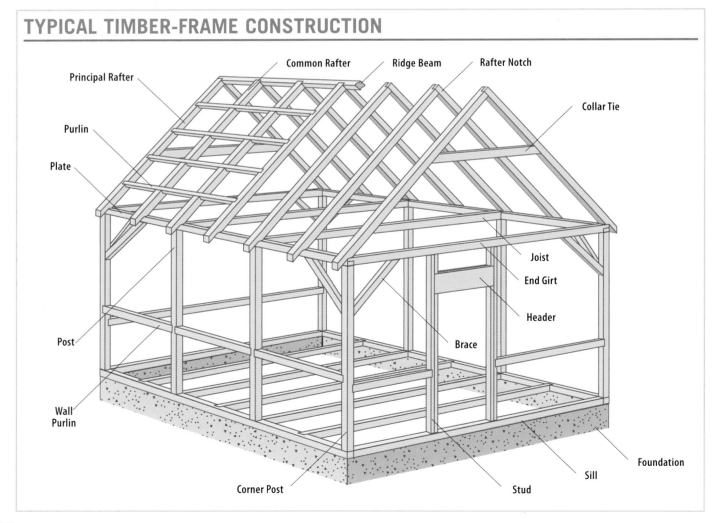

Principal Rafter · Common Rafter · Ridge Beam · Rafter Notch · Collar Tie · Purlin · Plate · Joist · End Girt · Header · Post · Brace · Wall Purlin · Corner Post · Stud · Sill · Foundation

Basic Construction

Most connections in a timber frame are mortise-and-tenon joints. They have to be cut precisely and often are trimmed to final shape with large and extremely sharp chisels. Tenons must fit snuggly into mortises, and they have shoulders that fit tightly against the mortised piece. When the tenon is in place, drill a hole through the joint and drive a peg into the hole to secure it. While most timber frame joints are mortise-and-tenon joints, there are several other types of joints used, as shown on page 94.

Once the bents are constructed, one after another is raised into place. Then bracing is installed, and finally permanent cross timbers are installed on the walls and roof that tie the building components together. The distance between each is dictated by the size and strength of the lumber used in the frame itself.

Timber-frame barns are built more like furniture than modern buildings. The heavy framing members are held together with fitted joints and pegs rather than nails or screws.

The exposed timbers direct the load of the roof down to the posts. Some bents can be designed with additional cross members that allow you to add storage space above the plates.

Each bent has its own set of components, namely the diagonal braces; the plate, which spans the bent where the posts meet the rafters; the girts, which span from post to post; the posts; and the knee braces, which reinforce the girt-and-post joint. Timbers that span from rafter to rafter parallel to the ground are called purlins. Timber frames do share some common terms with stick-built structures. For example, the timbers that rest on the foundation are called sills. But you will find some variation in the nomenclature; there is no one way to name all the parts of a timber frame, and even some professional timber-frame builders use different terms.

BENT CONFIGURATIONS

THE ILLUSTRATIONS BELOW show six common bent configurations. The design that you can use on your structure may vary depending on your region and the intended use of your building. In areas of heavy snow load, for example, it may be most efficient to use a queen post design instead of a king post with struts. Some designs allow for more headroom in second floors, while others increase the strength of a roof.

But these are only some of the options. The basic bent design for your structure can be any of a dozen or more configurations that tailor the space to your needs. Some, such as the hammer beam, require very complex joinery.

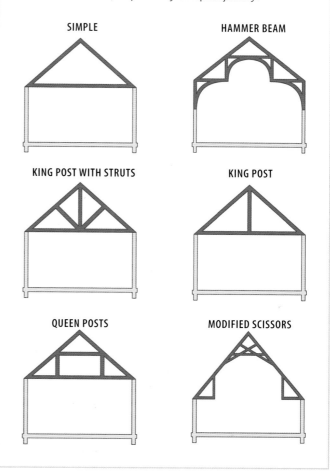

SIMPLE

HAMMER BEAM

KING POST WITH STRUTS

KING POST

QUEEN POSTS

MODIFIED SCISSORS

TIMBER-FRAME JOINERY

WHEN ASSEMBLING THE ELEMENTS of a timber frame, you have to cut a tenon in the ends of many timbers and a corresponding mortise in adjoining timbers, for example, where a strut meets a plate or rafter.

When cutting any part of a timber-frame joint, keep in mind that the frame joinery in a timber-frame structure will be visible. Unlike stick-built structures, which have the frame concealed in the walls, timber-frame structures generally reveal the frame, at least on the inside. So when laying out and cutting joints, remember to face the timber's best sides toward the inside.

When laying out a timber for cutting, remember to figure the shoulder-to-shoulder distance, or clear span of the timber, and also the extra length needed for joints, such as tenons. The shoulder-to-shoulder distance is what establishes the distance between your bents, not the tenon-to-tenon distance.

Also bear in mind that a sloppy shoulder cut or tenon cut too long will substantially compromise joint strength. These three-dimensional connections must fit snugly on all sides to create a strong joint.

Joint Variations

The mortise-and-tenon joint cut in the sequence opposite is a square joint, which is the type of joint you would cut where a girt meets a post. Where a strut meets a rafter, a knee brace meets a post at an angle, or where you are cutting scarf joints, housed dovetails, or many of the joints called for in a timber frame, the joinery becomes considerably more complicated. To get a taste of the requirements, you may want to attempt a complex joint, such as a dovetail lap joint, in short scraps of 4x4 material.

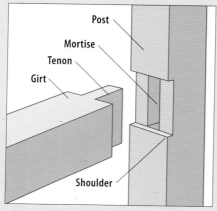

A housed mortise-and-tenon joint can be cut with the tenon extending into the post or extending all the way through so that the end grain of the tenon is visible. The tenon always has shoulders. In the case of girts, the mortise may also have shoulders to share the load with the tenon.

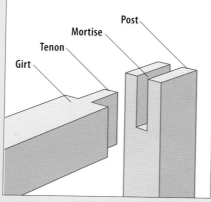

An open mortise-and-tenon joint is often found at the peaks of rafters that join together without a ridgeboard in between. This connection is not as strong as a housed joint but is more easily cut.

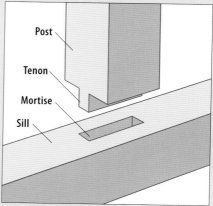

A stub mortise-and-tenon joint is found where posts are attached to sills. Here the mortise doesn't pass completely through the framing member. Gravity keeps the short tenon from pulling out of the mortise.

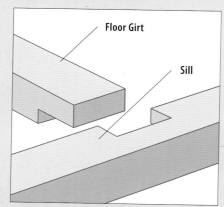

The lap joint—simpler to build than a mortise and tenon—is often used at sill beam corners and splices, or (as shown here) where floor girts meet the sill. It should be pegged particularly at corners.

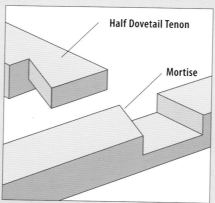

A dovetail lap joint is used to join timbers at right angles. It is harder to separate a dovetail lap joint than a standard lap. The half-dovetail shown above is easier to make than a full dovetail.

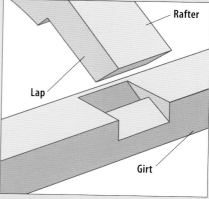

A step-lapped rafter seat is used to connect the rafter to the girt. This rather complicated joint does not need to be pegged, except at the ends of the plates to keep it from sliding off.

PROJECT: CUTTING A MORTISE & TENON

TOOLS & MATERIALS

- 2 rough-cut timbers
- Framing square
- Circular saw
- Combination square
- Measuring tape
- Handsaw
- Heavy-duty framing chisels (min. 5-inches long and 1½-inches wide, with a 25° bevel
- 30-ounce hardwood mallet
- Block plane or belt sander

1 Always start with square ends to your timbers. Check the ends with a combination square, and cut away any excess with a circular saw set to maximum depth of cut.

2 Determine your shoulder-to-shoulder distance and the tenon length, and mark them on one of the timbers. Mark the tenon and an X on the wood to be removed around it.

3 Using a circular saw, cut away the waste wood, keeping the blade kerf to the waste side. If the saw blade isn't large enough to cut the full tenon, you can finish these cuts with a handsaw.

4 Clean the tenon with a chisel to make sure all the sides are flat and square. Then put a slight chamfer on the edges of the tenon using a block plane, chisel, or belt sander.

5 The mortise will be the same dimensions as the tenon. Mark its outline, drill out the bulk of the wood, and clean up the four sides of the mortise with a sharp chisel.

MORTISE & TENON TIPS

REDUCE CHISELING WORK on a mortise by drilling out the bulk of the wood. For best results, use a Forstner bit (left) with a depth stop or depth mark to be sure that the floor of the mortise is flat. Then trim the corners and side walls with a sharp chisel.

After you cut the tenon and clean up the faces of the cut, use a chisel to shave a small chamfer along the edges. This helps the tenon slide into the mortise without compromising the strength of the joint.

PROJECT: 🐦🐦🐦 ASSEMBLING & RAISING A BENT

TOOLS & MATERIALS

- Varies widely according to scale of job
- Timbers cut according to plan
- Hardwood pegs

SMART TIP

In almost all cases, bents of even modest-size barns are raised by a professional crew, and your main job is to prepare the site and make sure that the foundation is ready for the installation.

WORKING WITH A TIMBER FRAME means handling large pieces of wood. Assembling timbers into a bent often includes using brute force to draw them together. You can gain a lot of mechanical advantage using a come-along, which has cables and a ratchet to pull on timbers with more force than you can muster by hand. You may find that it's handy to use more than one come-along to pull together components of a bent from several directions at once. Check for square and plumb as you would with a stick-framed wall, and check diagonal measurements to see if the bent is square. Once the bent is assembled and the joints are snug, you can drill and peg the joints.

1 Once all the timbers and joints have been cut and delivered to the site, the components can be assembled into bents right on the deck or slab.

2 Bents are often assembled on top of one another to save space and to be sure that they match each other. The profiles have to be the same for the walls to be square.

3 Here, the final bent has been assembled and is being braced in preparation for being strapped to a hook and raised into place by a crane.

4 The first bent has been strapped to the crane and is raised into place. The stub tenons at the bottom of the posts need to be guided into the mortises by crew members.

5 When the second and third bents have been raised, the side girts and purlins are raised into place. The final step is the two-piece ridge beam.

SHEDS FROM KITS

If you don't need a custom shed, just a utilitarian box for storing tools and equipment, a shed kit is a cost-efficient alternative. Typical kits are simple buildings with gabled roofs and 6 or 7 feet of clearance inside, sized anywhere from 5x4-feet to 10x17-feet for equipment sheds.

Wood kits generally come with all the lumber precut as well as enough fasteners to complete the project. Many styles are available. You can choose the cheapest, finished with T1-11 siding, or pick a kit with a similar siding to your house. Kits with metal siding and roof panels—usually steel with baked-on enamel finish—are also available in a variety of styles. There are even sheds that look like a miniature version of a typical red-and-white gambrel barn.

Metal kits are designed to be simple to assemble. Most parts snap together and are further strengthened with sheet-metal screws. The kits include prehung doors and other fixtures, but you still have to build the foundation. Because small metal buildings are light, they must be anchored to the foundation. In many regions, these sheds are considered permanent structures, and you will need to check installation details with your building department.

Small tool shed kits can be purchased at many lumberyards and home centers. They include the entire shell, but generally don't include materials for building a foundation or interior floor.

BASIC SHEDS

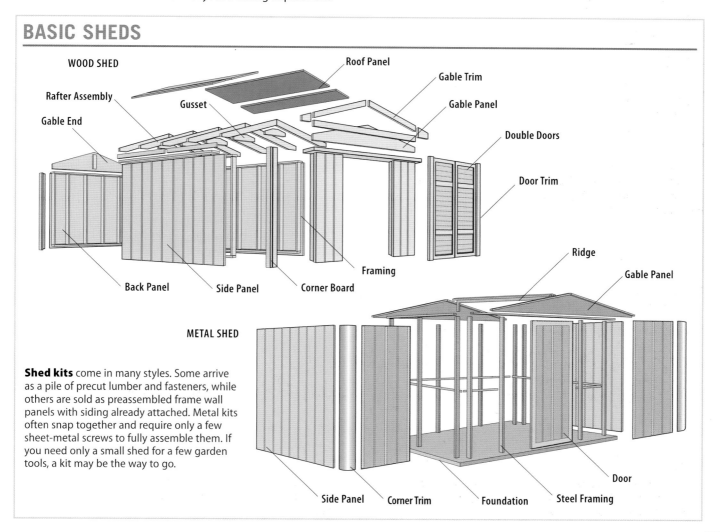

WOOD SHED — Roof Panel — Gable Trim — Rafter Assembly — Gusset — Gable Panel — Gable End — Double Doors — Door Trim — Framing — Back Panel — Side Panel — Corner Board — Ridge — Gable Panel

METAL SHED — Side Panel — Corner Trim — Foundation — Steel Framing — Door

Shed kits come in many styles. Some arrive as a pile of precut lumber and fasteners, while others are sold as preassembled frame wall panels with siding already attached. Metal kits often snap together and require only a few sheet-metal screws to fully assemble them. If you need only a small shed for a few garden tools, a kit may be the way to go.

STAIR CONSTRUCTION

Depending on its design, your barn may need stairs on the inside to access a second floor, loft, or attic; or on the outside for an exterior door that's a few feet above grade.

The easiest staircase to build is a set of straight-run stairs with no turns or intermediate landings. In most circumstances, a straight-run design will be your first choice. For a barn, you will probably want to build open-riser stairs.

All the steps in a flight of stairs must be the same size. The most critical calculation is the ratio between unit rise and unit run and their consistency from one step to the next. Local building codes regulate the acceptable dimensions. For most people, a 7-inch rise and 11-inch run are the most comfortable. An 11-inch run also makes it easier to build the treads—it works out to two 2x6s or three 2x4s.

The maximum rise generally allowable is 7⅞ inches; the minimum run is 9 inches. On the first riser, you need to subtract the thickness of the tread from the riser, so that the rise is uniform throughout the stairs.

Building codes also address landings and the room people need to get onto and off of the stairs safely. Headroom is another important issue. It's defined as the vertical distance measured from an imaginary line connecting the front edge on all of the treads up to overhead construction. Again, most codes establish a minimum (80 inches) from that line to any object above. This is required to prevent you from knocking your head against the ceiling or another obstruction.

Parts of a Staircase

Stringers are the diagonal elements that support the treads. You generally need to use 2x12s for your stringers. If your treads are more than 36 inches wide, you'll need a third stringer, called a carriage, to support them in the middle. Stringers can be notched into a sawtooth pattern to support the treads, but it is easier to leave them uncut and support the treads on stair brackets. For a utility building, regular two-by boards are fine for the treads. If the stairs are going to be outside or near a dirt floor, use pressure-treated wood.

UTILITY STAIRS

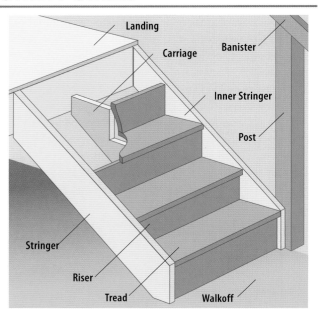

Utility stairs consist of the same parts as other stairs in your home. You may not need to include riser boards as you would inside. Treads can be made of dimensional lumber.

CALCULATING STAIR DIMENSIONS

- Measure the total rise from one finished floor surface to the other. Even if the finished floor hasn't been installed, you must include it in your calculations.
- The maximum riser height is 7⅞ inches. Divide your total rise by 7.75. This number, when rounded up to the nearest whole number, gives you the total number of risers you'll need. Then divide the total rise by this number to determine the actual unit rise.
- The minimum tread depth (called the run) is 9 inches; however, 10 or 11 inches is safer. Two simple formulas to match the tread depth to the riser height are rise + run = about 17 to 18, or, alternatively, rise x run = about 70 to 75. By the first formula, a riser of 7⅞ inches can have a tread depth anywhere from 9¾ to 10¾ inches.
- Calculate the total run by multiplying the number of steps by the tread depth. Check to make sure that you'll have sufficient head clearance for the entire run. Typical code requirements specify a minimum of 80 inches of headroom in all parts of a stairway.

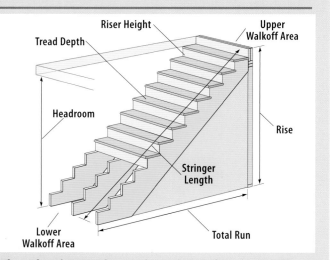

When planning a staircase, the total rise is the only given. The measurements of treads and risers must fall within parameters; the total run can be anything that won't cause an obstruction.

PROJECT: 🐾🐾🐾
BUILDING UTILITY STAIRS

TOOLS & MATERIALS
- 2x12s for stringers
- Calculator
- Measuring tape
- Framing square with stair tabs
- Circular saw
- Plumb bob
- Angle brackets
- Power drill with screwdriver bit
- Screws Stair brackets
- Newel post (if at least one side of the stairs is open)
- PT stair tread
- Hammer
- 4d, 8d, and 10d nails 1x8s for risers
- Balustrade

1 Starting at the top of the stringer, position a framing square with the rise measurement on one leg and the run measurement on the other leg aligned to the edge. Lay out each rise and run; stair buttons, shown here, can be fastened to the square to speed the work.

2 As an extra guide to your installation, also mark the thickness of the treads on the stringer. For a cut stringer, test the stringer in place before making any saw cuts.

3 Attach the top ends of your stringers with brackets and screws. Even when you have access to drive fasteners into the stringer end grain, brackets make a stronger connection

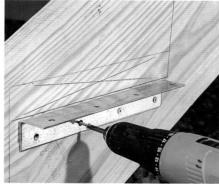

4 Screw galvanized metal stair brackets to the insides of your stringers following your layout lines. Allow for the tread thickness and a slight overhang at the front of each step.

5 After you've installed all the stair brackets, measure the stair frame opening, and center the low end of the middle support. Double-check the position using a framing square.

6 Cut square ends on the stair tread boards. Treads mounted on brackets should be cut at least ⅛ in. short of the overall space to allow room for expansion and drainage.

7 Predrill treads to avoid splits, and nail or screw the boards to the brackets. For designs with a cut stringer or for landings (shown above), extend treads past the stringer or joist.

8 Hidden fasteners can reduce splits on treads. On low treads, you can fasten the brackets to the treads first, and then screw the assembly to the stringers with deck screws.

5 ROOF FRAMING

The type of roof you select for your barn or outbuilding will depend on the style of the building you have decided to build. The most popular types of roofs are shown in "Choosing a Roof Type," opposite. When selecting a building type, remember that the roof bears the brunt of the natural elements; choose a style that fits your region of the country. For example, roofs with steep slopes are well suited for areas that receive a lot of snow. The techniques covered in this chapter will help you build the most popular types—gable, shed, and gambrel roofs.

ROOF BASICS

The gable roof is perhaps the most common roof profile. It has two sloping sides (not necessarily the same size) that meet at a center ridge. If the roof pitch isn't too low, gable attics can be spacious. Steep-pitched gables are ideal in areas with heavy winter snows. There are several other roof shapes, including shed, gambrel, saltbox, and hip, and many variations on the basic configurations.

Spans & Loads

Rafters must be able to span distances safely and according to code. Many factors bear on the allowable span, but the basic idea is that a large piece of lumber, such as a 2x10, has more strength and can span a greater distance than a 2x6, assuming the same type of wood species and grade of lumber. But at a low angle (one closer to level) there is more strain on a rafter than at a high angle (one closer to vertical). So a steep roof with a high angle creates less rafter load.

On-center framing distances also affect rafter span. Rafters placed 16 inches on center can take on a greater load than rafters of the same size set at 24 inches on center. That means you can use a smaller size (or a lesser grade of lumber in some cases) if you set rafters at 16 instead of 24 inches.

The grade of the lumber also affects allowable rafter span. No. 1 Douglas Fir will have a greater span than No. 2 Douglas Fir, for example, because the wood has more strength. That's why span tables used by architects, engineers, and building departments take wood species and grades into account.

When referring to tables, which are available from your local building department, make sure it's a rafter table and not a joist table. On a rafter table, you'll notice that there are two categories of span, not a listing for every possible angle. The tables typically break down the slopes into steep-sloped roofs, with slopes of 4 in 12 or more, and low-sloped roofs, with slopes of 4 in 12 or less. Remember that the building department has the final say on the design and construction.

CHOOSING A ROOF TYPE

THE KIND OF ROOF YOU USE will depend on your architectural taste, the climate, and the building's function. Shed roofs are often used on barns and wood sheds. These roofs are easy to build and the easiest type of roof to shingle. Gambrel and mansard roofs also can be practical in the long run because their rafter configuration provides extra second-floor space, which can be handy for storage in a barn. But these roofs are more difficult to frame because they have more surfaces that meet at angles. The same goes for hip roofs, which are used more on houses than on barns. But this design allows a deep overhang on all four sides of the building, which offers the most weather protection.

In any case, consider the option of using trusses, which are available in almost every style. You can order these locally, erect them yourself on a small structure, or hire a contractor with a crane to set trusses on a large building.

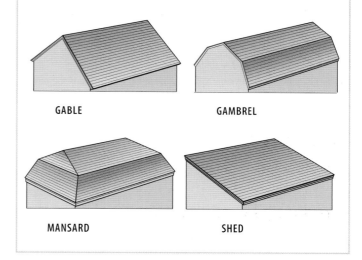

GABLE   GAMBREL

MANSARD   SHED

ENGINEERED COMPONENTS

Metal stirrups, or hangers, are used to fasten composite joists and rafters, such as wood I-beams, to support beams.

Engineered wood framing often needs special fasteners, but this system offers benefits over conventional framing.

Spans & Loads

If you know the slope of a roof but don't know the total rise, you can determine that dimension using the total run on a symmetrical roof. First, divide the span in half to get the total run. Let's say your structure has a span of 20 feet. The total run is 10 feet. Now multiply the unit rise by the number of feet in the total run. A roof with a slope of 8 inches in rise for every 12 inches of run (8-in-12 slope) and a total run of 10 feet has a total rise of 80 inches (8 x 10), or 6 feet 8 inches. If you increase the run, the slope doesn't change, but the total rise increases. For example, if you have a 12-foot run with an 8-in-12 roof, the total rise is 96 inches (8 x 12), or 8 feet.

When you determine rise, you use a measurement along a line from the cap plate's top outside edge to the ridge's centerline. The point at which the rafter measuring line and the ridgeboard centerline intersect is known as the theoretical ridgeboard height. The rise is the distance from the plate to the theoretical ridgeboard height.

But if math is not your strong point, there is another option (shown step by step on page 106). You erect braced posts at each end of the ridge; adjust the ridge up or down as needed with clamps; and test rafters for length, angle, and end cuts. This may be the best system for do-it-yourselfers working on an addition and trying to match an existing roof line.

ROOF TERMINOLOGY

- **RISE** is the height of the roof at its ridge measured from the top plate of the end wall below the ridge.
- **SPAN** is the horizontal distance from wall to wall. A roof's span does not include the overhang at the eaves.
- **RUN** is the horizontal distance from one wall to a point under the ridge, or typically half the span.
- **PITCH** is the angle of a roof as a ratio of the rise to the span. A 24-foot-wide structure, for example, with a gable roof that rises 10 feet from side wall to ridgeboard has a pitch of ¹⁰⁄₂₄, or ⁵⁄₁₂. A pitch of ¼ or ⅓ is common for gable roofs. A Cape Cod–style roof might have a ½ pitch.

- **SLOPE** is expressed as the rafter's vertical rise in inches, or unit rise, per 12 inches of horizontal run, or unit run. If a slope has a unit rise of 4 and a unit run of 12, the roof surface rises 4 inches for every 12 inches along the run line. This is expressed as 4/12 or 4 in 12. On most building plans, you'll notice a right triangle off to the side—for example, 4 in 12 with a 12 at the top of the triangle on one leg of the right angle and a 4 on the other leg. The hypotenuse of the triangle shows you the angle of slope. The higher the number of inches in unit rise, the steeper the roof. A 12-in-12 roof, common in Cape Cod-style roofs, rises a foot in elevation for every foot of run (a 45-degree angle).

ROOFING MEASUREMENTS

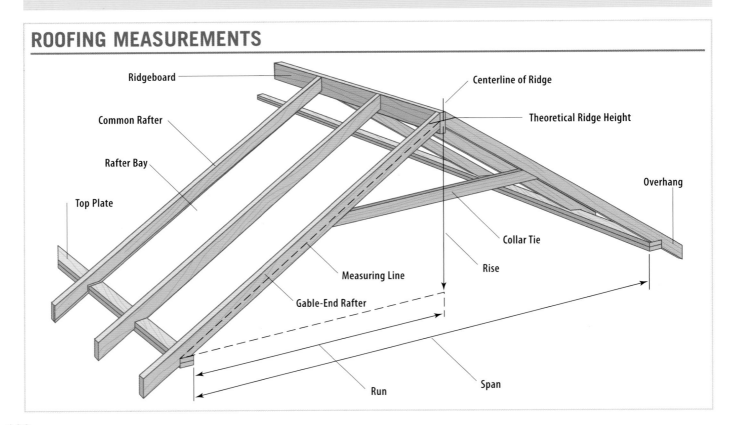

Ridgeboard
Common Rafter
Rafter Bay
Top Plate
Measuring Line
Gable-End Rafter
Run
Span
Rise
Collar Tie
Overhang
Theoretical Ridge Height
Centerline of Ridge

THREE METHODS FOR CALCULATING RAFTER LENGTH

THERE ARE THREE WAYS TO CALCULATE RAFTER LENGTH, aside from the trusted do-it-yourself method of holding a board in place and marking the cuts. The calculations used here are an example and are not meant for all rafters, but you can use the principles for any common gable rafter.

#1: Using the Pythagorean Theorem

Determine the roof slope. Here, assume a slope of 8 in 12, which means the roof rises 8 inches for every 12 inches it runs. Then determine the building width. For this example, assume the building is 30 feet wide. Next, determine the run. The run is one-half the building's width, in this case, 15 feet. Finally, determine the rise. Once you know the slope and run, you know the roof will rise 10 feet (8 x 15 = 120 inches, or 10 feet).

You're now ready to figure the rafter length for an 8-in-12 roof on a building 30 feet wide. If you think of half the roof as a right triangle, you already know the base (15) and altitude (10). You need to figure the hypotenuse of this right triangle, which represents the rafter length. Using the Pythagorean theorem:

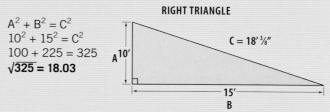

RIGHT TRIANGLE

$$A^2 + B^2 = C^2$$
$$10^2 + 15^2 = C^2$$
$$100 + 225 = 325$$
$$\sqrt{325} = 18.03$$

$C = 18' \frac{3}{8}''$

A 10'

15'
B

The square root of 325 feet is 18.03 feet, which equals 18 feet ⅜ inch. If your rise and/or run are not in whole feet but in feet and inches, then convert the whole figure to inches; do the math; and convert it back to feet. Use decimals of a foot rather than inches when you divide the resulting number of inches by 12 on a calculator to arrive at feet.

#2: Using a Rafter Table

The rafter table found on a framing square contains work-saving data and is useful for many calculations. You need only look at the first line of the table, which gives unit rafter length for common gable rafters. To find the unit length you need, look on the blade below the inch designation that corresponds to your slope. If, for example, you're framing a 6-in-12 roof, look at the number below the 6-inch mark on the framing square's blade. You'll find it reads 13.42. If your total run is 14, multiply 13.42 by 14 to get 187.88 inches. Divide 187.88 by 12 to get 15.656 feet, or 15 feet ⅝ inches.

RAFTER TABLE

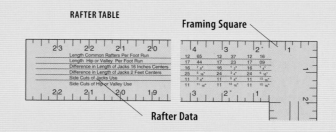

Framing Square

Rafter Data

#3: Stepping Off with a Framing Square

You can also accurately measure a rafter by stepping off dimensions with a framing square in 12-inch units of run.

Lay a straight piece of rafter stock across two sawhorses. Sight down the edge of the rafter, and position yourself on the crowned side, which will be the top of the rafter. To make accurate marking easier, attach adjustable stops called stair nuts or stair buttons to the square to set the rise and run positions.

Let's say you want to lay out a roof with an 8-in-12 slope. Lay the square on the left end of the stock. Hold the square's tongue in your left hand and its blade in your right. Pivot the square until the edge of the stock near you aligns with the unit rise mark (8 inches in this example) on the outside of the tongue and the 12-inch mark on the outside of the blade. Mark along the outside edge of the tongue for the ridge plumb line. You'll use this mark as the reference line for stepping off full 12-inch units.

If the span is an odd number of feet, say 25, with a run of 12½ feet, you'll have to include a half-step to accommodate the extra length. Mark off the partial step first, and then go on to step off full 12-inch units. Holding the square in the position in which you had it to mark the ridge cut, measure and mark the length of the odd unit along the blade.

Shift the square to your right along the edge of the stock until the tongue is even with the mark you just made. Mark off a plumb line along the tongue of the square. When you begin stepping off full units, remember to start from the new plumb line and not from the ridge cut line.

Testing a Template

Whatever system you use, take the time to test a rafter in place to be sure that the cuts are correct. Check the ridge cut, the overall length, and the overhang. Then you can use that rafter as a template to make others in the roof.

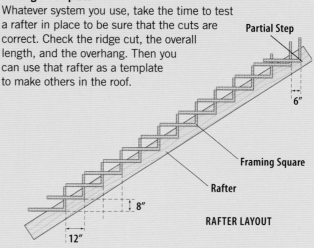

Partial Step

6"

Framing Square

Rafter

8"

RAFTER LAYOUT

12"

GABLE ROOFS

Calculating rafter length and the angles at the ridge and rafter tail is more complex than framing walls. But the job is doable using only basic math if you break down the task into smaller, simple steps. On gable roofs, you can either run the rafters individually to a center ridgeboard or assemble gable-style trusses on the ground and lift them into position. Some lumberyards carry prefabricated trusses for several common roof spans and pitches.

Measuring Gable Rafters

Because all common rafters in a gable roof are the same, you can mark and cut one, test the fit, and use it as a template.

Number of Rafters. If it's not included on your plans, you'll need to calculate the total number of rafters you'll need. For 16-inch-on-center framing, multiply the length of the building by three-quarters, and add 1 (L x 0.75 + 1 = X rafters). For 24-inch-on-center framing, multiply the building length by one-half and add 1 (L x 0.5 + 1 = Y rafters). If your plans include a gable-end overhang to match the eaves overhang, you'll need to add four pieces of lumber for the barge, or fly, rafters that extend beyond the gable-end walls.

Estimating the Size. Before you order rafter lumber, you must know what size boards to get. You can approximate the sizes using a framing square and measuring tape. To determine the exact rafter lengths, you can use any of three methods: work with rafter tables; use the Pythagorean theorem; or step off the rafters with a square.

To mark rafters, you have to find the roof slope indicated on the building plans. The rafter length will be determined by the roof slope and the building width. The rafter-length measurement will determine where you'll make the cuts on the rafters. The rafter length is the distance from the ridge to the edge of the building.

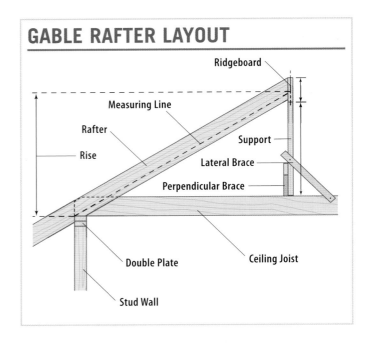

GABLE RAFTER LAYOUT

Ridgeboard
Measuring Line
Rafter
Rise
Support
Lateral Brace
Perpendicular Brace
Double Plate
Ceiling Joist
Stud Wall

Remember that the rafter size (and wood species and grade) will have to be approved by your local building department.

Subtracting the Ridgeboard Thickness. You start by calculating the length of the rafter to the center of the ridgeboard. Then you must shorten the rafter to accommodate the width of the board. Measure back from the center of the ridge line a distance of one-half the thickness of the ridgeboard. If you're using a two-by ridgeboard, the distance will be 3/4 inch. Mark another plumb line at this point as the cut line.

Calculating the Overhang. The overhang (sometimes called projection) is the level distance from the edge of the building. But the actual rafter length is longer because of its slope. You can use the Pythagorean theorem to figure out the dimension you'll have

THREE BASIC CUTS

MOST COMMON RAFTERS GET THREE CUTS: a plumb cut at the ridge where the rafter rests against the ridgeboard; a plumb cut at the tail, which makes the shape of the bottom end; and a bird's-mouth notch where the rafter seats on the plate of the outside wall. Sometimes you need a fourth cut, a horizontal cut at the tail, which is often used with an overhang and soffit.

The simplest way to mark these cuts is to hold the lumber up to the ridgeboard, which you can temporarily install on vertical supports. Once the rafter is aligned with the top of the ridgeboard at one end and resting against the top plate at the other, you can scribe the ridge cut and the bird's-mouth notch directly onto the rafter.

You can also measure these cut lines using a framing square. If you've stepped off the rafter, the first mark you make will be your plumb or ridge cut, the cut that rests against the ridgeboard.

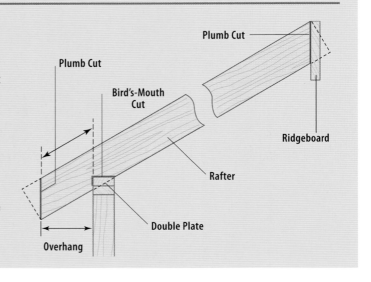

Plumb Cut
Bird's-Mouth Cut
Plumb Cut
Ridgeboard
Rafter
Double Plate
Overhang

to add to the rafter length for the overhang. If you want an 18-inch overhang on the same 8-in-12 roof, for example, you must envision the overhang area as a miniature roof. The run is 18 inches (the horizontal dimension of the overhang) and the rise is 12 inches (8 x 1.5 = 12). Therefore,

$$12^2 + 18^2 = C^2$$

144 inches + 324 inches = 468 inches

The square root of 468 inches is 21.63 inches, which is 1.80 feet, or 1 foot 9⅝ inches.

The gable end of a roof may also need an overhang to match the eaves overhang. You can create a slight overhang without adding extra rafters. You simply add blocking to the side wall, and add a trim board, often called a rake board. To build a deeper overhang, you can add fly rafters.

Framing a Gable Roof

After you lay out and cut the first rafter, use it as a template to lay out the second one. You can test the two rafters for fit on the ground by placing the bird's mouths over each end of a 2x4 you have cut to a length equal to the width of the building measured across the top plate. But it's best to test the rafter against the ridgeboard. If you're installing ceiling joists, nail these in place before erecting the rafters. This also stiffens the side walls against push-out as you install rafters and provides a working platform.

Cutting the Ridgeboard. Cut the ridgeboard to length, and mark the rafter positions on it and on the top plates. If the roof will overhang at the gable ends, allow for the overhang at each end when you cut the ridgeboard. In many cases, it pays to let the ridgeboard run long and trim it to exact length after the last rafters are installed and the layout is checked.

Preassembling End Rafters. On small sheds, you may be able to assemble some components on the ground. For example, you might attach two end rafters to the ridgeboard, adjust the spread of the rafters, and nail a temporary cleat to hold them in position securely as you raise the assembly into place. In most cases, you need to fix the ridgeboard in its final position ahead of time and brace it very securely so that it doesn't move as you nail up rafters one at a time.

Adding the Remaining Rafters. Once the end rafters are nailed in place, you can add the remaining rafters. On most projects, you can face-nail through the ridge to set the first rafter only. You have to toenail the second rafter. Codes may require hangers.

PROJECT:
STEPPING OFF RAFTER LENGTH

TOOLS & MATERIALS
- Rafter (to serve as a template)
- Framing square with stops
- Pencil

SMART TIP

No matter how you lay out and cut rafters, always check the first one in place before using it as a template to make others.

1 Before marking a rafter, sight down its length to see which side is crowned or raised in a slight bow shape. Always lay out and install all the rafters with the crowns facing up.

2 Pivot the square until the edge of the stock near you aligns with the unit rise mark on the tongue and the unit run mark on the blade. You can attach stops to capture the correct position.

3 Step along the rafter, laying out in 12-in. units of run. When the layout reaches the centerline of the ridgeboard, you need to deduct half its width from the overall rafter length.

MARKING RAFTER CUTS

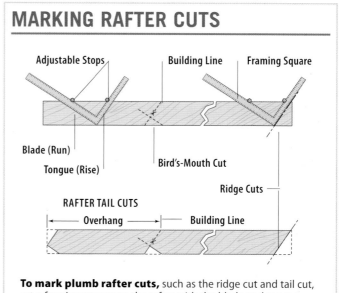

Adjustable Stops · Building Line · Framing Square

Blade (Run)

Tongue (Rise)

Bird's-Mouth Cut

Ridge Cuts

RAFTER TAIL CUTS

Overhang · Building Line

To mark plumb rafter cuts, such as the ridge cut and tail cut, set a framing square on the rafter with the blade and tongue measurements set at the rise and run of your roof.

Adding Strapping. Before you add any other framing, be sure that the rafter layout is correct. On all but small sheds, you should add strapping perpendicular to the rafters at midspan to keep the rafters square and prevent bowing. You can remove the strapping as you nail down the roof decking.

Framing the Gable End. Now you can add studs along the gable-end walls. They provide support for the roof, and they serve as nailing bases for both interior and exterior finishes. (See "Framing the Gable End," opposite.) Each stud gets two cuts to make a lap onto the rafter. The depth of the cut is equal to the thickness of the rafter so that the stud face is flush with the rafter face. The base cut in the lap has to be angled to match the angle of the rafter. You can use a sliding T-bevel to judge the angle of the cut. Hold a plumb stud in place to judge the height of the stud. At the bottom, toenail the base to the top plate of the first floor wall. At the top, nail through the rafter into the lapped portion of the stud.

Attaching Collar Ties. Some roof designs also require collar ties. These short horizontal timbers turn the inverted V-shape of rafters into an A-shape. Collar ties hold opposite rafters so that they can't spread apart. To provide the extra strength where required by code, the collar ties generally should be installed in the lower one third of the rafter span.

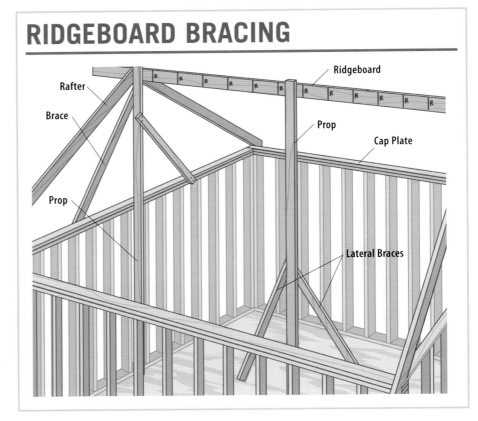

RIDGEBOARD BRACING

Rafter

Brace

Prop

Ridgeboard

Prop

Cap Plate

Lateral Braces

PROJECT:
INSTALLING THE RIDGEBOARD & RAFTERS

TOOLS & MATERIALS
- Measuring tape, pencil, and safety goggles
- Two 2x4 posts to support ridgeboard
- Circular saw and handsaw
- 4-foot level
- 2x4 bracing
- Two-by ridgeboards
- Clamps
- Hammer and common nails
- T-bevel square and framing square

1 For maximum safety, build a plumb post with a cleat extension to temporarily support the ridgeboard. Tack or clamp two braces at right angles; check the post for plumb; and nail the braces.

2 Set the ridgeboard on the brace post, leaning it temporarily on the 2x4 cleat. Then clamp it in position. A few screws will also work. Check to make sure that it is level and parallel with the building line.

FRAMING THE GABLE END

AFTER YOU'VE FRAMED THE ROOF with common rafters, use a plumb bob (or level against a straight 2x4) to find the center of the gable-end plate under the ridgeboard. If you'll be installing a gable-end vent, measure one-half its width to each side of center and mark for the first full studs. Continue to mark along the plate at your stud spacing. Set a stud at a full stud position; plumb it; and mark where it intersects the end rafter. Set the stud

at the next stud position, and mark it again. The difference in height is the common difference between studs. Cut notches 5 to 6 inches long and 1½ inches deep into the tops of several studs, matching the bottom of the notch to the rafter angle. Cut the studs to fit between the top plate and the end rafters, using the difference determined earlier, or one at a time if need be. Toenail the studs to the cap plate, and then nail through the rafters with 16d nails.

Vent Frame

Notched Studs

Rafter

Side Wall   Top Plate   Gable-End Stud Wall

INSTALLING GABLE-END OVERHANG RAFTERS

ON MOST ROOFS, the gable ends have an overhang that matches the eaves overhang. Gable overhangs are often constructed as a ladder-like set of boards called barge rafters or fly rafters.

There are two ways to attach them. For overhangs 12 inches wide or less, you can build a rake ladder made of two identical rafters attached to each other with two-by blocking. The inner side of the ladder is face-nailed to the end rafter, and the outer side is stabilized by nailing it to the extended ridgeboard. This system works best for roofs finished with relatively lightweight material, such as asphalt shingles.

The other method involves notching out the end rafter for lookouts. In some cases these boards sit on edge like rafters, but extend out past the gable-end wall at right angles to the main rafters. Another option is to recess lookouts on the flat into the end rafter and butt one end into a common rafter and the other into the barge rafter.

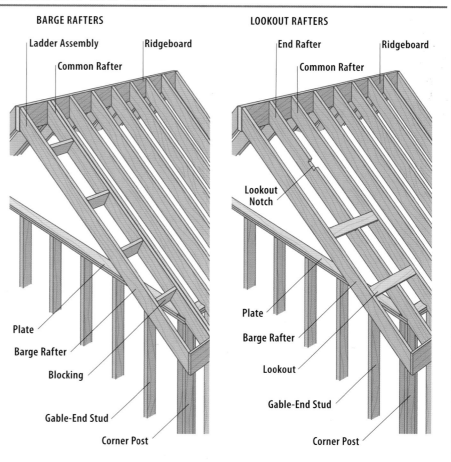

BARGE RAFTERS

Ladder Assembly   Ridgeboard

Common Rafter

Plate

Barge Rafter

Blocking

Gable-End Stud

Corner Post

LOOKOUT RAFTERS

End Rafter   Ridgeboard

Common Rafter

Lookout Notch

Plate

Barge Rafter

Lookout

Gable-End Stud

Corner Post

FINISHING THE OVERHANG

THE EAVES SECTION OF THE ROOF generally is called the overhang, or cornice. There are a number of different ways to finish the area. You can take the simple approach and leave the overhang open for ventilation. The roof sheathing is left exposed between the rafter tails, and the siding stops below the rafters. You can add a fascia—a long board that covers the ends of the rafter tails. This addition is wise on overhangs of more than a few inches because it keeps the rafter tails square, and provides a support surface for gutters, among other things.

Overhangs can also be soffited or boxed. In these types of designs, horizontal siding material or sheets of plywood (usually with some kind of ventilation added) is fastened in place between the fascia and the wall.

INSTALLING THE FASCIA

Before installing a fascia, snap a chalk line across the ends of the rafter tails, and check the end of each with a framing square (for square-cut ends) or a level (for plumb-cut ends). Trim any rafter tails that are not even.

The simplest fascia is a continuous piece of two-by lumber. The outside top corner of the fascia should be even with the top of the rafter so the roof sheathing can cover it. Or the top edge of the fascia can be beveled to meet the underside of the sheathing, thus creating continuous support for sheathing. Often, the two-by fascia is covered with one-by boards to match the trim on the rest of the building. Small sheds may have fascia consisting of one-bys only.

SOFFITED AND BOXED OVERHANGS

A boxed cornice generally is blocked out slightly from the wall and doesn't use soffit joists. This detail is more than adequate on basic sheds where you want the look of an overhang or the chance to provide a narrow strip of ventilation.

A soffited cornice has additional framing that connects the fascia to the shed wall. The framing creates a flat area, called a soffit, that generally is covered with plywood. Most soffits include vents to allow air to sweep up into the roof along the entire overhang on both sides of the building. You can use plug vents between rafters, strip-grill vents that extend along the overhang, or perforated panels instead of solid sheets of plywood.

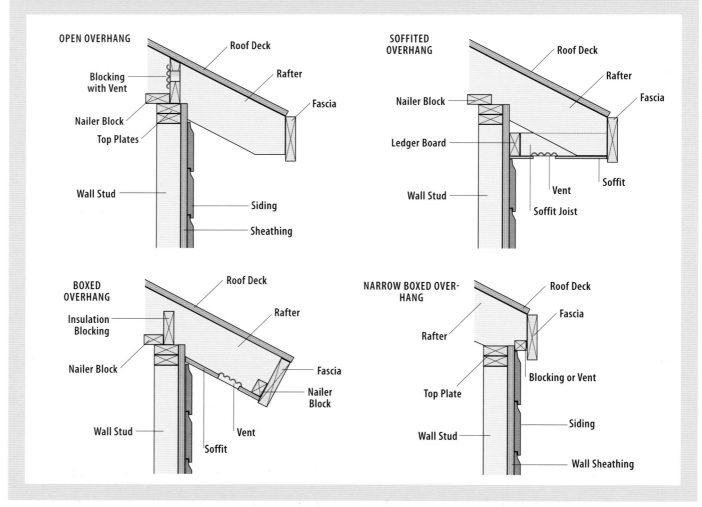

SHED ROOFS

Shed roofs are like one half of a gable roof. They are easy to design and build because they have only one shallow slope with basic rafters that notch over the low wall and the high wall in a straight run. Before cutting, be sure to make sure the crown edge is facing up.

If you're framing the building walls with 2x4s, the bird's-mouth seat cuts on the rafters should be 3½ inches wide. Using the framing square, line up the blade with the building line and move the square up or down until the 3½-inch mark on the tongue intersects the underside edge of the rafter. Draw the 3½-inch-long seat-cut line.

The bird's-mouth plumb-cut line runs from where the seat-cut line intersects the building line (inside line for the top of the rafter and outside line for the bottom of the rafter) down to the rafter edge. The depth of the bird's-mouth plumb cut should not exceed one-third the width of the rafter.

SHED RAFTER CUTS

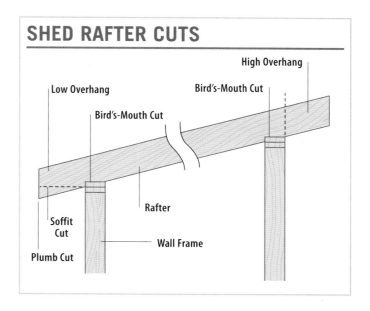

PROJECT: 🐾🐾🐾
MARKING AND CUTTING SHED RAFTERS

TOOLS & MATERIALS
- Rafter lumber
- Carpenter's pencil
- Circular saw and handsaw
- Hammer or drill-driver with screwdriver bit
- 12d nails or 2-inch galvanized deck screws

SMART TIP

To use a fascia board the same size as your rafters, you need to make a heel cut parallel with the ground at the base of each rafter. This shortens the plumb cut at the rafter tail.

1 To mark the bird's-mouth cuts on the lower wall, have a helper hold the rafter at the roof peak. Typically, the cut will be at least 1½ in. deep. Outline the position of the cap plates with a pencil.

2 Remove the rafter, and use a circular saw to make a bird's-mouth cut at the marks. Don't overcut the marks; this will weaken the rafter. Instead, finish the cut with a handsaw to make the notch area drop out.

3 Test-fit the shed rafter against the high- and low-wall top plates. If the rafter fits, use it as a template to mark and cut the rest. Then toenail the rafters at their on-center locations on the plates over the studs below.

ROOF TRUSSES

If you're nervous about cutting rafters from scratch and you don't mind losing the open attic space, roof trusses are a good option. On small sheds, trusses are usually 2x4s held together by gussets, which are flat metal or plywood plates that cover and reinforce the joints. The two top chords and one long bottom chord form the shape of a gable roof. Internal framing members, called webs, tie the chords together. Cutting any one of the members compromises the structural integrity of the entire truss.

There are many different truss configurations and sizes. End trusses often don't have the same webs as the trusses for the interior of the roof. Instead, the webs are vertical two-by studs.

Order trusses from a truss manufacturer by specifying the length of the bottom chord, which should include the span, wall thicknesses, and soffits.

Trusses for small buildings, such as this 12-ft. truss for a 4-in-12 gable-roofed barn, can easily be carried and raised into position by two strong people. Larger trusses will need special equipment.

PROJECT: 🐿🐿🐿
ERECTING TRUSSES

TOOLS & MATERIALS
- Stepladders or scaffolding
- Trusses Hammer
- 16d nails or metal anchor plates
- 4-foot spirit level
- Measuring tape
- 2x4s for braces, blocking & strapping

SMART TIP
Trusses make roof framing easy, but don't try to install trusses that are too large. Have a professional install larger trusses.

1 Place the first truss on one end of the building and its ends on the cap plate with the top pointing downward. Two or more people will be needed to raise it upright, depending on its size.

2 Fasten the truss to the cap plate using 16d nails or metal anchor brackets. Plumb the truss with a level, and nail it off to 2x4s that brace it securely to stakes in the ground.

3 Mark the positions of all the trusses on the cap plates. Nailing 2x4 spacer blocks between the truss locations will make it easier to hold a truss straight while it is toenailed into place.

4 Set the second truss in place against its spacer, and toenail it to the cap plate with four 16d nails or fasteners specified by the truss manufacturer. Brace each truss in position.

5 With three trusses installed, tack strapping across the top on each side. Nail strapping on additional trusses as you set them in position to tie the trusses together.

SETTING TRUSSES

LIGHTWEIGHT 2X4 TRUSSES for a small shed are easy to set up. The key is to add braces and strapping to trusses as you set them in position. But the only way to erect large trusses is with a crane, which is an expensive and potentially hazardous proposition best left to a professional.

THE FIRST TRUSS. Before lifting up the first truss, nail short two-by boards on the gable ends of the structure to act as stops so that the truss doesn't slip off the end of the plate. These can be removed when the sheathing is in place.

The best approach is to set the truss upside down, hanging from the wall plates peak down. Then walk it into place and turn it upright after calculating where the bottom chord will land on the plate. You need to work carefully.

BRACING THE FIRST TRUSS. Positioning the first truss is relatively easy on a small shed. It's more time consuming to brace it securely. You'll need several long 2x4s that reach down to the ground, and lateral braces that pin the truss in place on the gable-end wall. Because the rest of the trusses will depend on the stability of this first truss, you should include at least two braces running from the truss down to cleats on the floor of the building.

ADDING STRAPPING. With strapping passed up from below, tie trusses together with at least one line of strapping on each side of the ridge. Use a strong material, such as 2x4 boards or ¾ furring. You can stagger the strapping temporarily and use short boards in a pinch to secure the next truss in line. Another option is to leave some strapping extended into the next bay before you tip up the truss. But after several trusses are installed, you should go back to the end wall; double check for plumb; and install a continuous strip of strapping on each side of the ridge.

THE LAST TRUSS. Setting the last few trusses in place can be difficult if you do not have a crane because there isn't much room to maneuver them. You often have to raise them peak up. Set the last truss against two-by stops on the gable-end plate to keep it from slipping off during positioning. For safety, you need to have braces at the ready to lock the last truss securely in place.

FINAL CHECKING AND FASTENING. Go back and check for plumb on the trusses, and adjust them accordingly. It's wise to tack strapping so that you can easily pull the nails to make small adjustments. Then follow with nails into the plates, and add sheathing with staggered joints to cover the roof. If possible, sheath the trusses the same day you erect them.

BASIC TRUSS TYPES

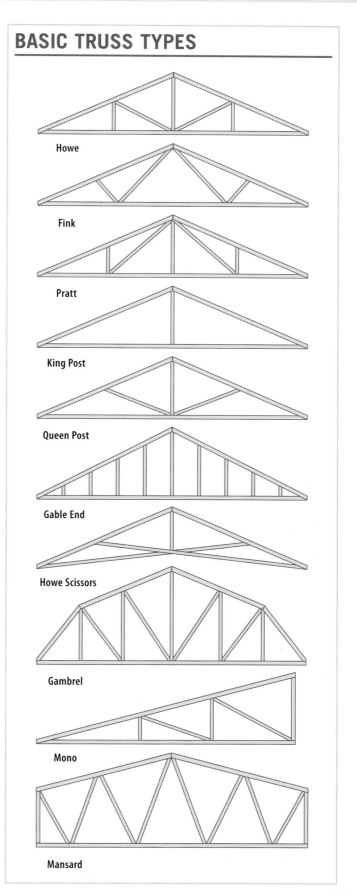

Howe

Fink

Pratt

King Post

Queen Post

Gable End

Howe Scissors

Gambrel

Mono

Mansard

GAMBREL ROOFS

Gambrel roofs are often found on barns and utility buildings because the design allows for more usable room on the topmost floor. Remember that you need to take this area into account when you plan the building. Adding second-floor joists suitable for heavy-duty storage can increase the load on exterior walls and foundations.

Basic Gambrel Design. A gambrel roof is really a combination of two gable roofs with different slopes. The part of the gambrel roof that rises directly off the top plates—the first gable—usually has a severe slope, such as 16 in 12, which is a 2/3 pitch. The part of the gambrel roof that rises to the ridge—the second gable roof—has a less severe slope—often something like 8 in 12, which is a 1/3 pitch.

With stick framing, you need a support such as a wall or a horizontal beam, possibly with posts, wherever the rafters on one slope meet the rafters on another. These cuts and joints can be tricky. In a true gambrel roof, the two parts of each side of the roof have rafters of the same length, and all four rafters describe chords of a semicircle. (See this type on the far right at the top opposite.) Not all gambrel-style designs fit this pattern, however. A common layout—easier to calculate and measure—has the upper and lower roof angles at 30 and 60 degrees respectively. (See this type on the left at the top opposite.)

Making Gambrel Trusses

The easiest approach is to build trusses on the deck or slab.

One option is to make what amounts to a full-scale drawing of the truss on the slab using a chalk-line box. Start by snapping a baseline across the short dimension of the floor so that you won't run into the anchor bolts that are sticking out of the concrete. Find the center of your baseline, and snap a perpendicular line. Measure and mark a point above the baseline to define the peak. Then snap diagonals running from the peak to each end of the baseline as if you were defining the bottom edge of two gable rafters.

Next, snap a mid-line that runs above and parallel with the baseline, and two lines running from the midpoint of the baseline through the intersections with the diagonals. There are no hard rules governing the offset of the two gambrel roof planes. Once the offset points are established, snap the bottom edges of the gambrel lines, running the chalk line from the peak to the offset point and from the offset point to the end of the baseline on both sides.

MEASURING FOR A GAMBREL ROOF

FOR MEASURING PURPOSES, a gambrel roof is divided into two different roofs with two different rises and runs. The total run for the lower part of the gambrel roof is found by measuring the distance from the cap plate of the building wall to the center of the cap plate of a mid-pitch supporting wall. The total rise is the distance the roof section rises from the floor to the top of the wall. The total run for the top part of the gambrel roof is found by measuring from the cap plate of the mid-span supporting wall to the center of the ridgeboard. The total upper-portion rise is the distance from the support wall's cap plate to the center of the ridge.

It's important to plan for the wall or other support system where the two slopes meet, unless you use a code-approved truss design that does not require additional support.

You can build standard gambrel rafters that join over the double plate of a support wall, buy gambrel roof trusses, or, for a small-scale project, build your own trusses on-site.

PREFABRICATED GAMBREL TRUSS

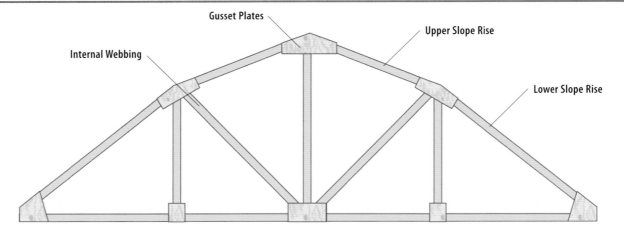

Gambrel roofs are the shape many people think of when they think of barns. They consist of two different sets of rafters or different slopes, often joined together by a plywood or metal gusset plate.

GAMBREL ROOF LAYOUT

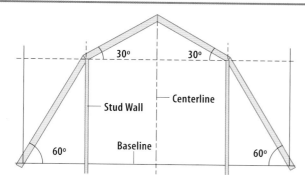

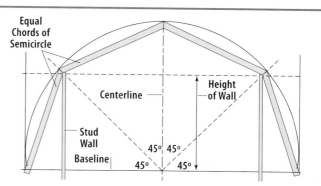

A simple layout for a gambrel roof has the first set of rafters at a 60° angle to the baseline and the second set of rafters at a 30° angle. In gambrel designs you need to support the joint at rafter segments with a beam (like a low-set ridgeboard) or a bearing wall.

A true gambrel roof—one that will give you more space in the second story—has rafters of equal lengths that describe chords of an imaginary semicircle. The intersections of the rafters and the peak of the roof will be the same distance from a central point.

PROJECT:
MARKING & CUTTING TRUSSES

TOOLS & MATERIALS
- Chalk-line box
- Pencil
- Two-by lumber for rafters and chord
- Sliding T-bevel
- Circular saw
- Plywood for gusset
- Dril-driverl with screwdriver bit
- 1½-inch screws

1 Obtain the roof slope and run from the plans, and then determine the rise. Snap chalk lines on a concrete slab (or driveway) marking the roof outline, including an overhang at the eaves.

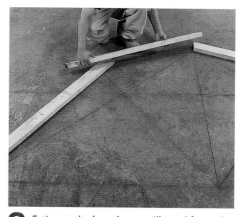

2 Estimate the length you will need for each of the four rafters in the truss, leaving a few inches extra. Lay the trusses down with the horizontal bottom chord over your chalk lines.

3 Mark the cut lines onto the rafters with a sliding T-bevel. The two cuts should align with the radius line that intersects with the center of the layout. Cut the marks with a circular saw.

4 Lay the rafters back on the chalk-line layout to make sure they fit. If they do, trace a plywood gusset to fasten them together. The gusset needs to be cut flush with the tops of the rafters.

5 Before you attach the gussets, trace both gussets and all four rafters to assemble the next truss. Then fasten the gussets together with construction adhesive and 1½-in. screws.

The roofing and siding materials you choose for your barn or shed will determine the finished appearance of the structure and protect the inside of the building from the elements. This chapter covers the most common types of siding and roofing used on outbuildings and explains how to install them. It also details different options for windows and doors, including directions for building a Z-braced door that you hang in homemade jambs. There is also a section on installing roof, gable, and soffit vents.

WALL SHEATHING

With the exterior walls plumb, square, and braced, it's time to add sheathing. You can apply sheathing vertically or horizontally. Horizontal sheathing is generally a better choice, although some building codes require that you put 2x4 blocking behind the horizontal seams.

Vertical sheathing is a good choice on 8-foot-high walls where you have a nailing surface along all four edges of the plywood. But on walls where the inside height is 8 feet, the outside wall may be higher, and you will need to extend sheathing over ceiling joists (if there are any).

If you sheathed these walls vertically, you would need to fill in strips at the top. That could compromise the superb racking resistance of plywood or oriented-strand board. Installing fill strips between full horizontal sheathing panels in the middle of the wall is a better approach and maintains better racking resistance.

Also, most wall designs call for the bottom edge of sheathing to overlap the sill plate and cover some of the foundation or slab. This overlap provides the wall with shear resistance and helps to seal out drafts and insects.

When sheathing walls, it's often easiest to sheath right over the rough openings that you created within your stud framing. When you're finished sheathing, you can drive nails from inside to mark the corners of the opening, then mark the openings and cut them from the outside with a reciprocating saw or a circular saw.

Material Choices

Most buildings today are sheathed either with ½-inch CDX plywood or ½-inch oriented-strand board. Your plans will probably specify the kind of sheathing to use. Textured 1-11 is a sheathing that also serves as siding. It's an economical approach that is often used for sheds and other outbuildings.

PROJECT:
INSTALLING SHEATHING

TOOLS & MATERIALS
- 2x4s for blocking (if required by code)
- Sheathing material (plywood or OSB)
- Measuring tape
- Chalk-line box
- Hammer or drill-driver
- Screwdriver bit
- 6d or 8d common nails or 1½-inch screws
- Circular saw
- Handsaw or reciprocating saw

1 Vertical sheathing should be installed with its edges centered on studs. The exception is corners, where the sheathing panel on one wall should butt into the back of the panel on the other wall. It's helpful for nailing to snap vertical chalk lines to mark stud locations.

2 Screw or nail the sheathing panels into the studs, spacing the fasteners every 6 in. along the edge and every 12 in. in the interior. Leave a ¹⁄₁₆-in. gap between the panels for expansion.

3 In horizontal applications, if two sheathing panels don't reach the top of the wall, you'll need a filler strip of plywood. It's best to install this strip in the middle of the wall's height.

4 For each rough opening, drive a nail or drill small holes from inside through the sheathing at the four corners. Use these to snap chalk lines on the outside of the sheathing.

5 Cut the rough openings using a circular saw. Plunge-cut into the sheathing, and continue cutting to the corners of the box. Finish the cuts with a handsaw or reciprocating saw.

VERTICAL SIDING SUPPORTS

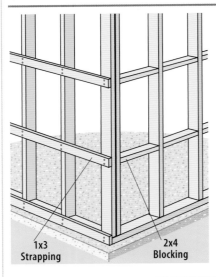

Unless installed over sheathing, vertical siding needs strapping, sometimes called nailers, or blocking for support between studs and to prevent the building from racking. Strapping consists of furring strips (such as 1x3s or 2x4s, depending on the span between studs) nailed across the studs every 24 inches. Blocking consists of 2x4s cut to fit and toenailed between the studs every 24 inches.

1x3 Strapping

2x4 Blocking

VERTICAL SIDING

There are several types of vertical siding. The most commonly used are board-on-board, board-on-batten, and batten-on-board. In three methods siding boards overlap each other so that expansion and contraction of the boards won't open gaps in the siding.

Vertical siding is ideal for barns—particularly pole barns and timber-framed barns that aren't sheathed with plywood but stand simply as framed walls. These are usually unheated, uninsulated structures. Vertical siding is typically installed on 1x3 or larger strapping set 24 inches on center or flush against the frame, nailed to the studs and to blocking installed between studs, 24 inches on center. The siding will stand out a bit from the frame. In the case of pole buildings, board siding can be installed on 2x4 girts and skirt boards spaced 24 inches apart. Vertical siding can also be installed over sheathing, which eliminates the need for blocking or strapping. Of course, the sheathing adds significantly to the cost and so is more often done in residential buildings.

PROJECT:
INSTALLING BOARD & BATTEN SIDING

TOOLS & MATERIALS

- 1x3 strapping
- Measuring tape
- Circular saw or power miter saw
- 4-foot spirit level
- Drill-driver and screws
- One-by boards (optimally the full height of the wall)
- 1x2 battens (optimally the full height of the wall)
- Hammer
- 10d galvanized nails

1 Install strapping, across studs or horizontal blocking between studs to provide a nailing surface for the boards and battens. Be sure straps are level as you screw them in place.

2 Start at one end of the frame, and nail a board onto the face of the corner studs. Leave about ½ in. between boards. Use a full-length spacer to gauge the gap.

3 Cover the gaps between the wide boards with 1½-in.-wide battens the same length as the boards beneath. Drive nails through each batten to penetrate into the blocking or strapping.

BOARD SIDING TYPES

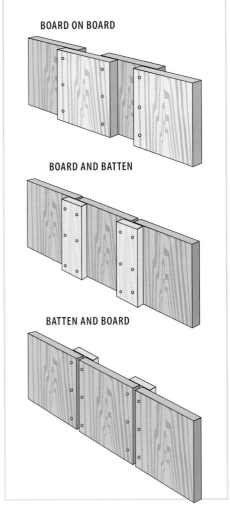

BOARD ON BOARD

BOARD AND BATTEN

BATTEN AND BOARD

Board-and-Batten Siding

Board-and-batten siding is the most popular vertical siding because it is economical and can be installed properly with basic skills and tools. Board widths come 1x6, 1x8, 1x10, and 1x12. Each board width gives a different look to the barn, so choose carefully. Most builders use the same width boards for the entire barn. Random widths generally look sloppy in board-and-batten siding, although you may have success with a repeating pattern of different sizes.

For the board stock, low-cost, rough-milled boards cut from spruce, pine, or fir are widely available, and they need not be kiln-dried before installation. In theory, board-and-batten siding can be installed the day it is milled. This is because, as mentioned, the battens overlap the boards by ½ inch or more, so even severe shrinkage will not expose gaps. However, severe shrinkage can loosen nails, so it is a good idea to use wood that has at least been air-dried. Although board siding is usually installed with thinner 1x2s nailed on top of the seams between wider boards, other variations include those shown in the illustration opposite right, "Board Siding Types."

METAL SIDING

NOT AS COMMON AS THE METAL ROOFING PANELS often used on barns, metal siding is nevertheless becoming a popular covering for utility buildings. Steel panels are generally available in widths from 24 to 36 inches. They come in a variety of baked-enamel finishes, including barn red, of course. Most siding panels are galvanized, or covered with a coating of zinc to prevent them from rusting.

Metal siding needs to be ordered directly from the manufacturer. Most manufacturers will deliver panels cut to a specific length to minimize the amount of cutting you will have to do. The manufacturer will also provide you with their minimum requirements for support. Keep in mind that barn animals can and will dent metal siding, as will normal activity around the barn. Dented metal panels are unsightly and difficult to replace, especially if they were custom sized.

Metal Siding Types

Many metal siding panels come 38 inches wide. After lapping at least one rib or corrugation, this yields 36 inches of coverage. Panels are usually ribbed along the face to add strength.

A high-quality metal siding will have ribs every 9 inches or so, and they will be ¾ inch high. (Metal siding panels are designed to interlock.) The ribs act as a stiffener, which adds durability, but they also keep the siding from crumpling during transportation and installation. The ideal thickness range is 24 to 26 gauge in galvanized steel.

There is a wide range of accessories you can buy with metal siding. It may be best if you choose a single metal siding manufacturer because they have attachments, caps, corners, and other fittings that are designed for use with their particular siding. Using compatible parts makes trimming out windows and doors much easier.

Metal buildings don't need to look like commercial storage facilities. Until you see the siding close up, you may not realize that the barn is sided in enamel-coated steel instead of wood.

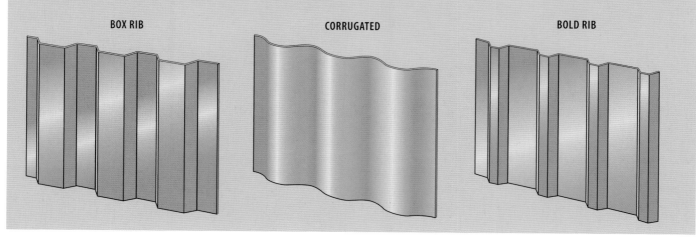

BOX RIB   CORRUGATED   BOLD RIB

WOOD PANEL SIDING

Many lumberyards carry Texture 1-11 panels. These 4x8-foot sheets have grooves cut into their face 4, 8, or 12 inches apart to simulate the look of separate planks. But many other styles and surface treatments of wood panel siding are available. It is important to understand the difference between plywood rated for exterior use versus exposure. An "Exterior" stamp means the plywood is designed to be used as siding—it can withstand permanent exposure to the elements. An "Exposure" stamp means the plywood is intended for use as sheathing—it can stand up to temporary exposure to the weather during construction, but is not intended as permanent siding.

Panel siding can be particularly economical because it sometimes can serve as wall sheathing and siding (check local codes), and be attached directly to the studs.

WOOD PANEL JOINTS

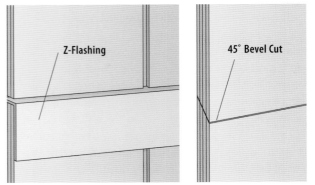

The joints between stacked wood siding panels can be protected from water with a piece of Z-flashing, left. If you don't want to see a metal strip, join panels with a 45-deg. cut.

PROJECT: 🐾🐾🐾
INSTALLING PANEL SIDING

TOOLS & MATERIALS

- Work gloves and eye protection Chalk-line box
- 2x4 ledger boards and corner boards
- 4-foot level and plumb bob
- Hammer and galvanized nails
- Plywood siding panels
- Circular saw or saber saw
- Sawhorses and ladders
- Drill-driver
- Combination square
- Z-flashing
- Saber saw (if needed)

1 Establish a level line on the foundation, and snap a chalk line to mark it. Then nail a 2x4 ledger in place to support heavy siding panels as you plumb them and nail them.

2 Start at an inside or outside corner, and hold the sheet up to the framing, making sure the sheet is plumb. Nail it into the studs using fasteners specified by the manufacturer.

3 On panels with shiplap edges, tack the edge of the last panel; then install the next sheet, aligning it so that the groove has the same width as the others. Nail through the lapped section.

4 To install corner boards over siding panels, mount the first board flush and the second board lapping the first to cover its edge.

5 To accommodate protrusions, such as hose bibcocks, measure out from the corner and up from the level base-line to mark your cutout. Then carefully cut the siding using a saber saw.

Install wood panel siding just as you would plywood sheathing, with nails every 6 inches around the perimeter and every 12 inches in the interior of the panel. Metal or fiberglass panels typically have proprietary fasteners, such as nails or screws with gaskets. Check with the manufacturer for installation recommendations.

Panels are usually installed vertically and stacked as needed to cover high walls. If you install them horizontally, blocking between the studs may be required by local codes where the panel edges meet. This blocking provides a continuous nailing surface along the edges, which is important for siding that doubles as sheathing.

Protecting the Joints. While the wood-panel surface will be coated with stain or paint for appearance and protection against the weather, panel edges often are not coated. They are the weak links because layers of thin plywood laminations are exposed along the edges. If the layers soak up water, the panel is likely to delaminate, which can pop nails and create an array of repair problems.

You can protect against this deterioration by brushing a primer coat on the edges prior to installation or by concealing the edges with trim, such as vertical corner boards. It's also important to caulk or flash seams around windows and doors and on two-story projects where one sheet rests on top of another.

On horizontal joints between sheets of siding on high-wall or two-story jobs, there are two good ways to protect the seams from the weather. (See the illustration opposite.) One method is to cut 45-degree angles along the mating edges and apply a bead of caulk to the seam. Water would have to run uphill to get behind the siding. But this kind of joint is difficult to make on panel siding without the use of a table saw.

The other method calls for a piece of Z-flashing tucked up behind the top panel and extended onto the face of the bottom panel. No 45-degree cuts are needed, but you will see the flashing. Do not be tempted to simply caulk a butt seam on vertically stacked panels because they will eventually leak.

WOOD PANEL TYPES

SURFACED PANEL

SURFACED PANELS come in a variety of patterns and surface textures depending on how the wood was sawed or sanded. The surface texture can be smooth, rough-sawn, striated, or brushed. These panels are often stained or covered with clear sealer for a rustic look, and exposed edges at corners are covered with trim.

COMPOSITE PANELS are engineered for extra strength by combining and gluing together sawdust, wood chips, and other waste materials. Without a natural grain to twist one way or another, the panels are very stable. Many manufacturers sell either solid-wood or engineered trim pieces matched to the panels to finish off the job.

GROOVED PANELS offer a variety of looks, depending on the groove profile. A wide spacing between grooves generally looks best on a big wall, while narrower spacing fits the scale on smaller buildings. These panels are built to join at a lap at the last groove so that seams between the panels aren't noticeable.

BATTEN-AND-BOARD PANELS have a wide, flat groove cut at regular intervals along the panel length. This configuration is designed to resemble a somewhat unusual twist on the typical board-and-batten design, called a reverse batten or batten-and-board, where a narrow board is set behind the simulated planks.

COMPOSITE PANEL

GROOVED PANEL

BOARD-AND-BATTEN PANEL

HORIZONTAL SIDING

Horizontal siding comes in a wide variety of configurations including clapboards, tongue-and groove, log cabin, shiplap, channel rustic boards, and more.

Clapboard Siding

If you install clapboards instead of panels, you take a step up in material price, workload, skill level, and sheathing requirements. Clapboard siding doesn't provide the required rigidity so it is always installed over sheathing panels. House wrap, felt paper, or some other protective layer is used between the sheathing and siding.

Choices vary widely among grades of siding, from premium products like clear vertical-grain all-heart cedar to spruce. You get what you pay for, though spruce, with proper caulking and careful attention to painting, can last a long time.

Clapboards typically range from 4 to 10 inches, generally with 1 inch covered by the course above. Most clapboards are around ½ inch thick at the bottom. Some types also take two nails per course, so be sure to check nailing specs with the manufacturer and local building inspector.

SIDING DETAIL

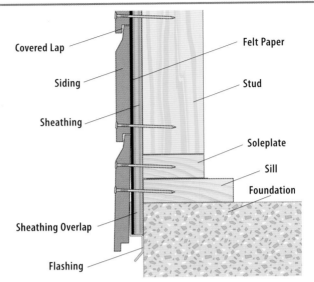

Covered Lap
Siding
Sheathing
Sheathing Overlap
Flashing
Felt Paper
Stud
Soleplate
Sill
Foundation

Horizontal board siding should overlap the sheathing. Flashing will further protect the sheathing and framing from moisture and insects. You may also need a termite shield.

HORIZONTAL SIDING STYLES

Rabbeted-edge siding has a lap between each board, dictated by the way the edge is milled. Fasten it with 8d nails.

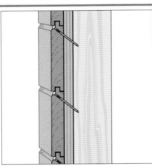

Tongue-and-groove siding should be set with the tongues firmly in the grooves. It also can be set vertically. Use 8d nails.

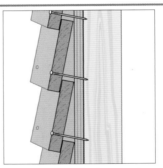

Board-on-board siding needs to be lapped so that the top board covers about 1 in. of the bottom board. Use 10d nails.

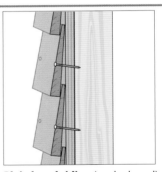

Plain bevel siding (or clapboard) has a wedge shaped profile that dictates a 1-in.-minimum lap. Use 6d nails to attach it.

Log-cabin–style siding looks similar to the exterior of a log home. It usually has no revealed lap. Attach it with 10d nails.

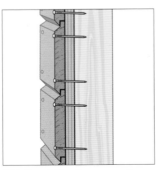

Shiplap siding has a reveal dictated by the profile, though extra space may be left. Use 8d nails to fasten it.

Channel rustic siding usually has a ½-in. lap. Fasten the siding with 8d nails. It may also be hung vertically.

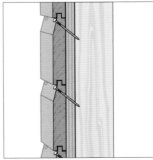

Drop tongue-and-groove (also called novelty siding) is available with cupped, beveled, or beaded upper edges. Use 8d nails.

CORNER OPTIONS

CORNER BOARDS PROTECT leak-prone siding joints at the corners of a building. Mitered joints look neat and elegant but aren't as durable as other options, and the technique requires laborious hand-fitting. Butted outside corner boards are easier to install. You nail them in place and simply cut the siding to butt against them. On outside corners, you must account for the thickness of the adjoining boards, which means that one will be narrower. At inside corners, one square board will do.

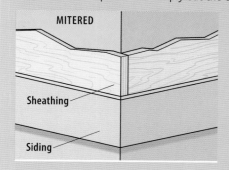

MITERED

Sheathing

Siding

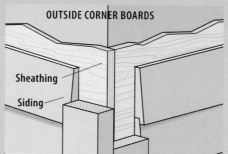

OUTSIDE CORNER BOARDS

Sheathing

Siding

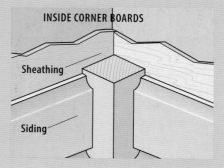

INSIDE CORNER BOARDS

Sheathing

Siding

PROJECT: INSTALLING CLAPBOARDS

TOOLS & MATERIALS

- House wrap
- Measuring tape
- Corner boards
- Circular saw
- Drill-driver
- Ladder
- 4-foot level
- Chalk-line box
- Starter strip
- Clapboards
- Hammer 6d nails
- Saber saw, caulk (if needed)

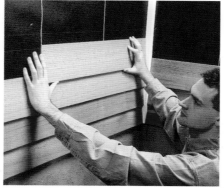

1 Install prefinished inside and outside corner boards to provide square edges against which the siding can butt. Using lumber that has been primed will save you time finishing later on.

2 Snap a level line for the base course, and nail a starter strip along the bottom edge of the sheathing. This will give the bottom of the first row of siding the proper pitch.

3 Overlap the starter strip with the first board, and drive nails high enough to be covered by the next course. Be careful not to split the thin top edge of the clapboard when you nail.

4 Stagger joints between siding lengths at every course. Place joints at random intervals spaced a minimum of 16 in. apart. This way, any water that seeps through a joint will be shed by the board below.

5 Cut around any obstructions as you come to them. Always overlap boards and fittings so that any rainwater will run off of the siding. Caulk around vents and electrical boxes.

METAL ROOFING

Metal standing-seam roofs look good, and are often guaranteed for 30 years or more. But they are expensive and generally installed by pros using special tools required to bend adjoining seams. Creating watertight valleys in these roofs can be difficult. But some modern systems simply snap together, are held to the roof with clips, and are easy to install for savvy do-it-yourselfers.

Agricultural-panel roofs, commonly called ag-panel, also can be installed by someone with average building skills. Ag-panels have ribs pressed into the panels to give them strength. Most ag-panels are galvanized steel, and they can easily last 15 years or more, though in wet climates or on low-sloped roofs where snow can build up, rust can form in as little as five years. They are an excellent low-cost roofing choice for most barns.

Ag-panels come in various lengths, typically from 8 to 16 feet in 2-foot increments, and are between 32 and 38 inches wide. Be sure to buy the required nails or screws (and sealing washers) at the same time. Attributes to look for in quality ag-panel roofing panel include the following.

- **26-Gauge Thickness.**
- **Watertight Fittings.** Practical designs accommodate watertight ridge caps, drip flashing, closure strips at the eaves, and sometimes a sealant or tape that seals the ag-panel overlaps along their lengths. These features will give you a watertight roof as opposed to a water-shedding roof, although that is not always needed in a barn.
- **Factory-Applied Enamel Coating.** When choosing color, note that you will get the largest lateral thermal movement with darker colored roofs, which absorb the most solar heat.
- **Flexible Washers.** These keep the fastener holes sealed. Because metal panels expand and contract with heat and cold, fasteners can shift and admit water.

Installation Techniques

Ag-panel roofs are installed over purlins, typically 2x4s, that run on edge across the rafters, normally every 2 feet on center. (See page 124.) The first row of purlins should be at the outermost eaves end of the rafters. Purlins can overhang the gable ends if you want the roof to overhang the walls.

Because ag-panels overlap, figure that the net coverage of your ag-panel will be between 30 and 36 inches. Multiply the net width of the ag-panel coverage in feet by the length of the rafter bay in feet, and then count the rafter bays. For instance, if your ag-panel's net coverage is 36 inches and your rafters are 12 feet long, each rafter bay will require 36 square feet of ag-panel. Of course, remember to order for both sides of the roof.

METAL ROOFING TYPES

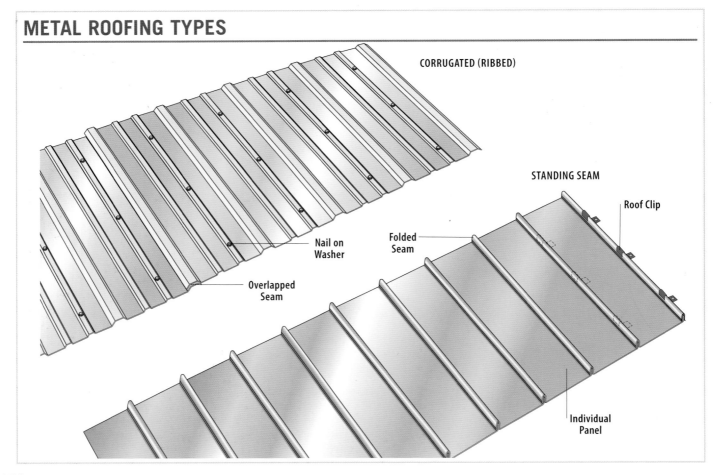

CORRUGATED (RIBBED)

STANDING SEAM

Roof Clip

Folded Seam

Nail on Washer

Overlapped Seam

Individual Panel

TYPICAL COMPONENTS OF METAL ROOFING & SIDING

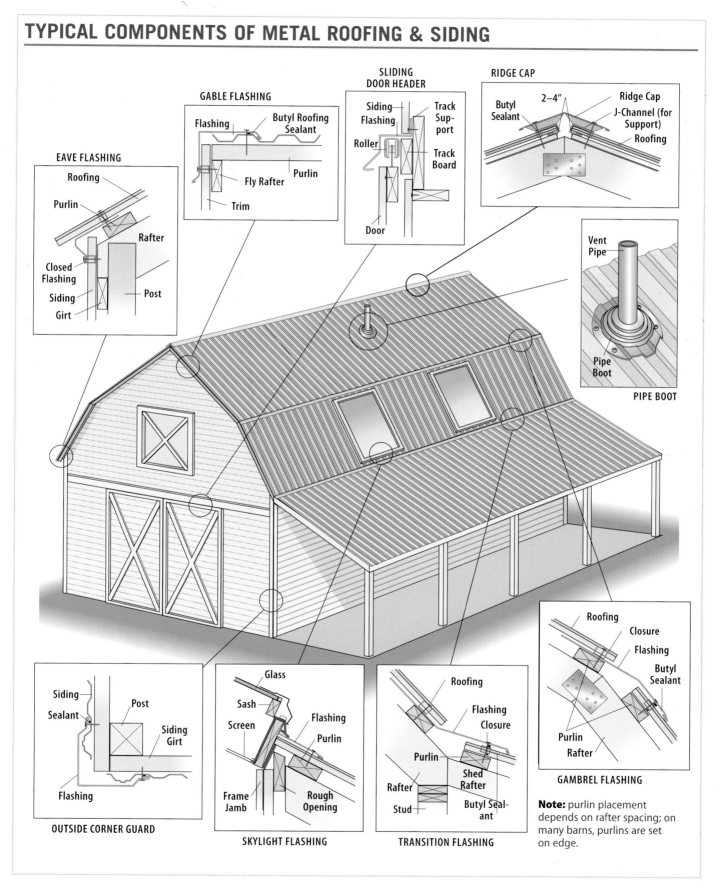

GABLE FLASHING

Flashing
Butyl Roofing Sealant
Fly Rafter
Trim
Purlin

SLIDING DOOR HEADER

Siding Flashing
Track Support
Roller
Track Board
Door

RIDGE CAP

Butyl Sealant
2–4"
Ridge Cap
J-Channel (for Support)
Roofing

EAVE FLASHING

Roofing
Purlin
Rafter
Closed Flashing
Siding
Post
Girt

Vent Pipe
Pipe Boot

PIPE BOOT

OUTSIDE CORNER GUARD

Siding
Post
Sealant
Siding Girt
Flashing

SKYLIGHT FLASHING

Glass
Sash
Screen
Flashing
Purlin
Frame Jamb
Rough Opening

TRANSITION FLASHING

Roofing
Flashing
Closure
Purlin
Shed Rafter
Rafter
Butyl Sealant
Stud

GAMBREL FLASHING

Roofing
Closure
Flashing
Butyl Sealant
Purlin
Rafter

Note: purlin placement depends on rafter spacing; on many barns, purlins are set on edge.

CORRUGATED ROOFING PANELS

CORRUGATED PANELS made of plastic or fiberglass can provide a watertight yet translucent covering for part of the roof. If you're installing a corrugated metal roof, you can add a few panels between the metal ones to admit light into your barn. Panels are typically sold along with manufacturer-specific nails or screws, filler strips, and caulk—everything you need for a proper installation. The filler strips fit the contours of the panel and are installed along the eaves. The fasteners are compatible with aluminum or steel panels. Use panels that interlock with the metal panels. To prevent leaks at the fastener holes, set every nail or screw with a rubberized washer. The trick is to set fasteners just firmly enough to seat the washer without deforming it and causing a leak. To prevent leaks, overlap panels along the edges by at least one corrugation.

PANEL ROOFING

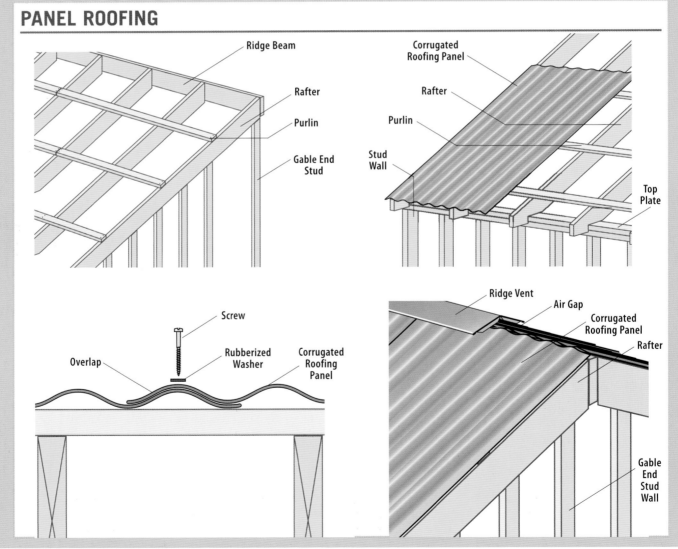

ROOF SHEATHING

If you don't install a metal roof attached to purlins, you need to install plywood decking. The sheets stabilize the rafters and provide a nailing surface for shingles or other roofing. Most areas require ½-inch-thick plywood rated for exterior use, although some codes allow less-expensive materials such as oriented-strand board (OSB).

When you install sheathing over rafters, stagger the end joints so that the seams don't line up. If you start with a full 4x8 sheet along the eaves, use a half sheet to start the next course. Prolonged exposure to the weather can damage the framing, so waterproof the roof sheathing as soon as possible.

Plan any panel cutting so that you can use the cutoff portions on the opposite side. You can start at the eaves with a full 4-foot-wide panel, provided you don't end up at the top having to use a strip less than 16 inches wide. A narrow strip may be too weak to support a person or provide a solid backing for the roofing. Trim the panels

of the first row as needed to adjust the width of the last row. Also plan to stagger panels in succeeding rows so that the ends fall on different framing members.

In general, roof slope dictates the method of felt paper installation. In temperate climates, apply one layer of 15-pound felt on roofs having a 4-in-12 or greater slope. Lap the felt at least 2 inches horizontally and 6 inches vertically to shed water. Overlap the ridge by at least 6 inches. On roofs having less than a 4-in-12 slope, start with a 19-inch-wide sheet along the eaves. Lay a 36-inch-wide sheet over that, and then lap each subsequent sheet 19 inches horizontally and at least 12 inches vertically.

Use caution working on the roof at all times. Remember, the greater the roof slope, the more hazardous the job. On steep roofs, nail down 2x4 cleats for footing support as you work up the roof and always use appropriate safety gear.

PROJECT: 🐦🐦🐦
SHEATHING THE ROOF

TOOLS & MATERIALS
- Plywood sheathing
- Circular saw
- Hammer
- Measuring tape
- ⅞-inch roofing nails
- Panel clips (for 24-inch-on-center framing)
- Chalk-line box

1 To allow for a fascia to be nailed across the rafter tails, the bottommost course of roof sheathing should be installed so that its top edge does not protrude past the rafter's tail cut.

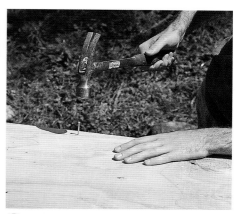

2 Begin installation at a bottom corner, placing the long side perpendicular to the rafters, with the end joint over the center of a rafter. Use 8d nails every 6 in. along the edges and 12 in. in the field.

3 To support the panel seams where they fall between rafters, use plywood panel clips in the center of the joint. Insert one end onto an installed sheet, and slide the next sheet onto the support

4 Start the second course with a half (4 x 4-ft.) panel so that the seams will not fall in the same places. Stagger the panel ends on several different rafters as you work up the roof

5 Mark the plywood at the eaves and ridge, and snap a chalk line to help guide nailing into the centers of the rafters. If you miss a rafter, pull the nail so that it won't work up into the singles.

ROOF FLASHING

Flashing is used to keep a roof watertight wherever it is punctuated by an opening such as a vent, chimney, or skylight. Roofs are also flashed along valleys, eaves, and rakes.

Flashing can be made from galvanized sheet steel, aluminum, copper, or flexible plastic in some cases. Generally, you need to use nails made of the same material as the flashing. Copper nails may be hard to find, but you should use them if you are going to be installing copper flashing. Other metals may cause chemical reactions which might undermine the strength of the copper and eventually cause leaks.

In some cases you can cut and bend flashing yourself. Step flashing, for example, is simply a small sheet of aluminum bent in half. But for most applications you can use preformed flashing, sometimes with a complex series of bends, to fit the particular installation.

Drip Edge

Drip edge covers the ends of eaves and rakes, which often need to be protected by more than just the overhang of the roofing material. Install preformed drip flashing along the eaves of the roof before you place the underlayment (generally felt paper) and along rakes on each side after the underlayment is down.

Cut the corners with metal-cutting shears, both for the sake of appearance and for better coverage. Work carefully and wear gloves, as cut sheet metal is extremely sharp. Use roofing nails every 8 to 10 inches to secure the drip edge to the sheathing. Do not nail the drip edge to the fascia.

Vent Collars

Projections through the roof, such as plumbing vent pipes, are best sealed with flashing sleeves. These sleeves are available in a variety of styles and materials, including lead, sheet metal, rubber, and plastic. The most modern type (it's also the easiest to install) has a flexible rubber collar that makes a tight seal around the pipe. Below the collar, a piece of metal flashing makes the watertight connections to the roof. On the high side, the flashing tucks under shingles. On the low side, it rests on top of them. You can trim shingles to make a neat fit around the flashing.

Step Flashing

Step flashing joins shingles to the sloping side of a wall or a chimney. Step flashing requires that each piece of flashing overlaps the one below it. The flashing is interlaced with the shingles as well. You can purchase step flashing precut, or you can cut the flashing into shingle-like pieces 10 inches long and 2 inches wider than the exposure of the roofing. You have to remember to insert a piece at the end of every course of shingles. You nail the high side against the adjacent structure, such as a dormer where it will be covered by siding, but do not nail the low side on the roof.

Valley Flashing

Valley flashing is installed on top of the sheathing and felt paper but beneath the roofing. The two basic types of valley treatments are called open and closed. If the flashing material is visible after the roof is finished, it is considered open. If the roofing material covers or even replaces the flashing, it is considered closed.

Open flashing works for all types of roofs. On the other hand, closed flashing is used only with asphalt shingles that are flexible enough to be woven together across the angle created by a valley. Open valleys are essential for wooden shingles, slate, and tile because the materials will not bend and overlap to make a closed valley. Open valleys also are commonly used with asphalt shingles because the design provides greater protection, especially from torrential downpours and the slow melt of heavy snow.

Valley flashing should extend 6 inches or more on each side of the valley centerline. (For low-slope roofs, make that 10 inches.) Valley flashing can be galvanized steel or aluminum, center-crimped or painted. (If you crimp the flashing after it is painted, retouch the paint at the crimp line.) When you are using cedar roofing, underlay valley metal with 15-pound builder's felt (minimum). Double-coverage with a strip of felt paper or heavier roll roofing is a good idea for backup protection under all open valleys.

TYPES OF FLASHING

Nail drip edge along the rakes and eaves before installing your first course of shingles.

Vents are best sealed with formed flashing. A rubber vent collar seals the pipe.

Step flashing is short angled pieces of flashing that seal between shingles and walls.

Counterflashing is sealed into mortar to cover the top edge of standard flashing below.

TYPICAL FLASHING FOR ROOFING & SIDING

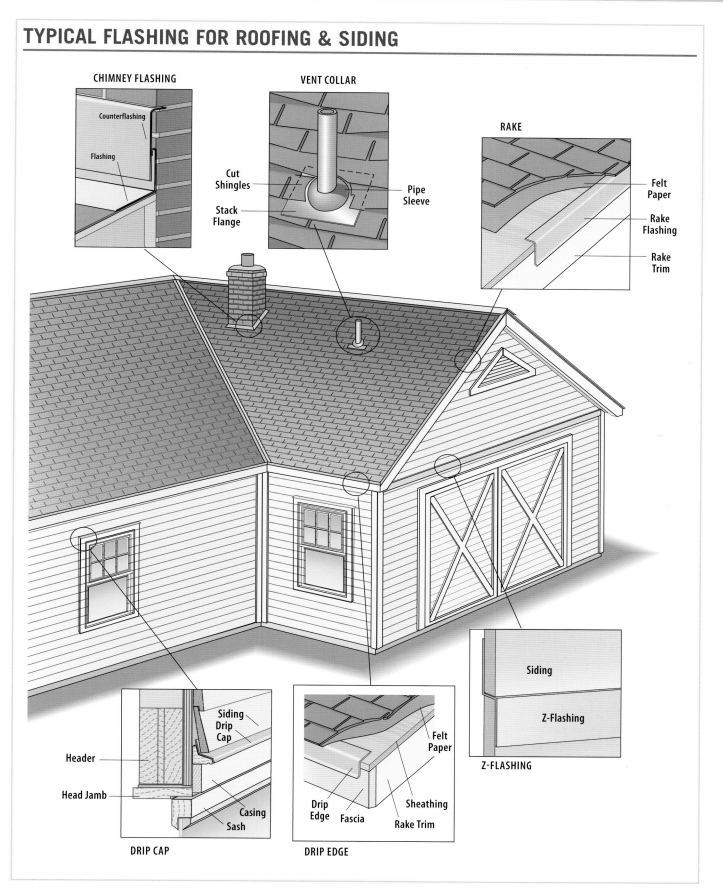

CHIMNEY FLASHING

Counterflashing

Flashing

VENT COLLAR

Cut Shingles

Stack Flange

Pipe Sleeve

RAKE

Felt Paper

Rake Flashing

Rake Trim

Siding

Z-Flashing

Z-FLASHING

Siding Drip Cap

Header

Head Jamb

Casing

Sash

DRIP CAP

Felt Paper

Drip Edge

Fascia

Sheathing

Rake Trim

DRIP EDGE

ROOFING MATERIALS

There are many materials you can use to finish a roof aside from ag-panels and other traditional barn coverings.

Asphalt-based shingles are relatively simple to apply and will last 20 to 40 years or more depending on their rating and the roof slope—they last longer on steeper slopes. They come in a variety of colors and shapes and several different styles. These shingles have a fiberglass mat impregnated with asphalt and coated with mineral granules. Asphalt shingles have adhesive beneath the tabs to keep them from curling or blowing back. They are suitable for every climate and can be applied to any roof that has a slope of 4 in 12 (4 inches of vertical rise for every 12 inches of horizontal run) or more. With double felt underlayment, they generally can be applied to a roof with a slope as low as 2 in 12 if shingle tabs are sealed down.

Roll roofing is an excellent choice for roofs with very shallow slopes. It's the least expensive roofing material, and while not as attractive as shingles, shallow roofs can't be seen from the ground anyway. Different types of roll roofing are made to be installed with different amounts of overlap. Single-coverage rolls are overlapped only a few inches. With double-coverage rolls, half of each course is covered by the next course. By increasing coverage, you can use rolls on slopes as low as 1 in 12 (1 inch rise per 12 inches of run). Roll roofing is 36 inches wide and is available in a variety of colors. Surface granules may be dark or light.

Wood shingles and shakes have twice the insulation value of asphalt shingles, are lighter in weight than most other roofing materials, and are very resistant to hail damage. They are also well suited to withstand the freeze-thaw conditions of variable climates. Wood shingles are machine-cut and smoothed on both sides. Shakes are thicker and rough on at least one side because they are split on one face and machine smoothed on the other. They vary in thickness and have a rustic appearance. A layer of felt paper sometimes is used between each course.

Both shingles and shakes require 1x4 strapping, often called skip sheathing, spaced to suit the desired exposure. Some modern wood roofs are laid over a mesh mat (instead of skip sheathing) that allows air to circulate under the wood and reduces the chance of rot and other problems. Pressure-injected fire retardant, as indicated by the industry designation "Certi-Guard," conforms to all state and local building codes for use in fire hazard regions. Given periodic coatings of wood preservative, shingles and shakes may serve for as long as 50 years. The drawbacks of using them include their high cost and slow application time.

Hardboard shingle panels are suitable for roofs with a slope of at least 4 in 12. With scored nailing and alignment lines, these 12 x 48-inch panels are installed in half the time it takes to apply cedar shakes. The panels do not crack with age, and they weather to a light gray.

Installing Composition Shingles

Roofers often have their own methods of applying strip shingles, but in most cases all applications follow a few key guidelines. One of the most important guidelines is to double up the first row with a starter course. These starter shingles are set with the keys up instead of keys down. Some roofers also install an extra layer running lengthwise along the gable ends to reduce drips and help channel water back into the main roof and down to the gutters.

Roofers also sometimes stay in one place on the roof and install a few shingles stacked with overlaps for many courses. Do-it-yourselfers generally are better off installing only a few courses all the way across the roof, regularly checking straightness with a string line and measuring up from the starter course to keep the courses even.

It's also important to be safe during roof work. In that regard, the best guideline is to work only on walkable roofs, and even then only wearing nonslip shoes in good weather. If you have any misgivings about working on the roof, you should leave the job to a professional.

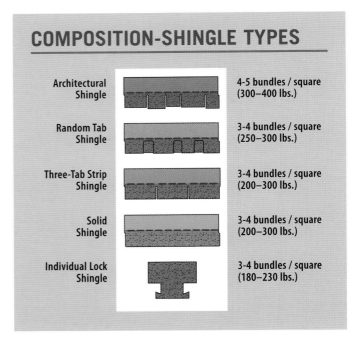

COMPOSITION-SHINGLE TYPES

Architectural Shingle	4-5 bundles / square (300–400 lbs.)
Random Tab Shingle	3-4 bundles / square (250–300 lbs.)
Three-Tab Strip Shingle	3-4 bundles / square (200–300 lbs.)
Solid Shingle	3-4 bundles / square (200–300 lbs.)
Individual Lock Shingle	3-4 bundles / square (180–230 lbs.)

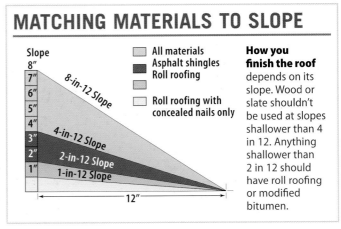

MATCHING MATERIALS TO SLOPE

Slope
8"
7"
6"
5"
4"
3"
2"
1"

8-in-12 Slope
4-in-12 Slope
2-in-12 Slope
1-in-12 Slope
12"

☐ All materials
■ Asphalt shingles
■ Roll roofing
☐ Roll roofing with concealed nails only

How you finish the roof depends on its slope. Wood or slate shouldn't be used at slopes shallower than 4 in 12. Anything shallower than 2 in 12 should have roll roofing or modified bitumen.

INSTALLING SHINGLES

TOOLS & MATERIALS
- Work gloves
- Hammer
- Metal drip edge
- Roofing felt and shingles
- Chalk-line box
- Shears and utility knife
- Roofing nails
- Roofing cement

SMART TIP

When installing drip edge, the nails should be snug, but don't drive them so tight that you deform the drip edge.

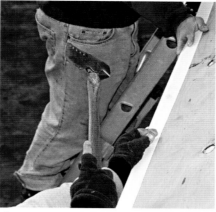

1 Nail on a metal drip edge at the edge of the eaves and the rake (on top of felt) with galvanized roofing nails. This helps keep water from the fascia boards and rake boards, preventing rot.

2 Roll out roofing felt on top of the roof decking. Secure the felt with staples every 10 or 12 inches, keeping them about 3 inches from the edges. Overlap adjacent rows by several inches.

3 For the starter course of shingles, snap a chalk line and lay the shingles with the tabs pointing toward the peak. Put one galvanized roofing nail through each tab.

4 The first visible course covers the starter course, with the tabs pointing away from the peak. Each shingle should be nailed just above the top of each key slot.

5 Start each new course at a 6-in. offset to stagger the seams in adjacent courses in a water-shedding layout. Make sure that the black adhesive strip is covered by the next course.

6 To shingle around a vent stack, trim to overlap only the upper half of the vent collar. Add roofing cement underneath this shingle. Do not drive nails through the shingles into the vent collar.

7 To shingle the ridge, cut single, slightly tapered tabs from whole shingles and wrap them across the ridge, nailing them on both sides in the area that will be covered by the next shingle.

8 To save time, you can let full shingles extend past the roof overhang. Come back later, and trim all of them at once with shears. This is much easier than cutting each to a specific length.

Installing Roll Roofing

Roll roofing, built-up roofing, and seam-sealed modified bitumen are the most common materials used to cover very low-slope roofs. Most roofs that appear flat actually have some slope to encourage drainage. While some types of roll roofing may be suitable, the material of choice today for flat roofs is a rubbery sheet material generally called modified bitumen or single-ply. Its seams are sealed with heat to form watertight seals. Single-ply also is widely used today instead of old fashioned built-up roofs that involve multiple layers of roofing material and hot tar. Both single-ply and built-up roofs should be installed by contractors.

On appropriate slopes, you can install roll roofing quickly. But the life of roll roofing is typically only 5 to 10 years. Given its plain appearance and short life, single-layer roll roofing is best used on sheds or in places where the roof is not visible. Think of roll roofing as a utility products that has little aesthetic value and whose only purpose is to keep water from entering the building. It may be used on slopes that are less angled than those normally covered by shingles, especially if a concealed nail application is used. Double-coverage roll roofing is best for roofs with a very low slope.

Roll roofing is more fragile than other roofing options. In temperatures below 45 degrees F, the material may crack, although you can work in colder conditions if you warm the rolls first. The roofing cement used at seams must be kept at a temperature above 45 degrees F, so store it indoors if you are working in cold weather.

Make sure the roofing has not curled at the edges or puckered in the middle. If it has, cut it into pieces 12 to 18 feet long and stack the pieces on a flat surface. Depending on the air temperature, they will take an hour to one full day to flatten. Felt paper may not be required, but is commonly installed over sheathing because it is inexpensive and worth the extra effort. Even small pebbles can eventually poke through roll roofing, so sweep the surface carefully.

PROJECT:
INSTALLING ROLL ROOFING

TOOLS & MATERIALS
- Work gloves
- Chalk-line box
- Builder's felt
- Roll roofing
- Broom
- Roofing cement
- Hammer
- Roofing nails
- Mason's trowel

1 Use a chalk-line box to snap a guideline 35½ in. from the eaves. Roll out the first layer of roofing on top of the felt paper, and nail it to the decking at 12-in. intervals.

2 After you install the first layer, spread roofing cement on it. This will help the second layer stick to this one. It's a messy job. Wear gloves, and keep the cement off of your shoes.

3 Roll out the second layer in a straight line, nailing it in place every 12 in. with roofing nails. Don't overdrive these nails, as this will puncture the roofing and could cause leaks.

4 Trowel on roof cement at course overlaps. Some roll roofing is designed to overlap up to half the previous layer. Be sure to read the instructions for the product you're using.

5 Cover each strip of roof cement with successive courses. Many brands of roll roofing are available with light-colored granules. Be sure your color matches roll for roll.

Installing Wood Shingles

Wood shingles and shakes are usually made of western red cedar, a long-lasting straight-grain wood. Even after years of weathering, wood does a much better job of shedding water than might be expected. In addition, wood shingles and shakes resist heat transmission twice as well as composition shingles. However, wood shingles often require more maintenance than other roofing materials, especially if you live in a harsh climate. In such areas it is advisable to treat wood shingles and shakes with a preservative every five years or so. Regular cleaning is also recommended to clear away debris that traps moisture and breeds fungus, mildew, rot, and insect borers.

Wood shingles and shakes are not naturally fire resistant, and some local codes may require that the wood be treated with fire retardant. In the past few years, some localities have banned wood roofing altogether, so be sure to check your local codes before deciding to use wood shingles or shakes. In addition, check with your insurance company to see whether your insurance premiums will be affected if you install wood roofing.

Shingles and shakes are not recommended for roofs with less than a 4-in-12 slope and exposure must also be limited for low slopes. For example, with a 4-in-12 slope, 16-inch shingles have a maximum of 5-inch exposure (6¾ inches on a 5-in-12 slope). Shingles that are 24 inches long can have the greatest exposure (7½ inches on a 4-in-12 slope and 9¼ inches on a 5-in-12 slope).

Synthetic-fiber panels are an alternative to shingles. They are embossed with deep shadow lines and random-cut grooves to look like shakes. These 12x48-inch panels are applied lengthwise across the roof. Because they are so large, installation goes quickly. The panels overlap with a shiplap joint between courses and a lap joint between panels in the same course. Use the panels for both reroofing and new roofing. If installing panels over an existing room, apply a layer of roofing felt first.

PROJECT:
INSTALLING WOOD ROOFING

TOOLS & MATERIALS

- Roofing felt
- Plastic mesh
- Staple gun
- Heavy-duty staples
- Chalk-line box
- Hammer
- Roofing nails
- Shingles or shakes
- Step flashing
- Carpenter's pencil
- Spacing jig

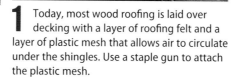

1 Today, most wood roofing is laid over decking with a layer of roofing felt and a layer of plastic mesh that allows air to circulate under the shingles. Use a staple gun to attach the plastic mesh.

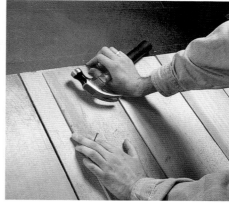

2 Install two layers of shingles at the eaves. Be sure to stagger their seams so that water can't penetrate to the roof beneath. Drive nails so that they will be covered by the next course.

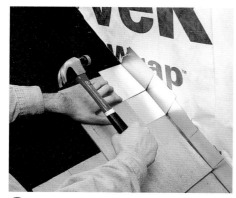

3 Nail on step flashing in any seams where roofs meet walls. Apply a length of flashing under each shingle at these joints as you go along. Also install a drip edge at the rakes and eaves.

4 As you add courses, keep about ¼ in. of space between shakes by holding a pencil between them. This will help channel water off the surface and allow for expansion and contraction.

5 Build a T-shape jig to provide consistent distance between the bottoms of each course. This will help make the process move a lot faster because you won't have to keep measuring.

TYPES OF DOORS

All door openings require a built-up horizontal pieced called a header. In bearing walls, the header transfers the load to jack studs, which are nailed to full-length king studs. Nonbearing walls have less beefy headers. The jacks and the headers form the rough opening.

Houses and more finished-looking outbuildings have one-by boards called jambs lining the rough openings. There's a little space between jambs and framing so you can shim the jambs perfectly square to fit the door. The space and the edges of the jam are covered with trim called door casing. Most lumberyards carry a "jamb set" consisting of a head jamb and two side jambs.

Many utility building have more rustic door openings with no finished jambs or casing, often fitted with homemade doors.

Making Your Own Door

If you need a door to fit an odd-size opening or simply want to save money, you can build your own door from rough-cut boards or plywood. Some of the possibilities are shown in "Door Framing," opposite top. Doors up to 3 feet wide by 6 feet 8 inches tall can be made of ½- to ⅝-inch plywood reinforced with a surface-mounted frame and braces made of 1x4s. You can use the same one-by stock to make the trim to frame the opening. Because you install these somewhat rough-looking doors with surface-mounted hinges, no jamb is needed. For taller or wider doors, you often need firmer bracing. To install large doors, it's wise to prop them up slightly during installation to account for a bit of sagging, even after mounting three hinges to carry the weight.

DOOR FRAMING

Cripple Stud
Header
Casing
Jamb
Jack Stud
King Stud

Shim
Jamb
Stop
Door
Casing
Jack Stud
King Stud

Shims
Drywall

DOOR STYLES

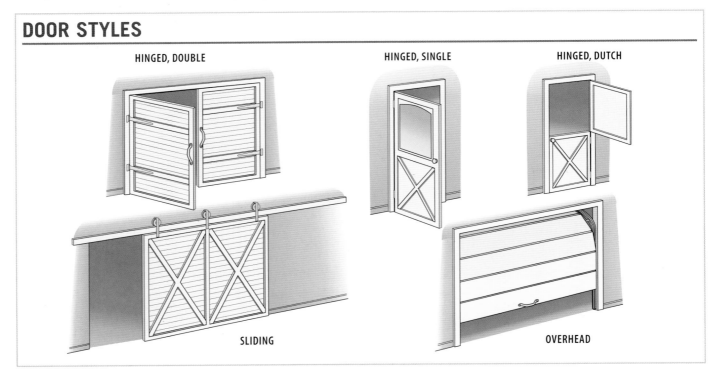

HINGED, DOUBLE

HINGED, SINGLE

HINGED, DUTCH

SLIDING

OVERHEAD

DOOR FRAMING

BRACE AND FRAME   HORIZONTAL BRACE ONLY   FULL Z-BRACE   DOUBLE Z-BRACE   FULL X-BRACE

PROJECT:
BUILDING A Z-BRACE DOOR

TOOLS & MATERIALS
- Circular saw
- 1x4 or 1x6 boards
- Drill-driver
- Screwdriver bit
- 1¼-inch deck screws
- Sliding T-bevel
- Clamps
- File or sandpaper
- Carpenter's glue

1 Use a circular saw to cut 1x4 or 1x6 boards to length. If full-width boards won't fit the width of your rough opening, rip two boards to identical widths, and use those boards at the sides.

2 Align the boards on a worktable, and attach them with two lengths of 1x4 strapping near the top and bottom. Make sure that the fasteners don't poke through to the other side.

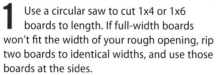

3 Lay a 1x4 for the Z-brace between the two straps. Use a sliding T-bevel to determine the angle at which to cut the brace to make it flush with the top and bottom straps.

4 Make the angled cuts in the Z-brace using a circular saw.

5 After applying some carpenter's glue, fasten the Z-brace between the straps. Put one or more screws through the Z-brace into each of the boards that make up the door.

HANGING A DOOR

A variety of hinge and latch styles are available for hanging exterior doors. Some of the most common are surface-mounted butt hinges, strap hinges, and T-hinges. On utility buildings, three factors are key to making a sturdy installation. First, make sure the hinges are large enough to support the weight of the door. Second, use galvanized or other rust-resistant hinges and hardware. Third, use screws long enough to reach well into the wall framing.

For most utility buildings, a homemade door will be surface-mounted to the siding, and the hinges will be left exposed. You can install the hinges on the door first and have a helper hold it in position. It's helpful to use shims to position the door with the proper spacing, including a slight rise on the opening side against sagging. If the door doesn't fit perfectly into the opening, you can use a block plane to shave down edges that scrape.

Once the door is properly mounted and swinging freely, close the door with the exterior face flush with the building, and install 1x2 stops directly to the header and jack studs inside the rough opening. If you're installing double doors, you can install a door stop at the bottom of the opening, or use hardware to keep the doors flush.

If you want to have the hinges on the inside of the door (as with a pre-hung exterior door), you'll have to install a doorjamb into the rough opening and mortise the hinges. Although there are exterior-mounted hinges with one-way screws and sealed pins that are difficult to remove, conventional leaf hinges are completely concealed from the outside and generally more secure.

Installing a doorjamb into the rough opening is not a difficult task, although it's easier to buy a pre-hung door. The process involves nailing jambs to the studs while using shims to make the jamb plumb and straight. Be sure to insert shims directly beneath all hinge locations. Hinges are attached directly to the jamb, generally in mortises.

PROJECT:
SURFACE-MOUNTING A HOMEMADE DOOR

TOOLS & MATERIALS
- Galvanized steel hinges
- Drill-driver
- Screwdriver bit
- Galvanized screws
- Block plane
- Level
- Shims

1 Attach the hinges to the outside of the door about 8 in. from the top and bottom. A heavy door may require three or more hinges. Align them with the barrel of the hinge just outside the door.

2 Set the door into the rough opening, and check its fit. If it is too large, plane one or more edges. When it fits properly, use shims to create an even space all around.

3 As a helper holds the door in place, mark the holes where the hinges fall.

4 Fasten the hinges to the siding and jack studs using 2 in. or longer galvanized flathead screws. Screws must be long enough to reach well into the studs to support a heavy door.

5 If the door binds on the rough opening, mark the area with chalk to highlight contact points, and use a sharp block plane to shave down that section of the door.

PROJECT: 🐾🐾🐾
HANGING A DOOR WITH JAMBS

TOOLS & MATERIALS
- Hammer
- One-by jamb stock
- Finishing nails
- Shims
- Measuring tape
- Hinges
- Galvanized screws
- Pencil
- ½-inch wood chisel
- Rubber mallet

1 Jambs should be the same width as the framing lumber plus the thickness of drywall and sheathing. Side jambs in pre-cut jamb kits have a dado that the head jamb fits into. Assemble the jambs and screw them together.

2 Tip the assembled jamb into the rough opening, and shim it so that it is plumb and level with square corners. The jamb should be flush with the finished surface around the opening.

3 Use finishing nails to nail the jamb to the jack studs through the shims. This will hold the shims in place and fasten the jamb to the wall. Use screws to help support a heavy door.

4 Attach the hinges to the door, oriented so that the leaves of the hinge are on the inside and the pins are outside of the building. Set the door into the jambs to check its fit.

5 Temporarily attach the hinge to the jamb with one screw, if need be. Be sure the door is in the correct position. Then trace the hinge outline onto the jamb for mortising.

6 Use a sharp wood chisel to cut a shallow mortise in the jamb for each of the hinges so that they will sit flush with the surface of the jamb. This will allow the door to close smoothly.

7 Set the hinges into the mortises, and screw the hinges into the jambs and the studs. Adjust the shims if needed as you work so that the door is plumb and level.

8 Add a stop to the latch side of the door to keep it from swinging through. Then add interior and exterior door casing to cover the jamb, shims, and jack studs.

INSTALLING A PREHUNG DOOR

Most prehung doors come squared up and braced. It's wise to leave the braces on as long as you can during the installation to keep the door from racking. Most interior prehung doors are built to allow for thick carpeting, so you may need to cut both jamb legs if the bottom of the door is too high off of an uncarpeted floor.

Center the unit in the opening, and check that the top is level. Insert shims in the gaps between the doorjambs and rough framing to square and plumb the unit. Use prepackaged shims sold for this purpose, tapered wood shingles, or homemade shims. Set a pair of shims with opposing tapers between the frame and stud at each hinge location—and if there are only two hinges, in the middle. Increase or decrease the overlap of the shims to adjust the frame until it is plumb. Drive a finishing nail through the jamb, each shim set, and partially into the stud. Then install three sets of shims on the other side jamb and one set above the head jamb. When all

shims are in place, the frame should be plumb and square, and there should be a uniform gap between the door and the jamb unless the framing is askew. Add a second nail at each shim, and drive all nails home.

After installing an exterior door in an insulated structure, stuff fiberglass insulation behind and above the jamb before installing the casing. Another option is to use a spray-in foam insulation. This is a simple and more thorough method of insulating between a doorjamb and framing, but there are some drawbacks. Foam can expand dramatically and deform your jamb if it is not securely attached. To avoid this, use low-expansion foam. Also, the process can be fairly messy. Polyurethane foam is difficult to remove; wear disposable gloves to avoid getting it on your hands. Allow any excess to dry, and then scrape or cut it away with a sharp blade.

PROJECT:
HANGING A PREHUNG INTERIOR DOOR

TOOLS & MATERIALS
- Prehung interior door
- Framing square
- Shims
- Cross brace
- Spirit level
- Hammer
- Nails
- Trim
- Carpenter's glue

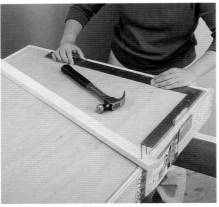

1 Although a prehung door is hinged in its frame, it pays to check to be sure it's square using a framing square. Once it's squared up, lock it into position with a cross brace if it doesn't have one.

2 Set the prehung unit on the sill and tip it into place. You can hold it in position temporarily with wood shims. Cross braces will keep the frame flush with the wall surface as you work.

3 Working from the inside of the wall, use more wood shims and a level to adjust the door until it is exactly plumb in the rough opening. Check both sides of the door.

4 When the door is plumb, drive 10d finishing nails through both the jamb and wood shims into the 2x4 wall framing. It's wise to double check for plumb and level as you work.

5 To use standard interior trim, cut mitered corners for a finished look, and install the pieces with glue and finishing nails. You can also use more rustic trim with butt joints.

PROJECT:
HANGING A PREHUNG EXTERIOR DOOR

TOOLS & MATERIALS
- Caulk or flashing
- Caulking gun
- Prehung door & lockset
- 2x4 brace
- Spirit level
- Shims
- Utility knife
- Hammer Nails
- Drill
- Putty knife
- Wood putty

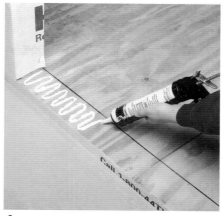

1 You can install flashing under the sill, although many manufacturers suggest using a waterproof caulk instead. Apply caulk liberally to the floor where the door sill will rest.

2 Set the prehung exterior door from the outside of the building. The door already has exterior molding attached to the frame. The molding around the door should fit tightly against the exterior wall.

3 Tack a brace across the outside to keep the door from falling out of the opening. Don't fasten the frame to the wall yet. Working from the inside, use a level to plumb the door.

4 As you plumb the door, insert wooden shims in the gaps between the frame and the 2x4 studs. The shims will not go through to the outside because the door molding is in the way.

5 When the door is in the correct position, predrill holes through the door frame and nail through the frame (and hidden shims) into the wall framing. Then you can remove the braces.

6 Also drive finishing nails through the face of the door's exterior molding well into the wall framing. Set the nailheads, and fill the holes with exterior-grade putty.

7 You can order most prehung doors with locks already installed or with the holes predrilled so that you can install your own. Follow the directions provided for installation.

8 A lockset plus dead bolt provides extra security. Use long screws in the strike plates that reach through to the house framing to improve the overall security of the opening.

INSTALLING WINDOWS

The most popular types of residential windows, double-hungs and casements, are suitable on more finished utility buildings. More rustic barns often have what amounts to one half of a double-hung—a large single sash, called a barn sash, that swings out awning style.

Windows usually come with specific installation instructions, including a rough opening size. Generally, the rough opening is ½ to ¾ of an inch larger than the unit itself. This allows room for plumbing and leveling the window even if the frame is out of square.

Some windows come with an exterior casing, called brick molding, on the outside. You have to install this type from the outside, nailing through the brick molding into the siding and framing. Whatever type of window you use, always shim the windows plumb and level before nailing.

Many modern windows come with a nailing flange around the frame. Nail these windows to the outside of the framing or sheathing. Depending on the look you want, you can cover the flange with casing and bring the siding to the casing, or cover the flange with siding, using no casing at all.

Insulating and Sealing a Window

Stuff fiberglass insulation into the gaps between the window and framing (or fill it with foam insulation from a pressure can). Patch the vapor barrier (if one exists) with 6-mil polyethylene sheet. Seal the polyethylene to the existing vapor barrier with polyurethane caulk. Then apply a bead of caulking around the inside edge of the window, and staple the polyethylene patch into the bead.

On any window installation you need to protect the top seams from the weather with flashing. This drip cap, generally made from either aluminum or plastic, must be installed to form a barrier between the window and the sheathing to prevent water from seeping inside the wall. *(continued on page 140)*

BASIC WINDOW TYPES

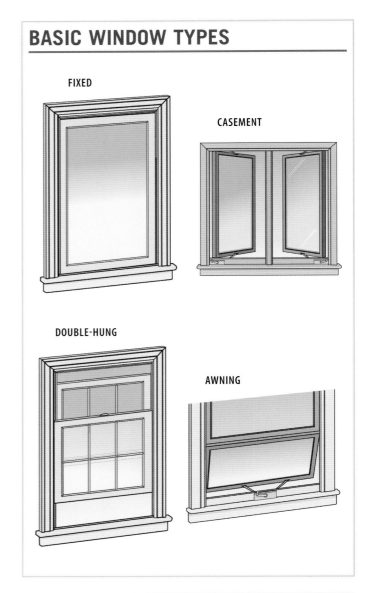

FIXED

CASEMENT

DOUBLE-HUNG

AWNING

TYPICAL WINDOW COMPONENTS

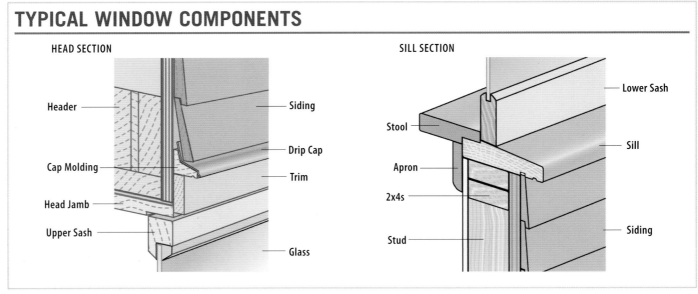

HEAD SECTION

Header · Siding · Drip Cap · Cap Molding · Trim · Head Jamb · Upper Sash · Glass

SILL SECTION

Lower Sash · Stool · Sill · Apron · 2x4s · Siding · Stud

PROJECT:
INSTALLING NEW WINDOWS

TOOLS & MATERIALS

- Safety glasses
- Measuring tape
- Circular saw
- Building felt or house wrap
- Staple gun
- Exterior-grade caulk
- New window
- Hammer
- Nails
- Shims
- Level
- Insulation
- Caulking gun
- Trim

1 After laying out and marking the rough opening, set a circular saw slightly deeper than the depth of your sheathing (typically ½ in.). Plunge the blade into the surface to begin the cuts.

2 Install roofing, running it right over window and door openings. Then cut through the material with a utility knife and staple it to the inside of the opening before trimming off excess.

3 To make a weathertight seal, add a bead of exterior-grade caulk to the back of the nailing flange before you install the unit. This will reduce the likelihood of moisture penetration.

4 Set the window unit into place, resting it on the sill so that you can tip the top into place. Temporarily tack a nail through the nailing flange to secure it while you adjust it.

5 Use pairs of tapered shingle shims to adjust the window on all sides in the opening. Next, use a level to check for plumb and level. This process should go quickly if the opening is properly framed.

6 Stuff insulation into gaps between the studs and the window frame. This will help eliminate drafts and improve energy efficiency. Or you can spray polyurethane foam into the spaces.

7 Once you have plumbed and leveled the window, fasten it to the wall by nailing all sides through the holes in the perforated flange into the rough window framing. Use roofing nails.

8 With the window fastened, you can add caulk and trim, J-channel for vinyl siding, or a variety of wood trim for clapboards or shakes. Using 1x4 pine works well for barns and sheds.

(continued from page 139)

The upper flange of the L-shaped flashing is installed underneath the siding above the window. The other side extends over the window frame. Install the drip cap with a downward slope to deflect rainwater. Be sure not to crimp or stress the flashing when you install siding or trim.

You can also install drip molding or cap molding above a window. This type of molding forms a projection past the casing and can add decorative detail as well as water-shedding protection.

It helps to seal the gaps between the window casing and the sheathing with an exterior-grade caulk. This bead of caulk will prevent water from seeping between the window and the wall, where it can cause rot. If your building is heated, the caulk will help save energy by reducing airflow into the building. After you've installed the window trim, run a second bead of caulk between the trim and the siding. Check the caulk around the windows periodically and replace it as needed.

Trimming and Finishing Windows

For most barns and outbuildings, 1x4 pine makes a good rustic casing. Fasten it with galvanized casing nails long enough to extend well into the framing. You can take the time to miter corner joints, creating a tight fit by slightly undercutting the edges. This allows the visible surfaces of the boards to meet and close tightly.

But on barns and other outbuildings it usually looks fine to use a rougher style. For example, you can mount the lower and side casings with square-edged butt joints, and let the head casing run long. On unfinished interiors you can use the same approach. If you plan to finish the interior, nail the trim around the window after the drywall is in place.

Prime and paint (or stain) the trim to protect it from the weather and prevent excessive shifting. If you want the trim to have a contrasting color, coat the edges ahead of time to save yourself the trouble of cutting in a second color.

PROJECT:
INSTALLING WINDOW TRIM

TOOLS & MATERIALS
- Casing, stool, and apron trim
- Power miter saw
- Wood glue
- Hammer
- Finishing nails
- Saber saw
- Power drill

1 Cut the top and side pieces of trim at 45-deg. angles to make mitered joints. Test the fit, and nail the top trim with finishing nails. Add glue to the miters and nail the side pieces.

2 Use a saber saw to cut the deep, interior sill, called a stool, where it extends beyond the window frame. The extensions of the stool will provide a base for the vertical trim pieces.

3 Add glue to mating edges, and drive finishing nails at an angle through the stool into the window frame. To avoid splitting the stool near the edge, you can predrill for nailholes.

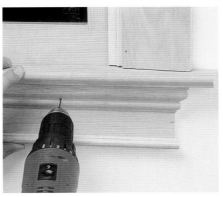

4 Add an apron under the stool for support and architectural decoration by cutting 45-deg. angles at the ends (to install small returns), and predrilling before nailing in place.

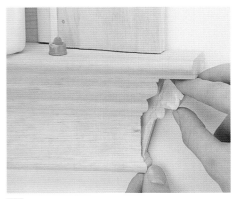

5 Cut complementary 45-deg. angles on short return pieces. Cut them on a power saw from a long piece to be safe. Glue these pieces in place, as they are too small to nail without splitting.

ADDING VENTILATION

If your utility building is not going to be finished for use as living space, proper ventilation may seem like an unnecessary worry. That's true if you're building a wood shed or a small equipment barn. But even an uninsulated potting shed is going to need some ventilation to make it comfortable and safe to work in.

If you're building a barn to house animals, proper ventilation is extremely important. You should check special agricultural requirements for venting and other livestock matters with local code agencies.

Even if your building has operating windows (which are generally essential to satisfy health and safety codes), you may need to provide additional ventilation to keep the interior cool and dry during hot and humid weather. You may want to install screened eave or gable vents, roof turbine vents, ridge vents, or even a louvered cupola on the roof peak to exhaust air.

Vents should generally be used in a balanced combination of inlets and outlets. Intakes, such as plug and strip vents at the eaves, let air in, and outlets, such as a gable-end vent or a ridge vent, let air out. If your building has few (or no) windows, you may want to install wall vents at floor level.

To create good cross ventilation (either horizontally, vertically, or both) you need about the same amount of vent square footage to let air in as you do to let air out. If the mix is out of balance—for example, with large vents along both eaves but only a small gable-end vent at one end of a barn— fresh air won't flow freely into the building because there won't be enough vent area to exhaust it. It's also important to install combinations of vents that keep air moving in all parts of the building, and do not leave stagnant areas.

TYPE OF VENTILATION

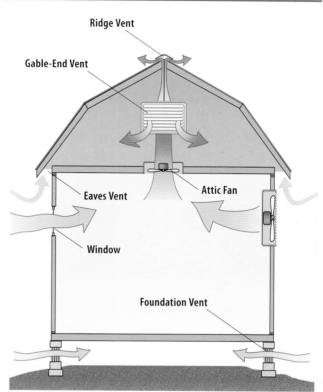

A **building's ventilation system** generally consists of inlets and outlets. The inlets, such as windows, wall, foundation, and eave vents, bring fresh air into the building. Typical outlets include ridge and gable vents.

ADDING A CUPOLA

BARN ROOFS are often ventilated with cupolas—small structures on the roof with louvered sides to allow for airflow and a shingled roof to keep out the weather. Some companies sell ready-to-assemble cupolas, or you can design and make your own.

A typical cupola has four side panels, consisting of two miter-cut 2x4 corner boards and 1x2 louvers glued into routed mortises in the corner boards. Louvers should be spaced close enough together to block light when viewed straight on.

To mount a cupola you cut a hole in the roof and join the two structures with framing hardware. Some may require flashing. When installed on finished barn structures, you can staple screening to the back of the side pieces to keep insects from entering.

Ready-made cupolas in kit form are available through many specialty and lumber supply stores.

A cupola can be used to ventilate a building, or it can be installed as a purely decorative element.

REQUIREMENTS OF LIVESTOCK

A BARN HOUSING LIVESTOCK needs to have an efficient ventilation system to replenish the air supply and remove heat, moisture, and odors. A mature dairy cow, for example, may exhale 4 to 5 gallons of water vapor a day and produce over 2,000 Btu of heat per hour.

It helps to locate the building on high ground with the long axis perpendicular to prevailing summer winds, and to keep the building at least 50 feet from other buildings or windbreaks. Any building housing livestock should have continuous ridge vents, as well as eaves or sidewall vents that can be closed to keep in heat in the cold weather. Also, a roof slope of 4 in 12 to 6 in 12 is recommended for good air mixing.

Whether or not you will need electric exhaust fans to properly ventilate a barn will depend on your climate and the animals you are keeping. The table below, "Exhaust Fan Performance," will give you an idea of the fan size and horsepower you will need for your space. Ventilation systems may operate under positive or negative static pressure, which is measured in "inches of water." For the purposes of this table, a static pressure of ⅛ inch of water is assumed. Fans don't work in closed spaces. A fan must work in conjunction with properly sized vents leading to and from the outdoors.

EXHAUST FAN PERFORMANCE

Fan Diameter (in.)	Fan Speed (rpm)	Motor Size (hp)	Airflow (cubic ft./min. at normal static pressure*)
8	1,650	⅟₅₀	289
8	3,500	⅟₁₅	509
10	1,550	⅟₅₀	413
10	3,416	⅙	1,209
12	1,600	⅟₁₂	1,035
16	1,140	⅟₁₂	1,374
16	1,670	¼	2,854
18	1,140	⅙	2,395
18	1,648	⅓	4,003
24	855	⅓	4,180
24	1,140	⅞	5,920
36	460	½	7,850
36	851	½	8,533
48	363	1	15,892
48	495	1	16,758

*Assuming a static pressure measured at ⅛ inch of water. Actual results will vary.

Adapted from "Fan Performance and Efficiency for Animal Systems" (University of Minnesota Extension Service).

Roof Vents

A well-vented roof keeps a structure from becoming too hot in the summer, helps to prevent the formation of ice dams and condensation in the winter, and prolongs the life span of asphalt shingles.

One of the most practical barn vents is a continuous ridge vent. This waterproof cap along the building peak helps to create a natural flow of air up through the building and out the roof. It is effective in venting an open-plan utility building without leaving any hot spots. The ridge vent covers a slit that runs along the ridge. It caps the opening with screening and a small roof of plastic that keeps rain from entering. Many types can be covered with shingles to blend in with the roof.

Install a ridge vent by snapping a chalk line a few inches from the top of the ridge on each side of the roof, as specified by the manufacturer. Cut out the sections with a circular saw set to the depth of the roof sheathing. Attach the ridge vent with caulking and roofing nails. On new construction you can anticipate the installation and install sheathing a few inches short of the ridge on both sides.

Gable Vents

Other common types of vents include fixed grilles (usually installed high on the wall near the ridge), which allow air to pass through louvers, and a variety of power fans. The venting ability of these systems depends on the size of the opening and on the capacity of the fan. Building codes usually require the area of attic vent openings to equal at least ⅟₃₀₀ of the total square feet of attic space being ventilated, and ⅟₁₅₀ with no vapor barrier in the ceiling.

Soffit Vents

Soffit vents come in three basic configurations: round, rectangular, and perforated panels. The round variety, called plug vents, are easier to install than the other types. You need only a power drill and a bit or hole saw to cut the hole for plug vents, whereas continuous vents require a circular saw to cut the opening. It is easier and safer to drill an overhanging section than it is to cut it with an upside-down circular saw—especially if you're working on a ladder.

Another option for installing soffit vents is to remove the plywood, cut the holes (circular or rectangular) while the plywood is secured to a worktable, insert the vents, and reinstall the panels. This is a viable option if the soffit is delaminated and is in need of replacing anyway. If you're planning to install rectangular strip-grille vents, this approach is probably the most practical.

Continuous perforated soffits are manufactured in preformed sheets of vinyl or aluminum, and can be installed once the old soffits have been ripped out. Perforated soffits eliminate the need for cutting plywood, but they may not come in the size or color that you require. However, perforated panels let in air all along the overhang. Home centers usually have manufacturers' catalogs listing the sizes and colors of their products.

PROJECT: INSTALLING A ROOF VENT

TOOLS & MATERIALS
- Caulk-line box
- Circular saw
- Ridge vent
- Hammer
- 8d galvanized nails
- Utility knife
- Asphalt roofing

PROJECT: INSTALLING A GABLE VENT

TOOLS & MATERIALS
- Hammer
- 10d nails
- Circular saw
- Drill-driver
- Gable vent
- 2–inch galvanized screws

PROJECT: INSTALLING A SOFFIT VENT

TOOLS & MATERIALS
- Circular saw
- Hammer
- Chisel
- Soffit vent
- Drill-driver
- 1–inch galvanized screws

1 Use a chalk line to mark a straight line across the sides of the ridge. Cut along both lines using a circular saw. Set the blade to the depth of the plywood decking to avoid cutting the framing.

1 Frame the opening for the vent in the gable. This may require you to remove and relocate studs. They are not load bearing, so you don't have to worry about installing structural headers.

1 Mark the outline of the vent on the soffit. Begin the cuts by plunging the circular saw with the front of the saw base against the soffit. Set the blade depth to the soffit thickness.

2 Nail the ridge vent to the roof using 8d nails. Some ridge vents come in sections, and others roll out across the ridge. Nail the vent about every 8 in. using nailing holes if they are provided.

2 Nail into the sheathing at each corner of the opening to provide reference for the cut lines you will draw on the outside. Plunge a circular saw to begin your cuts.

2 After you make the long side cuts with the saw, use a hammer and chisel to cut across the grain between the two saw cuts, and remove the piece of wood in the middle.

3 Cut full shingles into thirds, separating the three tabs. Install them over the ridge vent, lapping each over the previous one. Set one nail into each shingle on each side of the ridge.

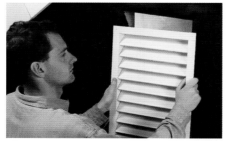

3 Install the vent in the opening. Secure it using a drill with a screwdriver bit and galvanized screws. Apply a bead of exterior caulk around the vent after you have attached it.

3 Insert the vent into the opening. Use galvanized screws to secure the vent to the soffit. Fastener holes are usually provided. Caulk around the edges of the vent if needed.

WIRING & PLUMBING

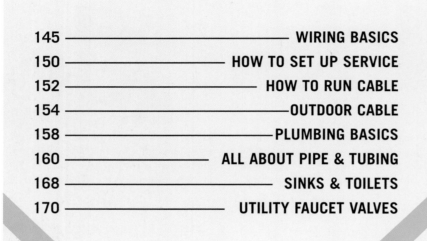

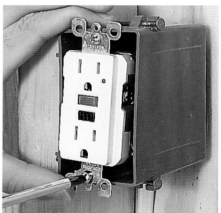

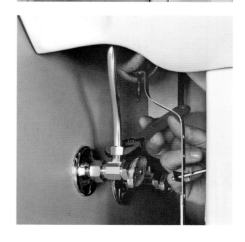

Providing your new barn or shed with electric power and running water will improve the functionality of the building. In many areas, building codes require that a licensed professional do the actual work. However, some building inspectors may allow you to do some of the simpler work, such as pulling cable and laying pipe, while the overall design and final connections are made by the professional. The information in this chapter can serve as a planning guide and help you check the work of the professional.

WIRING BASICS

Electricity can be dangerous, but if you use common sense, you can work with it safely. The most important things to remember are to always, without fail, turn off the power at the main service panel before working on a circuit, only use one hand to disconnect or reactivate a fuse or circuit breaker, and before starting work, check the circuit with a voltage tester to make sure that the power is off.

All electrical procedures and materials are governed by local building or electrical codes. Some municipalities won't let anyone but a licensed electrician do any wiring work. Some will allow DIYers to rough in their wiring as long as an electrician inspects it and makes the final hookup to the service panel. You need to check.

Understanding Electricity

Electricity enters your home through overhead or underground wires, where it passes through a meter before entering the main service panel. The meter measures how much electricity you use. At the main service panel, the electricity is divided into branch circuits, each of which is protected by a fuse or circuit breaker. Power travels in a closed loop through the circuit's hot wires to outlets or fixtures and returns to the service panel via neutral wires, unless it is interrupted by an open switch or short circuit. The fuses or breakers protect these circuits from overloading (drawing more power than the wires can handle). Always use the proper fuses or circuit breaker.

For an outbuilding, you have the choice of running wiring from your house through cables connected to your main panel box or having the building served by separate power lines. The option you choose depends on how much electricity you will consume, the capacity of the existing service panel at the house, and to some extent the distance from your house to the outbuilding.

BASIC ELECTRICAL TERMS

- **Amperes,** or amps, measure current flow. The amp rating is marked on many appliances. The rating for your house's circuits will be marked on the circuit breaker or fuse—generally 15 or 20 amps for most room circuits, and 30 amps or more for heavy-duty circuits supplying large appliances.
- **Volts** measure the force of electrical pressure that keeps the current flowing through the wires. Products are marked with a voltage capacity, usually 120 or 240 volts. You can't hook up a product designed to operate at 120 volts to a 240-volt electrical outlet. It's dangerous, and the product will burn out.
- **Watts** equal volts multiplied by amps. The wattage rating of a circuit is the amount of power the circuit can deliver safely, determined by the current-carrying capacity of the wires. Wattage also indicates the amount of power that a fixture or appliance needs to work properly.

WIRING LAYOUT

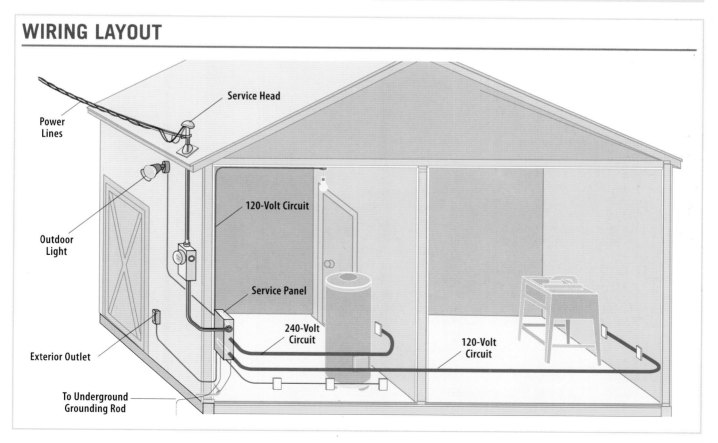

Power Lines

Service Head

Outdoor Light

120-Volt Circuit

Service Panel

240-Volt Circuit

120-Volt Circuit

Exterior Outlet

To Underground Grounding Rod

Grounding

Electricity always seeks to return to a point of zero voltage (the ground) along the easiest path open to it. If you touch an electric fence, electricity will flow from the fence through your body to the ground, and the electrical path is grounded through you. A short circuit in wiring is a similar situation. Electricity is able to leave the closed loop of the circuit—maybe because a hot wire is off its terminal and touches the metal box of a light fixture—and return to the source by some other means. If the system is properly grounded, this short will be a fault to ground and pose no hazard. If it's improperly grounded, the electricity will seek to ground itself through your body.

To guard against this, your house's electrical system has grounding wires, which give the electricity a permanent alternative path for its return to the source. Each receptacle and fixture has its own grounding wires that return electricity to the main panel. The entire system is also grounded to your metal cold-water pipes or (if you have plastic plumbing) to one or more grounding rods buried underground next to your foundation—or to both.

Another way to protect against the danger of shock is by using a ground-fault circuit interrupter, or GFCI. This device detects minute amounts of current leakage in a circuit. If the amperage flowing through the black and white wires is equal, then the circuit is operating properly. But if there is as little as a 0.005-amp difference detected between the two wires, then the circuit is internally broken fast enough to prevent a severe shock. This is much faster than the typical circuit breaker can shut down a circuit. Codes require GFCI outlets in outbuildings or in any spot less than 6 feet away from a source of water, such as a faucet or a sink.

WORKING WITH WIRE & CABLE

SINGLE WIRES are insulated to carry electricity or bare for grounding. Most household wiring is contained in cable, inside flexible metal (such as BX) or plastic insulation (such as NM). Individual wires have size numbers based on the American wire gauge (AWG) system, which expresses wire diameter as a whole number. For example, No. 14 wire is 0.0064 inch in diameter; No. 12 is 0.081 inch. Smaller numbers indicate larger diameters that can carry more power. The National Electrical Code requires a minimum of No. 14 wire for most house wiring.

Wires have color-coded plastic insulation to indicate their function in your house's wiring system. Hot wires carrying current at full voltage are usually black or red but can be other colors. Neutral wires are white or gray. Grounding wires can be bare copper or in green plastic insulation. But you should always use a tester to confirm wire applications. Don't rely on color codes, particularly in older buildings.

CONDUIT

Insulated wires are sometimes run through metal or plastic pipe called conduit. Metal conduit comes in three types: rigid (preferred for outdoor applications), intermediate, and EMT (electrical metal tubing). Plastic conduit (preferred for underground locations) comes in two types. They are schedule 40 and schedule 80. Standard conduit diameters are ½, ¾, 1, and 1¼ inches. There are fittings to join conduit for straight runs and at 45-degree angles, and a special tool (called a hickey) for making more gradual bends in metal tubing. You may be required by code to use conduit for wires run underground or in open, unfinished walls. Even if you aren't, it's a good idea if you're running cable in areas where they can be damaged, such as a horse barn.

Both metal and plastic conduit can be cut with a pipe cutter or a hacksaw. A pipe cutter is the best tool—the shoulders of the cutter keep the pipe square in the device and ensure an even cut. When cutting with a hacksaw, remove any burring, which can damage the wires' insulation when they are pulled through.

ESTIMATING WIRE NEEDS

To estimate the amount of wire or cable you will need, add an extra foot for every run you will make, and add about 20 percent to this figure. This will give you plenty of cable to make connections. For example, if you measure 12 feet between a new and existing receptacle, add another 2 feet for the two connections, and then add 20 percent (about 3 feet) to the total. To do the job, start working with 17 feet of cable.

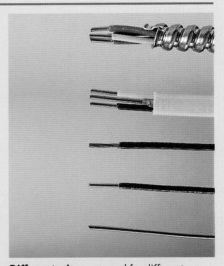

Different wires are used for different purposes. Most homes are wired with the second cable from the top. It is called NM, or nonmetallic sheath.

Conduit can be made of metal or plastic. It can be cut with a pipe cutter or a hacksaw. Use conduit or tubing when you need to run wires underground.

CREATING A WIRING PLAN

BEFORE YOU MAKE YOUR PLAN, you need to estimate the overall demand on your system to determine the size of the service entrance cable and the individual circuits. A 100-amp service is considered the minimum for even moderate-size buildings. If you're building a workshop that will hold a lot of high-powered tools, or if you want to install electric heat, you might want to consider 150- or 200-amp service.

There are three options for setting up service in an outbuilding. If your house's service panel has the capacity and room for new circuits, you can run them directly from the panel. If it has the capacity but not the room, you need to install a subpanel for your outbuilding. Otherwise, the outbuilding will need its own main service panel. This is also a good idea if the building will be for a business and you want to keep the bills separate for tax purposes.

BASIC ELECTRICAL NEEDS

The National Electrical Code (NEC) requires that houses have a base of 3 watts per square foot of living area for lighting. Use this as a guide. A good rule of thumb would be at least one light fixture (of 40–100 watts) and one outlet for every 100 square feet of floor space. This means you need at least one 15-amp circuit for every 600 square feet (which can supply up to 10 outlets) or a 20-amp circuit every 800 square feet (which can supply up to 13).

Ordinary power tools that you plug into the wall can be run off these standard 120-volt, 20-amp outlets. Larger equipment may require separate 120- or 240-volt circuits. For motorized

appliances, you should supply 125 percent of the ampere rating for your estimate.

Lights should be controlled by switches. It's less important for outlets but can be a convenience in some circumstances. A basic outbuilding wiring plan will include one circuit for overhead lighting, switch-controlled from one or more locations, and at least one circuit for power receptacles.

Note that the number and location of outlets is controlled by codes. You should draw up a wiring plan before starting work. Mark where you want lights, outlets, switches, and other fixtures, and where each room's wiring is connected to the cable coming from the main service panel. This will provide a rough estimate of the materials that you will need for the project.

AMERICAN WIRE GAUGES		
Wire Gauge	**Current Capacity (amps)**	**Typical Use**
No. 6	60	large appliances (240V), service ground wires
No. 8	40	large appliances (120V–240V)
No. 10	30	large appliances (120V–240V)
No. 12	20	small appliance branch circuits
No. 14	15	general-purpose house wiring
No. 16	10	extension/fixture cords
No. 18	7	low-voltage systems

TYPICAL ELECTRICAL LOADS	
Appliance	**Watts**
Air conditioner, central	2500–6000
Air conditioner, room	800–2500
Clothes dryer (electric)	4000–5800
Clothes dryer (gas)	500
Clothes washer	600–1000
Electric heat	250/baseboard foot
Fan, attic	400–500
Fan, ceiling	50
Fan, window	275
Freezer	500
Heater, portable	1000–1500
Motor, ¼ hp	600
Motor, ½ hp	840
Motor, 1 hp	1140
Motor, 2 hp	2400
Motor, 3 hp	3360
Refrigerator	300–600
Water heater	4500/element

CIRCUIT BREAKERS & FUSES

When a short circuit or ground fault occurs, a massive amount of current will surge through a circuit breaker, causing it to trip. You can reset it once. But if it trips again, call in a licensed electrician.

Overloads in older systems with fuses cause the metal strip to melt and create a break. Short circuits cause the metal element to vaporize, which leaves a distinctive sooty cloud on the fuse window.

PROJECT: STRIPPING CABLE

TOOLS & MATERIALS
- Cable ripper
- Cable

1 Slide the blade of the cable ripper onto the cable, and squeeze it 8 to 10 in. from the end. Squeeze the tool until the point penetrates through the plastic sheath covering the cable.

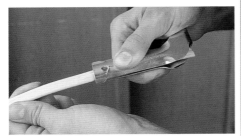

2 Grip the cable ripper in one hand and the cable in the other, and pull your hands apart so that the cable ripper moves toward the end of the cable, leaving a split in the plastic sheath.

3 Expose the wires by peeling back the plastic sheathing and paper wrapping. These can be cut off so that they don't get in the way. A cable ripper won't damage individual wires.

PROJECT: ATTACHING WIRES

TOOLS & MATERIALS
- Combination tool
- Wire
- Needle-nose pliers
- Insulated screwdriver
- Switch or outlet

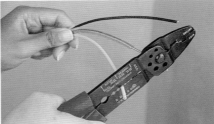

1 Insert the wire in the proper gauge slot of a combination tool, and clamp the jaws onto the wire. Strip ¾ in. of insulation from the end of each wire by pulling the tool away from the wire.

2 Insert the wire in the proper gauge slot of a combination tool, and clamp the jaws onto the wire. Strip ¾ in. of insulation from the end of each wire by pulling the tool away from the wire.

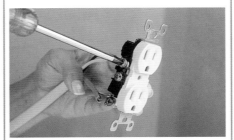

3 Hook each of the looped wire ends onto the correct screw terminal so that the wire goes around the screw in a clockwise direction. The wire loop will close as you tighten the screw.

PROJECT: CAPPING WIRES

TOOLS & MATERIALS
- Combination tool
- Needle-nose pliers
- Wire
- Wire connector

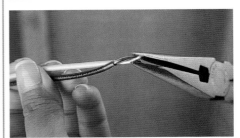

1 To join wires, strip ½ in. of insulation from the wires using a combination tool. Hold the wires parallel, and twist them together with pliers. Turn the pliers in a clockwise fashion.

2 The twisted part should be long enough to engage the wire connector, and short enough to be covered completely by the wire connector when the wires are inserted into it.

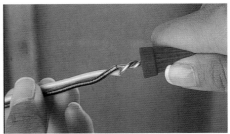

3 Screw the wire connector onto the wires until it feels tight and the exposed wires are covered completely. Use hand pressure only. Do not use pliers to tighten the connector.

RECEPTACLES & ELECTRICAL BOXES

A RECEPTACLE IS A DEVICE into which you plug appliances and lamps. It's housed in a metal or plastic box attached to the framing. Behind a faceplate, the receptacle is held by two screws to the box. When these screws are removed, the receptacle may be pulled from the box.

Some receptacles are designed exclusively for use outside. Some are made to handle heavy-duty appliances, such as air conditioners, dryers, and ranges, and have distinctive faces that won't accept ordinary two- or three-prong plugs. The most common receptacle is a duplex receptacle rated at 15 amps and 120 volts. The latest National Electrical Code requires receptacles used in living areas to be tamper-resistant. Ground-fault circuit interrupter (GFCI) receptacles, code-required for outbuildings, have a safety device that compares the amount of current flowing in the black and white wires of the circuit and breaks the circuit if it detects as little as a 0.005-amp difference.

All receptacles must be properly grounded to prevent short circuits. Metal receptacle boxes require that a grounding wire is pigtailed to the grounding screws of the receptacle and to the box. With plastic boxes, the cable grounding wire attaches directly to the receptacle's grounding screw. Wiring configurations differ from receptacle to receptacle, however, and you should always follow local codes.

INSTALLING RECEPTACLE BOXES

Cable running to outlet boxes must be anchored to the framing within 12 inches of the box. Also, on a 120-volt circuit, you should have at least one junction box to accommodate the circuit wiring, as there will be a different number of wires going to and from the outlet boxes. A 4 x 4 x 2⅛ inch box provides enough space for these additional wires.

Connect wires to terminals by looping the end around the terminal screw in the direction the screw tightens. The best way to loop the wire for terminal screws is with needle-nose pliers. Strip about ½ to ¾ inch of insulation off the end of the wire, and bend the bare wire around the jaws of the pliers. Then hook the loop onto the terminals in the direction the screws turn down, and tighten the screws. As the terminals are tightened, the wire is forced under the screwheads and clamped.

To install a receptacle with the lower outlet always on but the upper outlet controlled by a switch, you must break off the metal link between the terminal screws. This system makes it possible to control table lamps from a wall switch, which is practical in a room that has no overhead fixture. Use a screwdriver to pry the link up; then break it off with pliers. Connect the incoming hot (black) wire and one switch wire to the lower outlet terminal. Connect the white wire and other switch wire to the upper outlet terminal.

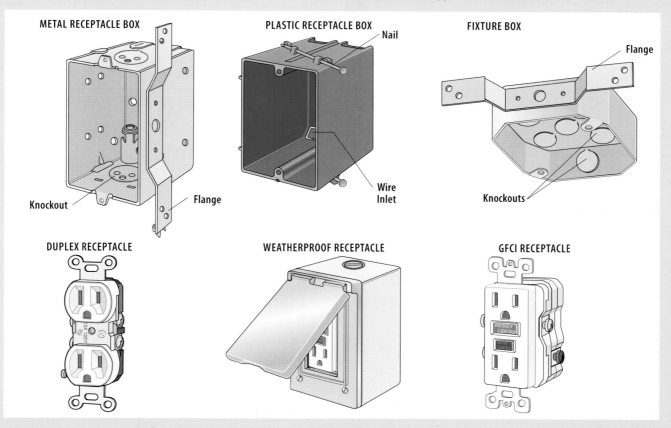

METAL RECEPTACLE BOX

Knockout

Flange

PLASTIC RECEPTACLE BOX

Nail

Wire Inlet

FIXTURE BOX

Flange

Knockouts

DUPLEX RECEPTACLE

WEATHERPROOF RECEPTACLE

GFCI RECEPTACLE

HOW TO SET UP SERVICE

If you are wiring your barn for new electric service, you will surely have a service panel, the gray metal box that holds the circuit breakers. The service panel for a sizable structure takes the utility power coming into the barn, typically a $^{120}/_{240}$-volt, 100-amp service delivered through three wires. The two hot service wires (usually black) each deliver 120 volts, and they attach to two corresponding terminals of the main disconnect. The 120-volt circuits deliver power to the individual barn circuits through a "hot bus," which is typically the chassis into which the breakers plug. Most common appliances run on 120 volts, but heavier machinery often requires 240 volts.

Before working on or even checking an existing service, turn off the power with the main breaker switch mounted at the top of the service panel. With the power off, remove the cover plate and note the breaker arrangement. Each breaker in use is connected to a cable; a label on the cover should identify each. Check whether there are any breakers not in use or spare slots for additional breakers. If there are no spares but there are empty slots, generally there is room to add a new circuit. If all of the slots are in use, you may be able to add a double (twin) breaker, which puts two breakers in the space of one.

NEW CIRCUITS

New circuits can be added to a service panel if there are spare breakers or empty slots along the bus bars. If there are no empty slots, new circuits should be added by a licensed electrician.

HOW TO ADD A CIRCUIT

TO ADD A NEW CIRCUIT to your house's main service panel, first be sure the main breaker is turned off. Remove the panel's cover plate, and then use a screwdriver to pry out a perforated knockout from the side or top of the panel box. Attach a cable clamp and thread 12 inches of the cable through the connector, the hole in the box, and the locknut. Tighten the two screws against the cable, and tighten the locknut. Remove about 8 inches of the outer sleeve of the end of the cable, and strip the wire ends. Insert the ends of the white (neutral) wire and the bare ground wire into holes along the bus bars intended for these wires at the side or bottom of the panel (note how the other circuits are connected), and tighten the setscrews.

If a spare breaker is not already in place, snap one into its slot on the panel board. Loosen the screw of the breaker, and insert the black wire of the cable into the hole below. Then retighten the screw to secure the wire end. Screw the cover back on the panel, and record the new circuit on the panel door. To prevent a power surge, turn off all the individual breakers and then turn on the main breaker. Turn the individual breakers back on one by one.

The main breaker, mounted at the top of the panel, controls power entering the hot buses. Begin by moving the double handle to the off position.

A new breaker can be added to a spare slot in the panel. If there are no spare slots, you'll need to have a licensed electrician add a subpanel.

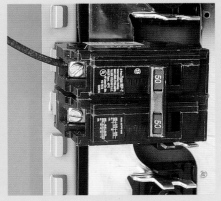

A circuit's hot wire is secured beneath a circuit-breaker screw. You insert the bare wire end in the terminal hole and tighten down the screw.

WIRING LAYOUTS

THE DIAGRAM ON THIS PAGE indicates the elements of a basic wiring plan for a typical barn (top) and shows how those basic individual elements are wired into the cables (bottom). In this plan, three separate circuits are run from the main service panel: a series of GFCI-protected power receptacles (illustrated in green); two overhead lights that are controlled by two switches (in red); and an exterior weatherproof receptacle with a switch-controlled floodlight (in blue).

Local building codes will dictate how many receptacles or fixtures can be put on each 20-amp circuit, as well as what variety and gauge of wire you must run. The illustration below shows how each item is wired in these three circuits. The black and white lines represent the black (hot) and white (neutral) wires in the cable; the green lines represent the grounding wires, which are usually bare copper but sometimes have a green covering.

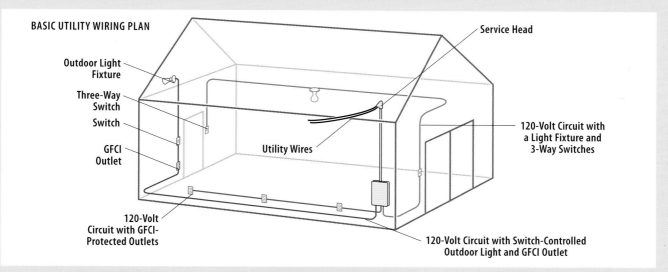

BASIC UTILITY WIRING PLAN

- Service Head
- Outdoor Light Fixture
- Three-Way Switch
- Switch
- GFCI Outlet
- Utility Wires
- 120-Volt Circuit with a Light Fixture and 3-Way Switches
- 120-Volt Circuit with GFCI-Protected Outlets
- 120-Volt Circuit with Switch-Controlled Outdoor Light and GFCI Outlet

WIRING GFCI RECEPTACLES

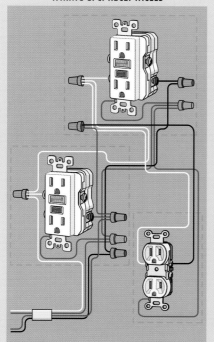

For a circuit that needs more than one GFCI-protected receptacle, wire as shown. This requires two- and three-wire cables.

WIRING THREE-WAY SWITCHES

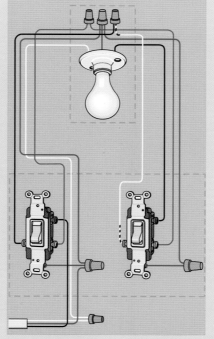

These two switches can be installed at opposite ends of a room so that whichever way you enter, you can turn on a light.

WIRING A RECEPTACLE AND SWITCH

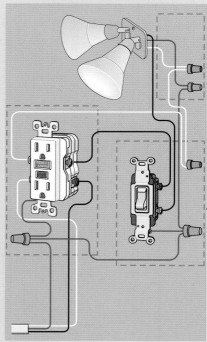

A switch need only be wired to the positive or "hot" wire of a circuit to be effective. Cutting the power loop here turns off the light.

HOW TO RUN CABLE

If you're running cable from your house's service panel to an outbuilding, you can do it either aboveground or underground. Aboveground is less work, but it's unsightly, and there's always the danger that wires will be blown down by the wind, pulled down by ice, or knocked down by a big delivery truck. Running cable underground means digging a trench, generally 18 to 24 inches deep, from your house to the outbuilding.

Wiring in unfinished outbuildings should be considered outdoor wiring, which must be installed with special weatherproof switches, outlets, and light fixtures. Generally, local codes require that wiring inside an unfinished building be NM cable protected by rigid nonmetallic conduit or special NMC (corrosion-resistant) cable whenever it is installed aboveground. If you'll be finishing the interior of your outbuilding, you should run the cable through the framing without conduit. Most codes allow buried cable to be Type UF (underground feeder); some require that Type TW (thermoplastic—wet) wire and conduit be used. Always check and observe your local codes when planning an outdoor wiring project.

Installing the Cable

Once new framing is ready to be wired and electrical boxes have been put in place, carefully begin pulling the cable through the framing. When you insert a cable end into an electrical box, leave about 8 inches of extra cable. Using a wire staple, secure the cable at a maximum of 8 inches above the box. After all of the cables have been run through the framing and into their respective electrical boxes, rip back and remove the sheathing from the cable ends in each box, and then strip the ends of the wires. Before a typical rough-in inspection is made, you must also splice together the grounding wires, using either green wire connectors or wire crimping ferrules. Be sure to include a bare copper wire pigtail that will be connected to the green grounding screw of a device, and neatly push all the wires back into the box for protection.

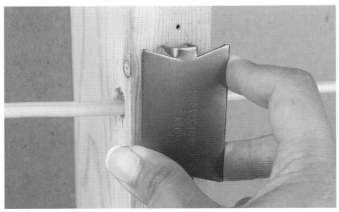

Steel plates are used to protect wires that run through holes drilled through studs. They prevent you from drilling, nailing, or screwing into the wire, causing damage to the wire and potential electrical shock.

Installing Switches & Receptacles

After a rough-in inspection is performed, the receptacles and switches may be installed. However, it is best to wait until the wallboard is in place before doing this work. When the walls are completed and all of the boxes wired, install cover plates and turn on the power. Be certain to check each receptacle using a plug-in receptacle analyzer to verify that all of the wiring has been properly done. Install the light fixtures, and then confirm that they are all in working order. Once you have completed this work, the job will be ready for final inspection.

PRO TIP

MAKING TURNS

When pulling cable through framing, make gradual, wide-angle turns. Sharp angles can damage wire insulation.

PREPARING THE FRAMING

IF LOCAL CODES PERMIT, consider running the new wiring in the framing yourself and letting a professional electrician make the hookups at the power source. Also, pay the pro to check your work so that you will be assured that it is safe and up to code.

You'll need a power drill or hand brace and a ⅝- or ¾-inch bit to make holes through studs. The edge of the hole should be no less than 1¼ inches from the facing edge of the stud. If this is not possible and you can't leave 1¼ inches of space between the hole and the edge of the framing member, put a steel plate on the framing member for the necessary protection. Nailing plates, which are available at electrical supply stores, work as a shield to prevent punctures from surface nails driven through drywall and paneling.

Electricians don't measure and mark each cable hole but create an unobstructed path through framing. Holes are centered to stay clear of nails driven through drywall or paneling.

PROJECT:

RUNNING CABLE

TOOLS & MATERIALS

- Measuring tape and pencil
- Plastic receptacle box
- Hammer
- Power drill with spade bit
- NM cable
- Cable staples
- Service panel
- Clamp connectors
- Receptacle
- Insulated screwdriver

1 Use a measuring tape and a pencil to measure and mark the height where utility boxes will be situated; generally this is 12 in. off the floor for receptacles and 44 in. for switches.

2 Nail utility boxes in place on the stud. Set the box out from the stud to account for the thickness of the drywall. Be sure that the boxes will be flush with the finished wall surface.

3 Using a power drill with a spade bit, drill holes through wall studs at the same height to run the electrical cable through. Drill in the center of the stud to avoid compromising its strength.

4 For vertical runs, attach the cable to the side of the stud using staples designed for use with the cable. These staples are attached by hammering them into the stud, over the cable.

5 Where the cable passes into a device box, use a clamp connector. This not only protects the cable from chafing, it clamps it in place so that it can't be easily pulled out.

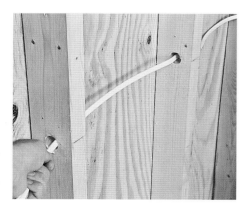

6 To run the cable horizontally, fish it through the studs, one at a time, using the holes you have drilled with a spade bit. Avoid kinking the cable or tearing the insulation.

7 Pull the cable up into the device boxes you have mounted. Be sure to pull an ample amount through, as the cable access ports on device boxes act as traps, making it hard to retract.

8 After connecting the proper wires to the proper terminals, mount switches or receptacles securely to the device box. A tight physical connection is essential for safety.

OUTDOOR CABLE

Underground feeder and branch-circuit cable, known as UF cable, is designated for outdoor wiring because it is weatherproof and suitable for direct burial. UF cable looks somewhat like ordinary NM cable, so be sure that the UF designation is clearly written on the sheathing. The wires are molded into plastic rather than wrapped in paper and then sheathed in plastic as NM cable wires are. Aboveground UF cable must be protected with conduit where subject to damage.

Direct-burial cable must be buried deeply enough to be protected from routine digging. The NEC specifies minimum depth requirements for underground cable: 24 inches for direct-burial cable; 18 inches for rigid nonmetallic conduit; and 6 inches for rigid and intermediate metal conduit.

If your cable is protected by a GFCI, you may be permitted to trench less deeply, but this is not recommended—you might someday plant a tree or shrub over the cable and risk cutting it while digging. Though the ground-fault circuit interrupter will prevent shocks, it's not going to save you the time needed to dig up and replace the line.

Any special characteristics of newer types of cable insulation will be identified on the sheathing, such as sunlight and corrosion resistance. Note that the plastic sheathing on UF cable encases the insulated conductors inside it, making the individual wires somewhat difficult to strip.

Outdoor Electrical Boxes

There are two main types of outdoor boxes, raintight and watertight. Raintight boxes typically have spring-loaded, self-closing covers, but they are not waterproof. This type of box has a gasket seal and is rated for wet locations as long as the cover is kept closed. It is best to mount a raintight box where it is not subject to water accumulation or flooding. Watertight boxes, on the other hand, are sealed with a waterproof gasket and can withstand a soaking rain or saturation. These boxes are rated for wet locations.

BURIED CABLE

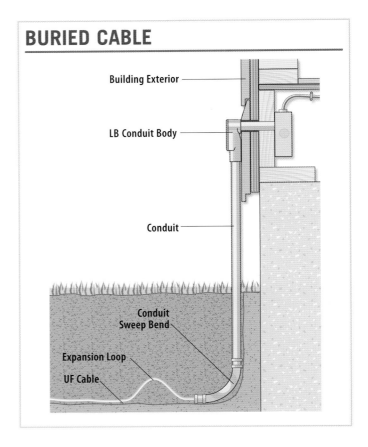

Building Exterior

LB Conduit Body

Conduit

Conduit Sweep Bend

Expansion Loop

UF Cable

CONDUIT, CONNECTORS & FITTINGS

OUTDOOR WIRING is typically protected by rigid conduit—both aboveground and wherever it enters or emerges from underground trenching. Rigid and intermediate metallic conduit (IMC) are most commonly used, but many local codes permit the use of rigid nonmetallic conduit, which is made of polyvinyl chloride (PVC). Regardless of which type of rigid conduit you are permitted to use, you will have to make a variety of connections. These are available for metal and nonmetallic conduit, including bushings for straight pieces and elbow connections, locknuts, offsets, and various couplings. Be sure that the connectors you select match the material of conduit.

At the point where cable runs through the exterior wall of your home, you will need a special L-shaped connector called an LB conduit body. An LB encloses the joint between your indoor cable and the outdoor UF cable (UF cable is also permitted for indoor use) that runs down the side of your house and into an underground trench. LB conduit bodies are fitted with a gasket that seals the cable connection against the weather.

Another type of fitting that you may find useful is a box extension, which is used to increase the volume of an existing outdoor receptacle or junction box when you need to tap into it to bring power where it is required. This is often done to avoid extensive rewiring and renovation work.

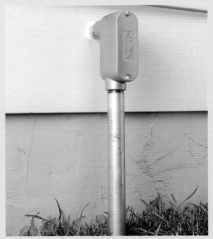

Outdoor cable run underground must be protected in rigid conduit where it enters or emerges from the trench.

PROJECT:
RUNNING CABLE UNDERGROUND

TOOLS & MATERIALS

- Power drill-driver with spade or masonry bit
- Junction box
- Conduit nipple
- LB fitting
- Rigid conduit
- Mounting bracket
- Conduit sweep bend
- Plastic bushing
- Wooden stakes and string
- Shovel
- UF Cable
- Knockout punch
- 12-3 or 12-2 with ground NM cable
- Needle-nose pliers
- Caulking gun

1 Make a mark for the access hole at least 3 in. from any structural framing. Using a spade or masonry bit, drill an access hole through the exterior wall or header joist.

2 Mount the junction box over the access opening with screws, and run the branch-circuit cable from the breaker box through the hole on the side of the box.

3 Use a short length of conduit, called a conduit nipple, to make a connection between the LB fitting and junction box. Turn the long end of the LB fitting down toward the ground.

4 Begin a trench through which the cable can travel. Connect a length of conduit from the LB fitting into the cable trench. Fasten it to the wall just above the point that makes contact with the ground.

5 A conduit sweep bend is attached below the first length of conduit. It safeguards the cable as it goes underground. A bushing at the end prevents the cable from chafing.

6 Stake out a trench, running from the LB fitting to wherever your outdoor box or fixture will be located. Carefully set aside the sod as you dig the trench so that you can replace it when you're done.

7 Feed exterior UF cable up the sweep bend, through the conduit and LB fitting, to the junction box inside. If you need to run conduit through the entire trench, you can do it now.

8 Splice the NM cable and exterior UF cable inside the interior junction box, or you can continue the run of cable because UF cable can be used indoors as well.

Outdoor Receptacles

Weatherproof receptacle boxes must be used when installing outdoor receptacles. They are made of a variety of materials, both metal and plastic. Check your local code for any variations in these basic rules.

An outdoor receptacle box must be completely weatherproof, regardless of whether it will be mounted on a wall, post, or length of rigid metal conduit. Attach special brackets, called mounting ears, to the back of the receptacle box if it will be attached to a wooden post; then screw the box securely in place. For a conduit mounting, first anchor a conduit sweep bend and a vertical section of rigid conduit at the end of your underground cable trench. Next, using a compression fitting, mount the receptacle box on top of the vertical section of conduit. Be sure the box is between 12 and 18 inches above the ground.

Attach a plastic bushing to the end of the conduit sweep; then fish the UF cable from the trench up through the pipe to the receptacle box. Pull the cable into the box; then secure it in place. Split and pull back about 10 inches of the cable sheathing to expose the inside wires. Cut away the peeled-back sheathing; then strip the wires using a multipurpose tool. Wire the GFCI-protected receptacle as you would any receptacle, connecting the wires to their proper terminals. Place the foam gasket over the box, and then screw the waterproof box cover over the gasket to complete the installation.

SMART TIP

FREESTANDING ELECTRICAL BOXES

Mount freestanding boxes on two rigid metal conduits. The receptacles should be at least 12 inches, but no more than 18 inches, above the ground.

PROJECT:
INSTALLING AN OUT-DOOR RECEPTACLE

TOOLS & MATERIALS

- Measuring tape
- Power drill-driver
- Fish tape
- Combination tool
- Weatherproof box
- Screwdriver
- Galvanized screws
- GFCI receptacle or GFCI-protected circuit

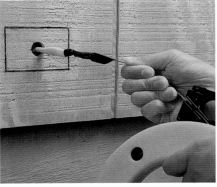

1 Use a fish tape to run the cable from inside the house to the spot where you plan your outdoor receptacle to be. This usually means drilling a hole through the stringer joist, sheathing, and siding.

2 Knock out the metal or plastic blocking the hole in the back of the box so that you can run the cable through it. Secure the cable, and screw the box to the outside of the building.

3 Screw the white wire to the silver screw and the black wire to the brass screw on either side of the receptacle. Standard receptacles should be connected to a GFCI-protected circuit.

4 A typical cover plate will only protect a receptacle from dust and nuisance contact. To seal the receptacle against weather, use a UL-listed weatherproof box.

5 A weatherproof receptacle box will need a gasket between the box and the cover plate. The spring-loaded cover will close tightly enough to keep out the weather.

OUTSIDE LIGHTS

FOR OUTDOOR LIGHTING, either type R (reflector) or type PAR (parabolic aluminized reflector) lamps are suitable. These long-lasting lamps have a reflective interior surface that maintains a bright light and resists weathering. Although PAR lamps are not affected by inclement weather, not all type R lamps are acceptable for outdoor use; check the package labeling. To mount lamps of this kind, you must install weatherproof lamp sockets. Outdoor sockets for single-, double-, and triple-lamp installations are available. Some mounts can also accommodate a motion-sensor control switch.

You can also install 120-volt or low-voltage (12-volt) exterior accent lighting. Mount a light fixture on a post to provide general lighting or on a ground spike pointing upward to show off a beautiful part of your landscape. If you choose low-voltage lighting, then you will also need to install a voltage transformer.

Exterior lights can be fitted with 24-hour timers or with motion sensors that turn on the lights automatically whenever someone comes within the range of the sensor.

PROJECT:
INSTALLING A FLOODLIGHT

TOOLS & MATERIALS
- Screwdriver
- Cable
- Staples
- Hammer
- Power drill-driver
- Weatherproof fixture
- box
- Floodlight
- Screws
- Wire connectors
- Caulking gun
- Caulk

1 To bring power to your new floodlight, break one of the knockout tabs out of an opening in an existing ceiling electrical box. Be sure the power to the circuit has been turned off.

2 Extend power from this box to the switch box that will house the switch you will be using to control the floodlight. Then run cable from the switch box to the fixture.

3 Most fixtures have two lamp holders that swivel to cover a large area. Many also have motion sensors and timer switches that provide security and make it easier to find your keys at night.

4 Connect wire leads from the lamps to the power leads (and ground) in the box with wire connectors. Caulk the top of the box to keep water from collecting and rotting the siding.

5 Mount the box cover, and adjust the lights to suit. The beams can be pointed in almost any direction. Use bulbs rated for outdoor use, even under a roof overhang.

PLUMBING BASICS

A modern plumbing system has two basic parts: water pipes that supply water, and a system that carries wastewater out (the DWV, or drain-waste-vent, system). Country houses draw water from underground wells, but most houses today are supplied by municipal water pipes. A water meter keeps track of how much is used.

Inside the structure, the main supply line splits, with one branch feeding all the cold-water pipes and the other supplying water to the water heater. The hot-water line coming out of the water heater branches, paralleling cold-water lines throughout the structure. Many barns need only a utility sink, a few outdoor hose-bibcock faucets, and perhaps a floor drain.

Drains & Vents

One part of the DWV system channels water to the main drain. The other part consists of pipes (called vents) that rise up out of the drainpipes to the roof. Vents allow in outside air to replace the air displaced by flowing water. Without them, the negative pressure would suck the water out of the traps. The trap's main purpose is to prevent noxious and potentially lethal sewer gases from rising up through the drains. Because of their shape, traps always have water in them, which provides an airtight seal. The traps are always near a drain opening, although some may be hidden below the floor (such as those on floor drains) or out of sight in the basement.

Each drain must be vented. Vent pipes are usually located near the drain opening after the trap; sometimes multiple drains are served by one vent, a system called wet venting. Vents connect to a drainpipe and run either directly to the roof or horizontally to another vent. Without them, wastewater flowing down the drain would empty the trap due to siphoning action. Instead, vents allow outside air to flow into the pipe, breaking the siphon action.

Plumbing an Outbuilding

The most basic plumbing setup consists of cold-water supply pipes (from your house's municipal or well system) providing water at faucets and utility sinks, and drainpipes bringing waste to the sewer system or septic tank. Pipes from your house will need to be buried underground below the local frost line so that they don't freeze and burst—it may be 4 or even 5 feet in some Northern locations. Because of this digging, you should have a plumbing plan drawn up before you start construction on the foundation.

If you want to have hot water, you'll need to install a separate water heater in the barn—preferably, close to its main point of use.

BASIC UTILITY PLUMBING PLAN

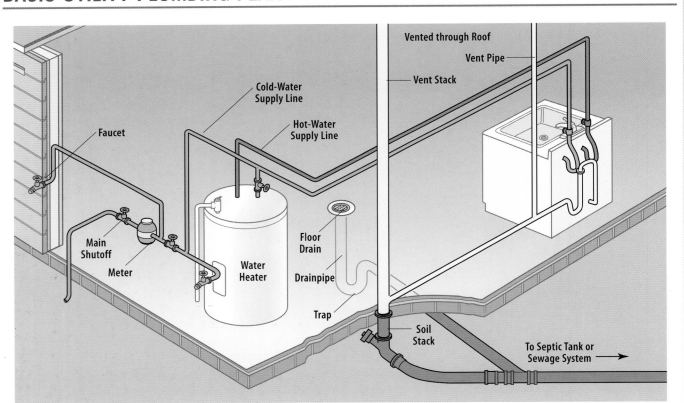

The supply and drainage system for any structure is a system that works together to supply fresh water and get rid of waste. Vent pipes allow air in at the appropriate junctures to allow for proper drainage.

SEPTIC SYSTEMS

WATER THAT LEAVES YOUR HOUSE must be separated from solid wastes and treated before it can be returned to the environment. Most urban and suburban areas channel waste water to waste-treatment plants. The plumbing in most barns, however, will be connected to septic systems.

A septic system has three main sections: the septic tank, the distribution box, and the leach field (also called the drainfield). As sewage enters the tank, it is poured into a mix of waste and anaerobic bacteria. Most of the solids are quickly broken down, and the liquid effluent leaves the tank and enters the distribution box, from which it flows into the leach field's perforated pipes and drains into the ground. What remains behind in the tank are solids, which sink to the bottom, and grease, which rises to the top. If not cleaned out, eventually new solids in the tank won't have enough room to settle properly and can infiltrate the leach field, clogging its pipes. The grease layer, if left to accumulate, can flow past the tank's outlet baffle and out into the leach field, where it limits absorption. If the sludge or grease gets this far, the entire leach field may have to be replaced.

To keep this from happening, you should have a septic tank professionally pumped out periodically. How often depends on the tank capacity and how many people use the system. Typically two people using a 1,000-gallon tank only need to pump it out every six years or so, but six people using a 2,000-gallon tank should have it pumped out every three years.

In some regions, you can install a graywater system. This allows you to channel water from dishwashers, clothes washers, and other nonseptic systems into the yard.

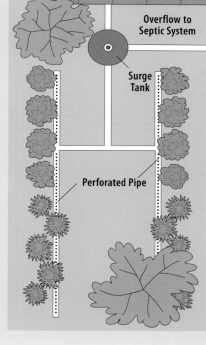

TYPICAL SEPTIC SYSTEM PLAN

Grease Trap (optional)

Septic Tank

Distribution Box

Main Drain-pipe

Outlet Pipe

Perforated Pipe

Leach Field

TYPICAL GRAY-WATER SYSTEM

Overflow to Septic System

Surge Tank

Perforated Pipe

Making a Plan

The most compelling reason to bring water to a barn is livestock. After all, you're not going to want to haul dozens of gallons of water from a spigot on your house to your barn or trip over a hundred feet of hose all summer (and have it freeze solid in the winter).

Some livestock operations, such as dairying, have very specific plumbing code requirements (particularly for manure removal in confinement buildings), and will need hot water to clean equipment. For other buildings, such as a workshop or potting shed, you need to weigh the convenience of water versus the expense. Your plumbing layout should be as efficient as possible, with the shortest possible pipe runs and a minimum of fixtures. Of course, one of the main expenses will probably be the digging of the trench for the supply lines and the cost of having a professional make the hookups to your supply and waste systems.

With this expense in mind, note that ripping apart your foundation and walls in order to retrofit a barn with a toilet and shower to convert it to living space isn't going to be cheap, either.

If you suspect you may want to convert part of your barn into living space at a later date, you can rough in the plumbing into the foundation and beneath the finished floor and walls and leave the installation for another time.

In any case, once the basic plan has been prepared (along with a list of parts and materials), get a copy of your local plumbing code from the office of the municipal plumbing inspector. You will find important information regarding such things as the required size and type of supply and DWV pipes, the slope required for horizontally positioned soil and waste pipes, allowable venting methods, and the placement of soil- and waste-pipe cleanout plugs.

After deciding where new fixtures and appliances are to go, make a drawing to show how you're going to get new water distribution and soil/waste pipes from here to there. Sketch in obstacles that are in the path. Do the roughing-in procedure to pinpoint the exact spots where water and soil/waste pipes will come into the room to align with the new fixture or appliance.

ALL ABOUT PIPE & TUBING

Water supply lines usually range from ½- or ¾-in. diameter (common in houses) up to 1-in. piping for main supply lines. The pipe walls have to be reasonably thick because the water these pipes carry is under pressure. Structures built before the 1960s may have galvanized steel water pipes, while newer buildings have copper or plastic pipes. Local codes regulate what kinds of supply lines you can use.

Waste pipes, usually at least 1⅛ inches in diameter, carry wastewater from sinks, showers, and appliances. Soil pipes, which handle solid wastes from toilets and serve as the main drain, are 3 or 4 inches in diameter. Most drain lines lead to the building's main drain, called the soil stack. Soil pipes and their vents are made from cast iron or plastic. Waste drain lines and vents are usually iron or plastic, with plastic being the most common in newer buildings. Vent pipes tend to be slightly smaller than the drains to which they connect.

Plastic Pipe

Lightweight plastic pipe ranges in diameter from 1⅛ to 6 inches. Plastic waste pipes are made of ABS (black) or PVC (white) plastic. Check with the local plumbing inspector to find out which type is acceptable for your project. Most plastic DWV lines are installed with just a few simple tools. You join them with solvent cement. Be sure to match the solvent cement to the type of plastic used in the pipe. You can even join a new section of plastic pipe to an existing cast-iron waste line with compression clamp fittings consisting of flexible gaskets and metal band clamps.

Measure the lengths required, allowing for the fittings. Unless you are cutting pipe already in place, put the lengths you're planning to cut in a miter box. Cut the pipe with a backsaw or hacksaw. Use a utility knife or emery cloth to remove burrs so that it will slide smoothly into the fitting. After cutting the pipes, test-fit the parts. Use PVC primer to clean the ends of PVC pipe and fittings. Coat the ends of each pipe and the inside of the fittings with the solvent cement. Then insert the pipe into the fitting, and twist the two parts against each other about one-quarter turn. Hold the pieces together for about ten seconds. If you fit the joint properly, the solvent cement will form a continuous bead around the joint. Once the cement sets, you cannot adjust the joint. Wipe off any excess cement around the pipe and fitting with a cloth.

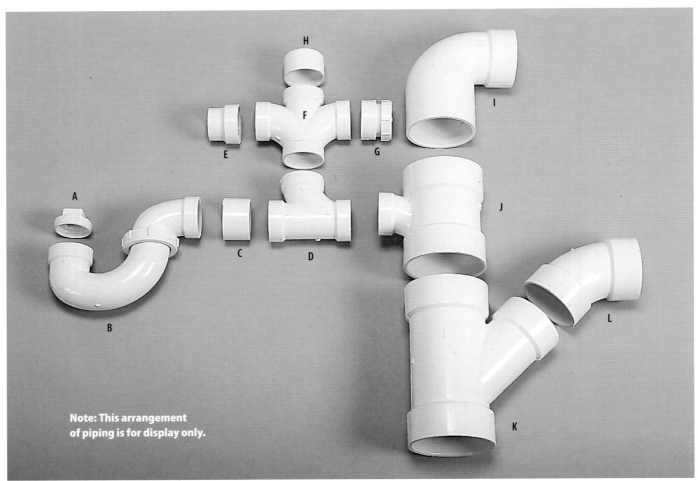

Note: This arrangement of piping is for display only.

PVC DWV fittings include: A—cleanout plug, **B**—P-trap, **C**—coupling, **D**—sanitary T-fitting, **E**—reducer, **F**—cross, **G**—ground-joint adapter, **H**—cap, **I**—90-deg. elbow, **J**—sanitary reducing T-fitting, **K**—sanitary Y-fitting, **L**—45-deg. elbow

ELECTRICAL GROUNDING AND PLASTIC

FEW HOMEOWNERS UNDERSTAND THE RELATIONSHIP between a home's plumbing and electrical systems. In many jurisdictions, the electrical panel is grounded through metallic water piping. Because the metallic piping inside the house connects to a metallic water service pipe that is buried underground, most codes require that the electrical system use this piping for all or part of its path to ground in order to have a safe installation.

If you cut out a section of cold-water trunk line and splice a length of plastic piping in its place, you'll interrupt this path to ground. That's a dangerous situation. If you decide to splice plastic into a cold-water trunk line, install a heavy grounding conductor across the span. This jumper wire should be the same size as the service panel's existing grounding wire, usually 6 gauge. Attach the wire to the metallic pipes using code-approved grounding clamps, one on each side of the splice. You won't need a jumper where the grounding wire connects directly to the water service pipe on the street side of the meter.

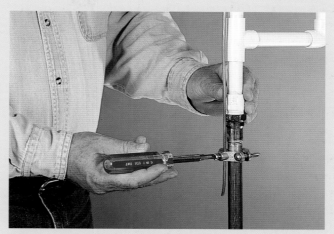

When splicing plastic into copper piping, you may need to install a copper jumper wire to maintain an unbroken ground for the home's wiring system.

PROJECT: CONNECTING PLASTIC PIPE

TOOLS & MATERIALS

- Rigid plastic pipe & fittings
- Fine-tooth saw or tubing cutter
- Utility knife
- Felt pen (for marking)
- Primer
- Solvent glue

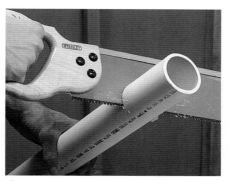

1 You can cut plastic pipes (supply lines, drains, and vents) with almost any saw, but a fine-tooth blade makes a cleaner cut. For cuts close to a wall you can use a flexible wire saw.

2 When you cut through plastic, even a fine-tooth saw can leave burrs and small shavings. Trim them off with a utility knife inside and out. A medium grit sandpaper also works well.

3 You can use one coat of adhesive in many cases, but it's best to start with a primer that cleans the surface for better adhesion. Use the primer and adhesive in a well-ventilated area.

4 Apply liquid cement for plastic pipe to mating surfaces. Be sure to read and follow all label cautions. Avoid contact between your hands and the cement. It can cause serious skin irritation.

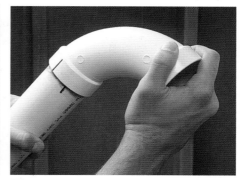

5 Plastic pipe cement softens mating surfaces. They become one when the surfaces harden. You need to work quickly. Always make a one-quarter turn when you mate pipe fittings.

Copper Tubing

Copper tubing is often available in 20-foot-long lengths of rigid tubing or coils of flexible tubing. The advantage of flexible tubing is that you can bend it to snake through curves in existing walls and floors without making joints. The downside is that curves have to be gentle and without kinks. Making the bends requires a little practice. By contrast, each turn in rigid tubing requires a joint with a soldered or threaded coupling, which can be hard to make in tight spots.

Copper tubing is available in several different grades. Rigid tubing is sold in three types: K (the thickest-walled), L, and M (the thinnest-walled). Type K is most often found in municipal and other underground lines. Type L is required by code for most commercial systems; type M, which is easiest to work with, is usually acceptable for homes.

Flexible tubing comes in two types: K and L. Another grade, DWV, generally has been replaced by plastic pipe, for the most part. Always consult with the local building inspector to find out which types they accept before planning any additions to your plumbing system.

In any system you may also want to include special fittings, such as an anti-hammer device to prevent pipe noise, and a freeze-proof exterior spigot. These have an exterior handle but turn off the water supply inside.

You can join rigid copper using soldered, compression, and push-fit fittings. Threaded adapters are available for joining copper to other threaded materials, such as steel or CPVC plastic.

SOLDERING PROBLEMS & SOLUTIONS

NOT ALL SOLDERING JOBS ARE SIMPLE. Propane torches produce intense heat, and if you are careless, you could injure yourself or damage your property. Sometimes the soldering project may take place in a confined area or on fittings installed too closely to structural timbers. To avoid damage, you can often pre-solder fittings that must rest against structural timbers or be installed deep inside cantilevers or walls. Do as much of the work as you can out in the open. **A.**

When you can't avoid soldering against studs or joists, you can keep from scorching the wood by sliding a double thickness of sheet metal between the fitting and the structural member to use as a shield. **B.**

It's handy to keep a 6-inch fold of sheet metal in your toolbox for this purpose. The sheet metal shield must have two layers in order to absorb the heat properly. For something that is a little more flexible, choose squares of woven fireproof fabric that plumbing outlets sell. **C.**

Solder deep-set fittings, like this freeze-proof sillcock, to their pipes before installing them.

Use a double thickness of sheet metal to keep from scorching the wood.

You can also use a flame shield of fireproof woven fabric to protect larger areas.

CUTTING COPPER TUBING

USE A WHEEL-TYPE CUTTER to cut copper pipe. It is possible to make cuts with a hacksaw, but it can be difficult on existing pipes where there isn't much room. Fit the cutter around the pipe, and tighten the handle. After you rotate the cutter around the pipe once or twice, you'll feel less resistance as the wheel deepens its cutting groove. Tighten the handle again to make the wheel bite in. Continue rotating and tightening until the wheel cuts all the way through. With some practice, you'll get the knack of tightening the handle gradually while you're rotating the cutter. If the wheel is biting in too deeply, you should back off on the handle a bit.

Sometimes even a relatively clean cut needs smoothing around the inner edges. This additional step will improve water flow and prevent buildup of mineral deposits on the pipe's inner wall. There are reaming tools for cleaning up burrs; many wheel cutters have fold-out reamers. You can also use a small piece of carbide sandpaper or a round metal file.

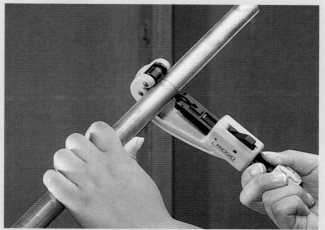

A pipe cutter can be used to cut many kinds of pipe. Just twist the tool around the pipe, tightening the blade.

PROJECT: 🐿🐿🐿
CONNECTING COPPER TUBING

TOOLS & MATERIALS
- Safety goggles or glasses
- Work gloves
- Copper tubing and fittings
- Hacksaw or tubing cutter
- Wire brush or sandpaper
- Flux
- Flux brush
- Propane torch
- Spark lighter
- Solder
- Rags

1 Plumbers use a small tool with metal wires inside to brighten copper for the best solder bond. Use sandpaper or a regular wire brush in a pinch. The surface of the copper should appear bright.

2 To brighten the interior surfaces of a connection, use a wire brush that looks similar to a bottle brush. Rotate it several times inside the fitting to remove any tarnish.

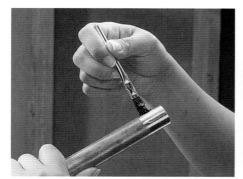

3 To draw solder completely into the joint (even uphill against gravity), coat mating surfaces with soldering paste, called flux. Use a brush to apply flux to the mating surfaces.

4 Assemble the connection, and apply heat evenly to the entire fitting. Wear gloves and use clamps to handle heated pipes. Test the heat by touching the solder to the pipe opposite from the flame.

5 When the copper is hot enough to melt solder, remove the flame and move the solder around the joint until it's filled. Also be careful of molten solder drips.

ROUGHING IN PLUMBING

TO EXTEND THE EXISTING copper-pipe water system to a new plumbing fixture, turn off the water supply and drain the system. If you are tapping into the existing pipe at an elbow, rather than cutting the pipe, use a propane torch to heat the elbow until solder melts. Then free the pipe from the elbow. Discard the elbow. (Wear thick gloves and use adjustable pliers to avoid burning your hands. Also be sure to protect building materials from the torch flame.) After the pipe cools, use an abrasive, such as sandpaper or steel wool, to clean residue from the ends of the pipe.

Solder a copper T-fitting between the two ends of the original copper pipe, and use the open end of the T-fitting as the supply source for your line. You can add adapters to copper and other types of pipe to continue the run in plastic where codes allow.

SUPPORTING PIPES

To prevent sagging, water pipes should be supported with hangers at the time they are installed, generally against floor joists, at minimum 32-inch intervals. If copper pipe is used to bring water to a new plumbing fixture or plumbing appliance,

be sure the hangers are of the same metal to avoid a galvanic reaction.

DWV pipes also need to be supported. You can use riser clamps to support vertical runs of DWV pipe. Supported horizontal runs of DWV pipe are at intervals of at least 3 feet. Don't forget to provide support at the fittings as well. This can be done by bracing the pipe with cinder block, brick, or strap hangers nailed to the foundation wall. If a DWV pipe runs overhead, parallel with the joists, it can be braced with wooden supports nailed between the joists. Provide some free play to allow for expansion so that the pipes will not bind as they expand, causing them to make noise.

To give water pipes maximum support, bore holes in joists and studs. Holes in joists should stay at least 2 inches from the edges of the joist. Never cut a hole larger than one-third or a notch deeper than one-sixth the depth of the joist. Any notches on the edge of a joist should be no longer than one-third of the depth of the joist and should never be put in the middle one-third of a joist. This is where the force is greatest on the joist through studs.

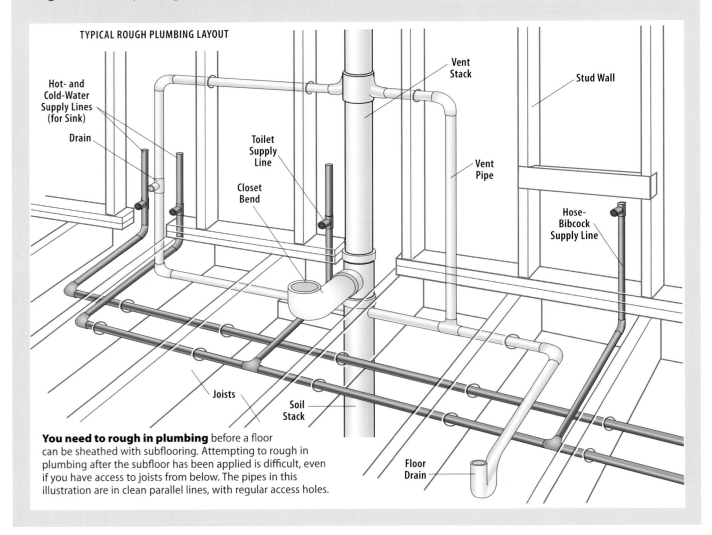

TYPICAL ROUGH PLUMBING LAYOUT

Hot- and Cold-Water Supply Lines (for Sink)

Drain

Toilet Supply Line

Closet Bend

Vent Stack

Stud Wall

Vent Pipe

Hose-Bibcock Supply Line

Joists

Soil Stack

Floor Drain

You need to rough in plumbing before a floor can be sheathed with subflooring. Attempting to rough in plumbing after the subfloor has been applied is difficult, even if you have access to joists from below. The pipes in this illustration are in clean parallel lines, with regular access holes.

PEX Water Tubing

Cross-linked polyethylene, or PEX, water tubing has been allowed in some locations for 20 years and pointedly disallowed in most others, but with the recent volatility in copper prices, resistance has begun to melt away.

Advantages: PEX has a lot going for it. It's easy to install using crimp and barbed fittings. Water flows through PEX silently, which is a big plus. PEX can take a freeze, and it's impervious to acidic soils, which destroy copper pipes. It will never rust or corrode, and internal turbulence is less likely to erode tubing walls. You can install main branch and trunk lines as you would with copper, but you can also establish a manifold system where each manifold supplies a number of fixtures throughout the house. And finally, soft water won't leave traces of copper in your drinking glass.

On the down side, PEX installations often require more tubing and hangers than copper, and some manifold installations can waste hot water because you'll have to wait for it at each fixture instead of fixture group. You'll also need one or more crimping tools, which run around $100. And finally, installations look messy, which bothers old plumbers a lot and young plumbers not at all. Put another way, PEX is the future.

Requirements: Some codes allow water-supply installations made entirely of PEX, while others require copper in the initial stages of the system—for its rigidity—usually at connections at the water meter and the water heater. Manufacturers make all sorts of copper-to-PEX conversion fittings for both ends of a line. Another place for rigidity is at the fixture stub-outs.

As most household electrical systems are grounded, at least in part, through the home's metal water piping, an alternative ground needs to be established when converting to non-conducting plastics.

PEX tubing comes in 20-foot sticks and 100- and 300-foot coils. PEX is made in a variety of colors, plus clear, but most companies are gravitating toward red and blue, to signify hot and cold water.

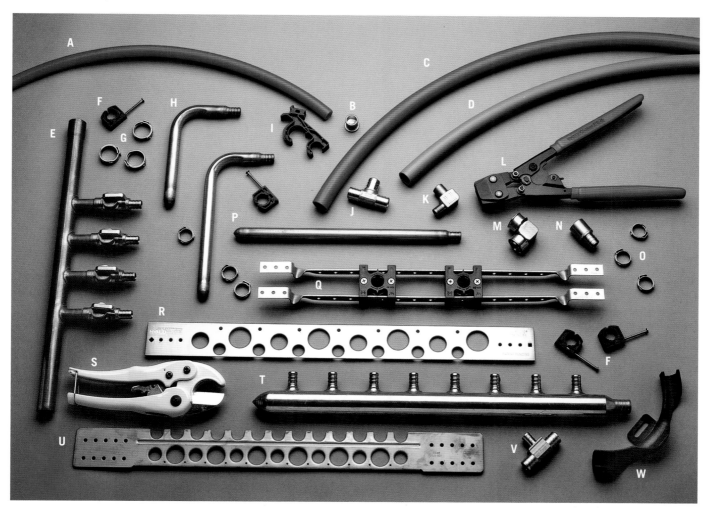

Tools and equipment for PEX tubing: A—½ PEX, **B**—plug, **C**—¾-in. PEX hot, **D**—¾-in. PEX cold, **E**—copper manifold with shutoffs, **F**—tubing hangers, **G**—¾-in. crimp rings, **H**—copper stub-outs, **I**—dual tubing hanger, **J**—brass T-fitting, **K**—brass 90-deg. elbow, **L**—crimping tool, **M**—elbow with crimp collar, **N**—sweat x PEX coupling, **O**—½-in. crimp rings, **P**—straight stub-out, **Q**—carriage stub-out bracket, **R**—copper stub-out bracket, **S**—tubing cutter, **T**—manifold without shutoffs, **U**—alternate copper bracket, **V**—¾ x ¾ x ½-in. T-fitting, **W**—90-deg. tubing bracket.

PROJECT:
RUNNING PEX THROUGH WALLS

As with other types of pipe, PEX runs are hidden in walls, ceilings, and floors. If you must run PEX through structural lumber, be sure to install the material in the center one-third of the stud or joist to protect the tubing from nails and screws during the drywalling process. In general, PEX requires more anchoring than rigid copper, and there are a variety of anchors and brackets to help you do the job. One of the advantages of PEX is the ability to bend for a change of direction; use 90-degree brackets for that purpose.

TOOLS & MATERIALS
- PEX tubing
- Hammer
- Drill
- Screwdriver
- Anchors and brackets

1 PEX is available in many colors, including clear, but many people are settling for blue for cold-water lines and red for hot. When running hot and cold water together, these dual tubing brackets are handy. Place one about every 2 ft. or at every stud or joist space.

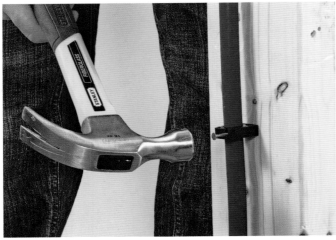

2 Don't forget to anchor PEX within wall spaces as well. PEX can take on a wavy look, especially on the hot water side. Plastic tubing brackets work well here and are inexpensive.

3 These 90-deg. brackets are used inside a wall. Center the holes in the stud width to prevent punctures by drywall nails, and nail the brackets in place. They have a bendable tab on one side, which allows you to lock the tubing into the bracket.

CUTTING & MAKING CONNECTIONS

Cut PEX tubing using a plastic tubing cutter for a square, burr-free cut.

Conversion fittings allow you to tap into existing plumbing materials.

This brass plug just slides into the tubing and is secured by a crimp ring.

PROJECT:
INSTALLING PEX STUB-OUTS

There are a variety of ways to terminate PEX tubing runs at plumbing fixtures, and a number are shown in the sequence that follows. For two stub-outs as you would use for a sink, there are brackets that allow you to set the stub-outs and the valves attached to them at precise locations. You can attach the valves directly to the PEX material or terminate the PEX run at copper stub-outs that are held in a copper bracket. In both cases, crimp rings seal the connection. For toilet stub-outs, use specially designed copper or galvanized brackets.

TOOLS & MATERIALS
- Stud-out brackets
- PEX tubing
- Tubing holders
- Hammer and screwdriver
- Crimping rings
- Crimping tool

1 Water stub-outs need to be rigid and properly spaced at the fixture, typically 4 or 8 in. apart. This carrier bracket provides ample support. Just nail it to the wall studs using galvanized nails, and slide the tubing fasteners for proper spacing.

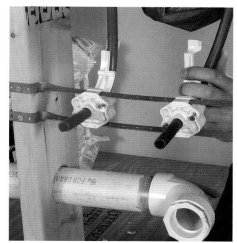

2 Feed the tubing into the holders from the back. Bend the PEX to fit into the 90-deg. elbows, leaving the tubing stubbed away from the wall 3 to 4 in.

3 Use a screwdriver to secure the tubes in the fittings. Two Philips-head screws compress the tubes in their holders.

4 Install a ½-in. PEX x ⅜-in. compression stop clamping a ½-in. crimp ring over the tube. Leave about ¼ in. of tubing showing at the end.

Brass ball valves allow direct connection to PEX tubing.

Here is a reducing T-fitting with barbed connections.

Barbed PEX tubing fittings allow you to join tube lengths end-to-end.

SINKS & TOILETS

According to most regional codes, sinks and lavatories must have a device to retain water in the basin and to trap matter floating in the water so that it can't flow into the waste pipe and cause a clog. Most lavatories have pop-up stoppers that are controlled by liftrods. Older lavatories and utility sinks use plain rubber or metal stoppers that you insert into and remove from drain inlets by hand. The drain inlets of these lavatories and sinks are outfitted with cross bars that will trap much of the debris floating in the water so that it can't run into the waste pipe.

Drain Inlets

The drain inlets of a kitchen sink and that of a sink in a utility room must be at least 1½ inches in diameter. The drain inlets of bath sinks are at least 1¼ inches in diameter. Although not required by most regional codes, bath sinks may also have one or more openings called an overflow. The overflow is located approximately three-quarters of the way up on one wall of the basin. It allows water to drain so that it doesn't overflow, flooding the countertop or floor.

Supply & Drain Lines to Sinks

Running supply and drain lines from your roughed-in plumbing to sinks is relatively easy, because these parts often come in a kit that you assemble. Someone else has engineered the pipe assembly for you and made sure that all the pipes and fittings are the same size and that all the bolts, nuts, and washers are in place.

The drains are typically PVC, arranged to form a water-filled P-trap that keeps foul gases from reaching the living area. The trap is attached to the sink drain, often by screwing a collar-type fixture onto the drain of the sink. Below the sink drain, the trap joins the pipes that take the wastewater to the septic system.

The supply line is usually not plastic (CPVC), but copper or flexible stainless-steel-mesh tubing. Here too, the fittings and

---

PROJECT: 🐾🐾🐾
INSTALLING A SINK

TOOLS & MATERIALS
- Adjustable wrench
- Groove-joint pliers
- Sink
- Faucet kit
- Drain kit
- Plumber's putty

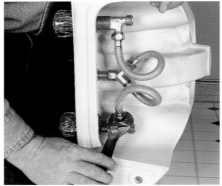

1 A counterset faucet has an 8-in. spread between valves. Join the control valves to the spout with flexible tubing. Some faucets mount differently. This one is probably the most difficult.

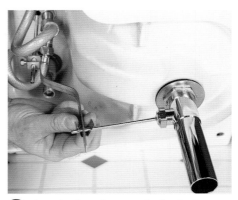

2 Coat the drain flange with plumber's putty. Tighten the nut on the drain tube from below, and attach the pop-up lever to the lift rod. This controls the drain mechanism.

3 The trap for a pedestal lavatory is hard to reach later, so attach it to the basin drain before setting the basin. You probably won't use a chrome trap in your barn. A PVC one is more appropriate.

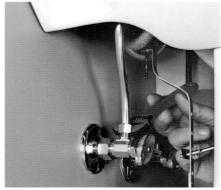

4 Set the basin on the pedestal, and join the faucet to the valves with supply tubes. Tighten the compression nuts to make a solid connection between the water supply and the faucet.

5 To connect the trap, slide a compression washer and nut onto the trap arm. Insert the arm into the drain, and tighten. Open the supply valves under the sink, and try the faucet.

tubing lengths will be part of an integral kit that links to your faucet. The only real challenge here is linking the kit fittings to your hot- and cold-water rough-ins.

Supply & Drain Lines to Toilets

Running supply lines to toilets is as easy as running supply lines to sinks. Drain lines to toilets are not, as with sinks, sold as kits. Indeed, they take some real skill and know-how to install. Call in a plumber on this one (or consult a more detailed specialty book) if you are doing this for the first time. Here a mistake can be a terrible mess to clean up. Toilets come with a built-in trap.

The toilet drain is nothing more than a pipe with a flange on top. The pipe optimally drops straight down from the toilet and connects to the main drain line of the building. The flange is called a closet flange. The lip of the flange screws in place to the subfloor of the bathroom. Be sure to make elevation accommodations for tile or other finished flooring. If you screw a closet flange to the subfloor and then improperly finish the floor with tile or wood, the finished flooring may lift the toilet away from the flange and prevent a proper seal, which will lead to a leak.

Once the closet flange and drain line are in place, they dictate the placement of the toilet because the two bolts that hold the toilet in place are attached to the closet flange. The distance to the wall from the back of the toilet is crucial (the tank must fit snugly), so it is imperative that you situate the closet flange properly. Too far from the wall, and you have a gap between the tank and the wall; too close to the wall, and your tank won't fit. Position your flange carefully in accordance with your toilet's requirements.

Once the closet flange is in place and you are ready to set the toilet, a wax seal is typically placed between the closet flange and the toilet. When the seal in in place, you can use it to keep the toilet closet bolts upright when you set the toilet. When cinched tight, the bolts will pull the toilet down snug against this seal to keep leaks from forming at the toilet's base.

PROJECT:
INSTALLING A TOILET

TOOLS & MATERIALS
- Closet bolts
- Wax gasket
- Adjustable wrench
- Groove-joint pliers
- Toilet
- Water supply tube
- Pipe joint compound

1 Insert the heads of closet bolts into the grooves in the flange so that the threads of the bolts stick up out of it. If the bolts have plastic washers, use them to hold the bolts in place.

2 Install the new gasket on the flange, and stick it in place between the bolts. If you prefer, you can insert the gasket into the drain hole on the underside of the bowl.

3 Using the closet bolts as guides, set the bowl onto the flange gasket. Site through the China bolt holes. Tighten the nuts onto the threaded ends of the closet bolts.

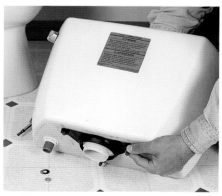

4 Prepare the tank by inserting the tank bolts through the tank and securing them with nuts and washers, if provided. Do not overtighten the nuts because the porcelain may break.

5 Carefully set the tank into position on the back of the bowl, and tighten the tank bolts. Level the tank by loosening and tightening the nuts, but don't over-tighten them.

UTILITY FAUCET VALVES

Some valves are intended to control water for utility purposes (to a yard hose, for example) or for occasionally draining appliances like water heaters.

Hose Bibcocks

A hose bibcock is a drain valve with external hose threads on its spout. While it may be connected to its piping via male or female threads or through a compression fitting, a hose bibcock's identifying feature is its hose threads, which are larger and coarser than iron-pipe threads. You can use hose bibcocks to join permanent water piping to clothes-washer hoses and garden hoses. Because you must occasionally drain water heaters and boilers, you'll also find hose bibcocks used as drain fittings for these appliances. For this reason, these valves are sometimes called boiler drains.

Most hose bibcocks are brass and use a compression mechanism for controlling water. A hose bibcock used as an outdoor sillcock (a wall-mounted outdoor faucet) usually has female threads and a brass flange that is predrilled to accept screws. In this case, a threaded water pipe extends through the exterior wall about ½ inch, and the valve is threaded onto the pipe. The flange is then screwed to the exterior wall.

Freeze-Proof Sillcocks

In areas with cold winter weather, sillcocks need some form of freeze protection. Traditionally, this has meant a two-valve assembly. You installed a hose bibcock valve outside, on the exterior wall, and an in-line valve just inside the building, in the joist space. When it began to get cold, the homeowner dutifully shut off the inside valve and drained the outside valve.

While this setup works well enough, it has two disadvantages. First, the faucet can't be used during the winter months. Second, homeowners are generally not good at routine maintenance like this. They either don't know that the second valve exists, don't know what it's for, or don't get around to draining the line before the first hard freeze occurs.

First Freeze-Proofing Attempts. The freeze-proof sillcock, introduced more than 30 years ago, was an attempt to correct the freezing problem, with generally good results. The trick was to move the stop mechanism well inside the building, where it could stay warm, while maintaining the handle and spout outside, where you could use them year-round. Those first freeze-proof sillcocks had a long stem that extended through an oversize tube, or drain chamber. Because the washer and seat operated in a warm environment and any water left in the chamber drained out when you shut off the faucet, it was a truly all-weather faucet.

These faucets would have been perfect but for one flaw: they only drained when the hose was removed. An attached hose created an air lock, which held water in the chamber. This water then froze and ruptured the sillcock. Because the freeze occurred in the chamber, on the downstream side of the stop mechanism, the leak only appeared when the sillcock was used again, usually the following spring. By then, of course, the hose had been stored away for months and the homeowner had forgotten last fall's early cold snap. Because an attached hose was about the only way to rupture a freeze-proof sillcock—and an attached hose voids the warranty—these sillcocks have been the source of a good many disputes between homeowner and plumber.

Modern Solution. Most new freeze-proof sillcocks have a vacuum breaker threaded onto the spout to solve the hose-related freeze problem and prevent back siphonage. The vacuum breaker

HOSE BIBCOCKS

Male threads on some hose bibcocks allow you to attach the faucets to elbows and other appropriate fittings.

Female threads on other hose bibcocks allow you to thread the units onto supply pipes.

releases the air lock created by the attached hose and drains the chamber. Some new so-called freeze-proof sillcocks include a top-mounted backflow preventer instead of a vacuum breaker. These prevent contaminating backflows, but they're not always freeze-proof with a hose attached. Nevertheless, codes now require sillcocks with either backflow preventers or vacuum breakers. When installing a freeze-proof sillcock, always prop up the rear of the chamber so that water can drain through the spout.

Freeze-proof sillcocks come in lengths ranging from 6 to 36 inches. Choose a length that places the stop a foot or so inside the house. If you are installing a sillcock in a cantilevered floor or wall, it will need to be longer, of course, as will those you install through brick or stone facades. While you usually install sillcocks through the band joist of a home, you can also use them on houses that are built on concrete slabs. In these cases, an interior wall houses the drain chamber, keeping it reasonably warm.

FREEZE-PROOF SILLCOCKS

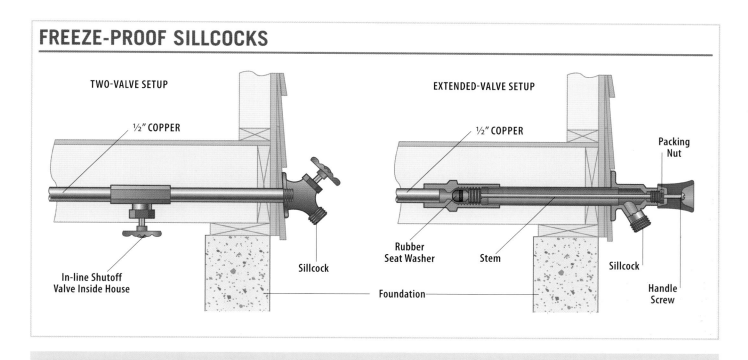

TWO-VALVE SETUP

½" COPPER

In-line Shutoff Valve Inside House

Sillcock

Foundation

EXTENDED-VALVE SETUP

½" COPPER

Packing Nut

Rubber Seat Washer

Stem

Sillcock

Handle Screw

FREEZE-PROOF SOLUTIONS

Aftermarket vacuum breakers can be installed on existing sillcocks.

Press plumber's putty around the freeze-proof sillcock mounting flange to seal the opening.

The way you plan on using your new barn, shed, or other building will determine how it should be finished. Finishing a utilitarian barn can be as easy as nailing up rough pine boards around doorjambs and windows or as difficult as mitering trim around openings and installing precisely cut corner boards. If the building will contain living space, such as a studio or guest room, you'll want to spend a few extra dollars and put in the additional time to trim out the space so that it looks more finished and attractive.

STORAGE

Because a barn or outbuilding is generally not a finished space, you don't want to put huge amounts of time or money into building storage systems. Finished one-by pine boards are expensive, and it can cost as much as $200 to put up 150 running feet of shelving.

But shelf space is nice to have, especially if you've finally built a storage shed to house all those boxes and who-knows-what-else you've been storing in the basement, attic, and back hallway all these years.

Basic shelf systems are easily adaptable to nearly any structure or area. These shelves and table systems are framed using principles similar to those used to frame partition walls. It might be tempting to screw steel L-brackets into the studs and place inexpensive ½-inch CDX plywood on top of them to create shelves.

But these types of shelves don't hold much weight. An inexpensive alternative is to create a 2x4 frame that you can deck with plywood. Run 2x4s floor to ceiling, tied into the floor and the joists above, and hang the framed shelves between them. This makes a sturdy, strong alternative to either lightweight steel L-brackets or shelf kits.

You can build a basic benchtop from a frame of 2x4s screwed together on edge and a piece of ¾-inch plywood screwed on top of the frame. (Using liberal amounts of construction adhesive also helps.) Use 2x4s or 4x4s for legs. You can use regular wood screws to attach the legs to the benchtop, or for extra durability, use hex-head lag screws. After the legs are attached, screw some cross bracing between the legs. You can add a shelf below the tabletop by securing plywood to the cross bracing.

This shelf and work surface is angle-braced to the wall below a series of sunny windows, providing a perfect place for growing and caring for potted plants.

Shallow storage shelves can be made of 2x4s (or 2x6s depending on the width of your studs) set on blocks that are screwed to the inside of the stud bay.

A sturdy workbench can be made from common dimensional lumber and one or two sheets of ¾-in. plywood. The height, width, and depth can be manipulated to suit your needs.

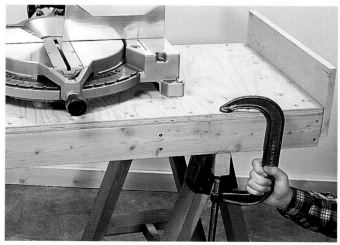

A portable workbench makes sense if you have limited workspace. This chop-saw table is made of plywood screwed to a 2x4 frame. The end panel supports long boards.

STALLS & PARTITIONS

IF YOU WANT A MULTIPURPOSE BARN where you can handle car and truck repair, keep a few animals, and have a large workshop and storeroom, you may need some walls, partitions, and stalls.

In most barns, the outside walls are load-bearing, although there are often interior posts. But most walls that divide space within a barn are nonload-bearing walls, better known as partition walls. You might build them by screwing a two-by top plate to the underside of the bottom webs of the trusses or the underside of the joists, and then shooting a two-by into the slab with power-actuated fasteners or screwing a two-by plate to the wood floor for a sill plate. With these two plates in place, you can simply frame walls as you would when building any structure.

Half-walls for stalls are framed the same way, but because each stud doesn't run all the way to the top plate, it's good to have a post or double stud at each end.

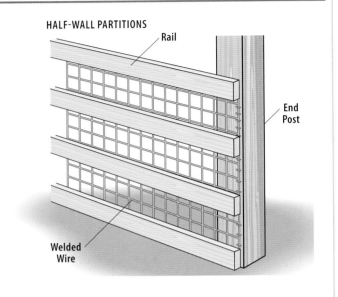

HALF-WALL PARTITIONS

- Rail
- End Post
- Welded Wire

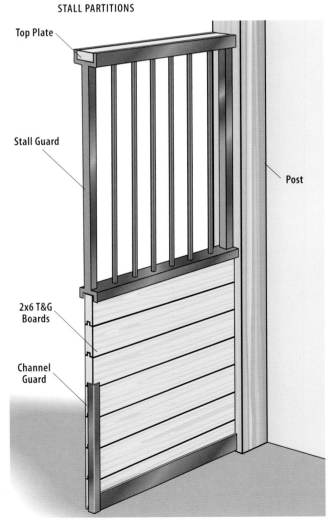

STALL PARTITIONS

- Top Plate
- Stall Guard
- Post
- 2x6 T&G Boards
- Channel Guard

Raising horses requires a large barn with individual stalls designed for each animal. Unique gable-end framing can contain combinations of windows to let in light and air.

Planning Animal Stalls

The best information on what type of area and square footage is required for animals is available from your state or university agricultural extension service or from a local 4-H group. You will find that large animals need a lot of room, and stalls that run 10 x 10, or 12 x12 feet can eat up an enormous amount of space in a 24 x 50 barn. Even smaller stalls can gobble up space. For instance, a cow under 1,400 pounds generally requires a stall at least 4 feet wide by 5½ feet long. For heavier cows, the recommended stall size grows to 5 feet wide and 6 feet long. A horse that's 14 hands needs a 10 x 10-foot stall, and a 16-hand horse needs stall 12 x 12 feet. Stalls for two 16-hand horses can take up the entire width of a 24-foot-wide barn.

You can build stalls with wide rough-cut boards such as 2x6s or 2x8s. Many suppliers offer treated 2x6s that add strength to partitions with single and sometimes double tongue-and-groove joints. You need to check carefully about the wood treatments that will be safe for animals in stalls. For example, you should not paint partitions because many animals will chew on the materials. Some livestock barns also need to be fitted with watering systems. There are basic containers you fill by hand and automatic systems connected to supply piping.

Feeders

The kind of hay feeder or grain feeder you have in your barn will depend on the type of animals you keep. The hay feeder shown below can provide food for many different kinds of animals.

Feeders need not be made of wood. Depending on the type of animals you are feeding, there are a number of metal feeders in round, oblong, and rectangular shapes that you can buy from feed and grain supply centers. Some of these feeders are on wheels and can be brought in and out of a barn, depending on access and weather.

PROJECT: BUILDING A FEEDER

TOOLS & MATERIALS

- 2x4s
- Circular saw
- Power drill-driver
- Galvanized deck screws
- ¾–inch plywood
- 2x8s
- 2x2s

1 Cut 2x4 legs, and build the two end sections by adding two supports. Then connect the two sides with longer 2x4 supports; notch the plywood corners; and fasten the sheet with screws.

2 Screw down a 2x6 cleat on top of the plywood. This will hold one end of the spokes. Use screws short enough so that they will not stick out of the other side and harm the animals.

3 Screw angled blocks at the tops of the front legs. The blocks should be angled with the lower part pitching toward the back of the feeder. Screw a wide board, such as a 2x8, to the blocks.

4 Screw 2x2 spokes to the inside of the front plate. Space them equally with about 3 to 4 in. between each spoke. The bottom end of each spoke is placed behind the cleat on the plywood deck.

5 After all of the spokes have been screwed in place, screw a section of plywood to the rear of the back legs to act as a back for the feed bin. This type of feeder is meant to back up to a wall.

LIVING SPACE

If you plan to use part of a barn for living space, you'll need to insulate part of the structure and make a plan for heating, plumbing, wiring, and other residential features.

One possible scenario is to have a living loft with a work area below. This will take a substantial amount of planning, as you will have to furnish the loft with hot water, heat, and a stairway.

You will also have to install some kind of bathroom and accommodate sewer lines to a new or existing septic system. Drain and supply lines will have to be run not only for a bathroom but possibly to a kitchen area as well, escalating the cost and complexity of the design. Even modest mechanical systems for basic conveniences can double construction costs.

You also have to consider that motorized vehicles or fume-producing paints or solvents used in a work area below will seep into a loft living area above unless you create an entirely separate space in the barn for those activities and provide substantial ventilation. You may need extra sheets of plastic or foil to completely isolate living spaces.

A more likely scenario is that the entire barn is used for living area or that the barn has some of its space for living and the remaining space for low-impact activities in a pottery or painting studio, workshop, carpenter's shop, or gardening space.

One drawback to turning a barn into a living space is that barns tend to be either squares or rectangles. Structures designed and built for living often have sections of walls that are offset to admit light and air, and to add some variety to the interior traffic patterns. You are dividing up a box when you partition a barn for living.

Sealing up Living Space

To cut heat loss while gaining moisture and preventing damage, it is necessary to reduce the passage of air and moisture through walls and ceilings. Selecting and applying the appropriate caulks, gaskets, or sheet materials is an important part of the process.

Air-Barrier House Wrap. This lightweight house-wrap sheeting stops the bulk of air movement through walls. Apply it over the outer walls beneath the siding. Materials used for house wraps allow water vapor to escape to the outside, but they also keep out wind.

Some materials, such as spun polyester, are able to do this because of their porosity. Other nearly impermeable materials, such as polyethylene, are perforated with many tiny holes to make them moisture permeable. Air-barrier house wrap is available in rolls 9 feet wide for large wall surfaces and in shorter widths for wrapping sill and head plates.

Vapor Barriers. Vapor-barrier sheeting blocks both air and water vapor. To do this, it must be impermeable to moisture. To be acceptable as a vapor barrier, the permeance rating should be less than 1. Unpainted drywall has a permeance rating of 50 and is not considered a vapor barrier. The asphalt-backed kraft paper used to face some blanket and batt insulation has a permeance rating of 1; it is a marginal vapor barrier. Two excellent vapor barriers are polyethylene sheeting, which has a permeance rating of 0.08 to 0.04, and aluminum foil, which has a rating of 0.

Weather Stripping. Weather stripping is made with many different materials and comes in many shapes. Its purpose is to create an effective barrier at openings between the inside of a structure and the outdoors. You can choose packaged kits that contain rigid strips intended for average-size doors or windows, or rolls of flexible material you cut yourself. You apply some types simply by sticking them to the window or door while others have to be tacked to the frame.

INSULATION OPTIONS

TWO MAIN FACTORS affect your choice of insulation: the configuration (for instance, loose fill or rigid foam board) and the R-value. But you should also consider ease of application, how the material is packaged, and potential drawbacks such as possible skin irritation. But many lumberyards and home centers stock only fiberglass and a few types of foam boards.

Insulation is commonly available in four forms: batts to fit between 16- or 24-inch-wide framing, either paper- or foil-faced; loose fill to blow or pour into structural cavities; and foam boards, used mainly on roofs and on the outside of walls and foundations. The other type, sprayed-in-place foam, is more expensive and not as widely used.

To create a thermal envelope around your living space, particularly in the framing compartments of an existing building, you may want to use more than one type of insulator. Smaller spaces, such as where pipes enter walls, can be more easily filled with foamed-in-place urethanes; partially closed walls can be filled with loose cellulose; open walls can get batts of fiberglass; and walls and ceilings with exposed framing are easier to insulate with rigid foam.

Spraying loose fill is one of the easiest ways to add insulation in an attic. Typically, this work is done by contractors with special equipment that delivers loose fill from a supply truck.

Venting Options. While typical barn venting consists only of louvers and a natural draft-through construction that is not intended to be airtight, living spaces require more complex systems. Aside from interior venting systems, usually with strong discharge fans, near moisture sources such as kitchens and baths, you'll also need to ventilate the space between the finished ceiling and the roof. Typically, you can do this with a balanced combination of soffit vents along the eaves and ridge vents, attic gable-end vents, or through-roof vents, just as you would in a house.

Rigid foam insulation adds significant R-value to the exterior walls of your barn or other structure but adds only a 1- to 2-in. layer of material.

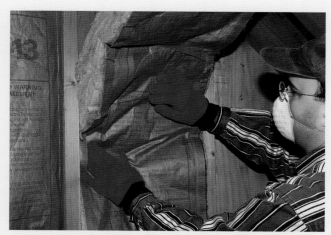

Fiberglass batt insulation is made to fit between studs. Its thin strands of glass can irritate skin, so be sure to wear gloves, a long-sleeve shirt, and a dust mask when handling it.

TYPES OF INSULATION

Fiberglass is the most common wall and ceiling insulation material. It has an R-value that ranges (depending on thickness) from R-11 to R-38, and is available in many sizes with different types of backing.

FIBERGLASS

Extruded Polystyrene Board is a dense board that offers R-5 per inch. Expanded polystyrene is made of a material similar to that used to make foam coffee cups. It has an R-value of about 3.5 per inch.

EXTRUDED POLYSTYRENE

Cellulose Fiber is a paper-based product and has roughly the same R-value as fiberglass, about R-3.5 per inch. Typically, it is made from shredded recycled paper combined with a fire retardant. Loose fill can be blown in using a pressurized air hose. Several newer insulating materials use a mix of about 75 percent recycled cotton fiber (even scraps of old blue jeans) with 25 percent polyester to bind the fibers together. The material comes in batts and as loose fill.

CELLULOSE LOOSE FILL

Polyurethane Foam can be sprayed by contractors into open framing cavities where it provides a thorough seal against air leaks and a thermal rating of about R-6.0 per inch. It also comes in pint-sized quantities—in a spray can with a nozzle so that you can use foam for small jobs, like filling openings in the building envelope.

POLYURETHANE FOAM

Polyisocyanurate Board is a rigid foam board rated at about R-6.3 per inch—double the thermal resistance of fiberglass.

POLYISOCYANURATE

DRYWALL

Also known as plasterboard, wallboard, and often by the registered trade name Sheetrock, drywall provides a solid foundation for interior finishes such as wallpaper, paneling, or tile. Because its paper-covered face can easily be painted, drywall often serves as the finished surface.

Drywall sheets are quickly cut and installed using a hammer and nails, or screws and a power drill-driver with a Phillips head screwdriver bit. Pros generally use a special drill with a torque limiter and other features that allow them to load a screw and just pull the trigger. The drill stops when the screw is set just into the panel surface with a neat and easily spackled dimple.

On wall studs spaced 16 inches on center, fasteners should be spaced every 8 inches for nails and 12 inches for screws. Use screws if possible to prevent nail pops.

The standard drywall panel for new construction and remodeling is ½-inch thick. Drywall is generally available in 4-foot widths and 8-, 10-, 12-, and 14-foot lengths. It may seem easiest to hang 4 x 8 sheets vertically, running the long dimension from floor to ceiling. And it's true that a 4 x 8 sheet, which weighs about 54 pounds, is easier to maneuver and install than longer sheets—especially on ceilings. But whenever possible, you should install sheets horizontally on walls. Choose the longest practical length to minimize the number of joints. You'll probably need a helper, but horizontal installation saves work during the time-consuming process of taping and finishing.

When you handle drywall during installation, remember to treat it gently because it breaks easily if dropped or hit. You can quickly crush a corner and ruin an entire panel if you put the full weight of a sheet on it. Stack drywall flat to prevent warping if you don't plan on using it right away.

PROJECT: INSTALLING DRYWALL

TOOLS & MATERIALS

- Eye protection
- Measuring tape
- Drywall panels
- T-square
- Utility knife
- Stepladder and/or scaffolding
- Drywall hammer or drill-driver
- Drywall nails or screws
- Panel lifter
- Joint compound
- Mud tray or hawk
- 3-, 6-, and 12-inch taping knives
- Drywall tape
- Tape dispenser (optional)
- Sanding pole
- Sandpaper

1 To cut drywall, score the surface with a utility knife against a straightedge such as a drywall T-square. Snap-break the panel along the cut, and slice through the paper backing.

2 Install the top wall panel first, butting it against the ceiling. If you're working alone, a few nails under the panel can support it. If you have a partner to help, things will go faster.

3 Butt the bottom panel against the top by pushing down on a panel lifter with your foot. If there is a small gap near the floor, it will be covered by the baseboard trim.

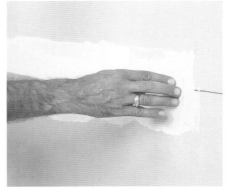

4 Spread the first coat of joint compound over the seam. Embed a length of paper drywall tape in the first coat of compound by smoothing it against the wall with a drywall knife.

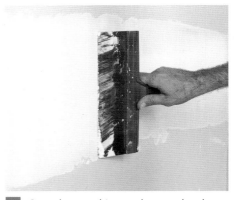

5 Once the coat dries, apply second and third coats of compound with a wider taping knife. Smooth compound carefully to reduce sanding time. Sand lightly between coats as needed.

TRIMWORK

Most of the trimwork you'll do in your barn will be with rough-cut 1x4 or 1x6 pine. The same material works quite well inside and out. For doors and windows, you can either miter the joint, butt the joint, or use corner blocks. For a more-finished appearance, use the same type of trimwork and molding you would find in your home.

For exterior trim you can usually use No. 2 lumber. This type of spruce, pine, or fir is a medium-grade stock. You'll find a lot of minor defects, such as knots in the wood. Treat them and exposed end grain with a stain-killing, shellac-based primer. This will keep the pitch in the knots from bleeding through after you paint the trim. Omit this step if you plan to use a better grade of lumber and will apply a stain or clear sealer. Finishing exterior trim is important because this kind of lumber is very susceptible to damage caused by insects and weather.

Over rustic barn siding, butt joints generally look fine, although you can dress up the the trim by mitering.

PROJECT: 🐀🐀🐀
INSTALLING BASE TRIM

TOOLS & MATERIALS
- Measuring tape
- Base trim
- Carpenter's pencil
- Power miter saw or backsaw and miter box
- Power drill and bits
- Hammer
- 8d finishing nails
- Nail set
- Wood putty

1 Scribing is more accurate than measuring. Set molding in position to mark where a miter will meet the corner. Mark the direction of the miter cut to avoid confusion.

2 For accurate miter cuts, use a power miter saw or a miter box. Use finishing nails to attach base trim, but drill pilot holes near the edges of the board to avoid splitting.

3 Begin installation by driving 8d finishing nails almost, but not quite, flush with the wood surface to avoid marring the wood with hammer blows. Accuracy is important here.

4 Use a nail set to drive nails below the surface of the wood. Fill holes with wood putty.

5 Inside corners require a coped joint where two sections of base trim meet. Square cut the first board, and cut an open miter in the second. Use a coping saw to cut along the exposed profile.

Exterior Trim

A rake board is basically a trim board, often used with one or more strips of smaller trim, that covers the outermost gable-end rafters. Its main functions are to conceal the rough lumber of the end rafter, which generally is construction-grade material, and to cover the top edges of siding on the gable-end walls. But you can also mount a rake board on blocking, and use trim along the top and bottom edges to increase its overall thickness and add detail to the roof line.

■ **Rake board lumber** is typically 1x6 or 1x8 pine. But you may need a different size depending on the depth of the rafters. Generally, the rake follows the lines of the rafters. For example, it will have the same plumb cut at the ridge where one rake board joins another. But to trim the roof neatly, the rake board should extend a bit below the rafter. This can allow sheathing and siding, in some cases, to tuck underneath the lower edge. You also need to plan the cuts on the downhill side where the gable-end rake often joins a one-by fascia made of the same material. The fascia covers the rafter tails. On more finished barn designs, fascias and rakes form a continuous belt of trim around the edges of the roof.

■ **Boxed-out rake boards** can create a soffit along the gable ends. But this requires extra labor, such as nailing up and venting a soffit in an area that is difficult to work in comfortably and safely without a fairly elaborate setup of ladders or scaffolding. Don't attempt this work from the roof, even if it has a shallow slope.

■ **Rake board thickness** can be several inches in a design where the board is blocked out and away from the rafters. But even when the rake board is attached directly to the outer rafter, overall roof width is increased by at least 1½ inches due to rakes on both gable ends. So it's important to plan and install the rakes and the rake flashing before you shingle the roof. If you jump the gun and shingle first, you're likely to discover that the shingles fall short of covering the rake.

PROJECT:
FINISH TRIM

TOOLS & MATERIALS
- Corner boards
- Hammer
- Circular saw
- Finishing nails
- One-by stock casing trim
- Caulking gun
- Paintable exterior caulk

1 Corner boards give siding something to butt into. The two boards can be mitered, but it is easier and just as attractive to set one flush with the wall and set the other so that it caps its edge.

2 Nail boards to cover the undersides of rafters. This will keep flying insects and birds from making their homes in your building. If you plan to finish the interior, these boards should be vented.

3 Case moldings around windows and doors also give the siding something to butt into. These can be made of one-by stock or any molding you prefer. Many windows are made with trim attached.

4 One way to build out a rake is to nail doubled 2x4s flush with the top of the roof and then cover the 2x4s with a 1x6 or 1x8. Finish the soffit with a 3-inch-wide board nailed to the bottom of the 2x4.

5 Run a bead of caulk along any seam that might let air or insects through to the inside. A good time to do this is after you have primed your siding and trim. This way all the wood gets primed.

GUTTER SYSTEM ASSEMBLY

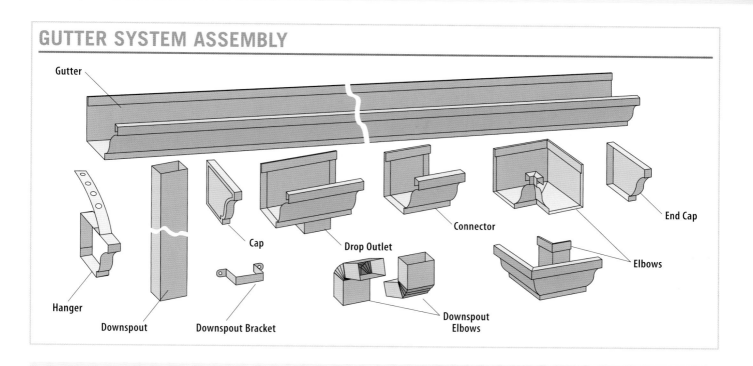

Gutter

Hanger

Downspout

Downspout Bracket

Cap

Drop Outlet

Connector

End Cap

Elbows

Downspout Elbows

GUTTER CLEANERS

A wire basket that rests in the gutter, over the downspout opening, will keep debris out of the pipe.

Screens that cover the entire gutter are designed to trap wet debris where it can dry and blow away.

Some systems replace standard gutters with louvers that disperse the flow onto the ground.

GUTTER HANGERS

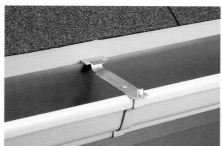

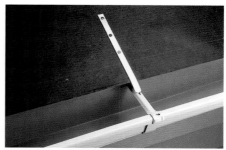

Spikes and ferrules are the standard hanging system. The ferrule (a tube around the spike) prevents crimping.

Brackets nail into the fascia board and clip into the gutter edge. Space brackets about 3 ft. apart.

Straps wrap around the gutter and are nailed to the roof deck under the first course of shingles.

PAINT & STAIN

Painting or staining your barn or outbuilding will not only protect and preserve the new siding but also add color and accent. How well your paint or stain stands up over time depends on a number of factors, including which finish you use and what quality you buy. It also depends on how well you prepare the wood and apply the finish.

Paint Types

Paint is a mixture of solids, pigments, solvents, and binders that sit on the surface of the wood when dry. It protects the wood as long as there are no cracks to admit water, sun, or insects. For paint, your choice is either latex (water-based) or alkyd (oil-based) products. Most recent research shows that a top-quality latex paint will outlast a top-quality alkyd paint. That's because the latex paint is flexible and permeable, so it doesn't crack as often when stressed with the movement of the siding or continuous assaults by water. Oil-based paints, though stiffer and more brittle when dry, are still the best when you want the paint to really penetrate, as is the case when painting bare wood.

Also, water-based paints are much easier to clean up (use water), and they have a lower volatile organic compound (VOC) content, making them marginally safer for the environment and for the painters applying them.

High-gloss paints (enamels) are shiny and reflective. They produce a strong water-resistant coating, but surface flaws show up readily. Semigloss paints (eggshell or satin) leave a somewhat shiny surface that doesn't resist moisture as well as high-gloss paint. Flat, or matte-finish, paints leave no gloss or shine. This paint is great for siding with imperfections, such as No. 2 spruce. A flat siding paint with semigloss trim is a good traditional combination.

FINISHING OPTIONS

THE SAME BOARDS can look dramatically different depending on the type of protection you apply. The most practical are clear sealers and semitransparent stains. They do not crack or chip like paint and some heavy-bodied stains. And as they fade over time, the surfaces will look slightly weathered but retain some of their color. Best of all, these coatings are easy to renew. Clear sealers in particular require no preparation work. These pictures show a series of different applications made on the same kind of Douglas fir. Before you select a finish, it's wise to test it on some of your scrap lumber.

Semitransparent stains allow some grain to show but add an overall tone to the boards. The stains come in many colors, in water-based or oil-based solutions.

Solid-body stains cover the wood grain completely the way paint does. They can also unify cheaper grades of lumber that have surface blemishes as well as different hues.

Paint provides the most opaque finish but lies on the surface instead of penetrating the wood. When a paint film cracks and begins to peel, it is more difficult to touch up than stain.

Oil-based clear sealers are the easiest to apply because they are so thin and easy to spread. You will need more than one coat on raw wood, particularly on rough-grained barn siding.

Latex-based clear sealers feature easy cleanup, but the sometimes milky-looking finish may not be as durable as a comparable oil-based finish. Be sure to test finishes on scrap lumber.

DIFFERENT TOOLS FOR PAINTING

Wall brushes are usually 4, 5, or 6 in. wide. Use smaller brushes for trim—angled bristles are good for cutting in.

Rollers apply coats of paint quickly and easily. They leave a stippled surface that is more pronounced with longer naps.

Paint sprayers apply a fine mist. Using one requires some practice, but it can greatly speed up application.

PROJECT: 🖌🖌🖌
FINISHING NEW SIDING

TOOLS & MATERIALS
- Ladders
- Scaffolding (optional)
- Wood putty
- Putty knife
- Sandpaper
- Sanding block
- Primmer and brush
- Caulking gun
- Exterior-grade caulk
- Exterior paint (or stain)
- Drip rags, dropcloths
- 1 ½-inch sash brush
- 4-inch exterior wall brush

1 Fill holes with exterior-grade putty. Deep holes will need two or more coats. Allow the putty to dry, and then sand it. Prime the dry patch so that it doesn't show under paint or stain.

2 Apply a weather-resistant caulk around window and door openings and where siding butts against corner trim. This will help keep out drafts, water, and insects.

3 There is no set application rule for paint or stain. But it works well to cover seams before brushing out the surface. Don't miss the underside of clapboards, or other hidden edges.

4 On the finish coat of paint or stain, work on small sections between trimmed borders. Start by cutting in the edges. A sash brush is the best tool for this job, even if you're using a sprayer.

5 Work from the top of the wall down to the bottom so that you can pick up any drips before they dry, or scrape them away with a paint scraper or joint compound knife.

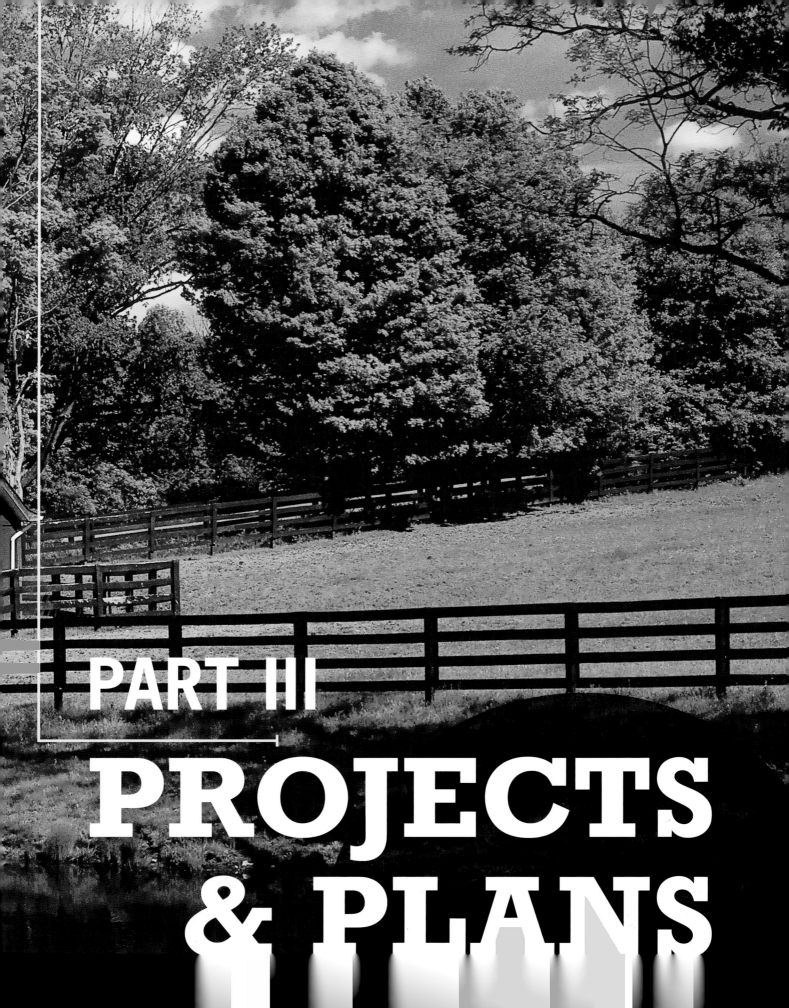

PART III
PROJECTS & PLANS

Up to this point, *Ultimate Guide: Barns, Sheds & Outbuildings* has provided the general construction information you need to build a storage building. You can place a barn or shed on your property by designing one from scratch, buying a barn or shed kit, or building from one of the designs shown here. This section contains a number of designs. As the photographs show, the first 10 designs have been built and continue to serve the needs of their owners. There are also four simple sheds that would improve your home storage. The section ends with 109 designs for which blueprints are available.

CASE STUDIES

The first projects are grouped in four categories, according to the complexity of their construction: simple framing, standard framing, pole framing, and advanced framing. The photos, drawings, and descriptions can serve as case studies to inform your own projects.

Depending on your needs, however, you will want to vary the dimensions, floor layouts, rooflines, or window and door placements. For all buildings except perhaps a simple shed, you should probably hire a professional to draw up plans for you. A pro will be able to create the floor plan and elevations required by most building inspectors, as well as framing plans that specify key structural elements, such as diagonal bracing, headers, and beams. If you hire a licensed architect or engineer to draw plans for you, the projects can be completed in several days. Be sure to check your design plans with the local building department.

Simple Framing Projects. The first three projects are simple framing projects that can be completed in a few days. All are constructed with simple 2x4 wall, floor, and roof frames. Although these sheds are relatively small structures, all the projects resemble the larger structures described later in their basic outlines. If you can build one of these, you are well on your way toward building any of the other projects.

Each shed project described here has been built on a different foundation. The Garden Tool Shed rests on a small pier-and-beam foundation. The piers are formed in 6-inch-diameter form tubes filled with concrete, leveled off, and tied together with a doubled 2x6 pressure-treated grade beam.

The Backyard Storage Shed uses a simple post foundation made by sinking 4x4 pressure-treated posts in concrete. The tops of these posts are tied together with pressure-treated 2x6s that lap the outside of the posts. In both cases, the floor is framed with pressure-treated 2x6 joists nailed into the grade beams. The third project—the Gambrel Shed—is built on a small structural slab.

Standard Framing Projects. The three projects described in this section qualify as full-scale buildings, with large wall and roof areas that exert wind and snow loads equal to those of a full-size house.

These projects all exemplify the standard framing procedures described in Chapter 4. In many cases, this is the method of framing you will find in modern wood-framed houses.

Pole Framing Projects. Pole construction often proves to be an economical alternative for large agricultural structures. The building projects described in this section all use 6x6 or 6x8 pressure-treated timber posts—a type commonly available at a lumberyard or building-supply center. These pressure-treated posts, encased in concrete pilings and extending all the way to the top of the walls, serve as both the foundation and the skeleton of the structure.

For any of these projects, you can substitute round pressure-treated poles for dimensioned timbers. Round treated poles can be less expensive, but they can also complicate the building process. It's usually much easier to build with square-edged timbers.

Three-Bay Garage

Advanced Framing Projects. The two projects described in this section represent the largest and most ambitious projects in this book. The first project—a large gambrel barn—combines many of the standard framing practices discussed in the text with traditional gambrel roof framing. The second project uses traditional timber joinery to create an elegant timber-framed garage. Timber framing calls for expert carpentry skills and a sound knowledge of construction.

Basic Sheds

The four sheds shown here are designed for the typical residential yard. Use them to store lawn and garden tools and equipment or as a general-purpose storage shed. Each design includes a detailed materials list and step-by-step building instructions.

Three of the sheds—shed-roof shed, gable-roof shed, and barn-style shed—are based on classic shed designs. The attached shed offers the opportunity to create a unique storage area. Because it is attached to the house, it requires less material than a typical shed.

Although the design shown here is only 24 inches deep and 72 inches wide, it provides ideal storage space for garden tools, pool and spa equipment and chemicals, or sports equipment.

Outbuilding Plans

Adding a barn, shed , or detached garage to your property can increase the value of the property substantially. The 82 designs shown at the end of this section cover a range of outbuilding plans that you can purchase to build.

Many of the designs include outbuildings with second-floor living spaces. Some offer the opportunity to turn the space into a workshop or studio of some kind. Other designs include plans for complete apartments, including living rooms, bedrooms, kitchens, and bathrooms. Complete with dormer windows, these spaces are ideal for guests or as mother-in-law apartments.

Many of the garages follow the latest trend for new homes: three-car garages. Of course, you can use the space any way that suits your needs, but with three bays you can devote one to a workshop and still have two left for your cars.

Livestock Barn

1

SIMPLE FRAMING   GARDEN TOOL SHED

LOCATED NEAR AN ORCHARD and a large garden plot, this shed provides much-needed storage for a range of yard and garden tools, hoses, and apple-storage bins. The large double doors provide easy access for a riding lawn mower. This is the simplest project in this group, and once the materials have been delivered, you will probably be able to build it over the course of a few days.

MATERIALS

6	80-pound bags concrete (for 3-ft.-deep piers)
6	6-in. diameter x 4 ft. form tubes
6	½-in. x 3-ft. #4 rebar
4	2x6 x 16-ft. grade beams
1	2x6 x 8-ft. grade beams and joists
4	¾-in. x 4x8 ft. CDX plywood for floor
85	2x4 x 8 ft. walls, gables, and rafters and rafter ties
16	1x8 x 8ft. sheathing pine sheathing boards
1	22-in. x 22-in. fixed window
2	24-in. x 30-in. screened awning windows
14	2x6 joist hangers
108	rough-sawn 1x6x8-ft. siding, doors, soffits, and rakes
100	rough-sawn 1x2x8-ft. siding and doors
3	rough-sawn 1x8x8-ft. for hinge side of doors
1	louvered gable vent
12	8-ft. agricultural metal roofing panels
6 lbs.	16d common nails
3 lbs.	8d common nails
6 lbs.	6d galvanized ring shank nails for siding
10 lbs.	8d galvanized ring shank nails for siding
3 lbs.	8d spiral nails for floor
6	136-in. metal let-in braces
4	3-in. leaf hinges for window shutters
9	4-in. galvanized strap hinges for doors
3	door handles

Foundation. Six concrete piers, poured into form tubes, support the shed. Make sure the piers extend below the frost line to prevent frost heaving, and bring the tops of the tubes several inches above grade so that they can be cut level with each other. Although concrete piers by themselves are fine, you can add a few inches of gravel in the base of the hole to improve drainage before filling the form with 2,000-psi concrete.

The tops of the piers are tied together with a double 2x6 grade beam made from pressure-treated lumber. After filling each form tube with concrete, run strings to mark the centerlines of the grade beams 1½ inches in from the outside of the building wall.

At each corner where two string lines intersect, embed an anchor bolt in the fresh concrete so that it extends at least 4 inches above the concrete between the two 2x6s of the grade beams. You can add a washer and nut at each location to lock each beam in place.

Framing. Once the grade beam has been built, frame conventional 2x4 walls with studs 24 inches on center. Use a single sill plate and two top plates that overlap at corners. (One option is to build the long walls as two 8-foot walls to avoid using 16-foot-long lumber that may be hard to handle or transport.) The doubled top plate will provide sufficient support above the door and window openings along the front elevation, but the local building department may require headers.

Install at least one horizontal row of blocking to support the siding; stand up the walls; check them for plumb; and temporarily brace the corners with diagonal 2x4s. Because the building is sided with vertical boards with no sheathing, it's a good idea to install let-in bracing at the corners (refer to page 81).

The shed has a steep 12-in-12-slope gable roof. (Refer to the gable framing section of Chapter 5, pages 104 to 108.) Once you have cut the rafters and positioned them along the top plates in line with the studs, install 2x4 collar ties and sheathe the top of the roof with 1x8 rough-sawn boards spaced approximately 12 inches apart.

Roofing & Siding. You can let the sheathing boards run a few inches past the gable-end walls, add supporting blocking, and nail a rough-sawn 1x8 along the rake to create an overhang and cover the tops of the siding boards. Finish the roof with agricultural metal roofing panels. (See Chapter 6, pages 122 to 124.) Cut the panels to length with a metal-cutting blade in a circular saw.

This shed is sided with vertical rough-sawn 1x6 boards and 1x2 battens. Space the boards about ½ inch apart and fasten each board with one vertical column of 6d galvanized ring shank nails. Then install the battens with vertical columns of 8d ring shanks. This will allow the boards to expand and contract with humidity changes.

FOUNDATION VIEW

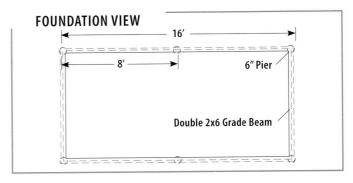

16'

8'

6" Pier

Double 2x6 Grade Beam

PLAN VIEW

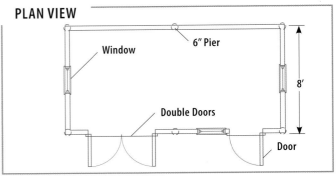

6" Pier

Window

8'

Double Doors

Door

SIDE ELEVATION

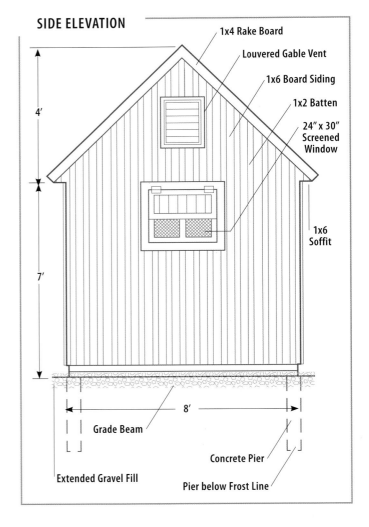

1x4 Rake Board

Louvered Gable Vent

1x6 Board Siding

1x2 Batten

24" x 30" Screened Window

1x6 Soffit

4'

7'

8'

Grade Beam

Concrete Pier

Extended Gravel Fill

Pier below Frost Line

BACK ELEVATION

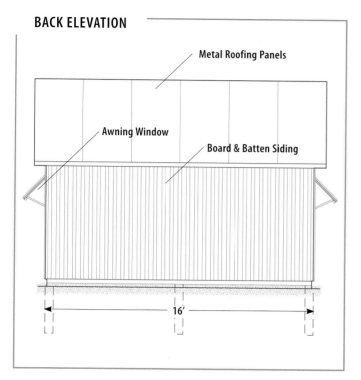

Metal Roofing Panels

Awning Window

Board & Batten Siding

16'

FRONT ELEVATION

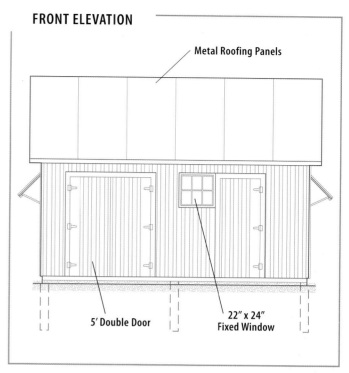

Metal Roofing Panels

5' Double Door

22" x 24"
Fixed Window

FRONT AND SIDE WALL FRAMING

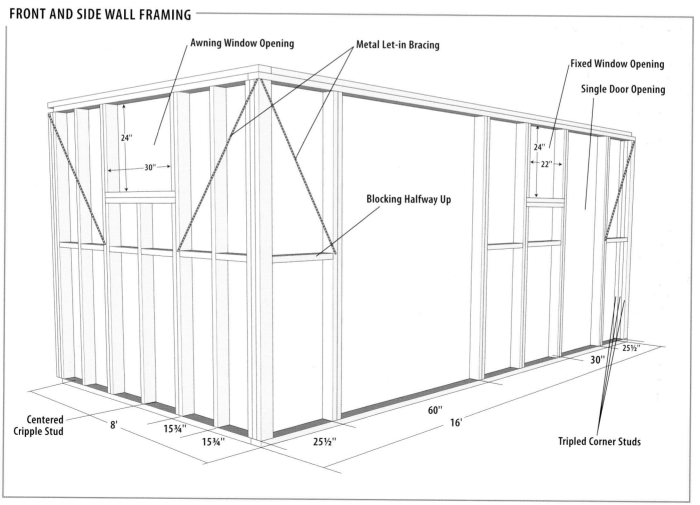

Awning Window Opening

Metal Let-in Bracing

Fixed Window Opening

Single Door Opening

24"

30"

24"

22"

Blocking Halfway Up

25½"

30"

Centered
Cripple Stud

8'

15¾"

15¾"

25½"

60"

16'

Tripled Corner Studs

BACKWALL FRAMING

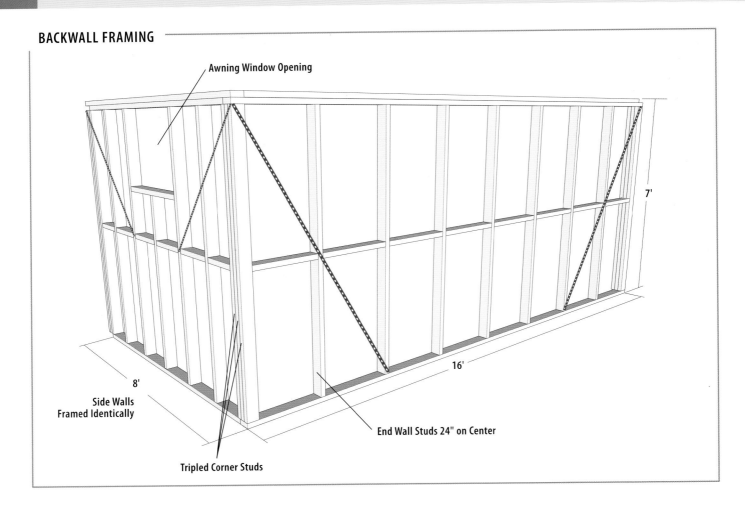

Awning Window Opening

7'

8'

16'

Side Walls
Framed Identically

End Wall Studs 24" on Center

Tripled Corner Studs

GABLE END FRAMING

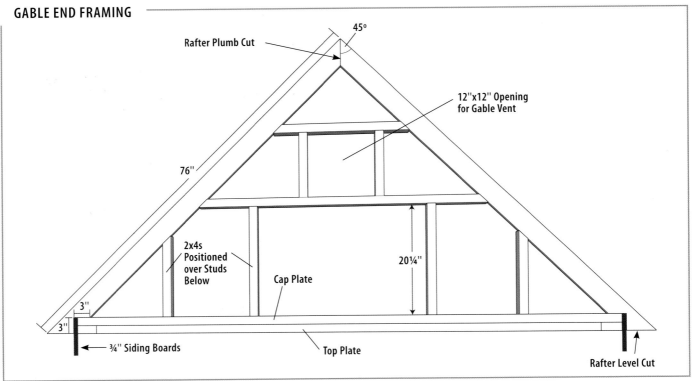

45°

Rafter Plumb Cut

12"x12" Opening
for Gable Vent

76"

2x4s
Positioned
over Studs
Below

Cap Plate

20¼"

3"

3"

¾" Siding Boards

Top Plate

Rafter Level Cut

Windows & Doors. You can add windows and vents anywhere, as long as they fit between the framing. A louver vent under the ridge will help air out the shed during summer months.

The gable-end windows are actually top-hinged shutters backed with screening. Box in the opening with 2x4s and a beveled 2x6 sill, as shown in the detail drawing below. No headers are required in the gable end, where roof loads are distributed to the side-wall top plates.

The double doors are constructed with 1x6 siding laid edge to edge. Use a 1x8 on the hinge side to provide anchorage for strap hinges, as shown in the front elevation drawing opposite. The boards are held together by a 1x6 Z-frame on the interior. Screw the door together using 1½-inch galvanized screws. Finish it off by nailing battens over the edge joints to mimic board-and-batten siding.

FRAMING SECTION

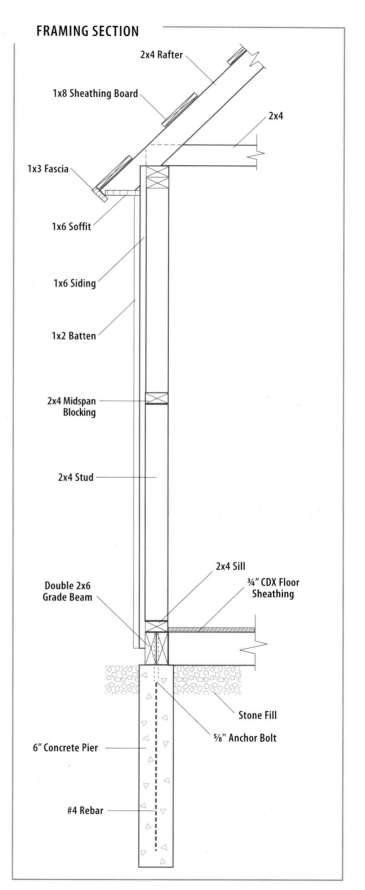

WINDOW DETAIL

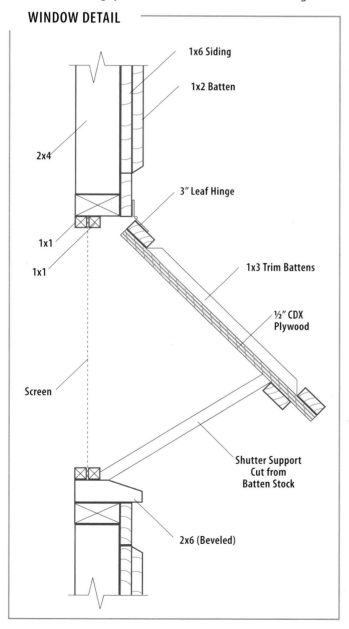

2

SIMPLE FRAMING   BACKYARD STORAGE SHED

THIS SMALL SHED is used for storing yard and garden tools. It is essentially a smaller version of the larger Garden Tool Shed but with two open storage wings that the owner uses for keeping his firewood dry. But it would also make a good place for keeping bikes, play equipment, or a garden tractor out of the weather.

This shed is supported on a post foundation. Four 4x4 pressure-treated posts support the floor of the main shed. Four more posts extend 3 feet above the ground to support the storage wing roofs and floors. (See Plan View, below.) The four posts for the main shed structure are tied together with pressure-treated 2x6s that

PLAN VIEW

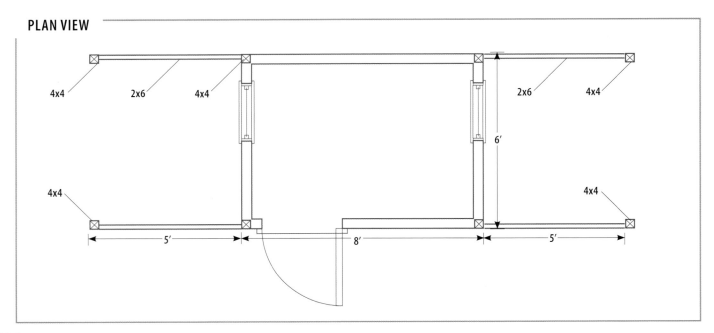

4x4   2x6   4x4   2x6   4x4

6'

4x4   4x4

5'   8'   5'

MATERIALS

6	4x4 x8-ft. pressure-treated for posts
14	2x6 x8-ft. pressure-treated for shed joists
4	2x6x10-ft. pressure-treated for wing joists
4	2x6x12-ft. pressure-treated for floor ledgers and header joists
2	1x6x12-ft. for wing roof ledgers
24	2x4x8-ft. for plates, long studs, rafter ties, blocking
12	2x4x10-ft. for short studs, rafters, blocking, gable cripples
3	¾-in. x 4-ft. x 8-ft. panels CDX plywood for floors
4	½-in. x 4-ft. x 8-in. CDX plywood for roofs
50	1x8x8-ft. shiplap
1	¼-in. 4-ft. x 8' exterior grade plywood for door
3	1x2x8-ft. for door trim
1	8-ft.-long aluminum flashing for wing roofs
8	10-ft.-long aluminum drip edge
1	roll roofing felt
1 lbs.	8d common nails
3 lbs.	12d common nails
2 lbs.	1-inch roofing nails
4	bundles (1 ⅓ squares) asphalt shingles
3	8-in. strap hinges
1	door handle
1 lbs.	8d common nails
3 lbs.	12d common nails
2 lbs.	1-inch roofing nails
1 box	⅜-in. staples for roofing felt

BACK ELEVATION

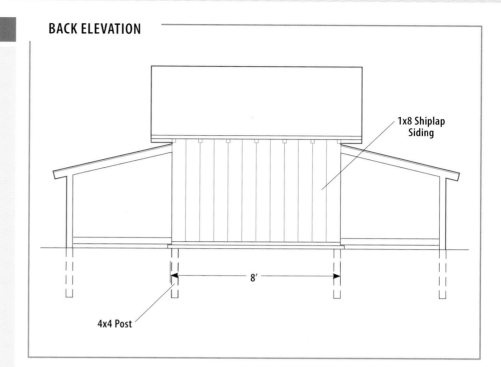

FRONT ELEVATION

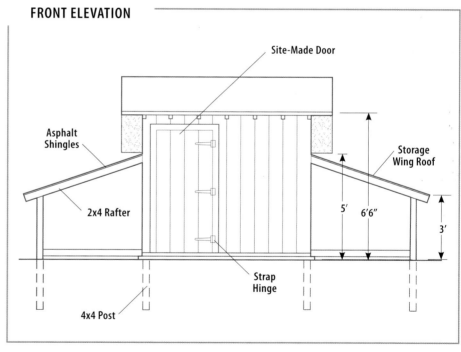

box in the tops of the posts, as shown in the foundation perspective drawing, page 196. Because the 2x6s lap over the face of the posts, the posts must be aligned 1½ inches inside the outside walls. It's important that all the posts extend below the frost line for your area so that heaving ground will not displace the main shed from the storage wings.

Framing. When using a simple post-and-beam foundation, the easiest way to install floor framing is by nailing 2x6 joists running the short dimension of the building to the grade beams. The grade beams function as the rim joists and headers. Attach the joists to the grade beams with joist hangers. Before framing the floor, lay down some gravel if necessary to help drainage. Frame the walls with 2x4s spaced 24 inches on center, and install horizontal blocking as a nailer for the siding. Because interlocking shiplap siding is used, no let-in bracing is needed even though there are no sheathing panels. Stand the walls with the outsides flush with the 2x6 ties on the post

LEFT SIDE ELEVATION

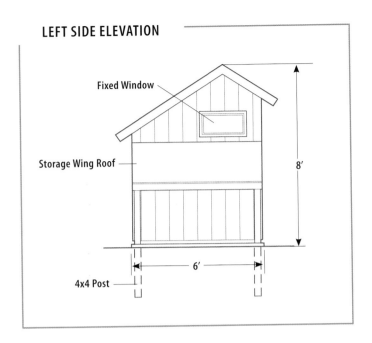

Fixed Window

Storage Wing Roof

8'

6'

4x4 Post

RIGHT SIDE ELEVATION

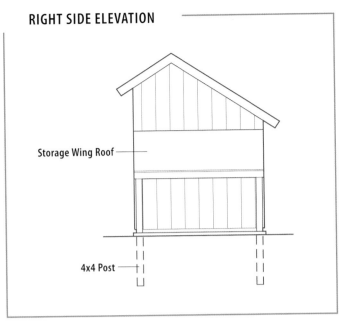

Storage Wing Roof

4x4 Post

FOUNDATION/ FLOOR PERSPECTIVE

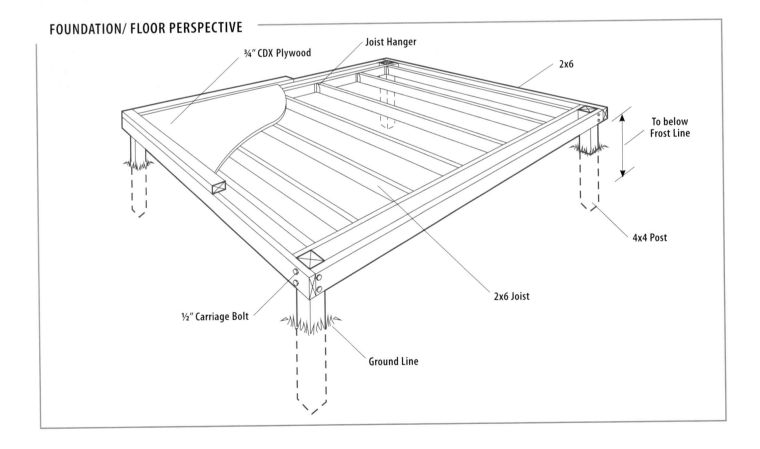

¾" CDX Plywood

Joist Hanger

2x6

To below Frost Line

4x4 Post

2x6 Joist

½" Carriage Bolt

Ground Line

FRAMING SECTION

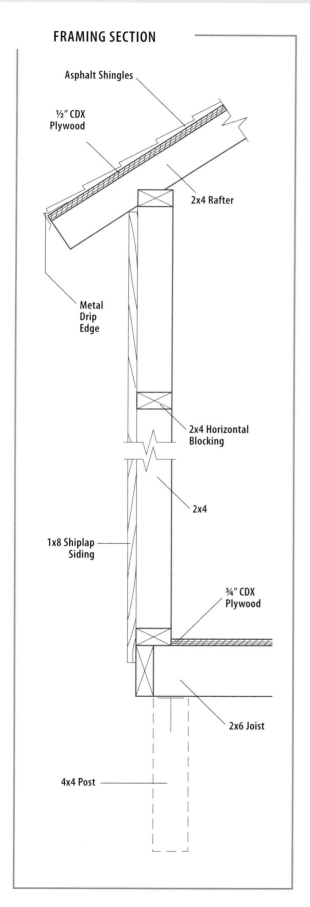

Asphalt Shingles

½" CDX Plywood

2x4 Rafter

Metal Drip Edge

2x4 Horizontal Blocking

2x4

1x8 Shiplap Siding

¾" CDX Plywood

2x6 Joist

4x4 Post

foundation. Sheathe the floor with ¾-inch plywood and the roofs with ½-inch CDX plywood.

The storage wing floor joists are supported by a ledger against the shed and a header joist between the posts. The end joists are nailed to the inside of the posts and connected to the ledger with inside corner brackets. Joist hangers connect inside joists to ledger and header joist with joist hangers.

All shed short and long rafters have an 8/12 pitch (see Roof Framing, page 100). To lay out the storage wing rafters, simply set the a 2x4 against the top plate and rafter ledger and scribe the bird's mouth and flush cuts shown in the drawing Storage Wing Framing on page 199.

Roofing and Siding. This shed was sided with 1x8 vertical shiplap siding. The eaves were left open. Use flashing where the wing roofs meet the siding and run metal drip edge on the roof edges. Staple down roofing felt, and cover it with asphalt roofing shingles.

Window and Door. It's useful to have a little natural light in any small shed to make it easy to find things during the day. This shed was built with one fixed-pane window placed in the gable end above the roof line of one storage wing. You can frame out the opening and mount a fixed-frame window on hinges to provide extra ventilation.

The door has two layers—a sheet of ¼-inch exterior-grade plywood faced with siding boards—and is framed with 1x2s. Bond the two layers with panel adhesive and ¾-inch-long galvanized screws, placed 6 inches on center along the door edges and 12 inches in the field.

SHED FRAMING

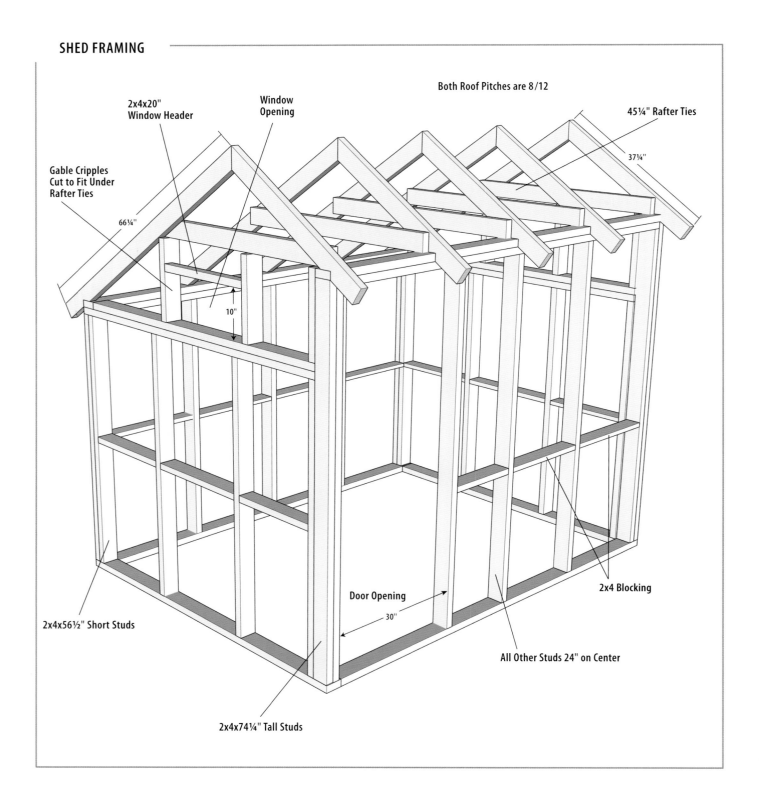

2x4x20" Window Header

Window Opening

Both Roof Pitches are 8/12

45¼" Rafter Ties

37¼"

Gable Cripples Cut to Fit Under Rafter Ties

66¼"

10"

2x4 Blocking

2x4x56½" Short Studs

Door Opening

30"

All Other Studs 24" on Center

2x4x74¼" Tall Studs

STORAGE WING FRAMING

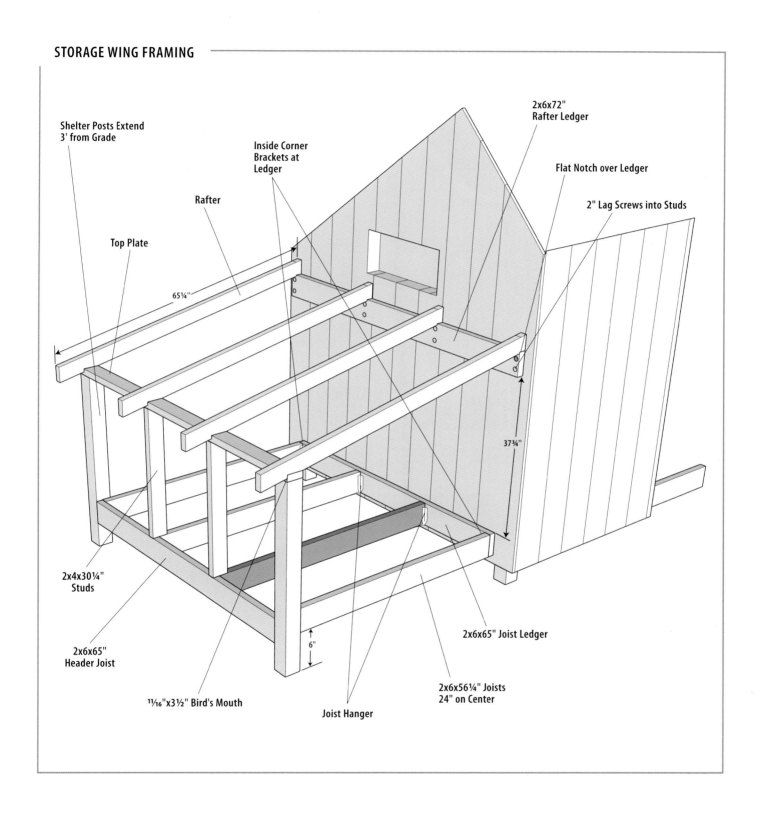

Shelter Posts Extend
3' from Grade

Inside Corner
Brackets at
Ledger

2x6x72"
Rafter Ledger

Rafter

Flat Notch over Ledger

Top Plate

2" Lag Screws into Studs

65¼"

37¾"

2x4x30¼"
Studs

6"

2x6x65" Joist Ledger

2x6x65"
Header Joist

2x6x56¼" Joists
24" on Center

¹¹⁄₁₆"x3½" Bird's Mouth

Joist Hanger

3

SIMPLE FRAMING　　GAMBREL SHED

THIS RUGGED STORAGE SHED serves as a garage for a small tractor and provides ample storage for supplies in the upper loft. You could build this shed with common rafters, but the gambrel design offers greater storage area below the roof than a gable roof does. You can site build the trusses for the gambrel or you can order factory-built trusses.

Slab Foundation. This shed was built in a location that is subject to little frost heave, so it has a monolithic foundation as described in "Trenches" on page 67. Because the shed is small, the footing portion of concrete is only 8 inches wide and 3 feet deep, while the slab area is 4 inches thick. If your area is subject to frost heave, build a wall foundation as described on page 67.

MATERIALS

1	13-ft. x 15-ft. 6-mil polyethylene for foundation	5	1x2 x8 for door trim
54 ft.	#4 rebar for footing	1	roll roofing felt
68 sq. ft.	6x6-in. ¹⁰⁄₁₀ welded-wire mesh	2	squares asphalt shingles
94	chairs with tie wires for rebar and mesh	7	10-ft. pieces drip edge
5 cu. yds.	3,000 psi concrete for monolithic pours	12-ft.	Z-flashing
2	2x4 x 12-ft. pressure-treated sills	28 ft.	aluminum soffit
2	2x4 x 14-ft. pressure-treated sills	28 ft.	f-channel for soffit
74	2x4 x 8-ft. studs, jacks, window frame, rake blocking	10 lbs.	16d common nails
26	2x4 x 10-ft. truss rafters and loft header	1 lbs.	8d common nails
24	2x4 x 12-ft. plates, truss rafters, collar ties	3 lbs.	8d galvanized button head nails for siding
6	2x4 x 14-ft. plates	2 lbs.	1 1 ½-in. deck screws for loft floor and gussets
6	¾-in. x 4-ft. x8-ft. CDX plywood loft floor sheathing, gussets	4 ½ lbs.	1 ½-in. roofing nails
10	⅝-in. x 4-ft. x8-ft. CDX plywood roof sheathing	1 box	⅜-in. staples for roofing felt
18	¾-in. T-1-11 siding	10	anchor bolts
4	1x6 x10 ft. for rake boards	10	4-in. strap hinges
6	1x4x8 ft. for soffit fascia and corner boards	1	locking latch for bottom door
		1	latch bolt for inside of latch door
		1	door handle for bottom door

After excavating for the footings, spread gravel below the slab area, and cover with 6-mil polyethylene before laying down 6 x 6-inch 10/10 welded-wire mesh. Make sure this mesh is supported on chairs so that it rests in the lower third of the slab. Place two lengths of #4 rebar, supported on chairs, at the bottom of the footing trench. For both rebar and mesh, space the chairs about 2 feet apart. Use 2x10 form boards, staked into the ground, to define the perimeter of the slab. Check to be sure that the form boards are square by measuring equal diagonals before pouring concrete. Pour the slab with 3,000-psi concrete specified for monolithic pours. Set anchor bolts in the midspan of the walls (and about 10 inches from each corner and to either side of the door opening) along the perimeter to receive a 2x4 pressure-treated sill plate.

Trusses. Build (or order) your trusses before framing the walls. The easiest way to lay out these trusses is to sweep the slab clean, and snap out a full-scale drawing of the truss on the slab as shown in the drawing Typical Gambrel Truss Design using a chalk-line box with nonpermanent blue chalk. Start by snapping a base line (12 feet, 6 inches) across the long dimension of the slab, about 18 inches in from one end so that you won't run into the anchor bolts that are sticking out of the concrete.

Find the center of your baseline (6 feet, 3 inches from each end in this case), and snap a line perpendicular to the baseline. Measure and mark a point 6 feet above the baseline to define the peak. Then snap diagonals running from the peak to each end of the baseline, as if you were defining the bottom edge of two gable rafters. Next, snap a line that runs about 3½ feet above and parallel with the baseline, and snap two lines running from the midpoint of the baseline through the intersections with the diagonals (gable lines).

There are no hard-and-fast rules governing the offset of the two gambrel roof planes. This roof has a 6-inch offset. This provides enough room for the loft doors. Once the offset points are established, snap the bottom edges of the gambrel lines, running the chalk line from the peak to the offset point and from the offset

PLAN VIEW

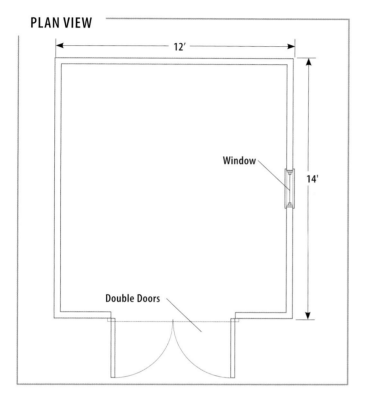

TYPICAL GAMBREL TRUSS DESIGN

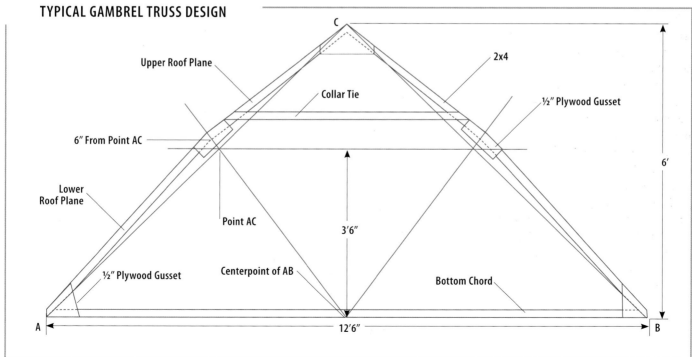

point to the end of the baseline on both sides. Lay down 2x4s along these gambrel lines, and mark the top edges to complete the full-scale plan of the truss.

Use this full-scale plan as a pattern to cut the 2x4 pieces of the trusses. Lay 2x4s on your full-scale drawing to mark the cut angles at the peak and at each offset point. Extend the lower roof plane by 6 inches to create the soffit shown in the drawing Framing Section.

Once you have the pieces for the upper and lower roof planes, you need a bottom chord, cut from one long, straight 2x4. Mark and cut the angle on each end of this 2x4 to match the angle of the lower roof plane members. You'll also need to cut a collar tie.

Cut enough pieces to build 12 trusses—one at each end and 10 trusses in between, spaced 16 inches on center. (One bay will be less than 16 inches.) Cut gussets from ¾-inch plywood as shown in the drawing Gusset Layouts and use them with 1 ½-inch deck screws and yellow glue to join the truss pieces. Use gussets on both sides of each truss except for the outer trusses, which will have gussets only on the inside.

Framing & Siding. Now you can lay out, cut, and bolt down the pressure-treated sill plates. Lay out the walls with 2x4 studs 16 inches on center; sheathe the walls with T1-11 siding; and attach them to the sill plate. Frame two 34½-inch-wide walls to stand on each side of the large door opening. The sill plates below these narrow walls will extend an additional 1½ inches beyond the wall to support jack studs in the door opening. The jack studs end 5 ½ inches below the top of the top plates. These jacks support a double header consisting of a 2x6 directly below the bottom chord of the first truss and a 2x8 nailed to 2x6 and the inside of the bottom chord (see the drawing Door Frame Detail).

This shed had one 30-inch-wide by 36-inch tall window in one side. After you have framed and erected the walls and trusses, install the plywood floor over the bottom chords. Frame the opening for the loft door, using a double 2x4 header. Cut the ends of the 2x4s at an angle to fit under the truss and under the collar tie. Double the

FRONT ELEVATION

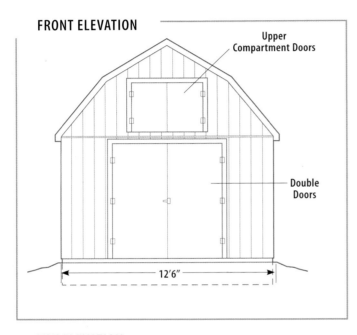

Upper Compartment Doors

Double Doors

12'6"

SIDE ELEVATION

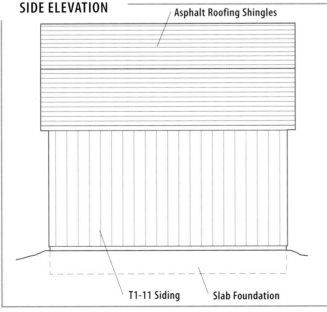

Asphalt Roofing Shingles

T1-11 Siding   Slab Foundation

FRAMING SECTION

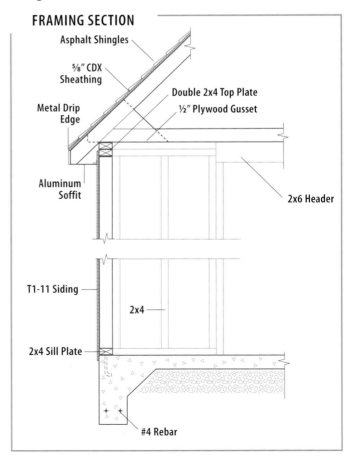

Asphalt Shingles

⅝" CDX Sheathing

Metal Drip Edge

Double 2x4 Top Plate

½" Plywood Gusset

Aluminum Soffit

2x6 Header

T1-11 Siding

2x4

2x4 Sill Plate

#4 Rebar

FRAMING PERSPECTIVE

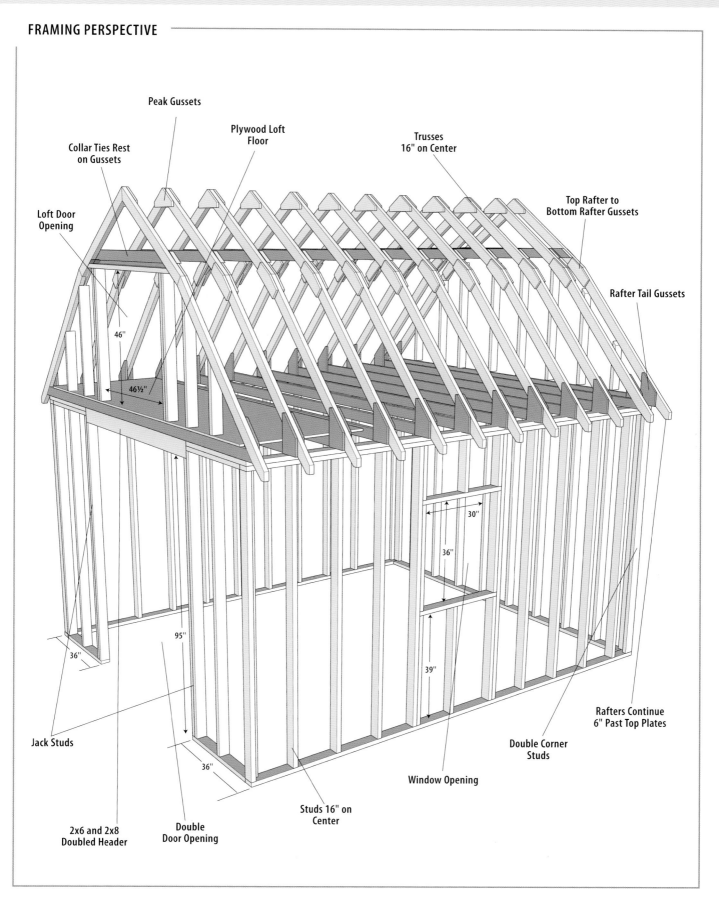

Peak Gussets

Collar Ties Rest on Gussets

Plywood Loft Floor

Trusses 16" on Center

Loft Door Opening

Top Rafter to Bottom Rafter Gussets

Rafter Tail Gussets

46"

46½"

30"

36"

39"

95"

36"

36"

Jack Studs

Rafters Continue 6" Past Top Plates

Double Corner Studs

Window Opening

2x6 and 2x8 Doubled Header

Double Door Opening

Studs 16" on Center

studs at the opening and then add two shorter studs to each side as shown in the drawing Framing Perspective. At the opposite end truss fill in studs 16 inches on center to fit under the rafter chords. Before applying the T1-11 siding above the top plates on each end, run a length of Z-flashing (available at building-supply centers) along the top edge of the plywood on the walls.

Exterior Trim & Roofing. Install a 1x4 fascia along the truss ends, and nail F-channel to the siding to hold the aluminum soffit. Also install vertical 1x4s at the gable sides of each corner. Over the sheathed end trusses, nail 2x4 blocking in line with the upper and lower chords of the end trusses. Over this blocking, install 1x6 rake boards. Install aluminum vented soffit material below the truss ends. You can also use plywood sheeting cut for plug vents or strip vents.

Sheathe the roof, and install metal drip edge on all sides. Now tack down your roofing felt, and complete with asphalt shingles.

Doors. All the doors on this gambrel shed have been built from T1-11 siding laminated to ½-inch exterior-grade plywood and trimmed with prepainted 1x2 pine.

GUSSET LAYOUTS

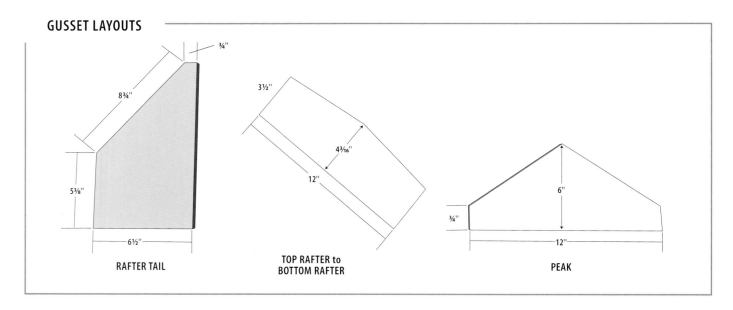

RAFTER TAIL

TOP RAFTER to
BOTTOM RAFTER

PEAK

DOOR FRAME DETAIL

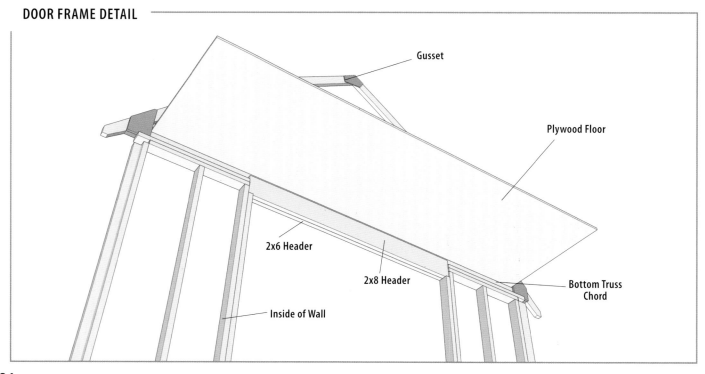

Gusset

Plywood Floor

2x6 Header

2x8 Header

Bottom Truss
Chord

Inside of Wall

4

STANDARD FRAMING   ALL-PURPOSE GARAGE

THIS LARGE GARAGE offers ample work area for a small mechanic's shop, for storing tools, or parking a small tractor. Its structural integrity depends on metal cross-bracing in the walls, a large built-up beam for the garage-door header, and factory-made W roof trusses with a 6 in 12 slope.

Slab Foundation. This building needs a full-size structural slab with a minimum 12-inch-wide footing around its perimeter, as described in Chapter 3, pages 60 to 64. After excavating for the footings, spread gravel below the slab area, and cover it with 6-mil polyethylene before laying down 6 x 6-inch 10/10 welded-wire mesh. Make sure this mesh is supported on chairs so that it will sit in the middle of the 4-inch slab section. Place two lengths of #4 rebar, supported on

MATERIALS

	3,000-psi concrete specified for monolithic pours
3	2x4 x 8-ft. pressure-treated sill plates
2	2x4 x 10-ft. pressure-treated sill plates
2	2x4 x 12-ft. pressure-treated sill plates
86	2x4 x1 0-ft. rough-sawn full dimension lumber for plates, studs, jacks, blocking
4	2x4 x 12-ft. rough-sawn full dimension lumber for plates
2	2x10 x 16-ft. header
2	2x4 x 10-ft. for gable end blocks
21	2x3 x 10-ft. for door construction
154	1x8 x 10-ft. rough sawn for siding and eaves and rake trim
158	1x2 x 10-ft. for battens
2	½-in. x 4-ft. x 8-ft. CDX plywood wall bracing

10	6/12 W roof trusses
20	⅝-in. x 4-ft. x8-ft. CDX plywood roof sheathing
12	anchor bolts
9	metal wall braces
8	10-ft. drip aluminum drip edge
285 sq. ft.	metal roofing with fasteners
8 lbs.	16d common nails
3 lbs.	8d common nails
25 lbs.	8d galvanized common nails for siding and trim
11	12-in. strap hinges
1	door handle
1	locking handle for entry door
1	latch bolt for interior of garage doors

PLAN VIEW

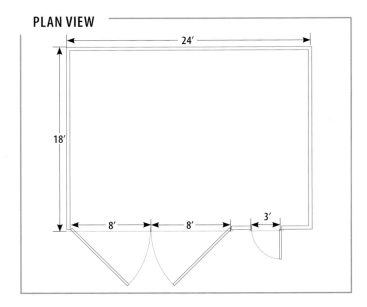

FRAMING SECTION

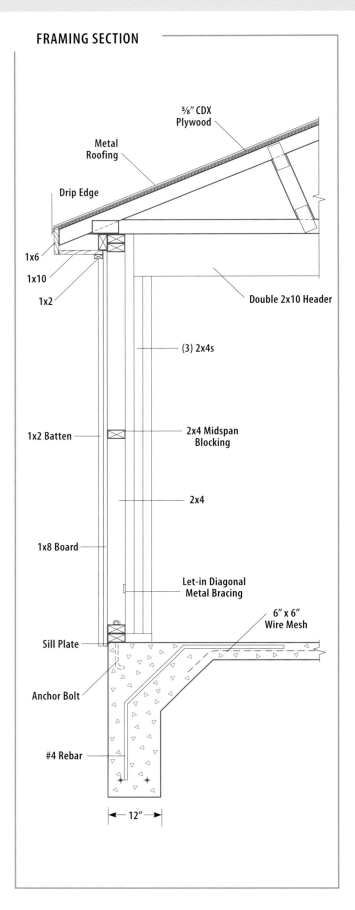

chairs, at the bottom of the footing trench. Use 2x10 form boards, staked into the ground, to define the perimeter of the slab. Measure diagonals to check that the form boards are square before pouring concrete. Pour the slab using fortified 3,000-psi concrete specified for monolithic pours. Set anchor bolts every 6 feet (and about 10 inches from each corner, and to either side of the door openings) around the perimeter to receive a 2x4 pressure-treated sill plate.

Wall Framing. This shed was framed using full-dimension rough-sawn 2x4s spaced 16 inches on center, but common dimensional 2x4s will work just as well. Install midspan blocking and let-in diagonal bracing. Run the metal bracing from near the top plate at each corner at about a 45-degree angle down to the sill plate of the walls.

Garage Door Framing. Build a garage door header using two 16-foot-long 2x10s, nailed every 12 to 16 inches with a row of four 16d common nails. This heavy beam should be supported by double jack studs on each end, as shown in the drawing Framing Section.

Because of the large opening, the front wall can't be braced with metal strapping. But this wall still requires bracing to prevent racking, especially around the two garage doors. Do this by sheathing the inside face of the wall with ½-inch CDX plywood. The strength of the plywood bracing will come from its nailing. Nail it off every 4 inches along the edges and 6 inches in the fields with 8d common nails.

FRAMING PERSPECTIVE

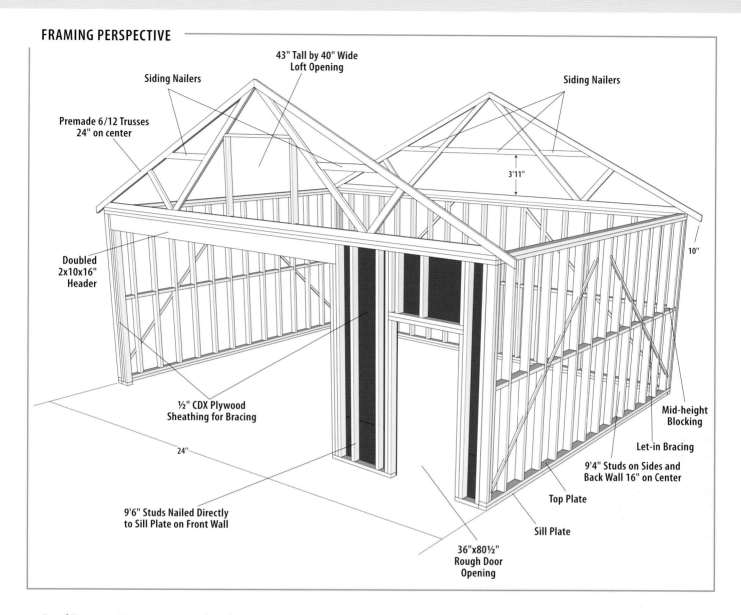

43" Tall by 40" Wide
Loft Opening

Siding Nailers

Siding Nailers

Premade 6/12 Trusses
24" on center

3'11"

Doubled
2x10x16"
Header

10"

½" CDX Plywood
Sheathing for Bracing

24"

Mid-height
Blocking

Let-in Bracing

9'4" Studs on Sides and
Back Wall 16" on Center

Top Plate

9'6" Studs Nailed Directly
to Sill Plate on Front Wall

Sill Plate

36"x80½"
Rough Door
Opening

Roof Trusses. Trusses were used on this project to create a clear span over the floor without interruption from supporting walls or posts. Trusses should be ordered before you begin construction, to allow time for them to be made and delivered to the site. A total of 10 trusses were ordered and spaced 24 inches on center. The trusses on this garage were ordered with a 24-foot-long bottom chord and 10-inch plumb cut overhang. In this case, the open webs of the truss were going to be used to store lumber (with access through the loft door), and the truss manufacturer had to be aware of these loading conditions. Follow the guidelines for erecting trusses found in Chapter 5, pages 110 to 111. Another option is to pay for delivery and installation, which often is cost effective if you have the building prepared for trusses.

To provide adequate nailing for the siding, add a vertical row of 2x4 nailers between the gable-end truss chords. Locate the nailers halfway between the peak and the bottom truss chord as shown in

the drawing Framing Perspective. At the front, frame the loft door opening instead of the middle nailer used on the back wall. Sheathe the roof with ⅝-inch CDX plywood. Hang the sheathing about 6 inches over the gable-end rakes, and support this overhang with short 2x4 blocks nailed to the end trusses as shown in the drawing Rake and Eaves Framing Detail.

Siding & Roofing. Install vertical 1x8 rough-sawn board siding covered by 1x2 battens. Space the boards about 1/2 inch apart to allow for seasonal movement. Battens should overlap the seams to avoid any gaps when the large boards lose moisture and shrink. Because this is an unheated garage with open-wall framing, a vented roof is not necessary. You can box the eaves with rough-sawn one-by material, and run this same material up the rakes, nailed to the support blocks. Run metal drip edge around the entire perimeter of the roof, and install metal roofing panels.

BRACING DETAIL

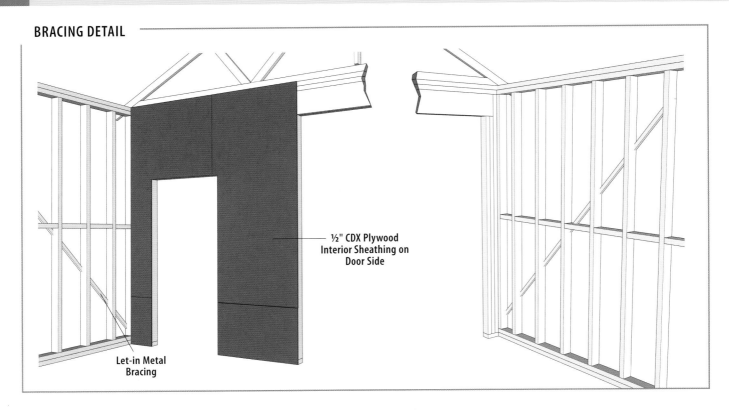

½" CDX Plywood
Interior Sheathing on
Door Side

Let-in Metal
Bracing

Doors. These large, swinging garage doors have been framed like small wall sections, using dimensional 2x3s and metal bracing. Be sure to run the bracing from the top hinge-side corners on a diagonal down to the corners where one door meets the other. The exteriors of all the doors have been sheathed with board-and-batten material, and box-trimmed with batten stock. You will need to notch the batten trim to allow long strap hinges to pass underneath. For large doors, you will need at least four very large strap hinges per side. As an alternative, you may prefer to buy and install an over-head style garage door. It may take some looking and possibly special ordering to get a 16-foot-wide overhead door, but it may still prove to be easier than building and hanging these large barn doors yourself. The entry door is constructed in a similar fashion to the garage doors. Alternately, you could install a conventional entry door in this standard-sized opening.

RAKE AND EAVES FRAMING

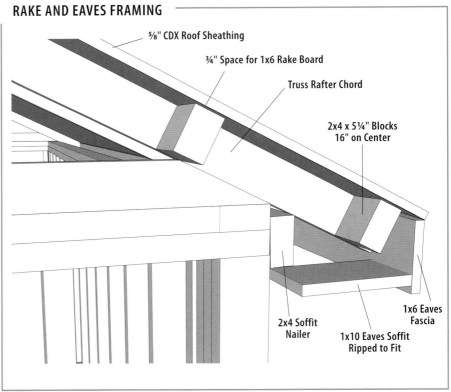

⅝" CDX Roof Sheathing

¾" Space for 1x6 Rake Board

Truss Rafter Chord

2x4 x 5¼" Blocks
16" on Center

2x4 Soffit
Nailer

1x10 Eaves Soffit
Ripped to Fit

1x6 Eaves
Fascia

FRONT ELEVATION

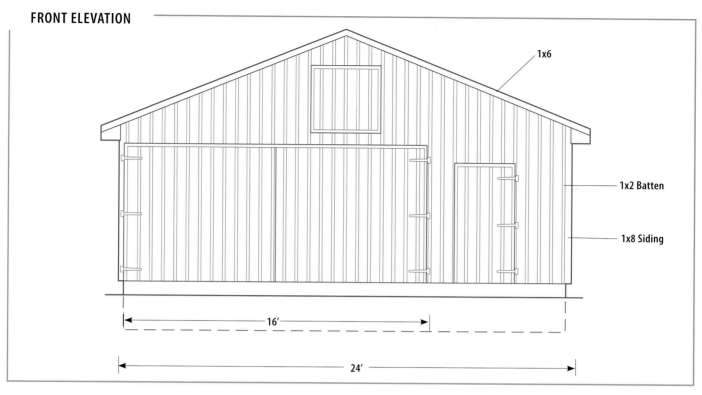

1x6

1x2 Batten

1x8 Siding

16'

24'

SIDE ELEVATION

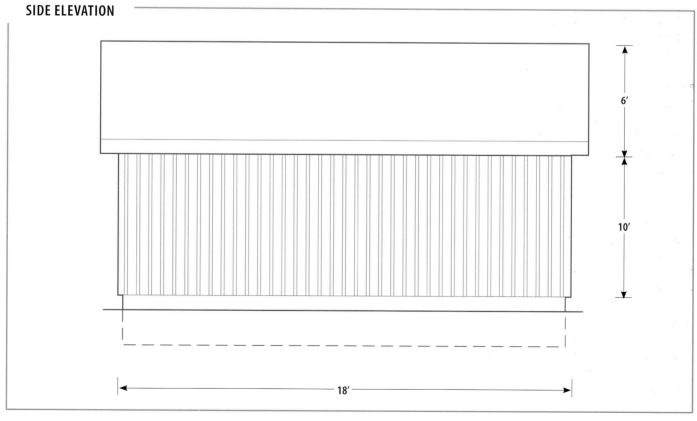

6'

10'

18'

5

HYBRID FRAMING   LIVESTOCK BARN

BUILT FOR A COMMERCIAL SHEEP FARMER, this livestock barn provides space for animals as well as storage for farm implements. The walls are constructed of 4x4s, similar to a pole barn. However, the poles don't extend into the ground. Instead the barn has a conventionally framed floor consisting of joists supported by piers and covered with planks. There are no wall studs, except as needed for framing around doors and windows. Horizontal nailers attached to the 4x4s provide attachment for the vertical board siding. Diagonal braces at the corners are nailed inside the horizontal nailers. These braces, along with the vertical siding boards, keep the building square.

MATERIALS

MAIN BARN

1.3 cu. yds.	concrete (for 4-ft.-deep holes)
25	8-in. for tubes
46	2x4 x 8' for studs, nailers, collar ties, and studs
10	2x4 x 10' for nailers, cap plates, headers
68	2x4 x 12' for diagonal braces and purlins
8	2x4 x 14' for nailers
14	2x6 x 8, for ridge beam
2	2x6 x 10 for gable end beams and nailers
88	2x6 x 12' for joists and beams
8	2x6 x 14' for nailers and rafters
10	2x8 x 8' for ridge beam and headers
218	1x8x10' rough-sawn siding
8	1x10' rough-sawn for rafter blocking
4	1x6x 14' fascia
8	1x4x8' window and door casing
2	1x4x 10' large door header casing
16	4x4 x 8' posts
7	4x4 x 14' posts
25	12" J-bolts
76	2x6 joist hangers
16 lbs.	16d nails
6 lbs.	8d nails

10 lbs.	8d galvanized nails for siding
3 lbs.	6d galvanized button-head nails for trim
16	2 ½" all-purpose screws for diagonal braces
1040 sq. ft.	metal agricultural roofing panels plus nails as specified by manufacturer

OPTIONAL ADDITION

5	4x4x8' posts
24	2x4x10' for purlins
8	2x4x12' for nailers
19	2x6x10' for rafters
12	2x6x12' for nailers and diagonal brackets
2	2x8x10' for beam
2	2x8x12' for beam
8	1x4x8' window and door casing
2	1x4x10' large door header casing
14	1x8' rough-sawn for siding
86	1x8x10' rough-sawn for siding
8	1x10' rough-sawn for rafter blocking
2 lbs.	8d nails
4 lbs.	8d galvanized nails for siding
2 lbs.	6d galvanized button-head nails for trim
16	2 ½" all-purpose screws for diagonal braces
400 sq.ft.	metal agricultural roofing panels plus nails as specified by manufacturer

PLAN VIEW

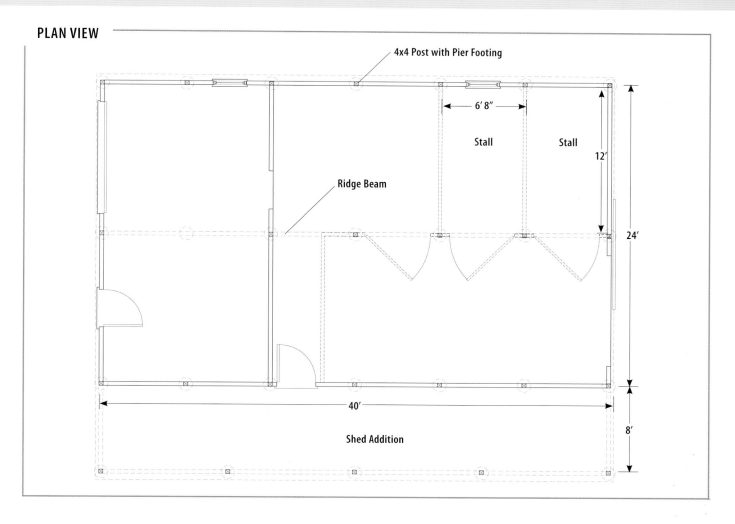

4x4 Post with Pier Footing

6' 8"

Stall   Stall

12'

Ridge Beam

24'

40'

8'

Shed Addition

Also, there are no ceiling joists, which in a conventionally framed roof resist the tendency of rafters to push the top of eaves-end wall outward. Instead, this barn employs a structural ridge beam that shares the load of the rafters. This beam, in addition to collar ties, eliminates the outward thrust so that the rafters bear directly down on the walls.

The barn shown in the photo has an optional shed addition that's also supported by 4x4 posts but has no floor. Instead, the posts are attached directly to piers.

Foundation. The foundation for the main barn consists of 25 piers spaced 6 feet 8 inches on center apart along the 40-foot length of the building and 6 feet apart along the width. This includes a row of 8-inch diameter piers along the center of the barn's length to support 4x4 posts that in turn support the structural ridge beam. If you choose to add the addition, you'll need five more piers spaced 10 feet apart as shown in the Plan View. Form the piers by digging holes with a power auger and inserting 8-inch diameter form tubes. Make sure the piers extend below your local frost line to prevent frost heaving and add a few inches of gravel in each pier for drainage. Extend the tops of the forms above grade as necessary to set them all level with each other. A laser level is the easiest way to do this. In most cases, you simply pour concrete into the tubes once they are braced or backfilled. Before pouring concrete, run string lines to mark the center of each pier. After filling each form, embed a J-bolt at the intersection of the string lines allowing 5 inches of the bolt to protrude from the concrete.

MAIN BARN FRAMING PERSPECTIVE—ADDITION SIDE

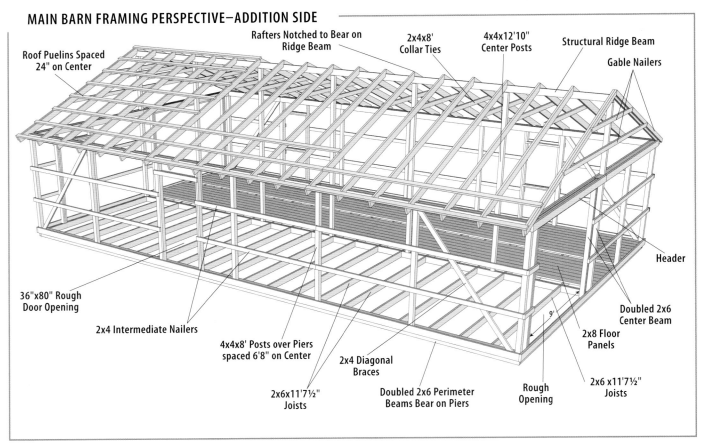

Roof Puelins Spaced 24" on Center

Rafters Notched to Bear on Ridge Beam

2x4x8' Collar Ties

4x4x12'10" Center Posts

Structural Ridge Beam

Gable Nailers

Header

Doubled 2x6 Center Beam

36"x80" Rough Door Opening

2x4 Intermediate Nailers

4x4x8' Posts over Piers spaced 6'8" on Center

2x4 Diagonal Braces

2x6x11'7½" Joists

Doubled 2x6 Perimeter Beams Bear on Piers

Rough Opening

2x8 Floor Panels

2x6 x11'7½" Joists

9'

MAIN BARN FRAMING PERSPECTIVE—WINDOW SIDE

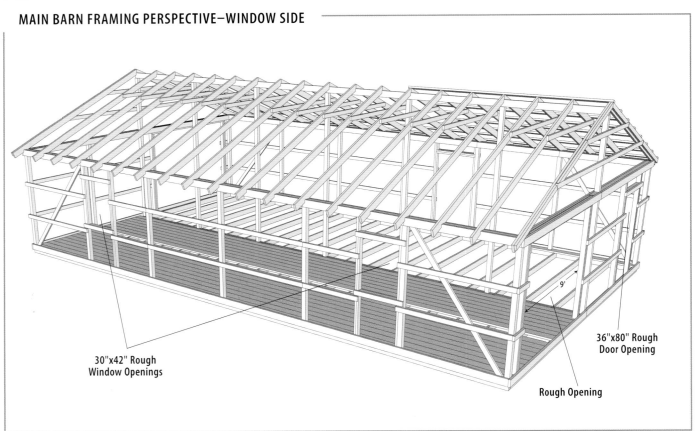

30"x42" Rough Window Openings

36"x80" Rough Door Opening

Rough Opening

9'

Floor framing. Three rows of beams consisting of doubled 2x6s span between piers along the length of the barn. The J-bolts will be sandwiched between the 2x6s, so you'll need to notch the beams slightly at bolt locations. Stagger butt joints between 2x6s at least 1 foot. To complete the floor framing, use joist hangers to install 2x6 joists between each outside wall and the center beam.

Wall framing. The lowest horizontal nailers consist of 2x6s. Install them 3 ½ inches up from the bottom of the beams. Next install the perimeter posts, plumbing each one before nailing it through the bottom horizontal nailers. Now install the uppermost 2x6 nailers with their top edges 1 ½ inches above the top of the posts.

This barn has a conventional overhead garage door on one gable end and a sliding gate of the same size on the other end. The rough openings shown here are 9 feet wide—use the rough opening specified for your garage door. The sides of the large door rough openings will be framed with tripled 2x4s. Mark the outside of this framing on the 2x6 uppermost nailer—for the 9-foot rough opening these marks will be 9 foot, 9 inches apart. Install 2x4 cap plates on top of the posts all around the perimeter except between these marks. Nail the cap plates to the top of the posts and through the topmost nailers.

Corner braces. Make angle cuts on the ends of the four 2x4 diagonal corner braces so they will butt into posts just below the top plate and along the beam. Fasten the braces to the inside of all the nailers with 2 ½-inch screws. (They'll bounce around too much if you try to nail them.)

HEADER AND CAP PLATE DETAILS

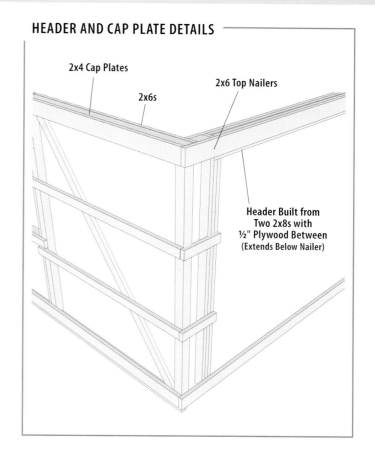

2x4 Cap Plates

2x6s

2x6 Top Nailers

Header Built from
Two 2x8s with
½" Plywood Between
(Extends Below Nailer)

RAFTER LAYOUTS

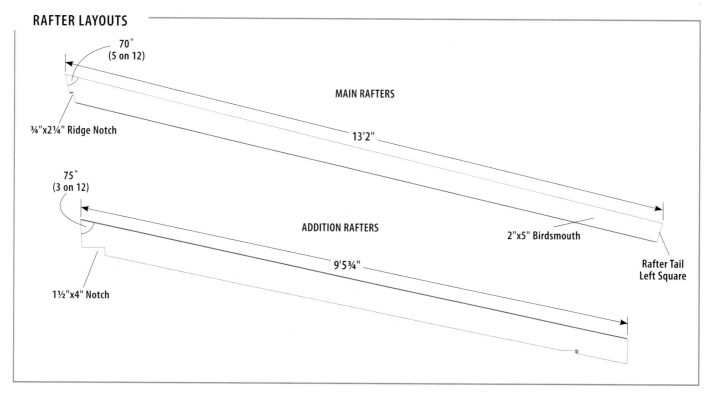

70°
(5 on 12)

MAIN RAFTERS

¾"x2¼" Ridge Notch

13'2"

75°
(3 on 12)

ADDITION RAFTERS

2"x5" Birdsmouth

9'5¾"

Rafter Tail
Left Square

1½"x4" Notch

Door and window framing. For the large door openings, cut the outermost studs to fit between the floor and the top of the uppermost nailer. Install them at the marks you made. A header consisting of doubled 2x8s with ½-inch plywood sandwiched between runs between these two studs. Install the top of this header flush to the top of the uppermost nailer. See the drawing Header and Top Plate Details.

This barn also has two entry doors. The framing for these doors consists of two 2x4 jack studs that support the header. One of these jacks is nailed to the side of a post, the other is nailed to a 2x4 stud cut to fit between the floor and the bottom of the cap plate. No cripple studs are needed over the header. There are two windows on one side of the barn. These are framed in the same way as the entry doors except that you'll add sill plates and instead of jacks, you'll cut pieces of 2x4 to fit between the floor and sills, the sills and the bottom of the header, and the header and cap plate. Now install the inner row of horizontal 2x6s flush to the top of the top plates. To complete the wall framing, install the two intermediate rows of 2x4 nailers. Space them evenly between the top and bottom nailers.

Floor and center post installation. The floor is made of 2x8 planks. Install these across the joists, notching as necessary to fit around perimeter posts. Stop installing about 5 feet from the center beam. Install the 12-foot, 10-inch center posts centered over piers. Plumb them and hold them in place with temporary 2x4 braces nailed to the posts and into the sides of joists.

Roof framing. Install the 2x6 structural ridge beam across the top of the center posts. Cut the rafters as shown in the drawing Rafter Layouts. Note that the rafters don't have plumb cuts on the top and bottom. Rather, the tops of the rafters are notched to fit over the ridge beam and the rafters are left square on the bottom end. Install the rafters in opposing pairs. In general, install the rafters 24 inches on center. However, when a rafter lands at a post, adjust its position so that one side is flush to the post. This will allow you to nail collar ties to the posts as well as opposing rafters. Install each collar tie as you install each pair of rafters. Install 2x4 purlins 24 inches on center across the rafters and then install agricultural panel roofing as described on page 122.

SIDING AND FASCIA DETAILS

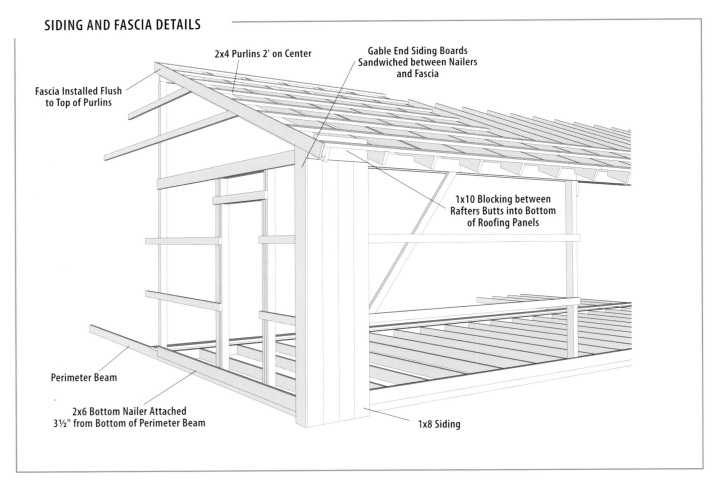

2x4 Purlins 2' on Center

Gable End Siding Boards Sandwiched between Nailers and Fascia

Fascia Installed Flush to Top of Purlins

1x10 Blocking between Rafters Butts into Bottom of Roofing Panels

Perimeter Beam

2x6 Bottom Nailer Attached 3½" from Bottom of Perimeter Beam

1x8 Siding

OPTIONAL ADDITION FRAMING PERSPECTIVE

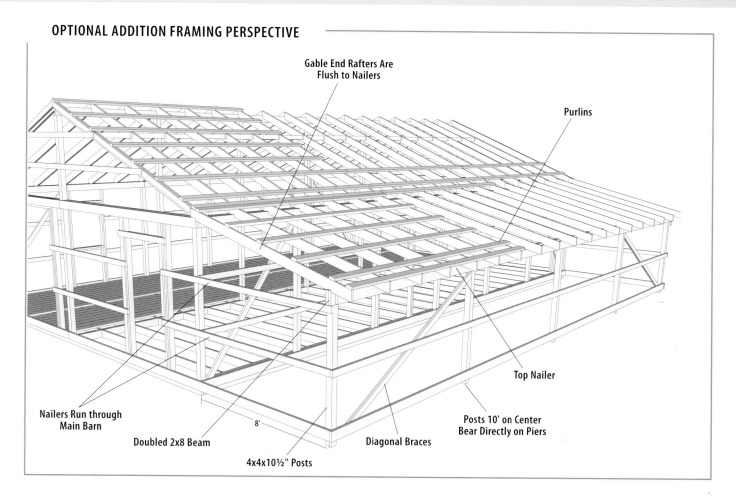

Gable End Rafters Are Flush to Nailers

Purlins

Nailers Run through Main Barn

Doubled 2x8 Beam

8'

4x4x10½" Posts

Diagonal Braces

Top Nailer

Posts 10' on Center Bear Directly on Piers

Siding and trim. Each gable end gets two 2x4 horizontal siding nailers equally spaced between the top plate and the roof peak. Install these nailers, and then install 2x4 nailers running flush to the top of the gable end rafters. The siding consists of rough-sawn 1x8 boards. Install these vertically using two nails into each nailer that the boards cross. At the gable ends, cut the boards off at an angle so they are flush with the top of the rafters. In the barn shown here, siding boards are cut at an angle at the top corners of the large door openings. This is an optional decorative detail. Cut 1x10 blocking to fit between rafters. Butt the blocks against the bottom of the roofing panels and nail them to the top nailer. Install 1x6 fascia boards on the gable ends. Position the top of the boards flush to the top of the purlins.

Windows and doors. The window openings hold single plastic glazing panels held in place with 2x2 stops. The entry doors are vertical board siding supported by a Z-frame as described in Chapter 6, page 133. The large opening on the back elevation has an overhead garage door to keep equipment secure, while the large front opening has a sliding gate, which uses heavy-duty sliding hardware available from agricultural supply centers.

Optional addition. If you'll be adding the optional addition, cut the rafters on the addition side of the main barn so that they end flush to the 2x6 top nailers. Pour five additional piers 10 feet

apart and located to support posts that will be 8 feet on center away from the main barn. Embed post anchors in these piers. Install the posts without cutting them to final height yet. Plumb the posts and support them with temporary braces. Next install a bottom 2x6 nailer and the lowest intermediate 2x4 nailers at the same levels as the main barn nailers. For added stability it's a good idea to make the nailer boards continue from the main barn through the addition as shown in the drawing Optional Addition Framing Perspective.

Now cut the posts off at 5 feet 1 ½ inches from the top of the bottom nailer. Add another 2x4 nailer to the gable ends. Add doubled 2x8 beams atop the posts making them flush to the outside of the posts and the faces of the gable-end nailers, and then add two diagonal 2x4 braces as shown in the drawing.

The drawing Rafter Layouts shows the hypothetical dimensions for the addition rafters. However, your framing is likely to vary a bit from these dimensions, so it's best to hold a rafter in place to scribe the cuts and then use that rafter as a pattern for all the others. Cut and install the 19 rafters nailing them to the main barn top plate and the sides of the main barn rafters as well as the addition beam. Attach 2x6 top nailers to the side of the beams butting them under the rafters. Add siding, fascia blocking, and purlins as you did for the main barn.

FRONT ELEVATION

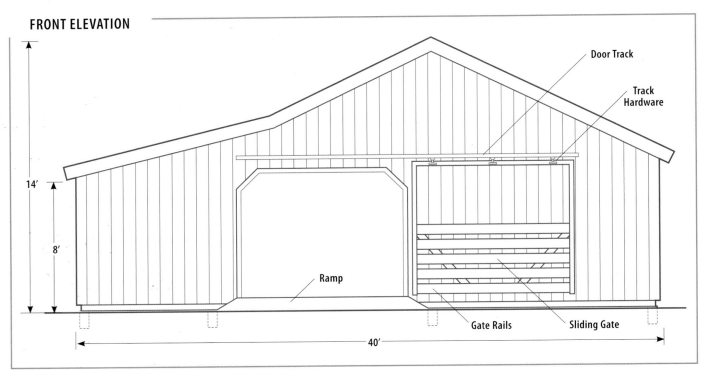

14'

8'

Door Track

Track Hardware

Ramp

Gate Rails

Sliding Gate

40'

BACK ELEVATION

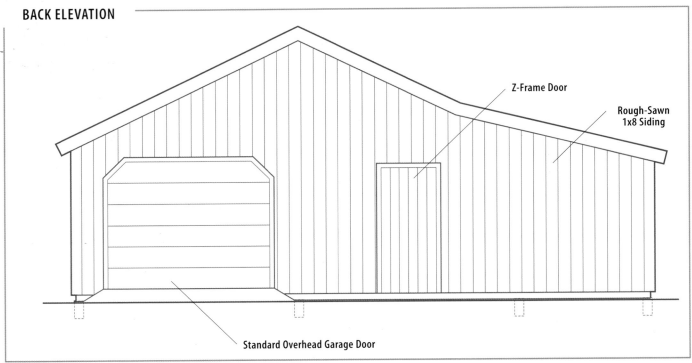

Z-Frame Door

Rough-Sawn 1x8 Siding

Standard Overhead Garage Door

6

STANDARD FRAMING ARTIST'S STUDIO

THIS SIMPLE BUT ELEGANT CERAMICS STUDIO offers good light and ample loft storage for a working artist. It is built much the same as a small house would be and, in fact, could make a charming guesthouse. Insulated walls and a drywall interior make it suitable for use year-round with the addition of a heat source. An optional rear porch extends both work and storage areas in the summer months.

MATERIALS

5 cu. yds.	gravel	4	1x6 x 12' rake fascia
10.5 cu. yds.	concrete	2	1x8 x 8' fascia
5 cu. yds.	gravel	2	1x8 x 10 fascia
300 sq.ft.	concrete reinforcing mesh	5 lbs.	16d common nails
600 ft.	#4 rebar	3 lbs.	8d common nails
14	2x4 x 8' purlins	4 lbs.	8d galvanized common nails for siding
2	2x4 x 10' for soffit framing	342 sq. ft.	metal roofing with fasteners approved by manufacturer
14	2x8 x 10'purlins		
85	2x6 x 8' walls	**OPTIONAL PORCH**	
16	2x6 x 10' platesA, collar ties	4	8" dia. x 4' concrete tube forms
20	2x6 x 12' rafters	6	cubic feet concrete
5	2x8 x 16 joists	4	4x4 x 8' posts
23	¾"x 4' x 8' CDX plywood sheathing	12	2x4 x 8' purlins
2	½" x 4' x 8' AC exterior grade plywood for soffits	9	2x6 x 12' rafters
36	1x6 x 14' siding boards	1	2x6 x 16' ledger
104	1x6 x 8' siding boards	2	2x6 x 16' beams
32	1x6 x 14' battens	2lbs.	8d galvanized nails
104	1x6 x 8' battens	2 lbs.	16d galvanized nails
10	1x4 x 8' window and door trim	160 sq. ft.	metal roofing with fasteners approved by manufacturer

PLAN VIEW

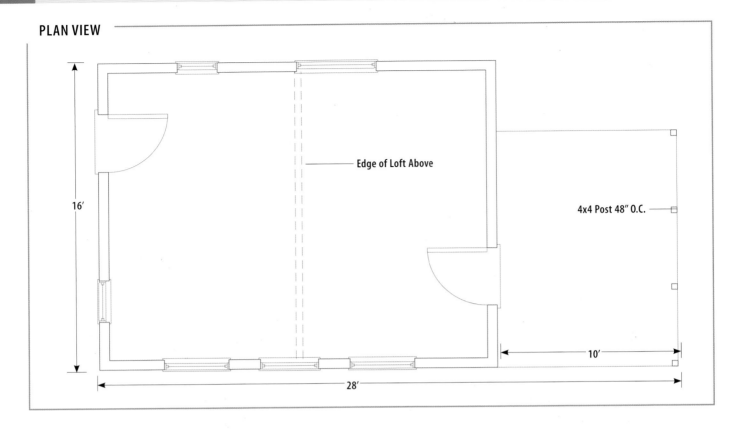

Slab Foundation. This building needs a full-size structural slab with a minimum 12-inch-wide footing around its perimeter, as described in Chapter 3, pages 60 to 61. The Materials List gives the amount of concrete needed for a 4-inch thick slab with 4-foot deep footings. Check with your building department for local footing and slab requirements. After excavating for the footings, spread gravel below the slab area, and cover it with 6-mil polyethylene sheeting before laying down 6 x 6-inch 10/10 welded-wire mesh.

Make sure this mesh is supported on chairs so that it will sit in the lower third of the 4-inch slab. Place two lengths of #4 rebar, supported on chairs, at the bottom of the footing trench. Use 2x10 form boards, staked into the ground, to define the perimeter of the slab. Measure diagonals to check that the form boards are square before pouring concrete. Pour the slab with a fortified 3,000-psi concrete specified for monolithic pours. Set anchor bolts every 6 feet and about 10 inches from each corner and to either side of the door opening around the perimeter to receive a 2x6 pressure-treated sill plate.

Framing. Lay out, cut, and bolt down the sill plates. Frame the walls with 2x6 studs spaced 24 inches on center, and sheathe them with ½-inch CDX plywood. Stand the walls, and add a second top plate to tie them together.

Frame a conventional roof with an 8-in-12 slope, using a 2x8 ridge beam and 2x6 rafters spaced 24 inches on center, as described in Chapter 5, pages 104 to 108. Sheathe the roof with ⅝-inch CDX plywood.

Half of this one-room structure is open all the way up to the rafters. Tie together the rafters over this area with 2x6 collar ties as shown in the drawing Front Framing Perspective. The other half of the space is covered by ceiling joists covered with ¾-inch CDX plywood to form a storage loft.

Porch. Four concrete piers, poured into fiber tubes and spaced 4 feet apart, support a shed porch along the back wall of the studio. Make sure the piers extend below the frost line to prevent frost heaving, and bring the tops of the fiber tubes several inches above grade so that they can be cut level with each other.

Erect 4x4 posts, and install a doubled 2x6 beam to support the lower end of the shed rafters. The upper end of the rafters are notched into a 2x6 ledger nailed over the exterior sheathing on the back wall of the studio. Nail down 2x4 purlins spaced 24 inches on center. Remember to check the support requirements with the ag-panel manufacturers. You will find that the size of the purlins can be altered, depending on the spacing of the rafters among other variables.

Siding & Roofing. This shed has been sided with vertical rough-sawn 1x6 boards and 1x2 battens. Before installing the siding, cover the exterior walls with housewrap or felt paper. Space the siding boards about 1 inch apart so that the battens have ample support and provide coverage should the main boards shrink.

Because this is an insulated, heated space, the roof must be ventilated. This means building ventilated soffits and a ridge vent

FRONT FRAMING PERSPECTIVE

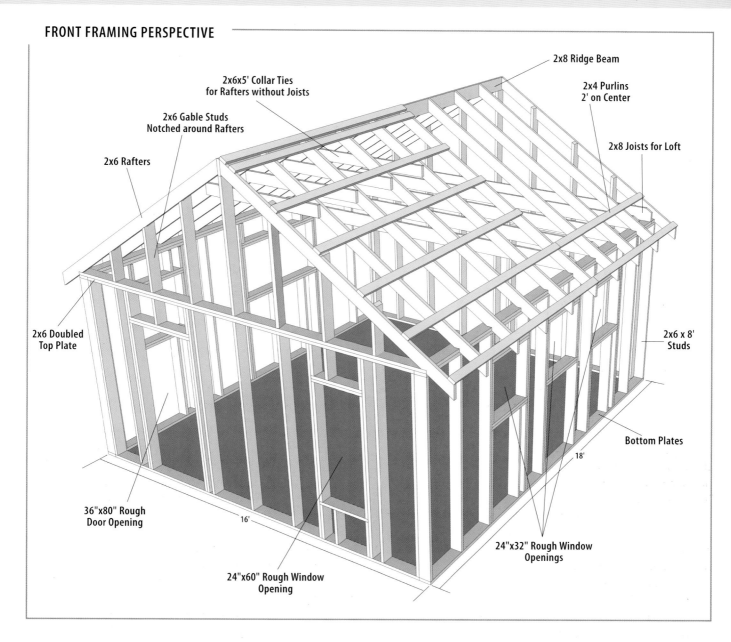

2x8 Ridge Beam

2x6x5' Collar Ties
for Rafters without Joists

2x4 Purlins
2' on Center

2x6 Gable Studs
Notched around Rafters

2x8 Joists for Loft

2x6 Rafters

2x6 Doubled
Top Plate

2x6 x 8'
Studs

Bottom Plates

36"x80" Rough
Door Opening

18'

16'

24"x32" Rough Window
Openings

24"x60" Rough Window
Opening

approved by the manufacturer of your metal roofing. Before installing the siding, run short lengths of 2x4 from the lower edges of each rafter, and toenail them into the walls, as shown in Framing Section, above. Next, install vent channel (available from building-supply centers), and piece in ½-inch exterior-grade plywood as a soffit. Install a 1x8 fascia to the rafter ends, allowing it to hang down slightly below the soffit, and then nail up a 1x2 drip fascia. Run metal drip edge around the entire perimeter of the roof, and install metal roofing panels as described in Chapter 6, pages 122 to 124.

Windows & Doors. The windows in this studio were purchased from a salvage yard. Each one is different, which lends a unique charm to the building. When using salvaged windows, purchase them before you begin framing the walls so that you can be sure to frame the correct rough openings. Bear in mind that some regions have strict energy codes and may not allow old,

single-pane glazing. The door is a standard prehung insulated steel entry unit.

Insulation & Drywall. Once you have closed in the studio, you are ready for insulation and drywall. This building was insulated with R-19 fiberglass batts, though other insulation choices are available. The rafter cavities should also be insulated, but first you must install vent channels. These plastic channels staple to the underside of the roof sheathing to prevent the insulation from blocking air flow. Finish the interior with ½-inch drywall.

REAR FRAMING

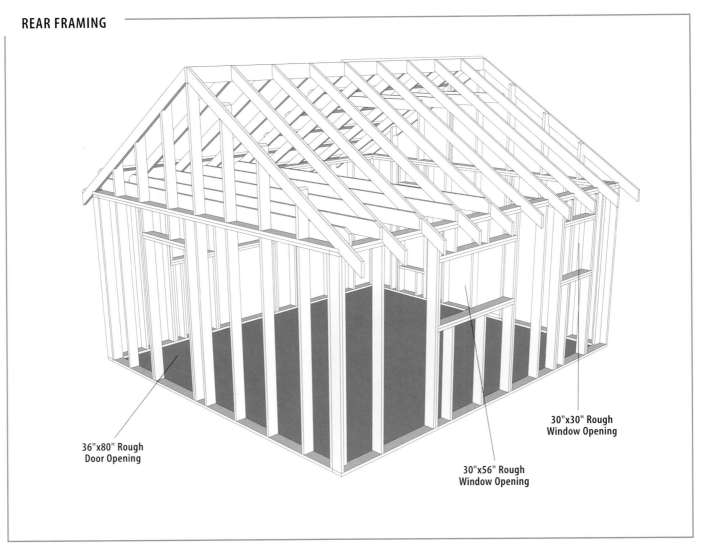

36"x80" Rough Door Opening

30"x56" Rough Window Opening

30"x30" Rough Window Opening

SIDE ELEVATION

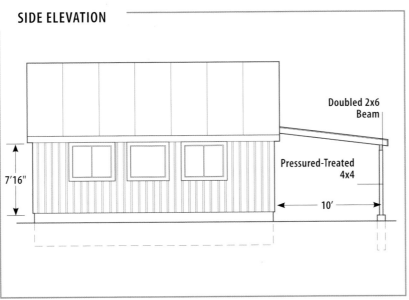

Doubled 2x6 Beam

Pressured-Treated 4x4

7'16"

10'

BACK ELEVATION

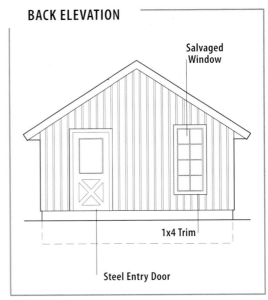

Salvaged Window

1x4 Trim

Steel Entry Door

FRONT ELEVATION

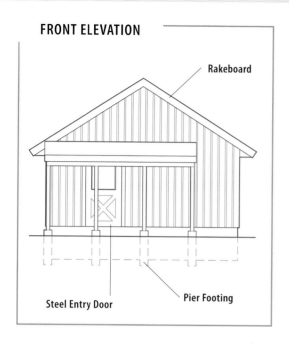

Rakeboard

Steel Entry Door

Pier Footing

SIDE ELEVATION

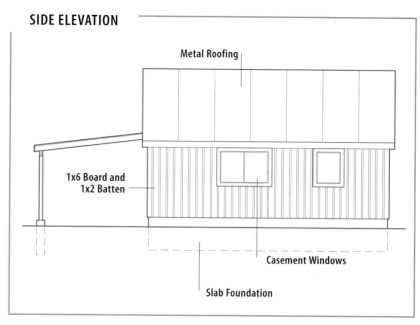

Metal Roofing

1x6 Board and
1x2 Batten

Casement Windows

Slab Foundation

PORCH ROOF CONNECTION DETAIL

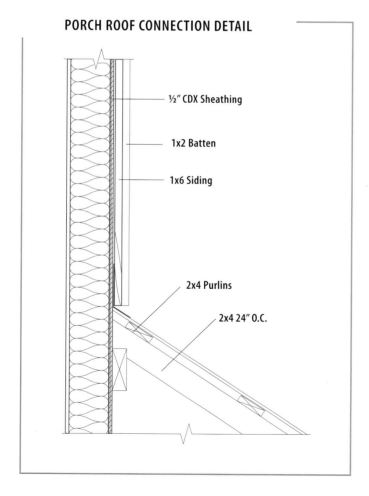

½" CDX Sheathing

1x2 Batten

1x6 Siding

2x4 Purlins

2x4 24" O.C.

FRAMING SECTION

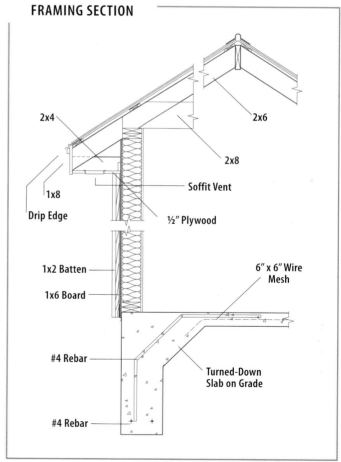

2x4

2x6

2x8

1x8

Soffit Vent

Drip Edge

½" Plywood

1x2 Batten

1x6 Board

6" x 6" Wire
Mesh

#4 Rebar

Turned-Down
Slab on Grade

#4 Rebar

7

POLE FRAMING POLE BARN

This large barn includes a livestock pen, poultry house, and small workshop. A large second-story hay loft provides ample dry storage. Although the design is a pole barn, this structure has square-edged timbers.

MATERIALS

1 yard	concrete for 3-foot deep holes
17	6x6x20' posts
5	6x6x20' center ridge posts
58	2x4x8' for gable end nailers, door studs, purlins
7	2x4x10' for window openings
103	2x4x 12' for window openings, door headers, thresholds
9	2x4 x 14' for nailers
3	2x4 x 16' for nailers
3	2x4 x 20' for nailers
12	2x6 x 10' for braces, and gable end nailer
56	2x6 x 16' for rafters
6	2x8 x 10' for ridge beams, loft header, support girts

4	2x8 x 12 for girts
248	1x4 x 8' rough sawn for siding
48	1x4 x 16 rough sawn for siding
20	1x4 x 10' rough sawn for window and door trim
248	1x2 x 8' rough sawn for siding battens
48	1x2 x 16' rough sawn for siding battens
10lbs.	16d common nails
4 lbs.	8d common nails
6 lbs.	8d galvanized nails for siding
28	¼" x 8" carriage bolts
1,500 square feet of metal roofing with fasteners approved by manufacturer	

PLAN VIEW

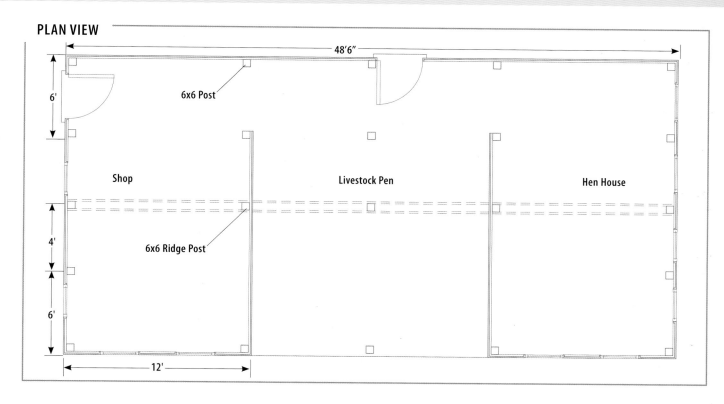

48'6"

6'

6x6 Post

6x6 Ridge Post

4'

6'

12'

Shop

Livestock Pen

Hen House

FRONT FRAMING PERSPECTIVE

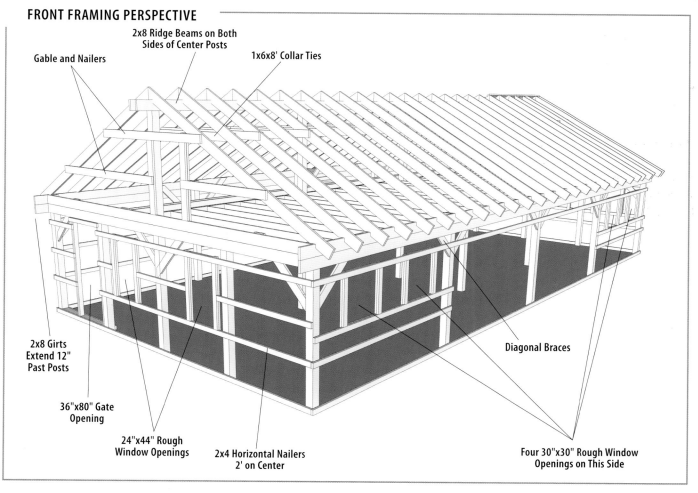

2x8 Ridge Beams on Both Sides of Center Posts

Gable and Nailers

1x6x8' Collar Ties

2x8 Girts Extend 12" Past Posts

Diagonal Braces

36"x80" Gate Opening

24"x44" Rough Window Openings

2x4 Horizontal Nailers 2' on Center

Four 30"x30" Rough Window Openings on This Side

REAR FRAMING PERSPECTIVE

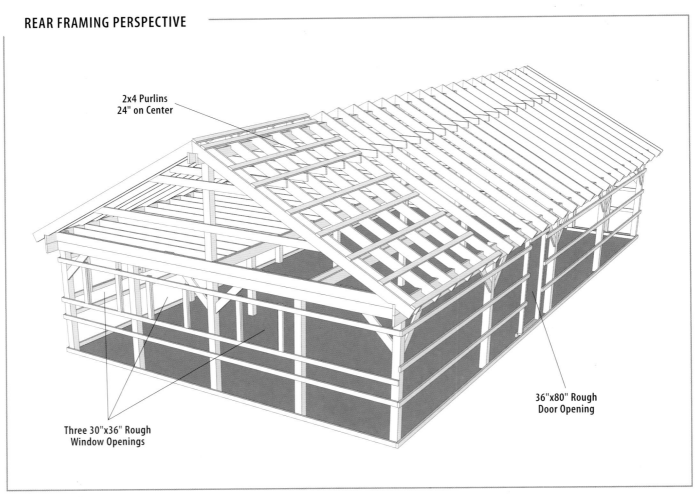

2x4 Purlins
24" on Center

Three 30"x36" Rough
Window Openings

36"x80" Rough
Door Opening

RAFTER LAYOUT

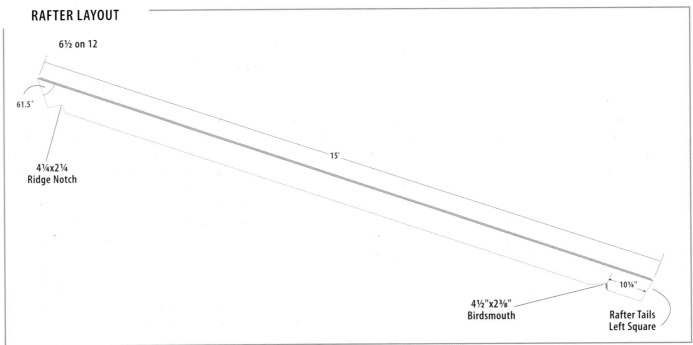

6½ on 12

61.5°

4¼x2¼
Ridge Notch

15'

4½"x2⅜"
Birdsmouth

10¼"

Rafter Tails
Left Square

FRONT ELEVATION

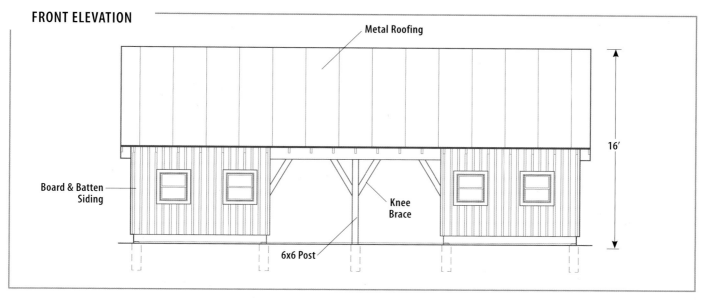

BACK ELEVATION

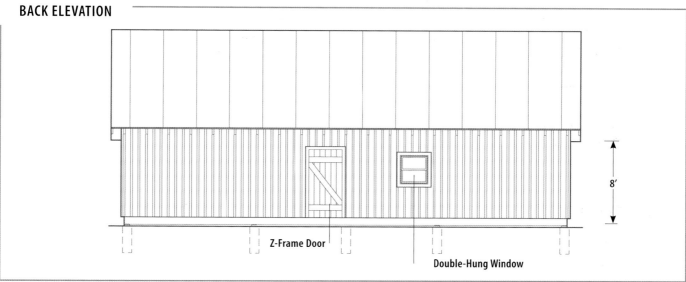

Framing. The structure for this barn consists of a grid of 6x6 pressure-treated timbers embedded in 2,000-psi concrete to below frost depth. There are 22 posts in all. The quantity of concrete and post lengths in the Materials List assumes you will bury the posts to a depth of 3 feet. Through the center of the barn, a row of ridge posts rises to 16 feet to support a ridge beam. The exterior wall posts rise 9 feet above grade. An interior row of posts that help support the loft is cut at 8 feet 4 ½ inches to be flush with the top of the loft joists; these five posts include two at the perimeter. Let the posts run long when you set them so you can cut them all off at the right heights after the concrete sets.

Girts. Tie the tops of the exterior walls together with girts consisting of two 2x8s stacked on edge. Note the drawing Front Framing Perspective that on the long walls these girts extend 1 foot beyond the posts on both gable ends. Secure each girt with pairs of 8-inch carriage bolts through the posts.

Loft. Next, install the loft header beam. This is a 2x8 nailed to the far side of the center posts as shown in the drawing Loft Framing Detail. On the near side of the center posts, 7¼ inches lower than the header, nail another 2x8 beam. The joists will rest on this beam. At that same level, attach another joist support beam against the remaining row of interior posts. Install the 2x8 joists 16 inches on center using joist hangers on both ends. Adjust joist spacing as necessary to get around posts. Deck the loft with ¾ in. CDX plywood.

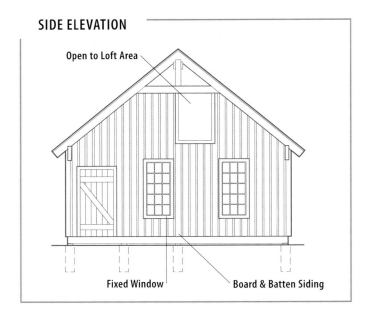

SIDE ELEVATION

Open to Loft Area

Fixed Window

Board & Batten Siding

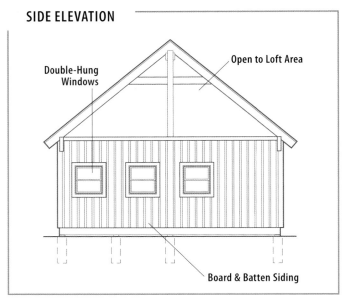

SIDE ELEVATION

Double-Hung Windows

Open to Loft Area

Board & Batten Siding

Siding & Roofing. This structure was sided with vertical rough-sawn 1x6 boards and 1x2 battens. Space the siding boards about ½-inch apart to allow for seasonal movement, and attach the battens.

Because this is an unheated barn with open wall and roof framing, a vented roof is not necessary. The rafter ends have been cut square and left open. Run metal drip edge around the entire perimeter of the roof, and install metal roofing panels as described in Chapter 6, pages 122 to 124.

Windows & Doors. The windows for this barn were purchased in a salvage yard. When using recycled windows, purchase them before framing so you will know exactly what the rough opening sizes will be. After framing these openings, install horizontal nailers across the exterior of the building, adjusting nailer height as necessary to form the bottom of window openings as shown in the drawing Window and Door Framing Detail. This barn has two door openings. One has a partial gate as shown in the photo. The other has a door made from the same rough-sawn 1x8 material as the siding with a Z-frame construction as described in chapter 6, page 133.

Ridge beam & rafters. The ridge beam consists of two rows of 2x8s attached to opposite sides of the center posts. Like the girts, the beam runs 1 foot past the gable end center posts. Position the beam flush with the top of the posts. As shown in the drawing Rafter Layout, the rafters are notched to fit over the ridge beam and the tops of the posts. Install rafters between the ends of the girts and the ends of the ridge beam to create gable overhangs. Then install sets of rafters in the same plane as the horizontal wall nailers. Cut gable-end nailers to fit under these rafters, nailing them to the bottom of the rafters and the side of the center posts. Now install the remaining rafters 24 inches on center. Nail 8-foot 2x4 collar ties to the rafters with their top outside corners just below the top of the rafters. To complete the roof framing add 2x4 purlins 2 feet on center across both sides of the roof.

LOFT FRAMING DETAIL

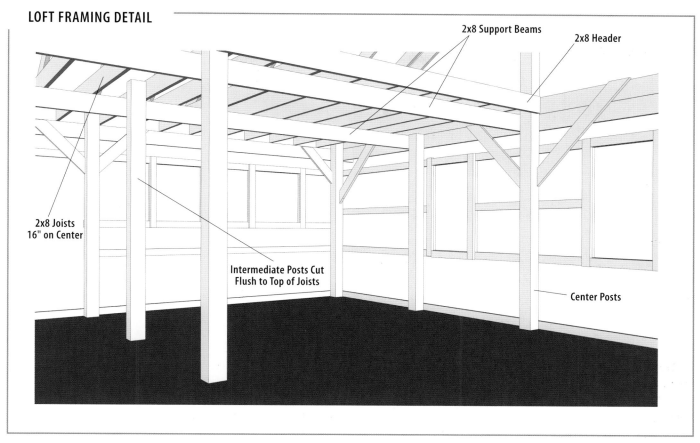

2x8 Support Beams

2x8 Header

2x8 Joists
16" on Center

Intermediate Posts Cut
Flush to Top of Joists

Center Posts

WINDOW & DOOR FRAMING DETAIL

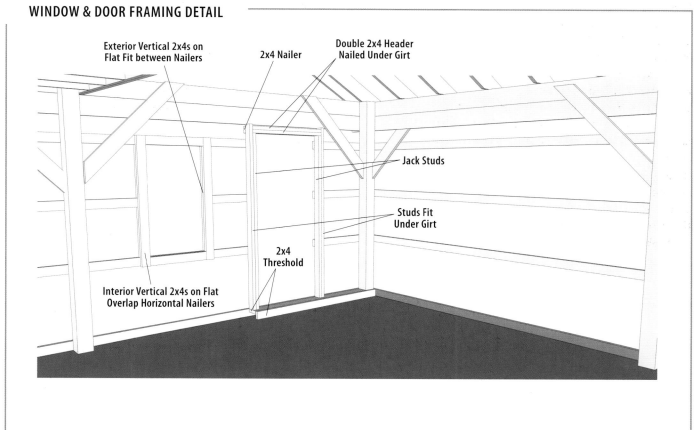

Exterior Vertical 2x4s on
Flat Fit between Nailers

2x4 Nailer

Double 2x4 Header
Nailed Under Girt

Jack Studs

Studs Fit
Under Girt

2x4
Threshold

Interior Vertical 2x4s on Flat
Overlap Horizontal Nailers

8

POLE FRAMING   THREE-BAY GARAGE

THIS LARGE THREE-BAY GARAGE provides ample storage for a variety of vehicles, from automobiles to farm equipment such as tractors and trucks. The structure also includes an insulated room that can serve as a carpenter's or machinist's shop. The garage has a saltbox-style roof.

MATERIALS

41	2x4 x 8' for nailers, barge rafters, diagonal braces	14	1x4 x 8' window and door casing, rake fascia, and rake trim.
28	2x4 x 12' for nailers	8	1x8 x 12' for fascia
8	2x4 x 14' for nailers	57	⅝" 4x8' CDX plywood for roof
35	2x6 x 8' for shop wall framing	6	½" x 4 x 8' CDX plywood for soffits
6	2x6 x 10' for shop wall framing	9	¾"x 4 x 8' plywood floor underlayment
22	2x6 x 12' for plates	5 rolls	#15 roofing felt
37	2x6 x 22' for rafter ties	18	squares of asphalt roofing shingles
23	2x8 x 12' for joists	1 box	⅜-inch staples for roofing felt
37	2x8 x 14' for rafters	140 ft.	aluminum drip edge
40	2x8 x 18' for rafters and ridge boards	10 lbs.	16d common nails
24	2x10 x 12' girts	4 lbs.	8d common nails
5	4x4 x 12' posts	4 lbs.	8d galvanized nails for siding
10	4x4 x 14' posts	22 lbs.	1-inch roofing nails
236	1x6 x 8' shiplap siding boards		

Framing. This building is framed around three rows of 6x6 pressure-treated posts embedded in 2,000-psi concrete to below the local frost depth, in this case 3 feet. There are 15 posts in all. The back exterior wall posts rise 8 feet above grade to the top wall plates. The front wall posts and the posts that support the center beam rise to 10 feet above grade. To make sure posts end up at the proper heights, run the posts long and cut them off in place after the concrete has set.

Girts. After setting and cutting the posts to height, nail 2x10 girts to the outside of the perimeter posts. Make these girts flush to the top of the posts. Cut 2x6 diagonal braces to 3 feet long with 45-degree angles on each end. Nail these to the posts and the inside of the girts, positioning them flush to the top of the

PLAN VIEW

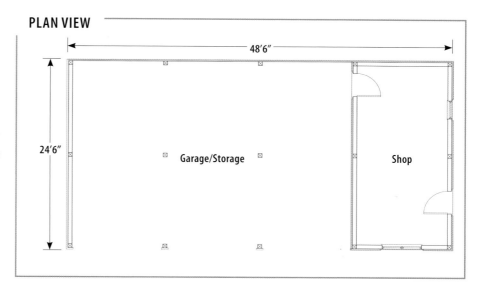

48'6"

24'6"

Garage/Storage

Shop

FRONT PERSPECTIVE

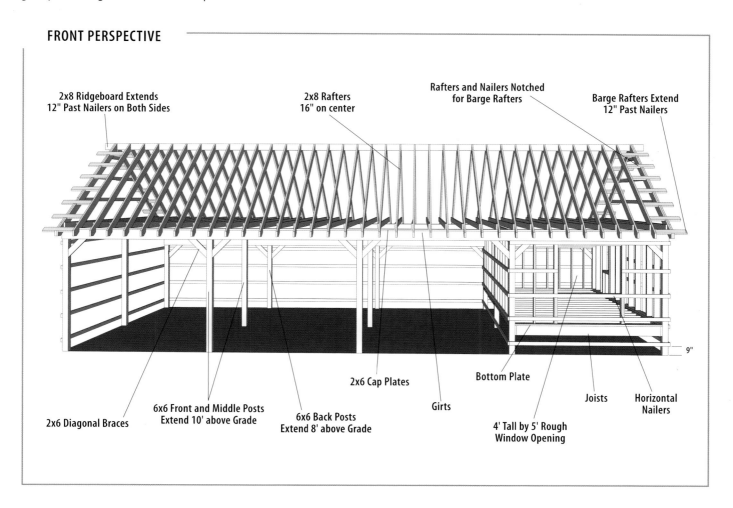

2x8 Ridgeboard Extends 12" Past Nailers on Both Sides

2x8 Rafters 16" on center

Rafters and Nailers Notched for Barge Rafters

Barge Rafters Extend 12" Past Nailers

2x6 Diagonal Braces

6x6 Front and Middle Posts Extend 10' above Grade

6x6 Back Posts Extend 8' above Grade

2x6 Cap Plates

Girts

Bottom Plate

4' Tall by 5' Rough Window Opening

Joists

Horizontal Nailers

9"

SHOP GABLE WALL FRAMING

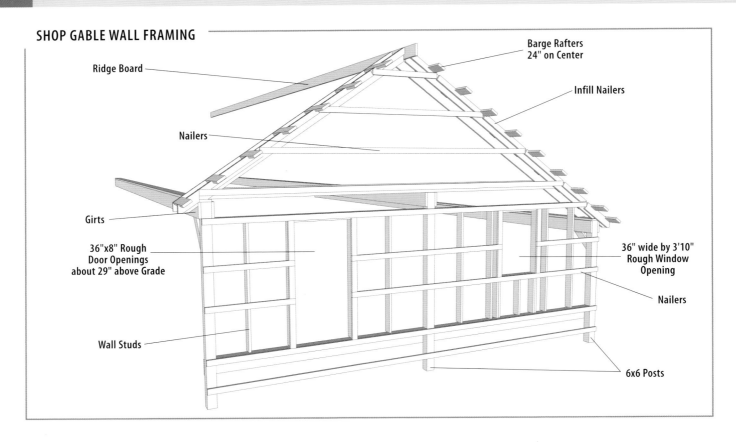

Ridge Board

Barge Rafters
24" on Center

Infill Nailers

Nailers

Girts

36"x8" Rough
Door Openings
about 29" above Grade

36" wide by 3'10"
Rough Window
Opening

Nailers

Wall Studs

6x6 Posts

SHOP FRAMING DETAILS

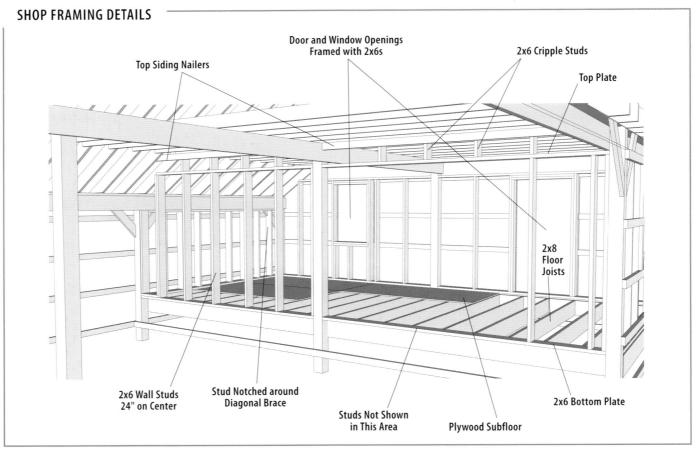

Top Siding Nailers

Door and Window Openings
Framed with 2x6s

2x6 Cripple Studs

Top Plate

2x8
Floor
Joists

2x6 Wall Studs
24" on Center

Stud Notched around
Diagonal Brace

Studs Not Shown
in This Area

Plywood Subfloor

2x6 Bottom Plate

RAFTER LAYOUTS

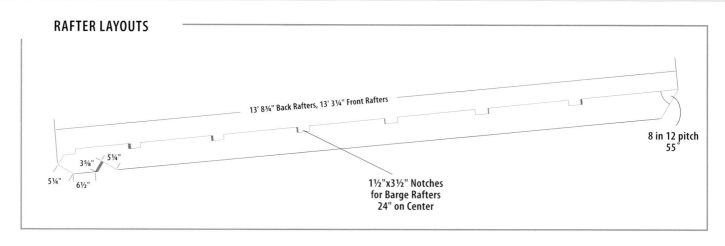

13' 8¾" Back Rafters, 13' 3¼" Front Rafters

8 in 12 pitch
55°

1½"x3½" Notches
for Barge Rafters
24" on Center

3⅝"
5¼"
5¼"
6½"

FRONT & BACK ELEVATIONS

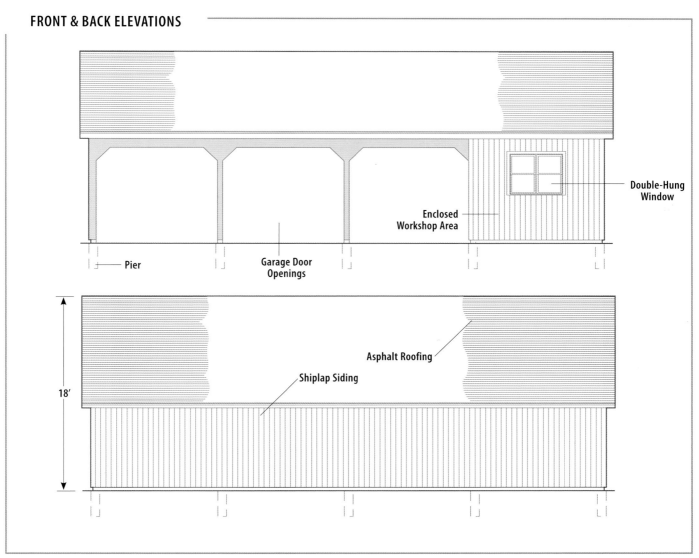

Double-Hung
Window

Enclosed
Workshop Area

Pier

Garage Door
Openings

Asphalt Roofing

Shiplap Siding

18'

girts. Nail another row of girts to the inside of the posts, also flush to the top. Then through-bolt the girts to the post using two 9-inch-long carriage bolts at each connection. Nail a 2x8 top plate over the tops of the posts, aligned with the outside as shown in the drawing Framing Section.

Center beams. Next, install the center beam, which is made of a pair of 2x10s bolted to both sides of the center posts with pairs of 9-inch carriage bolts. Brace the perimeter posts with diagonal 2x4s, and run horizontal 2x4s every 2 feet on center on the outside of the exterior walls.

Shop framing. The shop area has a floor with 2x8 joists installed 16 inches on center. Before you install the floor, lay down 6-mill plastic covered by a couple of inches of gravel to contain ground moisture. As shown in the drawing Shop Framing Details, the tops of the joists are 28 inches above grade. Install the header joists and then use joist hangers to attach the spanning joists. Install R-22 batt insulation between the joists, and then install a ¾-inch plywood subfloor. The four walls of the shop are framed with 2x6s spaced 24 inches on center. The shop has two windows, one at the front and one on the shop gable end. There is also a door on the gable end that's about four steps above grade. Frame these openings as you install the wall studs. The shop walls also will be insulated with R-22 batts, but wait until the roofing and siding are installed to protect the insulation from wet weather.

Nailers. Horizontal 2x4 nailers for siding are installed on all the walls, including the wall that separates the shop from the three garage bays. Install nailers about 9 inches from grade and about every 2 feet above that. Add pieces of 2x4 to the exterior of the window and door openings to bring the openings flush to the horizontal nailers.

Rafters & collar ties. The rafters have the same 8 in 12 pitch on both sides, but because of the saltbox design, the rear rafters are longer and the ridge is closer to the front of the of the building. See the drawing Rafter Layouts. Note that the gable end rafters have notches to accept the barge rafters. The rafter pairs meet at a 2x8 ridgeboard that extends 13½ inches beyond both gable end rafters. To raise this beam, build temporary posts as described in Installing Ridgeboard & Rafters (page 106). Cut the barge rafters so that they will butt into the second-to-last rafters at each gable and overhang the 13 ½ inches beyond the gable end rafters. Install the barge rafters.

The horizontal pieces that tie the rafter pairs together are a hybrid between collar ties and ceiling joists. At the front they rest on the top plate like joists and they'll be nailed to the rafters. At the rear, because the back wall is 2 feet below, they are nailed to the rafters only like collar ties. Add horizontal nailers every 2 feet across the gable end rafters and then install infill nailer pieces flush to the top of the gable end. You'll have to notch some of these infill pieces to fit around the barge rafters. Also add nailers to the rafters that define the outside wall that the shop shares with the garage bays.

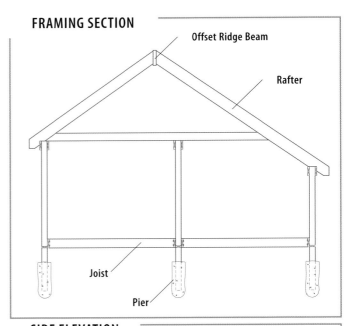

FRAMING SECTION

Offset Ridge Beam
Rafter
Joist
Pier

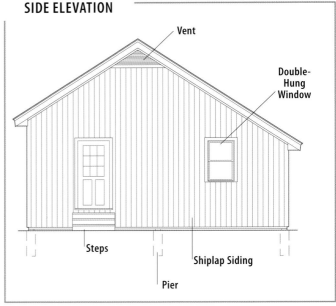

SIDE ELEVATION

Vent
Double-Hung Window
Steps
Shiplap Siding
Pier

Windows & doors. The shop door is a standard pre-hung insulated entry unit. You can order it with a lockset already installed. The windows are double-hung units. Install the windows and doors and then cover the outside of the four shop walls with 15-pound roofing felt.

Roofing & ventilation. The roof is covered with standard three-tab asphalt roofing. Sheathe the roof with ⅝-inch CDX plywood. Install 1x8 fascia against the rafter tails. Then nail a 1x2 drip strip to the top of the fascia as shown in the drawing Framing Section. Add a drip edge and 15-pound felt before installing the shingles as described in Chapter 6, pages 128–129. Because the shop is insulated and heated, the rafters above it must be

FRAMING SECTION

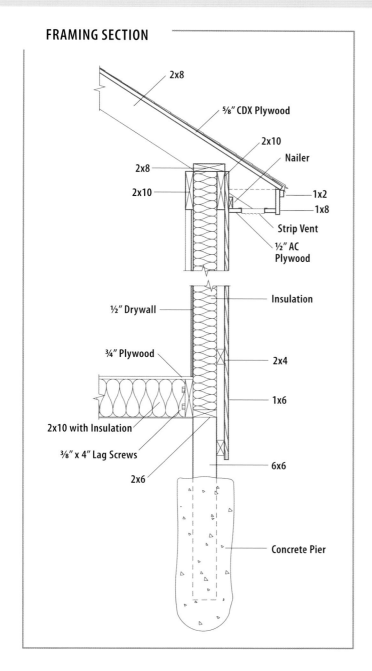

2x8

⅝" CDX Plywood

2x10

Nailer

2x8

2x10

1x2

1x8

Strip Vent

½" AC Plywood

Insulation

½" Drywall

¾" Plywood

2x4

1x6

2x10 with Insulation

⅜" x 4" Lag Screws

2x6

6x6

Concrete Pier

ventilated. Install a vent channel along these rafter bays and then batts of R-22 insulation.

Siding & trim. The siding is vertical 1x6 shiplap. Nail the siding to the nailers with 8d galvanized nails. Add vents to the shop gables. Trim the windows and doors with 1x4s. Cover the bottom of the barge rafters with ½-inch AC plywood and run a 1x4 trim board against the siding and butted into the bottom of the plywood. Then nail 1x4 rake boards to the end of the barge rafters.

Clad the three exterior posts that define the garage bays with one-bys. For each of these posts you'll need two 1x6s and two 1x8s trimmed to 7 inches to be flush to the outside of the 1x6s. To build the ventilated soffit, start by running 2x4s against the siding with their bottom edges at the same level as the bottom of the rafters. Then install soffits consisting of strip vents supported on both sides by strips of ½ AC plywood. Cut triangular "pork chops" to fit under the rake boards, and close off the ends of the soffits as shown in the opening photo.

9

ADVANCED FRAMING GAMBREL BARN

GAMBREL ROOF FRAMING on this barn affords two floors of usable space with a minimum of framing. Originally built as a horse barn, this traditional gambrel now provides first-floor storage for farm implements with an insulated second-story artist's studio.

Slab Foundation. This building needs a full-size structural slab with a minimum 12-inch-wide footing around its perimeter, as described in Chapter 3, pages 60 to 61. After excavating for the footings, spread gravel below the slab area, and cover it with 6-mil polyethylene before laying down 6 x 6-inch 10/10 welded-wire mesh.

MATERIALS

62	2x4 x 8' for gable overhangs, wall framing	22	½"x 4x8' sheets CDX plywood for wall sheathing
21	2x4 x10' for gable-wall end plates, ceiling joists	38	⅝" x 4x8 sheets CDX plywood for roof sheathing
16	2x4 x 12' for wall plates		
72	2x6 x 8' for wall framing, ridge board	5	rolls 15-lb. roofing
2	2x6 x 10' for ridge board	12	squares of asphalt shingles
79	2x6 x 12' for rafters, skylights, and wall plates	8 lbs.	16d common nails
9	2x8 x 8' center beam	6 lbs.	8d common nails
42	2x8 x 8' for joists	18 lbs.	1 ½-inch roofing nails
2	2x12 x 8' for door header	140 ft.	aluminum drip edge
3	4x4 x 10' for center posts	5 squares 16x8" No. 1-grade cedar shingles	
9	¾" x 4x8' sheets plywood floor underlayment	5 lbs.	3d galvanized siding nails.

PLAN VIEW

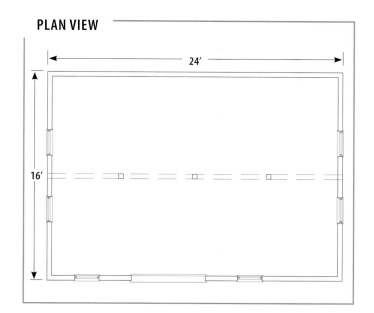

24'

16'

Make sure this mesh is supported on chairs so that it will sit in the lower third of the 4-inch slab section. Place two lengths of #4 rebar, supported on chairs, at the bottom of the footing trench. At the locations of the interior support posts, excavate for a 2-foot-square pad to the same depth as the thickened edge. Place short pieces of #4 rebar to make a square, supported on chairs at the bottom of these pads. Use 2x10 form boards, staked into the ground, to define the perimeter of the slab. Measure diagonals to check that the form boards are square before pouring concrete. Pour the slab with a fortified 3,000-psi concrete specified for monolithic pours. Set anchor bolts every 6 feet (and about 10 inches from each corner and to either side of the door openings) around the perimeter to receive 2x6 pressure-treated sill plates. Set a metal post anchor in the center of each pad to receive the 4x4 center posts.

FRAMING PERSPECTIVE

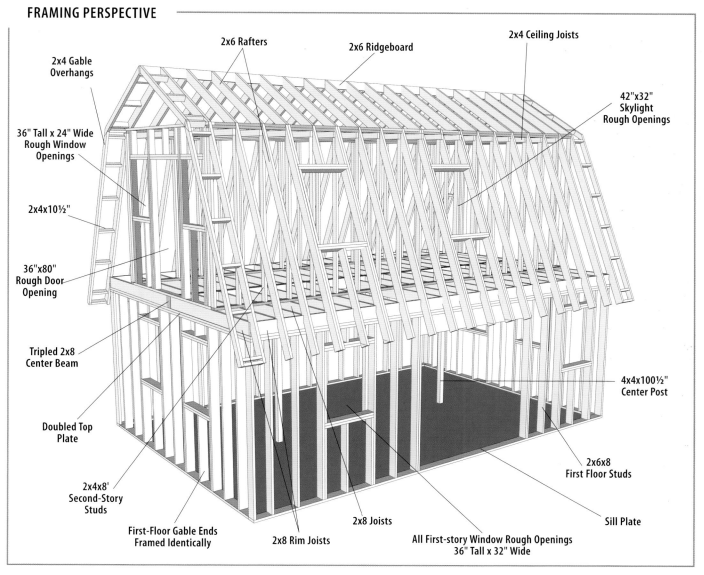

2x4 Gable Overhangs

2x6 Rafters

2x6 Ridgeboard

2x4 Ceiling Joists

42"x32" Skylight Rough Openings

36" Tall x 24" Wide Rough Window Openings

2x4x10½"

36"x80" Rough Door Opening

Tripled 2x8 Center Beam

Doubled Top Plate

2x4x8' Second-Story Studs

First-Floor Gable Ends Framed Identically

2x8 Rim Joists

2x8 Joists

All First-story Window Rough Openings 36" Tall x 32" Wide

4x4x100½" Center Post

2x6x8 First Floor Studs

Sill Plate

Wall & Floor Framing. Lay out, cut, and bolt down the pressure-treated 2x6 sill plates. Frame the walls with 2x6 studs spaced 16 inches on center. Frame the window openings and second-story door as shown in the drawing Framing Perspective, using a doubled 2x12 header for the 8-foot-wide first-story door. Stand the walls, and add a second, overlapping top plate to tie them together. Sheathe the walls with ½-inch CDX plywood.

Set 4x4 center posts in the metal post anchors letting them run long. Brace the posts with temporary 2x4s, then cut them all off at the same level 8 feet 4 ½ inches above the slab. Build the center beam from three 2x8s, and set it on the posts. Set 2x8 rim and header joists on the top wall plates, and install 2x8 joists spaced 16 inches on center. These joists butt into the center beam and are supported by metal joist hangers.

Next, frame the second-story walls with 2x4 studs spaced 16 inches on center. Measure in 38 ½ inches from the outside of the rim joists, and snap a line across the tops of the floor joists. Stand

the second-story walls along the inside of this chalk line, and tie the walls together with a second top plate. Nail 2x4 ceiling joists to the sides of the studs below the top plates, as shown in the drawing Framing Section. Install a ¾-inch plywood floor between the second story walls.

Gambrel Roof Framing. Once the walls are up, you are ready to frame the gambrel roof. Start by installing the 2x6 rafters for the lower roof plane, spaced 16 inches on center. As shown in the drawing Rafter Layouts, these are conventional rafters with a steep 24-in-12 slope. They have a plumb cut at the top that butts the top of the second-story walls, and a bird's-mouth that sits on the header joists of the second floor. Square cut the ends of the rafters, and run 2x6 fascia across the ends. Note in Framing Perspective how rafters are headered off and doubled to create a skylight opening.

Before raising the rafters for the upper roof plane, install a 2x8 ridgeboard. Support the ridgeboard about 4 feet above the second-floor ceiling joists using temporary 2x4 posts and bracing. These rafters run at a 7-in-12 slope from this ridgeboard down to the top plate of the second-story walls, intersecting with a bird's-mouth. A level cut instead of a birds'-mouth is used for the gable-end top rafters that sit atop the gable-end walls. Sheathe the roof with ⅝-inch CDX plywood.

Shingle Siding. This barn has been sided with durable cedar shingle siding. Start by applying a layer of felt paper over the exterior wall sheathing. The shingle exposure depends on the length of the shingles you'll use.

The barn as shown has 16 x 8-inch No. 1-grade cedar shingles installed with a 7 ½-inch exposure. To install the shingles, snap a level chalk line on the building felt 15 inches above the bottom edge of the wall sheathing, so that the first course of shingles hangs an inch below.

Nail each shingle with a pair of 4d galvanized siding nails about 8 inches above the bottom edge. Apply a second layer over these to create the starter course. Subsequent courses will have just one layer of shingles. Leave a ⅛-inch gap between adjacent shingles. Corners are overlapped in alternate courses to create a woven corner, as shown in the detail drawing on page 237.

Roofing. Cover the sheathing with building felt, and install metal drip edge along the perimeter. The intersection between the upper and lower roof planes must be flashed with 16-inch aluminum coil stock. Complete the roof by installing asphalt shingles.

Windows & Doors. The windows in this barn—large double-hungs with divided lights—add an elegant traditional flair. The large sliding door is built of 1x6 tongue-and-groove vertical siding boards secured by an overlapping grid of 1x6, 1x8, and 1x10 boards. It hangs from a 2x6 ledger nailed to the inside of the wall, using heavy-duty sliding-door hardware, available from agricultural supply centers.

RAFTER LAYOUT

5'5½"

60°

7 in 12
Top Rafters

4¼"x3½"
Bird's-Mouth

Top Plates

Stud Wall

10'9½"

1½x3¾"
Bird's-Mouth

Rafter
Tails Left
Square

SIDE ELEVATION

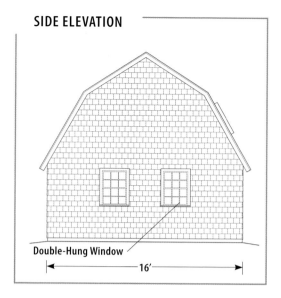

Double-Hung Window

16'

FRONT ELEVATION

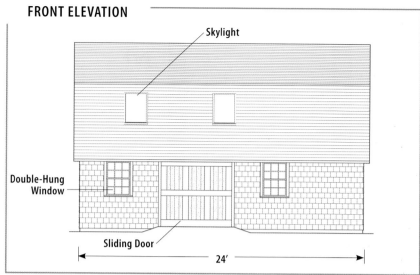

Skylight

Double-Hung Window

Sliding Door

24'

WOVEN CORNER DETAIL

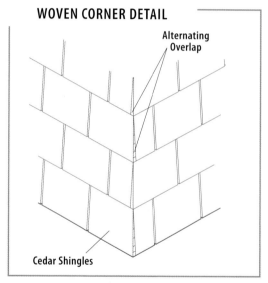

Alternating Overlap

Cedar Shingles

BACK ELEVATION

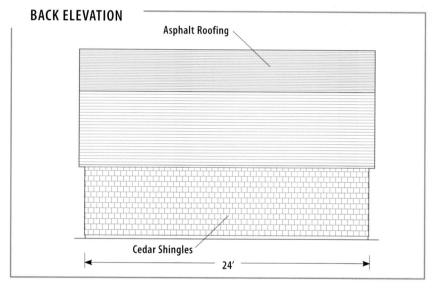

Asphalt Roofing

Cedar Shingles

24'

SIDING & FOUNDATION SECTION

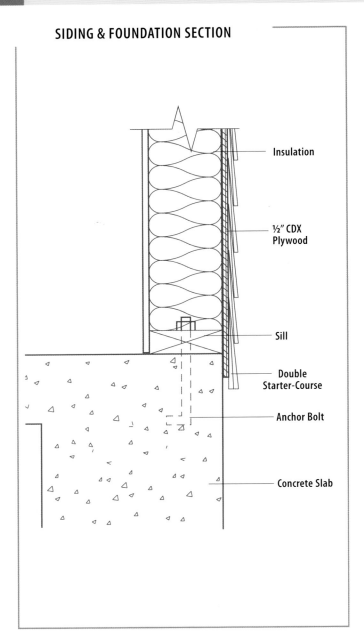

Insulation

½" CDX Plywood

Sill

Double Starter-Course

Anchor Bolt

Concrete Slab

FRAMING SECTION

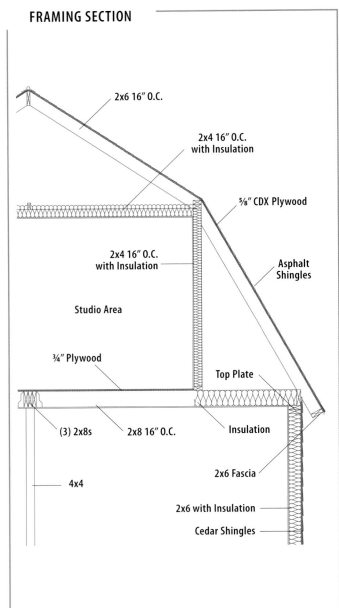

2x6 16" O.C.

2x4 16" O.C. with Insulation

⅝" CDX Plywood

2x4 16" O.C. with Insulation

Asphalt Shingles

Studio Area

¾" Plywood

Top Plate

(3) 2x8s

2x8 16" O.C.

Insulation

2x6 Fascia

4x4

2x6 with Insulation

Cedar Shingles

10

ADVANCED FRAMING   TIMBER-FRAME GARAGE

THIS ELEGANT OPEN-BAY GARAGE with an enclosed garden shed relies on traditional timber-framing techniques combined with modern framing. The skeleton structure consists of four saltbox-style timber bents that stand parallel with each other, forming three bays. The bay on the left is enclosed with walls on all four sides to create a shed, shop area, or studio.

The other two bays are open in the front, and serve as the garage. The four bents are tied together by crossbeams joining the tops of the three upright posts in each bent and by a sill beam running along the back. Between the bents of this skeleton structure, conventional rafters complete the roof structure, while a conventionally framed floor structure supports a loft storage area.

Bear in mind that timber framing techniques are among the most challenging in the building trades. This project description will give you a sense of the steps involved. However, it's best not to attempt such ambitious building without the assistance of an experienced timber framer who will know how to specify the

PLAN VIEW

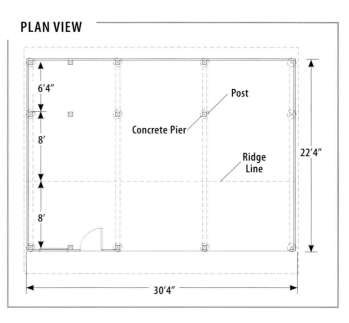

6'4"

Post

Concrete Pier

8'

Ridge Line

22'4"

8'

30'4"

proper timber sizes for the wood you want to use as well as know how to accomplish the sophisticated joinery required. This project assumes that you have ordered precut bents or will cut the timber joints with an experienced joiner who can be sure that the structure is sound and that the framing will pass local code inspection.

Foundation. The timber bents will be supported on concrete piers located below each post in the timber bent. These piers should be excavated for 8-inch fiber form tubes. (You may need larger-diameter forms to support the weight of some timber-frame materials.) Make sure the piers extend below frost line to prevent frost heaving, and bring the tops of the form tubes several inches above grade so that they can be cut level with each other.

Timber Bents. The Building Perspective shows the locations of the timber bents. Begin by laying out and mortising the sill beams. Assemble the bents, and brace across the face of each joint with temporary 2x4s to stabilize it as the bents are lifted into place. Lift the bents with a crane, and brace them with temporary two-by material. Lift the cross-tie running between the bents near the tops of each vertical post, and place the sill beams along the back as you go.

BUILDING PERSPECTIVE

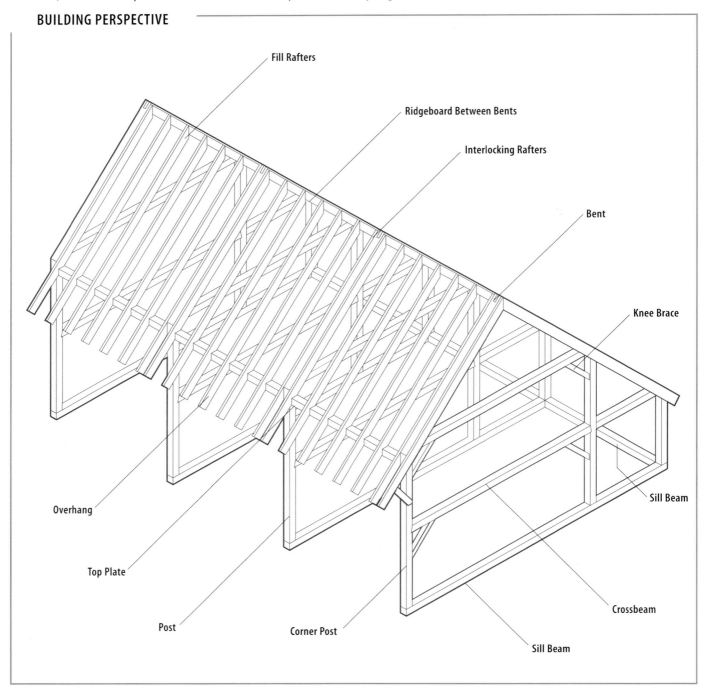

Fill Rafters

Ridgeboard Between Bents

Interlocking Rafters

Bent

Knee Brace

Sill Beam

Overhang

Top Plate

Post

Corner Post

Crossbeam

Sill Beam

FRONT ELEVATION

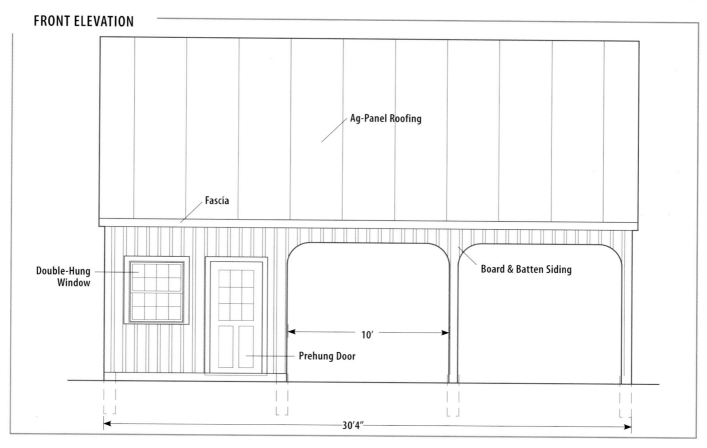

Ag-Panel Roofing

Fascia

Double-Hung Window

Board & Batten Siding

10'

Prehung Door

30'4"

BACK ELEVATION

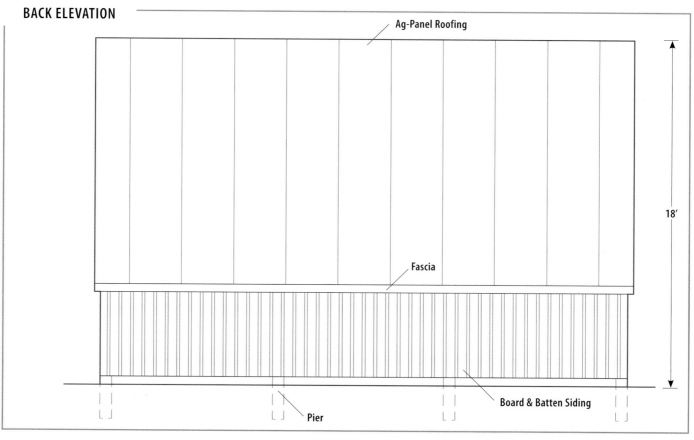

Ag-Panel Roofing

Fascia

18'

Board & Batten Siding

Pier

Once the skeleton structure is up, you will begin framing in the roof. Nail blocks to the face of each bent at the peak to support a 2x8 ridgeboard. Cut rafters for a 12-in-12-slope roof, as described in Chapter 5, pages 104 to 108, and install these with the bird's-mouth sitting on the front crossbeam. Square-cut the ends of the rafters so that the ends extend 32 inches horizontally from the outside wall line.

Frame the loft by running a 2x6 rim joist around the perimeter and in-filling with 2x6 joists over the tops of the center girts of each bent.

Enclosed Shed. The left-hand third of the garage has been enclosed for use as a garden shed. Begin the enclosure by framing an elevated floor. Before framing the floor, however, lay down 6-mil polyethylene sheeting, weighted down with gravel to prevent ground moisture from rising. Cut a 2x6 header joist to sit on top of the timber sill, flush with the outside on each side. In-fill the floor with 2x6 joists, and deck them with 3/4-inch CDX plywood.

Frame wall sections to fit between the bents on all four sides of the shop area using 2x6 studs spaced 24 inches on center. Note that the walls fitting inside the bents will sit between the knee braces. Stand these walls on the framed floor.

Siding & Roofing. Nail a horizontal 1x6 every 2 feet on center to the exterior as a nailing base for the siding. On the tall gable-end walls, run 2x4 horizontal nailers above the 8-foot line instead of the one-by nailers. This allows you to break the siding in an even line. Make the upper siding boards overlap the lower boards by at least ½ inch to create a more weather-resistant joint between boards.

This garage has been sided with vertical rough-sawn 1x6 boards and 1x2 battens. Space the siding boards about ½ inch apart to allow for seasonal movement.

Because this is an unheated garage with open wall and roof framing, a vented roof is not necessary. The rafter ends have been cut square and left open. Nail blocks over the siding along the roofline, and install a 1x8 fascia down the rake and over the ends of the rafter tails.

Note the attractive curve where the siding on the end walls meets the wide front overhang. (See Side Elevation, below.) These pieces of siding are supported by a 2x6 diagonal brace that extends from the rafter end to the front post of the bents each end. (See Building Perspective, page 240.) Nail the siding pieces so that they hang well below the brace, and cut the gentle arc using a saber saw.

Run metal drip edge around the entire perimeter of the roof, and install asphalt shingles as described in Chapter 6, pages 128 to 129.

Windows & Doors. The door into the shed area is a standard prehung entry unit that you can purchase at any home center or lumber yard. The windows are prebuilt double-hung units. Frame the window rough openings in the loft area of the gable-end walls with 2x4s nailed into the horizontal 2x4 nailers. The window and door rough openings in the shed area can be box-framed with 2x4s. These do not need structural headers above the openings, because the timber bents support the loads.

SIDE ELEVATION

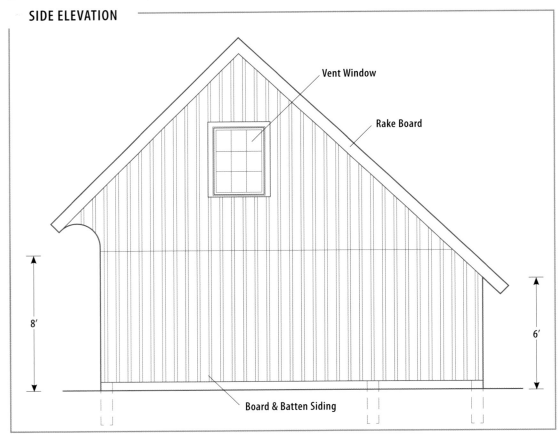

Vent Window

Rake Board

8'

6'

Board & Batten Siding

A new garage should complement the style of the main house.

11

BASIC SHEDS SHED-ROOF SHED

plate at a 15-degree angle to conform to the slope of the sidewall. To do this, cut the pieces slightly longer than their finished length, then hold them in position. Use a T-bevel and pencil to transfer the angle to the top end of the studs and both ends of the top plate. Set your circular saw to make a 15-degree cut. Cut the single top plate to fit; then attach it to the end studs. Cut the remaining studs individually to fit between the top and bottom plates (on 16-inch centers). The tops of the intermediate studs are also cut at a 15-degree angle. If desired, frame a rough opening in one of the sidewalls at this time.

CORNER DETAIL

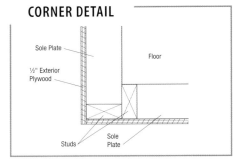

WALL SECTION

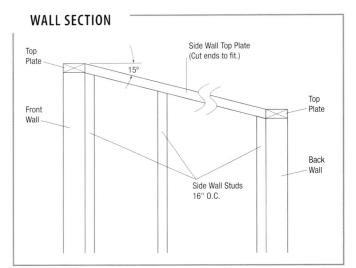

THE DRAWING ON THE OPPOSITE PAGE shows a shed 8 feet wide by 8 feet long. The overall height of the front wall is 8 feet, and the back wall is 6 feet tall. Be sure to subtract the thickness of the top and bottom plates when cutting studs to length. Each of the four walls has a single top plate.

The materials list on page 245 does not include foundation materials, windows, doors, siding, or extra lumber for building steps or a ramp to the shed. Refer to appropriate sections of this book for options.

Building the Floor Platform. Refer to the sections on foundations, pages 52 to 67, and framing, pages 68 to 82, for various options. Whether you choose a wood-frame floor or poured-concrete slab floor, the length of the finished floor platform and framing for the front and back walls is 3 inches shorter than the overall shed length (7 feet, 9 inches for an 8-foot-long shed, for example). This allows for the two 2x4 end rafters to be nailed to the outside of the top plate to accommodate 4x8-foot sheets of sheathing on the roof.

Erecting the Front and Back Walls. To assemble the 6-foot back wall, cut studs to 69 inches; for the 8-foot front wall, cut studs to 93 inches. Frame in the rough opening for the door (calculating by the door width plus 3 inches).

Erecting the Side Walls. On both sides of the shed, measure between the sole plates of the front and back walls; then cut the sidewall sole plates to fit between them. Attach the sole plates; then cut and attach the sidewall end studs, as shown in the detail drawing left. Cut the tops of the sidewall end studs and the ends of the top

RAFTER DETAIL

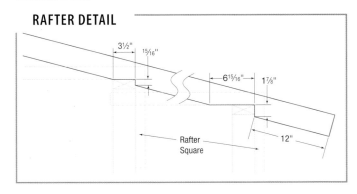

Installing the Roof. See page 109 for rafter framing details. After installing the rafters, attach 1x4 fascia to the rafter ends, roof sheathing, and roof shingles. Bird blocking between the rafters is optional.

Finishing the Shed. Install wall sheathing (if used), siding, door, and windows (optional). Refer to the appropriate sections in this book for installing these items. (See Chapter 6, pages 114–143 for information.)

PERSPECTIVE VIEW

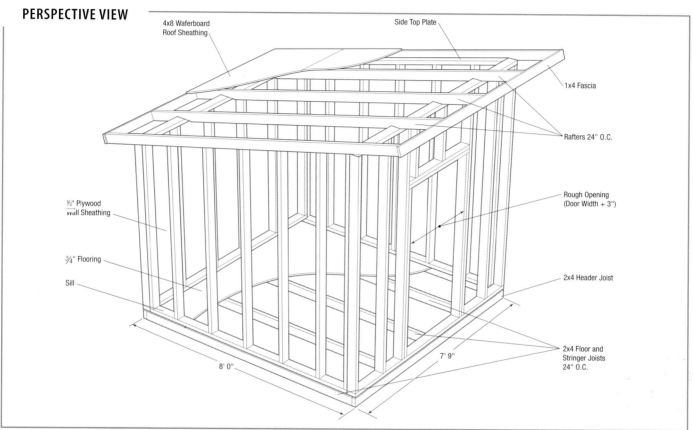

MATERIALS

8 X 8 SHED

5	2x4 x 8' floor joists
2	2x4 x 8' headerjoists
8	2x4 x 8' sole/top plates
9	2x4 x 6' studs
16	2x4 x 8' studs
5	2x4 x 12' rafters
2	¾" plywood sheets (flooring)
3	⁷⁄₁₆" waferboard sheets (roof sheathing)
2	1x4 x 8' pine or fir fascia
8	½" plywood sheets (wall sheathing)
96 sq. ft.	Roofing felt, shingles
11 ½ lbs.	16d nails
1 lb.	8d nails
2 ½ lbs.	8d spiral nails (flooring, roof)
2 ½ lbs.	6d galvanized nails (siding)
1 ½ lbs.	1 ½" roofing nails

8 X 10 SHED

6	2x4 x 8' floor joists
2	2x4 x 10' header joists
4	2x4 x 8' sole/top plates
4	2x4 x 10' sole/top plates
11	2x4 x 6' studs
18	2x4 x 8' studs
6	2x4 x 12' rafters
2 ½	¾" plywood sheets (flooring)
4	⁷⁄₁₆" waferboard sheets (roof sheathing)
2	1x4 x 10' pine or fir fascia
9	½" plywood sheets (wall sheathing)
120 sq. ft.	Roofing felt, shingles
2 lbs.	16d nails
1 ½ lbs.	8d nails
3 lbs.	8d spiral nails (flooring, roof)
3 lbs.	6d galvanized nails (siding)
2 lbs.	1 ½" roofing nails

8 X 12 SHED

7	2x4 x 8' floor joists
2	2x4 x 12' header joists
4	2x4 x 8' sole/top plates
4	2x4 x 12' sole/top plates
12	2x4 x 6' studs
19	2x4 x 8' studs
7	2x4 x 12' rafters
3	¾" plywood sheets (flooring)
4 ½	⁷⁄₁₆" waferboard sheets (roof sheathing)
2	1x4 x 12' pine or fir fascia
10	½" plywood sheets (wall sheathing)
144 sq. ft.	Roofing felt, shingles
2 ½ lbs.	16d nails
2 lbs.	8d nails
3 ½ lbs.	8d spiral nails (flooring, roof)
3 ½ lbs.	6d galvanized nails (siding)
2 ½ lbs.	1 ½" roofing nails

12

BASIC SHEDS   ## ATTACHED SHED

THIS SMALL, ATTACHED SHED is perfect for storing a variety of garden tools and implements. Although you can make the shed as long or as deep as you want, the dimensions shown here make best use of standard plywood and lumber sizes. Because the shed is only 2 feet deep, flooring and foundation requirements are minimal. The back of the floor is supported by a 2x4 ledger attached to the house; the front, by 4x4 pressure-treated posts set in concrete, like fence posts. You can substitute a poured concrete slab for the wood-framed floor shown here.

The back edge of the roof is attached to the house by means of a horizontal ledger; the shed sidewalls tie into the house via vertical ledger supports. We recommend ½-inch exterior plywood for the floor and roof sheathing; use plywood siding for the walls.

Building the Floor Platform. Cut the floor ledger 2'9" long. Level it and attach it to the house wall so that the bottom edge is 3 to 4 inches above ground level. Next locate and dig footing holes for posts at the front corners of shed. Cut the posts to length (add the depth below ground to the height above ground); then set them loosely in the holes (do not add concrete yet). Typically, posts should be set a minimum of 2 feet into the ground, and deeper in areas with severe frost heave.

Next, cut the two stringer joists and header joists to length. Attach the stringer joists to the post and ledger; then attach the header joist to the posts, as shown in the drawing Floor Platform. The top edge of the joists should be flush with the post top. With a framing square and level, make the platform square and level by adjusting the post height and location in the hole and backfilling with gravel, while keeping the posts plumb. Carefully backfill the holes with concrete. Check again for level and square; make any adjustments while the concrete is still wet. After the concrete sets, install the two intermediate 2x4 joists and ½-inch plywood floor.

Attaching the Vertical Ledger Supports and Roof Ledger. Cut the two vertical ledger supports to length, and attach them to the house at the back corners of the floor platform. Use a level to

PERSPECTIVE VIEW

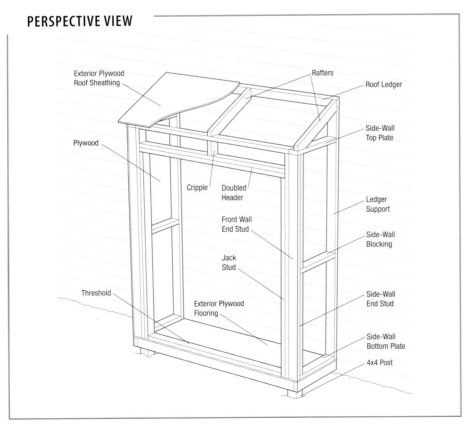

Exterior Plywood Roof Sheathing

Rafters

Roof Ledger

Plywood

Cripple   Doubled Header

Side-Wall Top Plate

Ledger Support

Front Wall End Stud

Jack Stud

Side-Wall Blocking

Threshold

Exterior Plywood Flooring

Side-Wall End Stud

Side-Wall Bottom Plate

4x4 Post

plumb them vertically; the distance between the outside edges of the supports at the top should be exactly 6 feet. Attach the ledger supports to the house wall with 16d nails and construction adhesive (for wood siding) or power-driven concrete nails (for masonry siding). Cut the roof ledger to length and bevel the top edge at a 27-degree angle, as shown in the drawing Ledger Supports. Attach the roof ledger to the house wall, and toenail it into the ledger supports.

MATERIALS

1	2x4* x 5' 9" floor ledger
2	4x4* x 3' posts
2	2x4* x 2' stringer joists
1	2x4* x 5' 9" header joist
16	2x4* x 1'9" joists
1	2'x6' x ½" ext. plywood (flooring)
2	2x4* x 7' 8 ½" ledger supports
1	2x4 x 6' roof ledger
1	2x4 x 5'5" front-wall top plate
1	2x4 x 1' 10 ½" sidewall top plate
1	2x4 x 5 ½" cripple
2	2x4 x 1' 9" sidewall bottom plate
2	2x4 x 6' 8 ½" sidewall end studs
2	2x4 x 6' 8 ½" front-wall end studs
2	2x4 x 5' 2" doubled header
2	2x4 x 6' jack studs
2	2x4 x 1' 9" sidewall blocking
3	2x4 x 25 ¼" rafters
4	½" plywood siding (siding, doors)
1	2' 6" x 6' 4" x ½" ext. plywood sheet (roof sheathing)
1	1x4 x 6' 1" fascia
1	1x4 x 6' 1 ½" skirt board, front wall
2	1x4 x 2' skirt board, sidewalls
2	90-lb. sacks ready-mix concrete, gravel
16 sq. ft.	Roofing felt, shingles
1	Hasp and lock (shed door)
2 lbs.	16d nails
2 lbs.	8d nails
2 lbs.	6d galvanized nails (siding, sheathing)
2 lbs.	4d roofing nails
6	4" strap hinges or T-hinges
* Treated lumber	

FLOOR PLATFORM

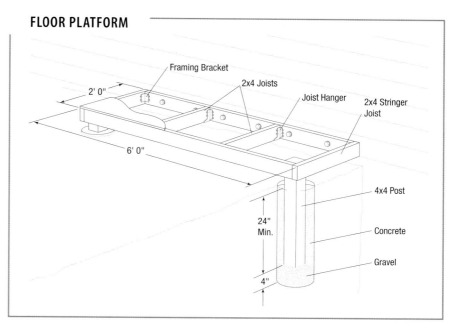

LEDGER SUPPORTS

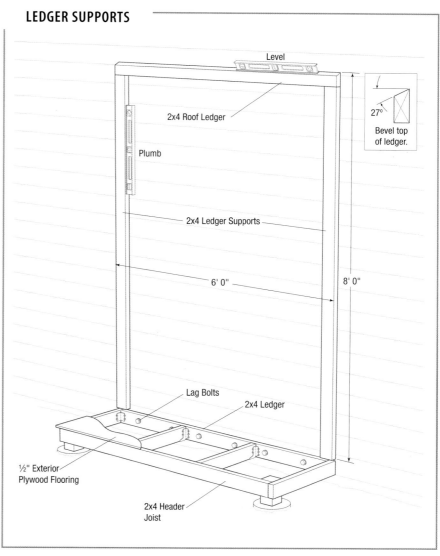

Framing the Walls and Roof. Refer to the framing drawings, but pay particular attention to the Corner Detail below. The corner framing will support the large double doors on the front of the shed. Cut all the framing pieces to the lengths indicated in the Material List on page 247. Frame the sidewalls first; then attach the full studs, jack studs, top plate, header, and cripple to complete the front wall and door opening. Finally, cut and attach the rafters to the front-wall top plate and roof ledger.

Installing the Siding, Roof Sheathing, and Roof. Cut and attach the ½-inch plywood siding to the side walls using 6d

FRONT & SIDE ELEVATIONS

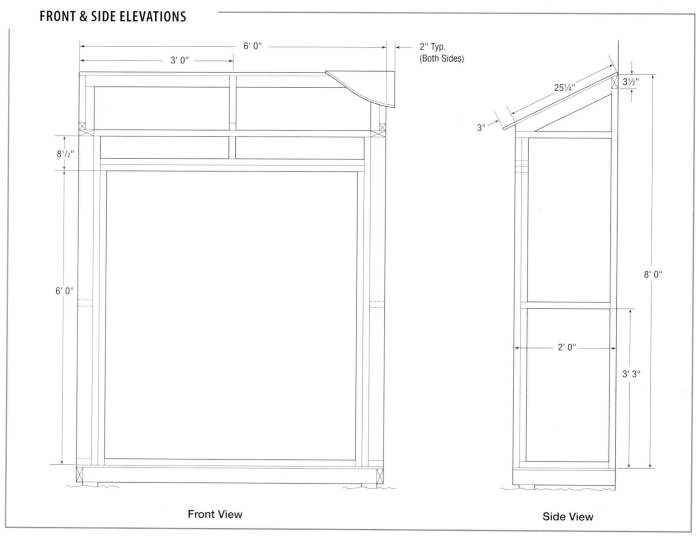

Front View

Side View

CORNER DETAIL

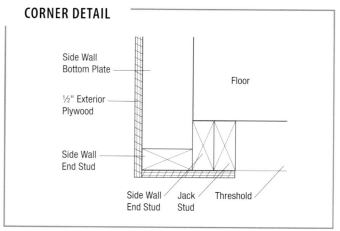

RAFTER LAYOUT

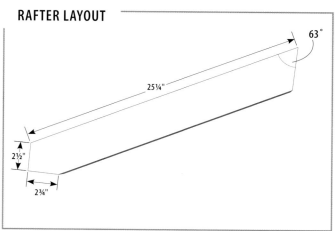

galvanized nails; then attach the siding around the door opening in the front wall. The siding should be flush with the sides of the framed door opening and flush with the bottom edge of the top 2x4 in the doubled header. The bottom 2x4 in the header serves as a doorstop.

Cut the roof sheathing so that it overlaps the front wall by 3 inches and the sidewalls by 2 inches. Using 8d galvanized finishing nails, attach the 1x4 fascia board across the top of the front wall just under the roof overhang, as shown right. Then install the 1x4 skirt around the base of the shed. As an option, you can install 1x4 trim strips to cover exposed plywood edges at the front corners of the shed, under the eaves on the sidewalls, and at the back corners of the shed where it meets the house wall.

Installing the Roofing. Install metal flashing under the shingles of the house where it meets the top of the roof. Caulk the joint where the roof sheathing meets the house wall. Apply a metal drip cap to the front edge of the roof deck. Cut and staple 15-pound roofing felt over the sheathing, overlapping the joints if necessary. Install asphalt shingles starting at the bottom of the roof. Begin by laying out a starter strip of shingles along the bottom edge. Cover this strip with another layer of shingles and proceed up the roof. Be sure to offset any joints. Any metal flashing at the joint where the house meets the shed should rest on top of the top course of shingles. To make the job go quickly, overlap shingles at the edge of the roof and go back when the entire roof is completed and trim with shears.

Marking and Hanging the Doors. From ½-inch siding material, cut doors to the dimensions shown on the drawing Door Detail. If the dimensions of your shed are different from the one shown here, be sure to leave a ¹⁄₁₆-inch clearance between each door and the rough opening (top, sides, and bottom) and a ⅛-inch gap where the two doors meet. Hang the doors in the opening using at least three large strap hinges or T-hinges placed at the top, bottom, and middle of the door.

ROOFING DETAIL

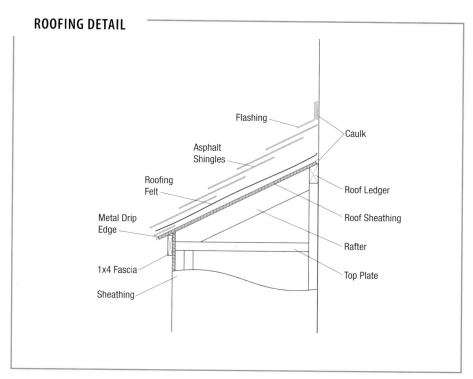

DOOR DETAIL

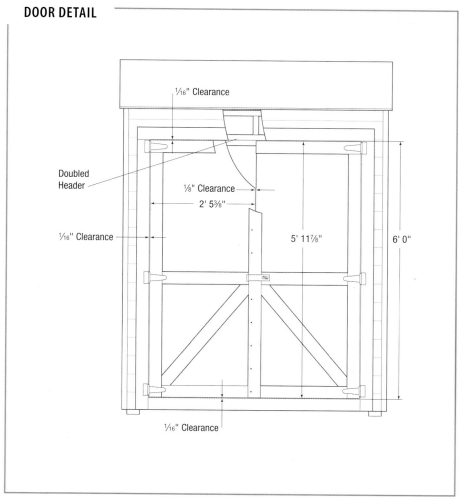

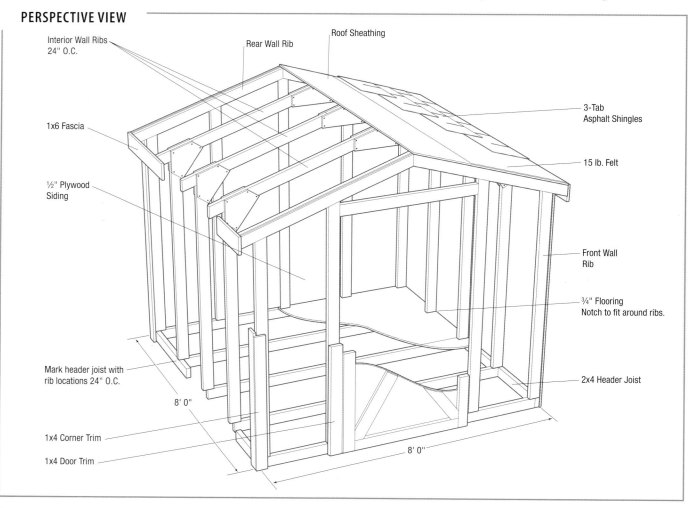

THIS SECTION shows how to frame a gable-roof shed. Unlike platform framing used to build houses and some types of large barns, the directions shown here are for framing sheds with rib-type construction. It consists of a front-wall rib, a rear-wall rib, and as many interior ribs as desired for the shed length you want, spaced on 2-foot centers. Each interior rib consists of two rafters, two studs, and a floor joist, reinforced with plywood gussets; the front- and rear-wall ribs include additional framing members as shown. They are made structurally stable by the plywood siding attached to them. The ribs are connected at the bottom with 2x4 stringer joists.

Cutting and Assembling the Ribs.
The drawings on pages 251 to 252 show rib details for 8- and 10-foot-wide sheds. Cut all of the rib members to the lengths and angles shown in the drawing. Assemble

13

BASIC SHEDS GABLE-ROOF SHED

PERSPECTIVE VIEW

Interior Wall Ribs 24" O.C.

Rear Wall Rib

Roof Sheathing

3-Tab Asphalt Shingles

1x6 Fascia

15 lb. Felt

½" Plywood Siding

Front Wall Rib

¾" Flooring Notch to fit around ribs.

Mark header joist with rib locations 24" O.C.

8' 0"

2x4 Header Joist

1x4 Corner Trim

1x4 Door Trim

8' 0"

GUSSETS

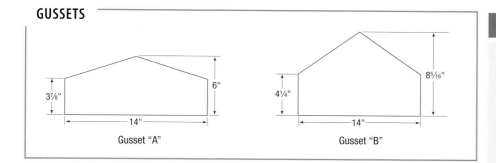

Gusset "A"   Gusset "B"

MATERIALS

8 X 8 SHED

2	2x4 x 8' header joists
1	2x4 front-wall rib assembly
1	2x4 rear-wall rib assembly
3	2x4 interior-wall rib assemblies
2	¾" plywood sheets (flooring)
2½	⁷⁄₁₆" waferboard sheets (roof sheathing)
4	1x4 x 10' pine or fir fascia/trim
2	1x4 x 14' pine or fir fascia/trim
6½	½" plywood siding (walls, door)
2	bundles of asphalt shingles
1	1x4 x 10' pine or fir door trim
2	1x4 x 14' pine or fir door trim
1½ lbs.	16d nails
1 lb.	8d nails
2½ lbs.	8d spiral nails (flooring, roof)
2½ lbs.	6d galvanized nails (siding)
1½ lbs.	1½" roofing nails
½ lb	3d galvanized finishing nails
3	Surface-mounted door hinges

10 X 10 SHED

2	2x4 x 10' stringer joists
1	2x4 front-wall rib assembly
1	2x4 rear-wall rib assembly
4	2x4 interior-wall rib assemblies
3¼	¾" plywood sheets (flooring)
4	⁷⁄₁₆" waferboard sheets (roof sheathing)
2	1x4 x 10' pine or fir fascia/trim
4	1x4 x 14' pine or fir fascia/trim
8	½" plywood siding (walls, door)
5	bundles of asphalt shingles
1	1x4 x 10' pine or fir door trim
2	1x4 x 14' pine or fir door trim
2 lbs.	16d nails
1 ½ lbs.	8d nails
3 lbs.	8d spiral nails (flooring, roof)
3 lbs.	6d galvanized nails (siding)
2 lbs.	1½" roofing nails
½ lb.	3d galvanized finishing nails
3	Surface-mounted door hinges

the front-wall rib, rear-wall rib, and as many interior ribs as desired (three ribs for an 8-foot shed, four ribs for a 10-foot shed, etc.). Each rib is assembled on the ground then lifted into position. (See Rib Details, page 252.)

Erecting the Ribs. Cut two header joists to the length of the shed, and mark the rib locations on each. Have a helper hold each rib upright while you nail it to the header joists with two 16d galvanized nails. After you've installed all of the ribs, use a level to plumb them vertically; then tack 1x4 braces across the upper rib members to keep them in position. Remove the braces when you attach the sheathing.

Installing the Flooring. Use 6d nails to attach the plywood flooring to the joists; notch the panels, as shown in the drawing on page 250, to fit around the ribs.

Adding Siding, Roofing, and Trim. Attach the ½-inch plywood siding and waferboard or plywood roof sheathing with 6d galvanized nails. Then attach the 1x4 corner trim, door trim, and fascia where shown in the drawing. Staple building felt on the roof sheathing and attach three-tab asphalt shingles with the roofing nails.

Building the Door. Make the door using the same material as used for the siding. Cut the door to provide ¹⁄₁₆-inch clearance on all sides between the door and the rough opening. Attach 1x4 door trim around the perimeter of the plywood door with screws or 3d galvanized finishing nails and construction adhesive. Cut sections of 1x4 and attach them to form an "X" design as shown in the drawing. Install 1x4 trim around the opening, as shown, then attach the door using sturdy hinges.

RIB MEMBERS

Use alternate dimensions shown in italic for 10-foot shed. Match with page 252.

1
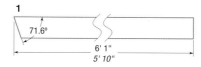

2

3

4

5

6

7

8
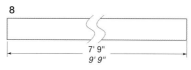

RIB DETAILS

Use alternate dimensions shown in italic for 10-foot shed. Match with Rib Members, page 251.

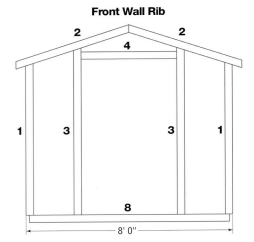

Front Wall Rib

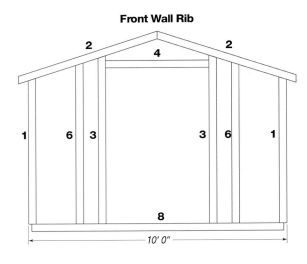

Front Wall Rib

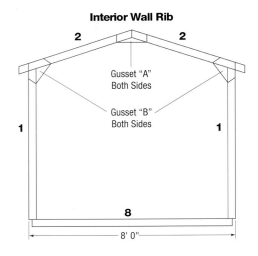

Interior Wall Rib

Gusset "A" Both Sides

Gusset "B" Both Sides

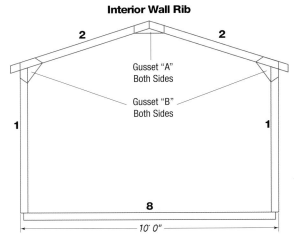

Interior Wall Rib

Gusset "A" Both Sides

Gusset "B" Both Sides

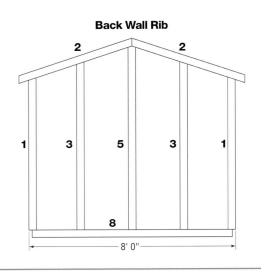

Back Wall Rib

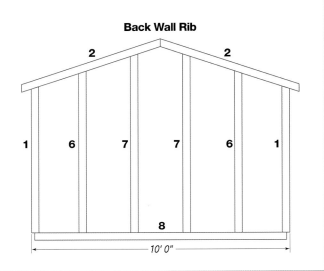

Back Wall Rib

THIS BARN-STYLE SHED uses simple rib construction. It consists of a front-wall rib, a rear-wall rib, and as many interior ribs desired for the shed length you want, spaced on 2-foot centers. Each interior rib consists of upper and lower roof chords (four total), two studs, plywood gussets, and a floor joist. Front- and rear-wall ribs include additional framing members as shown and are made structurally stable by the plywood siding attached to them. The ribs are connected at the bottom with 2x4 header joists.

Making the Assemblies. The drawings on pages 254 to 255 show the details for 8- and 10-foot-wide sheds. It's a good idea to cut the pieces that form the outside of each rib assembly and join them with gussets before you cut the square-cut pieces. Then you can measure in case the lengths of the square-cut pieces need to vary a bit from the dimensions given in the drawing Rib Members. Cut all of the rib members to the lengths and angles shown. Assemble the front-wall rib, rear-wall rib, and as many interior ribs as desired (three

14

BASIC SHEDS   BARN-STYLE SHED

PERSPECTIVE VIEW

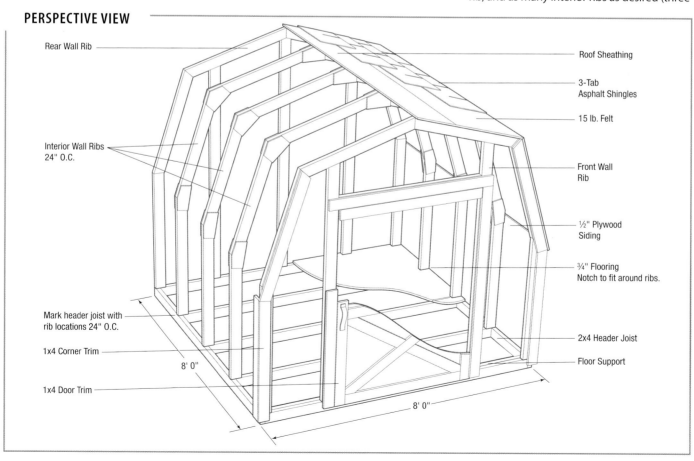

Rear Wall Rib

Interior Wall Ribs 24" O.C.

Mark header joist with rib locations 24" O.C.

1x4 Corner Trim

1x4 Door Trim

8' 0"

Roof Sheathing

3-Tab Asphalt Shingles

15 lb. Felt

Front Wall Rib

½" Plywood Siding

¾" Flooring Notch to fit around ribs.

2x4 Header Joist

Floor Support

8' 0"

MATERIALS

8 X 8 SHED

2	2x4 x 8' header joists
1	2x4 front-wall rib assembly
1	2x4 rear-wall rib assembly
3	2x4 interior-wall rib assemblies
2	¾" plywood sheets
4	⁷⁄₁₆" waferboard sheets (roof sheathing)
1	1x4 x 8' pine or fir fascia/trim
6	1x4 x 12' pine or fir fascia/trim
6	½" plywood siding (walls, door)
4	bundles of asphalt shingles
1	1x4 x 10' pine or fir fascia/trim
2	1x4 x 12' pine or fir fascia/trim
4 lbs.	2d nails (gussets)
½ lb.	16d nails
½ lb.	8d nails
2½ lbs.	8d spiral nails (flooring, roofing)
2½ lbs.	6d galvanized nails (siding)
1½ lbs.	1½" roofing nails
3	Surface-mounted door hinges

10 X 10 SHED

2	2x4 x 10' header joists
1	2x4 front-wall rib assembly
1	2x4 rear-wall rib assembly
4	2x4 interior-wall rib assemblies
3 ½	¾" plywood sheets (flooring)
5	⁷⁄₁₆" waferboard sheets (roof sheathing)
1	1x4 x 8' pine or fir fascia/trim
6	1x4 x 12' pine or fir fascia/trim
7 ½	½" plywood siding (walls, door)
5	bundles of asphalt shingles
1	1x4 x 10' pine or fir door trim
2	1x4 x 12' pine or fir door trim
4 lbs.	2d nails (gussets)
½ lb.	16d nails
½ lb.	8d nails
3 lbs.	8d spiral nails (flooring, roofing)
3 lbs.	6d galvanized nails (siding)
2 lbs.	1½" roofing nails
3	Surface-mounted door hinges

ribs for an 8-foot shed, four ribs for a 10-foot shed, etc.). Make cardboard templates of the gussets to make sure they fit. Approximate sizes and shapes are shown at right on page 255. Assemble each rib on the ground, and then lift it into position.

Erecting the Ribs. Cut two header joists to the length of the shed, and mark the rib locations. Have a helper hold the ribs upright. Plumb them while you connect them with 1x4 braces. (Remove the braces as you install the siding.) Nail the header joists to the rib joists with 16d nails, and add a joist to the front and rear ribs.

Installing the Flooring. Use 6d nails to attach the plywood flooring to the joists; notch the panels, as shown opposite, to fit around the interior ribs.

Adding the Siding, Roofing, and Trim. Attach the ½-inch plywood siding and roof sheathing with 6d galvanized nails. Then attach the 1x4 corner trim, door trim, and fascia. Staple roofing felt on the roof sheathing, and attach the asphalt shingles with the roofing nails.

Building the Door. Make the barn-style door from the same material you used for the siding. Cut the door to provide a ¹⁄₁₆-inch clearance on all sides. Attach 1x4 door trim around the perimeter of the plywood door with the galvanized finishing nails; then cut sections of 1x4 and attach them to form the "X" design. Install 1x4 trim around the opening, as shown, and then attach the door using sturdy hinges.

GUSSETS

Use alternate dimensions shown in italic for 10-foot shed.

A — 1⅜", 5", 8"
D — 1¼", 4⅞", 10"
B — 1⅜", 6", 8"
E — 2¼", 6", 10"
C — ¾", 4½", 9"
F — 1¼", 4¾", 10"

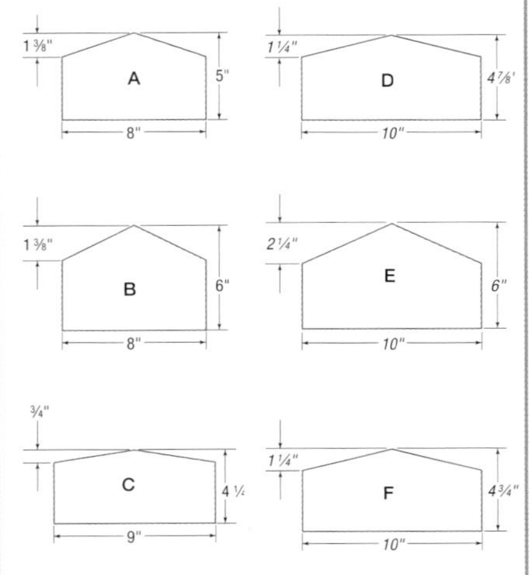

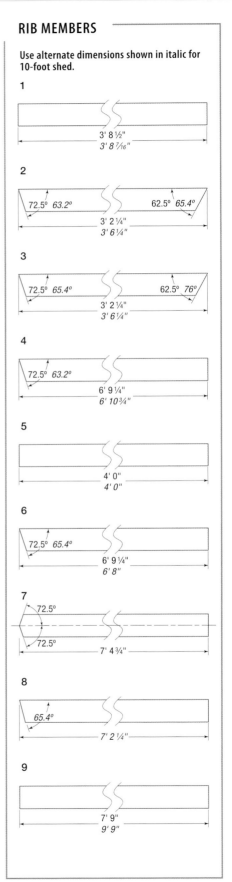

RIB MEMBERS

Use alternate dimensions shown in italic for 10-foot shed.

1 — 3' 8½", *3' 8⁷⁄₁₆"*

2 — 72.5° 63.2°, 62.5° 65.4°, 3' 2¼", *3' 6¼"*

3 — 72.5° 65.4°, 62.5° 76°, 3' 2¼", *3' 6¼"*

4 — 72.5° 63.2°, 6' 9¼", *6' 10¾"*

5 — 4' 0", *4' 0"*

6 — 72.5° 65.4°, 6' 9¼", *6' 8"*

7 — 72.5°, 72.5°, 7' 4¾"

8 — 65.4°, 7' 2¼"

9 — 7' 9", *9' 9"*

RIB DETAILS

Use alternate dimensions shown in italic for 10-foot shed.

Front Wall Rib

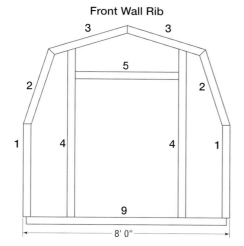

8' 0"

Front Wall Rib

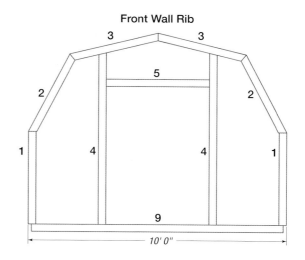

10' 0"

Interior Wall Rib

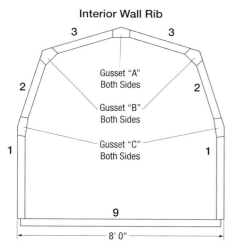

Gusset "A" Both Sides

Gusset "B" Both Sides

Gusset "C" Both Sides

8' 0"

Interior Wall Rib

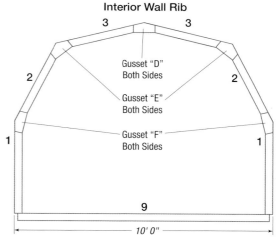

Gusset "D" Both Sides

Gusset "E" Both Sides

Gusset "F" Both Sides

10' 0"

Back Wall Rib

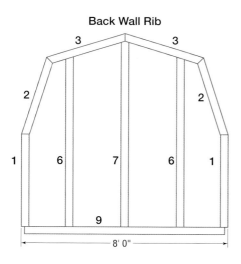

8' 0"

Back Wall Rib

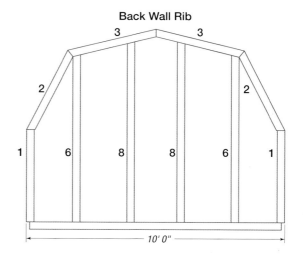

10' 0"

WHAT KIND OF PLAN DO YOU NEED?

Now that you've found the plan you've been looking for, determine the plan package best for your particular situation by reading the descriptions below. To order, visit houseplansandmore.com and type the plan number into the plan search to see specific plan options and current pricing. Then, easily order online!

PLEASE NOTE: Not all plan packages listed below are available for every plan. Please refer to houseplansandmore.com for a specific plan's current plan package options and pricing. For questions, visit houseplansandmore.com, or call 1-800-373-2646.

Your choices are:

1-SET PLAN PACKAGE is one full set of the construction drawings. A 1-set package is copyrighted, so therefore it can't be reproduced. Keep in mind, if you have to submit the plan to your local building department in order to obtain a building permit, then you would have to order additional sets.

3-SET PLAN PACKAGE is three full sets of the construction drawings. A 3-set package is copyrighted, so therefore it can't be reproduced. Keep in mind, if you have to submit the plan to your local building department in order to obtain a building permit, then you may need to order additional sets.

5-SET PLAN PACKAGE includes five complete sets of construction drawings. Besides one set for yourself, additional sets of blueprints will be required for your lender, your local building department, your contractor, and any other tradespeople working on your project.

8-SET PLAN PACKAGE includes eight complete sets of construction drawings. Besides one set for yourself, additional sets of blueprints will be required for your lender, your local building department, your contractor, and any other tradespeople working on your project.

REPRODUCIBLE MASTERS is one complete paper set of construction drawings that can be modified. They include a one-time build copyright release that allows you to draw changes on the plans. This allows you, your builder, or a local design professional to make the necessary drawing changes without the major expense of entirely redrawing the plans. Easily make minor drawing changes by using correction fluid to remove small areas of the existing drawing, then draw in your modifications. Once the plan has been altered to fit your needs, you have the right to copy, or reproduce the modified plans as needed for building your project. Please note the right of building only one structure from these plans is licensed exclusively to the buyer. You may not use this design to build a second or multiple dwelling(s) without purchasing a multi-build license.

PDF FILE FORMAT is our most popular plan option because of how fast you can receive them and their ability to easily share via email with your contractor, subcontractors, and local building officials. The PDF file format is a complete set of construction drawings in an electronic file format. It includes a one-time build copyright release that allows you to make changes and copies of the plans. Typically you will receive a PDF file via email within 24-48 hours (Monday - Friday) allowing you to save money on shipping. Upon receiving, visit a local copy shop and print the number of plans you need to build your project, or print one and alter the plan using correction fluid and drawing in your modifications. Please note: These are flat image files and cannot be altered electronically. PDF files are non-refundable and not returnable.

CAD FILE FORMAT is the actual computer files for a plan directly from AutoCAD, or another computer aided design program. CAD files are the best option if you have a significant amount of changes to make to the plan, or if you need to make the plan fit your local codes. If you purchase a CAD File, it allows you, or a local design professional the ability to modify the plans electronically in a CAD program, so making changes to the plan is easier and less expensive than using a paper set of plans. CAD File Format also includes a one-time build copyright release that allows you to legally make your changes, and print multiple copies of the plan. CAD files are non-refundable and not returnable.

OTHER PLAN OPTIONS

MIRROR REVERSE SETS A mirror reverse set of plans is simply a mirror image of the original drawings causing the lettering and dimensions to read backwards. Therefore, when ordering a mirror reverse set of plans, you must purchase at least one set of the original plans to read from, and use the mirror reverse set for construction. Some plans offer right-reading reverse for an additional fee. This means the plan has been redrawn by the designer as the mirrored version and can easily be read.

ADDITIONAL SETS You can order additional plan sets for an additional fee. A 1-set, 3-set, 5-set, 8-set, or reproducible masters must have been previously purchased. Please note: Only available within 90 days after purchase of a plan package.

MATERIAL LIST Many projects in this book include a material list that gives you the quantity, dimensions, and description of the building materials necessary to construct your shed or outdoor structure. Some plans have a material list that can be purchased for an additional fee (see specific plan for availability and pricing at houseplansandmore.com). Keep in mind, due to variations in local building requirements, exact material quantities cannot be guaranteed. Note: Material lists are created with the standard foundation only. Please review the material list and the construction drawings with your material supplier to verify measurements and quantities of the materials listed before ordering supplies.

2" x 6" EXTERIOR WALLS Some plans have an upgrade to 2" x 6" exterior walls that can be purchased for an additional fee (see specific plan for availability and pricing at houseplansandmore.com).

BEFORE YOU ORDER

PLEASE NOTE: Plan pricing is subject to change without notice. For current pricing, visit houseplansandmore.com, or call 1-800-373-2646.

BUILDING CODE REQUIREMENTS At the time the construction drawings were prepared, every effort was made to ensure that these plans and specifications met nationally recognized codes. These plans conform to most national building codes. Because building codes vary from area to area, some drawing modifications and/or the assistance of a professional designer or architect may be necessary to comply with your local codes, or to accommodate your specific building site conditions. We advise you to consult with your local building official, or a local builder for information regarding codes governing your area prior to ordering blueprints.

COPYRIGHT Plans are protected under Copyright Law. Reproduction of copyrighted blueprints by any means is strictly prohibited. The right of building only one structure from all plan packages is licensed exclusively to the buyer and the plans may not be resold unless by express written authorization from the home designer, or architect. You may not use this design to build a second or multiple structure(s) without purchasing a multi-build license. Each violation of the Copyright Law is punishable in a fine.

LICENSE TO BUILD When you purchase a "full set of construction drawings" from Design America, Inc., you are purchasing an exclusive one-time "License to Build," not the rights to the design. Design America, Inc. is granting you permission on behalf of the plan's designer or architect to use the construction drawings one-time for the building of the project. The construction drawings (also referred to as blueprints/plans and any derivative of that plan whether extensive or minor) are still owned and protected under copyright laws by the original designer. The blueprints/plans cannot be resold, transferred, rented, loaned or used by anyone other than the original purchaser of the "License to Build" without written consent from Design America, Inc. or the plan designer. If you are interested in building the plan more than once, please call 1-800-373-2646 and inquire about purchasing a Multi-Build License that will allow you to build a design more than one time. Please note: A "full set of construction drawings" also includes CAD files and PDF files.

EXCHANGE POLICY Since blueprints are printed in response to your order, we cannot honor requests for refunds.

PLAN INDEX

SHIPPING & HANDLING CHARGES

U.S. SHIPPING
(AK and HI express only)

Regular (allow 7-10 business days)	$30.00
Priority (allow 3-5 business days)	$50.00
Express* (allow 1-2 business days)	$70.00

CANADA SHIPPING**

Regular (allow 8-12 business days)	$50.00
Express* (allow 3-5 business days)	$100.00

OVERSEAS SHIPPING / INTERNATIONAL**
Call, fax, or e-mail (customerservice@designamerica.com) for shipping costs.

* For express delivery please call by 11:00 am Monday-Friday CST

** Orders may be subject to custom's fees and or duties taxes.

PLEASE NOTE: Shipping and handling does not apply on PDF and CAD File orders. PDF and CAD orders will be emailed within 24-48 hours (Monday - Friday) of purchase.

URBAN STYLE SHED

Plan #F52-127D-4514

- 9 sizes available:

12' x 8'	14' x 8'	16' x 8'
12' x 10'	14' x 10'	16' x 10'
12' x 12'	14' x 12'	16' x 12'

- Foundation: Wood floor on concrete blocks
- Building heights:
  11'-4 1/2" with 8' depth
  11'-10 1/2" with 10' depth
  12'-4 1/2" with 12' depth
- Ceiling height: 7'-6"
- Construction prints are 8 1/2" x 11" in size

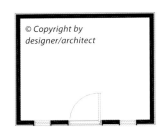

© Copyright by designer/architect

SALT BOX STORAGE SHEDS

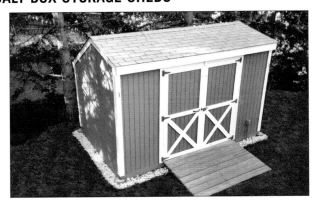

Plan #F52-002D-4500

- Includes 3 sizes:
  8' x 8'   12' x 8'   16' x 8'
- Foundation: Wood floor on gravel base or slab
- Building height: 8'-2"
- Front wall height: 7'
- Material list and step-by-step instructions included

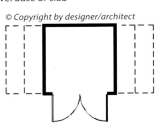

© Copyright by designer/architect

MODERN SHED

Plan #F52-127D-4512

- 15 sizes available:

8' x 8'	14' x 8'	12' x 12'
8' x 10'	16' x 8'	14' x 10'
8' x 12'	10' x 10'	14' x 12'
10' x 8'	10' x 12'	16' x 10'
12' x 8'	12' x 10'	16' x 12'

- Ceiling height: 7'-6" vaulted
- Construction prints are 8 1/2" x 11" in size

- Foundation: Wood floor on concrete blocks
- Building heights:
  12'-0 1/2" with 8' width
  12'-8 1/2" with 10' width
  13'-4 1/2" with 12' width
  14'-0 1/2" with 14' width
  11'-8 1/2" with 16' width

© Copyright by designer/architect

CHILDREN'S PLAYHOUSE

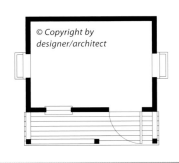

Plan #F52-002D-4505

- Width: 8'   Depth: 8'
- 64 square feet
- Foundation: Wood floor on 4x4 runners
- Building height: 9'-2"
- Ceiling height: 6'-1"
- Material list and step-by-step instructions included

© Copyright by designer/architect

BARN GARDEN SHED

Plan #F52-160D-4500

- Width: 19'   Depth: 14'
- 266 total square feet
  Garden storage: 168
  Lawn tractor shed: 98
- Foundation: Raised wood
  floor or slab
- Building height: 16'

© Copyright by
designer/architect

work bench

sink

lawn
tractor
shed
7' x 14'

garden
storage
12' x 14'

planter
box

6' double door opening

GARDEN SHED

Plan #F52-002D-4523

- Width: 10'   Depth: 10'
- 100 square feet
- Building height: 11'-3 1/2"
- Left wall height: 8'
- Foundation: Wood floor
  on 4x4 runners
- Material list and
  step-by-step instructions
  included

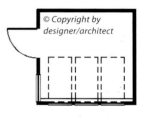

© Copyright by
designer/architect

DOG SHED

Plan #F52-142D-4505

- Width: 8'   Depth: 12'
- 96 total square feet
  Dog run: 64
  Dog room: 32
- Foundation: Wood floor joists
  over treated girders
- Building height: 11'-5"
- Ceiling height: 8'

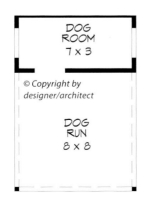

DOG
ROOM
7 x 3

© Copyright by
designer/architect

DOG
RUN
8 x 8

GARDEN SHEDS WITH CLERESTORY WINDOW

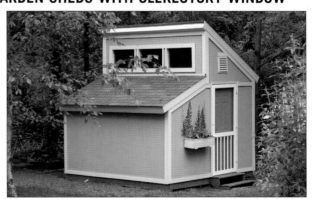

Plan #F52-002D-4515

- Includes 3 sizes:
  10' x 10'   12' x 10'   14' x 10'
- Foundation: Wood floor on 4x6 runners
- Building height: 10'-11"
- Rear wall height: 7'-3"
- Material list and
  step-by-step instructions
  included

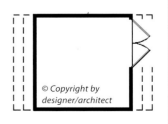

© Copyright by
designer/architect

INNOVATIVE SHED

Plan #F52-127D-4513

- 15 sizes available:

8' x 8'	14' x 8'	12' x 12'
8' x 10'	16' x 8'	14' x 10'
8' x 12'	10' x 10'	14' x 12'
10' x 8'	10' x 12'	16' x 10'
12' x 8'	12' x 10'	16' x 12'

- Foundation: Wood floor on concrete blocks

- Building heights:
  12'-0 1/2" with 8' width
  12'-8 1/2" with 10' width
  13'-4 1/2" with 12' width

- Ceiling heights: 7'-6" and vaults to:
  10'-2" with 8' depth
  10'-10" with 10' depth
  11'-6" with 12' depth

- Construction prints are 8 1/2" x 11" in size

© Copyright by designer/architect

SHED WITH COVERED PORCH

Plan #F52-125D-4502

- Width: 19'   Depth: 17'
- 151 square feet
- Foundation: Slab
- Building height: 16'
- Ceiling height: 9'

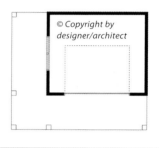

© Copyright by designer/architect

POTTING SHED WITH SINK

Plan #F52-125D-4503

- Width: 12'   Depth: 15'
- 180 square feet
- Foundation: Slab
- Building height: 14'-4"
- Ceiling height: 9'
- 2" x 6" wall upgrade available for a fee

© Copyright by designer/architect

Potting Shed
11⁴ x 14⁴

RUSTIC CRAFTSMAN SHED

Plan #F52-142D-4501

- Width: 15'   Depth: 15'
- 225 total square feet
  Shed: 150
  Porch: 75
- Foundation: Wood floor joists over treated girders
- Building height: 14'
- Ceiling height: 8'
- 2" x 6" wall upgrade available for a fee
- Foundation upgrade to slab available for a fee

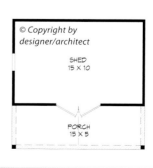

© Copyright by designer/architect

SHED
15 X 10

PORCH
15 X 5

STORAGE SHED WITH PLAYHOUSE LOFT

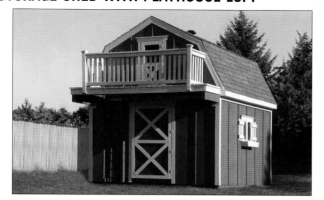

Plan #F52-002D-4514

- Width: 12'   Depth: 12'
- 144 square feet
- Foundation: Wood floor on concrete pier or slab
- Building height: 14'-1"
- Ceiling height: 7'-4"
- Material list and step-by-step instructions included

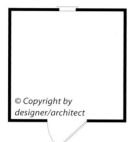

© Copyright by designer/architect

YARD BARN WITH LOFT STORAGE

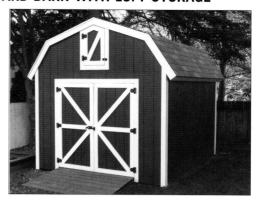

Plan #F52-002D-4520

- Width: 10'   Depth: 12'
- 120 square feet
- Foundation: Wood floor on 4x4 runners
- Building height: 10'-7"
- Ceiling height: 6'-11"
- Material list and step-by-step instructions included

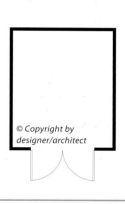

© Copyright by designer/architect

CONVENIENCE SHED

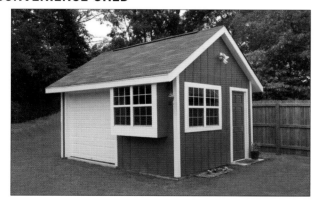

Plan #F52-002D-4506

- Width: 16'   Depth: 12'
- 192 square feet
- Foundation: Slab
- Building height: 12'-4 1/2"
- Ceiling height: 8'
- Material list and step-by-step instructions included

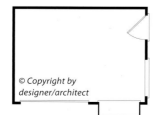

© Copyright by designer/architect

BARN STORAGE SHEDS WITH LOFT

Plan #F52-002D-4501

- Includes 3 sizes:
  12' x 12'   12' x 16'   12' x 20'
- Foundation: Wood floor on pier or slab
- Building height: 12'-10"
- Ceiling height: 7'-4"
- Material list and step-by-step instructions included

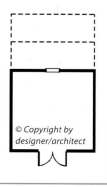

© Copyright by designer/architect

PRACTICAL GARDEN SHED

Plan #F52-127D-4516

- 9 sizes available:
12' x 10'	14' x 10'	16' x 10'
12' x 12'	14' x 12'	16' x 12'
12' x 14'	14' x 14'	16' x 14'
- Foundation: Wood floor on concrete blocks
- Ceiling height: 7'-6"
- Construction prints are 8 1/2" x 11" in size

© Copyright by designer/architect

GARDEN SHED GREENHOUSE

Plan #F52-127D-4517

- Width: 14'   Depth: 10'
- 140 square feet
- Foundation: Wood floor on concrete blocks
- Building height: 11'-8"
- Ceiling height: 7'-6"
- Construction prints are 8 1/2" x 11" in size

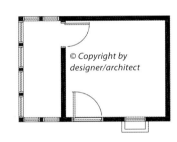

© Copyright by designer/architect

GABLE STORAGE SHEDS

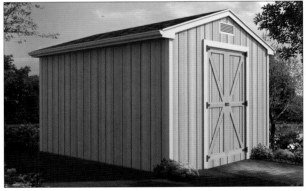

Plan #F52-002D-4504

- Includes 3 sizes:
10' x 12'	10' x 16'	10' x 20'
- Foundation: Wood floor on 4x4 runners
- Building height: 8'-8 1/2"
- Ceiling height: 7'
- Material list and step-by-step instructions included

© Copyright by designer/architect

YARD BARNS

Plan #F52-002D-4502

- Includes 3 sizes:
10' x 12'	10' x 16'	10' x 20'
- Foundation: Wood floor on 4x4 runners
- Building height: 8'-4 1/2"
- Ceiling height: 6'-4"
- Material list and step-by-step instructions included

© Copyright by designer/architect

GARDEN WORKSHOP WITH PORCH

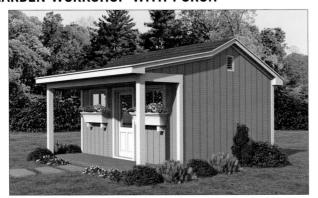

Plan #F52-142D-4500

- Width: 16'   Depth: 16'
- 256 total square feet
  Workshop: 192
  Porch: 64
- Foundation: Slab
- Building height: 11'-4"
- Ceiling height: 8'
- 2" x 6" wall upgrade
  available for a fee
- Foundation upgrade to
  pier/girder available for a fee

© Copyright by
designer/architect

WORKSHOP
15 X 11

PORCH
16 X 4

GABLED GARDEN SHED

Plan #F52-127D-4510

- Width: 14'   Depth: 13'
- 322 total square feet
  1st floor: 182
  2nd floor: 140
- Foundation: Wood floor
  on concrete blocks
- Building height: 15'-7"
- Ceiling height: 7'-6"
- Construction prints are
  8 1/2" x 11" in size

2nd Floor

© Copyright by
designer/architect

1st Floor

SHED WITH WINDOW BOX

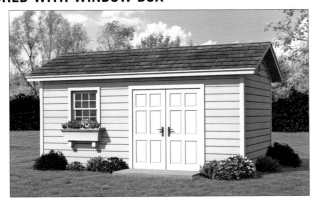

Plan #F52-142D-4504

- Width: 18'-4"   Depth: 10'-5"
- 191 square feet
- Foundation: Slab
- Building height: 10'-8"
- Ceiling height: 8'
- 2" x 6" wall upgrade
  available for a fee
- Foundation upgrade to
  pier/girder available
  for a fee

© Copyright by designer/architect

SHED WITH SHOP & PERGOLA

Plan #F52-142D-4502

- Width: 28'   Depth: 14'
- 352 total square feet
  Shed: 252
  Shop: 100
- Foundation: Slab or
  wood floor joists over
  treated girders
- Building height: 16'-4"
- Ceiling height: 12'
- 2" x 6" wall upgrade available for a fee
- Foundation upgrade to slab available for a fee

© Copyright by
designer/architect

SHED
17'3 X 13'3

SHOP
9'8 X 9'3

PERGOLA
10' x 4'

LAWN EQUIPMENT SHED

Plan #F52-142D-4506

- Width: 20'   Depth: 20'
- 361 total square feet
  Shop: 209
  Lawn Equipment: 120
  Storage: 32
- Foundation: Slab
- Building height: 14'-7"
- Ceiling height: 8'

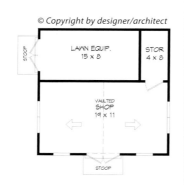

WORKSHOP SUITE WITH BATH

Plan #F52-142D-4503

- Width: 15'   Depth: 30'
- 450 total square feet
  Workshop: 383
  Bath: 67
- Foundation: Slab
- Building height: 13'-6"
- Ceiling height: 9'
- 2" x 6" wall upgrade
  available for a fee
- Foundation upgrade to pier/girder
  available for a fee

SHED WITH PORCH & FIREWOOD STORAGE

Plan #F52-125D-4501

- Width: 17'   Depth: 12'
- 122 square feet
- Foundation: Slab
- Building height: 16'-10"
- Ceiling height: 9'

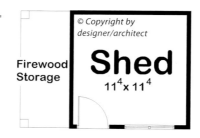

SHED WITH COVERED FRONT PORCH

Plan #F52-125D-4500

- Width: 14'   Depth: 17'
- 168 square feet
- Foundation: Slab
- Building height: 16'
- Ceiling height: 9'

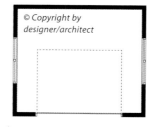

BARN STORAGE SHED WITH OVERHEAD DOOR

Plan #F52-002D-4521

- Width: 12'   Depth: 16'
- 192 square feet
- Foundation: Slab
- Building height: 12'-5"
- Ceiling height: 8'
- Material list and step-by-step instructions included

© Copyright by designer/architect

MINI BARNS

Plan #F52-002D-4524

- Includes 4 sizes:
  8' x 8'   8'x 10'   8' x 12'   8' x 16'
- Foundation: Wood floor on 4x4 runners
- Building height: 7'-6"
- Ceiling height: 6'
- Material list and step-by-step instructions included

© Copyright by designer/architect

BARN STORAGE SHEDS

Plan #F52-002D-4508

- Includes 3 sizes:
  12' x 8'   12' x 12'   12' x 16'
- Foundation: Wood floor on pier or slab
- Building height: 9'-10"
- Ceiling height: 7'-10"
- Material list and step-by-step instructions included

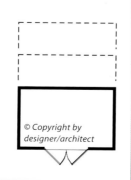

© Copyright by designer/architect

GABLE STORAGE SHED WITH CUPOLA

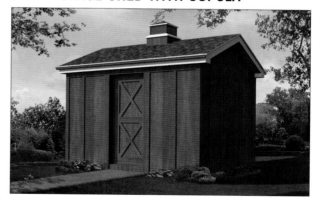

Plan #F52-002D-4511

- Width: 12'   Depth: 10'
- 120 square feet
- Foundation: Pier or slab
- Building height: 9'-8"
- Ceiling height: 7'-4"
- Material list and step-by-step instructions included

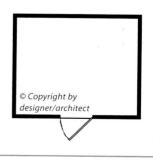

© Copyright by designer/architect

SHINGLE SIDING SHED

Plan #F52-125D-4504

- Width: 14'   Depth: 14'
- 196 total square feet
- Foundation: Slab
- Building height: 17'
- Ceiling height: 9'

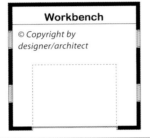

Workbench

© Copyright by designer/architect

STORAGE SHED

Plan #F52-063D-4514

- Width: 11'-11" Depth: 8'
- 95 square feet
- Foundation: Wood floor on concrete pier or slab
- Building height: 8'-6"
- Ceiling height: 6'-6"
- Material list included

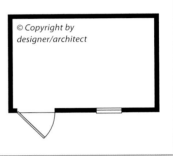

© Copyright by designer/architect

MODERN GARDEN SHED

Plan #F52-127D-4515

- 4 sizes available:
  8' x 8'   10' x 10'
  12' x 12'   14' x 14'
- Foundation: Wood floor on concrete blocks
- Building heights:
  12' with 8' depth
  12'-6" with 10' depth
  13' with 12' depth
  13'-6" with 14' depth
- Ceiling height: 7'-6"
- Construction prints are 8 1/2" x 11" in size

© Copyright by designer/architect

GREENHOUSE

Plan #F52-002D-4513

- Width: 8'   Depth: 12'
- 96 square feet
- Foundation: Gravel floor with concrete foundation wall
- Rear wall height: 7'-11"
- Building height: 8'-3"
- Material list and step-by-step instructions included

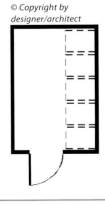

© Copyright by designer/architect

GARDEN SHED WITH ARCHES

Plan #F52-113D-4501

- Width: 14'   Depth: 14'
- 188 square feet
- Foundation: Pilaster
- Building height: 16'-4"
- Ceiling height: 7'-8"
- Material list available for a fee

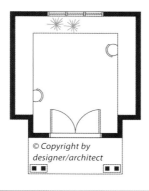

© Copyright by designer/architect

CHARMING GARDEN SHED

Plan #F52-127D-4507

- 4 sizes available:
  8' x 8'   10' x 10'
  12' x 12'   14' x 14'
- Foundation: Wood floor on concrete blocks
- Building heights:
  12'-10" with 8' depth
  13'-8" with 10' depth
  14'-6" with 12' depth
  15-4" with 14' depth
- Ceiling height: 7'-6"
- Construction prints are 8 1/2" x 11" in size

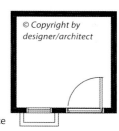

© Copyright by designer/architect

SHED GAZEBO

Plan #F52-127D-4502

- Width: 21'-7"   Depth: 21'-7"
- 466 square feet
- Foundation: Wood floor on concrete blocks
- Building height: 14'-6"
- Ceiling height: 8'
- Construction prints are 8 1/2" x 11" in size

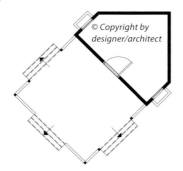

© Copyright by designer/architect

BARN WORKSHOP SHED

Plan #F52-136D-7501

- Width: 50'   Depth: 30'
- 1,420 total square feet
  Workshop: 900
  Shed Storage Area (ea.): 260
- Foundation: Slab
- Building height: 25'-6"
- Ceiling height: 12'

© Copyright by designer/architect

SHED STORAGE AREA   WORK SHOP 24 x 24   SHED STORAGE AREA

2-CAR GARAGE WITH LOFT

Plan #F52-002D-6001

- Width: 28'   Depth: 24'
- Foundation: Slab or floating slab
- Building height: 21'
- Ceiling heights
  Garage: 8'
  Loft: 7'-6"
- Material list and step-by-step instructions included

2nd Floor

© Copyright by designer/architect

1st Floor

GAMBREL BARN STYLE GARAGE

Plan #F52-125D-6010

- Width: 24'   Depth: 30'
- 669 square feet
- Foundation: Slab
- Building height: 23'
- Ceiling height: 9'

© Copyright by designer/architect

2-CAR BARN STYLE GARAGE

Plan #F52-142D-7513

- Width: 28'   Depth: 36'
- 1,647 total square feet
  Garage: 1,008
  Loft: 639
- Foundation: Slab
- 2" x 6" exterior walls
- Building height: 25'-1"
- Ceiling height: 9'

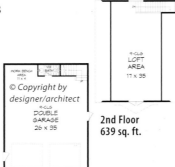

© Copyright by designer/architect

9'-CLG
LOFT AREA
17 x 35

2nd Floor
639 sq. ft.

9'-CLG
DOUBLE GARAGE
26 x 35

1st Floor
1,008 sq. ft.

CRAFTSMAN 2-CAR GARAGE & SHOP

Plan #F52-125D-6012

- Width: 32'   Depth: 32'
- 591 square feet
- Foundation: Slab
- Building height: 19'
- Ceiling height: 9'

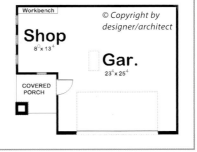

Workbench

Shop
8'⁴ x 13'⁵

Gar.
23'⁴ x 25'⁴

© Copyright by designer/architect

COVERED PORCH

2-CAR BARN GARAGE WITH LOFT

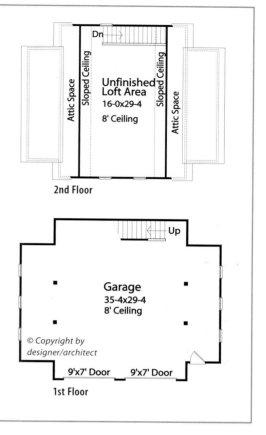

2nd Floor

Attic Space | Sloped Ceiling | Unfinished Loft Area 16-0x29-4 8' Ceiling | Sloped Ceiling | Attic Space

1st Floor

Garage 35-4x29-4 8' Ceiling

© Copyright by designer/architect

9'x7' Door 9'x7' Door

Plan #F52-059D-6109

- Width: 36' Depth: 30'
- 1,484 total square feet
  1st floor: 984
  2nd floor: 500
- Foundation: Footing and foundation wall
- Building height: 21'-6"
- Ceiling heights
  1st floor: 8'
  2nd floor: 8'
- Material list available for a fee
- 2" x 6" wall upgrade available for a fee

2-CAR GARAGE WITH LOFT & COVERED AREA

Plan #F52-059D-6086

- Width: 40' Depth: 30'
- 1,349 total square feet
  1st floor: 852
  2nd floor: 497
- Foundation: Footing and foundation wall
- Building height: 21'-6"
- Ceiling heights
  1st floor: 8' 2nd floor: 8'
- Material list available for a fee
- 2" x 6" wall upgrade available for a fee

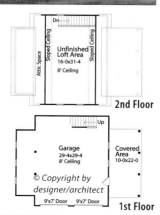

2nd Floor

Attic Space | Sloped Ceiling | Unfinished Loft Area 16-0x31-4 8' Ceiling | Sloped Ceiling

1st Floor

Garage 29-4x29-4 8' Ceiling

Covered Area 10-0x22-0

© Copyright by designer/architect

9'x7' Door 9'x7' Door

1-CAR GARAGE WITH LOFT & GAMBREL ROOF

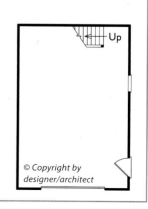

Plan #F52-002D-6043

- Width: 16' Depth: 24'
- 384 square feet
- Foundation: Floating slab
- Building height: 18'-9"
- Ceiling heights
  Garage: 8'
  Loft: 6'-7"
- Material list and step-by-step instructions included

Up

© Copyright by designer/architect

2-CAR GARAGE WITH SHOP & PARTIAL LOFT

Plan #F52-002D-6002

- Width: 32'   Depth: 24'
- 768 square feet
- Foundation: Floating slab
- Building height: 20'-2"
- Ceiling heights
  Workshop & Loft: 8'
  Garage: 9'-8"
- Material list and
  step-by-step instructions
  included

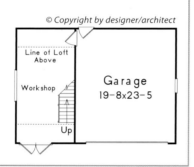

© Copyright by designer/architect

Line of Loft Above
Workshop
Up
Garage 19-8x23-5

COVERED PORCH GARAGE

Plan #F52-002D-6010

- Width: 24'   Depth: 22'
- Foundation: Slab
  or floating slab
- Building height: 13'
- Ceiling height: 8'
- Material list and
  step-by-step instructions
  included

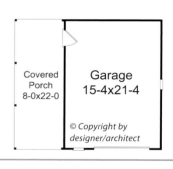

Covered Porch 8-0x22-0
Garage 15-4x21-4
© Copyright by designer/architect

MODERN GARAGE WORKSHOP

Plan #F52-012D-6015

- Width: 37'   Depth: 35'-6"
- 1,136 square feet
- Foundation: Slab
- 1 bath
- 2" x 6" exterior walls
- Building height: 17'-8"
- Ceiling heights
  Shop: 8' vaulted
  Garage: 10'

MECH./STOR 11/6 X 5/0 (10' CLG.)
WORK BENCH W/ 9" SOFFIT OVER
(8' CLG.)
STOR CABS BELOW WDWS
(9' CLG.)
VAULTED SHOP 34/0 X 29/0 +/-
(10' CLG.)
© Copyright by designer/architect

RV GARAGE WITH WORKSHOP

Plan #F52-117D-6002

- Width: 30'   Depth: 24'
- 636 total square feet
  Garage: 384
  Shop: 196
  Porch: 56
- Foundation: Slab
- Building height: 19'-6"
- Ceiling heights
  Garage: 10'
  Workshop: 8'
- Material list available
  for a fee

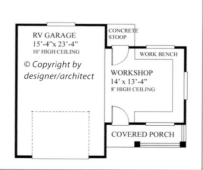

RV GARAGE 15'-4"x 23'-4" 10' HIGH CEILING
CONCRETE STOOP
WORK BENCH
WORKSHOP 14' x 13'-4" 8' HIGH CEILING
COVERED PORCH
© Copyright by designer/architect

2-CAR GARAGE WITH TRIO OF DORMERS

Plan #F52-059D-6013

- Width: 32'   Depth: 26'
- Foundation: Footing and foundation wall
- Building height: 26'
- Ceiling heights
  Garage: 9'
  Loft: 8'
- Material list available for a fee
- 2" x 6" wall upgrade available for a fee

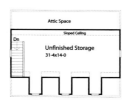

MULTI-SIZED GARAGE

Plan #F52-127D-6001

- Plan comes in multiple widths including 10'-8", 12', 14', 16', 18' and 20' and multiple depths of 20'-8", 22', 24' and 26', please specify when ordering
- Foundation: Poured concrete foundation wall 4'-6" deep in the earth (to support wall/roof structure) and a 6" slab on grade
- Construction prints are 8 1/2" x 11" in size

1-CAR GARAGE WORKSHOP & STORAGE

Plan #F52-142D-6021

- Width: 32'   Depth: 27' (including 3' awning)
- 848 total square feet
  Garage: 427
  Workshop: 347
  Porch: 37
- Foundation: Slab
- Building height: 16'
- Ceiling height: 7'
- 2" x 6" wall upgrade available for a fee

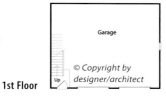

2-CAR GARAGE WITH CLERESTORY WINDOW

Plan #F52-162D-6007

- Width: 20'   Depth: 25'
- 500 total square feet
  Garage: 440
  Porch: 60
- Foundation: Slab
- 2" x 6" exterior walls
- Building height: 16'
- Ceiling height: 10' and 13'-10" at center tower

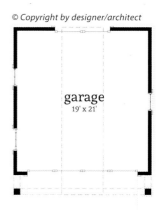

1-CAR GARAGE WITH STORAGE & PORCH

Plan #F52-107D-6004

- Width: 26' Depth: 24'
- Foundation: Slab
- Building height: 14'-3"
- Ceiling height: 8'
- Material list and step-by-step instructions included

2-CAR GARAGE WITH WORKSHOP & LOFT

Plan #F52-002D-6004

- Width: 32' Depth: 24'
- Foundation: Floating slab or slab
- Building height: 21'
- Ceiling heights
  Garage: 8'
  Loft: 7'-6"
- Material list and step-by-step instructions included

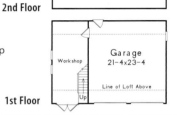

© Copyright by designer/architect

2nd Floor

1st Floor

2-CAR GARAGE WITH PORCH & STORAGE

Plan #F52-108D-6000

- Width: 38' Depth: 24'
- 664 square feet
- Foundation: Slab
- Building height: 24'-8"
- Ceiling heights
  1st floor: 8' 2nd floor: 9'
- 2" x 6" wall upgrade available for a fee
- Foundation upgrade to basement or crawl space available for a fee

2nd Floor
664 sq. ft.

© Copyright by designer/architect

1st Floor

2-CAR GARAGE WITH SHOP & STORAGE

Plan #F52-009D-6009

- Width: 38' Depth: 24'
- Foundation: Floating slab
- Building height: 21'-6"
- Ceiling heights
  Garage: 12'
  Other: 8'
- Material list available for a fee

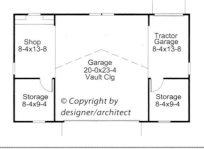

3-CAR GARAGE & WORKSHOP

Plan #F52-002D-6042

- Width: 24'   Depth: 36'
- Foundation: Floating slab or slab
- Building height: 14'-6"
- Ceiling height: 10'
- Material list and step-by-step instructions included

© Copyright by designer/architect

2-CAR GARAGE WITH WORKSHOP / STORAGE

Plan #F52-059D-6001

- Width: 40'   Depth: 30'
- Foundation: Footing and foundation wall
- 2" x 6" exterior walls
- Building height: 17'
- Ceiling height: 10'
- Material list available for a fee

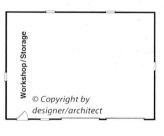

Workshop/Storage

© Copyright by designer/architect

2-CAR BARN GARAGE WITH LOFT

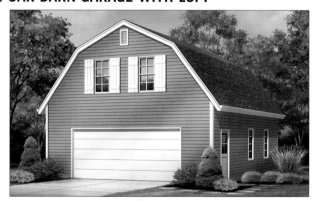

Plan #F52-059D-6083

- Width: 24'   Depth: 36'
- 1,301 total square feet
  Garage: 768   Loft: 533
- Foundation: Footing and foundation wall
- Building height: 21'-6"
- Ceiling heights
  1st floor: 8'
  2nd floor: 8'
- Material list available for a fee
- 2" x 6" wall upgrade available for a fee

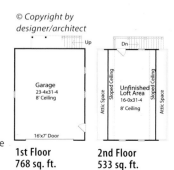

© Copyright by designer/architect

Garage
23-4x31-4
8' Ceiling

16'x7' Door

**1st Floor
768 sq. ft.**

Dn

Unfinished
Loft Area
16-0x31-4
8' Ceiling

Attic Space   Sloped Ceiling   Sloped Ceiling   Attic Space

Up

**2nd Floor
533 sq. ft.**

1-CAR BARN STYLE GARAGE WITH LOFT

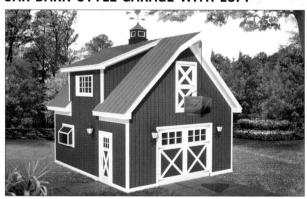

Plan #F52-142D-6008

- Width: 20'   Depth: 24'
- 865 total square feet
  Garage: 480
  Storage: 385
- Foundation: Slab
- Building height: 21'
- Ceiling heights
  1st floor: 9'
  2nd floor: 9'
- 2" x 6" wall upgrade available for a fee

© Copyright by designer/architect

STOR
14'x9'

GARAGE
19'x20'

**1st Floor
480 sq. ft.**

STOR
17'x21'

**2nd Floor
385 sq. ft.**

APARTMENT GARAGE WITH VAULTED INTERIOR

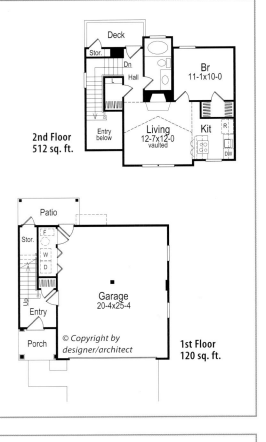

2nd Floor 512 sq. ft.

1st Floor 120 sq. ft.

© Copyright by designer/architect

Plan #F52-007D-0040

- Width: 28'   Depth: 26'
- 632 square feet of living area
  1st floor: 120
  2nd floor: 512
- Foundation: Slab
- 1 bedroom, 1 bath

- Building height: 26'-4"
- Ceiling heights
  1st floor: 9'
  2nd floor: 8'
- Material list available for a fee

APARTMENT GARAGE PLUS RV STORAGE

2nd Floor 351 sq. ft.

1st Floor 362 sq. ft.

© Copyright by designer/architect

Plan #F52-007D-0189

- Width: 39'-4"   Depth: 42'-4"
- 713 square feet of living area
  1st floor: 362
  2nd floor: 351
- Foundation: Slab
- 1 bedroom, 1 1/2 baths

- Building height: 25'
- Ceiling heights
  1st floor: 9'
  2nd floor: 8'
- Material list available for a fee

MOUNTAIN BARN GARAGE GUEST QUARTERS

2nd Floor
562 sq. ft.

© Copyright by designer/architect

1st Floor

Plan #F52-108D-7508

- Width: 24'   Depth: 28'
- 562 square feet of living area
- Foundation: Slab
- 1 bedroom, 1 bath
- Building height: 22'-5"

- Ceiling heights
  1st floor: 10'
  2nd floor: 8'
- Material List available for a fee
- Foundation upgrade to basement or crawl space available for a fee

GARAGE WITH ART STUDIO & WORKSHOP

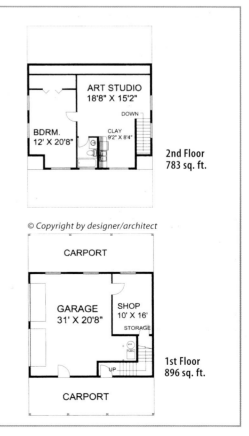

2nd Floor
783 sq. ft.

© Copyright by designer/architect

1st Floor
896 sq. ft.

Plan #F52-133D-7507

- Width: 28'   Depth: 32'
- 1,679 total square feet
  1st floor: 896
  2nd floor: 783
- Foundation: Slab
- 1 bedroom, 1 bath

- 2" x 6" exterior walls
- Building height: 24'-11"
- Ceiling heights
  1st floor: 9'
  2nd floor: 9'

3-CAR APARTMENT GARAGE

Deck

Living Rm
16-0x18-4

Br2
10-1x11-0

Dine

Hall

Kit
9-0x11-0

Mbr
14-0x11-1

vaulted

2nd Floor
819 sq. ft.

Patio

Garage
23-4x29-4

Entry

© Copyright by
designer/architect

Porch

1st Floor
110 sq. ft.

Plan #F52-007D-0070

- Width: 31'   Depth: 35'
- 929 square feet of living area
  1st floor: 110
  2nd floor: 819
- Foundation: Slab
- 2 bedrooms, 1 bath

- Building height: 27'-6"
- Ceiling heights
  1st floor: 9'
  2nd floor: 8'
- Material list available for a fee

3-CAR GARAGE APARTMENT

Plan #F52-002D-7529

- Width: 40'   Depth: 26'
- 1,040 square feet of living area
- Foundation: Floating slab
- 2 bedrooms, 1 bath

- Building height: 23'
- Ceiling heights
  1st floor: 8'
  2nd floor: 8'
- Material list included

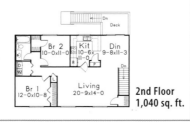

1st Floor

Garage
35-4x25-4

© Copyright by
designer/architect

Up

Dn

Deck

Br 2
10-0x11-0

Kit
10-6x
11-0

Din
9-8x11-3

Br 1
12-0x10-8

Living
20-9x14-0

2nd Floor
1,040 sq. ft.

2-CAR APARTMENT GARAGE

Plan #F52-136D-7500

- Width: 26'   Depth: 36'
- 807 square feet of living area
- Foundation: Slab
- 1 bedroom, 1 bath
- Building height: 28'-6"
- Ceiling heights
  1st floor: 9'
  2nd floor: 10'

Kit

DINING
AREA
17 X 15-4

GATHERING
AREA

BEDROOM
SUITE
14-5 X 18

BATH

CLOSET

2nd Floor
807 sq. ft.

2 CAR GARAGE
25 X 31-6

© Copyright by
designer/architect

1st Floor

CARRIAGE HOUSE WITH RV GARAGE

3rd Floor

2nd Floor
1,058 sq. ft.

© Copyright by
designer/architect

1st Floor
490 sq. ft.

Plan #F52-108D-7514

- Width: 57'-6"   Depth: 45'
- 1,548 square feet of living area
  1st floor: 490
  2nd floor: 1,058
- Foundation: Slab
- 1 bedroom, 2 1/2 baths

- Building height: 24'-3"
- Ceiling heights
  1st floor: 9'
  2nd floor: 8'

2-CAR APARTMENT GARAGE

Plan #F52-002D-7510

- Width: 28'   Depth: 26'
- 746 square feet of living area
- Foundation: Floating slab
- 1 bedroom, 1 bath

- Building height: 22'
- Ceiling heights
  1st floor: 8'
  2nd floor: 8'
- Material list and step-by-step instructions included

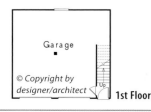

© Copyright by
designer/architect

1st Floor

2nd Floor
746 sq. ft.

2-CAR APARTMENT GARAGE

Plan #F52-002D-7528

- Width: 24'   Depth: 24'
- 576 square feet of living area
- Foundation: Floating slab
- 1 bedroom, 1 bath

- Building height: 21'-5"
- Ceiling heights
  1st floor: 8'
  2nd floor: 8'
- Material list and step-by-step instructions included

© Copyright by
designer/architect

1st Floor

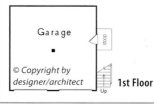

2nd Floor
576 sq. ft.

TWO-LEVEL BARN / STABLE WITH TACK ROOM STORAGE

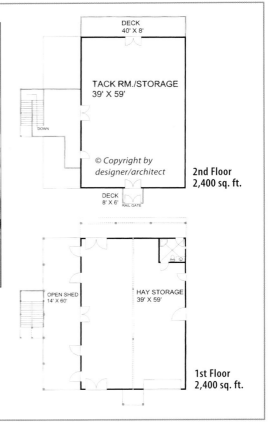

DECK
40' X 8'

TACK RM./STORAGE
39' X 59'

© Copyright by designer/architect

DOWN

2nd Floor 2,400 sq. ft.

DECK
8' X 6'   RAIL GATE

OPEN SHED
14' X 60'

HAY STORAGE
39' X 59'

1st Floor 2,400 sq. ft.

Plan #F52-133D-7510

• Width: 40'   Depth: 60'

• 4,800 total square feet
  Hay storage: 2,400
  Tack room/storage: 2,400

• Foundation: Slab

• 1 bath

• 2" x 6" exterior walls

• Building height: 34'-7"

• Ceiling heights
  Open shed: 11'
  Hay storage: 14'
  Tack room: 8' vaults to 12'

WORKROOM WITH COVERED PORCH

Plan #F52-002D-7520

• Width: 24'   Depth: 20'

• Foundation: Slab

• Building height: 13'-6"

• Ceiling height: 8'

• Material list and
  step-by-step instructions
  included

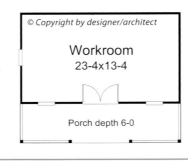

© Copyright by designer/architect

Workroom
23-4x13-4

Porch depth 6-0

4 STALL HORSE BARN

Plan #F52-002D-7522

• Width: 36'   Depth: 24'

• Foundation: Slab

• Building height: 13'-4"

• Ceiling height: 8'

• Material list included

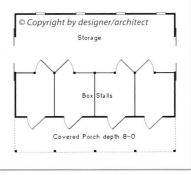

© Copyright by designer/architect

Storage

Box Stalls

Covered Porch depth 8-0

BARN WITH LOFT

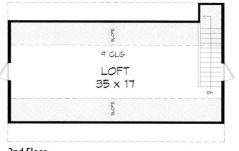

2nd Floor
626 sq. ft.

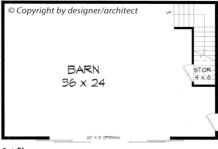

© Copyright by designer/architect

BARN
36 x 24

1st Floor
864 sq. ft.

Plan #F52-142D-7514

- Width: 36'   Depth: 24'
- 1,490 total square feet
  Barn: 864
  Loft: 626
- Foundation: Slab
- 2" x 6" exterior walls

- Building height: 26'
- Ceiling heights
  1st floor: 10'
  2nd floor: 9'

KENNEL / GARAGE WITH DOG RUN

Plan #F52-142D-6055

- Width: 36'-9"   Depth: 26'-9"
- 1,277 total square feet
  Kennel/garage: 983
  Dog run/porch: 294
- Foundation: Slab
- Building height: 15'-6"
- Ceiling height: 8'
- 2" x 6" wall upgrade
  available for a fee

DOG RUN / PORCH
37 x 8

© Copyright by designer/architect

KENNEL / GARAGE
36 x 26

WORKSHOP WITH STORAGE

Plan #F52-133D-7512

- Width: 44'   Depth: 30'
- 2,416 total square feet
  Shop/fishing room: 1,448
  Storage: 704
  Porch: 264
- Foundation: Slab
- 2" x 6" exterior walls
- Building height: 23'-4"
- Ceiling height: 10'

© Copyright by designer/architect

2nd Floor
704 sq. ft.

1st Floor
1,448 sq. ft.

HORSE BARN WITH APARTMENT

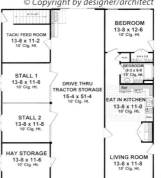

2nd Floor

HAY LOFT
15-4 x 51-4
9' Clg. Ht.

© Copyright by designer/architect

1st Floor

TACK/ FEED ROOM
13-8 x 11-2
10' Clg. Ht.

BEDROOM
13-8 x 12-6
10' Clg. Ht.

STALL 1
13-8 x 11-8
10' Clg. Ht.

DRIVE THRU
TRACTOR STORAGE
15-4 x 51-4
10' Clg. Ht.

BEDROOM
9-3 x 6-0
10' Clg. Ht.

EAT IN KITCHEN
13-8 x 11-0
10' Clg. Ht.

STALL 2
13-8 x 11-8
10' Clg. Ht.

HAY STORAGE
13-8 x 11-6
10' Clg. Ht.

LIVING ROOM
13-8 x 11-8
10' Clg. Ht.

Plan #F52-124D-7504

- Width: 44'   Depth: 52'
- 3,099 total square feet
  Unheated: 2,358
  Heated: 741
- Foundation: Slab
- 1 bedroom, 1 bath

- Building height: 26'-3"
- Ceiling heights
  1st floor: 10'
  2nd floor: 9'
- Material list available
  for a fee

2-STALL HORSE BARN

Plan #F52-002D-7521

- Width: 20'   Depth: 20'
- 400 total square feet
- Foundation: Partial slab
- Building height: 12'-8"
- Ceiling height: 8'
- Material list included

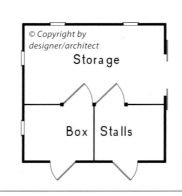

© Copyright by designer/architect

Storage

Box Stalls

3-STALL BARN WITH HAYLOFT, TACK & FEED

Plan #F52-075D-7512

- Width: 48'   Depth: 35'
- 2,372 total square feet
  1st floor: 1,588
  2nd floor: 784
- Foundation: Slab
- Building height: 25'-6"

2nd Floor
784 sq. ft.

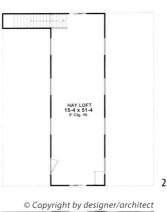

HAYLOFT
23-3 x 34-3

1st Floor
1,588 sq. ft.

STALL
12-0 X 10-0 (TYPICAL)

STALL
12-0 X 10-0 (TYPICAL)

STALL
12-0 X 10-0 (TYPICAL)

TRACTOR
AND/OR
STORAGE
23-3 x 34-3

FEED
11-7 X 15-0

TACK
11-7 X 15-0

© Copyright by designer/architect

RV GARAGE WITH WORKSHOP, OFFICE & STORAGE

Plan #F52-133D-7504

- Width: 58'   Depth: 46'
- 2,836 total square feet
  1st floor: 1,940
  2nd floor: 896
- Foundation: Slab
- 2" x 6" exterior walls

- Building height: 21'-6"
- Ceiling heights
  Garage: 10'
  1st floor: 8'
  2nd floor: 10'

2nd Floor
896 sq. ft.

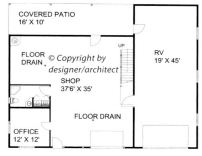

1st Floor
1,940 sq. ft.

BARN WITH RV PORT

Plan #F52-142D-7530

© Copyright by designer/architect

- Width: 60' (with 20' porch)
  Depth: 60'
- 3,600 total square feet
  Barn: 2,400
  RV Port: 1,200
- Foundation: Post & beam
- Building height: 30'-9"
- Ceiling heights
  Barn: 20'
  RV Port: 13' vaulted

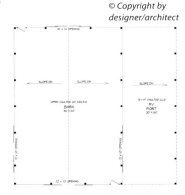

WORKSHOP WITH TACK ROOMS & GARAGE

Plan #F52-133D-6001

- Width: 64'   Depth: 48'
- 3,072 total square feet
  Shop/garage: 2,400
  Tack rooms: 672
- Foundation: Slab
- Building height: 23'-8"
- 2" x 6" exterior walls

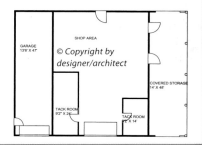

SCREEN PORCH / PLAYROOM

Plan #F52-124D-7501

- Width: 12'   Depth: 16'
- 192 square feet
- Foundation: Crawl space
- Ceiling heights
  Screen porch:
  7'-4" vaults to 9'
  Playroom: 7'
- Building height: 11'-4"
- Material list
  available for a fee

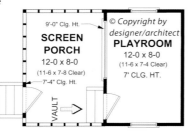

© Copyright by designer/architect

SCREEN PORCH
12-0 x 8-0
(11-6 x 7-8 Clear)
9'-0" Clg. Ht.
7'-4" Clg. Ht.
VAULT

PLAYROOM
12-0 x 8-0
(11-6 x 7-4 Clear)
7' CLG. HT.

POLE BUILDING

Plan #F52-002D-7506

- Width: 32'   Depth: 40'
- Foundation: Dirt floor
- Building height: 16'
- Ceiling height: 10'
- Material list and
  step-by-step instructions
  included

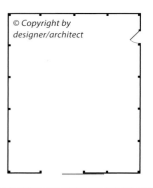

© Copyright by designer/architect

OUTDOOR LODGE

Plan #F52-142D-7506

- Width: 22'-6"   Depth: 21' (including 8' deck)
- 466 total square feet
  Lodge: 306
  Deck: 160
- Foundation: Slab
- Building height: 16'-5"
- Ceiling height: 9'
- 2" x 6" wall upgrade
  available for a fee

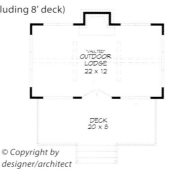

'VAULTED'
OUTDOOR
LODGE
22 x 12

DECK
20 x 8

© Copyright by designer/architect

MODERN FIREPLACE SHELTER

Plan #F52-162D-7500

- Width: 16'   Depth: 10'
- 160 total square feet
  Living area: 96
  Porch: 64
- Foundation: Slab
- Building height: 12'
- Ceiling height: 8'

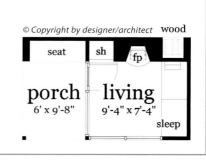

© Copyright by designer/architect   wood

seat   sh   fp

porch
6' x 9'-8"

living
9'-4" x 7'-4"

sleep

POLE BUILDING EQUIPMENT SHED

Plan #F52-002D-7505

- Width: 40'   Depth: 24'
- Foundation: Floating slab
- Building height: 14'-4"
- Ceiling height: 10'
- Material list and step-by-step instructions included

© Copyright by designer/architect

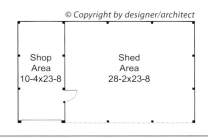

Shop Area 10-4x23-8

Shed Area 28-2x23-8

POLE BUILDING HORSE BARN WITH LOFT

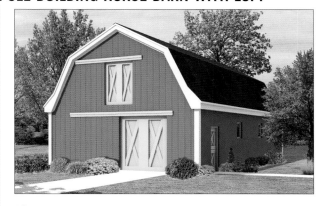

Plan #F52-002D-7511

- Width: 26'   Depth: 48'
- Foundation: Compacted clay floor in stalls or slab
- Building height: 22'
- Ceiling heights
  First floor: 9'
  Loft: 11'
- Material list and step-by-step instructions included

© Copyright by designer/architect

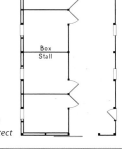

Box Stall

MODERN OFFICE GETAWAY

Plan #F52-162D-7501

- Width: 10'   Depth: 11'
- 99 square feet
- Foundation: Slab
- 2" x 6" exterior walls
- Building height: 12'
- Ceiling height: 9'

© Copyright by designer/architect

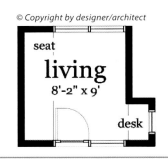

seat

living
8'-2" x 9'

desk

MID-CENTURY STYLE STUDIO

Plan #F52-152D-0079

- Width: 19'   Depth: 27'
- 513 total square feet
  Living/bath: 361
  Porch: 152
- Foundation: Slab
- 1 bedroom, 1 bath
- 2" x 6" exterior walls
- Building height: 14'
- Ceiling height: 8'

© Copyright by designer/architect

down

bath

shower

ref

sink

closet

stove

seat

living
18' x 10'

sliding doors

porch
19' x 8'

down

STUDIO / POOLHOUSE

Plan #F52-142D-7520

- Width: 18'   Depth: 24'
- 432 total square feet
  Studio/poolhouse/bath: 385
  Storage: 47
- Foundation: Slab
- 1 bath
- Concrete block exterior walls
- Building height: 14'-6"
- Ceiling height: 10'
- 2" x 6" wall upgrade available for a fee

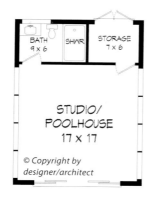

CLUBHOUSE

Plan #F52-075D-7503

- Width: 40'   Depth: 30'
- 1,134 square feet
- Foundation: Slab
- 2 half baths
- Building height: 25'-2"
- Ceiling height: 8'

CONTEMPORARY OFFICE / GUEST STUDIO

Plan #F52-011D-0603

- Width: 26'   Depth: 12'
- 312 square feet
- Foundation: Slab
- 1 bedroom, 1 bath
- 2" x 6" exterior walls
- Building height: 10'-6"
- Ceiling height: 8'

IN-LAW / GUEST SUITE

Plan #F52-012D-7510

- Width: 12'   Depth: 23'
- 276 square feet
- Foundation: Slab
- 1 bath
- 2" x 6" exterior walls
- Building height: 12'-10"
- Ceiling height: Vaulted

RUSTIC CABANA

Plan #F52-113D-7508

- Width: 28'   Depth: 20'
- 360 square feet
- Foundation: Monolithic slab
- 1 bedroom, 1 bath
- Material list available for a fee
- Foundation upgrade to floating slab or crawl space available for a fee

© Copyright by designer/architect

SUSTAINABLE WORK & OFFICE AREA

Plan #F52-108D-7507

- Width: 24'   Depth: 28'
- 503 square feet
- Foundation: Slab
- 6" SIP exterior walls
- Building height: 22'-5"
- Ceiling heights
  1st floor: 10'   2nd floor: 8'
- Material list available for a fee
- Foundation upgrade to basement or crawl space available for a fee

© Copyright by designer/architect

2nd Floor
503 sq. ft.

1st Floor

STUDIO HOME OFFICE

Plan #F52-063D-7501

- Width: 20'   Depth: 30'
- 432 square feet
- Foundation: Crawl space or slab
- 1 half bath
- 2" x 6" exterior walls
- Building height: 19'-6"
- Ceiling height: 9'
- Material list available for a fee

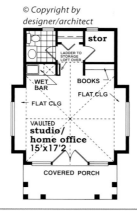

© Copyright by designer/architect

CRAFT COTTAGE

Plan #F52-063D-7505

- Width: 20'   Depth: 16'
- 288 square feet
- Foundation: Crawl space or slab
- 2" x 6" exterior walls
- Building height: 16'-8"
- Material list available for a fee

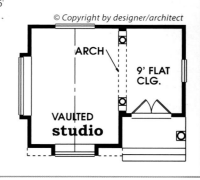

© Copyright by designer/architect

MUSIC STUDIO

Plan #F52-142D-7522

- Width: 22'   Depth: 18'-9"
- 413 square feet
- Foundation: Slab
- 1/2 bath
- Building height: 13'-6"
- Ceiling height: 8'
- 2" x 6" wall upgrade available for a fee
- Foundation upgrade to crawl space available for a fee

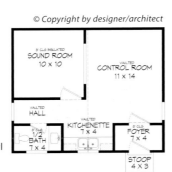

© Copyright by designer/architect

COUNTRY GUEST QUARTERS

Plan #F52-130D-0362

- Width: 16'   Depth: 24'-8"
- 395 square feet
- Foundation: Slab
- 1 bedroom, 1 bath
- Building height: 14'
- Ceiling height: 8'
- 2" x 6" wall upgrade available for a fee
- Foundation upgrade to crawl space or basement available for a fee

© Copyright by designer/architect

MODERN CABIN

Plan #F52-126D-1149

- Width: 24'   Depth: 22'
- 528 square feet
- Foundation: Pilings
- 2 bedrooms, 1 bath
- 2" x 6" exterior walls
- Building height: 18'
- Ceiling height: 8'
- Material list available for a fee

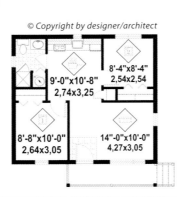

© Copyright by designer/architect

STYLISH GUEST OR IN-LAW SUITE

Plan #F52-011D-0431

- Width: 17'-6"   Depth: 23'
- 300 square feet
- Foundation: Slab
- 1 sleeping area, 1 bath
- 2" x 6" exterior walls
- Building height: 17'-5"
- Ceiling height: 8' vaulted

© Copyright by designer/architect

MODERN COTTAGE

Plan #F52-126D-1148

- Width: 22'   Depth: 18'
- 396 square feet
- Foundation: Pilings
- 1 bedroom, 1 bath
- 2" x 6" exterior walls
- Building height: 17'
- Material list available for a fee

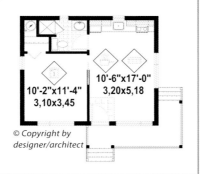

10'-2"x11'-4"
3,10x3,45

10'-6"x17'-0"
3,20x5,18

© Copyright by designer/architect

MODERN GUEST SPACE

Plan #F52-162D-7504

- Width: 21'   Depth: 21'
- 405 square feet
- Foundation: Slab
- 1 sleeping area, 1 bath
- 2" x 6" exterior walls
- Building height: 13'
- Ceiling height: 9'-4"

© Copyright by designer/architect

lin
shower **bath**
bed 9'-6" x 14'-2"
living 10'-6" x 14'-2"
sink stove
ref
patio 14' x 8'

COUNTRY COTTAGE

Plan #F52-077D-0084

- Width: 22'   Depth: 20'
- 640 total square feet
  Interior: 400
  Front porch: 120
  Screened porch: 120
- Foundation: Slab or crawl space
- 1 bedroom, 1 bath
- Ceiling height: 8'
- Material list available for a fee

© Copyright by designer/architect

Screened Porch
20 x 6

Bath
TubShwr

Kitchen
11-6 X 8-10
RANGE
RAISED BAR

W/D
P
Ref.

Bunk Room
7-6 X 13-10

Living Room
11-6 X 10-6
(CLEAR)
FIREPLACE

Front Porch
20 x 6

QUAINT COTTAGE

Plan #F52-156D-0008

- Width: 25'   Depth: 20'-6"
- 400 total square feet
- Foundation: Slab
- 1 bedroom, 1 bath
- Building height: 12'-1"
- Ceiling height: 8'
- Foundation upgrade to crawl space available for a fee

BATH
8'-4" x 5'

CLOSET
5'X9'

Kitchen/Living
11'-6" x 15'-4"

W/D

Clos.
2'-1" X 2'-9"

BEDROOM
10' X 10'

PORCH
11'-1" X 4'-2"

© Copyright by designer/architect

This list of manufacturers and associations is meant to be a general guide to additional industry and product-related sources. It is not intended as a listing of products and manufacturers represented by the photographs in this book.

Alcoa
201 Isabella St.
Pittsburgh, PA 15212-5858
Phone: 888-ALCOA-123
www.alcoa.com
Manufactures aluminum products.

American Lighting Association
P. O. Box 420288
2050 Stemmons Fwy., Ste. 10046
Dallas, TX 75342-0288
Phone: 214-698-9898
www.americanlightingassoc.com
Organization devoted to home and yard lighting, with safety, planning, and manufacturer information.

APA—The Engineered Wood Association
7011 S. 19th St.
Tacoma, WA 98466-5333
Phone: 253-565-6600
http://apawood.org
Nonprofit trade association whose primary functions include quality inspection and product promotion.

Better Barns Hardware & Plans
126 Main St. South (Rt. 61)
Bethlehem, CT 06751
Phone: 203-266-7989
www.betterbarns.com
Manufactures hardware and barn accessories.

Better Sheds
P. O. Box 995
Carbondale, CO, 81623
Phone: 800-276-0210
www.bettersheds.com
Makes ready-to-assemble steel, vinyl, and wood sheds.

Calgary Cupola & Weathervane
96 Havenhurst Crescent S.W.
Calgary, AB Canada T2V 3C5
Phone: 403-259-5571
www.cupola4me.com
Manufactures and sells handcrafted wooden cupolas.

Celotex, a div. of CertainTeed
750 East Swedesford Rd.
Valley Forge, PA 19482
Phone: 800-233-8990
www.certainteed.com
Manufactures building products.

Elmwood Reclaimed Timber
P. O. Box 10750
Kansas City, MO 64188-0750
Phone: 800-705-0705
www.elmwoodreclaimedtimber.com
Provides reclaimed timber and stone products.

Flood
15885 Sprague Rd.
Strongsville, OH 44136
Phone: 800-321-3444
www.flood.com
Makes a variety of paint-related products, including penetrating stains, sealers, wood renewers, and cleaners.

Georgia-Pacific LLC
133 Peachtree St., N.E.
Atlanta, GA 30303
Phone: 404-652-4000
www.gp.com
Manufactures building products and related chemicals.

Gerkin Windows & Doors
P. O. Box 3203
Sioux City, IA 51102
Phone: 800-475-5061
www.gerkin.com
Manufactures variety of types of windows and doors.

Handy Home Products
6400 East 11 Mile Rd.
Warren, MI 48091-4101
Phone: 800-221-1849
handyhome.com
Makes ready-to-assemble wooden storage buildings, gazebos, timber buildings, and children's playhouses.

HearthStone Homes
630 East Hwy. 25/70
Dandridge, TN 37725
Phone: 800-247-4442
www.hearthstonehomes.com
Manufactures quality logs, timber, projects, and custom-designed home plans.

Hyde Manufacturing Company
54 Eastford Rd.
Southbridge, MA 01550
Phone: 800-872-4933
www.hydetools.com
Makes a variety of hand tools, including those for masonry, drywall, and setting and finishing tile.

Louisiana-Pacific Corporation
805 Southwest Bdwy.
Portland, OR 97205-3349
Phone: 800-648-6893
www.lpcorp.com
Manufactures building products for the retail, wholesale, homebuilding, and industrial markets.

Metal Roofing Alliance
E. 4142 Hwy. 302
Belfair, WA 98528
Phone: 360-275-6164
www.metalroofing.com
Coalition of metal-roofing manufacturers and related companies in the metal-roofing industry, whose primary focus is to educate homeowners on the benefits of metal roofing for residential applications.

North American Insulation Manufacturers Association (NAIMA)
44 Canal Center Plz., Ste. 310
Alexandria, VA 22314
Phone: 703-684-0084
www.naima.org
Trade organization of manufacturers of fiberglass, rock wool, and slag wool insulation products.

Olympic Paints and Stains
PPG Industries
1 PPG Pl.
Pittsburgh, PA 15272
Phone: 800-441-9695
www.olympic.com
Manufactures paints and stains for professionals and do-it-yourselfers.

Porter-Cable Corporation
4825 Hwy. 45 N.
Jackson, TN 38305
Phone: 800-4-US-TOOL
www.deltaportercable.com
Manufactures portable electric and cordless power tools, nailers, compressors, and related accessories.

Ryobi North America
1424 Pearman Dairy Rd.
Anderson, SC 29625
Phone: 800-525-2579
www.ryobitools.com
Makes portable and bench-top power tools for contractors and DIYers. It also manufactures a line of lawn and garden tools.

Simpson Strong-Tie Company
5956 W. Las Positas Blvd./ P. O. Box 10789
Pleasanton, CA 94588
Phone: 800-925-5099
www.strongtie.com
Manufactures framing hardware.

Stanley Black & Decker
1000 Stanley Dr.
New Britain, CT 06053
Phone: 860-225-5111
www.stanleyblackanddecker.com
Manufactures hand and power tools for contractors and homeowners. Specialty products include a series of ergonomically designed products and a line of extra-durable contractor tools for the job site.

Summerwood Products
735 Progress Ave.
Toronto, ON Canada M1H 2W7
Phone: 866-519-4634
www.summerwood.com
Makes shed and gazebo designs, and sells precut kits that can be assembled at home.

Timber Frames by R.A. Krouse
46 Titcomb Ln.
Arundel, ME 04046
Phone: 207-967-2747
www.mainetimberframes.com
Specializes in timber-frame construction.

Western Wood Products Association
1500 SW First Ave., Ste. 870
Portland, OR 97201
503-224-3930
www.wwpa.org
Establishes standards and levels of quality for Western lumber and related Western softwood products.

Actual dimensions The exact measurements of a piece of lumber, pipe, or masonry. See *Nominal dimensions*.

Ampere (amp) A unit of measurement describing the rate of electrical flow.

Anchor bolt A bolt set in concrete that is used to fasten lumber, brackets, or hangers to concrete or masonry walls.

Apron Architectural trim beneath a window stool or sill.

Backfill Soil or gravel used to fill in between a foundation or retaining wall and the ground excavated around it.

Barge rafters The last outside rafters of a structure. They are usually nailed to outriggers and form the gable-end overhangs. Sometimes called fly rafters.

Battens Narrow wood strips that cover vertical joints between siding boards.

Batter board A level board attached to stakes and used to position strings outlining foundations and footings.

Beam A steel or wood framing member installed horizontally to support part of a structure's load.

Bearing post A post that provides support to a structure's framing.

Bearing wall A wall that provides structural support to the framing above.

Bent A complete cross-section frame assembly (typically including wall, ceiling, and roof components) in a timber-frame building.

Bird's mouth The notch made of a level and plumb cut near the tail end of a rafter where the rafter edge rests on a top plate or horizontal framing member.

Blocking Lumber added between studs, joists, rafters, or other framing members to provide a nailing surface, additional strength, spacing between boards, or firestopping within a framing cavity.

Board-and-batten siding A siding style that uses long siding boards installed vertically, with the gaps between them covered by one-by or two-by battens.

Cable Two or more insulated electrical wires inside a sheathing of plastic or metal.

Carriage bolt A bolt with a slotless round head and a square shoulder below the head that embeds itself into the wood as the nut is tightened.

Center pole In pole framing, the center ascending poles or posts that provide structural support for the roof and internal framing.

Chord The wood members of a truss that form the two sides of the roof and the base, or ceiling joist. (See also *Web*.)

Circuit breaker A protective device that opens a circuit automatically when a current overload occurs. It can be reset manually.

Cleat A small board fastened to a surface to provide support for another board, or any board nailed onto another board to strengthen or support it.

Collar tie A horizontal board installed rafter-to-rafter for extra support.

Concrete necklace The concrete that is poured around a post in the ground to provide support.

Conduit Metal or plastic tubing designed to enclose electrical wires.

Corner boards Boards nailed vertically to the corners of a building that serve as a stopping point for siding and as an architectural feature.

Cornice Generally called a roof overhang, the part of the roof that overhangs the wall.

Cupola Small ventilating stuctures built on top of the roof with louvered slides to allow for airflow.

Cripple studs Short studs that stand vertically between a header and top plate or between a bottom plate and the underside of a rough sill.

Curing The hardening process of concrete during which moisture is added or trapped under plastic or other sealer. Proper curing reduces cracking and shrinkage and develops strength.

Dead load The weight of a building's components, including lumber, roofing, and permanent fixtures.

Double top plate The double tier of two-by lumber running horizontally on top of and nailed to wall studs.

Drip cap Molding at the top of a window or door.

Drip edge A metal piece bent to fit over the edge of roof sheathing, designed to shed rain.

Dry well A hole in the ground filled with rocks or gravel, designed to catch water and help it filter into the soil. The outline of a dry well often is formed with concrete block or a perforated steel drum.

D-W-V Drain-waste-vent; the system of pipes and fittings used to carry away wastewater.

Easement The legal right for one person to cross or use another person's land. The most common easements are narrow tracts for utility lines.

Eaves The lower part of a roof that projects beyond the supporting walls to create an overhang.

Expansion bolt A bolt used to anchor lumber to masonry walls. The jacket of an expansion bolt expands to grip the side walls of a pilot hole due to wedge pressure at its base.

Face-nailing Nailing perpendicularly through the surface of lumber.

Fascia One-by or two-by trim pieces nailed onto the end grain or tail end of a rafter to form part of a cornice or overhang.

Flashing Thin sheets of aluminum, copper, rubber asphalt, or other material used to bridge or cover a joint between materials that is exposed to the weather—for example, between the roof and a chimney.

Floor joists The long wooden beams generally set horizontally 16 inches on center between foundation walls or girders.

Footing The part of a foundation that transmits loads to the soil; also, the base on which a stone wall is built. Typical footings are twice as wide as the wall they support and at least as deep as the wall is wide.

Foundation The whole masonry substructure of a building upon which the rest of the structure stands.

Frost heave Shifting or upheaval of the ground resulting from alternate freezing and thawing of the moisture in soil.

Frost line The maximum depth to which soil freezes in the winter.

Full stud Vertical two-by lumber that extends from the bottom plate to the top plate of a wall.

Gable roof A roof in the shape of an inverted V with two triangular ends.

Gable end The triangular wall section under each end of a gable roof.

Gambrel roof A roof design common on barns and utility buildings that combines two gable roofs of differing slopes. The lower slope on each side is steep, which provides more usable space in lofts.

Girder A horizontal wood or steel member used to support part of a framed structure. Also called a beam.

Girder pocket The recessed seat created in a foundation wall in which the end of a girder sits.

Girt Horizontal perimeter timbers used in timber framing that function as nailers for vertical sheathing or siding.

Grade The identification class of lumber quality. Also shorthand for ground level—the finished level of the ground on a building site.

Ground The connection between electrical circuits or equipment and the earth. Designed to reduce shock hazards.

Ground-fault circuit interrupter (GFCI) A device that detects a ground fault or electrical line leakage and immediately shuts down power to that circuit.

Gusset plates Metal or plywood plates used to hold together the chords and webs of a truss.

Header The thick horizontal member that runs above rough openings, such as doors and windows, in a building's frame.

Header joist A horizontal board, installed on edge, that is secured to the ends of the floor joists.

Heartwood The inner, nonliving part of the tree that is typically more durable due to denser wood grain.

Hip roof A roof with a central ridge and slopes in four directions creating an overhang on all sides of the building.

Jack rafters Short rafters, typically in a hip roof, that run at an angle between a rafter and a top plate.

Jack stud A stud that runs from the bottom plate to the underside of a header. Also called a trimmer.

Jamb The upright surface forming the side in an opening, as for a door or window.

Joist Horizontal framing lumber placed on edge to support subfloors or hold up ceilings.

Joist hanger Bracket used to strengthen the connection between a joist and a piece of lumber into which it butts.

Junction box Metal or plastic box inside which all standard wire splices and wiring connections are made.

Kerf The narrow slot a saw blade cuts in a piece of lumber, usually about ⅛ inch thick.

Lag screw A large screw with a pointed tip and a hex head, generally used for bolting large timbers to posts.

Live load All the loads in and on a building that are not a permanent part of the structure—such as furniture, people, and wind.

Miter A joint in which two boards are joined at angles (usually 45 degrees) to form a corner.

Mortise-and-tenon Wood joint where a protrusion (tenon) fits into a recess (mortise), usually at a right angle.

Nailing flange An extension attached to a building component, usually predrilled for nails or screws—for example, around the sides of a window and on the edges of beam hanging hardware.

Nominal dimensions In lumber, the premilling measurement for which a piece of lumber is named (i.e., 2x4); in masonry, the measured dimensions of a masonry unit plus one mortar joint.

Nonload-bearing wall Partition or wall that does not carry a load from above.

O.C. An abbreviation for "on center," typically referring to layout measurements taken from the center of one stud to the center of the next stud in line.

Oriented-strand board (OSB) Panel material made of wood strands purposely aligned for strength and bonded together with adhesive.

Outrigger A projecting framing member run out from a main structure to provide additional stability or nailing for another framing component.

Overhang Typically, the extension of a roof beyond the perimeter walls; also any projection, such as a deck platform that extends beyond its supporting girder.

Particleboard Panel material made from wood flakes held together by resin.

Partition wall A nonload-bearing wall built to divide up interior space.

Penny (Abbreviation: d.) Unit of measure for nail length, such as a 10d nail, which is 3 inches long.

Pier A concrete base used to support columns, posts, girders, or joists.

Pigtail A short piece of wire used to make a short connection between electrical components.

Pilot hole A hole drilled before a screw is inserted to defeat splitting.

Pitch Loosely, the slope or angle of a roof; technically, the rise of a roof over its span.

Platform framing The framing method in which walls are built one story at a time on top of decked platforms over the story below.

Plumb Vertically straight. A line 90 degrees to a level line.

Point load The downward force exerted by a single heavy object inside or on top of the structure, such as a fireplace, hot tub, or water heater.

Pole class Rating by the American Wood Preservers Association, which puts poles into one of ten classes depending on their load-bearing capacity (for loads delivered on a vertical pole) and for span (for loads on a horizontal pole or girt).

Pole framing Structures without standard masonry foundations that consist of construction poles set in the ground in select locations and regular intervals. Popular on barns, especially livestock barns designed to have large open central spaces.

Prehung door A door that's already set in a jamb, with hinges (and sometimes a lockset) preassembled, ready to be installed in a rough opening.

Pressure treated Wood that has preservatives forced into it under pressure.

Pump jack A working platform system that is raised and lowered along vertical 4x4s using a pumping action.

Purlin Roof timbers spanning between principal rafters, typically set on edge to derive maximum strength in the unsupported span.

Quality mark An ink stamp or end tag label that is applied to pressure-treated lumber (and some other lumber). The quality mark provides important information, including the type of preservative used and the water retention level.

Quarter-round molding Molding whose section is that of a quarter of a circle.

Rake trim Trim boards applied to the fascia along the gable ends of a roof projection.

Rafter Any of the parallel framing members that support a roof.

R-value The measure of a substance's resistance to heat flow. An R-value is a number assigned to insulation and printed on all insulation products. The higher the number, the greater the insulating value.

Rebar Short for reinforcement bar, or metal bars laid in a grid used to reinforce concrete.

Ridge The horizontal crest of a roof.

Ridgeboard The horizontal board that defines the roof frame's highest point, or ridge.

Ridge cut The cut at the uphill end of a rafter, along the ridge plumb line, which allows the rafter's end grain to sit flush against the ridgeboard.

Rim joists Joists that define the outside edges of a platform. Joists that run perpendicular to floor joists and are end-nailed to joist ends are also known as header joists.

Rise In a roof, the vertical distance between the supporting wall's cap plate and the point where a line, drawn through the outside edge of the cap plate and parallel with the roof's slope, intersects the centerline of the ridgeboard.

Riser In plumbing, a water-supply pipe that carries water vertically; in carpentry, the vertical part of a stair installed on edge, across the front of the step.

Run In a roof with a ridge, the horizotal distance between the edge of an outside wall's cap plate and the centerline of the ridgeboard.

Sapwood The living wood near the outside of a tree trunk that carries sap.

Scarf joint Where the end grain of two pieces of lumber meet in the same plane at a 45-degree angle, or in a jagged, overlapped cut, typically backed up by another board or hardware to secure the joint.

Setback A local building code that requires structures to be built a certain distance from the street, sidewalk, or property line.

Shakes Similar to cedar shingles, but rougher in texture because they are split rather than sawn.

Sheathing Panel material, typically plywood, applied to the outside of a structure. Siding is installed over it.

Shed roof A roof that slopes in one direction only.

Sill anchor Threaded metal anchors set in concrete to which sills are attached with washers and nuts.

Sill The horizontal two-by lumber attached directly to the masonry foundation. It supports the building's walls.

Skirt boards In pole framing, pressure-treated 2x6s that run along the ground of the structure.

Slope The rise of a roof over its run, expressed as the number of inches of rise per unit of run (usually 12 inches). For example: 6-in-12 means a roof rises 6 inches for every 12 inches of run.

Snow load The downward stress on a structure's roof from accumulations of snow.

Soffit The boards or plywood panels that run the length of a wall on the underside of the rafters, covering the space between the wall and the fascia.

Soil-cement mixture An equal-parts combination of soil and cement that is used to provide support for a pole or post being set into the ground.

Soleplate The horizontal two-by lumber that forms the base of framed walls, also called a shoe.

Span Distance between supports, such as the outside walls of a building or a structural wall and a beam.

Spikes 8-inch (or larger) ring nails usually grouped in fours, used to attach lumber to a pole.

Spread load The outward force on walls caused by the downward-and-outward force of rafters.

Spring brace A piece of wood that is wedged diagonally between two cleates—one on the floor and one on the wall—used to fix a bow in a stud wall.

Stool A narrow shelf that butts against a windowsill.

Stringer On stairs, the diagonal boards that support the treads and risers.

Subfloor The flooring underneath a finished floor, usually plywood or OSB decking installed on floor joists or sleepers.

Through-bolt A bolt that extends completely through material, typically secured with a nut.

Timber framing A traditional building system that uses a skeletal framework of large wooden members, often joined together with strong intricate joints.

Toenailing Driving a nail at an angle into the face of a board so that it penetrates another board beneath or above it.

Top plate The horizontal two-by board nailed to the top of wall studs, almost always consisting of two boards that overlap at corners.

Total rise The ridge height of a roof measured from the top plate of the structure's wall.

Total run One half the building span, used in the calculation of roof angles.

Trap The water-filled curved pipe that prevents sewer gas from entering the house through the drainage network.

Trim Typically one-by lumber used as siding corner boards or as finish materials around windows and doors, under eaves, or with other architectural elements.

Trimmer Another term for a jack stud, or the short stud (nailed onto a full stud) that supports a header.

Truss A rigid assembly of timbers relying on triangulation to span distances impractical for a single member.

Valley flashing Material used to prevent leaks at the intersection of two pitched roofs that form an internal angle.

Water hammer A knocking in water pipes caused by a sudden change in pressure after a faucet or water valve shuts off.

Watt Unit of measurement of electrical power required or consumed by a fixture or appliance.

Web The inner members of a truss that carry loads from the chords, or perimeter members.

Wind load The stress on a structure due to gusting winds.

Z-brace door Door construction typically consisting of boards joined together and strengthened by a series of braces screwed to the backs of the boards in a Z-shaped pattern.

INDEX

Note: Page numbers in *italics* indicate outbuilding designs and plans available to order on pages 189–287.

A

ABS pipe, 160–61
anchor bolts, 49, 62
animals/livestock. *See also specific livestock*
    barns for, 18–19, *210–16. See also* outbuilding plans (available to order)
    feeders, 175
    guidelines for, 18–19
    Kennel / Garage with Dog Run, *279*
    plumbing plan for, 159. *See also* plumbing
    space requirements, 19
    stalls and partitions, 174–75
asphalt-based shingles, 128

B

barns. *See also* outbuilding plans (available to order)
    cupolas, 141
    gambrel, *234–39*
    girders for floors, 74. *See also* floors
    livestock, 18–19, *210–16*
    pole, 84–91, *222–27*
    stalls and partitions, 174–75
    storage space, 173
    timber-frame, 92–96
    vents/ventilation, 32
base trim, 179
batter boards, making, 56
blueprints, 22–25. *See also* outbuilding plans (available to order)
board-and-batten siding, 116–17
bolts, 49
book (this), overview and use, 10–11
building permits and codes, 15

C

cable. *See* wiring
capping wires, 148
carriage bolts, 49, 89
cattle, guidelines for, 18–19
cellulose fiber insulation, 177
chickens (poultry), guidelines for, 19
circuit breakers, 145, 147, 150. *See also* electrical; wiring
circular saw, 38, 39
clapboard siding, 120–21
climate considerations, 57
codes and permits, 15
concrete
    block, wall foundations, 66
    building footing forms, 60
    curing, 58, 59
    estimating, 63, 65
    finishes, 59
    footings, 60–61, 62, 66, 86, 218
    mixing, 58–59
    piers and posts, 64–65
    pouring, 60–61, 63
    sill installation, 73
    slabs, 53, 62–63
conduit, 146
construction drawings, 15, 21
copper tubing, 162–63
corners, squaring, 56
corrugated roofing (metal), 122
corrugated roofing (plastic/fiberglass), 124
corrugated siding (metal), 117, 123
cupolas, 141

D

designing buildings, 16–19
designs. *See* outbuilding designs; outbuilding plans (available to order)
doors
    building Z-brace, 133
    exterior prehung, 137
    framing, 82, 132
    hanging, 134–37
    with jambs, hanging, 135
    making your own, 132–33
    prehung, 136–37
    surface mounting, 134
    types/styles, 132–33
    weather stripping, 176
drainage of soil, 28
drains. *See* plumbing
drawings, construction, 21
drills and bits, 36, 37
drip edge, 126, 127
drywall, 178
dust masks, 35

E

electrical. *See also* wiring
    adding circuits, 150
    basic needs/loads, 147
    boxes, types and installation, 149, 154, 156
    circuit breakers, 145, 147, 150
    foundation plan and, 53
    freestanding boxes, 156
    fuses, 145, 147
    grounding, 146, 161
    outdoor connections, 154–57
    power to site, 30–31
    receptacles, 149, 151, 152, 156
    service panels, 31, 145, 147, 150
    setting up service, 150
    switches, 151, 152
    temporary service panel, 31
    terms defined, 145
    understanding electricity, 146
elevation drawings, 15, 21
equipment shed, 16
expansion, accommodating, 17
extension-cord wire gauges, 31
extruded polystyrene board, 177

F

fall-arrest systems, 40
fasteners, 48–49
feed storage, 18, 19
feeders, 175
fiberglass insulation, 177
finishing buildings and spaces, 172–83
    about: overview of, 172
    drywall, 178
    feeders, 175
    insulation options, 176, 177
    living space, 176–77
    paint and stain, 182–83
    sealing up living space, 176–77

PHOTO CREDITS

Illustrations by Ian Worpole & Clarke Barre.
Front cover: shippee/Shutterstock; **bottom back cover:** only background/ Shutterstock; **page 1 background:** alina_danilova/Shutterstock; **page 4:** Nadia Yong/Shutterstock
pages 1–2: *both* Daniel Dempster **page 6:** Harpur Garden Images, design: Jonathan Baillie **page 7:** *top* Tony Giammarino/Giammarino & Dworkin; *bottom* T. Algire/H. Armstrong Roberts/Roberstock.com **pages 8–10:** *all* Jerry Pavia **pages 11–13:** *all* Tony Giammarino/Giammarino & Dworkin **page 14:** Jack Schiffer/Dreamstime.com **page 17:** Tony Giammarino/Giammarino & Dworkin **page 18:** Richard Gunion/Dreamstime.com **page 19:** Brian C. Nieves **page 20:** Jerry Pavia **page 23:** Tony Giammarino/ Giammarino & Dworkin **page 24:** Ken Cole/Dreamstime.com **page 27:** Tony Giammarino/Giammarino & Dworkin **page 28:** *both* John Parsekian/ CH **page 30:** Harpur Garden Images **page 31:** *both* Brian C. Nieves/CH **page 32:** *top* Tony Giammarino/Giammarino & Dworkin; *bottom* Happyvalley2/Dreamstime.com **page 33:** *top* Jerry Pavia; *bottom both* Tony Giammarino/Giammarino & Dworkin **page 34:** Donna Chiarelli/ CH **page 35:** *top left* & *top right* John Parsekian/CH; *center* & *bottom* Brian C. Nieves/CH **page 36:** *top left* & *bottom right* Brian C. Nieves/CH; *top right* John Parsekian/ CH; *bottom left* courtesy of Paslode **page 37:** *top row* & *bottom right* Brian C. Nieves/CH; *bottom left* John Parsekian/CH **page 38:** *top row* John Parsekian/CH; *bottom* Brian C. Nieves/CH **page 39:** *all* John Parsekian/CH **page 41:** *top* Robert Anderson; *center* courtesy of Pro-Trim; *bottom* courtesy of Werner Ladder Company **page 43:** Brian C. Nieves/CH **page 44:** John Par-sekian/CH **page 45:** *top left* & *bottom row* courtesy of APA–The Engineered Wood Association; *top right* courtesy of Louisiana Pacific **page 46:** *all* John Parsekian/CH **page 47:** courtesy of APA–The Engineered Wood Association **pages 50–51:** Maria Dryfhout/Dreamstime.com **pages 52–62:** *all* John Par-sekian/CH **page 63:** *top right* & *bottom row* Brian C. Nieves/CH; *top left* John Parsekian/CH **pages 64–66:** *all* John Parsekian/CH **page 67:** *all* Brian C. Nieves/CH **page 68:** John Puleio/CH **page 73:** *all* John Parsekian/ CH **pages 75–79:** *all* Brian C. Nieves/CH **pages 80–82:** *all* John Parsekian/ CH **page 83:** courtesy of Better Barns **pages 85–91:** *all* Brian C. Nieves/ CH **page 93:** *both* Deanna Ricketson/Hearthstone, Inc. **page 95:** *all* Brian C. Nieves/CH **page 96:** *all* Joan Reilly/Timber Frames by R.A. Krouse **page 97:** courtesy of Handy Home Products **page 99:** *all* John Parsekian/ CH **page 100:** Donna Chiarelli/CH **page 101:** *both* courtesy of Better Barns **page 105:** *all* Brian C. Nieves/CH **page 106:** *all* John Parsekian/CH **page 109:** *all* Brian C. Nieves/CH **page 110:** *top* Brian C. Nieves/CH; *bottom all* courtesy of Better Barns **page 113:** *all* Brian C. Nieves/CH **page 114:** Ken Cole/Dreamstime.com **page 115:** *all* Brian C. Nieves/ CH **page 116:** *all* courtesy of Handy Home Products **page 117:** Brian C. Nieves **pages 118–121:** *all* John Parsekian/CH **page 124:** courtesy of Suntuff **page 125:** *top left* & *bottom right* Dan Lane/CH; *top right, bottom left* & *bottom center* Brian C. Nieves/CH **page 126:** *top row* & *bottom left* John Parsekian/CH; *bottom right* courtesy of C & J Metal Products **pages 129–131:** *all* John Parsekian/ CH **pages 133–135:** *all* Brian C. Nieves/CH **pages 136–139:** *all* John Parsekian/ CH **page 140:** *all* Brian C. Nieves/CH **page 141:** *both* courtesy of Calgary Cupola **page 143:** *left* & *center column* John Parsekian/CH; *right column* Merle Henkenius **page 144:** *left* Merle Henkenius/CH; *right* Brian C. Nieves/CH **pages 146–155:** *all* Brian C. Nieves/CH **page 156:** *all* John Parsekian/CH **page 157:** *top* & *bottom row* Brian C. Nieves/CH; *center row* Merle Henkenius **page 160:** Brian C. Nieves/CH **page 161:** *top* Merle Henkenius/CH; *bottom rows* John Parse-kian/CH **page 162:** *all* Merle Henkenius/CH **page 163:** *all* John Parsekian/CH **pages 165–171:** Merle Henkenius/CH **page 172:** courtesy of Summerwood **page 173:** *top left* courtesy of Handy Home Products; *top right* & *bottom left* Brian C. Nieves; *bottom right* John Parsekian/ CH **page 174:** courtesy of Hearthstone Homes **page 175:** *all* Brian C. Nieves/CH **page 176:** John Parsekian/CH **page 177:** *top left* courtesy of Owens Corning; *bottom left* courtesy of Timber Frames by R.A. Krouse; *right all* Stephen Munz/CH **page 178:** *all* courtesy of Celotex **page 179:** *top right* Brian C. Nieves; *center* & *bottom rows* John Parsekian/CH **page 180:** *all* Merle Henkenius **page 181:** *top left* & *top center* courtesy of Amerimax; *top right* courtesy of Rainhandler; *bottom row* John Parsekian/CH **pages 182–183:** *all* John Parsekian/CH **pages 184–185:** Bonnie Sue **page 186:** *bottom* Brian C. Nieves/CH *center & top* Andrew Kline/CH **pages 188-194:** Andrew Kline/CH **page 200:** Brian C. Nieves/CH **pages 205-239:** Andrew Kline/CH **page 243:** Tony Giammarino/Giammarino & Dworkin **page 293:** Ken Cole/ Dreamstime.com **page 298:** Jerry Pavia

Metric Equivalents

Length

1 inch	25.4mm
1 foot	0.3048m
1 yard	0.9144m
1 mile	1.61km

Area

1 square inch	645mm^2
1 square foot	0.0929m^2
1 square yard	0.8361m^2
1 acre	4046.86m^2
1 square mile	2.59km^2

Volume

1 cubic inch	16.3870cm^3
1 cubic foot	0.03m^3
1 cubic yard	0.77m^3

Common Lumber Equivalents

Sizes: Metric cross sections are so close to their U.S. sizes, as noted below, that for most purposes they may be considered equivalents.

Dimensional lumber	1 x 2	19 x 38mm
	1 x 4	19 x 89mm
	2 x 2	38 x 38mm
	2 x 4	38 x 89mm
	2 x 6	38 x 140mm
	2 x 8	38 x 184mm
	2 x 10	38 x 235mm
	2 x 12	38 x 286mm
Sheet sizes	4 x 8 ft.	1200 x 2400mm
	4 x 10 ft.	1200 x 3000mm
Sheet thicknesses	¼ in.	6mm
	⅜ in.	9mm
	½ in.	12mm
	¾ in.	19mm
Stud/joist spacing	16 in. o.c.	400mm o.c.
	24 in. o.c.	600mm o.c.

Capacity

1 fluid ounce	29.57mL
1 pint	473.18mL
1 quart	0.95L
1 gallon	3.79L

Weight

1 ounce	28.35g
1 pound	0.45kg

Temperature

Fahrenheit = Celsius x 1.8 + 32
Celsius = Fahrenheit - 32 x 5⁄9

Nail Size and Length

Penny Size	Nail Length
2d	1"
3d	1¼"
4d	1½"
5d	1¾"
6d	2"
7d	2¼"
8d	2½"
9d	2¾"
10d	3"
12d	3¼"
16d	3½"

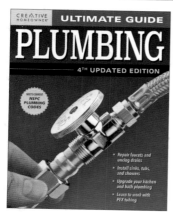
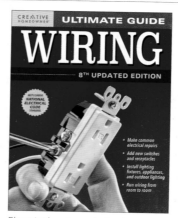
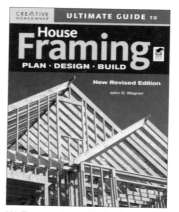

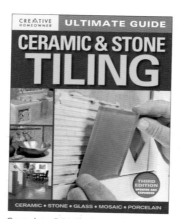
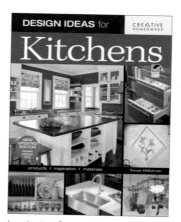

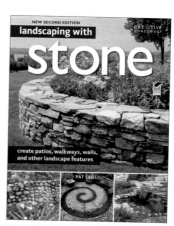

THE GIRL OUTDOORS

TO MY FABULOUS FAMILY – *my parents, Marina and Spencer, and my brother Matthew, for all the adventures.*

THE GIRL
OUTDOORS

THE WILD GIRL'S GUIDE TO ADVENTURE, TRAVEL AND WELLBEING

SIAN ANNA LEWIS

CONWAY

LONDON · OXFORD · NEW YORK · NEW DELHI · SYDNEY

CONWAY
Bloomsbury Publishing Plc
50 Bedford Square, London, WC1B 3DP, UK

BLOOMSBURY, CONWAY and the
Conway logo are trademarks of
Bloomsbury Publishing Plc

First published in Great Britain 2018

A catalogue record for this book is
available from the British Library

Library of Congress Cataloguing-in-
Publication data has been applied for

ISBN: PB: 978-1-8448-6533-8
ePub: 978-1-8448-6532-1
ePDF: 978-1-8448-6530-7

2 4 6 8 10 9 7 5 3 1

Designed by Austin Taylor
Printed and bound in China
by C&C Offset Printing Co

Bloomsbury Publishing Plc makes every
effort to ensure that the papers used in
the manufacture of our books are natural,
recyclable products made from wood grown
in well-managed forests. Our manufacturing
processes conform to the environmental
regulations of the country of origin

To find out more about our authors and
books visit www.bloomsbury.com and
sign up for our newsletters

A ship in harbour is safe, but that's not what ships are for.

GRACE MURRAY HOPPER

CONTENTS

INTRODUCTION

Welcome, my friends, to a wilder way of life. In these pages you'll find the inspiration and the information you need to get outside and get happy. *The Girl Outdoors* is a bible of all the good things the wide, wild world has to offer. It's an introduction to the crazy fun of action sports, a tome of inspiration for weekend adventures and far-flung travels, a girl's guide to feeling fit, a cookbook of hearty dinners to chow down on round the campfire with your mates. All rolled into one lovely package – good, eh?

The freedom, if not the desire, to explore the planet has been a long time coming for women. The playing field is a lot more even now than when the first female pioneers of mountaineering and derring-do were on the scene, yet when I am up a mountain peak, in the line-up or on a climbing wall I often find myself in a very male-dominated world. I reckon it's time to change that.

I hear again and again from girls who would love to try surfing, go hiking or travel alone but feel they lack the confidence to get out and give those things a go. Perhaps because there's still a perception of adventure as an extreme pursuit, a living-off-urine, round-the-world-on-a-unicycle tough club open only to the hardiest grizzled explorer. That's not what this book, or the outdoors, is about. It is about being your own have-a-go heroine, embracing new experiences and the simple, low-key pleasures of camping, walking, grilling fish over a fire you built with your own fair hands. It's about stepping away from the stresses of modern life, too. Getting outdoors is the easiest route I know to feeling happy and healthy, although there's no bollocks about diets and calories in this book – I'm far too fond of red wine and chocolate biscuits for that.

I've loved a little adventure since I was a nipper, when my grandmother would take me swimming in the cold Irish sea and my dad would cart us off on walks in the woods. As an outdoors journalist I've followed my love for fresh air around the world, camping on its cliffs, diving its oceans, getting extremely lost on its rain-sodden hills. And if I've learned anything, it's that there are three steps to living a full and happy life: 1. Get outdoors 2. Repeat as often as you can 3. In the words of Bill and Ted, be excellent to each other.

So what's our first adventure going to be? In Section One you'll find introductions to sports that get you out in the back of

beyond – mountain biking, climbing, hiking, skiing and their adrenaline-fuelled ilk. Feeling a bit sweaty? Cool off with a wild adventure – we'll be swimming in rivers, road tripping in campervans and setting up tents to sleep under the stars in Section Two. Section Three is all about feeling good – scrumptious eats you can whip up round a fire, crafty things to make, green-fingered advice for growing your own garden goodies and wellbeing advice for wonder women. And in Section Four we're on the road less travelled, exploring the four corners of the globe with guides to joyful travel and guides to planning trips of all shapes and sizes.

Jump on in – the water's lovely.

*Courage is resistance to fear,
mastery of fear, not absence of fear.*

MARK TWAIN

SECTION ONE
ACTIVE OUTDOORS

READY FOR AN ENDORPHIN BOOST? In Section One we're diving straight into the world of action sports, trying out eight adrenalin-fuelled ways to get fit and explore the great outdoors.

These short guides introduce each discipline, giving you an insight into what to expect and inspiring you to zip up a wetsuit or stick on some climbing shoes and try them out. Each chapter includes advice for beginners, fitness ideas, safety tips and all the essential kit you'll need. I've also listed three epic places around the world where you can put your newfound addiction into practice.

The only element standing in the way of the skills you want to learn and the experiences you'd love to try is the confidence to take the first step. The sometimes elitist representation of extreme sports can make starting out feel quite intimidating, and the word 'extreme' is misleading, implying that only the fittest or bravest can take part. That's not true – these sports are both safe and tremendous fun for the greenest beginner. But the only way to learn is to take the plunge, to jump into the water or hop onto a bike and get going. The more you practise, the more you'll achieve, and your confidence in your ability will grow.

We'll start our adventure on land, conquering dirt tracks on mountain bikes and trail runs, climbing up rocky cliffs, hiking merrily over hill and dale, and exploring winter wonderlands on skis and snowboards. Worked up a sweat? Jump into the water with a surfboard tucked under your arm, paddle your way down a winding river in a canoe or a kayak, and then dive beneath the surface of the ocean to see what mesmerising worlds wait below the surface.

Time to be your own have-a-go heroine – you have nothing to lose but your fear.

DIRT, ROCK AND SNOW

Let's go get muddy. Make tracks on a mountain bike, clock up the miles on a racer, climb a cliff face and hike or ski into the hills with my guides to five active sports that turn planet Earth into an epic playground.

1 ROAD CYCLING AND MOUNTAIN BIKING

INTRODUCTION

Whether you want to speed down tarmac on a slick road bike, take on a remote forest trail on a rugged mountain bike or just ride around town on a sit-up-and-beg Duchess with a baguette tucked into a wicker basket, owning a bicycle will open up a new world in which you can travel far under your own steam and get fit while you do it. Be careful – cycling can quickly morph from just a sport into an intrinsic part of your personality. You're a cyclist now – welcome to the club of bike-loving keenos. You'll recognise us by the helmet hair and the chain marks on our legs.

In this chapter we're exploring fast-paced road cycling and adventurous mountain biking. Road cycling as a term also includes commuters on two wheels and bikers-about-town. Road or racing bikes, with drop handles and myriad gears, are specifically designed for cycling for fitness, in a race, say, or up a painfully steep hill, as opposed to trundling to work along a canal path.

Mountain biking is essentially off-road biking with added thrills and spills – it takes cycling into the great outdoors, on rugged-wheeled bikes that can eat up bumpy terrain for breakfast.

STARTING OUT

Switching up to a smart road bike from a run-around hybrid is a big step, and one that can feel like graduating from riding a Shetland pony to a racehorse. Road bikes go fast. They want to eat up miles. They want you to keep up. And you will, eventually, but don't push yourself too hard at first. You need to get used to a lot of new feelings on a road bike, including your newfound speed, wobbliness and the rather scary move of dropping down onto low handlebars when going downhill. When you've chosen your new bike and brought it home, head out on a dry, sunny day on the quietest road you can find and put your new steed through its paces.

Mountain bikes are far more forgiving for beginners to try, and feel really comfy when ridden around town or on flat dirt roads. The best way to see if mountain biking is your thing is to head to a trail centre and rent a bike to take out for a session (mountain bike trails, like ski pistes, are usually colour coded, with green and blue for beginners, red for intermediates and black for the insane). Trails call for a different riding technique to road bikes. When climbing, keep your weight towards the front of the saddle. When descending, try

What the hell are cleats?

The little twist-locks on the bottom of cycling-specific shoes clip into pedals and are theoretically a great idea, as they mean that when you cycle you're pulling up as well as pushing down, and thus much faster. They can be tricky to master, though – get used to riding your bike first, and then invest in cleated shoes and pedals and try clipping in and out somewhere quiet, like an empty car park, as you'll inevitably mess it up and slowly fall over sideways the first few times.

standing off your pedals and hovering above or slightly behind the saddle. When you aren't pedalling, keep your feet parallel to avoid catching a pedal on a rock or a protruding root. Look ahead at where you're going and keep up a good speed – as tempting as it is to inch at snail slowness over a rocky bit or a drop, you'll be much better balanced if you ride at a brisk pace. Keep practising and see if you can find the 'flow' – that feeling when everything suddenly clicks into place and you and your bike are tearing down a hill in perfect sync. It's pretty addictive once you get there.

You'll often see cyclists kitted up in matching shiny Lycra, but all you really need to try road cycling or mountain biking are a helmet and well-padded shorts, on their own in summer and worn over leggings in winter. Add a waterproof jacket and you're good to go. If you get serious and want to go for the Tour

de France look, short-sleeved cycling jerseys and long-sleeved cycling jackets are a good place to start – pick ones with roomy pockets on the back for storing water and jelly babies – and bib shorts (the dungarees of the Lycra world) are a comfy option to wear underneath. Lycra is tight, so pick kit designed specifically for women. Mountain bikers get to look a lot less geeky than cyclists, and usually wear big baggy shorts (best to still stick padded shorts underneath) and T-shirts, plus base layers and leggings on cold days. Wear knee and elbow pads to save your extremities if you're prone to falling off. For both kinds of cycling, a bottle cage is the easiest way to carry water – avoid taking a backpack if possible, so you don't feel weighed down.

Both road and mountain cycling can feel quite male dominated at first glance, but don't let the boys' club put you off. There are

plenty of women out there taking to the road or getting muddy in the woods – you might just have to seek them out. Look around for a local ladies' cycling club (britishcycling.org.uk lists clubs in the UK) or check noticeboards at bike shops – my local trail centre, for example, offers weekly ladies-only rides. Let's get more women out in the saddle – liberty, equality, velocity!

PICKING THE RIGHT BIKE

Bike money burning a hole in your pocket? It's hard to resist the urge to pick the shiniest, most badass model in your local cycle shop, especially if there's an eager shop assistant whispering lovely words like 'titanium' and 'carbon fork' in your ear. But resist, and do your research. There are always myriad new models on the market, but if you're investing in your first bike you aren't going to need a race-ready beast with souped-up specs. My advice

is to avoid this year's models altogether, and look out for last year's on sale at better prices. It's definitely worth spending as much as you possibly can on your bike, especially if you plan to use it every day, and looking into insurance for at least a year or two.

Make a list of where and how you'll realistically use your bike. Are you going to commute on it? Build up to events or triathlons? I chose mine because it was compatible with panniers, so I could take it bikepacking. Oh, and because it was really, really pretty. Ask for advice in a few different shops and test-ride the bikes they suggest – the more bikes you can try out, the better. Online, bikes can look temptingly cheap, but make sure that they're returnable, and be aware that you often have to assemble them yourself. If you're a cycling newbie then buying a new bike in person is definitely worth the extra cash, as you'll get properly measured for it and have the saddle and handlebars correctly adjusted to your height. You don't need to pick a female-

specific bike unless you're on the short side, but you may prefer a wider saddle for more comfortable nether regions. If you're after something versatile that you can ride around town but also take exploring on the weekend, a mountain bike is a really good choice. Top-of-the-range mountain bikes have as many bells and whistles as racing bikes, but if you're a beginner you really don't need something with high specs. A hardtail bike (a bike with a solid frame and a front suspension fork) will definitely suffice, and if you get hooked on trail riding you can upgrade to something with full suspension later on.

If the price of a new bike is going to make a big dent in your bank account, see if your work offers a Cycle to Work scheme – this means your company will buy the bike and you'll pay it off in monthly instalments. Or look for well-treated second-hand bikes in independent bike shops. You might see second-hand bikes listed on Gumtree or Craigslist – treat these with a lot of caution, and take someone with you who really knows their stuff if you do go to see one.

Ride your bike as much as possible for the first few months and then get it serviced to iron out any kinks (this is sometimes included in the price). Sign up to a day's bike maintenance course and learn how to service your bike yourself – you'll get to understand its ins and outs and save hundreds in workshop repair fees.

CYCLING FITNESS

Incorporate a cycle into your day, and bang – you've worked out on your daily commute, you multitasking queen. Cycling is one of the most efficient ways to work out there is, and will tone you up fast without much risk of injury, as your bike takes most of the load. It's also satisfyingly

easy to see progress from the start. That big, sweaty hill you can't make it to the top of? Come back after a month in the saddle and it'll be toast. Steep climbs on a mountain bike will whip your legs, core and bum into shape, and you get the lovely reward of an adrenalin-fuelled ride back downhill for your hard work.

WINTER TRAINING

Say the word 'winter' to even a hardened cyclist and watch them recoil in horror. It's true that cold-weather cyclists need to take much more care. If it's raining heavily or the roads are filmed with ice it's not really worth the risk of a fall. If it's just bloody cold outside, be brave and tog up in heavier Lycra and lots of layers. The first few miles might hurt, but I promise you'll feel amazing afterwards. If you want to keep your training up for summer

rides, invest in a turbo trainer – a static platform you can lock your bike into so you can clock up miles from the warmth of your garage. Weight training, jogging and swimming will all keep your fitness up over winter, too. Mountain bikes are hardier and can be ridden on the muddiest of days, but it's best to give the trails a miss in rain, to avoid both eroding the land and slipping all over the place.

SAFETY IN TRAFFIC

One of the biggest stumbling blocks for would-be cycling commuters is dealing with traffic. It's worth remembering that cycling is usually safe, will get you fit, and in the average city's rush hour can take half the time that driving would. But you do need to be sensible, alert and careful at all times, so save chatting to your mate and pedalling along without a care for cycle paths. In traffic, wear a well-fitting helmet, use a decent set of working lights and

DIRT, ROCK AND SNOW

How to change an inner tube

Punctures happen to the best of us, but when you're on the side of a busy road it's far easier to just switch your inner tube (a separate inflatable rubber tube inside the tyre) for a new one than faff about trying to fix a tiny hole with rubber solution. You can then just cycle home and fix the old one at your leisure.

YOU WILL NEED

▶ Spare tube of the right size. Tyres have the correct size (700x23c, for example) embossed on them. It's worth always carrying one in your jersey pockets when you're riding
▶ Tyre levers
▶ Allen keys
▶ Cup of tea (if available)

1 Remove the afflicted wheel from your bike using an Allen key. Deflate the tyre completely by letting all remaining air out of the valve. Valves, by the way, come in two types – Presta valves are narrower and longer; Schrader valves are shorter and fatter. Most road bikes and mountain bikes are Prestas; touring bikes are usually Schraders. Annoyingly, you need to use a valve-specific pump for your tyres, but pumps are often convertible.

2 Using two tyre levers, hook the tyre away from the wheel's metal rim and remove it completely.

3 Remove the punctured tube (I keep mine, as they make good bungey cords for securing bags when you're bikepacking).

4 Check the inside of the tyre for any sharp objects which might have caused the puncture – if they're still stuck in there then changing the inner tube just will lead to another puncture.

5 Take the new inner tube and find the valve. Pop this into the valve hole in the metal rim.

6 Thread the inner tube into the tyre and inflate it with enough air to make it sit in it nicely.

7 Push the tyre back onto the rim, using the tyre levers to coax it into place. This is the tough bit – you especially need to make sure you don't pinch the inner tube between the tyre and the metal rim.

8 Wipe brow, and inflate the new tube fully. Again, your tyre will helpfully have the best pressure level printed on it in PSI or BAR – if your pump has a pressure gauge you can get it pretty exact.

1

2

5

7

HOW TO KEEP YOUR BIKE CLEAN AND IN GOOD SHAPE

If your bike isn't riding properly and you don't know what's wrong, just get it serviced by a bike mechanic. It's definitely worth the money you'll spend getting a pro to fix it properly, especially if it's your main mode of transport. However, a bit of love and care will keep your two-wheeled baby in good nick for longer and help avoid costly snags in the future. Try following this quick cleaning checklist once every week or two.

wear a high-visibility tabard or a reflective jacket to make sure you're picked up in headlights. Obey all the same rules of the road as cars (even if other cyclists are ignoring the lights. You are a better person than them). It just isn't worth rushing, even if you're running late for work. Ride positively, and remember you're just as entitled to use the space as cars – it's tempting to shrink into the kerb but it's much safer to ride carefully and confidently in the lane.

▶ Give your bike a good wash with a hose, soapy water and a sponge, and rinse clean with water.
▶ Wipe down rims and brake pads with an alcohol-based product or hot soapy water.
▶ Keep your tyres well inflated (this helps avoid punctures).
▶ Wipe your chain down with an old cloth and a chain cleaner.
▶ Use a degreaser product on the frame, chain, gears and cogs.
▶ Lube up your chain and pedal your bike backwards to distribute it.

8

Whenever you're planning a ride, give your bike a once-over first, to check for any niggles. To check your brakes, squeeze the brake lever one or two centimetres inwards and make sure the brake blocks touch the rim when you do so. Check that your brake cables aren't frayed or rusty, and that the brake pads have lots of material left (some have indicator lines to show when they need replacing). Check that your tyres are fully inflated, with no damage, and if you have quick-release wheels, that these are fully tightened.

ESSENTIAL CYCLING KIT

▶ Jersey
▶ Long-sleeved jersey jacket
▶ Helmet – helmets aren't compulsory, but my view is that it's worth wearing one. Pick one which feels as light and comfy as possible to stop it feeling restrictive
▶ Bib shorts – they're comfy, warm in cold weather and stay put
▶ Cycle shorts – go for some with generous padding to literally save your arse
▶ Waterproof socks
▶ Trainers or clip-in cycle shoes
▶ Waterproof jacket – pick one with reflective panels as a less geeky-looking alternative to a fluorescent tabard
▶ Water bottle
▶ Snacks – I favour jelly babies
▶ Bike lights
▶ Pump adaptor – this little brass tool converts between the two types of inner valve
▶ Spare inner tubes
▶ Tyre levers
▶ Set of Allen keys
▶ Spare cash
▶ Mobile phone
▶ Portable pump

Three places
to go cycling

1 Black Mountains, Wales

The northeast corner of the Brecon Beacons National Park is a glorious mix of heather-clad hills, wild valleys, winding roads and cosy towns selling tea and cake. Skirt under the shadow of the Sugar Loaf and head straight up iconic Gospel Pass, a heart-pumping climb that rewards the puffing, red-faced cyclist with the glorious rolling landscape of Hay Bluff and an easy cycle down into the pretty, bookish town of Hay-on-Wye.

2 Sa Calobra, Mallorca

Two little words designed to spark fear and lust in equal parts into the heart of any road rider worth her salt. Often called the 'perfect climb', this 7% gradient route ascends a spanking 670m over 9.4 kilometres, reaching high above Mallorca's craggy coastline and the sparkling blue waters of the Mediterranean, hairpinning like crazy as it goes. Make sure you look up at the view as you strive for the top – you can always reward yourself with a dip in that inviting-looking ocean afterwards.

3 Whistler, Canada

Canada's favourite ski town becomes a mountain biker's mecca once the snow melts. Stick your bike in a gondola for an easy ride into the hills, then test your skills in the massive mountain bike park, packed with everything from gentle green routes to jump trails, or get fighting fit on the endurance trails that snake past waterfalls and over granite rock rolls. When you're done being queen of the mountain you can hit the lively bars for a well-deserved beer.

② CLIMBING

INTRODUCTION

We've come a long way from the days of Victorian lady climbers scrambling up mountains armed only with petticoats and a bit of pluck. Elite climbers now push the limits of the sport every day, scaling new heights both mentally and physically, and it's just as exciting when you're first starting out. Climbing is a brilliant way to tame a fear of heights, achieve tangible goals and get really ripped arm muscles in one neat package. It also takes you to some incredible, remote places (or indoor climbing walls that smell like sweaty boys, your call), it's fantastic for all-over fitness and

it's a huge confidence builder – while climbing is a very sociable sport, it's really all about overcoming solo challenges. There's something very mentally beneficial about setting your brain to work on a route – it clears your mind of workaday worries and lets you focus fully on something physical.

There are three main kinds of climbing for newbies to sample:

▶ BOULDERING is climbing on low rocks, close to the ground and without ropes. It's not about gaining a lot of height, but more about solving the problem of how to get to the final hold without falling off (if you do fall, it'll be safely onto a crash mat. Indoor bouldering walls have padded floors; outside, a friend will act as a spotter and guide you to the crash mat if you fall).

▶ SPORT CLIMBING is climbing with a harness and a rope, indoors or outdoors, and using the permanent anchors (or 'bolts') which have been established on set routes to tie yourself onto the wall (see image below). This is in contrast to 'trad' (traditional) climbing, which always takes place outdoors and which involves taking your own equipment, or 'gear', with you, and inserting it into gaps in the rock to secure your rope to. Bouldering and sport climbing are the most beginner-friendly ponies in the climbing stable, and it's easy to try both indoors, on a taster course with an instructor.

▶ If you've mastered the basics of sport climbing, TRAD CLIMBING (together with its crazy sister ice climbing, which involves using crampons and an ice axe to scale ice-clad

rock) is the next step, but definitely requires a lot more tuition (and isn't covered here). There's a lot to learn and a ton of jargon in all incarnations of climbing – be safe and ask if you don't understand.

Indoor climbing routes are colour coded. Outside, you'll have to figure out which holds to use on your own. You'll hear routes referred to by numbers, which are their grades of difficulty. There are lots of different grading systems in use – it's best to start with as easy a route as possible (this is also a good way to warm up) and progress from there until you find your own limit to work away at. Outdoor routes usually also have (very silly and often naughty) names – you'll find these listed in climbing guidebooks, along with the grade and key features of the climb. Wanna learn to scale Tufa King Hard, Pineapple Thunderpussy or, my personal favourite, John Craven's Willy Warmer? Read on.

BOULDERING

Pared back and simple, you could argue that bouldering is one of the purest ways to climb. Indoor bouldering walls have thick crash mats at the bottom of routes, so if you fall you'll get a cushioned landing. You still need to take care, but you can boulder indoors alone. Outdoors, boulderers use portable crash mats, and usually climb in pairs (see images on page 27). One is the climber and one acts as the spotter, watching the climber and staying ready to guide them safely to the mat if they do fall.

When bouldering indoors, you'll be following a coloured route. To complete a route you need to start from a sitting position with your hands on the first hold(s), climb up to the top hold, and touch it with both hands. When you've bagged it, climb down to a safe distance rather than just jumping off from the top, and watch out for other climbers near or below you.

Remember to use your toes as much as your arms, and try to keep your arms hanging straight to save energy. Think of it as putting your weight on your skeleton, not your muscles. Be open to trying different movements in order to complete the problem – a little like playing Twister. Look for a foothold, then a handhold, and progress upwards. Climbing shoes have tight rubber toes that you can work into surprisingly small footholds, or even smear across a featureless wall to get a bit of grip as you pull yourself up.

SPORT CLIMBING

Rope climbing takes all the elements of bouldering and adds one more fear factor – height. If this is what puts you off the idea of rock climbing, remember that it is completely normal, and in fact entirely sensible, to be aware of heights. This is just your brain doing

Climbing fitness

Climbing is an incredible all-body workout – just go to your local wall and eye up the muscle-clad bodies of the female regulars if you doubt me. It works the whole body in bursts of cardio energy but also relies on flexibility, core strength and grace. It can be very easy to injure muscles and fingers when rock climbing, though. Warm up properly before a climb, and stretch muscles out afterwards. If you strain a muscle, don't continue to climb on it – give it a rest for a week or two instead. Cross training will also help your climbing to improve in leaps and bounds – lifting weights will build strong arms, and yoga helps with better bendiness.

its damnedest to keep you out of what it thinks are dangerous situations. Climbing, however, is safe as long as you take the correct precautions – a 2010 study even found that you're more likely to injure yourself playing football than at a climbing wall. If you're nervous, try bouldering first, in order to master the basics of climbing, and then sign on to an induction course at an indoor climbing gym (find a list via the British Mountaineering Council, thebmc.co.uk. Many of them have bouldering and roped sections, so you can try both disciplines) or ask an experienced friend to teach you the ropes (hah).

When you're sport climbing, you are attached to the wall with a rope that is tied to your harness. Your climbing partner, also known as a belayer, stands at the bottom of the route and belays you from their own harness. Belaying involves pulling in rope and holding the climber tight if they fall. In essence, if you fall off (or just let go), nothing will happen – your belayer will keep you held in place and you'll just hang there like a potato. It's actually a useful way to have a rest if you can't finish a problem in one go. When you finish a sport route by reaching the top, your belayer will lower you down to the bottom. This involves letting go of the holds, leaning back and walking your feet down the wall while the belayer feeds out rope to bring you back to solid ground.

When you buddy up for a climb you will both need to know how to belay the other person. The easiest way to learn is to be shown, and then supervised as you belay your partner. A belayer keeps one hand on the rope at all times and pulls it through a belay device to take in slack as the climber ascends, then feeds it slowly out as they descend.

The two most common kinds of belay device you'll encounter are tubular-style belays and Grigris. Tubulars are easy to learn to use, but

require you to constantly hold the climber in place. Grigris run your rope around a pivoting cam that feeds out rope smoothly when open, but locks completely in the event of a fall. The benefit of a Grigri is that if a belayer lets go of the rope accidentally, the climber still gets caught, making them the safest option.

LEAD CLIMBING

Beginner climbers will usually be attached to the wall with a top rope, which, as the name suggests, is a rope threaded through an anchor at the very top of the route. Once you're confident on top rope, the natural progression in sport climbing is to try lead climbing. This is a whole new ballgame, and a point at which The Fear can come creeping back in. You'll still be attached to a rope, and via the rope to your belayer, but you won't be tied to the top of the route. Instead, you'll clip the rope onto bolts placed at intervals on the route whenever you draw alongside them. If you're indoors, you'll

clip into ready-prepared bolts threaded with a quickdraw (two carabiners connected by a fabric sling). If you're outdoors, you'll have your own set of quickdraws attached to your harness, and you'll clip one onto the bolt and then clip your rope onto the quickdraw. If this sounds confusing, scary or both, don't panic! Leading is a safe, and fun, form of climbing, and if you fall, you'll only drop a little way – to the height of the last place you clipped your rope. You don't need to try leading until you're feeling good on a top rope.

How to tie a figure-of-eight knot

This is the most basic of climbing knots, attaching your rope to your harness, and is standard practice because it's both easy and reliable. It's also something you'll have to know by heart before a climbing wall will let you climb without supervision. It attaches to either one or two tie-in loops on your harness, depending on the harness model.

1 Take the tail end of the rope and measure a length as long as your spread arms. Make a loop here, twist it and then thread the tail end through to make a figure of eight. Leave somewhat loose.

2 Feed the tail into your harness – most harnesses have two tie-in loops. Do not tie your knot in your belay loop.

3 Now follow the first figure-of-eight knot with the tail, threading around the first knot to create a double figure-of-eight knot. Pull tight.

4 You should have around six inches of leftover tail (if not, start again). Optionally you can secure this by wrapping around the rope twice and pulling through.

CLIMBING SAFETY

❱ Know your limits, and climb well within your ability when trying out new places.

❱ Check ropes and equipment are in good nick before every climb.

❱ If you aren't sure of a new technique or of taking the step to sport or outdoor climbing, take a course with an instructor (they'll be more patient than your mates, too).

❱ Retire your rope after a major fall.

❱ Warm up properly before a climb (try the yogi sun salutation on page 169).

❱ Always check your partner before a sport climb – the climber checks the belayer's device is being used correctly, and the belayer checks the climber's harness and knot.

❱ When bouldering, never jump from the top – climb down to a safe distance (or even all the way, it's a better workout).

❱ Don't walk underneath other boulderers.

SLACKLINING

Climbers all seem to love to slackline, as it really works your core balance, and you'll often see a line set up at climbing walls. You don't need to be a climber to give it a go, though.

Slacklining is like tightrope walking but uses a thicker, flatter line, usually strung between two trees. It's highly addictive and, once you own a line, a free and unlimited way to play outdoors in the summer. Buy a wide beginner line of around two inches thick – I like Gibbon lines (gibbon-slacklines.com), which you can usually pick up for under £50. A line comes in two parts, one each to wrap around each tree trunk, and they can then be ratcheted together to create a tense ribbon. Attach your line between two sturdy trees with a flat space clear of debris between them – when you're beginning, the line only needs to be a few feet off the ground. Ratchet as tightly as you can. Step onto the slackline and try to walk along the line to the other tree – it's a *lot* harder than it looks! The key is to place your feet straight, flat and one in front of the other, to look ahead, not down, and to use your arms to balance yourself by holding them out at right angles.

DEEP-WATER SOLOING

Deep-water solo climbing – which requires nothing but your swimmers and climbing shoes – involves scaling coastal cliffs with just the ocean below you as a safety net. If you fall, you simply plummet into the water. If you're a confident swimmer, it's a reasonably safe way to climb at lower levels, but deep-water soloing still poses a mental challenge for anyone who's never cast off the shackles of a harness and rope before, and is best tried with caution. If you want to have a go, seek out a route which progresses parallel to the water, so that you can easily fall in from an unscary metre or two. You absolutely need to check the water for any rocks or other obstacles, even if others are already climbing there, and be aware of changing tides.

ESSENTIAL CLIMBING KIT

▶ CLIMBING SHOES – they should be snug but not painful.

▶ LOOSE TROUSERS or leggings.

▶ CHALK BAG – tie this around your waist and fill with…

▶ CHALK – chalk wicks away sweat from your hands and improves friction.

▶ HARNESS – female-specific ones tend to offer a better fit. You can rent a harness for your first few sessions. If you're buying one, go to a decent outdoors shop to try a few on (some shops will let you try hanging from a rope to test a harness out).

▶ HELMET – essential if you're climbing outdoors. Ideally both the climber and the belayer should wear them, but the belayer is the most in danger from falling rocks dislodged by their mate above.

▶ ROPE – beginners should plump for a 10mm-wide, 30m rope for indoor climbing, and 60m long for outdoors. Always buy a brand-new rope.

▶ DOWN JACKET – now you look like a proper climber, especially if it is grubby and patched up with duct tape.

▶ WATERPROOF JACKET

▶ BELAY DEVICE

▶ CARABINERS – D-shaped metal loops with an opening gate, used to attach gear to your rope and harness.

▶ QUICKDRAWS – these are essentially two carabiners connected by a strong strip of material, and they attach your rope to the wall when clipped into bolts.

Three places
to go climbing

1 Swanage, Dorset, UK

The chilled-out, sun-drenched Dorset coast is a heavenly place to spend a few days sport climbing. Hike down to Dancing Ledge, where a wide expanse of dramatic quarried cliffs drops down to the crashing sea. Flex your fingers on the varied sport routes, and then have a dip in the cliffside swimming hole that fills up when the tide is low. No climbing weekend here is complete without a pie and a pint of honey-coloured cider at the marvellous Square and Compass pub.

2 Fontainebleau, France

Fifty kilometres from Paris you'll find the fairytale forests of Font. A boulderer's dream, the area features thousands of fat sandstone rocks scattered among the pine trees and a whopping 20,000 problems to get to grips with, ranging massively in style and difficulty. Go in summer and stay in the friendly nearby campsites – you can even pop to the local village bakery for morning coffee and croissants or a mid-boulder baguette.

3 Krabi, Thailand

Wannabe deep-water solo climbers will love flinging themselves off coastal crags and into the glittering turquoise waters of Krabi, a province of mangrove forests and magical limestone cliffs edged by postcard-perfect islands. Local boat owners will take you out to favourite climbing spots for the day, and you can always go for a snorkel when your arms start to ache. Or if you'd rather rope up, you'll never find a more beautiful backdrop for sport climbing than the white sands of Railay beach.

3 TRAIL RUNNING

INTRODUCTION

Get off the road and into the mud: trail running might just put you off tarmac for life. Taking to the trail is, for me, a million miles more interesting and engaging than pounding the pavement. Trails are beautiful, quiet and ever-changing with the weather and the seasons. Plus, negotiating mud, rocks, tree roots and the occasional squirrel keeps your brain engaged and your legs and feet working in a less repetitive way, which can lead to fewer injuries.

Flying through the forest or along the coast feels simple and free, but trail running does require a little more planning than a city run. If you want to try the road less travelled, my tip is to start out with a gentle jog along a coast path. As long as the ocean is on the right side of you, you'll always know exactly where you are, and if you knacker yourself out you can easily turn around and head home. Then build up your fitness and your confidence with runs in parks and on commons before you plunge into empty woodlands and the wider wilderness.

THE RULES
OF THE TRAIL

One of the joys of outdoor running is that you can be completely alone, surrounded by the wild world. The flipside is that you need to take safety precautions in case you manage to hurt yourself or get lost. Carry a fully charged phone and a waterproof map of your route, and let someone know where you're headed before you go. I usually plump for clearly marked walking routes and bridleways. Leave plenty of time before sunset, and carry a head torch in case you get caught out after dark. If you don't relish the idea of running solo then scout out a local runners' group to join – you'll gain some trail-mad mates and learn new local routes you can revisit together or alone.

Trail etiquette is pretty simple. Respect and give way to other trail users, and don't stray onto dedicated mountain bike tracks. Run through puddles, as opposed to around them, to protect the path. Drop no litter and leave no trace of your presence. If you encounter another runner, make sure you share a smug smile at how hardcore you both are.

Running fitness

Trail running is tough. If you're graduating from roads then be kind to yourself at the beginning – running off tarmac is far more exhausting than on, so don't beat yourself up if you can't breeze through a 5k the way you usually do. Build up your pace and distance over time, and don't be afraid to walk up hills. When navigating more challenging trails, look not at your feet but forwards, at where you want to go, and create a line of travel in your mind. You'll find this makes you faster and surer of yourself.

ORIENTEERING

If you like the idea of pretending to be Indiana Jones searching the jungle for treasure while also developing really good leg muscles, foot orienteering might be the running-meets-adventure sport for you. The aim is to navigate between a set of control points in sequence, choosing the best route between them in the fastest time possible. Brilliant for rekindling your love of running if you're feeling a bit burnt out, and for gaining some rad map-reading skills.

British Orienteering (britishorienteering.org.uk) lists events and local clubs to join, as well as permanent courses in forests and parks that are perfect for trying orienteering out.

ESSENTIAL RUNNING KIT

▶ Running tights
▶ Sports bra
▶ Vest
▶ Lightweight waterproof running jacket
▶ Hat or cap
▶ Head torch
▶ Waterproof trainers

▶ Water (a hands-free hydration rucksack is the best option)
▶ Phone
▶ Sunglasses
▶ Sun cream
▶ Small first aid kit
▶ Energy gels

Three places
to go trail running

1 Wales Coast Path, UK

An incredible 870 miles of uninterrupted coast path licked by churning sea hugs the whole edge of Wales. It makes for an easy-to-navigate and relentlessly lovely trail-running route you can dip in and out of. My favourite section stretches along wild Pembrokeshire. Try the Stackpole Head circuit, jogging past Barafundle Bay and Broadhaven beach and then heading inland across the lily ponds at Stackpole for coffee and cake in the Boathouse Tea Room.

2 Chamonix, France

In summer, the valleys at the heart of Chamonix-Mont Blanc are home to myriad wildflowers, grassy meadows and lots and lots of sweaty runners. The area even has its own dedicated trail-running valley called, you guessed it, *la Vallée du Trail*, with 18 dedicated running tracks winding far below distant snow-capped peaks, accessible using ski lifts. You can even run between remote mountain refuges and stay the night in them – a proper running adventure.

3 Table Mountain, South Africa

Hoerikwaggo, *Tafelberg*, the Table – whatever you want to call the lofty brooding presence which hangs over Cape Town, this diverse, ancient landscape 500 million years in the making is a joy to explore on foot. And if you don't fancy the route taken by the gruelling annual 43km Table Mountain Challenge Run *just* yet, you can just stride out along the mercifully flattish paths which criss-cross the top of the plateau.

4 HIKING

INTRODUCTION

Wandering with a knapsack on your back is one of the simplest, easiest and cheapest ways you can get outdoors on a human-powered adventure. Two legs is often the only form of transport that'll let you venture into some of the most remote and beautiful pockets of the world, and walking is also one of the most contemplative things I know – perhaps that's why there are quite so many poems and songs about the glories of the rambling life. Walking, hiking, hillwalking – it's hard to define clearcut edges between different kinds of perambulation, except that the walker and the rambler tend to take gentler strolls over rolling countryside with plenty of tea breaks, while the hiker and the hillwalker stride womanfully off into the high hills. However hardcore you want to make it, a walk will clear your mind, fill your lungs with fresh air and leave you calm and happy. It's worth the blisters.

Hiking Fitness

Hiking might not be the first activity that springs to mind when you're planning how to bump up your fitness levels, but regular walking is a brilliant way to get a great cardio and muscle workout without the extra strain and impact of running. Walking erect is one of the things that defines us as human beings – perhaps that's why it feels so good to just stride out and *go*. If you're clocking up a fair few miles, make sure you pace yourself. You should be able to hold a conversation as you walk – if you can't, you're going too fast. Endurance and stamina are your two keywords, and are best improved by building up the distance you walk over time. To improve your stamina when off the trail, try exercises that work your core and back, to ensure a strong posture. Running and swimming will also build up the aerobic fitness you'll need for more challenging hikes.

NAVIGATION AND ROUTE PLANNING

Does planning a hike make you worry you might get so horribly lost that you'll never return to civilisation and end up becoming a lonely woodland dweller living off grubs? Or is that just me? It's definitely sensible to be aware of your navigational ability before a walk, and to plan routes carefully before stepping out your front door. That said, there are plenty of beginner-friendly ways to get into walking which will build your confidence in navigation and your hiking ability.

Try downloading an easy, step-by-step walk from the internet and taking it, along with a map, to an area you already know to practise following the directions. Then try a new walk in countryside which is near civilisation – if you do get into a pickle there'll be someone around to ask for help. Or pick a coast path – they're my favourite choice of route for not having to think too much, because as long as you keep the sea on the right side of you, you'll know exactly where you are.

Never rely on your phone, or anything else electronic, for navigation – technology has a tendency to go wrong, or to die just when you need it the most. *Always* carry a map with you. A map is in essence a 2D representation of

the 3D world around you, drawn to a set scale such as 1:50,000 (or one centimetre of map for every 500 metres of ground). In Britain, Ordnance Survey (or OS) maps are the ones most commonly carried by walkers – they show footpaths, rivers, roads and, importantly, contour lines. These orange and brown squiggles show the map reader the lie of the land, and the closer together they appear, the steeper the hill or valley they represent. You can find detailed guides online to help you get to grips with contour lines, but it's even better to ask an experienced hiker to show you how to read them during a hike (then you get to play the sometimes frustrating game of guessing which real-life hill or gully corresponds to which contour line). Then take a map with you on a simple walk past easy-to-spot landmarks like towers or rivers and see what the contours are doing in the surrounding area. The more you practise simple navigation, the more confident you'll feel.

To work out how long it'll take you to walk a certain distance, allow one hour for every three miles you measure on a map (a 20-minute mile is the general rule of thumb) and add an extra 30 minutes for every 1,000 feet of elevation you climb.

Hiking safety

All hikers should follow the Countryside Code, or any other local rules and regulations.

RESPECT OTHER PEOPLE
▶ Be considerate towards the local community and other people enjoying the outdoors.
▶ Leave gates and property as you find them, and follow paths unless wider access is available.

PROTECT THE NATURAL ENVIRONMENT
▶ Leave no trace of your visit, and take your litter home.
▶ Keep dogs under control.
▶ You should always stick to paths if possible, but this is especially important on farms.
▶ Use gates and stiles where possible, to avoid damaging fences and hedges.
▶ Leave livestock alone.

ENJOY THE OUTDOORS
▶ Plan ahead and be prepared.
▶ Follow local advice and signs.

Public footpaths in Britain often run smack through fields full of cows. Cows are lovely big beasties with remarkably Disney-like dewy eyes. They mean you no harm. But you should still treat them with respect and give them a wide berth. Move quietly around the edge of the herd, sticking to the edge of the field, and never walk between cows and their calves.

When hiking and hillwalking in remote, mountainous areas you need to exercise a lot more caution than you would when swanning down a sunny canal path. Check the weather first, and make sure you have more than enough daylight hours for the route you're planning. Pack clothing for all weathers, and if conditions suddenly worsen it's best to just turn around and call it a day. Carry a survival bag – these keep your body insulated in the event of an emergency. Don't underestimate the dangers of mountains – just because other people walk up Snowdonia in flip-flops doesn't mean you aren't going to be sensible and properly prepared.

SCRAMBLING

The lovechild of hillwalking and climbing, scrambling is usually defined as using your hands as well as your feet to get up a hill or rock face. Some scrambles are so easy they aren't graded, but others are graded as one, two or three, with three verging on an easy rock-climbing route you might want a rope for, two possibly needing a rope to protect you on a tricky patch and one being basically an exposed walking route over terrain that will necessitate a bit of clambering. If you're a competent walker, you'll be able to manage level one. However, be aware that bad or cold weather

will hugely change how difficult a scramble feels, and how feasible it is to attempt. If you're keen to try scrambling, I suggest having a few climbing sessions first – it gets your brain used to dealing with heights and tuned into the importance of placing your feet carefully. Pick a warm, dry day to try your first scramble, and wear a helmet. If you want to try grades two or three, it's best to have a go with an instructor.

WINTER HIKING

Winter hiking is a whole new ballgame, my friends. Here the mercurial weather really could do you serious damage if you aren't careful.

Even the gentlest fells and hills you ambled up in the summer become very different places when rimed with ice or covered in snow, so check the weather conditions first. Snow and ice require crampons (metal overshoes with sharp spikes which give good grip on ice) and an ice axe (for balance and for self-arrest if you slip and start to slide). Both are extremely easy to hurt yourself with if you aren't used to using them – you're best signing on to a winter mountaineering course to be taught the basics.

If you just fancy a walk in the nippy air somewhere where the going is decent, there's nothing better for blowing away the winter cobwebs. But take precautions. Do your research, take emergency equipment and make sure someone knows your planned route.

NIGHT WALKING

Stars shining, owls hooting, a landscape wreathed in twilit blue – night walking is magical. The clearest in my memory is a moonlit walk near the Dorset coast on which I was both terrified (when I met a roaming white cow in a field and thought it was a bovine-shaped ghost) and utterly entranced (when I saw my first glow-worm, waving his fluorescent bottom proudly around in the grass). Walking or hiking in the witching hour heightens your senses to the beauty of the natural world around you and reveals a whole new nocturnal cast of wildlife.

Buy a decent head torch and start with an easy ramble with a friend. Pick a clear, moonlit night and follow an obvious landmark, like a road. You don't need to go far – you could always keep your car in sight if you're not feeling confident. Make sure you've got a fully charged phone, and if you want to venture further, take a tent or bivvy bag. That way, if you do find yourself hopelessly lost, you can just bed down for the night. Navigating by the stars sounds extremely cool, but it's pretty tricky, and there's no guarantee that clouds won't roll in and hide your astral map. Instead, take a map and a GPS system, and let someone know where you're going. A fluorescent jacket is also a good idea to help traffic (or your mates) spot you. And don't let any cows freak you out.

BUYING THE RIGHT HIKING BOOTS

First up, decide if you'd rather choose leather, which is naturally waterproof, long-lasting and good-looking, but stiffer, heavier and harder to wear in, or fabric boots, which tend to be lighter and comfier but less warm and not as durable. Pick a boot engineered with Gore-Tex, a reliable waterproofing system. Try on plenty of pairs and choose something that fits you perfectly, with enough room to wriggle your toes and no tightness anywhere.

ESSENTIAL WALKING KIT

- Waterproof trousers
- Waterproof jacket
- Hiking boots
- Hiking socks
- Rucksack
- Filtering water bottle
- Sunscreen
- Sunglasses
- Map in waterproof case (or an OS Active map, which is already waterproof)
- Survival bag
- Torch and batteries
- First aid kit

Three places
to go hiking

1 To a bothy, Scotland

The wild Scottish Highlands hold an extra pleasure for hikers – a network of remote bothies dotted among the hills. These basic stone huts are free to use as a place to bed down for the night, and walking to one and then back the next morning makes the perfect weekend adventure. Or you could plan an epic hike, stopping at a whole string of them. Some are extremely basic (I once stayed in one containing just a stone bench and a sheep's skull), some have fireplaces and some are positively posh, but all of them offer a wild night away.

2 Slovenia

Slovenia's magnificent alpine routes have been a bit of a secret until recently – go now before the whole world realises how wonderful this land of glimmering lakes, snowy peaks and friendly locals really is. The 500km-long Slovenian Mountain Trail makes for an epic challenge, beginning in the pretty valleys of Maribor and crossing the Kamnik, Karavanke and Julian Alps, home to ibex, chamois and soaring eagles. Be prepared for some self-sufficiency, interspersed with a warm welcome in old-fashioned mountain villages and farms.

3 Everest Base Camp, Nepal

The ultimate do-it-before-you-die hike has to be up, up, up from Kathmandu and through the Nepalese mountains to Everest Base Camp at 5,380m. If you can make the arduous 12-day trek and deal with the altitude, you'll get to cross rickety rope bridges, refuel at friendly teahouses, watch prayer flags flap in the wind and then stand in the shadow of the merciless mountain where so many legends have been made and lost.

5 SNOWSPORTS

INTRODUCTION

There's little more magical than racing through deep virgin snow and leaving a set of fresh tracks behind you as you swoosh past ice-clad trees and distant mountain ranges. Skiing and snowboarding open up otherwise remote and untouchable mountains and turn them into a playground. And few sports can boast a similar social scene to snowsports – the boozy joy of après-ski makes it very easy to ski hard by day and play hard by night.

Skiing's reputation as a sport strictly for the posh kids has, thankfully, been transformed in the last few decades by some amazing athletes and the advent of more affordable trips. It's still pretty expensive to head to the Alps for a week, but there are other ways you can get your fix if you aren't lucky enough to A) have oodles of cash or B) live within driving distance of a ski town, including seasonnaire work, cheap university and club trips or heading to indoor ski slopes and dry slopes. Snowsports are worth saving up or cleaning chalet toilets for – you can't get a more immersive day spent in the natural world than racing through fresh white powder.

Skiing (on two skis and usually with two poles) is still the default way to cane it down mountains, even if the equipment has moved on a bit from the days when elegant Austrian ladies would strap wooden planks to their boots and swish down the snow in long skirts. But modern skiing still doesn't have the coolest image on or off the pistes. That prize goes to...

Snowboarding, which has always been proud of its bad-boy image. Since its birth in the seventies, the art of riding a single board has been the naughty little brother of the pistes, although it's now so popular that in resorts favoured by younger crowds boarders and skiers are pretty much matched for numbers.

Which sport you pick is totally up to you, but it's definitely worth trying both skiing and boarding to see if you naturally prefer one or the other. If you surf or skateboard, then snowboarding's sideways stance might feel more natural. If you're in a rush to learn so you can keep up with your mates, skiing can be easier to get the hang of, and a little more forgiving when you inevitably fall over. On the other hand, snowboarding boots are WAY comfier than ski boots.

Not hooked on the thought of either? You can still play in the mountains – snowshoeing and cross-country skiing open up an otherwise impossible-to-navigate world of forest trails and pristine mountainsides, and are great ways to spot winter wildlife. Or you could just go tobogganing.

STARTING OUT

Ski resorts can feel like quite strange places if the closest you've been to the white stuff in your life is a winter snow fight in your local park. Ski towns can be centuries old and full of gorgeous old Alpine cabins, or they can be modern clusters of slick hotels and bars. Either way, if it's a skiing destination, the town will be clustered around or near a system of lifts (these can include chairlifts, gondolas, drag lifts and massive cable cars). Lifts carry skiers and boarders high into the mountains, so that they can careen back down different pistes, or ski routes, which are flattened (or 'groomed') into easy-to-ski paths. Pistes join together in a map a bit like a subway system, and some lead all the way back down to the bottom of the mountain, where you then get another lift up and do it all again (or, if it's a bit later in the day, begin drinking in earnest).

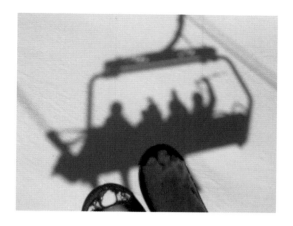

If you've never tried skiing or boarding before, then book yourself in for a set of lessons, where you'll get taught good basic techniques on gentle baby slopes and then shown how to ride on the lifts. A week of half-day lessons will have you off to a good start. You'll need to buy a lift pass – a plastic card that goes in your pocket and gives you a day (or a week or a season)'s entry onto all the lifts. Each lift has a gate which automatically reads your pass and lets you through. Grab a piste map, too. They show the network of routes you can ski as well as lifts, lookout spots, bars and restaurants. Lifts begin to run first thing in the

morning and close at around 4-5pm.

Bigger resorts can have other outdoor goodies too, most temptingly snow parks. These are playgrounds where skiers and boarders can practise freestyle jumps and tricks, and include snow jumps, boxes and rails you can perform manoeuvres on as you head down the hill. Stick to the beginner section if you're learning – you'll usually find small kickers (curved ramps) and jumps to pop over here. You might also spot massive, bouncy castle-style inflatable air bags in resorts – these are for practising ski jumps with a soft landing, and are seriously fun to play on.

Busier resorts will also have plenty of bars, restaurants and even rowdy clubs dotted around the slopes. The time-honoured ski holiday tradition is to head to an après party on the pistes after around 3pm – but be warned, you'll then have to ski down to town in a drunken state, trying not to crash into your equally tipsy friends.

Skiing is of course seasonal, and resorts usually open when snow begins to fall in earnest in December and close in April when the powder turns to slush. Avoid ski resorts at Christmas and in school holidays, when they're at their busiest and most expensive. January to March is the most snow-sure time to go, but prices are often low in December and April, so if you're a cash-strapped beginner these are good times to book a flight.

LEARNING TO SKI

If it's your first time on the slopes, head to a rental shop to get fitted out. First up, you'll need ski boots, which are clunky, plasticky horrors with special bottoms that clip onto your skis. Next you'll be fitted with skis, chosen to match your height and weight. Your skis will come with bindings attached to them – your boots clip into these to hold your feet in place on the snow. And finally, you'll be given ski poles, which help with both balance and propulsion.

Beginners are taught simple techniques, including how to clip into and out of skis, how to start and stop, and the famous, tasty duo of French fries (gliding down the hill with your skis parallel) and pizza (slowing down by pointing your toes inwards and your heels

Snowsports fitness

Skiing and snowboarding are brilliant ways to get fit while having so much fun you don't even notice that it's happening. They'll both tone your glutes and increase your heart rate, and tearing down pistes non-stop is great for endurance. A good level of base fitness before a trip will help you get the most out of a holiday, and keep you happily on the slopes from first lift to last lift. A spinning or high-intensity interval training (HIIT) class will mimic the on-off intensity of skiing, and leg stretches, squats and lunges will help your leg muscles cope.

out to make your skis into a pizza slice shape, also known as the Snow Plough). When you've mastered these, you'll learn how to turn with your skis kept parallel (it's all about balance and weight distribution).

LEARNING TO SNOWBOARD

There are two main snowboarding styles – freeriding, which is fast, off-piste snowboarding, and freestyle, which is all about performing tricks on man-made jumps and in snow parks. Snowboarders usually favour one style, and snowboards are built to suit one or the other, too. Freeride boards are longer and stiffer; freestyle boards are shorter and softer (ahem). If you're just beginning you can rent an all-mountain board, a good all-rounder to learn on.

You'll ride your board with one foot forward, just like when surfing, and depending on the foot you prefer to lead with, you'll be regular (right foot first) or goofy (left foot first). If you're renting a snowboard the rental shop will help you figure out which stance you prefer, as well as sorting you out with boots and the right size snowboard.

In your first lesson you can expect to strap in to your board, learn the basic stance, how to stand up when you fall down (surprisingly hard!) and side-slip using the edge of your snowboard to move down the slope safely. As you progress, you'll learn to side-slip diagonally and then to link the movements into the enticingly named falling leaf, a simple way of heading down the pistes.

How to read a piste map

Pistes are colour-coded, usually as follows. Difficulty is assigned purely on how steep the piste's gradient is, and doesn't take into account how narrow it might be. As with all sports, the best way to build confidence is to work up through each level.

● **GREEN:** suitable for learners and lessons, also known as baby or nursery slopes
● **BLUE:** beginners
● **RED:** intermediate
● **BLACK:** advanced
◆◆ **DOUBLE BLACK:** usually found in North America and Australia, and always hardcore
○ **YELLOW:** established off-piste/ungroomed routes

GOING OFF-PISTE

The amazing photos you see of pro snowboarders launching themselves down empty mountain passes are 'off-piste', also known as backcountry skiing if you're really heading into the mountains. Technically, you're off-piste if you go and play in the deeper snow on the edges of marked pistes – this is definitely the easiest and safest way to try it, but it's worth noting that often your insurance will only cover you if you manage to break your ankle on, not off, a piste. If you're a confident skier and want to try some proper off-the-grid off-piste, pay for a local guide to take you. Resorts issue avalanche warnings when the snow is dangerous – in those cases it's just not worth going off-piste.

PISTE ETIQUETTE

▶ Take on pistes within your ability and at speeds you can control.
▶ Look for people coming from above you before joining a piste.
▶ Watch out for skiers and snowboarders in front of you, especially wobbly beginners, and only overtake them if you have plenty of space. Skiers in front have right of way.

- Obey all posted signs and warnings.
- Never stop in the middle of the piste.
- If you're trying out the snowpark, only approach a jump if the coast is clear. Wait your turn, and announce clearly that you're about to head down to try a jump.

ESSENTIAL SKI AND SNOWBOARD KIT

Snowsports kit isn't cheap, so if you're trying it for the first time it's worth begging or borrowing a jacket, salopettes (waterproof ski trousers) and gloves. Most skiers and boarders who head off on one or two holidays a year just rent skis, boards, a helmet and boots in the resort, but if you're getting serious it's worth buying your own helmet and boots, and having them properly fitted. When shopping around for ski jackets, salopettes and gloves, search out last year's styles in outlet shops – you can find some massive bargains, especially at the end of the season. You can often get away with wearing men's kit, too. If all else fails you could always borrow your mum's pastel-stripe ski onesie from the '80s and pretend it's ironic.

your boots hit your calves. Your socks should be the only thing inside your ski boot to stop any rubbing.

▶ GOGGLES – if you're a beginner your best bet is to buy an orange- or brown-tinted pair, which will work well in both bright and low light. If you ski regularly, go for a pair of goggles with swappable lenses and invest in a few different tints for different weather conditions.

▶ HELMET – helmets were pretty non-existent on ski slopes up until about ten years ago, but have thankfully now become the norm. They're definitely worth wearing to protect your bonce and you can now buy decent lightweight ones which won't overheat. Helmets are usually obligatory if you want to ride in the snow park, too. If you're going sans helmet, wear a warm woolly hat instead.

▶ SUNCREAM – you'll burn tons faster up at altitude, so slap factor 50 on the lower half of your face if you don't want to get a gnarly goggle tan.

▶ SKI JACKET – pick a thick, fleece-lined waterproof one. Ski wear often comes in mad colours and patterns, and it's worth going for these as opposed to plain black or white as you'll be much easier to spot on crowded pistes. Don't buy anything you wouldn't wear back home, though – it makes more sense to buy an all-rounder jacket you wouldn't mind wearing on winter walks.

▶ SALOPETTES – cool boarders wear them baggy, posh skiers wear them high waisted, with attractive suspenders.

▶ THERMAL TOP

▶ THERMAL LEGGINGS

▶ BUFF – a lifesaver when you feel like your face is going to freeze off.

▶ WATERPROOF SNOW GLOVES – or mittens, your call.

▶ SKI SOCKS – hiking socks might do at a pinch, but ski socks have padding where

Three places
to go skiing and boarding

1 Scotland

You don't have to leave Britain to get your snow fix. If the conditions are right you can ski up a storm in Scotland's Glenshee, Glencoe or Cairngorms resorts, surrounded by the glorious peaks of the Highlands. They are most likely to get a good dump of snow between January and April – be prepared to drop everything and head to the mountains as soon as it happens. You could always combine a trip to the slopes with a few winter hiking routes (or just a whisky-tasting session).

2 St Anton, Austria

I have a soft spot for the host of the World Ski Championships and the heart of the Arlberg ski region. St Anton ticks all the boxes – fantastic, challenging skiing, tons of snow, a gorgeous historic town dotted with timber chalets and a friendly après scene all the way along the lovely main Dorfstrasse. The fine art of downhill skiing was born here too, so you're following in some distinguished tracks.

3 Japan

Ski world-class powder and discover a new culture at one of Japan's 600 small but perfectly formed resorts. Niseko is the best known internationally due to its wonderland of snow-covered trees (called *juhyo*, or ice monsters). This landscape is especially magical explored on skis or snowshoes. And when your legs are aching you can head down to town to relax in an *onsen* (hot springs bath) and to refuel with sushi and *sake* (rice wine).

FRESH AND SALT WATER

Ready for some vitamin sea? Learn to conquer the waves on a surfboard or stand-up paddleboard, grab a paddle for a canoe or kayak adventure and then dive in with a snorkel or SCUBA kit to explore the strange and wonderful world beneath the ocean's surface.

SURFING AND PADDLEBOARDING

INTRODUCTION

Salty hair, don't care. Who needs therapy when you can surf? Being out in the ocean is one of the most liberating things I know: sea water cures all aches and washes away worries, and surfing, the fine art of riding a wave, will give you great respect for the ocean, that mercurial beast which can be a calm playground or a furious monster at whim. The sea is no easy mistress, and you'll have to put the time in if you want to learn her ways. But it's all worth it the first time you stand up on a board and ride your first wave. Whether you try it on a lush tropical beach or under Britain's grey skies with a woolly jumper under your wetsuit, you might find you get immediately smitten by surfing's meditative rush.

PICKING YOUR FIRST SURFBOARD

When you first try surfing and rent a board you'll usually ride a 'foamie' or 'softie', a large and forgiving board that is easy to catch waves on. A rough rule is that the more advanced the surfer, the smaller the board, so as you progress and learn to pop up you'll probably graduate to the iconic and smaller Mini-Malibu (or Mini-Mal): a classic, beginner-friendly and affordable hard-surfaced board. Boards are measured in feet and inches – a foamie surfboard might measure 8ft, a massive longboard comes in at 9ft, and a tiny shortboard you might see the pros ride could be as small as 6ft.

If you live near enough to the sea to get into the ocean regularly it's worth buying your

own board to practise on without the hassle of renting. Surfboards aren't cheap, but decent second-hand boards abound. If you're going down the second-hand route, try surf shops for good deals.

PICKING THE RIGHT WETSUIT

A second skin made of tough, warm neoprene is essential unless you're only planning to surf on warm tropical beaches. Wetsuits are designed in different thicknesses for different water temperatures – a 5/3 is an all-seasons wetsuit, with a body 5mm thick and arms and legs 3mm thick, and a 3/2 is a summer wetsuit with thicknesses of 3mm and 2mm respectively. Wetsuit arms and legs are thinner so you have more flexibility while your core stays warm. Winter wetsuits cover you completely, with tight collars and cuffs to trap a layer of water around your body. Summer wetsuits, or shorties, usually have short arms and legs. They feel less restrictive to wear, but still offer more protection than a swimsuit.

The rumours are true – surfers usually wee in their wetsuits to warm them up, which is a good reason to buy your own rather than renting (eew). Female-specific designs are a must if you're blessed in the boobs and booty departments. Try on as many different

wetsuits as you can and pick one which you can get into and out of by yourself (wetsuits usually either zip up at the back or have a zip across the chest).

In winter, add neoprene gloves and booties. A hood can also be a big help, although I personally find them pretty claustrophobic. A rash vest (a light T-shirt-style layer) is useful worn underneath your wetsuit to protect your skin, or popped over a swimsuit in summer. Always wash your wetsuit in clean water after a dip in the ocean to prolong its life.

HOW TO CATCH A WAVE

When you're learning to surf you'll start in the white water, the area where waves have already broken, closest to the beach. Walk out into the sea with your board attached to you (a surfboard's leash wraps around your ankle with Velcro). When you're in waist-height water, lie on your board and use your arms to paddle forwards towards the waves – when you reach a breaking wave, push the front of your body up and you'll glide over it. When you want to try catching a wave, lie on your board and face towards the shore. Watch behind you for a wave. When one is about two metres away, face forward and paddle as hard as you can with alternate arms. Look forwards and when the wave catches you, push your chest up with your hands. The first few times you catch a wave, try staying on your board until you reach the shore, getting off when you get to shallow water. When you've caught a few waves, try coming up into a sideways standing position

with one foot forward and one back. Keep your knees bent and your feet slightly more than shoulder distance apart. Put your arms up for balance, and look forwards in the direction you want to go.

Reading the waves

To check if there are waves to ride on the beach you want to visit, have a look at a surf report (Magicseaweed.com lists reports for surf points across the globe). You're looking for indicators of the size of the waves and a rating of how good quality they are for surfers. Wind is the main factor here – if it's onshore, and coming from the sea towards the coast, it'll cause messy waves which aren't so good for surfing. If it's offshore, and heading towards the sea, it'll form lovely green waves. Any other direction is cross-shore, a combination of the two.

HOW TO POP UP

Popping up is the key to progressing from white water to green waves. Practise it on the sand first, so your muscle memory has the movement down. When you're in the water and a wave is approaching, turn your board so that the nose is facing towards the beach. Paddle to catch the wave as before. Then push your body up and, in one fluid movement (no knees on the board), bring your feet up and into a sideways standing position, one foot placed in front and one behind, with your knees a little bent. Try to look forwards to where you're going.

Popping up can be a bit of a learning curve, especially because it's actually easier to pop up on bigger green waves – as they drop you and your board down it's easier to find your feet. Once you can pop up you can practise turning your board to ride along the wave as opposed to straight to shore.

If you're a confident swimmer and have mastered regularly getting to your feet in the white water you can try getting out back behind the white water, where surfers sit in a line-up and wait for waves to catch. To get there, you'll need to get over the breaking waves. On a day with small surf you can paddle over them, but for bigger waves you'll need to learn to duckdive (this involves pushing under a wave, and requires a small board) or turtle roll, flipping your board under the wave and waiting until it passes over you.

WIPING OUT

The brilliant thing about surfing (compared with, say, snowboarding) is that when you fall off the board, you'll land in soft, forgiving ocean. The downside is that when you progress to bigger, unbroken green waves, you'll either catch one and ride it (hurrah!) or you won't, and the wave will crash over you. Wiping out is scary. However, if you're a beginner you'll be learning in shallow white water and you'll be able to stand up in the sea the whole time. When you do feel confident enough to try green waves, remember that you're only actually underwater for a few seconds – it just feels like a lot longer. The key to wiping out well is to keep calm, protect your head from your board with your arms and just wait it out.

Surf fitness

Surfing is a great all-over workout – paddling provides a cardio hit and popping up strengthens your arms and core. Swimming is the obvious way to improve your fitness for surfing, and will also help your confidence when out in the water. Out of the water, push ups and pull ups (not that I can do a pull up) are great for working your arms and back, and yoga and surfing go together like Bill and Ted – both tap into zenlike calm, and a spot of yoga before a surf will loosen up your muscles and make you ready to flex like a boss.

It's important to warm up properly before a surf, especially if the water is icy cold. If it's a really freezing day, go for a brisk run along the beach – it'll make the water seem (slightly) less like plunging into an ice bath.

HOW TO WAX YOUR BOARD

Wax on, wax off, *Karate Kid* style. A coat of wax creates a rough surface on your board that you can get a grip on with your hands and feet. A new board will need a complete coat of fresh wax, and boards need regular rewaxing when they stop feeling grippy. You can top up wax before each surf but you should periodically remove all wax and give your board a fresh coat.

Start with a clean board. If yours has a coating of old, grey wax, leave it in the sun to soften it and then scrape the wax off with a wax comb. Then sweep a new stick of wax generously over the board, first in large and then in smaller circles. Eventually it will start to form hard bobbles in an even pattern.

Make sure there's plenty of wax in the spots where you plant your feet and where your hands grip the board – you don't need to wax the nose. You'll probably need an entire block of wax for a base coat. Surf wax comes in different temperatures for different water (and it all smells delicious).

- Basecoat: hard wax used as a first layer before adding temperature-specific wax on top
- Tropical: for water above 23°C (73°F)
- Warm: for 17–22°C (62–72°F) water
- Cool: for 14–21°C (57–70°F) water
- Cold: for water below 14°C (57°F)

SURF ETIQUETTE

◗ Don't drop in on someone else's wave – the person closest to where the wave breaks has the right of way.

◗ Don't paddle into the heart of the line-up when you're learning – aim for a quieter section and be careful not to paddle out in front of someone as they catch a wave.

◗ Try to control your board – don't just let go and let it fly off; it's easy to injure yourself or others that way.

◗ If you mess up, smile and apologise.

◗ Leave no rubbish on the beach – you could even do a quick beach clean after a surf to leave the beach even better than you found it.

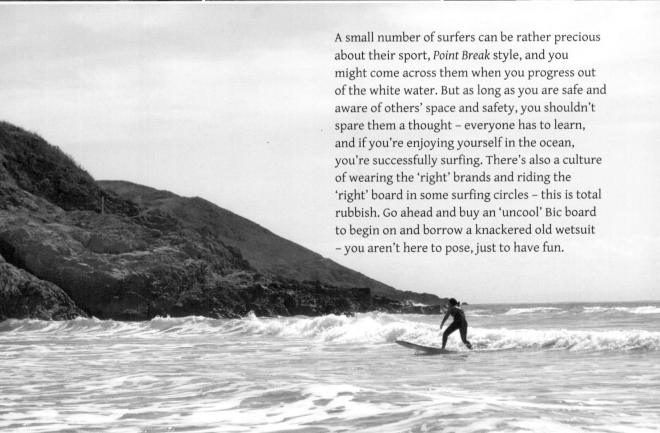

A small number of surfers can be rather precious about their sport, *Point Break* style, and you might come across them when you progress out of the white water. But as long as you are safe and aware of others' space and safety, you shouldn't spare them a thought – everyone has to learn, and if you're enjoying yourself in the ocean, you're successfully surfing. There's also a culture of wearing the 'right' brands and riding the 'right' board in some surfing circles – this is total rubbish. Go ahead and buy an 'uncool' Bic board to begin on and borrow a knackered old wetsuit – you aren't here to pose, just to have fun.

ESSENTIAL SURFING KIT

▶ SURFBOARD

▶ WETSUIT

▶ SUNCREAM – it's really easy to burn on a board, as the sun is reflected off the water and does double the damage to your skin. Stick some factor 50 on your face and hands if you don't want to get what one of my surfer mates attractively calls 'poo head' (a nut-brown head and neck and pasty white body).

▶ CHANGING ROBE – I'm often shameless and just get my bits out in beach car parks when changing, but if you fear the world watching you while you wrestle into a wetsuit, a towelling robe with a hood is a godsend.

▶ TOWEL – mainly to sit on during the car journey home.

▶ WATERPROOF POUCH for keys and money.

▶ WAX – see page 72 for which temperature to pick. My favourite is Sex Wax – it smells like a coconut-strewn Caribbean beach.

Three places
to go surfing

1 Ireland

Come for the coast, stay for the *craic*. Ireland's golden west coast offers big waves for seasoned surfers and plenty of sheltered beaches and surf schools for beginners. Head for the miles of sandy beaches around the friendly, laidback village of Strandhill in County Sligo (SUP-ers can paddle the calm waters of nearby Enniscrone Pier, too), then cast off that Atlantic chill in cosy Shells Café – they serve banging homegrown breakfasts and incredible coffee.

2 Morocco

Morocco's coast is as laid-back as its cities are bustling, and the fishing villages that line it have become small meccas for surfers. Pack your board and head to Taghazout, an original fixture on the fifties hippie trail. There are myriad surf camps to choose from, and local guides can drive you to the best breaks – they range from huge open beaches with camels being herded along the sand to tiny fishing villages lined with blue boats.

3 Costa Rica

As its name suggests, this South American jewel is rich in good things – lush rainforest, paradisical surfing on empty beaches and the Costa Rican lifestyle of *pura vida* (pure life). Oh, and you can surf the warm green waves in just a bikini. Tamarindo is the most built-up surf spot, but from here you can stick your board in a 4x4 and journey down the Pacific Coast in search of your dream tropical beach. You might even spot giant leatherback turtles.

Stand-up paddleboarding

SUP (or stand-up paddleboarding) might seem like one of the newest active sports on the block, but it has actually been around forever. Hawaiians have been practising what is now the fastest growing water sport for centuries – they just called it *Hoe He'e Nalu* instead. Paddleboarding involves standing up on a large board and using a paddle to propel yourself forwards. You can SUP on a flat river or lake, which is easy to get the hang of, or ride waves on the sea, which is trickier to master and involves a smaller board.

To get started on flat water, carry your board to the water's edge using the central handle and attach the leash to your ankle. Push your board out into shallow water

so the fin is clear of the ground, and then get on and kneel in the centre of the board – use the handle as a guide and place your knees on each side of it. Hold the paddle with the concave side of the blade facing towards you. To stand up, place your palms in front of you, draw your knees off the board and slowly come to standing, picking up your paddle as you do so. Keep a slight bend in your knees and your core centred over the board. Hold your paddle with one hand on the top and the other on the centre of the shaft. Insert the paddle in the water in front of you and then pull it back alongside your body. To keep your SUP on an even keel, take a few strokes on one side, then a few strokes on the other.

7 CANOEING AND KAYAKING

INTRODUCTION

Imagine steering yourself across the glassy surface of a misty Canadian lake, dipping into secret rocky archways and caves along the Cornish coast, or just pulling your canoe up on a sunny riverbank for a picnic. Canoeing and kayaking make exploring winding waterways and the wide ocean achievable. They are also both deeply calming ways to travel – there's something about the repetitive dip of a paddle into water that ebbs away stress.

Canoes are all about lazy days messing about on the water. They are open, and often built for more than one person. Canoeists kneel on the bottom of the boat or sit on a raised seat and use a paddle with one blade, swapping sides after a few strokes. Kayaks are the canoe's zippier cousins, originating in Greenland, where they were used for hunting. A kayak has

a smaller opening you slot your legs through, covered with a spray deck, and the paddle has two blades for alternate strokes.

Canoes are best used on gentle rivers and flat lakes, and can be packed with a lot

of gear, including a tent if you fancy a spot of camping. (There's more info on planning a canoe adventure on page 105.) A kayak is better suited to choppier waters such as river rapids or the ocean – though if you're taking to wilder waters, it's best to go with a guide.

To paddle your vessel, sit up with a straight back and lean slightly forward. Reach towards the nose of the boat with your paddle and push the blade into the water, then pull back. Keep your arms straight and pull the paddle to your body and then out of the water. If there are two of you in a canoe, the person in front sets the paddling rhythm and the person at the back is in charge of steering. To turn, paddle repeatedly on the opposite side (i.e. paddle right to turn left) and try pushing your paddle out in a sweeping semicircle rather than a straight line.

Paddle fitness

A brisk paddle is great for your health. Canoeing and kayaking are low impact, improve aerobic fitness and really strengthen your upper body and arms (which will definitely ache by the end of the day). Canoeing and kayaking do work your core and legs, but I find a cycle or a run the day after a heavy kayaking session makes me feel like I've had more of a balanced workout. Knowing how to swim at least 50 metres is a safety essential, and swimming sessions will improve both your fitness and your confidence.

CANOEING AND KAYAKING SAFETY

▶ Paddle with a buddy.
▶ Watch out for boats (they may not see you) and manoeuvre around them. The rule on rivers is that the smallest vessel (that'll always be you) yields and moves around the larger vessel.
▶ Stay to the right on rivers.
▶ Do not disturb wildlife.
▶ Be careful not to damage riverbanks when landing.
▶ Check the weather forecast before your journey.
▶ Always wear a lifejacket.
▶ Leave no trace of your paddle.

ESSENTIAL KIT

▶ Kayak or canoe
▶ Paddle(s)
▶ Dry bags
▶ Splash skirt
▶ Wetsuit
▶ Personal flotation device (lifejacket)
▶ Aquatic shoes
▶ Waterproof map

Three places
to go paddling

1 Wye Valley, England and Wales

The meandering Wye is the beginning paddler's dream – a gentle, wide river banked by lush green fields that curves past campsites and pubs to moor up at, over tiny, fun rapids and below the epic soaring cliffs of Symonds Yat. Plenty of canoe hire companies will sort you out with a big green Canadian canoe and a map, launch you into the river at Ross-on-Wye and pick you up at the end of the day, tired, sunkissed and happy.

2 Norwegian fjords

Sick of sitting in your office on a sunny Friday? Hop straight on a plane to the quaint city of Bergen in Norway and you could be kayaking in the fjords, spotting seals and paddling under waterfalls by Saturday. Paddling lets you explore far along the blue fingers of deep water which dip into the country's western coast, flanked on both sides by sharply cut mountains and rolling green landscapes.

3 Yukon Territory, Canada

Just the name of Canada's wildest frontier calls up a mental image of remote, forest-capped landscapes, of roaming black bears and of rough-and-ready frontier towns. Now the gold rush is over, most roamers come to the Yukon to paddle the astonishingly beautiful turquoise waters of the Yukon River. For an epic adventure, hire a guide and take on the 700km stretch between Whitehorse and Dawson City, camping under the stars on the riverbanks at night.

8 SNORKELLING AND DIVING

INTRODUCTION

'The sea, once it casts its spell, holds one in its net of wonder forever', wrote undersea explorer Jacques Cousteau. They say that we know less about the world beneath the waves than we do about outer space, but diving and snorkelling let us scratch the surface of the mysteries of the deep by venturing into a wonderful, alien landscape home to a whole cornucopia of colour and life – rainbows of coral, glittering shoals of iridescent fish, crayon-coloured anemones and wizened turtles bobbing by.

SCUBA (from 'self-contained underwater breathing apparatus') diving involves using a source of breathing gas, strapped to your back and taken in through a respirator in your mouth. This means you can swim far below the surface (recreational divers can swim as deep as 40m) and explore for as long as your air lasts – usually around an hour. Snorkelling, or swimming through water wearing a diving mask and a breathing tube that bobs on the ocean's surface, is less immersive, but has the advantage of being a lot cheaper and easier to try, and doesn't require a big leap out of your comfort zone.

SNORKELLING

If you can swim, you can snorkel. It's a lot less fuss and a hell of a lot cheaper than diving, and involves using a snorkel tube to breathe while you keep your head down and your gaze below the water. You can also dive deeper down, holding your breath and returning to the surface to expel water from your snorkel. Buy your own snorkel if you can – you'll get it properly fitted to your face, and you can bung it in your rucksack on any trip and never need to rent one. Snorkellers often use fins, too, to speed them up in the water. To try snorkelling, pick a beach you know has clear water and fish to observe, or head out to a deeper spot on a boat with a snorkel tour.

SNORKELLING SAFETY TIPS

▶ Swim with a buddy.
▶ Be aware of the ocean – what currents are present, the size of the waves and the swell, wind speed and any other hazards. Continue to check them periodically as you snorkel, as conditions can change fast.
▶ Be aware of boat traffic – they might not be able to see you in the water. An inflatable orange safety buoy tied to your leg is a good way to make you visible.
▶ If it's chilly or if there's strong sun wear a wetsuit to protect your skin.
▶ If your mask tends to fog up, rub a dab of baby shampoo or spit on the lenses before you stick it on.

Underwater fitness

Exploring the life aquatic is a great workout, and an hour-long dive can be as effective as a 10-mile bike ride. Warm up first – this is often forgotten in the excitement to get underwater, but it'll get your muscles ready for the chill of the ocean. Out of the water, exercises that work your back and core will help you to support the weight of your tank, and swimming regularly will strengthen your heart and lungs and boost your confidence in the sea. Yoga will also teach you to calm your breath and improve your lung function.

SCUBA DIVING

SCUBA diving is nothing short of magical when you think about it – it's a brief foray into an alien world where you can breathe just like the locals. It's also an expensive hobby, but I'd argue it's one worth spending your pennies on, given the wonders you get in return.

You can try diving on taster days, but it's absolutely worth getting an open water diving qualification (there are various authorities but PADI is the most recognised). This teaches you all the basics over a few days, both in the classroom and in the sea, and means you can dive wherever you want around the world without needing instruction. Learning to dive involves the big mental step of training your brain to stop freaking the hell out every five seconds when it realises afresh that you are BREATHING UNDERWATER. But you'll learn how to stay safe in progressively deeper water, as well as gaining a good understanding of your gear and how it works, and both will boost your confidence in your ability. Once you're certified, an underwater playground of caves, wrecks and sea slugs is your oyster. You can progress to further qualifications, such as adventure diving, try the bizarre world of night diving or make a diving wildlife bucket list (although if you see a whale shark before I do I'll be pretty upset).

Three places
to go diving and snorkelling

1 Isles of Scilly, UK

Dip into the clear blue waters off the tiny island of St Martin's, part of the Scilly archipelago, and you'll come face to face with a colony of friendly seals. Strap on a snorkel and head out on a boat to meet these gentle giants, who are fond of dancing around human visitors to their seaweed-filled stomping grounds, even nibbling on their fins. This is one of the most magical wildlife experiences you can dream up on these shores, and you get to explore the sub-tropical wonders of the Scillies afterwards, too.

2 Silfra fissure, Iceland

Swim between the shelves of two tectonic plates in Iceland's iconic Silfra fissure, found in the heart of Thingvellir National Park. This narrow channel cut through a giant lava field offers perfect visibility in water clear as glass. You'll need a dry suit to navigate the freezing glacial water of the ravine, but the island's natural hot springs are the perfect warming tonic post-dive.

3 Mozambique

The gentle whale shark is the biggest fish in the ocean (it's the size of a double-decker bus) and arguably the most lovely, with a huge flat back spotted white like a starry sky. You can dive with these big beauties off the unspoiled coast of Mozambique, where they like to congregate to chow down on plankton. They are often spotted off Tofo beach and at the deeper dive sites at Cabo San Sebastian.

SECTION TWO
WILD ADVENTURES

*I go to nature to be soothed and healed and
to have my senses put in tune once more.*

JOHN BURROUGHS

ROLLING STONES OF THE WORLD, UNITE! In this section we're packing up a tent and getting outward bound, spending lazy days riding bikes and jumping into swimming holes and nights sleeping out under a billion stars. These travelling adventures celebrate the simplest, slowest pleasures the wild world can offer.

You can't get a better impromptu *Famous Five* adventure than camping. Do you want to sleep wild in the remote hinterlands? Kip in a hammock? Take a canoe on an epic *Swallows and Amazons* river trip? Or simply dust down an old tent, load friends and duvets into the car and make for the hills to just, well, *camp*? Whatever you fancy this weekend, I've got all the advice for packing, playing and, erm, pooing you'll need to be a very happy camper.

I can forever wax lyrical over the soul-feeding pleasures of wild swimming. Take a single dip and you'll instantly feel connected to the natural world around you. Try it regularly and you'll see how ever-changing our little blue planet is, as spring wildflowers bloom on riverbanks, summer warms the water in sunny coves, autumn scatters pools with golden leaves and winter turns the temperature of lakes down to totally bloody freezing, even in a thick wetsuit (but your skin zings with health).

And hippies at heart will love the chapters on making a home on the move. Hit the open road with a couple of panniers on the back of your bike for a human-powered cycling adventure or pack up a campervan for an epic drive along lost lanes and winding mountain passes. The road awaits.

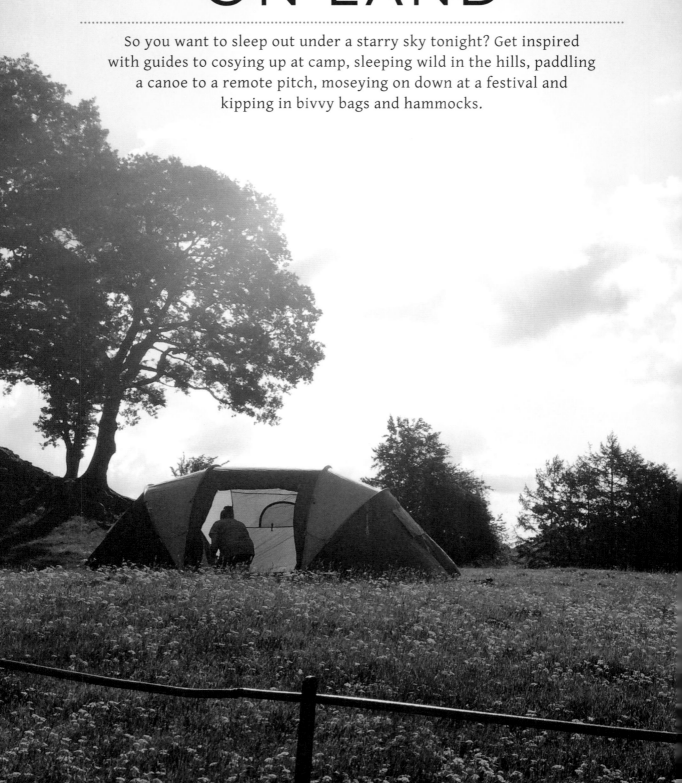

ON LAND

So you want to sleep out under a starry sky tonight? Get inspired with guides to cosying up at camp, sleeping wild in the hills, paddling a canoe to a remote pitch, moseying on down at a festival and kipping in bivvy bags and hammocks.

1 CAMPING

INTRODUCTION

Why do we feel the urge to spend the night in a tiny, stuffy canvas triangle, surrounded by a field of cowpats? Because camping is magical, that's why. The smell of tents takes me straight back to the extreme excitement of being allowed to sleep outdoors in a den of blankets and cushions as a little'un – even if it was just out in the back garden.

Camping is all about uncomplicated little pleasures. It's bare feet on grass, cooking toast over the fire, paddling in streams and drinking warm white wine out of a box. It's the joy of unzipping your tent in the morning to the smell of a wild meadow and the chirping of birds – you can't get further away from hectic city living than this.

In this chapter we're going to look at two kinds of camping – in a campsite, with showers, washing-up bowls and bacon butties, and wild camping, alone in the wilderness and probably thinking very deep thoughts about nature. They are very different, but equally awesome, ways to escape real life and sleep under the night sky. The wonderful thing about camping is that you can do what suits your mood. If you'd like a cosy duvet, jam jars full of wild flowers and a yurt strung with fairy lights, you can go proper posh camping. And if you want to feel alone in the landscape, far from fellow mortals, carrying your little portable home on your back and purifying your own water like a proper explorer, you can go wild camping.

Before we delve into the grubby delights of perfect pitching, a word for camping virgins.

The most common doubts I hear about camping are 1. Won't I be cold? and 2. Isn't it a lot of hassle? First, there is no shame at all in being a fair-weather camper. If you only ever camp in the hot haze of August, brilliant. If it's your first time sleeping in a tent I would most definitely pick a balmy and beautiful day to try it. Take a decent tent, sleeping bags, pillows and your duvet and set up in a meadow where you can frolic about in a bikini and barbecue under the stars. There's no need to rough it. As for the packing, assembling and disassembling side of camping – it's definitely true that there's a certain amount of faffing about, especially with big groups, but setting up your own mini hamlet of tents is extremely satisfying, and the

more you camp, the better (and faster) you'll get at having your mini home ready in a flash, so you can get on with the important things, like carbonising marshmallows.

PICKING A CAMPSITE

Where do you want to camp this weekend? On a beach? In the woods? With your mates? With other families? I usually have a look at CoolCamping (either the website or the guidebook), which curates some of the nicest sites across the UK and Europe, or Stephen Neale's lovely books, or just ask around to see if friends know of good sites near where I want to go exploring. Photos of campsites can look very similar to each other online, making it hard to choose. My tactic is to make a list of what I want (campfires permitted, hot showers, by a surf beach, etc.) and see if one site ticks all the boxes. Before you go, check opening times and rules – some campsites are only open for the summer months, others don't take big groups or dogs, some have a noise policy, and some sell bacon and eggs to hungry campers in the mornings (definitely pick those ones).

I wouldn't recommend assuming you'll just drive past a nice campsite on your travels. There are plenty of bog-standard, perfectly acceptable sites you can sleep at in a pinch, but what's the point of camping if you aren't

waking up somewhere really special? I avoid anywhere with lots of pitches, anywhere named a 'Holiday Park' and anywhere that accepts motorhomes, as they all tend to be big, busy and impersonal. Instead, plump for the tiny farmers' fields, the woodland groves with a handful of pitches and the hippie sites with wind chimes and hand-painted signs – they're always the most fun and friendly. Campsites run by the YHA (the Youth Hostels Association, yha.co.uk) or an overseas equivalent tend to be decent, too, and usually offer a hostel or

camping barn you can retreat to if the weather suddenly turns terrible. When you get to the site, you'll either be given a pitch or allowed to stick your tent wherever you fancy. The best pitching spot is on the edge of the site, and slopes very gently downwards to drain off any water. Hedges and walls make good windbreaks. Avoid camping close to the bogs, or by any communal spaces if you're a light sleeper. You've done the hard bit now – my motto is that if you choose a great campsite, everything else will look after itself.

PICKING A TENT

Buying your own little canvas fortress? There are some obvious but essential factors to look for in a shiny new tent. Make sure the model you buy has a completely waterproof rain fly (the outer layer) and a coated nylon floor, so you don't wake up in the middle of the night in a puddle. The more guy ropes a tent comes with the better (for added stability), and groundsheets are essential – they protect the tent's floor from rocks and debris and stop condensation forming if you're camping somewhere chilly and damp (like, say, Britain). It's tempting to spend piles of dosh on a huge, multi-roomed palace of a tent, but there's really no need – as long as it's well made and waterproof it'll treat you right. When figuring out how many people can fit into a tent, halve labels like 'two man' and 'four man' to get the real number they'll sleep in comfort if you're not a fan of living like a sardine. Second-hand tents can be a great bargain in my experience, but it's worth getting the seller to erect it for you and then checking it carefully for any damage before you take it home.

The size and weight of the tent you choose depends massively on how and where you'll be camping. Wild camping calls for tiny, lightweight one-man tents you can hike with. Week-long trips with a car and kids mean you can pick something mammoth with adjoining sleeping pods. Festivals are best served by a cheapie tent you don't mind your friend being sick in. It's a game of horses for courses, but the guide below should help – and my apologies if you end up getting overexcited and buying five different tents for different occasions.

A-frame or ridge tents

These tents are the traditional prism tent shape plucky Scouts used to use in the good old days. They are light and effective, but can feel very claustrophobic as there's barely room to sit up in them.

Dome tents
Probably the most common and popular tent on the market these days, domes usually use two poles crossed over the top as a frame, giving a feeling of more space than an A-frame. Small models are pretty stable and dome tents are usually well priced, so they're a good shout if you're buying your first all-rounder tent.

Pop-up tents
Cheap, cheerful and easy to use, pop ups are ideal for festivals. These tents have a rigid frame which coils into a big pancake and springs up magically into a tent shape once unleashed. Good for feeling smug when setting up camp in the pouring rain. Note that these tents do usually pop up as quickly as they promise, but can be a merry hell to put down again, especially when you are hungover.

Canvas tents
Tipis, bell tents, yurts, safari tents – these are the posh kids of the camping world. Canvas tents feel lovely to sleep in as they let in more light, often have more headroom and are more breathable than cheap plasticky tents. They smell amazing, too. However, if they don't have an inner tent they won't be very weather resistant. Perhaps that's why you only seem to see them at festivals and in summery pastures.

Geodesic tents
A tight criss-cross of poles make geodesic tents very good at withstanding strong winds and serious weather conditions. They are expensive, but usually great quality. Ideal for mountaineers and wild campers or just for looking like you know what you're doing.

Multi-room or family tents
Like a canvas palace among teeny hovels, massive multi-room tents rise high above all others in the campsite. These sprawling beasts often contain vestibules, living spaces, multiple bedrooms, powder rooms, maid's quarters... well, some of those. They tend to be painfully expensive but are brilliant for big families or long camping trips (but you'll need a big car). Usually hellish to put up because there are so many bloody bits.

STOVES

If you're camping for just one night and don't want the hassle of cooking you can always just pack cold or ready-made food. But if you're getting your tent out regularly for longer trips, a stove makes all the difference – you can have a hearty stew in the evening, then warm up in the morning with a hot cup of coffee. Stoves vary in size from dinky little ultralight burners which fit into your pocket to massive two-burner numbers complete with grill, side-wind protectors and a lid that are pretty much like bringing your cooker from home along with you.

FUEL

Always ensure you buy the right fuel canister for your particular stove. The most common use gas (propane or butane) or liquid fuel (paraffin, kerosene, etc.), and different canisters are designed to clip or screw on to different stoves. If I'm ever not sure which one I need, I take the stove into a hardware shop and ask them to check for me. Buy double the fuel you think you'll use, just in case – you can always keep an extra canister in the car. It's also worth taking a supply of fuel with you if you're off camping abroad, in case it isn't available.

Make sure you know how to use your stove (and that it works with the fuel you've bought) *before* you head outdoors. Most fuel canisters screw onto single burners or get slotted into or attached to bigger stoves. Turn the gas on and light with a match or lighter – some will burn with a bright, friendly blue flame; others are hard to see alight but make a bit of a roaring noise. If it's really windy, watch carefully to make sure the flame hasn't gone out. *Never* cook inside your tent – you could poison yourself with carbon monoxide fumes.

Camping packing list

If you're taking a car on your camping trip you might as well chuck anything you might possibly need in the boot. The basics for happy camping include:

- Tent (duh)
- Sleeping bag
- Groundsheet – if your tent doesn't have a built-in one. Even if it does, a spare one is a great shout for sitting outside on wet days
- Inflatable sleeping mats – don't scrimp on these, as cheap blow-up ones like to gently deflate overnight
- Sunscreen
- First aid kit
- Stove
- Lighter or matches

- Head torch – for midnight loo trips, and to use as a tent light
- Firewood, if campfires are allowed – often you can buy bags of firewood at campsites, but check first
- Marshmallows – obligatory
- Torch or lantern
- Wellingtons
- Loo roll
- Camping pots and pans
- Camp kettle
- Cutlery, plates and cups
- Washing-up bowl and liquid

FESTIVAL CAMPING

Camping at a festival is a rather different beast to a romantic woodland weekend. It's best to arrive as early as you can to find a decent pitch, or get a keeno mate who is getting to the festival early to snag you a spot. Camp as far as you can from showers, loos and taps. It's up to you if you want to be close to the stages for easy moshing or as far from the bands as possible – you'll have more of a walk into the

festival but you'll get more space, peace and quiet for your camp. My favourite trick is to nab a space next to one of the big ugly metal fences that get put up on the edges of festival camping fields. That way you can arrange your mates in a semicircle for a guaranteed bit of communal space and string bunting up on the fence to make your pad easy to find in the sea of tents. Towels and rained-on clothes can hang on the fence to dry, too. Another trick for happy festie camping is keeping your tent

neat and tidy, so you can find your obnoxious fancy dress outfits easily. I usually share a tent with a friend and take another tent to be the gear/dressing-up tent – it means you can keep your sleeping tent as a clean, cosy haven, and your other tent can be a glitter-strewn mess. Campsite lifesavers for festivals are earplugs (they cost about 50p a pair and have completely changed my life), wet wipes (a makeshift shower, but see 'Keeping clean' overleaf) and big bottles for water refills.

WILD LOOS

Everybody poops, but camping makes it a more interesting endeavour than usual. If your campsite has loos, you don't need this paragraph. If you're wild camping (or just hiking far from civilisation), there are other ways of doing the deed. You'll need a small shovel. Pick a spot far away from any water sources and downwind from other campers, then dig a hole at least a foot deep. Do your thing and then fill in the hole with earth. Voila! Now there are two ways to dispose of the loo roll you used. Some of my hardened outdoor

friends burn it. This is a valid option, but one I personally shy away from after an unfortunate incident involving heavy winds which I'd rather not share with you. So I prefer to stick mine (and any sanitary stuff) in a Ziploc bag and take it away with me to throw away when I reach a bin. Finish the whole operation off with some sanitising hand gel.

KEEPING CLEAN AT CAMP

You're going to have to accept that camping is intrinsically a bit grubbier than life at home – that's the beauty of it. You're free to get mud on your face, salt in your hair and sand between your toes, and after a few days of being a wild child you probably won't even notice that you pong a bit. But there are also lots of ways to freshen up at camp. Wet wipes, while extremely useful, are not an eco-friendly option – try bringing a flannel to stick under a tap for a makeshift shower instead. If you're near a river or a lake you can have a bracing morning swim, and if you're at a festival, force yourself to get up early – the showers have usually just been cleaned and tend to be quiet.

Summer campers can also try my friend Donna's amazing bin bag shower trick. Fill a black bin bag with water and leave it in full sun while you go off exploring. Then hang it from a tree (or ask patient friends to hold it over you) somewhere where the water will drain and punch holes in it with a pen. An instant, blissful shower.

WILD CAMPING

The romantic notion of sleeping in the mountains in a lone little canvas tent doesn't have to be a fantasy. Wild camping is the fine art of setting up your tent in the back of beyond and waking up in a pocket of nature that's all your own. Going back to basics does require a little more thought and preparation

than regular camping, though. To start with, no, wild camping in England and Wales is technically not legal. There are ways around this, though – you can ask the permission of a landowner, or camp in the mountains above the limits of farmed land. Or just head to Dartmoor, where you're free to set up camp on open moorland where you like, providing you keep to certain rules (check dartmoor. gov.uk for an interactive map of where you can wild camp). Scotland (with the exception of East Loch Lomond) is also a haven for those wild at heart, and you can sleep where you wish on unenclosed land, including (especially magically) on beaches, as long as you leave nothing behind and respect the landscape.

Pack as light as you can for a wild camp. Essentials include a small tent or a bivvy bag, a sleeping bag, an ultralight sleeping mat, water, food, a stove and fuel, a head torch and a map. Make sure you've let someone know where you'll be and when you expect to return. Set up tent late in the evening, dismantle it early in the morning and leave no trace of your visit. Use only stoves to cook on, never light a campfire and carry all rubbish away with you.

BIVVY BAG CAMPING

Bivvying is the hardcore, no-frills version of camping. Essentially, it's just wrapping your sleeping bag in a waterproof bag, known as a bivouac, and sleeping out in the elements. If you're feeling wimpy you can slide a comfy camping mat in there with you, too.

Bivvying may look chilly, but it's not significantly colder than camping. It's also a great way to feel a lot closer to nature – the last things you'll see before you shut your eyes are the stars and the first thing you see will be the sunrise, with no tent walls in between. If you're planning to wild camp this is the subtlest way to go about it, too. Zip your bag up and draw it tightly around your face if it's a bit nippy. If rain is forecast, your best bet is to string a tarpaulin up between two trees and kip under that, to avoid the Chinese water torture of rain dripping on your nose all night.

HAMMOCK CAMPING

Hammock camping has been given a bit of a
hipster image of late, and its popularity on
Pinterest attests to how brilliant a way to sleep
out in the wild it is. Hammocks are lightweight
and easy to carry, quick to hang from trees
and much, much comfier than a tent. Imagine
waking up without a crick in your back from
sleeping on a stony floor, and how wonderful
the glistening forest would look if a night of

camping hadn't made you feel like a hungover zombie. That's hammock camping. Rain doesn't need to stop play, either – you can buy rain covers to hang above you which work well (some hammocks also come with covers), or string up a tarpaulin. Hang your hammock as high as you can (while still being able to get into it) between two trees four to five metres apart. If your hammock didn't come with some, buy some tree protection straps. Pop your sleeping mat and sleeping bag inside your swinging bed and you're good to go.

I usually keep my belongings dry by leaving them in waterproof stuff bags tied to trees. The only real downside to hammock camping is that you need to be pretty sure that there are some handy trees at your planned campsite. Everything else about it is awesome.

CANOE CAMPING

For a wonderful weekend of wild living please follow this recipe. Take one canoe. Add two waterproof barrels and fill them with tent, sleeping bags, food, water and other camping goodies. Add a friend. Take a paddle each and proceed down a slowly snaking reed-lined river, stopping off to camp under the stars where the mood takes you. For best results, pick a sultry summer weekend.

Canoe camping. Just putting those two words together speaks to me of *Swallows and Amazons* adventures. If you're new to its delights, the easiest way to sample them is to find a canoe hire company happy to sort you out with canoe rental for two or three days. The river Wye in Wales and the Great Ouse in East Anglia are both beginner-friendly paddles, and local guides can drop you off with a map and pick you up at the other end of your trip. Or if you have an old canoe in the garage, dust it off, stick it on the roof and drive it to a lake. Scotland is perfect for beginner canoe camping,

as you can paddle across the glassy surface of one of its many lochs and then wild camp on its banks without worrying about tricky currents or getting lost. Wild About Scotland (wildaboutscotland.com) lists lovely camping spots and secret islands you can sleep on.

It can be tempting to pack loads of gear into a big Canadian canoe, but it's best to travel light, especially if you're not sure if you'll have to carry the canoe across land at any point of the journey (this is known as portage). Pack your camping essentials into waterproof barrels in the middle of the boat, and take precious gear and camera equipment in a waterproof dry bag tucked under your seat. Tie down anything that looks a bit wobbly with bungees. You'll also need personal flotation devices (lifejackets) for everyone in the canoe, plus plenty of fresh water and a filtering water bottle.

When you stop for the night make sure you carry your canoe well out of the water. As with any wild camping trip, leave no trace of your camp behind.

GLAMPING

Glamping is seen as a bit of a wussy option among the tough members of the outdoor community who like to spend each weekend bivvy bagging on snowy mountains. But if you ask me, anything that gets you outdoors is a very good thing. Glamping usually involves sleeping in a big, semi-permanent structure such as a tipi, yurt, bell tent, tree house, shepherd's hut or gypsy caravan, usually with a few more creature comforts than a tent (think showers, real beds, even hot tubs). A brilliant compromise between a cosy cottage and proper camping, glamping is a wonderful way to sleep out in nature without much hassle, and ideal if you have a fresh-air-phobic friend who you want to ease slowly into the great outdoors. Glamping weekends can be as expensive as a stay in a B&B (try canopyandstars.co.uk if you want to splash out on something special), but there's no reason why you can't have a bit of a glamp on your own on the cheap. Shop around for a canvas bell tent or a tipi – they have a hefty price tag, but if you care for them they'll last you for decades, and your canvas beauty will always be the party tent at festivals. Pack battery-operated fairy lights, solar-powered garden lights, bunting, a proper duvet and pillows, a big camp stove, a fire pit and my personal definition of luxury: some proper coffee.

Three places
to go camping

1 Cornwall, UK

There's nowhere in Britain like Cornwall. This is a land of duck egg blue ocean and gorse-strewn cliff sides, of secret coves and lost gardens, of pubs where plotting smugglers once gathered and of abundant pasties to stuff in your face. It has a wealth of gorgeous campsites to tempt the pirate-minded camper, and surfers will love the sites perched on the edge of the Atlantic. You can also pack your tent up and hop across to the magical, car-free Isles of Scilly to camp on a sub-tropical island haven.

2 Norway

Norwegians love and respect the incredible untamed wilderness they're so lucky to live in – perhaps that's why Norway is one of the most wild-camping-tolerant countries in the world. The *Allemannsretten*, or 'all man's right', enshrines in law the right to camp freely for two nights on uncultivated land, and you're even allowed to freely fish in salt water and pick berries and mushrooms for your dinner. Pitch up on the edge of a glittering fjord or on a beach on the wild Lofoten Islands and go to sleep under the midnight sun.

3 Patagonia

South America's southern tip is a mesmerising, ever-changing vista of green steppes, arid desert, rainforest and glacial mountains. Chile and Argentina's wildest corner has great campsites near its towns and villages, but once you're out trekking in the stunning Torres del Paine National Park in Chile or in the shadow of the Fitz Roy massif in Argentina you'll be more likely to come across *campings agrestres* (marked wild camps). They don't go for facilities much round here, but what you lose in comfort you gain in epic snow-capped mountain landscapes. You can rent camping equipment before you hit the trail, too. Just watch out for the pumas.

IN WATER

Outdoor swimming is the best therapy I know, but be warned –
a dip in wild waters may change you forever. Dive on in and find
your inner water baby by sea swimming, cliff jumping or
braving a liberating skinny-dip.

2 SWIMMING

WILD SWIMMING

Human beings are 60% liquid, so perhaps it is no surprise that stepping into water can feel like coming home. Immersing yourself in an empty lake or the rolling ocean frees your mind, stretches out your limbs and washes away the stress of the outside world. Of course, it can also feel bloody freezing, and like your nipples are about to fall off.

Honestly, though, despite all the times I have teetered on a riverbank or sat in a warm car looking with alarm at the frosty ocean, I have never, ever regretted a wild swim. Jumping off rocks in limpid Greek coves, night swimming surrounded by sparkling bioluminescence, losing all feeling in my toes in the Cornish sea on New Year's Day – they are all grouped together in my mind as the happiest of times. Once you start seeking out quiet reed-edged rivers and pellucid forest plunge pools

you'll be astonished at the beautiful wild spaces you'll find. Try the wonderful *Wild Swimming* book series from Wild Things Publishing, or wildswimming.co.uk, for suggestions. Even if you only ever stick to being a heatwave swimmer, round up your mates and give the life aquatic a try. You might just find your inner mermaid.

Wild swimming safety rules

▶ Only swim sober (save your picnic booze for afterwards).
▶ Always check the depth of the water first.
▶ Search out an easy exit point before entering the water.
▶ Avoid swimming alone.
▶ Wear aquatic sandals with a good grip when on rocks.
▶ Wear a wetsuit in colder weather.
▶ Have a plan for warming up as soon as you get out.
▶ If you encounter weeds, don't panic. They are easiest to navigate by floating gently through.
▶ Avoid swimming in city rivers – the water can carry harmful bacteria.
▶ Lakes and ponds can be home to nasties such as blue-green algae, a scum on the surface of the water that can make you sick. Avoid swimming anywhere with stagnant water or a greenish bloom on the surface of the water.

SEA SWIMMING

Ahh, vitamin sea, one of the best cures for the blues I know. The ocean, however, can be a cruel mistress, and one you must treat with respect and caution. The same safety rules as for general wild swimming apply to the sea, with the added advice that you check in advance to find out if there are dangerous currents present. Never swim anywhere with warning signs in place. Hypothermia and, ironically, dehydration are real risks when swimming, so drink lots of water, have a plan in place for warming up properly once you're out again (hello, hot chocolate) and get out well before you start to feel tired or cold. Treat her well, and the sea will reward you with a vast and fascinating space to explore.

Sea swimming for fitness

Swimming is utterly amazing for getting fit. It puts no pressure on your bones and muscles, yet still builds up strength and improves

cardiovascular (that's your heart) fitness really efficiently. It's also deeply calming, training your breath and endurance while it boosts your mood. If you don't feel you're a confident swimmer, sign up for lessons in the pool first and work on achieving a decent level of stamina before you consider a dip in the briny.

Making the step to sea swimming can be rather daunting. Deep water, a lack of visibility and dealing with changing tides and currents make it a very different kettle of fish to a nice safe swimming pool. A good first step is to find a placid lake you can swim the width of – you'll get used to guiding yourself without marked lanes. After that, I suggest beginning in shallow sea water and swimming parallel to the beach – you want to feel that you can easily stand up at any time. Wear a wetsuit

and decent goggles and try building up to completing an increasing number of laps along the shore. Before swimming anywhere, check if there are any currents or riptides to be aware of, as some are permanent features, although a rip can form on any beach with waves. Rip tides are fast-flowing bodies of water heading out to sea, spottable by looking for rippled and sometimes discoloured areas in an otherwise calm sea. If you do find yourself caught in fast-moving water, see if you can stand up. If you can, wade back to land. If you can't, try to relax and swim to the right or the left of the rip, parallel to the shore, as opposed to directly against it.

Feeling confident? The sea-swimming world is your oyster, and joining a swimming club such as the Outdoor Swimming Society (outdoorswimmingsociety.com) is the perfect way to find aquatic mates, group swims and local events.

CLIFF JUMPING

Springing off a cliff face and free falling into the sparkling ocean is one of my favourite ways to both delight and terrify myself. Cliff jumping is wild and joyous and makes you feel a little like James Bond when he has to do an epic dive to get away from the baddies. But it is also a pursuit to treat with a lot of respect. If you want to jump into water from any height, make sure you carefully check the depth of the water below first, including scouting for any submerged rocks and ledges. I recommend finding somewhere where you can build up height with each jump, such as stone steps – it'll help your confidence in your jumping skills, too. When you've mustered up the courage to jump, leap out well away from the cliff side, and then bring your body into a tight pencil shape. Aim to enter the water feet first. Lastly, remember to enjoy the rush, 007.

SKINNY-DIPPING

You aren't truly liberated till you've experienced the joy of freeing your bits from the confines of a swimming costume and splashing about wild and free in the nuddy pants. Skinny-dipping is way up there in the list of the most enjoyable (and hilarious) ways you can have fun with your kit off.

I often get asked if skinny-dipping is legal. The answer is that, in the UK, you are totally within your rights to swim naked, but it's worth avoiding upsetting bystanders by opting to swim in quiet places. Find an empty bit of beach or lake, and if other people are present, walk far enough away that it isn't hugely obvious you're butt-naked. In Europe, you'll find swimming nude positively encouraged on certain beaches, especially in the Mediterranean – ask around to find out which part of the coast is reserved for nudism and then just join the locals. In more reserved

countries, or if you feel a bit shy, get into the water with a costume on, then take it off and tie it to your wrist.

Be brave and try going bare-bottomed – up the skinny-dip revolution!

Three places
to go wild swimming

1 Fairy Pools, Isle of Skye, Scotland

If you're on the ethereal island of Skye, make a pilgrimage to one of the loveliest wild swimming spots I've ever encountered. Clear spring water flows from the foot of the Cuillin mountains and feeds deep, crystalline lagoons you can dive into, topped up with rushing waterfalls. These are the Fairy Pools, where the water is icy-cold but so enchanting you might not notice you've got a bad case of brain freeze when you take the plunge. There's even a submerged arch connecting two of the pools you can dive under if you're feeling brave.

2 Greek islands

Some of my happiest memories involve dips in the limpid blue waters of the Greek islands strewn like jewels across the Aegean and Ionian seas. Each one offers water so clear you can see little fish flitting around under your feet; rickety wooden piers to jump off; boats to take on snorkelling trips; and, rarest and most mesmerising of all, glowing bioluminescence glittering in the ocean after dark – a sea of stars you can bathe in.

3 Mexican cenotes

Troglodytes should pack their bathers for Mexico's Yucatán Peninsula and go in search of its famed cenotes (or sinkholes) for an otherworldly underground experience. Try Cenote X'keken, near Valladolid, a vaulted cave full of deep, still water with a ceiling of graceful limestone arches and spaghetti-like stalagtites. Narrow shards of light descend from the heavens through chinks in the roof of the cave, home to the cenote's other regular visitors – leathery little bats.

ON THE ROAD

Pack your bags and feel the wind in your hair on an
epic overland trip. Plan a human-powered adventure and go
bikepacking on two wheels or explore lanes less travelled
in a trusty campervan. Go make tracks.

3 BIKEPACKING

If real life makes you itch to down tools and
hit the open road with the wind in your hair
and home disappearing on the distant horizon,
bikepacking has your name on it. Cycling with
camping gear strapped to your bike is a wild
and free way to escape, with the added bonus
of being a lot speedier and farther reaching
than a hike. It's a cheap way to explore, too –
all you need is a trusty bike, a pair of panniers
and some lightweight camping kit and you're

sorted for a weekend biking adventure.

As with most things in this book, I definitely
recommend starting small and building up to
the wild intrepid trips of your dreams. Start by
planning an overnight cycle to a nice campsite
and back the next day, or try cycling to your
next festival (with the added bonus that cyclists
often get nicer campsites and showers in return
for saving the planet). Then you can start
eyeing up maps and thinking about cross-
country jaunts.

The key to happy cycle touring
is to pack as light as you can. You'll
need a rear bike rack and two
panniers to sling over it – this is a
much comfier option than taking a
sweaty backpack on your ride. You
can buy a lot of different nifty bags
to attach to your bike: triangular
frame bags are a good use of spare
space, and a small bag attached
to your handlebars is useful for
storing your bike repair kit. Don't
forget a map, ideally marked
with your route and stored in a
waterproof wallet. If you want to
cook you'll need a small stove, but

How to plan a route

Pull out a map of your surrounding countryside and see what local highlights you can weave together into a cycle route. Could you cycle to a river to swim in, and then head to a favourite campsite? Or can you create a route which ends up at a brilliant country pub? Don't make your first multi-day trip too ambitious – you're more likely to really enjoy it if it's within your abilities.

Avoid big roads as much as possible. Cycling isn't legal on motorways, of course, but it's also not fun on dual carriageways or busy roads. Cycling charity Sustrans (sustrans.org.uk) has a brilliant map showing National Cycle Network routes and car-free lanes criss-crossing Britain, and Cycle Streets (cyclestreets.net) has maps listing cafés, bike shops and other points of interest to factor in. Look for old railways, canal towpaths and forest paths if you'd rather have a traffic-free ride, or stick to the kind of quiet country lanes that pootle between villages. For more challenging routes, bikepacking.net lists epic trails to tackle across the wildest landscapes in America.

If you aren't leaving from your doorstep, think about how you'll transport your bike. If you've got a car you can stick your bikes on a rack on the back or on the roof. An easier option if there's a group of you is to stick your bike on a train. Check if you need to book a space for your wheels first, then make sure you get to the platform in good time and ask a guard where to stand to get your bike into the cycle carriage speedily.

I find 40 or 50 miles per day is more than enough cycling if, like me, you like to stop off at every sunny lake and cake shop you pass. It's best to be a fair-weather cyclist for your first few rides – pick a day with cool, clear weather and a tailwind rather than forcing yourself out in icy rain and gales. You don't have to camp – if the weather isn't looking too warm you could find a route which ends up at your mate's house in the next town. Take it slow, ride in an easier gear than normal and don't burn yourself out by worrying about speed or mileage at the beginning. Take lots of pit (cake) stops, admire the view, take photos, relax into the route and enjoy pretending you're in the Tour de France.

Dyrham 1
Doynton 2½

if you'll be near civilisation it's worth simply buying food each day to avoid the extra weight of carrying nosh and cooking supplies. You'll need plenty of snacks, as you'll constantly be burning calories in the saddle.

Dress in layers – it's the easiest way to cool off or warm up quickly, as you can shed or add one in a flash. Be prepared for changing conditions, even if you're hitting the road in summer. Always carry a thermal layer, a waterproof shell jacket, sunglasses and sun cream. The absolute musts are a good helmet and some decent padded shorts. Long distances on a hard bike saddle can make things pretty hot and all squished up in your lady bits (this is where you thank God you're not a bloke) – try applying a layer of chamois cream to avoid dreaded chafing.

If you're planning a long, multi-day route, don't scrimp on your bike and its maintenance. It's pretty essential to know how to fix a puncture (or at least how to change an inner tube) and how to recognise other bike aches and pains, mainly to save on costly visits to the mechanic. Make sure you've given your bike an MOT before the start of the ride. If you're buying or renting a bike for a cycling odyssey, think about the roads and surfaces you'll be riding on. Touring bikes are designed to be comfortable over long distances, and the thicker tyres on mountain and hybrid bikes are a good shout if you're planning on going off-piste down rough country lanes.

Bikepacking kit list

- Sleeping bag
- Bivvy bag or one-man tent
- Waterproof coat
- Insulated jacket
- Gloves
- Spare set of clothes
- Well-padded cycling shorts
- Medicines and wash kit
- Suncream
- Chamois cream (and massive, comfortable pants)
- First aid kit
- Sandals
- Bike tool kit
- GPS computer or map
- Snacks
- Spare inner tubes
- Bike lock
- Pump
- Bike lube
- Panniers
- Water cage

Three places
to go bikepacking

1 Coast to Coast, UK

If the very thought of a gruelling Land's End to John O'Groats ride up the length of Britain makes your thighs ache, try a shorter but no less epic bike tour across the width of England instead. The three-day, 140-mile Coast to Coast route meanders through some of England's wildest landscapes. Start in Whitehaven to the west and ceremoniously dip your back wheel in the sea, then hit the winding roads through the lovely (if hilly) Lake District and on to Tynemouth in the east, camping, bivvying or staying in B&Bs along the way.

2 Camino de Santiago, Spain

A pilgrims' route since the Middle Ages, the 480-mile-long Way of St James meanders along the whole top of Spain and through the green mountains of Galicia on the way to Santiago de Compostela. There are multiple possible routes to follow, but the well-signposted Camino Frances is the most famous, beginning in Roncesvalles and pit-stopping in Pamplona, Burgos and León on its way west. You can camp or stay in traditional *albergues*. One for your biker's bucket list.

3 Arizona Trail, USA

Imagine 800 epic, car-free miles stretching across the state of Arizona, reaching up from Mexico in the south-west to Utah in the north. That's the AZT. It links mountains, forests, the Sonoran Desert and the Grand Canyon, and is only passable in the friendlier temperatures of spring and autumn. The route is almost totally unpaved singletrack, and mastering it calls for a tough mountain bike. There are some campsites, but most of the time you'll be wild camping out in the desert with just your bike for company.

4 CAMPERVANS

INTRODUCTION

To the Mystery Machine! Campervans are the ultimate adventure-enablers, a ticket to the wide-open road with your bed ready in the back for when you get tuckered out from all that exploring. One of my happiest ever weekends was spent trundling down the coastline of Devon in a knackered green VW campervan called Alice. Alice couldn't do more than about 50 mph when putt-putting along the motorway, but that didn't really matter – pulling up in a campsite, making a cup of tea and sitting in her doorway watching the sun go down made me feel extremely fond of her. It poured with rain for most of the weekend we had Alice, but that was okay, too – we went surfing in the drizzle each day and then got back into the warm, welcoming van for tea and bacon sarnies.

A campervan lets you combine all the best bits of glamping (candles, duvets, kitchen sink, copious wine) with the ability to move your new home around and park up overlooking a beautiful new beach every day. Everyone on the road smiles at you in a campervan. Retro van drivers even wave to each other, like members of a secret club. It's definitely a special way to pootle around. And renting a home on wheels really comes into its own when you're planning a big road trip with designs on massive countries such as America or Canada.

Planning a route

When poring over a guidebook and a map of a brand-new country it can be easy to start dreaming of an ambitious, sweeping route taking in myriad cities, national parks and beauty spots. But I promise you'll have much more fun if you aren't sticking to a tightly stretched schedule. The best van trips are slow, with plenty of time to linger in the unexpected special places you find along the way. When you're plotting a route, leave yourself a few days of extra time and don't aim to get too far each day. Some van companies will let you collect a van from the airport and then drop it off in another city, which suits the keen road tripper perfectly.

RENTING A CAMPERVAN

Let's get the painful bit out of the way: RVs and campervans aren't cheap to rent. If you're looking for a really budget weekend you'd be better off driving your car and camping or wild camping each night, as on top of the cost of a week of van hire you'll also have to shell out to stay in campsites most evenings. It is possible, if not usually legal, to sleep by the roadside or in laybys in some places, but in reality it's a lot less hassle to just pay for a campsite (you'll get to hook up your van's electricity and have a shower, too). Some of the prettiest campsites don't accept vans, though, so check the rules before you arrive. Have a look online to see what other van drivers recommend in the country you're exploring. In Italy, for example, there are cheap or free *Aree di Sosta* (rest areas) where campervanners can kip for the night.

   If you're renting a van for just a weekend you can get away with something tiny and

sardine-like but cute, like a classic VW, but if you're after a home for a week or more you might be comfier splashing out on something big and packed with mod cons. If you're on a budget, try five-seater vans with separate pop-out tents on the roof or simple vans with just a bed in the back – if you're used to camping these will probably still seem pretty luxurious. If you want to road trip over really big distances, you're more likely to get along with a big, spacious RV (short for recreational vehicle, also known as a motorhome) complete with shower, heating and other bells and whistles. Some can sleep up to six people, which might be a bit crammed but will bring the cost down massively if you're sharing with a gang of friends (you could always take a tent along for extra storage, too). Don't go for the dirt-cheap option when comparing quotes from different rentals – instead, pick a reputable company with good online reviews, and check they offer

breakdown cover. Confused by all the different choices? A VW California is a brilliant modern all-rounder and is easy to drive and small enough to park in cities, but still large enough to sleep four. Look for vans with pop-top roofs with beds in – a space-saving extra, not to mention seriously cosy to sleep in.

When you pick up your rental make sure you get a full demonstration, pay close attention to all instructions (as opposed to daydreaming about your road-trip playlist) and go for a practice drive before you head off into the sunset.

VAN LIVING

Happy van life is all about being very clean, very tidy and very good at playing Tetris with your belongings. Pack as light as you possibly can – vans can take a lot of stuff, but the less you bring along, the more space you'll have to

live in. Stick heavy items at the bottom of the boot and lighter ones on top to keep things stable in transit. Always take the time to put away or tie down loose items before you drive off, if only so you don't go insane listening to your belongings crash around every time you

brake. Pack emergency supplies, extra fuel and plenty of water and snacks, plus extra layers and blankets – vans can get chilly when night falls.

Everything in vans has its own compartment and often doubles up into something else – a little sofa and table magic into a bed, a seat hides all the crockery beneath it, pull up a counter and there's a tiny hidden stove and a sink seemingly designed for pixies. After a few days you'll be a pro at converting the back of the van from kitchen to bedroom in a snap, and the lazy pace of van life will suddenly click into place. It's all worth it for the mornings when you wake up, slide open the door and sit cradling a hot coffee and watching dawn surfers riding waves or listening to the sound of the woods coming to life. Beware – you could find yourself hooked and set on saving all your pennies for your very own pastel-coloured VW bus.

Three places
to road trip in your campervan

1 Scottish Highlands

Here be monsters, mountains and magic. Pristine lochs, rugged peaks and plentiful whisky-stocked pubs make the Scottish Highlands the road-tripping vanner's Avalon. Make Inverness your starting point and go island-hopping by hugging the road along the shore of the dark, fabled waters of Loch Ness and then heading over the bridge to Skye for wild swimming and hiking, or driving down to Oban and catching a ferry over to the Isle of Mull or Islay for white sand beaches like something from the Caribbean. For a really epic challenge, take on Scotland's iconic North Coast 500 route, a circular jaunt around the wild northern tip of the United Kingdom.

2 France

Nothing beats *la belle France* for a few summery weeks of sheer campervan ease. Myriad charming campsites will let you park your van up (try Camping du Brec in the Alps, with its very own lake, or Camping Le Clapas in the south, with a private river beach) for a few days of sunbathing and swimming before you lazily decide to hop over to the next one, possibly with a stop in a picture-perfect medieval village to stock up on local wine and copious amounts of smelly cheese. Heaven (or perhaps that should be *paradis*).

3 Cape Breton, Canada

Hit the Cabot Trail around Nova Scotia's Cape Breton Island – the route makes a 185-mile loop, passing through the thick, empty forests of Cape Breton Highlands National Park and ribboning along the stunning, blustery coast. Go hiking on the plateau and keep your eyes peeled for moose, black bears and bald eagles, then drive south to the Bay of Fundy, where the highest tidal range in the world means you can join locals for a spot of mud sliding on the sea bed when the water has ebbed away.

SECTION THREE
WILD COOKING, CRAFTS AND WELLBEING

There is no cosmetic for beauty like happiness.
LADY BLESSINGTON

WHEN I TOLD MY MOTHER about this section of the book, she immediately requested I call it 'The Grill Outdoors'. Thanks, Mum. We're starting by diving fork-first into one of my favourite things in the entire world – food – and how to make it taste brilliant outdoors. I can't imagine a nicer dinner party than sitting under the stars around a crackling fire, nursing a camping mug full of red wine.

Why does all grub taste better when eaten outside? Perhaps because happy campers are always ravenous after a day of hiking, wild swimming and gallivanting. Or perhaps it's the excitement of watching and smelling something tasty as it bubbles and spits over the flames. Learn to build a fire and gut a fish like a badass, then feed the hordes with smoky stew and scrumptious s'mores. There's wild food for free, too – go foraging for goodies and try my recipes for hedgerow booze and meadow flower cookies.

I've dreamt up a clutch of nature-inspired projects for crafty foxes to try their hand at. I'm not suggesting you quit real life and become a spoon whittler, but it's seriously satisfying learning to make your own eco-friendly candles, build a shelter in the woods, knit your mate a bobble hat and set up a flourishing vegetable patch in the most minuscule of back gardens.

And finally, there are some thoughts for outward-bound ladies on staying happy and healthy. I'm pretty sure Wonder Woman never let periods, midges or altitude sickness stand in the way of her epic quests, and neither shall you.

FIRESIDE FOOD

Rustle up an al fresco feast to feed your hungry camping
hordes with my scrumptious ideas for great food from the fire,
including favourite recipes and guides to cooking on grills,
embers and stoves. Anyone for s'mores?

1 COOKING OUTDOORS

HOW TO BUILD A CAMPFIRE

YOU WILL NEED
- tinder – newspaper, firelighters, etc.
- kindling – dry sticks and twigs are best
- dry logs of varying thicknesses
- matches or a lighter

The holy trinity of a good fire are tinder, kindling and dry logs. Choose a dry spot on flat ground, away from tents and trees, and clear an area of around three feet in diameter. Enclose your spot with rocks if there are any handy – this prevents embers from scattering and offers a bit of wind protection. Make a pile of flammable materials (your tinder) in the centre of the circle, and over it create a tipi construction by leaning sticks of kindling together. Light the inner materials. When the kindling catches fire and begins to burn, start to slowly add bigger pieces of wood, taking care not to add too many and suffocate your beautiful new fire. When the larger logs are crackling away, slowly add progressively thicker logs. I find a fire usually needs careful tending for up to half an hour before you can leave it be and just add logs when it gets low.

When you've finished with your fire, spread the embers out and wait until they have gone completely cold. You can also douse them with water.

Whatever you do, don't leave the fire making to the boys.

CAMPFIRE COOKING ON A GRILL

Grilling is my go-to method for cooking over a fire. It does take time, but that means you get to sit and drink beer while tending to dinner, which is fine with me. First, you need to wait until the wood fire you lit blazes away for long enough to produce a glowing bed of hot coals – this usually takes an hour or so. When you've got some glowing coals, use a stick to spread them out to make an even base. Once that's done you can stick a grill over them. Old barbecue grills or grills with their own pop-out legs are ideal, otherwise you can balance a grill on two bricks or large rocks on either side of the fire. To gauge if a fire is hot enough to cook on, hold your hand about seven inches over it. If you have to draw it away after a few seconds, it's hot enough.

CAMPFIRE COOKING OVER A TRIPOD

My mate Matt loves a campfire stew, and can be relied upon to head off into the trees and return with three sturdy branches to lean together over the fire. He lashes these together and hangs a pot or a kettle from the middle. You can also buy ready-made tripods with built-in fire pits – a good option for cooking in your back garden or on a beach without having to make a fire on the ground.

Cooking in foil

Make your own mini oven by wrapping meat, veggies or potatoes in thick foil and burying the parcel in the coals to cook. I rub the inside of the foil with oil first, then sling in the grub and add sauces, herbs or just loads of butter. Make sure the parcels are well wrapped, and check them periodically to see if they're done. This is also a great way to package up food in your kitchen to take with you on a camping trip. Wrap up foil parcels, bung them in a plastic container and then pop on the fire for a zero-prep supper.

COOKING ON THE BEACH

Open fires are not usually legal on British beaches – it depends on who owns or looks after the land (it could be a local council or the National Trust, for example). If you want to cook up a beach barbecue, your best bet is to lug a small portable barbecue or a fire pit along with you. Make sure you've got a supply of wood and kindling with you if there isn't much dry driftwood around to collect. Grilled fish tastes especially good by the sea, and you can forage for seaweed for a salad or even for mussels picked from the rocks, and add a bit of salt water to season your beach feast. If you do have permission for an open fire, make sure to light it between the low and high tide line. Dig a shallow pit in the sand to light it in and when you leave, douse the ashes with seawater and take any large bits of debris with you.

COOKING ON A CAMP STOVE

The awesome thing about camping stoves is that they are essentially portable hobs, meaning that anything you can cook on your stove at home can be whipped up in the great outdoors by sticking a pot or frying pan on top. They're also the only way you can cook a hot meal if you're wild camping or staying at a campsite that doesn't allow campfires. Always have a go at setting your stove up at home first – there's little more frustrating than realising you brought the wrong fuel when you're desperate for a cuppa after a massive hike (see page 96, Section Two for more info on stoves). High winds can also be an issue – move your cooking station somewhere sheltered, or at a pinch use a coat or tarp to shield the flame. Always cook on a flat surface, and never fire up your stove inside your tent. Most of the (usually pretty disgusting) instant camping meals and ration packs you can buy are easy to cook, as you just stick the entire packet in boiling water. Couscous, instant noodles and stew are more palatable one-pot stove meals.

Four fire starters
Handy cheats to make lighting a fire that little bit easier.

1 Waterproof matches
It's one of the ironies of outdoor life that the conditions in which you need a fire the most (rain, wind, snow) are the hardest to get a flame to stay alight in. Waterproof matches can come to the rescue and are really useful if you've managed to drench the rest of your kit. You can buy them in outdoor shops or make your own by dipping the heads of regular matches in nail polish or candle wax and leaving to dry.

2 Flint and steel, or firestriker
This is a tool every outdoorswoman should have in her pocket, mainly because using flint and steel to make a shower of bright golden sparks will make you feel like you're Harry Potter. Strike steel against flint in sharp downwards motions to create sparks above very dry tinder, such as wood shavings or cotton wool dipped in wax, until they catch fire, then blow very gently to disperse the flames.

3 Newspaper plaits
These paper braids are a pleasingly old-fashioned way to start your fire. They burn for longer than loose balls of paper and are weirdly satisfying to make on a rainy evening. Twist three sheets of paper into long sausages, line them up and plait tightly together. Fold the plait over and tie the ends up with string. Make a stack of these plaits to keep by the woodburner or to take camping to use as kindling for a barbecue or campfire.

4 A feather stick
Use dead, dry wood to make these attractive easy burners. Remove the bark and then run a sharp knife down the stick's length, with the blade angled slightly inwards. It takes practice but you should be able to create fine, curling shavings after a few goes. Stop your blade just before the curls shave off the stick and repeat until your stick is covered in curly fronds. Feather sticks are fantastic tinder, and you can even make them if it's been raining – just take damp wood and cut down until you find its dry core, then feather that.

CAMPFIRE STEW
WITH DUMPLINGS

Feed the hordes with a hearty stew. The joy of having a big hotpot bubbling away on the fire is that you can do absolutely whatever you want to it – add baked beans, take away the meat for a veggie concoction, double the ingredients for a big gang or bring along leftovers from home to use up. This, however, is the basic recipe I usually cook as a winter warmer, and it does a lovely job on camping trips, serving around six ravenous tent dwellers.

Grab a big pan and chuck in two tins of chopped tomatoes, then add chopped carrots, mushrooms and courgettes, and let the whole pot simmer gently until all the veggies are soft. Add half a cup of water and a beef stock cube, and then stir in a few spoonfuls of pesto and a chorizo ring, chopped into slices. Season with lots of salt and pepper and let bubble away until it all reduces to a sticky mess.

To make your stew into a really filling dinner, try adding dumplings. Make a batter by mixing flour, water, salt and pepper and then shaping into egg-sized balls (you can get all posh and add chopped wild garlic leaves or a spoonful of bacon fat for really pimped-up dumplings). Bring the stew to the boil and then drop in the dumplings. Cover the pot and simmer for 10 minutes, or until the dumplings are cooked all the way through. Serve the stew in tin bowls or cups with a few dumplings popped on top. Yum.

How to gut and prepare a fish

Not a skill for the squeamish or the vegetarian, this, but knowing how to gut a raw fish and then setting it to sizzle on the campfire is extremely satisfying. Casually debone one in front of your mates and you'll always be named the most likely to survive a zombie apocalypse.

First, you'll need to rid your dinner of its scales. Take the blunt side of a knife and run it up and down your fish's sides – the scales will come off in an iridescent shower. Give your now naked fish a sluice with clean water and you're ready for the gory bit.

1 Using a sharp knife, make a cut in the belly of your fish, beginning from the tail and cutting through the skin all the way to the bottom of the head. You'll know when to stop as you'll hit bone and no longer be able to cut easily.

2 Open your fish's belly up wide and remove all the guts. Lovely.

3 Cut off the fish's head, tail and fins and discard, then give the body another wash.

4 To debone the fish, open up its sides wide, like a book. Carefully slip your fingers under the ribs and run them up and down to loosen the bones, then push your fingers down to the spine, and ease the ribs and spine out of the flesh. Check for and remove any remaining bones.

5 Ta-dah! A beautiful fillet of fish, ready to grill on the campfire. Drizzle with lemon, add salt and pepper and grill skin-down over the fire.

CAMPFIRE BREAD TWISTS

These helter-skeltery twists are brilliant if you want to graduate from toasting marshmallows over the fire to something more filling. They're an easy, fun and Scout-approved recipe, and cooking them up on sticks seems to be a big hit with big and little kids alike. Before you head off for a night of canvas and stars, sift together three cups of flour, one hefty pinch of salt, one pinch of baking powder and one of brown sugar. Add a tablespoon of oil and 200ml of water to your mix and chuck it all about until you have a firm dough. Roll the dough out flat, lay a sheet of baking parchment on top and roll the dough around the parchment, Swiss-roll style, to take with you. When you've got a happily burning campfire going, cut the unravelled, flat dough into inch-wide strips and wrap each strip around a clean stick. Bake over the fire, turning the twists regularly as they cook. The twists are ready when they're no longer doughy in the middle (check by tearing a bit off). Serve hot with butter and jam before bed, or with coffee and bacon to bleary-eyed campers in the morning.

BOBBY'S ALL-AMERICAN S'MORES

Here I will hand over to my American friend Bobby, and let him teach you how to make the most delicious and calorific fireside treat of all – s'mores, so named because you are guaranteed to want 'some more' (until you feel sick).

'In my eyes, the s'more's closest relatives are camping and childhood. In America, foods like Graham crackers, Hershey's chocolate, and party-sized bags of marshmallows are abundant, much like I imagine porridge-making supplies to be in England. I'm using Graham crackers, but if you're in the UK you could always use digestive biscuits, or make your own cinnamon biscuits.

STEP ONE: GATHER YOUR ESSENTIALS

The three ingredients to a s'more are Graham crackers, chocolate (preferably Hershey's) and marshmallows. In addition, you must light a fire and forage for a proper roasting stick (set your eyes on a long and thin twig). Also, if you're on a diet, forget it.

STEP TWO: GRAB TWO GRAHAMS

Think of the s'more as the caloric king of sandwiches, with the Graham cracker being the bread.

STEP THREE: PREPARE THE CHOCOLATE

A King Size Hershey's bar is separated into 12 rectangles, providing enough chocolate for three nicely sized s'mores. Stick a rectangle of chocolate between two crackers.

STEP FOUR: READY THE MARSHMALLOW

If you searched properly, you've found a nimble stick that can be easily rotated between your thumb, middle and index fingers. Place your white puff ball on the end of it. CAUTION: If you don't jam the stick far enough into the marshmallow, it can fall off during roasting.

STEP FIVE: ROAST THE MARSHMALLOW

A novice s'moremaker might thrust the marshmallow directly into the fire's golden heart, eager to make it soft and delectable. Resist temptation and hold it two or three inches from the flame, allowing the heat to soften its core. Wait a few more seconds until the mallow begins to droop slightly and then let the fire crisp the outer layer. Roast to preferred crispiness, and don't panic if your mallow goes up in flames. Remember, the heat from the marshmallow needs to melt your chocolate when you place it between the Grahams.

STEP SIX: ASSEMBLE THE S'MORE

Centre the mallow between the chocolate and the Grahams. Put light pressure on each side of the s'more and slowly slide the stick out of the mallow's centre.

STEP SEVEN: ADMIRE AND DEVOUR

Don't forget to observe the subtle-yet-overwhelming beauty of your s'more before you embark on your flavourful journey. Savour it. Cherish it. Devour it.'

MEXICAN HOT CHOCOLATE

I first tried this spiced, exotic stunner of a hot chocolate in the mountains of Mexico. It's the most comforting cold-weather campfire drink ever, and is also really simple to prepare before you head outdoors. This recipe will serve four happy campers.

Mix together 400g cocoa powder, 200g sugar, a teaspoon of cinnamon, ¼ teaspoon of chilli powder, four cinnamon sticks and half a bar of dark chocolate, broken into pieces. Pop the mixture in a Ziploc bag. Warm up four cups of milk (proper Mexican hot chocolate uses boiling water, but I'm a sucker for the comfort of hot milk) over the fire and add the mixture to the pan, mixing until the chocolate melts and making sure the milk doesn't boil. You could even lace your hot chocolate with rum if you really need warming up before bed.

HIKER'S BANANA BREAD

All hail the hiker's banana bread! This recipe isn't strictly one to make over the fire, but I couldn't leave it out because it makes the perfect mid-trek snack and it's easy to make the night before a mountain adventure. You can either use a loaf tin and slice it up, or make mini ones in a muffin tin. Hand them out to hungry walkers at the summit and you'll be crowned queen of the mountain. Banana bread is also great tucked in skiing rucksacks or cycling jerseys for a hit of carbs mid-workout. Plus, bananas are fruit, so technically this is good for you.

INGREDIENTS

- five mashed bananas
- 100g softened butter
- 250g muscovado sugar
- one egg
- 100g chopped walnuts
- 175g flour
- pinch of salt
- pinch of allspice

METHOD

1 Preheat the oven to 180°C (350°F). Grease a 4x8-inch loaf tin.

2 In a mixing bowl beat together the bananas, butter, sugar and egg. In a separate bowl, mix the walnuts, flour, salt and allspice. Add the dry ingredients to the main mixture and stir together.

3 Pour into the tin and bake for one hour, or until a skewer comes out clean.

4 Slice and wrap ready for the hills (or butter and eat while hot, I won't tell anyone).

FORAGING

The countryside is full of edible goodies all year round – you just have to know how to seek them out. My favourite seasonal finds are perfect for beginner foragers, and my handy recipes will help you transform your treasure into soups, liquors and sweet treats.

2 HOW TO GO FORAGING

Food for free! Foraging (the art of gathering wild food to eat) is thrifty, fascinating and a brilliant excuse for a ramble. Plus, imagine the smugness of serving up lip-smacking homemade sloe gin. Foraging can sound a bit scary if you've never tried it before, but if you're savvy and sensible about what you pick it's easy and satisfying, and you can come home with a bag full of tasty seasonal scoff to feed yourself with.

First, it's worth knowing that foraging is legal in England, but only if you're collecting for your own personal use. Private property and Sites of Special Scientific Interest are off-limits. If the apples you like the look of are on private land, they're no go unless you ask permission to pick them first. Whatever you collect, take only what you can eat and leave plenty behind for wildlife (and other hungry pickers). Don't forage near roads, to avoid

polluted plants. If you've never foraged before, I recommend sticking to very easily identifiable crops, such as blackberries or nettles, and then seeing if there's a local wild-food course you can take – it's much easier to recognise plants if someone shows you their characteristics, and you'll learn about secret foraging hotspots near you. Wildfooduk.com has clear photos and descriptions of commonly foraged British hedgerow fare.

You might automatically think of mushrooms when you see the word foraging. As much as I love them, my personal advice is not to pick fungus without someone who has years of experience standing right next to you checking what you pick. My fear comes mainly from realising that as well as the tasty chanterelles I confidently used to bring home it's possible to pick mega-dangerous and pretty much identical faux chanterelles. Those mushrooms are a wily bunch.

Seasonal foraging favourites

What to try foraging for each month:

JANUARY – Nettles
FEBRUARY – Seaweed (try laver or sugar kelp)
MARCH – Wild garlic
APRIL – Primrose
MAY – Sea cabbage
JUNE – Wild strawberries
JULY – Elderflowers
AUGUST – Blackberries
SEPTEMBER – Rosehips
OCTOBER – Sloes
NOVEMBER – Dandelions
DECEMBER – Chestnuts

3 EASY FORAGED GRUB

EASY WAYS WITH WILD GARLIC

The delicious, pungent leaves of wild garlic lend themselves perfectly to pesto. Collect a large bunch of wild garlic leaves and stems. Pop them into a food processer with a few handfuls of pine nuts, a grated chunk of Parmesan and a big slug of olive oil. Add salt, pepper and a teaspoon of garlic powder, then blitz into a rough sauce and serve with fresh pasta. Another favourite way with wild garlic comes from my mates Jenny and Mark – simply mix finely chopped leaves with mayonnaise and serve up with barbecued goodies.

ELDERFLOWER TEA

If you got a bit overexcited and came home with armfuls of delicate elderflowers, no problem. You can dry the flowers easily and keep them to make a delicious tea. Clean any bugs off your flowers and then spread them out in the sun on a sheet or a piece of cardboard. Once they've dried, make a refreshing, antioxidant cuppa by adding one teaspoon of the flowers per cup to a teapot, adding hot water and letting it steep. Serve with a little sugar or honey to taste.

BLACKBERRY ICE POPS

Is there anything better on a sizzling summer's day than a blackberry-picking session followed by an ice lolly? You can make these delicious treats with one of those ice-pop moulds you can buy in supermarkets. Simmer together a cup of sugar and two cups of water until dissolved, then let cool. Purée or mash up two cups of blackberries, then stir into the sugar water. You could add a squeeze of lemon juice, rosewater or some chopped mint leaves if you're feeling fancy. Fill the ice-pop moulds with the mixture and stick in the freezer until frozen. Eat with a daisy chain on your head and juice dripping down your chin.

DANDELION COOKIES

The poor old dandelion gets a bad rep as being a weed, but it's actually highly nutritious, abundant and tasty. Dandelion leaves are good in risotto or salads, but my favourite things to make with the beautiful yellow flowers are these pretty, summery cookies.

Collect dandelion flowers using gloves, as the stems can stain your hands, and pick off the petals. Blend half a cup of oil and half a cup of honey with two eggs, then stir in one cup of flour, one cup of oatmeal and half a cup of loose petals. You can add vanilla or allspice too. Drop spoonfuls of the batter on an oiled baking tray and bake for 15 minutes, or until golden.

NETTLE SOUP

Ah, the classic foraging favourite – the humble nettle. Cooking nettles removes their sting and makes them harmless, filling and very good for you, packing in more vitamins than spinach. Nettles are also around for most of the year, so they're ideal for picking in winter when other goodies are scarce. When picking nettles, wear thick gloves and pick only the young, healthy leaves. When you get home, wash the nettles and then drop them into boiled water to remove their sting. Fry up some garlic and chopped onion until softened, then add the nettles and any other veg you have to hand – I like adding potatoes, leeks and courgettes. When all the vegetables are tender, season well and then blend with a hand-held blender – you can add crème fraîche to bulk the soup up.

4 HOMEMADE FORAGED LIQUEURS

Use nature's bounty to make merry. These easy-peasy recipes for homemade tipples made from foraged finds are great fun to make and brilliant given as gifts.

PETE'S (VERY) SLOE GIN

Super simple, this one – it's mainly just picking a punnet of sloes and adding them to a bottle of gin. You'll have to wait a couple of months for the flavours to do their thing, but the result is worth being patient for. The beautifully plum-coloured final drink packs a punch – perfect poured into little bottles and given out as presents.

INGREDIENTS
- 450g sloes
- 225g caster sugar
- 1 litre of gin

METHOD

Wash the sloes, then prick each one with a fork or needle and put the whole lot into a large jar. Pour in the sugar and the gin and shake it up, baby. Store the bottle in a dark cupboard and shake every day for a week, then leave for two months, shaking once a week. Strain the liquid with a fine sieve and bottle up.

FLORENCE'S LIP-SMACKING BLACKBERRY LIQUOR

Coming across a blackberry bush heavy with fruit is one of the headiest delights of a British summer. Fill your boots with berries and then make this easy liquor: try it poured over ice cream or serve it chilled on warm evenings.

INGREDIENTS
- 250ml water
- 500ml brandy
- three cups caster sugar
- three cups ripe blackberries

METHOD

Dissolve the sugar in the water on the stove and let it cool, then add the brandy. Mix in the blackberries and bottle up the mixture. Leave for at least a week, then strain. If you fancy making more of a syrup for puddings you can use half the amount of water.

ELDERFLOWER CHAMPAGNE

Okay, it doesn't really taste like champers, but elderflower bubbly is still lovely, and makes me think of festival weddings. It's a bit fiddlier to make than the other recipes here but extra special as a result.

INGREDIENTS
- 750g caster sugar
- five handfuls of elderflower flowers
- two lemons, zested and juiced
- 2 tbsp white wine vinegar
- pinch of dried yeast

METHOD

Pick the elderflowers and use while fresh. Pour 4.5 litres of warm water into a clean bucket and add the sugar, stirring until dissolved. Then pour in a further 1.5 litres of cold water. Add the elderflower heads to the bucket along with the lemon juice, zest and vinegar. Cover the bucket with a cloth and leave in a cool place for two days. Check the mixture – if it is not starting to foam, add the pinch of yeast and mix again. Cover and leave for another four days, allowing the mixture to ferment (tiny bubbles will appear in the liquid). Then strain through a sieve lined with muslin and pour into glass or plastic bottles with champagne lids. The brew can produce gas, which may cause the bottles to explode, so you'll need to let off gas regularly to prevent this. Seal the bottles and leave to stand for a week before serving chilled.

GROWING YOUR OWN

There's nothing more satisfying than chowing down on fresh fruit and veggies that you grew with your own fair hands, and it's easier to get a little garden of your own flourishing than you might think, even in tiny spaces.

5 GROWING YOUR OWN FRUIT AND VEGETABLES

How does your garden grow? If the answer is not very much and in a very small space, never fear – you can still nurture delicious fruit, herbs and vegetables in minuscule back gardens or on the teeniest of patios, even if you're a complete beginner and so non-green-fingered you could kill a plastic cactus.

Tending your own patch is one of the most calming and rewarding activities there is, and the perfect antidote to a long day staring at a computer. Gardening can also be wonderful exercise for both your body and your brain – you can't use your phone, you get outdoors and a bit muddy, and there's just something amazing about watching green shoots spring to life under your tender care.

If you've got a bit of back garden, a tiny patio or even a sunny windowsill you can grow stuff, and even if you don't have any of those, you can apply for an allotment patch in your local area or just join a gardening club or association – many cities have volunteer gardening gangs who pitch in a few hours of work at a community garden in return for a bag of fresh veggies. This is also a good option if you aren't always at home to look after your new green babies, or if you fancy learning the ropes before setting up your own garden patch.

Got a garden? Your soil needs to be at least a foot deep to give plants room to grow, and reasonably stone free. If your house has a mega-stony back yard you could spend a zen-like afternoon patiently removing them, or just get some builder's bags and raised beds to grow in instead. Dry dusty land won't yield much, either, so try working some natural fertilisers such as eggshells, ground coffee, veg peelings and dried, crushed seaweed into the soil and covering them up with topsoil.

You can plant directly into the soil, but a nice option for small gardens is to have raised vegetable beds. These are easy to make using wooden pallets or old wooden planks. Push the wood well down into the ground and nail the sides together to make a square container, then fill with soil.

You'll need to think about how much sunlight you have to play with. Vegetables and herbs usually like as much sun as possible. If you've got a shady courtyard, you could try growing berries and Swiss chard, which don't mind getting fewer rays. The other big enemies of a little veg plot are weeds and pests. You can remove weeds by hand, making sure you pull them out from the roots, or kill them by dousing with vinegar. Slugs and snails can be deterred with crushed eggshells, a copper strip barrier, salt, a cup of beer, or if you have to, and don't have pets, slug pellets.

Ready to get green? Try these easy beginner crops, following the instructions either on the seed packet or on a ready-grown plant's label.

IN A VEGETABLE GARDEN

Potatoes

WHEN TO PLANT: April–May
WHEN TO HARVEST: June–July
If your garden hasn't sprouted veggies before, then potatoes are a great place to start, as your first crop will actually improve the soil. Grow in trenches or in builder's bags. Slugs, unfortunately, LOVE potatoes, so you'll need to be on mollusc watch.

Courgettes

WHEN TO PLANT: April–May, in direct sun
WHEN TO EAT: July–September
Probably my favourite vegetable to eat. Courgettes are amazing with pasta, in salads and even in cakes, and they are a doddle to grow either in soil or in containers, and easy to grow from seeds. Courgettes need good moisture, and prefer warm soil – a good choice if you're starting your patch in late spring. Pick them when they are still courgette sized, or you'll end up with massive marrows.

Swiss chard

WHEN TO PLANT: April–June in direct sunlight
WHEN TO EAT: August–November
Pretty pink Swiss chard is notoriously hard to kill and tastier than boring lettuce. It doesn't mind cooler weather, either. When you collect leaves for your supper make sure you leave smaller clusters behind to grow.

ON YOUR PATIO

Even a tiny courtyard can be a green oasis if you grow edible goodies in pots. If space is really tight, try sticking your plants on wooden ladders or up steps. Choose pots at least 20cm in diameter, to give your plants space to grow. You can also buy compact versions of some salads and herbs which are ideal for a container garden. Keep your plants well watered, and top up compost in pots periodically.

Tomatoes

WHEN TO PLANT: March–April
WHEN TO EAT: when ripe and red in August–September
Eat a home-grown tomato fresh from the stalk and warm from the sun and your supermarket-bought ones will pale in comparison. Tomatoes aren't fussy – they'll grow in any container you like in the sunshine. You can encourage more fruit with a high-potash fertiliser.

Mediterranean herbs

WHEN TO PLANT: plant when you like in pots, keep indoors in winter
WHEN TO EAT: pick in summer and leave to recover in winter
Hardy herbs such as rosemary, thyme and oregano grow naturally on dusty Mediterranean mountains, so they don't mind a little bit of neglect, and they go beautifully in salads and with meat or potatoes. You can also buy compact versions of lots of herbs for tiny spaces. Grow in big pots in well-drained, gritty compost and water sparingly. Herbs like to be picked, and this encourages them not to grow up too straggly.

Chillies

WHEN TO PLANT: February–March
WHEN TO EAT: When the chillies are mature
Fiery chillies grow happily in pots in the sun, and as a tiny bit goes a long way when cooking with them, one plant should sort out all your spice needs. If you're starting them from seed, grow your plant indoors. Mature plants can cope with the outdoors in summer. Your chilli might not make it through the winter but you can dry its fruits to use for curries.

Strawberries

WHEN TO PLANT: April
WHEN TO EAT: When berries are plump and red
These lovely berries don't mind growing in compact spaces, and do well in hanging baskets, pots and wooden planters. They like the sun, and if you grow them somewhere elevated slugs won't get at them. Starter plants are the easiest for reaping sweet rewards – water whenever the soil is dry, and cover the plants in netting if birds are trying to get at the fruit.

In a builder's bag

Builder's bags make fantastic growing containers. Usually used to transport debris and waste materials, they are very tough, cheap (you can pick them up for around £5) and can take loads of compost – enough to grow bigger plants and house small veggie patches and even fruit trees. Fold the sides down a few times, fill the bottom with rubble or broken-up pots (called crocks) for drainage, and then cover in a few feet of multipurpose compost and use as a mini vegetable bed.

CRAFTY FOXES

Ready, steady, make! Channel your inner *Blue Peter* presenter
with these crafty projects for nimble (and not-so-nimble) fingers, plus
homemade candles, knits and jewellery to give as presents; quirky
wild houses; and inspiring outdoor photography projects.

6 (GIMME) SHELTERS

Rudimentary shelters are extremely useful in survival situations and for escaping extreme weather in the great outdoors. They're also just brilliant fun to stick up in a corner of the garden, and take me back to the days of making impenetrable forts out of sofa cushions.

FOR SURVIVAL

TARP SHELTER: If you don't have a tent then a well-placed waterproof tarpaulin is a good substitute, and a tarp and a rope take up little space in a backpack. If you're in a wooded area, it's the work of minutes to string your rope up between two trees and hang your tarp over it in the style of a traditional A-frame tent, keeping it low enough so there's just room for you and your sleeping bag inside. If you're stuck outdoors somewhere without any trees, search for big rocks or boulders – or anything tall you can tie one end of your tarp to. Then peg the other end tightly in the ground with a stick. Out in the desert with absolutely no features in the landscape? Wrap the tarp around you and your sleeping bag as a makeshift bivvy bag for extra insulation and waterproofing – it's still much better protection than nothing.

WOODLAND SHELTER: A forest offers up all the components you need to make a decent shelter. Start by wedging a big stick against a tree fork to make a slanting roof beam (or if you're lucky, you might find a fallen tree ready to use), then rest smaller branches against your main beam, tent style. Weave foliage and bark between these branches for more protection – the more you cover the structure, the better insulated your makeshift cabin will be. Insulate the floor of the shelter with leaves or fern fronds.

FOR FUN

BEACH HOUSE: Next time you're on a big beach with a decent amount of driftwood, have a competition with your mates to see who can make the most bangin' abode. Split into teams, collect debris and driftwood and let your imagination run wild. Blue fishing rope is good for tying all the bits and pieces together. Added bonus – when you're finished, you can take all the plastic you found home with you for an instant beach clean.

POW-WOW IN A TIPI: Hang out in the garden on a balmy summer's day in your own boho tent. Tipis remind me of my mum making houses for us in the back garden by draping a sheet across the washing line. Start with three sturdy branches of the same length. Push their ends into the earth a little to stabilise them, then tie the tops together with twine. Cover the tipi with old blankets and fill the inside with more blankets, cushions, fairy lights, whatever you fancy. Then invite people round – I find dogs and kids are always especially keen to come over.

7 # CRAFTS

PINECONE DREAM CATCHER

You may believe, as the Ojibwe people do, that hanging an intricate weaved web over your bedroom window will catch any bad spirits coming to visit in the night, leaving you to sleep soundly. Or you may just think a homemade dream catcher looks really pretty. I like collecting pinecones and other bits and bobs when on a favourite hike and taking them home to make into a dream catcher that then serves as a memory of that walk. If you aren't sure about the weaving bit, try watching a YouTube tutorial – it's a lot easier to watch someone make a dream catcher than it is to follow written instructions. But anyway, here goes:

1 Find a long piece of bendy wood (willow is ideal) and shape into a hoop, tying the ends with string to secure. You can also use the string to make a hanging loop. Wrap the hoop in strips of bright material if you'd like.

2 Weave a piece of string around the hoop. Begin at the top and wrap it round five or six times, until you arrive back at the top of the hoop.

3 Begin to weave around again, but this time, thread the string into the loops of the first row of string instead of around the hoop itself.

4 Repeat this in decreasing circles until you end up in the middle of the hoop.

5 Add a bead or a shell to the end of the string and tie off in a knot.

6 Hang string or ribbons from the bottom of the dream catcher and attach found objects to them – I like adding pinecones and feathers.

SOY CANDLES

Whether they line the banks of a river during a summer's midnight swim or keep your camp cosy when the dark tendrils of winter threaten, candles are the nicest illumination for nocturnal adventures. Traditional paraffin wax candles are not the best for the environment – save the planet and your pocket by making your own scented candles from soy wax instead. It's a lot easier than it sounds, and watching wax flakes slowly melt is strangely therapeutic.

You can buy soy wax flakes, wicks and wick holders online, and a kilo of wax will make at least four jam jar candles. Add your favourite essential oils – lavender will help you sleep and citronella is a natural mosquito repellent.

INGREDIENTS
- 250g soy wax
- 50 drops of essential oil
- one wick
- one wick holder
- a clean, dry jam jar or tin can

METHOD
Melt the soy wax flakes in a saucepan on a medium heat. When fully liquid, leave the melted wax to cool for five minutes, then add 50 drops of your chosen essential oil and stir. Pop a wick in a wick holder and place in the centre of the bottom of your jar. Pour in an inch of wax and leave to set. Once the first layer of wax is completely solid, pour in the rest of the wax and leave the candle to cool. These babies make great gifts, too – for a botanical vibe you could line the inside of the jar with dried leaves and flowers before you add the wax, or just write out a label for the front in your best handwriting.

WILLOW STARS

A quick and easy craft for Christmas, taught to me by the lovely Rebecca of Honeywoods Camping. You'll need a pliable stem – willow and dogwood are the best. Gather fresh stems and soak them in water for a day or two to make them soft and easy to work with. Fold the willow into a star shape, beginning with the narrow end of the stem. When it's complete, use some of the remainder of the stem to weave in and out of the final point of the star to secure it. Hang from the Christmas tree or string a line of stars above the mantelpiece.

CHEAT'S BOBBLE HAT

I approach knitting rather like guitar playing. In the latter, I mastered four chords and realised via sheer laziness that I could botch my way through a lot of songs with them. And in knitting

I've only learned to knit basic plain stitch, but I still make scarfs, blankets and hats with it. The basic stich is very, very easy to master – you're guaranteed to have a mum, granny or friend who can teach you, or there are loads of beginner-friendly YouTube tutorials online. And once you can knit you can make brilliant things to wear outdoors or to give as presents to friends (who will be forced to wear them out of politeness). The easiest project to try is a tube scarf. I use massive needles, which is very quick, and thick wool, as it hides myriad flaws. Simply knit a rectangle a little wider than your head (measure with some string around your forehead) and as long as your neck, and then sew the ends together with matching thread.

Once you can make a tube scarf, you can make a bobble hat. Knit a rectangle as wide as your head and long enough so that there's a bit extra above the crown of your head. Sew the ends of the rectangle together. Now tightly sew one end of the tube together, drawing the edges in as you go. Flip the hat inside out. Tada! And if the top of the hat looks a bit messy you can pop a pompom on top to hide your terrible sewing skills.

SEASIDE JEWELLERY

Show off how much of a water baby you are by making trinkets from beach finds. Spend a day searching for treasure in the sand – look around the high-tide mark, where the most plentiful offerings brought in by the waves tend to lie. Shells with small holes in are surprisingly easy to find, and can be threaded onto a chain or a leather thong. You're also likely to find bright orange and blue fishing rope, which is easily plaited into bracelets.

Jewels of sea glass rubbed to a smooth jade translucency by the ocean are rarer but a thrill to find.

To make a sea glass pendant, you'll need a chunk of glass, jeweller's wire, a chain and a jump ring. You can use a craft drill to make holes in thinner bits of glass, but it's much easier to just wrap the glass tightly with wire and then attach it via the jump ring to the chain.

HOW TO PAINT YOUR SURFBOARD

Transforming a boring surfboard into your own work of art is easier than you think. If you're a dab hand at illustration you can cover your stick in intricate patterns, and even if you're about as artistic as a potato you can still spray-paint on bold colours and stripes. This project is perfect for sprucing up a tired second-hand board, or if your old beginner board is so dinged and broken it's time for retirement you could paint it and stick it on your wall or in the garden.

METHOD
Start by completely removing all the wax on your surfboard. If your board has stickers pasted on it, you can remove them very carefully with a razor blade, or try leaving the board in the sun to warm up and then picking them off. Rub white spirits all over your board to clean it, and then rinse with water. If the board has designs glassed in (i.e. below the surface level) to the deck they are there to stay, but you can just paint over them. There are two simple ways to paint your board (you can use them both together, too).

YOU WILL NEED
▶ a surfboard with a fibreglass surface
▶ spray paints or Posca pens
▶ clear varnish
▶ masking tape

1 **Posca pens:** These water-based colour pens let you paint on all surfaces. Simply draw straight on your board, and then cover your final creation with a coat of clear varnish.

2 **Spray paint:** I like using Montana spray paint, which you can get on Amazon. You'll need a few different colours as well as a clear varnish with UV protection. Pick a sunny day and stick your board on struts in the garden. Use masking tape to cover any sections of the board you don't want to paint, then shake it up and spray away. Leave each coat of paint to dry completely before spraying on a fresh one. When your masterpiece is completely dry, spray the whole board with varnish, let it dry fully and then go hang ten on your beautiful creation.

8 OUTDOOR PHOTOGRAPHY TIPS

Photography is an amazing medium to play with in the great outdoors. Capturing anything from action images to surreal underwater shots and hazy pictures of lazy summer days is a wonderful way to record and look back on your adventures – one day you can show your grandkids just how badass Granny was.

We live in a constantly documented world, and the pressure to snap everything from your dog to your dinner can make it tempting to just point and shoot your camera in automatic without thinking much about the photo you're taking. But if you take the time to experiment with photography you might rediscover quite how beautiful an art form it is, and come away with touching and unusual photos of the world as you explore it. If you're feeling stuck for inspiration in the great outdoors, try one of these tweaks and techniques.

FAKE A FILTER

Pick up a cheap second-hand film camera at a flea market or car boot sale and experiment with making your own retro-feel filters. A pair of beige tights stretched over the lens gives a seventies look, and blue and green translucent sweet wrappers give a cool under water hue to photos. Much more fun than just letting Instagram do the job for you.

TAKE IT UNDERWATER

Buy a disposable waterproof camera or charge up a GoPro and dive beneath the surface to see what you can shoot. I like trying to create optical illusions of people walking on water by shooting a swimmer mid-dive (warning: a *lot* of seawater goes up your nose attempting this), or capturing landscape-style shots of an underwater seabed. If you're out wild swimming, try holding your camera half in, half out of the water for surreal shots of the worlds above and below the surface.

LIGHT IT UP
AFTER DARK

If you have a digital camera, stick it on a tripod and dial it down to a slow shutter speed (if you don't feel confident in manual, try Shutter Priority Mode) at night. Then play with shots of crackling fires, or light up a tent with a lantern and shoot it glowing against the landscape.

WADE INTO THE SEA

Wrap your camera in a plastic bag or a soft waterproof camera case such as an Aquapac and stand in the shallows (this is safest on a day with small waves). Getting into the sea gives much better photos of surfers and cool abstract shots of waves.

GO FOR GOLD

Force yourself to get up at dawn and go shoot the golden hour. The magical, fleeting few minutes when sunrise floods the landscape with soft warm colour creates the most beautiful landscape photos you'll ever take. Or if you're like me and you struggle to even talk before 6am, sunset is often just as lovely, ephemerally bathing summer camping scenes in golden light.

CREATE A DOUBLE EXPOSURE

Shoot a portrait of a friend (a shot in profile works best, and it needs to be against a clear sky or a plain wall), then take a photo of your favourite landscape and then splice them together. Some cameras can do this automatically (look for Multiple Exposure Mode in settings), otherwise you'll need to use Photoshop – there's an easy, step-by-step tutorial on techradar.com. Or you could go really old school and use a disposable camera to create weird double exposures. Shoot using a roll of film, then wind the film back to the first few photos and shoot again.

HEALTH AND BEAUTY

Stay happy and healthy outdoors with tips for everything from simple yoga stretches and how to deal with blisters, sprains and periods to advice for mermaids on keeping skin and hair protected from sun and salt water.

9 NATURAL BEAUTIES

If I could give any message to the intrepid ladies of our planet, it would be this: your body is amazing. It can power you up mountains. It can push you through waves. It can grow an entire human being inside it. Your body is *awesome*. Your body is also alive at a time where there is a hell of a lot of pressure placed upon it to look a certain way. It's easy to buy into the idea that to be considered feminine you must be willowy thin and too weak to wrench the lids off jam jars. But I'm much more interested in the word 'woman' meaning someone powerful, strong and able to thrive in her environment.

The beauty of all the sports and activities I've covered in this book is that they are all excellent ways to get fit and healthy without really noticing that that is what is happening. No jogging on a treadmill facing a blank wall for an outdoors lady – a run in the woods or a swim in the sea will work your muscles and get your heart rate up brilliantly, as well as fulfilling you in a way that the gym never can. I'm all for wanting to look and feel your best, but I don't believe denying yourself pleasure is the way to get there. The happiest, glowy-est women I've met are the ones who run through woods, cycle up hills and swim in the sea for the joy of it, and then eat cake and drink wine.

Let's champion loving our bodies for the amazing things they can do, and help them a bit by keeping them happy and healthy. Get outdoors and get active as often as you can – you'll never regret it and you'll never be bored. Instead, your limbs will be powerful, your hair will be sun streaked and your mind will be calm. I promise.

10 YOGA AND PADDLEBOARD YOGA

Namaste, ladies! Whether or not you want to go deep into the mental benefits of yoga, its physical ones are not to be denied. Yoga means unity, and helps you to become aware of your body, of its ability and of any aches and pains, and to work towards strength and mental relaxation. A yoga session just once a week will make you feel calmer, happier and far more flexible. And if you're mad keen on a particular sport, try adding yoga to your training routine – I guarantee you'll see an improvement in your performance. If you're a surfer or a climber, yoga will really help your core, and I find its focus on breathing really beneficial for running.

There are a ton of amazing and free yoga tutorials on the internet, but if you've never tried this ancient form of exercise before it's definitely best to get yourself to a class to learn the poses from a pro and get help perfecting them. You'll see the names of different kinds

of yoga (hatha, flow, ashtanga, etc.) bandied around – I suggest starting with a beginner's hatha class. All you need is a yoga mat – a mega-cheap, one-time investment for a habit that'll keep you flexible and strong for life. If you've gotten into yoga and want to fit it in after work or when you're travelling, try a quick yoga video – my favourite is the free, friendly and often hilarious Yoga With Adriene series.

Yoga is best of all practised outdoors. Rolling out your mat in a sunny garden is enough to get some vitamin D, or to really dial up your workout and work your core, try paddleboard yoga (yep, yoga on a paddleboard on the water). Pick a placid lake on a day with zero wind and keep the centre of your body above the paddleboard handle. It's not as hard as it sounds if you stick to the basic moves – Downward Dog is a cinch, or if you're feeling brave and you don't mind falling in, see if you can master a Tree (standing on one leg) or even a headstand.

Yogi sun salutation

The basic yogi sun salutation (Surya Namaskar) is a great warm-up for all sports, and a good way to stretch out after a run.

1 Stand at the top edge of your mat with your feet together. As you breathe in, lift your arms up from your sides. As you breathe out, bring them to your chest and press your palms together as if in prayer.

2 Breathe in and lift your still-touching hands up and over your head, stretching your back.

3 Breathe out and fold your upper body forward over your legs, bringing your hands down to the floor next to your feet. You can bend your knees a bit if you can't reach.

4 Breathe in and send your right leg back behind you as far as possible, toes on the ground. Rest your right knee on the floor. Look up.

5 Send your left leg back too – lift your knees and you'll end up in a plank position.

6 Breathe out and lower your body to the floor, touching down first with your knees, then your chest, then chin to the floor.

7 As you breathe in, slide forward, keeping your tummy engaged, look forward and up and raise your upper body with your palms, keeping your shoulders down, opening your chest forward. Make sure you don't slump into your lower back.

8 Breathe out and lift your bottom to send your body into an inverted V shape (yoga's famous Downward Dog). Aim for straightening your legs, but soften them if it's too tight in your hamstrings – you can pedal your feet a bit to loosen them. Make sure your tailbone is lengthening up and your hips are reaching back.

9 Breathe in and bring the right foot forward between your hands, the reverse of 4.

10 Breathe out and bring the left foot forward and stretch down, the reverse of 3.

11 Breathe in and roll your body up, bit by bit, and bring arms up and over the head to stretch your back with hands pointing to the ceiling, as in 2.

12 Breathe out and bring your body back to standing with arms by your sides, and relax. Repeat as many times as your chakra desires.

11 NATURAL HEALTH AND BEAUTY BITES FOR WONDER WOMEN

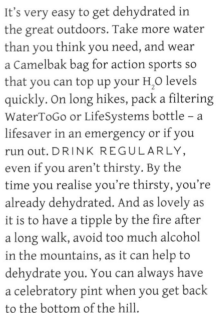

Any outdoors woman worth her salt should please, please WEAR SUNSCREEN. Pop it on in the mornings, even on overcast days. If you tend to be pretty active try P20, a clear spray which lasts all day. You're much more likely to burn at altitude and on snow or water, so be even more religious about sunscreen in those cases, and wear protective lip balm when snowboarding or surfing. If you burn very easily when you're doing sports, try a stick of zinc sunblock, cricket player-style – it's like wearing a layer of paint on your cheeks and nose, but no rays can penetrate it.

It's very easy to get dehydrated in the great outdoors. Take more water than you think you need, and wear a Camelbak bag for action sports so that you can top up your H_2O levels quickly. On long hikes, pack a filtering WaterToGo or LifeSystems bottle – a lifesaver in an emergency or if you run out. DRINK REGULARLY, even if you aren't thirsty. By the time you realise you're thirsty, you're already dehydrated. And as lovely as it is to have a tipple by the fire after a long walk, avoid too much alcohol in the mountains, as it can help to dehydrate you. You can always have a celebratory pint when you get back to the bottom of the hill.

Sea swimmers, surfers and mermaids, ahoy! TO LOOK AFTER YOUR FLOWING LOCKS, take a squirty bottle of conditioner with you to the beach and comb it into your hair before an underwater session. Honey is an effective natural conditioner, too.

Altitude sickness is hellish. Unfortunately, it can be all but inevitable if you're attempting to hike big peaks. The general rule is that if you're somewhere over 2,500 metres in altitude you should only ASCEND AROUND 300 METRES A DAY, to let your body adjust. Keep hydrated, take medication and don't ascend until your symptoms go away. The bad news is that altitude sickness seems to affect the young and fit the most. The plus side is that once you summit, you'll just feel better and better as you descend.

The ubiquitous COCONUT OIL really is wonderful slathered onto dry bits and frazzled hair, and also works brilliantly rubbed on the collar and cuffs of wetsuits to avoid chafing, and even as a chamois cream when you're on your bike.

Always WEAR LONG TROUSERS and closed shoes when walking anywhere ticks may be present (they tend to like woodland and grassy areas). If your trousers are loose, tie the cuffs tight with string. If you do get a tick bite, remove it by grasping near the head and pulling back. Tick remover tools and tweezers work too – just make sure the head doesn't stay in your skin. A small percentage of ticks carry Lyme disease. If after a tick bite you have symptoms including a red rash, a fever, a headache or nausea, go to see your doctor.

LAVENDER OIL and honey are both natural antiseptics and good for stings and scrapes.

Midge and mosquito bites are nasty little buggers at the best of times, and dangerous at the worst. COMBAT MIDGES with Avon Skin So Soft oil spray and a net over your face, and fight off mosquitoes with a spray containing at least 20% DEET. Always apply repellent *after* sunscreen, and be careful – it can lessen the protection sun cream gives your skin. If you're abroad, wear repellent both on exposed skin and on clothing, and sleep under a decent mosquito net.

Small injury from exercising? If it's a sprain or a strain, ICE IT AND ELEVATE IT. Heat is the best treatment for tired running muscles – try slapping a Deep Heat patch on the affected area, or just stick a tea towel in the oven on a low heat, then lay it on the aching muscle to help it loosen up.

You can SCRUB YOUR SKIN TO BABY-SMOOTH softness after a swim in the sea with wet sand, or by mixing sea salt and olive oil and rubbing all over, then showering off.

If you only pack one product for your next adventure, make it SUDOCREM (nappy rash cream). The antiseptic magic in each little pot works wonders on bites, rashes, spots and sunburn.

Got BIKE OIL all over your hands? Wash them with a mix of sugar and washing-up liquid for soft, clean mitts.

Yay, periods! Surfing the crimson wave is a bloody nuisance, pun intended. If it makes you want to crawl into bed and avoid the outdoors for a week, then I hear you. But I promise (backed by science and everything) that if you can FORCE YOURSELF OUTSIDE for a bit of exercise you'll feel better. Do not, I repeat, do not let periods get in the way of doing anything that you love. If Olympians can compete and Victorian lady explorers could navigate jungles on their periods, so can you. Pack some industrial-strength tampons and painkillers and go do it. It's astonishing how many women aren't sure if they can swim while Aunt Flo is in town. You most definitely can – wear a tampon or try a silicone cup, or if it's towards the end of your period and you're in the ocean or a lake just go in au naturel. Free bleeding is also an option if you don't feel comfortable using tampons when long-distance running.

Blisters are a bitch, and are better avoided than treated. Never go out on a long hike in boots you haven't tested (I discovered this to my chagrin 20 kilometres into the Welsh hills). BOOTS NEED TO FIT your feet perfectly, and some need wearing in before a big hike. Wear decent walking socks, and check your boots aren't too loose or too tight around your heels. The jury is out on whether to burst a blister once you've got one. I always burst mine and pop a bandage on them – you risk infection this way, but my logic is that if you're going to keep walking with a blister then it'll burst soon anyway. I also like to walk around barefoot as much as possible in the summer to harden my soles. Your feet will definitely not be auditioning for sandal adverts any time soon, but they'll be tough as nails.

Camping while surfing the crimson wave? WET WIPES ARE YOUR FRIEND for makeshift showers. Wrap used tampons up in a bit of bog roll and stick them in a Ziploc bag to carry out of the camp with you. Or try a Mooncup – they are far more eco-friendly (and cheaper) than other options. By the way, it's total rubbish that bears can smell blood and come to eat you if you're out camping in the USA or the Arctic, or, indeed, that sharks will want to eat you if you're swimming in the ocean on your period.

BE A PRO AT LONG-HAUL FLIGHTS by bringing the right kit to help you sleep in the sky. Before I board a plane, I like to slap on as much of the really posh overpriced moisturiser samples from Duty Free as I can (or as much as the beady-eyed sample ladies let me). Then I take off my shoes and pop on warm socks. I also pack moisturiser and lip balm (as aircraft air dries out your skin big-time), a neck cushion, an eye mask and earplugs. Sweet dreams!

SECTION FOUR
WANDERLUST

The purpose of life is to live it, to taste experience to the utmost,
to reach out eagerly and without fear for newer and richer experience.
ELEANOR ROOSEVELT

BROADEN YOUR HORIZONS and scratch your wanderlusting itch with this rip-roaring guide to the essentials of joyful travelling and trips of all sizes.

First, be prepared, Girl Scout style, by buying and packing the right gear. Stock up with my essential kit list for wild women, make a car-boot adventure box and a basic first aid kit and learn how to keep all your shiny new possessions in good nick.

Let's hit the road. At the start of our travel itinerary are easy weekends away and adventures with gangs of friends, including tips on where to stay and crowd-pleasing games to play. Anyone for a round of sardines?

Next, we'll boogie on into the ins and outs of that time-old summer staple, the music festival – their ambrosial delights, their terrible toilets, and how to stay bright-eyed and bushy-tailed while you dance up a storm in a muddy field.

Then spin the globe and leave on a jet plane with tips for happy global travelling, a little boost of bravery for women voyaging solo and plenty of ways to turn your trip into a whole new life by working or volunteering overseas. Get your passport ready and make sure you pack a diary to record all the wonderful sights you see. After all, you'll never be this young and free again.

1 BUYING THE RIGHT KIT

To quote famed fell-walker Alfred Wainwright, 'there's no such thing as bad weather – only unsuitable clothing'. After all, human beings manage to successfully explore some of the harshest environments on our planet, and you could argue that their accomplishments are as much down to good planning and good packing as to bravery and derring-do.

The ever-growing outdoor gear world is stuffed with choice and a *lot* of jargon (ultra-lightweight microporous polytetrafluoroethylene membrane, anyone?), and there's plenty of specialist equipment on offer that you simply don't need if you aren't planning on scaling K2 or crossing the Sahara any time soon. But it makes sense to own a basic amount of versatile, good-quality gear

and clothing you can use on most adventures, and I've put together a list of the essentials I reckon a keen outward-bound woman should arm herself with.

Adventure-appropriate kit can be painfully expensive, especially if you just walk into an outdoors shop and ask a sales assistant to fling at you everything you need for, say, a hiking trip. Shopping around will get you much better deals. Try outlet shops, look for lightly used second-hand gear on eBay, Gumtree and in army surplus stores, raid your friend's attic for a serviceable tent and your mum's wardrobe for an old ski jacket. Own-brand outdoor clothing from big warehouses like Decathlon and GO Outdoors can also be very cheap yet serviceable. Some items can be scrimped on (well-cared-for

second-hand layers, for example), but some simply cannot. If you're shopping for climbing kit, bike parts, waterproof clothing, hiking boots, sleeping bags or anything else you're going to have to depend on to keep you warm, dry or safe, cough up the money and go for something of good quality.

The easiest way to save money on kit is boring but obvious – look after the equipment you already own and you'll add years to its life. Clean, dry and air tents and camping kit after every trip. Let waterproofs dry before storing, and re-proof regularly with wax or with a waterproofing solution such as Nikwax. Muddy hiking boots should be scrubbed clean and regularly re-waterproofed or polished. Down jackets and sleeping bags are best washed only when really pongy. Use a down cleaning solution and then tumble dry on a low heat or dry outside on a hot day so they retain their puff. A lot of small rips and tears in fabric can be fixed by sewing with waterproof

thread or, at a pinch, patching with duct tape. And one benefit of buying well-made gear from eco-conscious companies such as Patagonia, Finisterre or Barbour is that they'll often repair your item for free or for a small fee.

Until very recently, most female-specific outdoors kit was a bit of an embarrassment, usually following the 'shrink it and pink it' maxim – taking a piece of men's gear, resizing it and selling it in a sickly shade of blush or purple (bleurgh). The market is changing fast, though, and brands are figuring out that women 1) do actually venture outside regularly, and 2) perhaps don't want to wear a fluffy, acid-pink fleece while they do so. Most outdoor companies can now be relied on to design clothing specifically for the female figure, and often pieces are so cool you'll wear them happily in the city as well as in the mountains (surf and snowboarding brands are especially good at this). If all else fails I'll often just buy a small size in men's gear – it usually fits fine.

2 THE WILD GIRL'S ESSENTIAL KIT LIST

If you're getting into regular adventuring, I suggest investing in a 'starter pack' of versatile kit that'll do you proud on camping trips, winter walks and weekends away. You can always rent or borrow anything else you need.

- Warm waterproof jacket (a lightweight ski jacket is a good all-rounder)
- A down or insulated jacket
- Waterproof trousers
- Waterproof hiking boots
- Wellington boots
- Snow boots
- Comfortable trainers
- Sports sandals

- A decent wetsuit (a 4/3 will see you through most seasons)
- A decent, sports-friendly swimsuit
- A tough, waterproof rucksack (or one with a good rain cover)
- A tough, waterproof duffel bag

- A dry bag (these are waterproof bags with tops you fold over to seal them)
- A sun hat
- A knitted beanie
- Sunglasses with a minimum UV protection of 99%
- Warm, ideally waterproof gloves
- Fluffy dog (optional)

CAR BOOT ADVENTURE KIT

Impromptu, last-minute adventures are probably my favourite of all. Be ever-ready by keeping a crate or a big tote bag full of outdoorsy basics in the boot of your car. That way you'll never come across a secret swimming hole or a shady camping spot and experience terrible FOMA (fear of missing adventures) when you realise you haven't packed your bathers or a tent.

- Tent (just a cheapie four-man will do)
- Sleeping bag
- Wetsuit
- Swimsuit
- Towelling changing robe (essentially towels with arm and head holes you can change under)
- First aid kit
- Small stove
- Spare gas canister
- Tin cups and bowls
- Packaged camping food (it keeps forever)
- A few big bottles of water
- A plastic bucket (great for storing damp wetsuits or for doing a quick beach clean)
- Chocolate biscuits
- Beer (don't judge me)

Build a first aid kit

First aid is an invaluable skill to have anywhere, but it's especially important in the back of beyond for treating yourself or others. Keep a kit in your car and pack a soft mini kit bag for overnight treks and travelling. Nag your work to see if you can get free first aid training, or pay for a course with a local college or the Red Cross (redcrossfirstaidtraining.co.uk). Useful components of a first aid kit include:

- Scissors
- Sterile gloves
- Non-adhesive dressing
- Sterile compress
- Medical tape
- Gauze bandages
- Sterile eye dressing
- Antibacterial ointment
- Disinfectant wipes
- Thermometer
- Tweezers
- Insect repellent
- Energy gel
- Painkillers
- Antihistamine tablets
- Distilled water
- First aid manual

A NOTE ON KNIVES

A decent sharp knife is a massive help on camping trips and for learning wilderness skills, but make sure you know the law before you whip one out for a spot of whittling. In England, carrying knives which lock open or fixed-blade knives with blades longer than three inches is illegal, unless you've got them out specifically for an appropriate reason, such as cooking or gutting a fish. Often-used

Opinel knives, for example, lock open, and are thus technically illegal, while Swiss Army Knives are legal (as their blades are smaller than three inches). Use good sense and don't carry one unless you really need to use it immediately.

Cheap and cheerful presents for free-ranging friends

Outdoorsy types are maybe the easiest people of all to buy presents for, as any bits and pieces of gear you give them will get them extremely excited for their next little adventure. But if you need a bit of inspiration, try buying or making your travel-mad mate one of these little beauties – they all usually cost under £20.

- Flint and steel
- Set of tin cups
- Hand-knitted neck warmer (see my tips on knitting on page 160)
- Citronella candle (these repel mosquitoes naturally, and you can make your own by adding citronella oil to my soy candle recipe on page 159)
- Homemade bunting or tent flags
- Towelling changing robe
- Keep Cup (plastic, reusable coffee cup for eco-warriors)

- Thermos
- Wetsuit booties
- Head torch
- Lip balm with SPF
- Waterproof wash bag
- Rash vest
- Small cycling tool kit

3 ADVENTURES WITH FRIENDS

Where do you want to explore this weekend? For me, poring over a map and a guidebook with a cup of coffee and dreaming up all the places I could go is arguably just as fun as the actual going bit. I start with the two big factors – transport and the weather. If you have your own car it's a lot easier to simply hit the road to somewhere new and play things by ear. If you're using public transport (a much more eco-friendly option, well done you!) then the wildest corners of the country might be a bit tricky to get to, and staying in a town or a village with a train station, or at least a bus stop, is going to make more sense. You can then use it as a base to walk or cycle off into the surrounding countryside.

What's the weather looking like? If the skies are clear then camping combined with the Wild Adventures from Section Two will be right up your street – you could research a campsite and find a nearby wild swimming

spot, or plan a lazy pub-hopping cycle. If it's freezing or pouring, you'll probably have more fun renting a little cottage via Airbnb (airbnb.co.uk) – that way you have a host on hand who you can pump for information on the local area,

GOOD TIMES!!

Siân! Jon Leo Flox Spacey x Fredx Lucyx Tom Arlene Peter ! WEST BAY APRIL 2013 too. Even if it is bucketing down it's always worth going for a walk, just so you can sit by a fire in a pub for the rest of the afternoon feeling all smug about how intrepid you are.

BIG GROUPS

Gathering up a gaggle of mates can feel like herding cats, but it's definitely worth the effort when everyone finally makes it to the countryside together for a weekend of picnics, games and gentle bickering. Figuring out where to stay is easier than you might think – although big houses and bunkhouses can look expensive at first glance, if you split the cost between 10 or 12 of you for a few nights it tends to work out to be reasonably affordable.

Try the Youth Hostel Association's Exclusive Hire (exclusive-hire.yha.org.uk) for lovely bunkhouses, coastal houses and big cottages, all cheap, cheerful and often sleeping bazillions of people – great if you're planning a massive reunion. For something smarter, the National Trust's bigger holiday cottages, sleeping up to 16 (nationaltrustholidays.org.uk) are all in beautiful pockets of the country and are uniformly gorgeous (and you get free shortbread). To really push the boat out for a special occasion you can't beat the Landmark Trust's quirky historic properties (landmarktrust.org.uk) – private sea fort for the weekend, anyone?

And, of course, a campsite is the cheapest way to get together of all – some will even rent out the whole site or a separate field to a group.

BACK GARDEN FESTIVALS AND MOVEABLE FEASTS

If you've got (or can borrow) a biggish garden, then throwing your own mini festival is a lot easier than you think, and definitely less hassle than trying to get Glastonbury tickets. Get creative with the space you have – favourites of mine include when Jake's dad's band set up in the garden polytunnel, strung up loads of fairy lights and invited the neighbours round for a summer gig, and when a cow barn was completely transformed into a party den complete with disco balls. Bunting, decorated sheets and outdoor lights will instantly transform a bog-standard back garden into something special. And watch out for rolls of old lino in skips – they make a surprisingly good dance floor. Even if your garden is minuscule, you could haul dining tables outside for an al fresco dinner party, or just set up a campfire in the middle and invite your friends round for an evening of marshmallow roasting. If you don't want to scorch the ground, invest in a fire pit – you can pick them up for around £40.

GAMES TO PLAY WITH LITTLE KIDS AND BIG KIDS

Sardines

This is my absolute favourite group game. You'll need a biggish house or an outdoor space with a lot of nooks and crannies to hide in. One person is the hider, and while they run off and ensconce themselves somewhere, everyone else counts to 100. The seekers then split up and hunt the hider out. When you find the hider, you have to hide with them, cramming yourself into the tiny space they've chosen and trying desperately not to give yourselves away by giggling too loudly. The next person to find you hides too, until you end up with 20 people crying silent tears of laughter and one poor person fruitlessly searching for you all (but they get to hide first next time).

French cricket and rounders

Easy, beach-friendly crowd pleasers from my childhood. All you need for French cricket are a bat and ball, and jumpers work as posts for rounders.

Treasure hunts

You can either nominate a hunt master to make up a series of clues leading to a treasure and then solve them as a group, or split into two teams – each one plans a treasure hunt for the other team using a certain amount of clues, and then both teams race to finish first.

The cardboard box game

This weirdly hilarious game was a favourite when I was at university. Place a cereal box on the floor. Each contestant has to stand over it and attempt to pick up the box with their teeth – no knees or elbows may touch the ground. When you've had a round of eliminations, cut an inch off the top of the box and go again, reducing the height of the box in stages until you've all fallen over in the attempt to pick it up and a winner is crowned. Careful not to rip your jeans.

Sock wars

Another game likely to cause extreme mirth. Sit opposite your contestant, both with socks on, and wrestle until one of you has denuded the other of both socks. Then another contender can take on the reigning sock champion.

Camping Olympics

Welcome, ladies and gentlemen, to Camping Olympics. Here you'll witness the astonishing sporting prowess of teams from different countries (or tents) taking on amazing challenges in their chosen sport – the long jump, the javelin, the tug of war, the three-legged race and, of course, the egg and spoon race. The more ridiculous your substitutes for proper sports, the funnier it is. You could even have an aquatic round if you're near somewhere safe to swim. Don't forget cardboard medals for the awards ceremony.

4 HOW TO SURVIVE A FESTIVAL

Ahh, the summer music festival. What an institution. They look so sunkissed and flower child-filled in photos that it can be a bit of a culture shock to arrive to a mud bath full of sweaty tents, dodgy-looking street food and hipsters in tiny shorts. That's not to say that you can't have a tremendous time at a festival. They tend to be places of wonderful highs, such as sitting around a campfire with daisies in your hair as the sun sets and a folk band strum their ukuleles ... and crushing lows, such as being violently sick on your friend's wellies, or having to visit any festival toilet there has ever been. You gotta take the rough with the smooth.

Not sure if festie life is your thing? Once strictly for the psychedelically inclined, these days there's a festival to cater for pretty much any music taste or lifestyle choice. You can embrace world music at Womad, flaunt your fashion credentials at Coachella, go nuts in the desert at Burning Man, or go dirty mosh-pit crazy at Reading or Leeds. You can live it up in style at genteel Port Eliot or Wilderness, get a literary fix at Hay, or even meet like-minded adventure folk at Base Camp Festival. My favourites are the teeny tiny festivals, the kind that cost about £50 for a weekend and have a lineup of bands you definitely haven't heard of, because they tend to be friendly, stress free and easy to navigate.

The trick to being a happy reveller is pacing yourself. Once you've seen the programme you'll want to pack as many band sets, theatre shows, swing dance classes and fire breathing demonstrations into your days as you can, especially at events with lots of different stages and areas, but that way exhaustion lies. My best festival experiences have always been when lost in a random healing field, or stumbling past an out-of-the-way circus tent or an impromptu ceilidh and ending up partying there all night. Explore the little fields and quiet corners – they tend to be more proper fun than trying to catch a glimpse of the Saturday headliner from a sea of jostling people.

Festival street food is usually delicious and often quite healthy, but it definitely isn't cheap. Bringing in your own fruit, snacks and alcohol (check the rules on booze first) will keep costs down, but do try to carry around a bottle of water even if you're on the cider – a hot sticky festival plus lots of alcohol is a fast route to getting sick. Take cat naps, especially in the heat of the day.

After a day or two you will be smelly, but so will everyone else. If you're feeling particularly grubby, search out a shower block, if there is one on site. My mate Flo and I used to deal with the Glastonbury morning horrors by washing each other's hair under the taps (that's friendship right there). If you aren't a fan of attempting to sluice your locks with fairy liquid in a sink every morning, then there are clever ways of disguising less-than-fresh festie hair. Well, there are essentially two options – plait, braid or wave your hair, or camouflage its misery with bright hats and headdresses.

The joy of being in a field full of bohemians is that you can wear pretty much anything you like and get away with it. In fact, it might make you new friends. If you fantasise about wearing gold jumpsuits, unicorn horns and rainbow face paints, but are hampered by the social norms of daily life, now is your time to shine.

FESTIVAL ESSENTIALS PACKING LIST

Bring the camping kit from Section Two (page 97), plus:

▶ **LOO ROLL**: take twice as much as you think you need

▶ **TENT AND SLEEPING BAG**: don't get precious about them. They will return home covered in graffiti and smelling like other people's wee – that is the festival law. If you have a lovely tent you take on chilled-out camping trips, buy a separate festival one that you won't cry over

▶ **PAINKILLERS**: essential for breakfast

▶ **WET WIPES** or a flannel in a wash bag: a makeshift shower

▶ **WELLIES**: if you take them, it'll be sunny. If you don't, it'll chuck it down

▶ **DEODORANT**: please

▶ **FANCY DRESS**: obligatory. Take some with you to avoid the temptation to spend £15 on a lime green jester's hat once you're there

▶ **MAC IN A SAC**: folds up small. Again, it won't rain if you bring one

▶ **FLAG OR BUNTING**: to mark out your camp in a sea of dark green tents

▶ **SUNSCREEN**: heatstroke ain't fun

▶ **TORCH**: avoid breaking your leg by tripping over someone else's guy rope at 3am

▶ **BIN BAGS**: incredibly useful for rubbish, storing dirty clothes, fixing holes in your tent…

▶ **SNACKS**: take cereal bars and peelable fruit (it may be the only vitamin C you have all weekend)

▶ **DRINKS**: but avoid anything in glass bottles, as it's usually prohibited – boxed wine and mixers in plastic bottles are the best

5 HAPPY TRAVELLING

Wherever you wander, try to embrace local culture as much as possible. Avoid tourist hotspots and venture further afield instead – it's usually a lot more interesting to explore the areas where locals actually live and work than busy city centres. Don't stay in posh hotels – you'll make a lot more friends in smaller hostels, or even better, in homestays. Be respectful and aware of local customs, including dress codes (sadly often stricter for women – it's a good idea to always carry long trousers and a scarf in some countries, especially if you're visiting any religious sites). Try the local food – life's too short not to eat

HOW TO BE A HAPPY TRAVELLER

Travelling will open your mind to colourful new cities, mesmerising wild landscapes, strange customs and the wonders of Imodium. There's nothing that'll leave you richer in experiences (if not in pocket) than a plane ticket to somewhere your eyes have never feasted on before. One warning, though: if you travel to try to sate your wanderlust, beware. It will only grow.

Take the plunge and buy that ticket. The first feeling is a warm glow of excitement, of exhilaration. You're really going! After that it's easy to start overthinking. Try not to worry about travel's inherent element of unknown – that's the whole appeal. Getting as clued-up as you can on your destination is an excellent idea; worrying that everything will go wrong is not. When I get nervous before a big trip I remind myself that I've voyaged to a lot of places, often on my lonesome, and have been mugged exactly once – in Bath, at one time voted the second-safest city on the planet.

delicious street cart goodies – and learn to say at least *hello*, *please* and *thank you* in the local tongue, even if you have to plunge into English after that.

Be prepared to be very patient, and very flexible. You're not in Kansas anymore, Toto. Other countries run to the beat of their own drum, and as hair-pullingly stressful as it can feel when travel plans get delayed or cancelled, it's not the end of the world if you don't stick to a strict itinerary. You'll have a much better time if you aren't trying to 'tick off' (a phrase I detest) a ton of places in just a few weeks. The best travel memories usually happen when you relax into your new home for at least a few days and start to learn how it ticks.

BEFORE YOU GO

▶ Check if you need, and book appointments for, travel vaccinations; fitfortravel.nhs.uk lists country-specific requirements

▶ Find out if you need to apply for a visa

▶ Make sure you have enough prescription medication for your trip

▶ Buy travel money

▶ Buy travel insurance. If you're travelling more than once a year, a 12-month policy is usually the best value for money

▶ Let your bank know you'll be abroad. Sometimes they'll cancel your card anyway, just to be difficult, but at least you'll have tried

▶ Buy a guidebook

▶ Check for local events and festivals, either so you can make sure you're there in time to party or so that you're aware of which places are likely to be busy and hard to get a room in

▶ Check your phone's roaming charges, and buy a travel package if you need one

What to pack for happy travels

▶ Passport
▶ Thick socks for kipping on the plane
▶ Earplugs for noisy hostels
▶ Tampons (not always available in other countries)
▶ Condoms (ditto)
▶ Painkillers and medication
▶ More spare pants than you think you need
▶ A decent hard suitcase
▶ A backpack and waterproof backpack cover
▶ Antibacterial hand gel
▶ Mini bottle of clothes detergent
▶ Filtering water bottle
▶ Plug adapters
▶ Cash (stored in different places)
▶ A spare set of clothes in your hand luggage, in case your main bag goes walkabout
▶ Physical photocopies of your passport

SOLO TRAVEL TIPS

6

Hey lone wolf! The pleasures and perils of travelling on your own are something I get asked about a lot. I am here to tell you that not only is going solo going to be FINE, you might even end up loving it. One-woman-band travelling offers something really special – the chance to see the world at your own pace. Explore a country or a city exactly how you'd like to and set your own agenda. Spend hours in galleries, sleep on beaches, trek in jungles, meet new mates or just find yourself, maaan. If you're taking the plunge and booking a ticket for one, I've got some practical advice for staying safe and feeling happy and at home.

It's totally okay to be nervous about heading to a new country. You are BRAVE. Put those nerves to good use by throwing yourself into research. Get a guidebook, figure out the in-country transport you want to take, give yourself a loose budget and look online for guides and information. It is worth checking for advice for women travelling alone to your destination, too (often you'll find this section in the back of guidebooks).

When I travel with a friend I'll happily get on any plane, rock up in a random city and assume it'll all work out in the wash. When I'm on my own I'm far more organised, and will

always book a decent, well-reviewed hostel for the first few nights so I have a safe, easy base while I get to know a new place.

If you aren't sure if a ticket for one is your cup of tea, try booking a long weekend in a city you've always wanted to visit. Make a list of lots of things to do – the time will fly by, and you won't even notice how much fun you're having, just doing you. Or if you're keen to

find a gang of like-minded lady travellers to hang out with, try a sports holiday for instant friends. For example, Surf Sistas (surfsistas.com) offer Costa Rican road trips for female surfers, and Girls for Sail (girlsforsail.com) will get you navigating a yacht with an all-girl crew in the limpid waters of the Caribbean.

TIPS FOR SOLO LADY EXPLORERS

▶ Try staying at hostels to meet other travellers
▶ Make yourself talk to new people – it gets easier and easier
▶ See your trip as a space to breathe and to learn to be alone with yourself
▶ Accept that you might not feel totally comfortable for a few days. Your imagination will eventually get tired and stop scaring you, promise
▶ Don't hide in the safety of your hotel in the evenings – go out and have dinner. Take a book if you need something to do
▶ Start slow, be kind to yourself and be proud of what you're doing. A weekend in Stockholm can be as big a solo adventure as backpacking through India

You're far less likely to get any unwanted attention from strangers than you may think, but if you do, stay calm and don't get angry. If it's in the street, just ignoring advances is safest. If you're already in a conversation, claiming to be married to a heavyweight boxer and the mother of four charming children is a good initial line. A solo traveller in India even told me that she found telling would-be admirers she was pregnant was a fast track to being left in peace

If you're walking around a busy city and feel a bit vulnerable, walk with purpose, even if you're lost. You can always duck into a café to regroup and figure out where you are

Need to look at a map? Don't walk around staring at your phone or carrying your guidebook up in front of your face – you may as well write 'tourist' on your forehead. My more subtle way of navigating new streets is to grab a free city map or rip out a street map from an unsuspecting guidebook, fold it small and carry it around in my pocket or my palm to check discreetly

If I'm in a safe, exciting new city my tactic for exploring is to deliberately lose myself in its streets and markets – you see a lot more by wandering away from the centre. Just remember the name of where you're staying and carry taxi money with you

Do what makes you feel safe. Trying new things is good, but so is just getting a taxi home if you find yourself somewhere dodgy, or bowing out of a mega-boozy night with travellers you just met and aren't sure about

When it comes to positive communication with people who don't speak your language, a smile goes a very long way

7

BIG ADVENTURES

See the world beyond the glossy pages of travel magazines on a long-term trip – it's likely to change everything, from your career direction to your confidence in yourself.

If you want to pack a lot into a month or two, ready-made itineraries and overland trips from companies such as STA Travel (statravel.co.uk) are easy, planning-free options – you could be crossing the heart of Africa on a Dragoman bus or island-hopping in Asia at the click of a button, although it won't come cheap. Adventure-minded travel companies often offer good deals on multi-stop flights if you want to plan your own planet-encircling journey. I defy you not to be seduced by the idea of buying a ticket labelled LA – New York – Bangkok – Sydney – Fiji – Auckland – London. Or save money (and the planet) with an epic train trip – Interrail's (interrail.eu)

Global Pass lets you hop in and out of no less than 30 European cities.

For a mental and physical challenge, seek out an expedition-style trip. World Challenge (world-challenge.co.uk) specialises in bucket-list adventures for young people, including trekking to Everest Base Camp and climbing up Mount Kilimanjaro, and specialist companies such as Secret Compass (secretcompass.com) take teams far from the beaten track to tackle remote river crossings, follow reindeer migrations and complete the first ascents of glacial peaks.

And for the adventurous of heart yet light of purse, there's always a classic backpacking trip. Taking overland transport in a slow, snaking route across a continent is an excellent way to get under the skin of it. If you're leaving with a knapsack on your back try to pack as light as possible, travel as the locals do and try Couchsurfing (couchsurfing.com) to keep your pennies going for longer.

VOLUNTEERING

Giving a little back by offering your skills for free is a wonderful way to travel. The right project will let you see your efforts lead to real change, and spending a few months based in one place really helps you integrate with local people and culture, too. When I volunteered in Bolivia I ended up dancing in costume in an island festival, staying with a tribe on the Amazon and even going to a local wedding. And if you've just graduated from university or are considering a new career, volunteering is also a fantastic way to take a sabbatical, gain new skills in a different field and add something special to your CV.

Be savvy when searching for somewhere to give your time to. There are a lot of dodgy companies looking to make a quick buck by offering 'volunteer' schemes that cost tons of money to take part in. Please don't pay out loads of dosh so you can spend a week cuddling baby lions in Africa (as nice as that sounds). Instead, pick a smaller organisation or charity which either hosts volunteers for free, or charges a small fee for bed and board. Then agree to an established amount of hours per day – six is usually the maximum, so that you also have time to enjoy exploring where you're staying. Look online for opportunities in the country you're headed to. In South America, for example, the simple website volunteersouthamerica.net offers a massive list of free volunteering placements you can start your research with.

WWOOFING (working on organic farms across the world, wwoof.net) is great for solo travel – you get bed and board in exchange for four to six hours of farm work a day in a beautiful rural location, and there are usually lots of other Wwoofers to make friends with. Join the WWOOF organisation of the country you're headed to – you could find yourself picking tomatoes on a Tuscan estate, or working on a horse ranch in Guatemala. HelpX (helpx.net) and Work Away (workaway.info) operate on a similar system, and placements are reviewed by past visitors. It's a good idea to pick a host who takes multiple workers at once, so you end up with a bevvy of friends to explore with.

There are also larger organisations offering well-run volunteer placements. I'm a big

advocate of the government-run International Service (internationalservice.org.uk), a scheme sending volunteers to disadvantaged countries for three-month placements. You work on established projects in the local community (helping women in Burkina Faso to set up new businesses, for example) and receive a living allowance. Professionals with teaching or medical experience can also head overseas with Voluntary Service Overseas (vsointernational.org) for similar long-term placements. And if you're over 25 you could work as a team leader for charities and organisations such as Raleigh International (raleighinternational.org) and the British Exploring Society (britishexploring.org), helping to take young people on international expeditions and volunteering trips around the globe.

WORKING ABROAD

Using your skills in another country and getting paid for it is the holy grail for wandering souls. Avoid any companies offering you gap-year 'work' or help with visas, as it often comes with hefty fees or terrible pay. You're better off searching for a legitimate job which suits your skills. Teaching English abroad is a failsafe and often decently paid way to see the world. If you have a university degree you could get a teaching job with the British Council (britishcouncil.org), or pay to train for the TEFL qualification (Teaching English as a Foreign Language – tefl.org.uk) – once you have it, it's a lot easier to bag a good job at a reputable international English school. Seasonal work in ski resorts is easy to come by and tremendous fun, and while the pay isn't great, you'll get to live in a winter wonderland and go skiing or boarding every day. Try Natives.co.uk for seasonal vacancies. Explorers Connect (explorersconnect.com) is a good resource for international jobs, and also lists opportunities to join expeditions and international adventures. I also like Escape the City (escapethecity.org), which posts paid opportunities of all kinds, filtered by where they claim to be on the spectrum from 'safe' to 'wild'. Sounds like a challenge.

ACKNOWLEDGEMENTS

This book would be little more than a vague idea in my head if it weren't for the amazing and adventurous people who've helped it come to life. Thank you all.

THANK YOU to all the FANTASTIC FRIENDS AND TRAVEL COMPANIONS who let me photograph them on our adventures big and small. What a roll call of inspiring, much-loved names.

In order of appearance: Valerie Hopkins, Mary Spender, Annie Brooks, Sarah Thain, Donna Ellen Jenkins, Helen Isaacs, Beren Neal, Peter Butler, Elyse Farhi, Malika Belhajjam, Leo Fortey, Matt Stott, Charlie Newman, Tom Anderson, Maria Hodson, Claire Gillo, Richard Welbirg, Gavin Kennard, Chris Morrell, Jillian Henderson, Angelica Sykes, Lauren Williams, Frankie Stott, Jacob Little, Florence Fortnam, Sam Little, Cara Richards, Sian Sykes, Cal Major, Emma Bell, Lisa McCarten, Sam Howard, Lydia Mawle, Rebecca Braund, Athene Gadsby, Drew Shwartz, Timmy the dog, Harry Neill, Lisa Worthington, Robert Downs Jr, Anni Kasari, Mark Fothergill, Yeliz Mert, Lula the dog, Jenny Ainscough, Florence Brockway, Katy Livesey, Rachel Verity, Alexandra Holyer, Clemmie Millbank, Lucy Thackray, Elsie Brockway, Roan Du Feu, Adam Millbank, Sarah Benett and Nadia Merdasi Caceres.

THANK YOU to my FABULOUS FAMILY for endless love and support, with a special mention to my grandmother BARBARA for giving me an enduring love of swimming in ice-cold lakes and oceans.
To the fantastic and ever-patient TEAM AT BLOOMSBURY – Liz, Clara, Holly, Penny and Austin – for making my dream a reality on proper paper.

To LUCY THACKRAY, platonic soul mate. Mr and Mrs Lewis forever. To FLORENCE BROCKWAY, travelling companion extraordinaire. To MARY SPENDER for countless motivational chats and a newfound love of road biking. To the ever-inspiring JOSIE COX for long runs and endless cheerleading. To the lovely CLEMMIE ROBINSON and ADAM MILLBANK for festival fun times and many pub dates. To PETER BUTLER for campervan adventures, surf sessions and for constantly calling me Sharon. To CHARLIE NEWMAN for cycling forays, hiking in the Lakes and momentous travel plans.

To MATT and FRANKIE STOTT for country walks and woodland games. To the BIRTHDAY COTTAGE GANG(S) for so many happy years. You are all amazing at sardines. To the totally rad CLIMBING GANG – Pete, Beren, Gav, Chris, Tiv, Helen, Rebecca, Jake, Malika and co for all the belays and all the magical wild camping weekenders. To the LASH GANG - Leo, Flo, Tom and Wally for foraging walks and pints of gin. To CAL MAJOR of PADDLE AGAINST PLASTIC for a day of paddleboarding hilarity and lots of eco advice. To ROBERT DOWNS JR for a truly excellent s'mores session in New York State. To blogging sista LAUREN

WILLIAMS of THE ENJOYABLE RUT for understanding the pain of typing alone in pyjamas. To GEORGE SPENDER for lots of practical book-writing advice. To MARIA HODSON for silly video shoots and meditative mountain walks. To IMMY TINKLER and KATE WILLIAMS for wild swimming weekenders. To REBECCA HUGHES, co-founder of WOMEN'S ADVENTURE EXPO, for girl power inspiration. To JAKE THOMPSETT of JT EXPEDITIONS for Brecon Beacons blisters and navigation tips. And, of course, to the always wonderful JACOB LITTLE. Thank you so much for everything.

Photo credits

All photos © Sian Anna Lewis except:

Cover image: © Jacob Little

Getty Images: *Pages* 1, 2-3, 4-5, 16, 18, 19, 22, 23, 25, 33, 36, 38-39, 50-51, 55, 58, 60, 63, 66, 68, 69, 72, 74, 84, 85, 86, 94, 105, 116, 119, 125, 126-127, 130, 133, 134, 148, 152, 153, 155, 162, 170, 171, 172, 174-175, 177, 194
Jacob Little: *Pages* 8, 13, 14, 47, 48, 49, 52, 64, 65, 67, 70-71, 78, 97, 103, 108, 120, 123, 135, 138, 139, 144, 150, 159, 163, 164, 179, 181, 200
Mary Spender: *Pages* 79, 110, 111, 114, 165
Rebecca Cork: *Page* 135
Peter Butler: *Pages* 27, 35
Beth Newman of Small Grey Cat and

Holly Lewis of Duchess Photography: *Pages* 120, 123, 178
Matthew Lewis: *Page* 129
Adam Millbank: *Page* 182
Angelica Sykes: *Pages* 57, 61
Jake Thompsett: *Pages* 48, 92-93
Florence Brockway: *Page* 199
Gavin Kennard: *Page* 113
Annie Brooks: *Page* 37
Katy Livesey: *Page* 167
Alexandra Holyer: *Page* 172
Sarah Thain: *Page* 169

INDEX